The Moral Life

AN INTRODUCTORY READER IN ETHICS AND LITERATURE

Louis P. Pojman
Lewis Vaughn

New York Oxford
OXFORD UNIVERSITY PRESS

Oxford University Press is a department of the University of Oxford. It furthers the University's objective of excellence in research, scholarship, and education by publishing worldwide. Oxford is a registered trade mark of Oxford University Press in the UK and certain other countries.

Published in the United States of America by Oxford University Press
198 Madison Avenue, New York, NY 10016, United States of America.

For titles covered by Section 112 of the US Higher Education Opportunity Act, please visit www.oup.com/us/he for the latest information about pricing and alternate formats.

CIP data is on file at the Library of Congress
978-0-19-761006-0

9 8 7 6 5 4 3 2 1
Printed by LSC Communications in the United States of America

CONTENTS

PREFACE

This seventh edition of *The Moral Life* continues the text's tradition of combining literature and philosophy to deepen students' understanding of moral concepts and issues. As those who have used *The Moral Life* know, the cross-pollination between fiction and philosophical writing can yield much fruit. Literature can show life in vivid relief and unnerving detail—and reveal how the moral life is, or could be, or should be lived. Philosophy can help us make sense of the complexities and conflicts of this moral experience, guiding us to moral principles, theories, or insights beneath the everyday muddle of emotion, prejudice, and custom. This text draws from both worlds, juxtaposing some of the finest writing and thinking of each to illuminate the essentials of ethics.

The additions and improvements in this edition include:

- Six new chapters with fifteen new readings, many of them newer voices or the most authoritative on a particular topic:
  - Sexism and Misogyny—Ann E. Cudd and Leslie E. Jones, "Sexism"; Kate Manne with Sean Illing, "What We Get Wrong About Misogyny"; Charlotte Perkins Gilman, "The Yellow Wallpaper."
  - Racism, Equity, and Privilege—Lawrence Blum, "Racism: What It Is and Isn't"; Naomi Zack, "Uses and Abuses of the Discourse of White Privilege"; Eduardo Bonilla-Silva, "Racism Without Racists"; Shannon Sullivan, "Good White Liberals."
  - Free Speech and Hate Speech—Sigal R. Ben-Porath, "Free Speech on Campus"; Richard Stengel and Conor Friedersdorf, "Two Views of Speech Laws"; Erwin Chemerinsky and Howard Gillman, "Hate Speech."
  - Pandemic Ethics—Michael Sandel with Colleen Walsh, "Why Some Americans Refuse to Social Distance and Wear Masks"; Ezekiel J. Emanuel, Govind Persad, Ross Upshur, et al., "Fair Allocation of Scarce Medical Resources in the Time of Covid-19."
  - Food Ethics—Alastair Norcross, "Puppies, Pigs, and People: Eating Meat and Marginal Cases."

   - The Ethics of Climate Change—Stephen M. Gardiner, "A Perfect Moral Storm: The Ethical Tragedy of Climate Change"; John Broome, "The Public and Private Morality of Climate Change."
- The above includes new readings by eight women writers, bringing the total in the text to nineteen.
- A revised chapter 9, "Does Life Have Meaning?" with a new reading by John Messerly, "The Ascent of Meaning."
- Altogether there are sixteen new readings, many of them newer voices or the most authoritative on a particular topic.
- A revised introduction to the Stoic philosophers (Chapter 6).
- New fiction: "The Yellow Wallpaper" by Charlotte Perkins Gilman.
- *The Moral Life*, 7e comes with a wealth of digital teaching and learning resources that will help your students excel in your course. For more information, visit www.oup.com/he/pojman-moral-life7e.

Many people helped Louis Pojman with the first two editions of this text, and a multitude lent their skilled hands to me with the third, fourth, fifth, sixth, and seventh. My greatest thanks for help with this edition goes to Andrew Blitzer, my distinguished editor at Oxford University Press, and his able assistants, Rachel Boland and Lacey Harvey.

For this new edition, I had the advice and counsel of numerous reviewers, including Olivia Bailey, Tulane University; David S. Brown, Lindenwood University; Connie Humphreys, Urbana University; Christopher Innes, College of Western Idaho; Julius-Kei Kato, King's University College; Paul LaChance, Northampton Community College; Glen A. Mazis, Penn State, Harrisburg; Louisa Moon, Mira Costa College; Andy Sanford, Southwestern Michigan College; Tammler Sommers, University of Houston; Aleksy Ivan Vasyl Tarasenko-Struc, Miami University; Travis Timmerman, Seton Hall University; and Daniel Zelinski, Richard Bland College.

Lewis Vaughn
March 2021

Dedicated to
my colleagues in the English Department
United States Military Academy
West Point

Where Philosophy and English
cross-fertilize each other
in a magnificent manner

INTRODUCTION

On the Nature of Morality

Ethics is about morality, and morality is about life. That is, *ethics* (also called moral philosophy) is the study of morality using the methods of philosophy, and *morality* concerns beliefs about right and wrong actions and good and bad persons or character.

Ethics is a systematic, rational search for answers to moral questions, often the hardest and most momentous questions we can ask. The moral issues that confront us are often difficult, contentious, and complex, yet ethics holds out the hope of making headway even in these turbulent waters. Through careful reflection, critical analysis, and the close examination of moral arguments, we can often make good progress. Ethics may not be easy, but neither is it futile.

Morality consists mostly of our moral judgments, principles, values, and theories; and ethics is the careful, philosophical examination of them. There are many ways to study morality, but the deepest and most enlightening is the philosophical way. Philosophy is the systematic exploration of life's big questions using critical thinking and logical argument. Using its methods, we can examine the heart of moral issues, judge the worth of moral judgments or principles, and—above all—work to ensure that our moral beliefs rest on the solid ground of good reasons.

Our distinction between morality and ethics seems clear enough, but everyday language sometimes blurs it. People often use *morality* and *ethics* as synonyms for moral beliefs or practices in general (as in "Morality is the foundation of civilization" or "Ethics cannot be ignored"). Or they may use the words to refer to the moral beliefs or practices of specific groups or persons (e.g., "Muslim morality," "Chinese ethics," or "the ethics of John Stuart Mill"). They may maintain our distinction and use the adjective forms *moral* and *ethical* accordingly. Or they may consider these terms equivalent to *right* or *good* ("That was the ethical thing to do") and use *immoral* or *unethical* as synonyms for *wrong* or *bad* ("abortion is immoral," "cheating on an exam is unethical").

We all sense that morality is somehow crucially different from other aspects of life. But how? For starters, it is *normative,* or evaluative. It provides us with norms, or standards, for judging actions and persons—standards in the form of moral judgments, principles, rules, or theories. With moral standards in hand, we decide whether an action is morally right or wrong and whether a person is morally good or bad. The main business of morality is therefore not to describe how things are, but to prescribe how things should be.

Morality, of course, is not the only normative realm. Just as morality is preoccupied with moral norms, other normative endeavors are concerned with nonmoral norms. The art world may use aesthetic norms to judge painting and sculpture. The law applies legal norms (laws and regulations) to judge the lawfulness of people's actions. Society insists on norms of etiquette to judge the politeness of social behavior.

But even in the crowded domain of the normative, morality is unique, deriving its distinctiveness from the combination of several characteristics. First, moral norms seem to have a much stronger hold on us than nonmoral ones do. The former are thought generally to dominate the latter, to have the property of *overridingness*. If a law enjoined us to commit a seriously immoral act, we would probably think the law illegitimate and might even flout it in an act of civil disobedience. If a rule of etiquette prevented us from performing an action that we regarded as morally obligatory, we would likely ignore the rule. Whatever we actually do when confronted with a conflict between a moral and a nonmoral norm, we tend to believe that the moral norm must override the nonmoral.

Second, moral norms have the feature of *impartiality,* the idea that they apply to everyone equally, that everyone should be considered of equal moral worth, and that each person's interests must be given equal weight. One familiar way to express this requirement is to say that equals should be treated equally unless there is a morally relevant reason to treat them differently. If we have a moral rule that says we must not assault innocent persons, then it applies to everyone, regardless of his or her social standing, income, race, skin color, gender, age, or occupation. We would consider it unjust—a clear-cut case of discrimination—to apply the rule to some people but not to others when there is no morally relevant difference between them. Social standing, race, gender, and the like mark differences among people, but they are not morally relevant differences, that is, they are not the sort of differences that affect individuals' moral standing as persons.

Some differences, of course, are morally relevant and may justify our treating people differently. Ordinarily we would think it unjust to single out a law-abiding person and forcibly take away her freedom of movement by confining her to a medical facility. But if she is a carrier of a deadly contagious disease, we might think her condition constitutes a morally relevant difference that justifies her being quarantined by public health authorities.

Third, like nonmoral norms, moral norms have *universality.* They apply not just in one unique circumstance, but in all circumstances that are relevantly similar. Logically, it makes no sense to say that Anne's deliberate injuring of someone in a particular situation is wrong but that Eduardo's deliberate injuring of someone in a nearly identical situation is right. Morality demands consistency among similar cases.

Fourth, morality is *reason driven.* To be fully involved in the moral life, to make informed moral judgments, and to use the resources of ethics to fathom the nature of morality itself is to engage in moral reasoning—critical thinking applied to the moral sphere. To "do" moral reasoning is to ensure that our moral judgments are not wrought out of thin air or concocted from prejudice or blind emotion but are instead supported by good reasons. The entire enterprise of ethics is devoted to the search for moral understanding, which can be attained only through careful reflection and the sifting of reasons for belief.

From the dictates of logic and our commonsense moral experience, we know that moral assertions that are uncoupled from reasons are usually suspect. What would we think of someone who declares that torturing innocent people is morally permissible (or impermissible) and that he has no reasons whatsoever for believing this? Or worse, he believes what he does because he wishes it to be true? We would likely not take him seriously and would not think much of his opinion, for he has given us no good reason to. He has told us something about himself—but nothing about the trustworthiness of his view.

None of this should lead us to conclude that moral reasoning is a mechanical process that is cut off from human emotion. Feelings are an essential element in the moral life. The kinds of moral issues that are discussed in this text—abortion, euthanasia, terrorism, animal rights, and others—are bound to evoke emotions in us. And that can be a good thing. Emotions can help us empathize with others and enlarge our understanding of the stakes involved in moral decisions. But our feelings are too often the product of our psychological needs, cultural conditioning, and selfish motivations. Critical thinking is the corrective, giving us the power to examine and guide our feelings to achieve a more balanced view.

What about our conscience—can we trust it? Our conscience is conditioned by our upbringing, cultural background, and other influences. At times, it seems to speak to us in an imaginary though authoritative voice, telling us to do or not do something. But conscience is like our feelings in that it may be the result of irrelevant influences and is therefore no infallible indicator of moral truth. In the name of conscience, people have done noble deeds—and committed horrible acts. Like our feelings, the voice of conscience should not be ignored; it can often alert us to something of moral importance—something that we need to submit to critical examination. Only through critical thinking can we rise above our feelings, our conscience, and our personal interests to see with moral clarity.

The moral norms that permeate our lives and to which we apply moral reasoning are of two kinds: norms of *obligation* and norms of *value.* The former refer to what we are obligated to do, our obligatory conduct or duty; the latter have to do with our estimations of moral worth, what we think is good or bad. We generally apply norms of obligation to *actions*, judging particular acts to be right or wrong according to a relevant moral concept, principle, or theory. Thus we say, "He should not have stolen the book" or "Breaking her promise was wrong." We use norms of value to judge the moral worth of *persons*, their *character*, or their *motives*, finding them to be good, bad, praiseworthy, or blameworthy. We say, "He was a good man," "She is compassionate," or "He acted out of greed." Acknowledging the complexity of the moral life, we sometimes insist that a right action was performed by a bad person or that a wrong action was performed by a good person.

We can also make some important distinctions about the seemingly straightforward terms *right* and *wrong. Right* can mean "permissible"; a permissible action is allowed, one that is not wrong to perform. Or *right* can mean "obligatory"; an obligatory action is required, one that it would be wrong *not* to perform. *Wrong* means "prohibited"; a prohibited action would be wrong to perform. An action that is "above and beyond" our duty—one that is not required but is praiseworthy—is *supererogatory.* Some believe that telling a "white lie" to spare a friend's feelings is right (permissible), some think the action is right (obligatory), and some insist that telling any kind of lie is wrong (prohibited). For many people, giving to charity is obligatory; for others, it is supererogatory.

Morality is both personal and social. It is personal in that it has to do with how we should live our lives, what we should strive to become. It is social in that it recognizes that we are not hermits or gods, independent beings with no need for each other. We are centers of conscious striving and desire, who have wills of our own but have to adjust the pursuit of our goals in the light of other people's desires and interests. How to reconcile and adjust these twin forces, the personal and the social, is the central domain of ethics. It is the central concern of this anthology. Many works of ethics emphasize the broader areas of social policy or social ethics: just-war theory, economic relations, punishment, political arrangements, and institutional justice. There is a place for that. But in this work we focus on the more personal dimension of ethics: its raison d'être, its fundamental purposes. We want to build from the ground up, for unless we get our foundations firmly laid, our structure will be in danger of capsizing. We will first study the nature of morality, beginning with a sizable selection from William Golding's moral allegory, *Lord of the Flies.* After a commentary, we will examine the philosophical analogue to Golding's work,

Thomas Hobbes's *Leviathan,* written three hundred years earlier. In Chapter 2 we examine the nature of good and evil. After this we raise one of the most crucial questions about morality: Is it universally valid or only relative to individual choice or one's culture?

In Part II we progress to the three classic moral theories: *utilitarianism,* which aims to maximize good consequences, usually defined in terms of pleasure or happiness; *deontological ethics,* which focuses on the individual act (its inherent rightness or wrongness) and the individual (his or her inherent dignity or value); and *virtue ethics,* which focuses on character, the kind of qualities we should inculcate, and the kind of people we should become. But all of these theories recognize the role of virtue and vice—morally significant character traits—so in Chapter 6 we examine several classic virtues and vices.

In Part III we consider theoretical issues that are implicit in our study of the nature of morality and moral theories, enlarging on what was said earlier. If the first two parts constituted the foundations and formal structure of moral theory, Part III deals with the materials in our building. First we examine the idea of the self in relation to others. Sometimes we can flout moral rules when it is in our perceived interest to do so. Should we do so? Why should we be moral whenever we can enhance personal gain by disregarding morality's requirements? This problem is related to a second question—what really is important about life? What, if anything, gives it meaning? Or is it merely "a tale told by an idiot, full of sound and fury, signifying nothing"? Here we look at various worldviews about the nature and destiny of humanity: Epicureanism, Stoicism, theism, Buddhism, existentialism, and others.

Finally, in Part IV we examine six practical moral issues. In Chapter 10 we think through the harsh social and moral realities of sexism and misogyny. In Chapter 11 we analyze the pervasive problem of racism and inequity. In Chapter 12 we look at free speech and hate speech, especially as they manifest themselves on campus and in popular culture. Chapter 13 wrestles with pandemic ethics—what do we owe each other in a time of national peril, and how should be allocate the resources we have to withstand the threat? Chapter 14 deals with food ethics—the morality of meat-eating and the treatment of animals. Finally Chapter 15 considers our moral duties in the face of climate change what, if anything, are we morally obligated to do about it, what do we owe future generations?

Generally, the readings take opposing stands on the issues at hand, though some are included simply to stimulate thinking. The main purpose of this work is to help you think through some of the most difficult and exciting issues of our time. Hence the use of literature to supplement philosophical analysis.

Literature particularizes the general problem and brings it home to us, enlivening the imagination so that we see and feel nuances that are vital to resolving difficult moral issues, possibilities that we might not have considered in our abstract thinking about moral dilemmas. But it is no substitute for philosophical analysis, so while many chapters begin with a literary work, the philosophical essays are where most of the necessary argument and theory take place.

PART I

The Nature of Morality

Good and Evil

In this part of our work, we consider three fundamental questions related to morality: What is the purpose of morality? What are good and evil? Is morality essentially relative, or are there objective moral truths? We begin each chapter with a literary selection and then go on to provide a philosophical analysis.

CHAPTER 1

What Is the Purpose of Morality?

What is the purpose of morality? What is morality for? It seems to have many purposes. These include enabling us to reach our goals in socially acceptable ways, enabling us to resolve conflicts of interest fairly, developing certain kinds of positive character, promoting human happiness, and enabling society to survive. You can probably think of others. But just as a picture is worth a thousand words, a good story may do more to illuminate the purpose of morality than a thousand disquisitions on the subject. So we begin our book with a sizable selection from William Golding's *Lord of the Flies,* a modern allegory on the nature and purpose of morality. A group of British private school boys are marooned on an island; detached from the constraints of civilization, they turn into savages. Whether or not human nature is as depraved as Golding makes it out to be, the significance of the book lies in the fact that it illuminates the need for and purpose of ethical codes. After the excerpt from Golding's novel, Louis Pojman gives an analysis on its meaning for our understanding of morality. This is followed by a selection from Thomas Hobbes's classic work *Leviathan* (1651), which, in seventeenth-century prose, poignantly sets forth a similar message to Golding's.

These three readings center on the foundational problems of moral philosophy. It is imperative that we think clearly about them before we tackle normative theories and applied ethics. Let us turn now to one of the great moral allegories of our time, William Golding's *Lord of the Flies.*

Lord of the Flies

A Moral Allegory

WILLIAM GOLDING

William Golding is considered one of the most profoundly insightful writers of our age. His works explore the human condition and the need for moral consciousness. In this work, published in 1954, Golding describes a situation in which the veneer of civilization is stripped away from children and a primordial evil emerges out of the depths of the human heart.

An indeterminate number of schoolboys, ranging in age from six to twelve, are cast adrift on an uninhabited island in the Pacific, after being evacuated from England during the next world war. They are forced to create their own social system. All begins well, as Ralph is democratically chosen leader of the group and appropriate rules are agreed upon: keep the fire going, use proper sanitation, obey proper authority and orderly procedures in the assembly. Bereft of modern technology, they must reinvent simple tools or use tools for innovative purposes: eyeglasses to focus the sun's light to start a fire, sticks for spears. They construct shelters and build a fire on the top of the mountain in order to signal their presence to passing ships. They miss simple conveniences: scissors to cut their long, knotty hair; toothbrushes; sanitary facilities; and clothes.

For a while the constraints of civilized society prevent total chaos. While the youngest children, "littluns," are frightened and homesick, the older boys entertain them. They seem ready to make the best out of their fate and recognize the necessity of substantive and procedural rules. Only he who has the white conch, the symbol of authority, may speak at an assembly, and the democratically chosen leader is invested with limited powers. Even the sadistic Roger, while taunting little Henry by throwing stones near him, manages to keep the stones from harming the child.

> Here, invisible yet strong, was the taboo of the old life. Round the squatting child was the protection of parents and school and policemen and the law. Roger's arm was conditioned by a civilization that knew nothing of him and was in ruins. (p. 78)

After some initial euphoria at being liberated from the adult world of constraints into an exciting world of fun in the sun, the children come up against the usual banes of social existence: filth, competition for power and status, neglect of social responsibility, failure of public policy, and escalating violence. Two boys—Ralph, the son of a naval officer, and Jack, the head

---

choirboy—vie for leadership and a bitter rivalry emerges between them. As a compromise, a division of labor ensues in which Jack's choirboy hunters refuse to help Ralph and a few others in constructing shelters. Piggy, the bespectacled asthmatic, acts as the wise and rational counselor, and Simon, an epileptic, is portrayed as possessing special spiritual insight, but these qualities of rationality and spirituality are tested by the Lord of the Flies. Freeloading soon becomes a common phenomenon as the majority of children leave their tasks to play on the beach. Sanitation becomes a problem, as the diarrheal children defecate all over the beach. Neglect of the fire causes it to burn out, which, in turn, results in failure to be rescued by a passing ship. We enter the novel as Jack returns with his choirboy hunters, having slain their first pig, only to be reprimanded by Ralph for not tending the fire.

The hunters were more silent now, but at this they buzzed again. Ralph flung back his hair. One arm pointed at the empty horizon. His voice was loud and savage, and struck them into silence.

"There was a ship."

Jack, faced at once with too many awful implications, ducked away from them. He laid a hand on the pig and drew his knife. Ralph brought his arm down, fist clenched, and his voice shook.

"There was a ship. Out there. You said you'd keep the fire going and you let it out!" He took a step towards Jack who turned and faced him.

"They might have seen us. We might have gone home—"

This was too bitter for Piggy, who forgot his timidity in the agony of his loss. He began to cry out, shrilly:

"You and your blood, Jack Merridew! You and your hunting! We might have gone home——"

Ralph pushed Piggy on one side.

"I was chief; and you were going to do what I said. You talk. But you can't even build huts—then you go off hunting and let out the fire——"

He turned away, silent for a moment. Then his voice came again on a peak of feeling.

"There was a ship——"

One of the smaller hunters began to wail. The dismal truth was filtering through to everybody. Jack went very red as he hacked and pulled at the pig.

"The job was too much. We needed everyone."

Ralph turned.

"You could have had everyone when the shelters were finished. But you had to hunt—"

"We needed meat."

Jack stood up as he said this, the bloodied knife in his hand. The two boys faced each other. There was the brilliant world of hunting, tactics, fierce exhilaration, skill; and there was the world of longing and baffled commonsense. Jack transferred the knife to his left hand and smudged blood over his forehead as he pushed down the plastered hair.

Piggy began again.

"You didn't ought to have let that fire out. You said you'd keep the smoke going——"

This from Piggy, and the wails of agreement from some of the hunters drove Jack to violence. The bolting look came into his blue eyes. He took a step, and able at last to hit someone, stuck his fist into Piggy's stomach. Piggy sat down with a grunt. Jack stood over him. His voice was vicious with humiliation.

"You would, would you? Fatty!"

Ralph made a step forward and Jack smacked Piggy's head. Piggy's glasses flew off and tinkled on the rocks. Piggy cried out in terror:

"My specs!"

He went crouching and feeling over the rocks but Simon, who got there first, found them for him. Passions beat about Simon on the mountain-top with awful wings.

"One side's broken."

Piggy grabbed and put on the glasses. He looked malevolently at Jack.

"I got to have them specs. Now I only got one eye. Jus' you wait——"

Jack made a move towards Piggy who scrambled away till a great rock lay between them. He thrust his head over the top and glared at Jack through his one flashing glass.

"Now I only got one eye. Just you wait——"

Jack mimicked the whine and scramble.

"Jus' you wait—yah!"

Piggy and the parody were so funny that the hunters began to laugh. Jack felt encouraged. He went on scrambling and the laughter rose to a gale of hysteria. Unwillingly Ralph felt his lips twitch; he was angry with himself for giving way.

He muttered.

"That was a dirty trick."

Jack broke out of his gyration and stood facing Ralph. His words came in a shout.

"All right, all right!"

He looked at Piggy, at the hunters, at Ralph.

"I'm sorry. About the fire, I mean. There. I——"

He drew himself up.

"—I apologize."

The buzz from the hunters was one of admiration at this handsome behaviour. Clearly they were of the opinion that Jack had done the decent thing, had put himself in the right by his generous apology and Ralph, obscurely, in the wrong. They waited for an appropriately decent answer.

Yet Ralph's throat refused to pass one. He resented, as an addition to Jack's misbehaviour, this verbal trick. The fire was dead, the ship was gone. Could they not see? Anger instead of decency passed his throat.

"That was a dirty trick."

They were silent on the mountain-top while the opaque look appeared in Jack's eyes and passed away.

Ralph's final word was an ungracious mutter.

"All right. Light the fire."

With some positive action before them, a little of the tension died. Ralph said no more, did nothing, stood looking down at the ashes round his feet. Jack was loud and active. He gave orders, sang, whistled, threw remarks at the silent Ralph—remarks that did not need an answer, and therefore could not invite a snub; and still Ralph was silent. No one, not even Jack, would ask him to move and in the end they had to build the fire three yards away and in a place not really as convenient. So Ralph asserted his chieftainship and could not have chosen a better way if he had thought for days. Against this weapon, so indefinable and so effective, Jack was powerless and raged without knowing why. By the time the pile was built, they were on different sides of a high barrier.

When they had dealt with the fire another crisis arose. Jack had no means of lighting it. Then to his surprise, Ralph went to Piggy and took the glasses from him. Not even Ralph knew how a link between him and Jack had been snapped and fastened elsewhere.

"I'll bring 'em back."

"I'll come too."

Piggy stood behind him, islanded in a sea of meaningless colour, while Ralph knelt and focused the glossy spot. Instantly the fire was alight Piggy held out his hands and grabbed the glasses back.

Before these fantastically attractive flowers of violet and red and yellow, unkindness melted away. They became a circle of boys round a camp fire and even Piggy and Ralph were half-drawn in. Soon some of the boys were rushing down the slope for more wood while Jack hacked the pig. They tried holding the whole carcass on a stake over the fire, but the stake burnt more quickly than the pig roasted. In the end they skewered bits of meat on branches and held them in the flames: and even then almost as much boy was roasted as meat.

Ralph dribbled. He meant to refuse meat but his past diet of fruit and nuts, with an odd crab or fish, gave him too little resistance. He accepted a piece of half-raw meat and gnawed it like a wolf.

Piggy spoke, also dribbling.

"Aren't I having none?"

Jack had meant to leave him in doubt, as an assertion of power; but Piggy by advertising his omission made more cruelty necessary.

"You didn't hunt."

"No more did Ralph," said Piggy wetly, "nor Simon." He amplified. "There isn't more than a ha'porth of meat in a crab."

Ralph stirred uneasily. Simon, sitting between the twins and Piggy, wiped his mouth and shoved his piece of meat over the rocks to Piggy, who grabbed it. The twins giggled and Simon lowered his face in shame.

Then Jack leapt to his feet, slashed off a great hunk of meat, and flung it down at Simon's feet.

"Eat! Damn you!"

He glared at Simon.

"Take it!"

He spun on his heel, centre of a bewildered circle of boys.

"I got you meat!"

Numberless and inexpressible frustrations combined to make his rage elemental and awe-inspiring.

"I painted my face—I stole up. Now you eat—all of you—and I——"

Slowly the silence on the mountain-top deepened till the click of the fire and the soft hiss of roasting meat could be heard clearly. Jack looked round for understanding but found only respect. Ralph stood among the ashes of the signal fire, his hands full of meat, saying nothing.

Then at last Maurice broke the silence. He changed the subject to the only one that could bring the majority of them together.

"Where did you find the pig?"

Roger pointed down the unfriendly side.

"They were there—by the sea."

Jack, recovering, could not bear to have his story told. He broke in quickly.

"We spread round. I crept, on hands and knees. The spears fell out because they hadn't barbs on. The pig ran away and made an awful noise——"

"It turned back and ran into the circle, bleeding——"

All the boys were talking at once, relieved and excited.

"We closed in——"

The first blow had paralysed its hind quarters, so then the circle could close in and beat and beat—

"I cut the pig's throat——"

The twins, still sharing their identical grin, jumped up and ran round each other. Then the rest joined in, making pig-dying noises and shouting.

"One for his nob!"

"Give him a fourpenny one!"

Then Maurice pretended to be the pig and ran squealing into the centre, and the hunters, circling still, pretended to beat him. As they danced, they sang.

"*Kill the pig. Cut her throat. Bash her in.*"

Ralph watched them, envious and resentful. Not till they flagged and the chant died away, did he speak.

"I'm calling an assembly."

One by one, they halted, and stood watching him.

"With the conch. I'm calling a meeting even if we have to go on into the dark. Down on the platform. When I blow it. Now."

He turned away and walked off, down the mountain.

[Things degenerate. The fire, the symbol of hope, is left unattended, and the conch, the symbol of orderly governance, is disdained by Jack's group. With the diminished symbols, Ralph's authority, and the rational procedures he stands for, become undermined. Frightened little Percival reports that he has seen the beast, a preternatural creature who bodes no good. Piggy dismisses such talk as superstitious and assures the group that life follows scientific laws that exclude the preternatural. Ghosts and beasts can't exist. Why not?

> *"'Cos things wouldn't make sense. Houses an' streets, an' TV—they wouldn't work."*
>
> *But Simon thinks differently. "Maybe there is a beast."*
>
> *The assembly cried out savagely and Ralph stood up in amazement. "You, Simon? You believe in this?"*
>
> *. . . "What I mean is . . . maybe it's only us."*
>
> *"Nuts" [responded] Piggy shocked out of decorum . . .*
>
> *Simon became inarticulate in his effort to express mankind's essential illness.*

Eventually Jack succeeds in winning all but five of the boys to his cause. Only Simon, Piggy, and the twins, Sam and Eric ("Samneric"), remain with Ralph in his project of keeping the fire burning and living by the rule of law, though Simon has gone off on a venture. The crowd has joined Jack and his hunters. Jack rules by charismatic might, livening their spirits with pig hunts and orgies but treating the littluns cruelly. Needing a magnifying glass to start their fire for the pig roast, three hunters, Jack, Roger, and Maurice, steal into Ralph and Piggy's shelter, attack Ralph and Piggy, and steal Piggy's glasses. We enter (Chapter 11) as Ralph and his friends are grieving the loss of the glasses and the fire. Piggy complains that without his glasses he can't see and demands that they confront Jack with his crime. He speaks:]

"I got the conch. I'm going to that Jack Merridew an' tell him, I am."

"You'll get hurt."

"What can he do more than he has? I'll tell him what's what. You let me carry the conch, Ralph. I'll show him the one thing he hasn't got."

Piggy paused for a moment and peered round at the dim figures. The shape of the old assembly, trodden in the grass, listened to him.

"I'm going to him with this conch in my hands. I'm going to hold it out. Look, I'm goin' to say, you're stronger than I am and you haven't got asthma. You can see, I'm goin' to say, and with both eyes. But I don't ask for my glasses back, not as a favour. I don't ask you to be a sport, I'll say, not because you're strong, but because what's right's right. Give me my glasses, I'm going to say—you got to!"

Piggy ended, flushed and trembling. He pushed the conch quickly into Ralph's hands as though in a hurry to be rid of it and wiped the tears from his eyes. The green light was gentle about them and the conch lay at Ralph's feet, fragile and white. A single drop of water that had escaped Piggy's fingers now flashed on the delicate curve like a star.

At last Ralph sat up straight and drew back his hair.

"All right. I mean—you can try if you like. We'll go with you."

"He'll be painted," said Sam, timidly. "You know how he'll be——"

"—he won't think much of us——"

"—if he gets waxy we've had it——"

Ralph scowled at Sam. Dimly he remembered something that Simon had said to him once, by the rocks.

"Don't be silly," he said. And then he added quickly, "Let's go."

He held out the conch to Piggy who flushed, this time with pride.

"You must carry it."

"When we're ready I'll carry it——"

Piggy sought in his mind for words to convey his passionate willingness to carry the conch against all odds.

"—I don't mind. I'll be glad, Ralph, only I'll have to be led."

Ralph put the conch back on the shining log.

"We better eat and then get ready."

They made their way to the devastated fruit trees. Piggy was helped to his food and found some by touch. While they ate, Ralph thought of the afternoon.

"We'll be like we were. We'll wash——"

Sam gulped down a mouthful and protested.

"But we bathe every day!"

Ralph looked at the filthy objects before him and sighed.

"We ought to comb our hair. Only it's too long."

"I've got both socks left in the shelter," said Eric, "so we could pull them over our heads like caps, sort of."

"We could find some stuff," said Piggy, "and tie your hair back."

"Like a girl!"

"No. 'Course not."

"Then we must go as we are," said Ralph, "and they won't be any better."

Eric made a detaining gesture.

"But they'll be painted! You know how it is——"

The others nodded. They understood only too well the liberation into savagery that the concealing paint brought.

"Well, we won't be painted," said Ralph, "because we aren't savages."

Samneric looked at each other.

"All the same——"

Ralph shouted.

"No paint!" . . .

They set off along the beach in formation. Ralph went first, limping a little, his spear carried over one shoulder. He saw things partially through the tremble of the heat haze over the flashing sands, and his own long hair and injuries. Behind him came the twins, worried now for a while but full of unquenchable vitality. They said little but trailed the butts of their wooden spears; for Piggy had found, that looking down, shielding his tired sight from the sun, he could just see these moving along the sand. He walked between the trailing butts, therefore, the conch held carefully between his two hands. The boys made a compact little group that moved over the beach, four plate-like shadows dancing and mingling beneath them. There was no sign left of the storm, and the beach was swept clean like a blade that has been scoured. The sky and the mountain were at an immense distance, shimmering in the heat; and the reef was lifted by mirage, floating in a kind of silver pool half-way up the sky.

They passed the place where the tribe had danced. The charred sticks still lay on the rocks where the rain had quenched them but the sand by the water was smooth again. They passed this in silence. No one doubted that the tribe would be found at the Castle Rock and when they came in sight of it they stopped with one accord. The densest tangle on the island, a mass of twisted stems, black and green and impenetrable, lay on their left and tall grass swayed before them. Now Ralph went forward.

Here was the crushed grass where they had all lain when he had gone to prospect. There was the neck of land, the ledge skirting the rock, up there were the red pinnacles.

Sam touched his arm.

"Smoke."

There was a tiny smudge of smoke wavering into the air on the other side of the rock.

"Some fire—I don't think."

Ralph turned.

"What are we hiding for?"

He stepped through the screen of grass on to the little open space that led to the narrow neck.

"You two follow behind. I'll go first, then Piggy a pace behind me. Keep your spears ready."

Piggy peered anxiously into the luminous veil that hung between him and the world.

"Is it safe? Ain't there a cliff? I can hear the sea."

"You keep right close to me."

Ralph moved forward on to the neck. He kicked a stone and it bounded into the water. Then the sea sucked down, revealing a red, weedy square forty feet beneath Ralph's left arm.

"Am I safe?" quavered Piggy. "I feel awful——"

High above them from the pinnacles came a sudden shout and then an imitation war-cry that was answered by a dozen voices from behind the rock.

"Give me the conch and stay still."

"Halt! Who goes there?"

Ralph bent back his head and glimpsed Roger's dark face at the top.

"You can see who I am!" he shouted. "Stop being silly!"

He put the conch to his lips and began to blow. Savages appeared, painted out of recognition, edging round the ledge towards the neck. They carried spears and disposed themselves to defend the entrance. Ralph went on blowing and ignored Piggy's terrors.

Roger was shouting.

"You mind out—see?"

At length Ralph took his lips away and paused to get his breath back. His first words were a gasp, but audible.

"—calling an assembly."

The savages guarding the neck muttered among themselves but made no motion. Ralph walked forwards a couple of steps. A voice whispered urgently behind him.

"Don't leave me, Ralph."

"You kneel down," said Ralph sideways, "and wait till I come back."

He stood half-way along the neck and gazed at the savages intently. Freed by the paint, they had tied their hair back and were more comfortable than he was. Ralph made a resolution to tie his own back afterwards. Indeed he felt like telling them to wait and doing it there and then; but that was impossible. The savages sniggered a bit and one gestured at Ralph with his spear. High above, Roger took his hands off the lever and leaned out to see what was going on. The boys on the neck stood in a pool of their own shadow, diminished to shaggy heads. Piggy crouched, his back shapeless as a sack.

"I'm calling an assembly."

Silence.

Roger took up a small stone and flung it between the twins, aiming to miss. They started and Sam only just kept his footing. Some source of power began to pulse in Roger's body.

Ralph spoke again, loudly.

"I'm calling an assembly."

He ran his eye over them.

"Where's Jack?"

The group of boys stirred and consulted. A painted face spoke with the voice of Robert.

"He's hunting. And he said we weren't to let you in."

"I've come to see about the fire," said Ralph, "and about Piggy's specs."

The group in front of him shifted and laughter shivered outwards from among them, light, excited laughter that went echoing among the tall rocks.

A voice spoke from behind Ralph.

"What do you want?"

The twins made a bolt past Ralph and got between him and the entry. He turned quickly. Jack, identifiable by personality and red hair, was advancing from the forest. A hunter crouched on either side. All three were masked in black and green. Behind them on the grass the headless and paunched body of a sow lay where they had dropped it.

Piggy wailed.

"Ralph! Don't leave me!"

With ludicrous care he embraced the rock, pressing himself to it above the sucking sea. The sniggering of the savages became a loud derisive jeer.

Jack shouted above the noise.

"You go away, Ralph. You keep to your end. This is my end and my tribe. You leave me alone."

The jeering died away.

"You pinched Piggy's specs," said Ralph, breathlessly. "You've got to give them back."

"Got to? Who says?"

Ralph's temper blazed out.

"I say! You voted for me for Chief. Didn't you hear the conch? You played a dirty trick—we'd have given you fire if you'd asked for it——"

The blood was flowing in his cheeks and the bunged-up eye throbbed.

"You could have had fire whenever you wanted. But you didn't. You came sneaking up like a thief and stole Piggy's glasses!"

"Say that again!"

"Thief! Thief!"

Piggy screamed.

"Ralph! Mind me!"

Jack made a rush and stabbed at Ralph's chest with his spear. Ralph sensed the position of the weapon from the glimpse he caught of Jack's arm and put the thrust aside with his own butt. Then he brought the end round and caught Jack a stinger across the ear. They were chest to chest, breathing fiercely, pushing and glaring.

"Who's a thief?"

"You are!"

Jack wrenched free and swung at Ralph with his spear. By common consent they were using the spears as sabres now, no longer daring the lethal points. The blow struck Ralph's spear and slid down, to fall agonizingly on his fingers. Then they were apart once more, their positions reversed, Jack towards the Castle Rock and Ralph on the outside towards the island.

Both boys were breathing very heavily.

"Come on then——"

"Come on——"

Truculently they squared up to each other but kept just out of fighting distance.

"You come on and see what you get!"

"You come on——"

Piggy clutching the ground was trying to attract Ralph's attention. Ralph moved, bent down, kept a wary eye on Jack.

"Ralph—remember what we came for. The fire. My specs."

Ralph nodded. He relaxed his fighting muscles, stood easily and grounded the butt of his spear. Jack watched him inscrutably through his paint. Ralph glanced up at the pinnacles, then towards the group of savages.

"Listen. We've come to say this. First you've got to give back Piggy's specs. If he hasn't got them he can't see. You aren't playing the game——"

The tribe of painted savages giggled and Ralph's mind faltered. He pushed his hair up and gazed at the green and black mask before him, trying to remember what Jack looked like.

Piggy whispered.

"And the fire."

"Oh yes. Then about the fire. I say this again. I've been saying it ever since we dropped in."

He held out his spear and pointed at the savages.

"Your only hope is keeping a signal fire going as long as there's light to see. Then maybe a ship'll notice the smoke and come and rescue us and take us home. But without that smoke we've got to wait till some ship comes by accident. We might wait years; till we were old——"

The shivering, silvery, unreal laughter of the savages sprayed out and echoed away. A gust of rage shook Ralph. His voice cracked.

"Don't you understand, you painted fools? Sam, Eric, Piggy and me—we aren't enough. We tried to keep the fire going, but we couldn't. And then you, playing at hunting. . . ."

He pointed past them to where the trickle of smoke dispersed in the pearly air.

"Look at that! Call that a signal fire? That's a cooking fire. Now you'll eat and there'll be no smoke. Don't you understand? There may be a ship out there—"

He paused, defeated by the silence and the painted anonymity of the group guarding the entry. The chief opened a pink mouth and addressed Samneric who were between him and his tribe.

"You two. Get back."

No one answered him. The twins, puzzled, looked at each other; while Piggy, reassured by the cessation of violence, stood up carefully. Jack glanced back at Ralph and then at the twins.

"Grab them!"

No one moved. Jack shouted angrily.

"I said 'grab them'!"

The painted group moved round Samneric nervously and unhandily. Once more the silvery laughter scattered.

Samneric protested out of the heart of civilization.

"Oh, I say!"

"—honestly!"

Their spears were taken from them.

"Tie them up!"

Ralph cried out hopelessly against the black and green mask.

"Jack!"

"Go on. Tie them."

Now the painted group felt the otherness of Samneric, felt the power in their own hands. They felled the twins clumsily and excitedly. Jack was inspired. He knew that Ralph would attempt a rescue. He struck in a humming circle behind him and Ralph only just parried the blow. Beyond them the tribe and the twins were a loud and writhing heap. Piggy crouched again. Then the twins lay, astonished, and the tribe stood round them. Jack turned to Ralph and spoke between his teeth.

"See? They do what I want."

There was silence again. The twins lay, inexpertly tied up, and the tribe watched Ralph to see what he would do. He numbered them through his fringe, glimpsed the ineffectual smoke.

His temper broke. He screamed at Jack.

"You're a beast and a swine and a bloody, bloody thief!"

He charged.

Jack, knowing this was the crisis, charged too. They met with a jolt and bounced apart. Jack swung with his fist at Ralph and caught him on the ear. Ralph hit Jack in the stomach and made him grunt. Then they were facing each other again, panting and furious, but unnerved by each other's ferocity. They became aware of the noise that was the background to this fight, the steady shrill cheering of the tribe behind them.

Piggy's voice penetrated to Ralph.

"Let me speak."

He was standing in the dust of the fight, and as the tribe saw his intention the shrill cheer changed to a steady booing.

Piggy held up the conch and the booing sagged a little, then came up again to strength.

"I got the conch!"

He shouted.

"I tell you, I got the conch!"

Surprisingly, there was silence now; the tribe were curious to hear what amusing thing he might have to say.

Silence and pause; but in the silence a curious air-noise, close by Ralph's head. He gave it half his attention—and there it was again; a faint "Zup!" Someone was throwing stones: Roger was dropping them, his one hand still on the lever. Below him, Ralph was a shock of hair and Piggy a bag of fat.

"I got this to say. You're acting like a crowd of kids."

The booing rose and died again as Piggy lifted the white, magic shell.

"Which is better—to be a pack of painted niggers like you are, or to be sensible like Ralph is?"

A great clamour rose among the savages. Piggy shouted again.

"Which is better—to have rules and agree, or to hunt and kill?"

Again the clamour and again—"Zup!"

Ralph shouted against the noise.

"Which is better, law and rescue, or hunting and breaking things up?"

Now Jack was yelling too and Ralph could no longer make himself heard. Jack had backed right against the tribe and they were a solid mass of menace that bristled with spears. The intention of a charge was forming among them; they were working up to it and the neck would be swept clear. Ralph stood facing them, a little to one side, his spear ready. By him stood Piggy still holding out the talisman, the fragile, shining beauty of the shell. The storm of sound beat at them, an incantation of hatred. High overhead, Roger, with a sense of delirious abandonment, leaned all his weight on the lever.

Ralph heard the great rock long before he saw it. He was aware of a jolt in the earth that came to him through the soles of his feet, and the breaking sound of stones at the top of the cliff. Then the monstrous red thing bounded across the neck and he flung himself flat while the tribe shrieked.

The rock struck Piggy a glancing blow from chin to knee: the conch exploded into a thousand white fragments and ceased to exist. Piggy, saying nothing, with no time for even a grunt, travelled through the air sideways from the rock, turning over as he went. The rock bounded twice and was lost in the forest. Piggy fell forty feet and landed on his back across that square, red rock in the sea. His head opened and stuff came out and turned red. Piggy's arms and legs twitched a bit, like a pig's after it has been killed. Then the sea breathed again in a long, slow sigh, the water boiled white and pink over the rock; and when it went, sucking back again, the body of Piggy was gone.

This time the silence was complete. Ralph's lips formed a word but no sound came.

Suddenly Jack bounded out from the tribe and began screaming wildly.

"See? See? That's what you'll get! I meant that! There isn't a tribe for you any more! The conch is gone—"

He ran forward, stooping.

"I'm Chief!"

Viciously, with full intention, he hurled his spear at Ralph. The point tore the skin and flesh over Ralph's ribs, then sheared off and fell in the water. Ralph stumbled, feeling not pain but panic, and the tribe, screaming now like the Chief, began to advance. Another spear, a bent one that would not fly straight, went past his face and one fell from on high where Roger was. The twins lay hidden behind the tribe and the anonymous devils' faces swarmed across the neck. Ralph turned and ran. A great noise as of sea-gulls rose behind him. He obeyed an instinct that he did not know he possessed and swerved over the open space so that the spears went wide. He saw the headless body of the sow and jumped in time. Then he was crashing through foliage and small boughs and was hidden by the forest.

The Chief stopped by the pig, turned and held up his hands.

"Back! Back to the fort!"

Presently the tribe returned noisily to the neck where Roger joined them.

The Chief spoke to him angrily.

"Why aren't you on watch?"

Roger looked at him gravely.

"I just came down——"

The hangman's horror clung round him. The Chief said no more to him but looked down at Samneric.

"You got to join the tribe."

"You lemme go——"

"—and me."

The Chief snatched one of the few spears that were left and poked Sam in the ribs.

"What d'you mean by it, eh?" said the Chief fiercely. "What d'you mean by coming with spears? What d'you mean by not joining my tribe?"

The prodding became rhythmic. Sam yelled.

"That's not the way."

Roger edged past the Chief, only just avoiding pushing him with his shoulder. The yelling ceased, and Samneric lay looking up in quiet terror. Roger advanced upon them as one wielding a nameless authority.

CRY OF THE HUNTERS

Ralph lay in a covert, wondering about his wounds. The bruised flesh was inches in diameter over his right ribs, with a swollen and bloody scar where the spear had hit him. His hair was full of dirt and tapped like the tendrils of a creeper. All over he was scratched and bruised from his flight through the forest. By the time his breathing was normal again, he had worked out that bathing these injuries would have to wait. How could you listen for naked feet if you were splashing in water? How could you be safe by the little stream or on the open beach?

Ralph listened. He was not really far from the Castle Rock, and during the first panic he had thought he heard sounds of pursuit. But the hunters had only sneaked into the fringes of the greenery, retrieving spears perhaps, and then had rushed back to the sunny rock as if terrified of the darkness under the leaves. He had even glimpsed one of them, striped brown, black, and red, and had judged that it was Bill. But really, thought Ralph, this was not Bill.

This was a savage whose image refused to blend with that ancient picture of a boy in shorts and shirt.

The afternoon died away; the circular spots of sunlight moved steadily over green fronds and brown fibre but no sound came from behind the Rock. At last Ralph wormed out of the ferns and sneaked forward to the edge of that impenetrable thicket that fronted the neck of land. He peered with elaborate caution between branches at the edge and could see Robert sitting on guard at the top of the cliff. He held a spear in his left hand and was tossing up a pebble and catching it again with the right. Behind him a column of smoke rose thickly, so that Ralph's nostrils flared and his mouth dribbled. He wiped his nose and mouth with the back of his hand and for the first time since the morning felt hungry. The tribe must be sitting round the gutted pig, watching the fat ooze and burn among the ashes. They would be intent.

Another figure, an unrecognizable one, appeared by Robert and gave him something, then turned and went back behind the rock. Robert laid his spear on the rock beside him and began to gnaw between his raised hands. So the feast was beginning and the watchman had been given his portion.

Ralph saw that for the time being he was safe. He limped away through the fruit trees, drawn by the thought of the poor food yet bitter when he remembered the feast. Feast to-day, and then to-morrow. . . .

He argued unconvincingly that they would let him alone; perhaps even make an outlaw of him. But then the fatal unreasoning knowledge came to him again. The breaking of the conch and the deaths of Piggy and Simon lay over the island like a vapour. These painted savages would go further and further. Then there was that indefinable connection between himself and Jack; who therefore would never let him alone; never.

He paused, sun-flecked, holding up a bough, prepared to duck under it. A spasm of terror set him shaking and he cried aloud.

"No. They're not as bad as that. It was an accident."

He ducked under the bough, ran clumsily, then stopped and listened.

He came to the smashed acres of fruit and ate greedily. He saw two littluns and, not having any idea of his own appearance, wondered why they screamed and ran.

When he had eaten he went towards the beach. The sunlight was slanting now into the palms by the wrecked shelter. There was the platform and the pool. The best thing to do was to ignore this leaden feeling about the heart and rely on their common sense, their daylight sanity. Now that the tribe had eaten, the thing to do was to try again. And anyway, he couldn't stay here all night in an empty shelter by the deserted platform. His flesh crept and he shivered in the evening sun. No fire; no smoke; no rescue.

> [Jack launches a murderous manhunt for Ralph, who hides in the forest. After a time, he hears "a curious trickling sound and then a louder crepitation as if someone were unwrapping great sheets of cellophane." Smoke is flowing through the branches "in white and yellow wisps." Jack has started a forest fire in order to smoke Ralph out into the open. What can he do? He begins to panic. He might find a place away from the fire and climb a tree or he could try to burst their line. A third idea is to find a hiding place somewhere and hope his pursuers will pass by him.]

A nearer cry stood him on his feet and immediately he was away again, running fast among thorns and brambles. Suddenly he blundered into the open, found himself again in that open space—and there was the fathom-wide grin of the skull, no longer ridiculing a deep blue patch of sky but jeering up into a blanket of smoke. Then Ralph was running beneath trees, with the grumble of the forest explained. They had smoked him out and set the island on fire.

Hide was better than a tree because you had a chance of breaking the line if you were discovered.

Hide, then.

He wondered if a pig would agree, and grimaced at nothing. Find the deepest thicket, the darkest hole on the island, and creep in. Now, as he ran, he peered about him. Bars and splashes of sunlight flitted over him and sweat made glistening streaks on his dirty body. The cries were far now, and faint.

At last he found what seemed to him the right place, though the decision was desperate. Here, bushes and a wild tangle of creeper made a mat that kept out all the light of the sun. Beneath it was a space, perhaps a foot high, though it was pierced everywhere by parallel and rising stems. If you wormed into the middle of that you would be five yards from the edge, and hidden, unless the savage chose to lie down and look for you; and even then, you would be in darkness—and if the worst happened and he saw you, then you had a chance to burst out at him, fling the whole line out of step and double back.

Cautiously, his stick trailing behind him, Ralph wormed between the rising stems. When he reached the middle of the mat he lay and listened.

The fire was a big one and the drum-roll that he had thought was left so far behind was nearer. Couldn't a fire out-run a galloping horse? He could see the sun-splashed ground over an area of perhaps fifty yards from where he lay: and as he watched, the sunlight in every patch blinked at him. This was so like the curtain that flapped in his brain that for a moment he thought the blinking was inside him. But then the patches blinked more rapidly, dulled and went out, so that he saw that a great heaviness of smoke lay between the island and the sun.

If anyone peered under the bushes and chanced to glimpse human flesh it might be Samneric who would pretend not to see and say nothing. He laid his cheek against the chocolate-coloured earth, licked his dry lips and closed his eyes. Under the thicket, the earth was vibrating very slightly; or perhaps there was a sound beneath the obvious thunder of the fire and scribbled ululations that was too low to hear.

Someone cried out. Ralph jerked his cheek off the earth and looked into the dulled light. They must be near now, he thought, and his chest began to thump. Hide, break the line, climb a tree—which was the best after all? The trouble was you only had one chance.

Now the fire was nearer; those volleying shots were great limbs, trunks even, bursting. The fools! The fools! The fire must be almost at the fruit trees—what would they eat to-morrow?

Ralph stirred restlessly in his narrow bed. One chanced nothing! What could they do? Beat him? So what? Kill him? A stick sharpened at both ends.

The cries, suddenly nearer, jerked him up. He could see a striped savage moving hastily out of a green tangle, and coming towards the mat where he hid, a savage who carried a spear. Ralph gripped his fingers into the earth. Be ready now, in case.

Ralph fumbled to hold his spear so that it was point foremost; and now he saw that the stick was sharpened at both ends.

The savage stopped fifteen yards away and uttered his cry.

Perhaps he can hear my heart over the noises of the fire. Don't scream. Get ready.

The savage moved forward so that you could only see him from the waist down. That was the butt of his spear. Now you could see him from the knee down. Don't scream.

A herd of pigs came squealing out of the greenery behind the savage and rushed away into the forest. Birds were screaming, mice shrieking, and a little hopping thing came under the mat and cowered.

Five yards away the savage stopped, standing right by the thicket, and cried out. Ralph drew his feet up and crouched. The stake was in his hands, the stake sharpened at both ends, the stake that vibrated so wildly, that grew long, short, light, heavy, light again.

The ululation spread from shore to shore. The savage knelt down by the edge of the thicket, and there were lights flickering in the forest behind him. You could see a knee disturb the mould. Now the other. Two hands. A spear.

A face.

The savage peered into the obscurity beneath the thicket. You could tell that he saw light on this side and on that, but not in the middle—there. In the middle was a blob of dark and the savage wrinkled up his face, trying to decipher the darkness.

The seconds lengthened. Ralph was looking straight into the savage's eyes.

Don't scream.

You'll get back.

Now he's seen you. He's making sure. A stick sharpened.

Ralph screamed, a scream of fright and anger and desperation. His legs straightened, the screams became continuous and foaming. He shot forward, burst the thicket, was in the open, screaming, snarling, bloody. He swung the stake and the savage tumbled over; but there were others coming towards him, crying out. He swerved as a spear flew past and then was silent, running. All at once the lights flickering ahead of him merged together, the roar of the forest rose to thunder and a tall bush directly in his path burst into a great fan-shaped flame. He swung to the right, running desperately fast, with the heat beating on his left side and the fire racing forward like a tide. The ululation rose behind him and spread along, a series of short sharp cries, the sighting call. A brown figure showed up at his right and fell away. They were all running, all crying out madly. He could hear them crashing in the undergrowth and on the left was the hot, bright thunder of the fire. He forgot his wounds, his hunger and thirst, and became fear; hopeless fear on flying feet, rushing through the forest towards the open beach. Spots jumped before his eyes and turned into red circles that expanded quickly till they passed out of sight. Below him, someone's legs were getting tired and the desperate ululation advanced like a jagged fringe of menace and was almost overhead.

He stumbled over a root and the cry that pursued him rose even higher. He saw a shelter burst into flames and the fire flapped at his right shoulder and there was the glitter of water. Then he was down, rolling over and over in the warm sand, crouching with arm up to ward off, trying to cry for mercy.

He staggered to his feet, tensed for more terrors, and looked up at a huge peaked cap. It was a white-topped cap, and above the green shade of the peak was a crown, an anchor, gold foliage. He saw white drill, epaulettes, a revolver, a row of gilt buttons down the front of a uniform.

A naval officer stood on the sand, looking down at Ralph in wary astonishment. On the beach behind him was a cutter, her bows hauled up and held by two ratings. In the stern-sheets another rating held a sub-machine gun.

The ululation faltered and died away.

The officer looked at Ralph doubtfully for a moment, then took his hand away from the butt of the revolver.

"Hullo."

Squirming a little, conscious of his filthy appearance, Ralph answered shyly.

"Hullo."

The officer nodded, as if a question had been answered.

"Are there any adults—any grown-ups with you?"

Dumbly, Ralph shook his head. He turned a half-pace on the sand. A semicircle of little boys, their bodies streaked with coloured clay, sharp sticks in their hands, were standing on the beach making no noise at all.

"Fun and games," said the officer.

The fire reached the coco-nut palms by the beach and swallowed them noisily. A flame, seemingly detached, swung like an acrobat and licked up the palm heads on the platform. The sky was black.

The officer grinned cheerfully at Ralph.

"We saw your smoke. What have you been doing? Having a war or something?"

Ralph nodded.

The officer inspected the little scarecrow in front of him. The kid needed a bath, a hair-cut, a nose-wipe and a good deal of ointment.

"Nobody killed, I hope? Any dead bodies?"

"Only two. And they've gone."

The officer leaned down and looked closely at Ralph.

"Two? Killed?"

Ralph nodded again. Behind him, the whole island was shuddering with flame. The officer knew, as a rule, when people were telling the truth. He whistled softly.

Other boys were appearing now, tiny tots some of them, brown, with the distended bellies of small savages. One of them came close to the officer and looked up.

"I'm, I'm——"

But there was no more to come. Percival Wemys Madison sought in his head for an incantation that had faded clean away.

The officer turned back to Ralph.

"We'll take you off. How many of you are there?"

Ralph shook his head. The officer looked past him to the group of painted boys.

"Who's boss here?"

"I am," said Ralph loudly.

A little boy who wore the remains of an extraordinary black cap on his red hair and who carried the remains of a pair of spectacles at his waist, started forward, then changed his mind and stood still.

"We saw your smoke. And you don't know how many of you there are?"

"No, sir."

"I should have thought," said the officer as he visualized the search before him, "I should have thought that a pack of British boys—you're all British aren't you?—would have been able to put up a better show than that—I mean——"

"It was like that at first," said Ralph, "before things——"

He stopped.

"We were together then——"

The officer nodded helpfully.

"I know. Jolly good show. Like the Coral Island."

Ralph looked at him dumbly. For a moment he had a fleeting picture of the strange glamour that had once invested the beaches. But the island was scorched up like dead wood—Simon was dead—and Jack had. . . . The tears began to flow and sobs shook him. He gave himself up to them now for the first time on the island; great, shuddering spasms of grief that seemed to wrench his whole body. His voice rose under the black smoke before the burning wreckage of the island; and infected by that emotion, the other little boys began to shake and sob too. And in the middle of them, with filthy body, matted hair, and unwiped nose, Ralph wept for the end of innocence, the darkness of man's heart, and the fall through the air of the true, wise friend called Piggy.

The officer, surrounded by these noises, was moved and a little embarrassed. He turned away to give them time to pull themselves together; and waited, allowing his eyes to rest on the trim cruiser in the distance.

For Further Reflection

1. What is the main idea about morality that you get out of this selection from *Lord of the Flies?*
2. Piggy tells Ralph that he is going to Jack to order him to return his glasses. "I don't ask for my glasses back as a favor . . . but because what's right's right. Give me my glasses. . . . You got to." What is Piggy presupposing about the situation and about the significance of morality? What is Jack's response? How does he further respond upon being called a thief? Why is he infuriated by that charge?
3. Compare Ralph's understanding of morality with Piggy's and Jack's. How do they exhibit different moral positions?
4. What, if anything, is the significance of the conch, and how do you interpret its destruction?

On the Nature and Purpose of Morality

Reflections on William Golding's Lord of the Flies

LOUIS P. POJMAN

Louis P. Pojman was a professor of philosophy at the United States Military Academy and the editor of this volume. In this essay he analyzes Golding's novel in terms of the nature and purpose of morality. He relates it to Hobbes's account in the Leviathan (see the next reading) and identifies the larger purposes of morality.

> Which is better—to have rules and agree, or to hunt and kill?
>
> —*Piggy*

> Morality is more honored in the breach than in the observance.
>
> —*Thomas Hobbes*

Why exactly do we need moral codes? What function do they play in our lives and in society in general? William Golding's classic novel *Lord of the Flies* (1954), a modern moral allegory, abridged in the previous reading, may provide us with a clue to the answer to these questions.

Golding's allegory is a response to a Victorian British children's classic, *The Coral Island* (1858), by Robert Ballantyne, in which three teenage boys are shipwrecked on an unidentified Pacific island: Ralph Rover, the fifteen-year-old narrator, Jack Martin, and the creative and wise Peterkin Gay. These boys prove to be ideal Englishmen and live in uninterrupted harmony, a utopia, until they encounter cannibals who capture them. But just when the cannibals are about to boil them for dinner, missionaries arrive who convert the cannibals and liberate them from heathen darkness and the boys from the dark cauldron. The book was written as a refutation of the prevailing Calvinist and Puritan doctrine of original sin, which holds that human nature is ineluctably perverse. In *The Coral Island,* human nature is essentially good.

Since then, two traumatic, cataclysmic world wars have disabused us of such Pollyanna-like humanism and the age of innocence. Golding transforms Ralph Rover into Ralph, the commonsensical, decent, and likable leader; Jack Martin into the rapacious and Dionysian Jack Merridew, redheaded rival of Ralph, who demands the position of leadership because he is head choirboy and can sing C-sharp; and creative and wise Peterkin into two persons, Simon, the clairvoyant, mystical epileptic, and Piggy, the asthmatic, myopic philosopher, the conscience of Ralph.

Lord of the Flies is the antithesis of *The Coral Island.* It portrays the very opposite of the Victorian utopia, a dystopia, a virtual hell. Jack overthrows Ralph as the leader, and with him, humane rules. The unbridled lust for excitement leads to the great orgiastic pig-kills, the sodomizing of a female pig, and finally, at its nadir, to the thirst for human blood. They turn into savages, sadistically hunting, "Kill the beast! Cut its throat! Spill its blood!" In their Dionysian frenzy, they mistake Simon for a beast and kill him. Piggy has his glasses stolen with impunity and is sadistically murdered. Ralph, who resists the depravity to the end, is hunted like a pig and is about to be destroyed when the British navy, seeing the smoke of the burning jungle, comes to the rescue.

What is Golding trying to tell us? E. L. Epstein comments on his work:

> The theme is an attempt to trace the defects of society back to the defects of human nature. The moral is that the shape of a society must depend on the ethical nature of the individual and not on any political system however apparently logical or respectable. The whole book is symbolic in nature except the rescue in the end where adult life appears, dignified and capable, but in reality enmeshed in the same evil as the symbolic life of the children on the island. The officer, having interrupted a manhunt [of Ralph], prepares to take the children off the island in a cruiser which will presently be hunting its enemy in the same implacable way. And who will rescue the adult and his cruiser?[1]

Civilization's power is weak and vulnerable to atavistic, volcanic passions. The sensitive Simon, the symbol of religious consciousness (as in "Simon Peter," the first disciple of Jesus), who prophesies that Ralph will be saved and is the first to discover and fight against the "ancient, inescapable recognition" of the beast in us, is slaughtered by the group in a wild frenzy. Only Piggy and

[1]E. L. Epstein, "Notes on *Lord of the Flies,*" in William Golding, *Lord of the Flies* (New York: G. P. Putnam, 1959), pp. 250–51.

Ralph, mere observers of the orgiastic homicide, feel vicarious pangs of guilt at this atrocity.

The incarnation of philosophy and culture—poor, fat, nearsighted Piggy, with his broken spectacles and asthma—becomes ever more pathetic as the chaos increases. The nadir of his ridiculous position is reached after the rebels, led by Jack, steal his spectacles in order to harness the sun's rays for starting fires. After Ralph, the emblem of not too bright but morally good civilized leadership, fails to persuade Jack to return the glasses, Piggy asserts his moral right to them:

> You're stronger than I am and you haven't got asthma. You can see. . . . But I don't ask for my glasses back, not as a favour. I don't ask you to be a sport . . . not because you're strong, but because what's right's right. Give me my glasses. . . . You got to. (p. 211)

Piggy might as well have addressed the fire itself, for in this state of anarchy moral discourse is a foreign tongue that only incites the worst elements to greater immorality. Roger, Jack's sadistic lieutenant, perched on a cliff above, finally liberated from the constraints which held back his arm from harming little Henry, responds to moral reasoning by dislodging a huge rock from a cliff that hits Piggy and flings him to his death forty feet below.

The title *Lord of the Flies* comes from a translation of the Greek *Beelzebub,* which is a name for the devil. The boys are frightened by shadowy figures which they imagine to be a supernatural beast, but, as the prophetic Simon points out, "Maybe [the beast] is only us." We need no external devil to bring about evil. We have found the devil and, in the words of Pogo, "he is us." Ubiquitous, ever waiting for a moment to strike out, he emerges from the depths of the subconscious whenever there is a conflict of interest or a moment of moral lassitude. As E. L. Epstein says, "The tenets of civilization, the moral and social codes, the Ego, the intelligence itself, form only a veneer over this white-hot power, this uncontrollable force, 'the fury and the mire of human veins.'"[2]

Beelzebub's ascendancy proceeds through fear, hysteria, violence, and death. A delegation starts out hunting pigs for meat. The hunters quickly find themselves enjoying the excitement, the violence, the bloody destruction of the pig, the symbol of the beast. In order to drown the incipient shame over bloodthirstiness, and take on a persona more compatible with their deed, the children paint themselves with colored mud. Their lusting for the kill takes on all the powerful overtones of an orgiastic sexual ritual, including ritual, sadistic sodomy, as they lunge the wooden spear up the rectum of the female pig. Liberated from their social selves, they kill without remorse whoever gets

[2]Op. cit., p. 252.

in their way. The death of Simon and Piggy (the symbols of the religious and the philosophical, the two great fences blocking the descent to hell) and the final orgiastic hunt with the "spear sharpened at both ends" signal for Ralph the depths of evil in the human heart.

Ironically, it is the British navy that finally comes to the rescue and saves Ralph (civilization) just when all seems lost. But the symbol of the navy is a Janus-faced omen. On the one hand it may symbolize the fact that a military defense is, unfortunately, sometimes needed to save civilization from the barbarians (Hilter's Nazis or Jack and Roger's allies), but on the other hand it symbolizes the quest for blood and vengeance latent in contemporary civilization. The children's world is really only a stage lower than the adult world whence they come, and that shallow civilization could very well regress to tooth and claw if it were scratched too sharply. The children were saved by the adults, but who will save the adults, who put so much emphasis on military enterprises and weapons systems—in the euphemistic name of "defense"? To quote Epstein:

> The officer, having interrupted a man-hunt, prepares to take the children off the island in a cruiser which will presently be hunting its enemy in the same implacable way. And who will rescue the adult and his cruiser?[3]

The fundamental ambiguity of human existence is seen in every section of the book, poignantly mirroring the human condition. Even Piggy's spectacles, the sole example of modern technology on the island, become a bane for the island as Jack uses them to ignite a forest fire that will smoke out their prey, Ralph, and that ends up burning down the entire forest and destroying the island's animal life. The spectacles are a symbol both of our penchant for misusing technology to vitiate the environment and of our ability to create weapons that will lead to global suicide.

Golding is trying to place his finger on a defect of human nature. What exactly is that defect? An older theological term for it is *original sin,* a certain tendency to assert one's ego against God and the social good. One need not be a theist with a concept of sin to accept this message: human nature has a tendency to selfishness, to a desperate egotism, which, in appropriate circumstances, is all too willing to harm others unjustly. Cut off from the sanctions of adult civilization, these preteens lack the resources to sustain the institutions that would mitigate the damage of unbridled egoism.

Ask yourself, What could make the difference between the dystopia of *Lord of the Flies* and the utopia of *The Coral Island*? Could you rewrite Golding's book in order to achieve an opposite ending? I had a conversation with a

[3]Op. cit., p. 251.

Bucknell University philosophy student, Coleen Zoller, who said that she thinks *Lord of the Flies* is a very male book, illustrating the worst kind of male behavior. "Women would typically act differently. They would stress cooperation and caring for one another. The process would be quite different." Do you think this is true? Can you imagine different young people acting better?

WHY DO WE NEED MORALITY? HOBBES'S ACCOUNT

Why do we need morality? What is its nature and purpose? What does it do for us that no other social arrangement does? There are many philosophical replies to these questions, but a classic reply, one relevant to the situation of *Lord of the Flies,* is that given by the English philosopher Thomas Hobbes (1588–1679) in his book *Leviathan* (1651). Hobbes believed that human beings always act out of perceived self-interest, that is, they invariably seek gratification and avoid harm. His argument goes like this:

Nature has made us basically equal in physical and mental abilities, so that while one person may be somewhat stronger or have a higher IQ than another, each has the ability to harm, even kill, the other, if not alone, then in confederacy with others. Furthermore, we all want to attain our goals, including sufficient food, shelter, security, power, wealth, and other scarce resources. These two facts, equality of ability to harm and desire to attain our goals, lead to an unstable state.

> From this equality of ability arises equality of hope in the attaining of our ends. And therefore if any two people desire the same thing, which nevertheless they cannot both enjoy, they become enemies; and in the way to their end, which is principally their own preservation and sometimes their enjoyment only, endeavor to destroy, or subdue one another. And from hence it comes to pass, that where an invader hath no more to fear, than another man's single power; if one plant, sow, build, or possess a convenient seat, others may probably be expected to come prepared with forces united, to dispossess, and deprive him, not only of the fruit of his labor, but also of his life or liberty. And the invader again is in the like danger of another.[4]

Given this state of insecurity, people have reason to fear one another. Hobbes calls this a "state of nature," one in which there are no common ways of life, no laws or moral rules which are enforced, no justice or injustice, for these concepts lack application. There are no reliable expectations about

[4]Thomas Hobbes, *Leviathan* (1651), chapter 13.

other people's behavior—except that they will follow their own inclinations and perceived interests, tending to be arbitrary, violent, and capricious.

> Hereby it is manifest, that during the time men live without a common power to keep them all in awe, they are in that condition which is called war; and such a war, as is for *every man, against every man.* For war consists not in battle only or in the act of fighting; but in a tract of time, wherein the will to contend in battle is sufficiently known: and therefore the notion of *time,* is to be considered in the nature of war; as it is in the nature of weather. For as the nature of foul weather lies not in the shower or two of rain, but in an inclination thereto of many days together; so the nature of war consists not in actual fighting, but in the known disposition thereto, during all the time there is no disposition to the contrary.

The consequence of the state of nature, this war of all against all, is described thusly:

> In such condition, there is no place for industry; because the fruit thereof is uncertain: and consequently no culture of the earth; no navigation, nor use of the commodities that may be imported by sea; no commodious buildings; no instruments of moving, and removing, such things as require much force; no knowledge of the face of the earth; no account of time; no arts; no literature; no society; and which is worst of all, continual fear, and danger of violent death; and the life of man solitary, poor, nasty, brutish and short.

But this state of nature, or more exactly, state of anarchy and chaos, is in no one's interest. We can all do better if we compromise, give up some of our natural liberty—to do as we please—so that we will all be more likely to get what we want: security, happiness, power, prosperity, and peace. So rational egoists that we are, according to Hobbes, we exchange some of our liberty for a *social contract* or *covenant,* wherein a ruler and rules are set over us, which we are to obey, since they are enforced by a mighty ruler, the State, the *Leviathan.* Only within this contract does morality arise and do justice, and injustice come into being. Where there is no enforceable law, there is neither right nor wrong, justice nor injustice.

So morality is a form of social control. We all opt for an enforceable set of rules which *if almost all of us obey almost all of the time almost all will be better off almost all of the time.* A select few, conceivably, might be better off in the state of nature, but the vast majority will be better off in a situation of security and mutual cooperation. It may turn out that some people cheat, renege on their contract, but so long as the adherence is widespread by most of us most of the time, we will all flourish.

Hobbes didn't claim that a pure state of nature ever existed or that humanity ever really formally entered into such a contract, though he notes that among nations such a state actually exists, so that a "cold war" keeps us all in fear. Rather, Hobbes is offering an explanation of the function of morality. He is answering the question, Why do we need morality. Why? Because without it existence would be an unbearable hell in which life was "solitary, poor, nasty, brutish and short."

THE PURPOSES OF MORALITY

What is the role of morality in human existence? What are little boys and girls and big men and women made of that requires ethical consciousness? Ralph answers these questions at the end of *Lord of the Flies.*

> And in the middle of [the children], with filthy body, matted hair, and unwiped nose, Ralph wept for the end of innocence, the darkness of man's heart, and the fall through the air of the true, wise friend called Piggy. (p. 248)

In this wise modern moral allegory, we catch a glimpse of some of the purposes of morality. Rules formed over the ages and internalized within us hold us back and hopefully defeat the "Lord of the Flies" in society, whether he be inherent in us individually or an emergent property of corporate existence. The moral code restrains even the sadistic Rogers of society from evil until untoward social conditions open up the sluice gates of sadism and random violence. Morality is the force that enables Piggy and Ralph to maintain a modicum of order within their dwindling society, first motivating them to compromise with Jack and then keeping things in a wider perspective.

In Golding's allegory, morality is "honored more in the breach than in the observance," for we see the consequences of not having rules and principles and virtuous character. As Piggy says, "Which is better—to have rules and agree, or to hunt and kill [each other]?" Morality consists of a set of rules which if followed by nearly everyone will promote the flourishing of nearly everyone. These rules restrict our freedom but only in order to promote greater freedom and well-being. More specifically morality seems to have these five purposes:

1. To keep society from falling apart.
2. To ameliorate human suffering.
3. To promote human flourishing.
4. To resolve conflicts of interest in just and orderly ways.
5. To assign praise and blame, reward the good and punish the guilty.

Let us elaborate these purposes. Imagine what society would be if everyone or nearly everyone did whatever he or she pleased, disregarding basic moral rules. I would make a promise to you to help you with your philosophy homework tomorrow if you fix my car today. You believe me. So you fix my car, but you are deeply angry when I laugh at you on the morrow when I drive away to the beach instead of helping you with your homework. Or you loan me money but I run off with it. Or I lie to you or harm you when it is in my interest or even kill you when I feel the urge.

In such a society parents would abandon or abuse their children and spouses betray each other whenever it was convenient. The very notion of a *spouse* would be meaningless, since it connotes commitment, loyalty, fidelity, all of which are *moral* notions. No one would have an incentive to cooperate or help anyone else because reciprocity (a moral principle) would not be recognized. Great suffering would go largely unameliorated and, certainly, people would not be very happy. We would not flourish or reach our highest potential. Under such circumstances society would break down. Even thieves must adhere to moral rules with each other, if they have any hope of robbing others.

In 1995 I visited the former USSR countries Kazakhstan and Russia, which are undergoing a difficult transition from communism to democracy (which hopefully will be resolved favorably). In this transition, with the state's power considerably withdrawn, crime is on the increase and distrust is prevalent. At night I had to navigate my way up the staircases in our apartment building in complete darkness. I inquired as to why there were no light bulbs in the stairwells, only to be told that the residents stole them, believing that if they did not take them, their neighbors would. Without a dominant authority, the former Communist authorities, the social contract has eroded and everyone must struggle alone in the darkness.

We need moral rules to guide our actions in ways that light up our paths and prevent and reduce suffering, that enhance human (and animal, for that matter) well-being, that allow us to resolve our conflicts of interests according to recognizably fair rules, and to assign responsibility for actions, so that we can praise and blame, reward and punish people according to how their actions reflect moral principles.

Even though these five purposes are related, they are not identical, and different moral theories emphasize different purposes and in different ways. Utilitarianism stresses human flourishing and the amelioration of suffering, whereas contractual systems rooted in rational self-interest accent the role of resolving conflicts of interest. A complete moral theory would include a place for each of these purposes. Such a system has the goal of internalizing the rules that promote these principles in each moral person's life, producing the virtuous person, someone who is "a jewel that shines in [morality's] own light," to paraphrase Kant. It is fair to say that morality is a necessary condition for happiness. Whether it is also a sufficient condition for happiness is more controversial, a question we shall consider in Part III. The goal of morality is to create happy and virtuous people, the kind that create flourishing communities. That's why it is the most important subject on earth.

For Further Reflection

1. What, according to Pojman, is the main message of *Lord of the Flies?* Do you agree? Explain.
2. How does Pojman relate Golding's novel to Hobbes's account of morality?
3. Discuss Pojman's five purposes of morality. Do you agree morality has all of these purposes? If not, explain. Can you think of other purposes it has?

On the State of Nature

THOMAS HOBBES

Thomas Hobbes (1588–1679), the greatest English political philosopher, set forth the classic version of the idea that morality and politics arise out of a social contract. He was born on Good Friday, April 5, 1588, in Westbury, England, the son of an eccentric vicar. On the day of his birth the Spanish Armada, the greatest naval fleet the world had then seen, was spotted off the coast of southern England. The chronicler John Aubrey reports that Hobbes's mother, only seven months pregnant, startled by the news, fell into labor and delivered him. Hobbes wrote of this experience, "Unbeknownst to my mother at that time she gave birth to twins, myself and fear. And fear has been my constant companion throughout life." Hobbes's lifetime was filled with the dangers of war, the invading Spanish Armada, the religious wars of Europe, and the series of civil wars in England. His political philosophy may be read as a defense against the fear and insecurity of people desperately in need of peace and tranquility. Hobbes was educated at Oxford University and lived through an era of political revolutions as a scholar and tutor (to the future Charles II).

From Thomas Hobbes, *Leviathan,* 1651.

Hobbes is known today primarily for his masterpiece in political theory, *Leviathan* (1651), a book written during the English civil wars (1642–1652), sometimes referred to as "the Great Rebellion," which pitted the forces of monarchy (the Royalists) under Charles I against those of Parliament under Oliver Cromwell. Hobbes's work was intended to support the Royalists, as he believed that the monarchy was the best guarantee for orderly and stable government. Yet the Royalists misconstrued his interpretation as supporting the rebels, no doubt because Hobbes rejected the usual grounds for the monarchy, the divine right of kings. For this reason, and because the book conveyed a materialist view of human nature that was thought to be dangerous to religion, it was suppressed or violently attacked throughout Hobbes's lifetime.

What are the doctrines his contemporaries found so controversial? First of all, Hobbes breaks from the medieval notion that the state is a natural organism, based on natural devotion and interdependence. He develops a moral and political theory based not on natural affection but on psychological egoism. Hobbes argues that people are all egoists who always act in their own self-interest to obtain gratification and avoid harm. However, we cannot obtain any of the basic goods because of the inherent fear of harm and death that result from the insecurity in an unregulated "state of nature," in which life is "solitary, poor, nasty, brutish and short." We cannot relax our guard, for everyone is constantly in fear of everyone else. In this state of anarchy the prudent person concludes that it really is in all our self-interest to make a contract to keep to a minimal morality of respecting human life, keeping covenants made, and obeying the laws of the society. This minimal morality, which Hobbes refers to as "the laws of nature," is nothing more than a set of maxims of prudence. In order to ensure that we all obey this covenant Hobbes proposes a strong sovereign or "Leviathan" to impose severe penalties on those who disobey the laws, for "covenants without the sword are but words."*

*The term *Leviathan* refers to the sea monster (or whale) referred to in the Book of Job:

> Let those curse the day who are skilled to rouse up Leviathan (3:8) . . .
> Can you draw out Leviathan with a fishhook or press down his tongue with a cord?
> Can you put a rope in his nose or pierce his jaw with a hook? . . .
> Will he make a covenant with you to take him for your servant for ever? . . .
> His sneezings flash forth light, and his eyes are like the eyelids of the dawn.
> Out of his mouth go flaming torches; sparks of fire leap forth.
> Out of his nostrils comes forth smoke, as from a boiling pot and burning rushes.
> His breath kindles coals, and flame comes forth from his mouth. . . .
> When he raises himself up the mighty are afraid; at the crashing they are beside themselves. . . .
> Upon earth there is not his like, a creature without fear.
> He beholds everything that is high; he is king over all the sons of pride. (Job 41)

OF THE NATURAL CONDITION OF MANKIND AS CONCERNING THEIR FELICITY, AND MISERY

Nature hath made men so equal, in the faculties of the body, and mind; as that though there be found one man sometimes manifestly stronger in body, or of quicker mind than another; yet when all is reckoned together, the difference between man, and man, is not so considerable, as that one man can thereupon claim to himself any benefit, to which another may not pretend, as well as he. For as to the strength of body, the weakest has strength enough to kill the strongest, either by secret machination, or by confederacy with others, that are in the same danger with himself.

And as to the faculties of the mind, setting aside the arts grounded upon words, and especially that skill of proceeding upon general, and infallible rules, called science; which very few have, and but in few things; as being not a native faculty, born with us; nor attained, as prudence, while we look after somewhat else, I find yet a greater equality amongst men, than that of strength. For prudence, is but experience; which equal time, equally bestows on all men, in those things they equally apply themselves unto. That which may perhaps make such equality incredible, is but a vain conceit of one's own wisdom, which almost all men think they have in a greater degree, than the vulgar; that is, than all men but themselves, and a few others, whom by fame, or for concurring with themselves, they approve. For such is the nature of men, that howsoever they may acknowledge many others to be more witty, or more eloquent, or more learned; yet they will hardly believe there be many so wise as themselves; for they see their own wit at hand, and other men's at a distance. But this proveth rather that men are in that point equal, than unequal. For there is not ordinarily a greater sign of the equal distribution of any thing, than that every man is contented with his share.

From this equality of ability, ariseth equality of hope in the attaining of our ends. And therefore if any two men desire the same thing, which nevertheless they cannot both enjoy, they become enemies; and in the way to their end, which is principally their own conservation, and sometimes their delectation only, endeavour to destroy, or subdue one another. And from hence it comes to pass, that where an invader hath no more to fear, than another man's single power; if one plant, sow, build, or possess a convenient seat, others may probably be expected to come prepared with forces united, to dispossess, and deprive him, not only of the fruit of his labour, but also of his life, or liberty. And the invader again is in the like danger of another.

And from this diffidence of one another, there is no way for any man to secure himself, so reasonable, as anticipation; that is, by force, or wiles, to master the persons of all men he can, so long, till he see no other power great enough to endanger him: and this is no more than his own conservation requireth, and is generally allowed. Also because there be some, that taking pleasure in contemplating their own power in the acts of conquest, which they pursue farther than their security requires; if others, that otherwise would be glad to be at ease within modest bounds, should not by invasion increase their power, they would not be able, long time, by standing only on their defence, to subsist. And by consequence, such augmentation of dominion over men being necessary to a man's conservation, it ought to be allowed him.

Again, men have no pleasure, but on the contrary a great deal of grief, in keeping company, where there is no power able to over-awe them all. For every man looketh that his companion should value him, at the same rate he sets upon himself: and upon all signs of contempt, or undervaluing, naturally endeavours, as far as he dares, (which amongst them that have no common power to keep them in quiet, is far enough to make them destroy each other), to extort a greater value from his contemners, by damage; and from others, by the example.

So that in the nature of man, we find three principal causes of quarrel. First, competition; secondly, diffidence; thirdly, glory.

The first, maketh men invade for gain; the second, for safety; and the third, for reputation. The first use violence, to make themselves masters of other men's persons, wives, children, and cattle; the second, defend them; the third, for trifles, as a word, a smile, a different opinion, and any other sign of undervalue, either direct in their persons, or by reflection in their kindred, their friends, their nation, their profession, or their name.

Hereby it is manifest, that during the time men live without a common power to keep them all in awe, they are in that condition which is called war; and such a war, as is of every man, against every man. For war, consisteth not in battle only, or the act of fighting; but in a tract of time, wherein the will to contend by battle is sufficiently known: and therefore the notion of *time*, is to be considered in the nature of war; as it is in the nature of weather. For as the nature of foul weather, lieth not in the shower or two of rain; but in an inclination thereto of many days together: so the nature of war, consisteth not in actual fighting; but in the known disposition thereto, during all the time there is no assurance to the contrary. All other time is PEACE.

Whatsoever therefore is consequent to a time of war, where every man is enemy to every man; the same is consequent to the time, wherein men live without other security, than what their own strength, and their own invention shall furnish them withal. In such condition, there is no place for industry; because the fruit thereof is uncertain: and consequently no culture of the earth; no navigation, nor use of the commodities that may be imported by sea; no commodious building; no instruments of moving, and removing, such things as require much force; no knowledge of the face of the earth; no account of time; no arts; no letters; no society; and which is worst of all, continual fear, and danger of violent death; and the life of man, solitary, poor, nasty, brutish, and short.

It may seem strange to some man, that has not well weighed these things; that nature should thus dissociate, and render men apt to invade, and destroy one another: and he may therefore, not trusting to this inference, made from the passions, desire perhaps to have the same confirmed by experience. Let him therefore consider with himself, when taking a journey, he arms himself, and seeks to go well accompanied; when going to sleep, he locks his doors; when even in his house he locks his chests; and this when he knows there be laws, and public officers, armed, to revenge all injuries shall be done him; what opinion he has of his fellow-subjects, when he rides armed; of his fellow citizens, when he locks his doors; and of his children, and servants, when he locks his chests. Does he not there as much accuse mankind by his actions, as I do by my words? But neither of us accuse man's nature in it. The desires, and other passions of man, are in themselves no sin. No more are the actions, that proceed from those passions, till they know a law that forbids them: which till laws be made they cannot know: nor can any law be made, till they have agreed upon the person that shall make it.

It may peradventure be thought, there was never such a time, nor condition of war as this; and I believe it was never generally so, over all the world: but there are many places, where they live so now. For the savage people in many places of America, except the government of small families, the concord whereof dependeth on natural lust, have no government at all; and live at this day in that brutish manner, as I said before. Howsoever, it may be perceived what manner of life there would be, where there were no common power to fear, by the manner of life, which men that have formerly lived under a peaceful government, use to degenerate into, in a civil war.

But though there had never been any time, wherein particular men were in a condition of war one against another; yet in all times, kings, and persons of sovereign authority, because of their independency, are in continual jealousies, and in the state and posture of gladiators; having their weapons pointing, and their eyes fixed on one another; that is, their forts, garrisons, and guns upon the frontiers of their kingdoms; and continual spies upon their neighbours; which is a posture of war. But because they uphold thereby, the industry of their subjects; there does not follow from it, that misery, which accompanies the liberty of particular men.

To this war of every man, against every man, this also is consequent; that nothing can be unjust. The notions of right and wrong, justice and injustice have there no place. Where there is no common power, there is no law: where no law, no injustice. Force, and fraud, are in war the two cardinal virtues. Justice, and injustice are none of the faculties neither of the body, nor mind. If they were, they might be in a man that were alone in the world, as well as his senses, and passions. They are qualities, that relate to men in society, not in solitude. It is consequent also to the same condition, that there be no propriety, no dominion, no *mine* and *thine* distinct; but only that to be every man's, that he can get; and for so long, as he can keep it. And thus much for the ill condition, which man by mere nature is actually placed in; though with a possibility to come out of it, consisting partly in the passions, partly in his reason.

The passions that incline men to peace, are fear of death; desire of such things as are necessary to commodious living; and a hope by their industry to obtain them. And reason suggesteth convenient articles of peace, upon which men may be drawn to agreement. These articles, are they, which otherwise are called the Laws of Nature: whereof I shall speak more particularly, in the two following chapters.

OF THE FIRST AND SECOND NATURAL LAWS, AND OF CONTRACTS

The right of nature, which writers commonly call *jus naturale,* is the liberty each man hath, to use his own power, as he will himself, for the preservation of his own nature; that is to say, of his own life; and consequently, of doing any thing, which in his own judgment, and reason, he shall conceive to be the aptest means thereunto.

By LIBERTY, is understood, according to the proper signification of the word, the absence of external impediments: which impediments, may oft take away part of a man's power to do what he would; but cannot hinder him from using the power left him, according as his judgment, and reason shall dictate to him.

A LAW OF NATURE, *lex naturalis,* is a precept or general rule, found out by reason, by which a man is forbidden to do that, which is destructive of his life, or taketh away the means of preserving the same; and to omit that, by which he thinketh it may be best preserved. For though they that speak of this subject, use to confound *jus,* and *lex, right* and *law:* yet they ought to be distinguished; because RIGHT, consisteth in liberty to do, or to forbear; whereas LAW, determineth, and bindeth to one of them: so that law, and right, differ as much, as obligation, and liberty; which in one and the same matter are inconsistent.

And because the condition of man, as hath been declared in the precedent chapter, is a condition of war of every one against every one; in which case every one is governed by his own reason; and there is nothing he can make use of, that may not be a help unto him, in preserving his life against his enemies; it followeth, that in such a condition, every man has a right to every thing; even to one another's body. And therefore, as long as this natural right of every man to every thing endureth, there can be no security to any man, how strong or wise soever he be, of living out the time, which nature ordinarily alloweth men to live. And consequently it is a precept, or general rule of reason, *that every man, ought to endeavour peace, as far as he has hope of obtaining it; and when he cannot obtain it, that he may seek, and use, all helps, and advantages of war.* The first branch of which rule, containeth the first, and fundamental law of nature; which is, *to seek peace, and follow it.* The second, the sum of the right of nature; which is, *by all means we can, to defend ourselves.*

From this fundamental law of nature, by which men are commanded to endeavour peace, is derived this second law; *that a man be willing, when others are so too, as far-forth, as for peace, and defence of himself he shall think it necessary, to lay down this right to all things; and be contented with so much liberty against other men, as he would allow other men against himself.* For as long as every man holdeth this right, of doing any thing he liketh; so long are all men in the condition of war. But if other men will not lay down their right, as well as he; then there is no reason for any one, to divest himself of his: for that were to expose himself to prey, which no man is bound to, rather than to dispose himself to peace. This is that law of the Gospel; *whatsoever you require that others should do to you, that do ye to them. And that law of all men, quod tibi fieri non vis, alteri ne feceris.*[1]

To *lay down* a man's *right* to any thing, is to *divest* himself of the *liberty*, of hindering another of the benefit of his own right to the same. For he that renounceth, or passeth away his right, giveth not to any other man a right which he had not before; because there is nothing to which every man had not right by nature: but only standeth out of his way, that he may enjoy his own original right, without hindrance from him; not without hindrance from another. So that the effect which redoundeth to one man, by another man's defect of right, is but so much diminution of impediments to the use of his own right original.

Right is laid aside, either by simply renouncing it; or by transferring it to another. By *simply* RENOUNCING; when he cares not to whom the benefit thereof redoundeth. By TRANSFERRING; when he intendeth the benefit thereof to some certain person, or persons. And when a man hath in either manner

[1] ["What you do not want done to you, do not do to others."—ed. note]

abandoned, or granted away his right; then is he said to be OBLIGED, or BOUND, not to hinder those, to whom such right is granted, or abandoned, from the benefit of it: and that he *ought,* and it is his DUTY, not to make void that voluntary act of his own: and that such hindrance is INJUSTICE, and INJURY, as being *sine jure,*[2] the right being before renounced, or transferred. So that *injury,* or *injustice,* in the controversies of the world, is somewhat like to that, which in the disputations of scholars is called *absurdity.* For as it is there called an absurdity, to contradict what one maintained in the beginning: so in the world, it is called injustice, and injury, voluntarily to undo that, which from the beginning he had voluntarily done. The way by which a man either simply renounceth, or transferreth his right, is a declaration, or signification, by some voluntary and sufficient sign, or signs, that he doth so renounce, or transfer; or hath so renounced, or transferred the same, to him that accepteth it. And these signs are either words only, or actions only; or, as it happeneth most often, both words, and actions. And the same are the BONDS, by which men are bound, and obliged: bonds, that have their strength, not from their own nature, for nothing is more easily broken than a man's word, but from fear of some evil consequence upon the rupture.

Whensoever a man transferreth his right, or renounceth it; it is either in consideration of some right reciprocally transferred to himself; or for some other good he hopeth for thereby. For it is a voluntary act: and of the voluntary acts of every man, the object is some *good to himself.* And therefore there be some rights, which no man can be understood by any words, or other signs, to have abandoned, or transferred. At first a man cannot lay down the right of resisting them, that assault him by force, to take away his life; because he cannot be understood to aim thereby, at any good to himself. The same may be said of wounds, and chains, and imprisonment; both because there is no benefit consequent to such patience; as there is to the patience of suffering another to be wounded, or imprisoned: as also because a man cannot tell, when he seeth men proceed against him by violence, whether they intend his death or not. And lastly the motive, and end for which this renouncing, and transferring of right is introduced, is nothing else but the security of a man's person, in his life, and in the means of so preserving life, as not to be weary of it. And therefore if a man by words, or other signs, seem to despoil himself of the end, for which those signs were intended; he is not to be understood as if he meant it, or that it was his will; but that he was ignorant of how such words and actions were to be interpreted.

The mutual transferring of right, is that which men call CONTRACT.

[2][That is, without right.—ed. note]

There is a difference between transferring of right to the thing; and transferring, or tradition, that is delivery of the thing itself. For the thing may be delivered together with the translation of the right; as in buying and selling with ready-money; or exchange of goods, or lands: and it may be delivered some time after.

Again, one of the contractors, may deliver the thing contracted for on his part, and leave the other to perform his part at some determinate time after, and in the mean time be trusted; and then the contract on his part, is called PACT, or COVENANT: or both parts may contract now, to perform hereafter: in which cases, he that is to perform in time to come, being trusted, his performance is called *keeping of promise,* or faith; and the failing of performance, if it be voluntary, *violation of faith.*

When the transferring of right, is not mutual: but one of the parties transferreth, in hope to gain thereby friendship, or service from another, or from his friends; or in hope to gain the reputation of charity, or magnanimity; or to deliver his mind from the pain of compassion; or in hope of reward in heaven, this is not contract, but GIFT, FREE-GIFT, GRACE: which words signify one and the same thing.

Signs of contract, are either *express,* or *by inference.* Express, are words spoken with understanding of what they signify: and such words are either of the time *present,* or *past;* as, *I give, I grant, I have given, I have granted, I will that this be yours:* or of the future; as, *I will give, I will grant:* which words of the future are called PROMISE.

If a covenant be made, wherein neither of the parties perform presently, but trust one another; in the condition of mere nature, which is a condition of war of every man against every man, upon any reasonable suspicion, it is void: but if there be a common power set over them both, with right and force sufficient to compel performance, it is not void. For he that performeth first, has no assurance the other will perform after; because the bonds of words are too weak to bridle men's ambition, avarice, anger, and other passions, without the fear of some coercive power; which in the condition of mere nature, where all men are equal, and judges of the justness of their own fears, cannot possibly be supposed. And therefore he which performeth first, does but betray himself to his enemy; contrary to the right, he can never abandon, of defending his life, and means of living.

But in a civil estate, where there is a power set up to constrain those that would otherwise violate their faith, that fear is no more reasonable: and for that cause, he which by the covenant is to perform first, is obliged so to do.

The cause of fear, which maketh such a covenant invalid, must be always something arising after the covenant made; as some new fact, or other sign of the will not to perform: else it cannot make the covenant void. For that which could not hinder a man from promising, ought not to be admitted as a hindrance of performing.

OF OTHER LAWS OF NATURE

From that law of nature, by which we are obliged to transfer to another, such rights, as being retained, hinder the peace of mankind, there followeth a third; which is this, *that men perform their covenants made:* without which, covenants are in vain, and but empty words; and the right of all men to all things remaining, we are still in the condition of war.

And in this law of nature, consisteth the fountain and original of JUSTICE. For where no covenant hath preceded, there hath no right been transferred, and every man has right to every thing; and consequently, no action can be unjust. But when a covenant is made, then to break it is *unjust:* and the definition of INJUSTICE, is no other than *the not performance of covenant.* And whatsoever is not unjust, is *just.*

But because covenants of mutual trust, where there is a fear of not performance on either part, as hath been said in the former chapter, are invalid; though the original of justice be the making of covenants; yet injustice actually there can be none, till the cause of such fear be taken away; which while men are in the natural condition of war, cannot be done. Therefore before the names of just, and unjust can have place, there must be some coercive power, to compel men equally to the performance of their covenants, by the terror of some punishment, greater than the benefit they expect by the breach of their covenant; and to make good that propriety, which by mutual contract men acquire, in recompense of the universal right they abandon: and such power there is none before the erection of a commonwealth. And this is also to be gathered out of the ordinary definition of justice in the Schools: for they say, that *justice is the constant will of giving to every man his own,* and therefore where there is no *own,* that is, no propriety, there is no injustice; and where there is no coercive power erected, that is, where there is no commonwealth, there is no propriety; all men having right to all things: therefore where there is no commonwealth, there nothing is unjust. So that the nature of justice, consisteth in keeping of valid covenants: but the validity of covenants begins not but with the constitution of a civil power, sufficient to compel men to keep them: and then it is also that propriety begins. . . .

For Further Reflection

1. Hobbes wrote, "The utility of morality and civil philosophy is to be estimated, not so much by the commodities we have by knowing these

sciences, as by the calamities we receive from not knowing them." What does he mean by this, and does the foregoing selection illustrate it?

2. Is Hobbes's view of human nature accurate? Do we always act out of the motivations of fear and distrust? Are people entirely self-interested egoists? Is psychological egoism, the view that we always do what we perceive to be in our best interest, too bleak and one-sided?
3. Hobbes thought that only an absolute sovereign could establish or ensure peace and civil society. Is he correct? What would his estimation of democracy be? Could democratic society make use of his analysis? How would democrats modify Hobbes's theory?
4. David Hume criticized the idea that contract theories provide a justification of political authority. First of all, there is no evidence of an original contract ever being made, and second, even if our ancestors did sign an original contract, why should that give us any reason for obeying the laws of the state? Even as we are not bound by the marriage or business contracts of our ancestors, why should we be obligated by their political contracts?

Further Readings for Chapter 1

Baier, Kurt. *The Moral Point of View.* Ithaca, N.Y.: Cornell University Press, 1958. This influential work sees morality primarily in terms of social control.

Frankena, William K. *Ethics.* 2nd ed. Englewood Cliffs, N.J.: Prentice-Hall, 1973. A succinct, reliable guide.

Gert, Bernard. *Morality: A New Justification of the Moral Rules.* 2nd ed. Oxford: Oxford University Press, 1988. A clear and comprehensive discussion of the nature of morality.

MacIntyre, Alasdair. *A Short History of Ethics.* New York: Macmillan, 1966. A lucid, if uneven, survey of the history of Western ethics.

Mackie, J. L. *Ethics: Inventing Right and Wrong.* New York: Penguin, 1976. This book takes a very different view of ethics from mine, viewing ethics from a skeptical perspective.

Pojman, Louis. *Ethics: Discovering Right and Wrong.* 4th ed. Belmont, Calif.: Wadsworth, 2002. An objectivist perspective.

Singer, Peter. *The Expanding Circle: Ethics and Sociobiology.* Oxford: Oxford University Press, 1983. A fascinating attempt to relate ethics to sociobiology.

Taylor, Paul. *Principles of Ethics.* Evanston, Ill.: Dickerson, 1975. This work covers many of the same topics as my book, usually from a different perspective. His discussion of the principle of universalizability (pp. 95–105) is especially useful.

Taylor, Richard. *Good and Evil.* Buffalo, N.Y.: Prometheus, 1970. A lively, easy-to-read work that sees the main role of morality as the resolution of conflicts of interest.

Turnbull, Colin. *The Mountain People.* New York: Simon & Schuster, 1972. An excellent anthropological study of a people living on the edge of morality.

Van Wyk, Robert. *Introduction to Ethics.* New York: St. Martin's Press, 1990. A clearly written recent introduction to the subject.

Warnock, G. J. *The Object of Morality.* London: Methuen, 1971. A clearly written, well-argued analysis of the nature of morality.

CHAPTER 2

Good and Evil

What are good and evil? In the general introduction we contrasted two classical notions of the good: Plato's transcendent notion that the good was the source of all being and morality, and the hedonic notion that the good is defined as pleasure (and, by extension, happiness). Plato and religious theories have a common thesis: that good is transcendent, that is, that it has a source beyond the empirical, in God or in a world of ideas. Similarly, for transcendentalists, the opposite of goodness, evil, is preternatural, inexplicable by ordinary understanding, and mysterious. The third-century Manicheans and Zoroastrians believed that good and evil were two independent, equally powerful forces, always in conflict. St. Augustine (354–430), partly in response to the Manicheans, a group to which he had formerly belonged, developed the idea that evil was not a real being at all, but merely an absence of the good. It is parasitic on the good, a state of deprivation. Others attribute evil to the devil. In contrast, the hedonist tradition rejects this transcendental approach and identifies the good with pleasure and happiness and evil with pain and suffering, purely empirical experiences. There is nothing mysterious about evil. It is, in the hedonist account, merely a problem of socializing human beings to take others into due consideration.

For many people, the hedonist account lacks sufficient explanatory power. Evil is a profound mystery, more perplexing than the nature of good, for it seems gratuitous. How could a good God permit evil? This is the question raised in our second reading, from Dostoevsky's *Brothers Karamazov,* where the cynical philosopher Ivan asks his religious brother Alyosha how he can explain the problem of evil in the world.

Something bewildering and fascinating does surround evil. We are shocked, even horrified, at the brutalities of the Nazis or Pol Pot's atrocities.

Shakespeare's Iago is one of the most frightening characters in literature, for he seems to carry sadism to an unprecedented height, or, at least, a point approaching that of Milton's Satan, who cries out in *Paradise Lost,* "Evil be thou my good." Is this ugly feature, malignity, in all of us to some extent? Is it a primordial force that civilization constantly represses? Or is it simply an outcome of frustrated endeavors, a result of a failed upbringing? Yet we sometimes discover families in which love and consideration are strong, though one child develops into a moral monster. This was apparently the case of the youth in Washington State who killed his two parents, both teachers, who, it is reported, gave him enormous love and care. Yet he was an ornery child from early childhood. Sometimes good children grow up in neglected environments and bad people grow up in good environments. What accounts for this?

We begin Chapter 2 with a selection from Herman Melville's *Billy Budd,* the story of a seemingly innocent, beautiful youth, Billy Budd, who becomes entrapped in evil, in the guise of master-at-arms John Claggart. It is Billy's inner nobility that brings out Claggart's venom and leads to the tragedy of the story. The third reading is from William Styron's *Sophie's Choice,* in which a young Polish mother, Sophie, is forced by a Nazi doctor at Auschwitz to make a terrible choice in sacrificing the life of one of her children.

The very opposite of the evil of John Claggart and the Nazi doctor are the Protestant Pastor Trocme and the people of La Chambon, France, who, at enormous personal risk, saved the lives of six thousand Jews from the Nazis. Philip Hallie analyzes the situation in our fourth reading. In our fifth reading, Philippa Foot argues that moral norms can be derived from "natural norms"—from our nature as humans.

In our sixth reading, the German philosopher Friedrich Nietzsche offers a radically different analysis of good and evil as constructions of a weak herd morality that is fearful of the superior ability of the natural aristocrat, whose master morality transcends what we now call good and evil. It is no accident that Nietzsche names his hero "Zarathustra," the name of the ancient Zoroastrian leader who believed that good and evil were independent, eternally co-present forces in the universe. Finally, in our last reading, Richard Taylor gives a thoroughly naturalistic account of the origin of good and evil, as based on our interests and preferences.

Billy Budd

HERMAN MELVILLE

Herman Melville (1819–1891), the American novelist, wrote *Billy Budd* late in life. It was not published until Melville had been dead more than thirty years. The story takes place in 1797, a time when the British Navy was threatened by mutinies, in which its very authority was at stake. It was the custom of naval ships to stop merchant vessels at sea and impress sailors into their service. Such occurs when men from the British man-of-war the HMS *Indomitable* go on board a merchant ship and impress one sailor into His Majesty's service. The sailor is Billy Budd, a handsome and guileless twenty-one-year-old orphan, known for his affable nature and inability to speak clearly. He is illiterate and stammers, but nevertheless communicates such genuine good will that he is the darling of his mates. When informed by his new masters that he will not be returning home but heading out to sea, Billy changes his plans cheerfully and devotes himself to his duties as a good citizen and sailor. He soon becomes immensely popular on board the *Indomitable*.

One man, however, despises Billy. He is John Claggart, master-at-arms. Perhaps Claggart is jealous of Billy's good looks and popularity. We are not told the exact reasons, but Claggart loathes Billy to the point of concocting a fantastic story of mutiny, supposedly instigated by Billy. Claggart goes to the captain of the *Indomitable*, Captain Vere, and reports an alleged meeting between Billy and another sailor discussing mutiny. There was such a meeting, but it was instigated by Claggart, and Billy renounced the suggestion of rebellion without hesitation.

Captain Vere is an honorable, fair-minded man of good will who likes Billy and suspects that Claggart is lying. He warns his master-at-arms that bearing false witness against a fellow sailor at sea merits the death penalty. Then he invites Billy into his office and instructs Claggart to face him with the charges. We enter as Billy is being accused of plotting to mutiny.

With the measured step and calm collected air of an asylum physician approaching in the public hall some patient beginning to show indications of a coming paroxysm, Claggart deliberately advanced within short range of Billy, and mesmerically looking him in the eye, briefly recapitulated the accusation.

Not at first did Billy take it in. When he did the rose-tan of his cheek looked struck as by white leprosy. He stood like one impaled and gagged. Meanwhile

---

From Herman Melville, *Billy Budd*. The manuscript of *Billy Budd* was found among Melville's possessions after he died. It was not published until 1924.

the accuser's eyes, removing not as yet from the blue, dilated ones, underwent a phenomenal change, their wonted rich violet color blurring into a muddy purple. Those lights of human intelligence losing human expression, icily protruding like alien eyes of certain uncatalogued creatures of the deep.

The first mesmeric glance was one of surprised fascination; the last was as the hungry lurch of the torpedo-fish.

"Speak, man!" said Captain Vere to the transfixed one, struck by his aspect even more than by Claggart's. "Speak! defend yourself." Which appeal caused but a strange, dumb gesturing and gurgling in Billy; amazement at such an accusation so suddenly sprung on inexperienced nonage; this, and it may be horror at the accuser, serving to bring out his lurking defect, and in this instance for the time intensifying it into a convulsed tongue-tie; while the intent head and entire form, straining forward in an agony of ineffectual eagerness to obey the injunction to speak and defend himself, gave an expression to the face like that of a condemned vestal priestess in the moment of being buried alive, and in the first struggle against suffocation.

Though at the time Captain Vere was quite ignorant of Billy's liability to vocal impediment, he now immediately divined it, since vividly Billy's aspect recalled to him that of a bright young schoolmate of his whom he had seen struck by much the same startling impotence in the act of eagerly rising in the class to be foremost in response to a testing question put to it by the master. Going close up to the young sailor, and laying a soothing hand on his shoulder, he said, "There is no hurry, my boy. Take your time, take your time." Contrary to the effect intended, these words, so fatherly in tone, doubtless touching Billy's heart to the quick, prompted yet more violent efforts at utterance—efforts soon ending for the time in confirming the paralysis, and bringing to the face an expression which was as a crucifixation to behold. The next instant, quick as the flame from a discharged cannon at night, his right arm shot out, and Claggart dropped to the deck. Whether intentionally, or but owing to the young athlete's superior height, the blow had taken effect full upon the forehead, so shapely and intellectual-looking a feature in the master-at-arms; so that the body fell over lengthwise, like a heavy plank tilted from erectness. A gasp or two, and he lay motionless.

"Fated boy," breathed Captain Vere, in tone so low as to be almost a whisper. . . .

Who in the rainbow can draw the line where the violet tint ends and the orange tint begins? Distinctly we see the difference of the colors, but where exactly does the one first blendingly enter into the other? So with sanity and insanity. In pronounced cases there is no question about them. But in some supposed cases, in various degrees supposedly less pronounced, to draw the exact line of demarcation few will undertake, though for a fee becoming considerate some professional experts will. There is nothing namable but that some men will, or undertake to, do it for pay.

Whether Captain Vere, as the surgeon professionally and privately surmised, was really the sudden victim of any degree of aberration, every one must determine for himself by such light as this narrative may afford.

That the unhappy event which has been narrated could not have happened at a worse juncture was but too true. For it was close on the heel of the suppressed insurrections, an aftertime very critical to naval authority, demanding from every English sea commander two qualities not readily interfusable—prudence and rigor. Moreover, there was something crucial in the case.

In the jugglery of circumstances preceding and attending the event on board the *Indomitable,* and in the light of that martial code whereby it was formally to be judged, innocence and guilt personified in Claggart and Budd in effect changed places. In a legal view the apparent victim of the tragedy was he who had sought to victimize a man blameless; and the indisputable deed of the latter, navally regarded, constituted the most heinous of military crimes. Yet more. The essential right and wrong involved in the matter, the clearer that might be, so much the worse for the responsibility of a loyal sea commander, inasmuch as he was not authorized to determine the matter on that primitive basis.

Small wonder then that the *Indomitable*'s captain, though in general a man of rapid decision, felt that circumspectness not less than promptitude was necessary. Until he could decide upon his course, and in each detail; and not only so, but until the concluding measure was upon the point of being enacted, he deemed it advisable, in view of all the circumstances, to guard as much as possible against publicity. Here he may or may not have erred. Certain it is, however, that subsequently in the confidential talk of more than one or two gun rooms and cabins he was not a little criticized by some officers, a fact imputed by his friends and vehemently by his cousin Jack Denton to professional jealousy of Starry Vere. Some imaginative ground for invidious comment there was. The maintenance of secrecy in the matter, the confining all knowledge of it for a time to the place where the homicide occurred, the quarterdeck cabin; in these particulars lurked some resemblance to the policy adopted in those tragedies of the palace which have occurred more than once in the capital founded by Peter the Barbarian.

The case indeed was such that fain would the *Indomitable*'s captain have deferred taking any action whatever respecting it further than to keep the foretopman a close prisoner till the ship rejoined the squadron and then submitting the matter to the judgment of his admiral.

But a true military officer is in one particular like a true monk. Not with more of self-abnegation will the latter keep his vows of monastic obedience than the former his vows of allegiance to martial duty.

Feeling that unless quick action was taken on it, the deed of the foretopman, so soon as it should be known on the gun decks, would tend to awaken any slumbering embers of the Nore[1] among the crew, a sense of the urgency of the case overruled in Captain Vere every other consideration. But though a conscientious disciplinarian, he was no lover of authority for mere authority's sake. Very far was he from embracing opportunities for monopolizing to himself the perils of moral responsibility, none at least that could properly be referred to an official superior or shared with him by his official equals or even subordinates. So thinking, he was glad it would not be at variance with usage to turn the matter over to a summary court of his own officers, reserving to himself, as the one on whom the ultimate accountability would rest, the right of maintaining a supervision of it, or formally or informally interposing at need. Accordingly a drumhead court was summarily convened, he electing the individuals composing it: the first lieutenant, the captain of marines, and the sailing master.

In associating an officer of marines with the sea lieutenant and the sailing master in a case having to do with a sailor, the commander perhaps deviated from general custom. He was prompted thereto by the circumstance that he took that soldier to be a judicious person, thoughtful, and not altogether incapable of grappling with a difficult case unprecedented in his prior experience. Yet even as to him he was not without some latent misgiving, for withal he was an extremely good-natured man, an enjoyer of his dinner, a sound sleeper, and inclined to obesity—a man who though he would always maintain his manhood in battle might not prove altogether reliable in a moral dilemma involving aught of the tragic. As to the first lieutenant and the sailing master, Captain Vere could not but be aware that though honest natures, of approved gallantry upon occasion, their intelligence was mostly confined to the matter of active seamanship and the fighting demands of their profession.

The court was held in the same cabin where the unfortunate affair had taken place. This cabin, the commander's, embraced the entire area under the poop deck. Aft, and on either side, was a small state-room, the one now temporarily a jail and the other a dead-house, and a yet smaller compartment, leaving a space between expanding forward into a goodly oblong of length coinciding with the ship's beam. A skylight of moderate dimension was overhead, and at each end of the oblong space were two sashed porthole windows easily convertible back into embrasures for short carronades.

All being quickly in readiness, Billy Budd was arraigned, Captain Vere necessarily appearing as the sole witness in the case, and as such temporarily

[1]The mutiny on the ship *Nore* shook the British navy's authority and created a spirit of insurrection among its seamen.

sinking his rank, though singularly maintaining it in a matter apparently trivial, namely, that he testified from the ship's weather side, with that object having caused the court to sit on the lee side. Concisely he narrated all that had led up to the catastrophe, omitting nothing in Claggart's accusation and deposing as to the manner in which the prisoner had received it. At this testimony the three officers glanced with no little surprise at Billy Budd, the last man they would have suspected either of the mutinous design alleged by Claggart or the undeniable deed he himself had done. The first lieutenant, taking judicial primacy and turning toward the prisoner, said, "Captain Vere has spoken. Is it or is it not as Captain Vere says?"

In response came syllables not so much impeded in the utterance as might have been anticipated. They were these: "Captain Vere tells the truth. It is just as Captain Vere says, but it is not as the master-at-arms said. I have eaten the King's bread and I am true to the King."

"I believe you, my man," said the witness, his voice indicating a suppressed emotion not otherwise betrayed.

"God will bless you for that, your honor!" not without stammering said Billy, and all but broke down. But immediately he was recalled to self-control by another question, to which with the same emotional difficulty of utterance he said, "No, there was no malice between us. I never bore malice against the master-at-arms. I am sorry that he is dead. I did not mean to kill him. Could I have used my tongue I would not have struck him. But he foully lied to my face and in presence of my captain, and I had to say something, and I could only say it with a blow, God help me!"

In the impulsive aboveboard manner of the frank one the court saw confirmed all that was implied in words that just previously had perplexed them, coming as they did from the testifier to the tragedy and promptly following Billy's impassioned disclaimer of mutinous intent—Captain Vere's words, "I believe you, my man."

Next it was asked of him whether he knew of or suspected aught savoring of incipient trouble (meaning mutiny, though the explicit term was avoided) going on in any section of the ship's company.

The reply lingered. This was naturally imputed by the court to the same vocal embarrassment which had retarded or obstructed previous answers. But in main it was otherwise here, the question immediately recalling to Billy's mind the interview with the afterguardsman in the forechains. But an innate repugnance to playing a part at all approaching that of an informer against one's own shipmates—the same erring sense of uninstructed honor which had stood in the way of his reporting the matter at the time, though as a loyal man-of-war's man it was incumbent on him, and failure so to do, if charged against him and proven, would have subjected him to the heaviest of penalties; this, with the blind feeling now his that nothing really was being hatched, prevailed with him. When the answer came it was a negative.

"One question more," said the officer of marines, now first speaking and with a troubled earnestness. "You tell us that what the master-at-arms said against you was a lie. Now why should he have so lied, so maliciously lied, since you declare there was no malice between you?"

At that question, unintentionally touching on a spiritual sphere wholly obscure to Billy's thoughts, he was nonplussed, evincing a confusion indeed that some observers, such as can readily be imagined, would have construed into involuntary evidence of hidden guilt. Nevertheless, he strove some way to answer, but all at once relinquished the vain endeavor, at the same time turning an appealing glance toward Captain Vere as deeming him his best helper and friend. Captain Vere, who had been seated for a time, rose to his feet, addressing the interrogator. "The question you put to him comes naturally enough. But how can he rightly answer it?—or anybody else, unless indeed it be he who lies within there," designating the compartment where lay the corpse. "But the prone one there will not rise to our summons. In effect, though, as it seems to me, the point you make is hardly material. Quite aside from any conceivable motive actuating the master-at-arms, and irrespective of the provocation to the blow, a martial court must needs in the present case confine its attention to the blow's consequence, which consequence justly is to be deemed not otherwise than as the striker's deed."

This utterance, the full significance of which it was not at all likely that Billy took in, nevertheless caused him to turn a wistful interrogative look toward the speaker, a look in its dumb expressiveness not unlike that which a dog of generous breed might turn upon his master, seeking in his face some elucidation of a previous gesture ambiguous to the canine intelligence. Nor was the same utterance without marked effect upon the three officers, more especially the soldier. Couched in it seemed to them a meaning unanticipated, involving a prejudgment on the speaker's part. It served to augment a mental disturbance previously evident enough.

The soldier once more spoke, in a tone of suggestive dubiety addressing at once his associates and Captain Vere: "Nobody is present—none of the ship's company, I mean—who might shed lateral light, if any is to be had, upon what remains mysterious in this matter."

"That is thoughtfully put," said Captain Vere; "I see your drift. Ay, there is a mystery; but, to use a scriptural phrase, it is a 'mystery of iniquity,' a matter for psychologic theologians to discuss. But what has a military court to do with it? Not to add that for us any possible investigation of it is cut off by the lasting tongue-tie of—him—in yonder," again designating the mortuary stateroom. "The prisoner's deed—with that alone we have to do."

To this, and particularly the closing reiteration, the marine soldier, knowing not how aptly to reply, sadly abstained from saying aught. The first lieutenant, who at the outset had not unnaturally assumed primacy in the court, now overrulingly instructed by a glance from Captain Vere, a glance more effective than words, resumed that primacy. Turning to the prisoner, "Budd," he said, and scarce in equable tones, "Budd, if you have aught further to say for yourself, say it now."

Upon this the young sailor turned another quick glance toward Captain Vere; then, as taking a hint from that aspect, a hint confirming his own instinct that silence was now best, replied to the lieutenant, "I have said all, sir."

The marine—the same who had been the sentinel without the cabin door at the time that the foretopman, followed by the master-at-arms, entered it—he, standing by the sailor throughout these judicial proceedings, was now directed to take him back to the after compartment originally assigned to the prisoner and his custodian. As the twain disappeared from view, the three officers, as partially liberated from some inward constraint associated with Billy's mere presence, simultaneously stirred in their seats. They exchanged looks of troubled indecision, yet feeling that decide they must and without long delay. For Captain Vere, he for the time stood—unconsciously with his back toward them, apparently in one of his absent fits—gazing out from a sashed porthole to windward upon the monotonous blank of the twilight sea. But the court's silence continuing, broken only at moments by brief consultations, in low earnest tones, this served to arouse him and energize him. Turning, he to-and-fro paced the cabin athwart; in the returning ascent to windward climbing the slant deck in the ship's lee roll, without knowing it symbolizing thus in his action a mind resolute to surmount difficulties even if against primitive instincts strong as the wind and the sea. Presently he came to a stand before the three. After scanning their faces he stood less as mustering his thoughts for expression than as one only deliberating how best to put them to well-meaning men not intellectually mature, men with whom it was necessary to demonstrate certain principles that were axioms to himself. Similar impatience as to talking is perhaps one reason that deters some minds from addressing any popular assemblies.

When speak he did, something, both in the substance of what he said and his manner of saying it, showed the influence of unshared studies modifying and tempering the practical training of an active career. This, along with his phraseology, now and then was suggestive of the grounds whereon rested that imputation of a certain pedantry socially alleged against him by certain naval men of wholly practical cast, captains who nevertheless would frankly concede that His Majesty's navy mustered no more efficient officer of their grade than Starry Vere.

What he said was to this effect: "Hitherto I have been but the witness, little more; and I should hardly think now to take another tone, that of your coadjutor for the time, did I not perceive in you—at the crisis too—a troubled hesitancy, proceeding, I doubt not, from the clash of military duty with moral scruple—scruple vitalized by compassion. For the compassion, how can I otherwise than share it? But, mindful of paramount obligations, I strive against scruples that may tend to enervate decision. Not, gentlemen, that I hide from myself that the case is an exceptional one. Speculatively regarded, it well might be referred to a jury of casuists. But for us here, acting not as casuists or moralists, it is a case practical, and under martial law practically to be dealt with.

"But your scruples: do they move as in a dusk? Challenge them. Make them advance and declare themselves. Come now; do they import something like this: If, mindless of palliating circumstances, we are bound to regard the death of the master-at-arms as the prisoner's deed, then does that deed constitute a capital crime whereof the penalty is a mortal one. But in natural justice is nothing but the prisoner's overt act to be considered? How can we adjudge to summary and shameful death a fellow creature innocent before God, and whom we feel to be so?—Does that state it aright? You sign sad assent. Well, I too feel that, the full force of that. It is Nature. But do these buttons that we wear attest that our allegiance is to Nature? No, to the King. Though the ocean, which is inviolate Nature primeval, though this be the element where we move and have our being as sailors, yet as the King's officers lies our duty in a sphere correspondingly natural? So little is that true, that in receiving our commissions we in the most important regards ceased to be natural free agents. When war is declared are we the commissioned fighters previously consulted? We fight at command. If our judgments approve the war, that is but coincidence. So in other particulars. So now. For suppose condemnation to follow these present proceedings. Would it be so much we ourselves that would condemn as it would be martial law operating through us? For that law and the rigor of it, we are not responsible. Our vowed responsibility is in this: That however pitilessly that law may operate in any instances, we nevertheless adhere to it and administer it.

"But the exceptional in the matter moves the hearts within you. Even so too is mine moved. But let not warm hearts betray heads that should be cool. Ashore in a criminal case, will an upright judge allow himself off the bench to be waylaid by some tender kinswoman of the accused seeking to touch him with her tearful plea? Well, the heart here, sometimes the feminine in man, is as that piteous woman, and hard though it be, she must here be ruled out."

He paused, earnestly studying them for a moment; then resumed.

"But something in your aspect seems to urge that it is not solely the heart that moves in you, but also the conscience, the private conscience. But tell me whether or not, occupying the position we do, private conscience should not yield to that imperial one formulated in the mode under which alone we officially proceed?"

Here the three men moved in their seats, less convinced than agitated by the course of an argument troubling but the more the spontaneous conflict within.

Perceiving which, the speaker paused for a moment; then abruptly changing his tone, went on.

"To steady us a bit, let us recur to the facts.—In wartime at sea a man-of-war's man strikes his superior in grade, and the blow kills. Apart from its effect the blow itself is, according to the Articles of War, a capital crime. Furthermore—"

"Ay, sir," emotionally broke in the officer of marines, "in one sense it was. But surely Budd purposed neither mutiny nor homicide."

"Surely not, my good man. And before a court less arbitrary and more merciful than a martial one, that plea would largely extenuate. At the Last Assizes it shall acquit. But how here? We proceed under the law of the Mutiny Act. In feature no child can resemble his father more than that Act resembles in spirit the thing from which it derives—War. In His Majesty's service—in this ship, indeed—there are Englishmen forced to fight for the King against their will. Against their conscience, for aught we know. Though as their fellow creatures some of us may appreciate their position, yet as navy officers what reck we of it? Still less recks the enemy. Our impressed men he would fain cut down in the same swath with our volunteers. As regards the enemy's naval conscripts, some of whom may even share our own abhorrence of the regicidal French Directory, it is the same on our side. War looks but to the frontage, the appearance. And the Mutiny Act, War's child, takes after the father. Budd's intent or non-intent is nothing to the purpose.

"But while, put to it by those anxieties in you which I cannot but respect, I only repeat myself—while thus strangely we prolong proceedings that should be summary—the enemy may be sighted and an engagement result. We must do; and one of two things must we do—condemn or let go."

"Can we not convict and yet mitigate the penalty?" asked the sailing master, here speaking, and falteringly, for the first.

"Gentlemen, were that clearly lawful for us under the circumstances, consider the consequences of such clemency. The people" (meaning the ship's company) "have native sense; most of them are familiar with our naval usage and tradition; and how would they take it? Even could you explain to them—which our official position forbids—they, long molded by arbitrary discipline, have not that kind of intelligent responsiveness that might qualify them to comprehend and discriminate. No, to the people the foretopman's deed, however it be worded in the announcement, will be plain homicide committed in a flagrant act of mutiny. What penalty for that should follow, they know. But it does not follow. *Why?* they will ruminate. You know what sailors are. Will they not revert to the recent outbreak at the Nore? Ay. They know the well-founded alarm—the panic it struck throughout England. Your clement sentence they would account pusillanimous. They would think that we flinch, that we are afraid of them—afraid of practicing a lawful rigor singularly demanded at this juncture, lest it should provoke new troubles. What shame to us such a conjecture on their part, and how deadly to discipline. You see then, whither, prompted by duty and the law, I steadfastly drive. But I beseech you, my friends, do not take me amiss. I feel as you do for this unfortunate boy. But did he know our hearts, I take him to be of that generous nature that he would feel even for us on whom this military necessity so heavy a compulsion is laid."

With that, crossing the deck he resumed his place by the sashed porthole, tacitly leaving the three to come to a decision. On the cabin's opposite side the troubled court sat silent. Loyal lieges, plain and practical, though at bottom they dissented from some points Captain Vere had put to them, they were without the faculty, hardly had the inclination, to gainsay one whom they felt to be an earnest man, one too not less their superior in mind than in naval rank. But it is not improbable that even such of his words as were not without influence over them, less came home to them than his closing appeal to their instinct as sea officers: in the forethought he threw out as to the practical consequences to discipline, considering the unconfirmed tone of the fleet at the time, should a man-of-war's man's violent killing at sea of a superior in grade be allowed to pass for aught else than a capital crime demanding prompt infliction of the penalty. . . .

In brief, Billy Budd was formally convicted and sentenced to be hung at the yardarm in the early morning watch, it being now night. Otherwise, as is customary in such cases, the sentence would forthwith have been carried out. In wartime on the field or in the fleet, a mortal punishment decreed by a drumhead court—on the field sometimes decreed by but a nod from the general—follows without delay on the heel of conviction, without appeal. . . .

The next morning Billy Budd was hanged. His last words were "God bless Captain Vere!"

For Further Reflection

1. Normally we think that one must intend to kill a victim before one can be guilty of murder, as opposed to involuntary manslaughter. But Budd

never intended to kill Claggart. Should he have been charged with murder?

2. Why did Captain Vere take the stance he did against Billy? Was he concerned with the deterrent effect an execution would have at a time when mutiny was a serious problem or did he think he was bound to carry out the letter of the law? What should he have done? Why?
3. Perhaps the most interesting thing about this story is the stark contrast between Claggart and Billy Budd. What are some of the moral lessons we may learn from this contrast and how they encounter one another?

Why Is There Evil?

FYODOR DOSTOEVSKY

Fyodor Dostoevsky (1822–1881), the great Russian novelist, was born in Moscow. His revolutionary sympathies and a penchant for gambling managed to keep him in constant danger. Among his famous novels are *Crime and Punishment* (1866) and *The Brothers Karamazov* (1880), from which our reading is taken.

In this scene, the philosophical cynic Ivan Karamazov explains to his devoutly religious brother Alyosha, a Christian monk, why the problem of evil prevents him from accepting God.

"Well, tell me where to begin, give your orders. The existence of God, eh?"

"Begin where you like. You declared yesterday at father's that there was no God." Alyosha looked searchingly at his brother.

"I said that yesterday at dinner on purpose to tease you and I saw your eyes glow. But now I've no objection to discussing with you, and I say so very seriously. I want to be friends with you, Alyosha, for I have no friends and want to try it. Well, only fancy, perhaps I too accept God," laughed Ivan, "that's a surprise for you, isn't it?"

"Yes of course, if you are not joking now."

From Fyodor Dostoevsky, *The Brothers Karamazov,* translated by Constance Garnett (London: Heinemann, 1912).

"Joking? I was told at the elder's yesterday that I was joking. You know, dear boy, there was an old sinner in the eighteenth century who declared that, if there were no God, he would have to be invented. . . . And man has actually invented God. And what's strange, what would be marvelous, is not that God should really exist; the marvel is that such an idea, the idea of the necessity of God, could enter the head of such a savage, vicious beast as man. So holy it is, so touching, so wise and so great a credit it does to man. As for me, I've long resolved not to think whether man created God or God man. . . . For what are we aiming at now? I am trying to explain as quickly as possible my essential nature, that is what manner of man I am, what I believe in, and for what I hope, that's it, isn't it? And therefore I tell you that I accept God simply. But you must note this: if God exists and if He really did create the world, then, as we all know, He created it according to the geometry of Euclid and the human mind with the conception of only three dimensions in space. Yet there have been and still are geometricians and philosophers, and even some of the most distinguished, who doubt whether the whole universe, or to speak more widely the whole of being, was only created in Euclid's geometry; they even dare to dream that two parallel lines, which according to Euclid can never meet on earth, may meet somewhere in infinity. I have come to the conclusion that, since I can't understand even that, I can't expect to understand about God. I acknowledge humbly that I have no faculty for settling such questions. I have a Euclidian earthly mind, and how could I solve problems that are not of this world? And I advise you never to think about it either, my dear Alyosha, especially about God, whether He exists or not. All such questions are utterly inappropriate for a mind created with an idea of only three dimensions. And so I accept God and am glad to, and what's more I accept His wisdom, His purpose—which are utterly beyond our ken; I believe in the underlying order and the meaning of life; I believe in the eternal harmony in which they say we shall one day be blended. I believe in the Word to Which the universe is striving, and Which Itself was 'with God,' and Which Itself is God and so on, and so on, to infinity. There are all sorts of phrases for it. I seem to be on the right path, don't I? Yet would you believe it, in the final result I don't accept this world of God's, and, although I know it exists, I don't accept it at all. It's not that I don't accept God, you must understand, it's the world created by Him I don't and cannot accept. Let me make it plain. I believe like a child that suffering will be healed and made up for, that all the humiliating absurdity of human contradictions will vanish like a pitiful mirage, like the despicable fabrication of the impotent and infinitely small Euclidian mind of man, that in the world's finale, at the moment of eternal harmony, something so precious will come to pass that it will suffice for all hearts, for the comforting of all resentments, for the atonement of all the crimes of humanity, of all the blood they've shed; that it will make it not only possible to forgive but to justify all that has happened with men—but though all that may come to pass, I don't accept it. I won't accept it. Even if parallel lines do meet and I see it myself, I shall see it and say that they've met, but still I won't accept it. That's what's at the root of me, Alyosha; that's my creed."

" . . . Do you understand why this infamy must be and is permitted? Without it, I am told, man could not have known good and evil. Why should he know that diabolical good and evil when it costs so much? Why, the whole world of knowledge is not worth that child's prayer to 'dear, Kind God'! I say nothing of the sufferings of grown-up people, they have eaten the apple, damn them, and the devil take them all! But these little ones! I am making you suffer, Alyosha, you are not yourself. I'll leave off if you like."

"Never mind. I want to suffer too," muttered Alyosha.

"One picture, only one more, because it's so curious, so characteristic, and I have only just read it in some collection of Russian antiquities. I've forgotten the name. I must look it up. It was in the darkest days of serfdom at the beginning of the century, and long live the Liberator of the People! There was in those days a general of aristocratic connections, the owner of great estates, one of these men—somewhat exceptional, I believe, even then—who, retiring from the service into a life of leisure, are convinced that they've earned absolute power over the lives of their subjects. There were such men then. So our general, settled on his property of two thousand souls, lives in pomp and domineers over his poor neighbors as though they were dependents and buffoons. He has kennels of hundreds of hounds and nearly a hundred dog-boys—all mounted, and in uniform. One day a serf boy, a little child of eight, threw a stone in play and hurt the paw of the general's favorite hound. 'Why is my favorite dog lame?' He is told that the boy threw a stone that hurt the dog's paw. 'So you did it.' The general looked the child up and down. 'Take him.' He was taken—taken from his mother and kept shut up all night. Early that morning the general comes out on horseback, with the hounds, his dependents, dog-boys, and huntsmen, all mounted around him in full hunting parade. The servants are summoned for their edification, and in front of them all stands the mother of the child. The child is brought from the lockup. It's a gloomy, cold, foggy autumn day, a capital day for hunting. The general orders the child to be undressed; the child is stripped naked. He shivers, numb with terror not daring to cry. . . . 'Make him run,' commands the general. 'Run! run!' shout the dog-boys. The boy runs. . . . 'At him!' yells the general, and he sets the whole pack of hounds on the child. The hounds catch him, and tear him to pieces before his mother's eyes! . . . I believe the general was afterwards declared incapable of administering his estates. Well—what did he deserve? To be shot? to be shot for the satisfaction of our moral feelings? Speak, Alyosha!"

"To be shot," murmured Alyosha, lifting his eyes to Ivan with a pale twisted smile.

"Bravo!" cried Ivan delighted. "If even you say so. . . . You're a pretty monk! So there is a little devil sitting in your heart, Alyosha Karamazov!"

"What I said was absurd, but—"

"That's just the point that 'but'!" cried Ivan. "Let me tell you, novice, that the absurd is only too necessary on earth. The world stands on absurdities, and perhaps nothing would have come to pass in it without them. We know what we know!"

"What do you know?"

"I understand nothing," Ivan went on, as though in delirium. "I don't want to understand anything now. I want to stick to the fact. I made up my mind long ago not to understand. If I try to understand anything, I shall be false to the fact and I have determined to stick to the fact."

"Why are you trying me?" Alyosha cried, with sudden distress. "Will you say what you mean at last?"

"Of course, I will; that's what I've been leading up to. You are dear to me, I don't want to let you go, and I won't give you up to your Zossima."

Ivan for a minute was silent, his face became all at once very sad.

"Listen! I took the case of the children only to make my case clearer. Of the other tears of humanity with which the earth is soaked from its crust to its center, I will say nothing. I have narrowed my subject on purpose. I am a bug, and I recognize in all humility that I cannot understand why the world is arranged as it is. Men are themselves to blame, I suppose; they were given paradise, they wanted freedom, and stole fire from heaven, though they knew they would become unhappy, so there is no need to pity them. With my pitiful, earthly, Euclidian understanding, all I know is that there is suffering and that there are none guilty; that cause follows effect, simply and directly; that everything flows and finds its level—but that's only Euclidian nonsense, I know that, and I can't consent to live by it! What comfort is it to me that there are none guilty and that cause follows effect simply and directly, and that I know it—I must have justice, or I will destroy myself. And not justice in some remote infinite time and space, but here on earth, and that I could see myself. I have believed in it. I want to see it, and if I am dead by then, let me rise again, for if it all happens without me, it will be too unfair. Surely I haven't suffered, simply that I, my crimes and my sufferings, may manure the soil of the future harmony for somebody else. I want to see with my own eyes the hind lie down with the lion and the victim rise up and embrace his murderer. I want to be there when everyone suddenly understands what it has all been for. All the religions of the world are built on this longing, and I am a believer. But then there are the children, and what am I to do about them? That's a question

I can't answer. For the hundredth time I repeat, there are numbers of questions, but I've only taken the children, because in their case what I mean is so unanswerably clear. Listen! If all must suffer to pay for the eternal harmony, what have children to do with it, tell me, please? It's beyond all comprehension why they should suffer, and why they should pay for the harmony. Why should they, too, furnish material to enrich the soil for the harmony of the future? I understand solidarity in sin among men. I understand solidarity in retribution, too; but there can be no such solidarity with children. And if it is really true that they must share responsibility for all their fathers' crimes, such a truth is not of this world and is beyond my comprehension. Some jester will say, perhaps, that the child would have grown up and have sinned, but you see he didn't grow up, he was torn to pieces by the dogs, at eight years old. Oh, Alyosha, I am not blaspheming! I understand, of course, what an upheaval of the universe it will be, when everything in heaven and earth blends in one hymn of praise and everything that lives and has lived cries aloud: 'Thou art just, O Lord, for Thy ways are revealed,' when the mother embraces the fiend who threw her child to the dogs, and all three cry aloud with tears, 'Thou art just, O Lord!' then, of course, the crown of knowledge will be reached and all will be made clear. But what pulls me up here is that I can't accept that harmony. And while I am on earth, I make haste to take my own measures. You see, Alyosha, perhaps it really may happen that if I live to that moment, or rise again to see it, I, too, perhaps, may cry aloud with the rest, looking at the mother embracing the child's torturer, 'Thou art just, O Lord!' but I don't want to cry aloud then. While there is still time, I hasten to protect myself and so I renounce the higher harmony altogether. It's not worth the tears of that one tortured child who beat itself on the breast with its little fist and prayed in its stinking outhouse, with its unexpiated tears to 'dear, kind God'! It's not worth it, because those tears are unatoned for. They must be atoned for, or there can be no harmony. But how? How are you going to atone for them? Is it possible? By their being avenged? But what do I care for avenging them? What do I care for a hell for oppressors? What good can hell do, since those children have already been tortured? And what becomes of harmony, if there is hell? I want to forgive. I want to embrace. I don't want more suffering. And if the sufferings of children go to swell the sum of sufferings which was necessary to pay for truth, then I protest that the truth is not worth such a price. I don't want the mother to embrace the oppressor who threw her son to the dogs! She dare not forgive him! Let her forgive him for herself, if she will, let her forgive the torturer for the immeasurable suffering of her mother's heart. But the sufferings of her tortured child she has no right to forgive; she dare not forgive the torturer, even if the child were to forgive him! And if that is so, if they dare not forgive, what becomes of harmony? Is there in the whole world a being who would have the right to forgive and could forgive? I don't want harmony. From love for humanity I don't want it. I would rather be left with the unavenged suffering. I would rather remain with my unavenged suffering and unsatisfied indignation, *even if I were wrong.* Besides, too high a price is asked for harmony; it's beyond our means to pay so much to enter on it. And so I hasten to give back my entrance ticket, and if I am an honest man I am bound to give it back as soon as possible. And that I am doing. It's not God that I don't accept, Alyosha, only I most respectfully return Him the ticket."

"That's rebellion," murmured Alyosha, looking down.

"Rebellion? I am sorry you call it that," said Ivan earnestly. "One can hardly live in rebellion, and I want to live. Tell me yourself, I challenge you—answer. Imagine that you are creating a fabric of human destiny with the object of making men happy in the end, giving them peace and rest at last, but that it was essential and inevitable to torture to death only one tiny creature—that baby beating its breast with its fist, for instance—and to found that edifice on its unavenged tears, would you consent to be the architect on those conditions? Tell me, and tell the truth."

"No, I wouldn't consent," said Alyosha softly.

For Further Reflection

1. There are three propositions involved in the traditional formulation of the problem of evil:

   God is all-powerful (including being all-knowing).
   God is perfectly good.
   Evil exists.

   These premises seem to be mutually incompatible, for if God is all-good, he will not allow evil if he can help it. And if he is all-powerful, he is able to prevent evil. But evil exists. Hence, the problem of evil. How does Ivan deal with these premises? Is there any way to resolve this problem that makes sense of all the premises?
2. Do you think that the existence of enormous evil, such as Ivan portrays, counts against the existence of God? Explain why or why not.

Sophie's Choice

WILLIAM STYRON

William Styron, the well-known American novelist, received the Pulitzer Prize in 1967 for *The Confessions of Nat Turner.* In this excerpt from *Sophie's Choice*, he describes a young Polish mother, Sophie, who with her two small children is being transported in a crowded train by German soldiers during World War II to Auschwitz, the Nazi concentration camp. There she is examined by a doctor, whom she calls *Jemand von Niemand* (literally, every man of no man), who first tries to seduce her but shortly after offers her a fateful choice. We enter the story with Sophie and her two children, Jan and Eva, on the train.

The name Oświęcim—Auschwitz—which had at first murmured its way through the compartment made [Sophie] weak with fear, but she had no doubt whatever that that was where the train was going. A minuscule sliver of light, catching her eye, drew her attention to a tiny crack in the plywood board across the window, and during the first hour of the journey she was able to see enough by the dawn's glow to tell their direction: south. Due south past the country villages that crowd around Warsaw in place of the usual suburban outskirts, due south past greening fields and copses crowded with birch trees, south in the direction of Cracow. Only Auschwitz, of all their plausible destinations, lay south, and she recalled the despair she felt when with her own eyes she verified where they were going. The reputation of Auschwitz was ominous, vile, terrifying. Although in the Gestapo prison rumors had tended to support Auschwitz as the place where they would eventually be shipped, she had hoped incessantly and prayed for a labor camp in Germany, where so many Poles had been transported and where, according to other rumor, conditions were less brutal, less harsh. But as Auschwitz loomed more and more inevitably and now, on the train, made itself inescapable, Sophie was smothered by the realization that she was a victim of punishment by association, retribution through chance concurrence. She kept saying to herself: I don't belong here. If she had not had the misfortune of being taken prisoner at the same time as so many of the Home Army members (a stroke of bad luck further complicated by her connection with Wanda, and their common dwelling place, even though she had not lifted a finger to help the Resistance), she might have been adjudged guilty of the serious crime of meat smuggling but not of the infinitely more grave crime of subversion, and hence might not be headed for a destination so forbiddingly malign. But among other ironies, she realized, was this one: she had not been *judged* guilty of anything, merely interrogated and forgotten. She had then been thrown in haphazardly among these partisans, where she was victim less of any specific retributive justice than of a general rage—a kind of berserk lust for complete domination and oppression which seized the Nazis whenever they scored a win over the Resistance, and which this time had even extended to the several hundred bedraggled Poles ensnared in that last savage roundup.

Certain things about the trip she remembered with utter clarity. The stench, the airlessness, the endless shifting of positions—stand up, sit down, stand up again. At the moment of a sudden stop a box toppling down on her head, not stunning her, not hurting too much, but raising an egg-size bulge at the top of her skull. The view outside the crack, where spring sunlight darkened into drizzling rain: through the film of rain, birch trees still tormented by the past winter's crushing snowfall, bent into shapes of white parabolic arches, strongbows, catapults, beautiful broken skeletons, whips. Lemon dots of forsythia everywhere. Delicate green fields blending into distant forests of spruce and larch and pine. Sunshine again. Jan's books, which he tried to read in the feeble light as he sat on her lap: *The Swiss Family Robinson* in German; Polish editions of *White Fang* and *Penrod and Sam.* Eva's two possessions, which she refused to park in the luggage rack but clutched fiercely as if any moment they might be wrested from her hands: the flute in its leather case and her *mís*—the one-eared, one-eyed teddy bear she had kept since the cradle.

More rain outside, a torrent. Now the odor of vomit, pervasive, unextinguishable, cheesy. Fellow passengers: two frightened convent girls of sixteen or so, sobbing, sleeping, waking to murmur prayers to the Holy Virgin; Wiktor, a black-haired, intense, infuriated young Home Army member already plotting revolt or escape, ceaselessly scribbling messages on slips of paper to be passed to Wanda in another compartment; a fear-maddened shriveled old lady claiming to be the niece of Wieniawski, claiming the bundle of parchment she kept pressed close to her to be the original manuscript of his famous *Polonaise,* claiming some kind of immunity, dissolving into tears like the schoolgirls at Wiktor's snarled remark that the Nazis would wipe their asses on the worthless *Polonaise.* Hunger pangs beginning. Nothing at all to eat. Another old woman—quite dead—laid out in the exterior aisle on the spot where her heart attack had felled her, her hands frozen around a crucifix and her chalk-white face already smudged by the boots and shoes of people treading over and around her. Through her crevice once more: Cracow at night, the familiar station, moonlit railroad yards where they lay stranded hour after hour. In the greenish moonglow an extraordinary sight: a German soldier standing in *feldgrau* uniform and with slung rifle, masturbating with steady beat in the half-light of the deserted yard, grinningly exhibiting himself to such curious or indifferent or bemused prisoners as might be looking through the peepholes. An hour's sleep, then the morning's brightness. Crossing the Vistula, murky and steaming. Two small towns she recognized as the train moved westward through the dusty pollen-gold morning: Skawina, Zator. Eva beginning to cry for the first time, torn by spasms of hunger. Hush, baby. A few more moments' drowse riven by a sun-flooded, splendid, heart-wrenching, manic dream: herself begowned and bediademed, seated at the keyboard before ten thousand onlookers, yet somehow—astoundingly—flying, *flying,* soaring to deliverance on the celestial measures of the Emperor Concerto. Eyelids fluttering apart. A slamming, braking stop. Auschwitz.

They waited in the car during most of the rest of the day. At an early moment the generators ceased working; the bulbs went out in the compartment and what remaining light there was cast a milky pallor, filtering through the cracks in the plywood shutters. The distant sound of band music made its way into the compartment. There was a vibration of panic in the car; it was almost palpable, like the prickling of hair all over one's body, and in the near-darkness there came a surge of anxious whispering—hoarse, rising, but as incomprehensible as the rustle of an army of leaves. The convent girls began to wail in unison, beseeching the Holy Mother. Wiktor loudly told them to shut up, while at the same instant Sophie took courage from Wanda's voice, faint from the other end of the car, begging Resistance members and deportees alike to stay calm, stay quiet.

It must have been early in the afternoon when word came regarding the hundreds upon hundreds of Jews from Malkinia in the forward cars. *All Jews in vans* came a note to Wiktor, a note which he read aloud in the gloom and which Sophie, too numb with fright to even clutch Jan and Eva close against her breast for consolation, immediately translated into: All the Jews have gone to the gas. Sophie joined with the convent girls in prayer. It was while she was praying that Eva began to wail loudly. The children had been brave during the trip, but now the little girl's hunger blossomed into real pain. She squealed in anguish while Sophie tried to rock and soothe her, but nothing seemed to work; the child's screams were for a moment more terrifying to Sophie than the word about the doomed Jews. But soon they stopped. Oddly, it was Jan who came to the rescue. He had a way with his sister and now he took over—at first shushing her in the words of some private language they shared, then pressing next to her with his book. In the pale light he began reading to her from the story of Penrod, about little boys' pranks in the leafy Elysian small-town marrow of

America; he was able to laugh and giggle, and his thin soprano singsong cast a gentle spell, combining with Eva's exhaustion to lull her to sleep.

Several hours passed. It was late afternoon. Finally another slip of paper was passed to Wiktor: *AK first car in vans.* This plainly meant one thing—that, like the Jews, the several hundred Home Army members in the car just forward had been transported to Birkenau and the crematoriums. Sophie stared straight ahead, composed her hands in her lap and prepared for death, feeling inexpressible terror but for the first time, too, tasting faintly the blessed bitter relief of acceptance. The old niece of Wieniawski had fallen into a comalike stupor, the *Polonaise* in crumpled disarray, rivulets of drool flowing from the corners of her lips. In trying to reconstruct that moment a long time later, Sophie wondered whether she might not then have become unconscious herself, for the next thing she remembered was her own daylight-dazzled presence outside on the ramp with Jan and Eva, and coming face to face with Hauptsturmführer Fritz Jemand von Niemand, doctor of medicine.

Sophie did not know his name then, nor did she ever see him again. I have christened him Fritz Jemand von Niemand because it seems as good a name as any for an SS doctor—for one who appeared to Sophie as if from nowhere and vanished likewise forever from her sight, yet who left a few interesting traces of himself behind. One trace: the recollected impression of relative youth—thirty-five, forty—and the unwelcome good looks of a delicate and disturbing sort. Indeed, traces of Dr. Jemand von Niemand and his appearance and his voice and his manner and other attributes would remain with Sophie forever. The first words he said to her, for example: "*Ich möchte mit dir schlafen.*" Which means, as bluntly and as unseductively as possible: "I'd like to get you into bed with me." Dreary loutish words, spoken from an intimidating vantage point, no finesse, no class, callow and cruel, an utterance one might expect from a B-grade movie Nazi *Schweinhund.* But these, according to Sophie, were the words he first said. Ugly talk for a doctor and a gentleman (perhaps even an aristocrat), although he was visibly, indisputably drunk, which might help explain such coarseness. Why Sophie, at first glance, thought he might be an aristocrat—Prussian perhaps, or of Prussian origin—was because of his extremely close resemblance to a Junker officer, a friend of her father's, whom she had seen once as a girl of sixteen or so on a summer visit to Berlin. Very "Nordic"-looking, attractive in a thin-lipped, austere, unbending way, the young officer had treated her frostily during their brief meeting, almost to the point of contempt and boorishness; nonetheless, she could not help but be taken by his arresting handsomeness, by—surprisingly—something not really effeminate but rather silkily feminine about his face in repose. He looked a bit like a militarized Leslie Howard, whom she had had a mild crush on ever since *The Petrified Forest.* Despite the dislike he had inspired in her, and her satisfaction in not having to see this German officer again, she remembered thinking about him later rather disturbingly: If he had been a woman, he would have been a person I think I might have felt drawn to. But now here was his counterpart, almost his replica, standing in his slightly askew SS uniform on the dusty concrete platform at five in the afternoon, flushed with wine or brandy or schnapps and mouthing his unpatrician words in an indolently patrician, Berlin-accented voice: "I'd like to get you into bed with me."

Sophie ignored what he was saying, but as he spoke she glimpsed one of those insignificant but ineffaceable details—another spectral trace of the doctor—that would always spring out in vivid trompe l'oeil from the confused surface of the day: a sprinkling of boiled-rice grains on the lapel of the SS tunic. There were only four or five of these; shiny with moisture still, they looked like maggots. She gave them her dazed scrutiny, and while doing so she realized for the first time that the piece of music being played just then by the welcoming prisoners' band—hopelessly off-key and disorganized, yet flaying her nerves with its erotic sorrow and turgid beat as it had even in the darkened car—was the Argentine tango "La Cumparsita." Why had she not been able to name it before? Ba-dum-*ba*-dum!

"*Du bist eine Polack,*" said the doctor. "*Bist du auch eine Kommunistin?*" Sophie placed one arm around Eva's shoulders, the other arm around Jan's waist, saying nothing. The doctor belched, then more sharply elaborated: "I know you're a Polack, but are you also another one of these filthy Communists?" And then in his fog he turned toward the next prisoners, seeming almost to forget Sophie.

Why hadn't she played dumb? "*Nicht sprecht Deutsch.*" It could have saved the moment. There was such a press of people. Had she not answered in German he might have let the three of them pass through. But there was the cold fact of her terror, and the terror caused her to behave unwisely. She knew now what blind and merciful ignorance had prevented very few Jews who arrived here from knowing, but which her association with Wanda and the others had caused her to know and to dread with fear beyond utterance: a selection. She and the children were undergoing at this very moment the ordeal she had heard about—rumored in Warsaw a score of times in whispers—but which had seemed at once so unbearable and unlikely to happen to her that she had thrust it out of her mind. But here she was, and here was the doctor. While over there—just beyond the roofs of the boxcars recently vacated by the death-bound Malkinia Jews—was Birkenau, and the doctor could select for its abyssal doors anyone whom he desired. This thought caused her such terror that instead of keeping her mouth shut she said, "*Ich bin polnisch! In Krakow geboren!*" Then she blurted helplessly, "I'm not Jewish! Or my children—they're not Jewish either." And added,

"They are racially pure. They speak German." Finally she announced, "I'm a Christian. I'm a devout Catholic."

The doctor turned again. His eyebrows arched and he looked at Sophie with inebriate, wet, fugitive eyes, unsmiling. He was now so close to her that she smelled plainly the alcoholic vapor—a rancid fragrance of barley or rye—and she was not strong enough to return his gaze. It was then that she knew she had said something wrong, perhaps fatally wrong. She averted her face for an instant, glancing at an adjoining line of prisoners shambling through the golgotha of their selection, and saw Eva's flute teacher Zaorski at the precise congealed instant of his doom—dispatched to the left and to Birkenau by an almost imperceptible nod of a doctor's head. Now, turning back, she heard Dr. Jemand von Niemand say, "So you're not a Communist. You're a believer."

"*Ja, mein Hauptmann.* I believe in Christ." What folly! She sensed from his manner, his gaze—the new look in his eye of luminous intensity—that everything she was saying, far from helping her, from protecting her, was leading somehow to her swift undoing. She thought: Let me be struck dumb.

The doctor was a little unsteady on his feet. He leaned over for a moment to an enlisted underling with a clipboard and murmured something, meanwhile absorbedly picking his nose. Eva, pressing heavily against Sophie's leg, began to cry. "So you believe in Christ the Redeemer?" the doctor said in a thick-tongued but oddly abstract voice, like that of a lecturer examining the delicately shaded facet of a proposition in logic. Then he said something which for an instant was totally mystifying: "Did He not say, 'Suffer the little children to come unto Me'?" He turned back to her, moving with the twitchy methodicalness of a drunk.

Sophie, with an inanity poised on her tongue and choked with fear, was about to attempt a reply when the doctor said, "You may keep one of your children."

"*Bitte?*" said Sophie.

"You may keep one of your children," he repeated. "The other one will have to go. Which one will you keep?"

"You mean, I have to choose?"

"You're a Polack, not a Yid. That gives you a privilege—a choice."

Her thought processes dwindled, ceased. Then she felt her legs crumple. "I can't choose! I can't choose!" She began to scream. Oh, how she recalled her own screams! Tormented angels never screeched so loudly above hell's pandemonium. "*Ich kann nicht wählen!*" she screamed.

The doctor was aware of unwanted attention. "Shut up!" he ordered. "Hurry now and choose. Choose, goddamnit, or I'll send them both over there. Quick!"

She could not believe any of this. She could not believe that she was now kneeling on the hurtful, abrading concrete, drawing her children toward her so smotheringly tight that she felt that their flesh might be engrafted to hers even through layers of clothes. Her disbelief was total, deranged. It was disbelief reflected in the eyes of the gaunt, waxy-skinned young Rottenführer, the doctor's aide, to whom she inexplicably found herself looking upward in supplication. He appeared stunned, and he returned her gaze with a wide-eyed baffled expression, as if to say: I can't understand this either.

"Don't make me choose," she heard herself plead in a whisper, "I can't choose."

"Send them both over there, then," the doctor said to the aide, "*nach links.*"

"Mama!" She heard Eva's thin but soaring cry at the instant that she thrust the child away from her and rose from the concrete with a clumsy stumbling motion. "Take the baby!" she called out. "Take my little girl!"

At this point the aide—with a careful gentleness that Sophie would try without success to forget—tugged at Eva's hand and led her away into the waiting legion of the damned. She would forever retain a dim impression that the child had continued to look back, beseeching. But because she was now almost completely blinded by salty, thick, copious tears she was spared whatever expression Eva wore, and she was always grateful for that. For in the bleakest honesty of her heart she knew that she would never have been able to tolerate it, driven nearly mad as she was by her last glimpse of that vanishing small form.

For Further Reflection

1. This is a classic moral dilemma in which both options are bad: either *actively* condemn one of your children to death or by *refusing to choose* have both killed. What should Sophie have done? What would you do? Why?

From Cruelty to Goodness

PHILIP HALLIE

Philip Hallie grew up in Chicago and earned his degrees at Grinnell, Oxford, and Harvard. For many years he was a professor of philosophy at Wesleyan University. Among his many works are *The Paradox of Cruelty* (1969) and *Lest Innocent Blood Be Shed* (1979).

In this essay Hallie examines the reality of cruelty, especially institutional cruelty, such as that of slavery and the Nazi treatment of Jews during World War II. Institutionalized cruelty involves the undermining of dignity by perpetrating a false inequality of worth and power. By degrading the victim, the victimizer exalts his own perception of self-worth, but in reality becomes evil. As an example of the kind of goodness necessary to defeat cruelty, Hallie describes the Protestant citizens, especially Pastor Trocmé, of the village of Le Chambon, who risked their lives to save six thousand Jews from the Nazis.

I am a student of ethics, of good and evil; but my approach to these two rather melodramatic terms is skeptical. I am in the tradition of the ancient Greek *skeptikoi,* whose name means "inquirers" or "investigators." And what we investigate is relationships among particular facts. What we put into doubt are the intricate webs of high-level abstractions that passed for philosophizing in the ancient world, and that still pass for philosophizing. My approach to good and evil emphasizes not abstract common nouns like "justice," but proper names and verbs. Names and verbs keep us close to the facts better than do our highfalutin common nouns. Names refer to particular people, and verbs connect subjects with predicates *in time,* while common nouns are above all this.

One of the words that is important to me is my own name. For me, philosophy is personal; it is closer to literature and history than it is to the exact sciences, closer to the passions, actions, and common sense of individual persons than to a dispassionate technical science. It has to do with the personal matter of wisdom. And so ethics for me is personal—my story, and not necessarily (though possibly) yours. It concerns particular people at particular times.

But ethics is more than such particulars. It involves abstractions, that is, rules, laws, ideals. When you look at the ethical magnates of history you see in their words and deeds two sorts of ethical rules: negative and positive. The negative rules are scattered throughout the Bible, but Moses brought down from Mount Sinai the main negative ethical rules of the West: Thou shalt not murder; thou shalt not betray. . . . The positive injunctions are similarly spread throughout the Bible. In the first chapter of the book of Isaiah we are told to ". . . defend the fatherless, plead for the widow." The negative ethic forbids certain actions; the positive ethic demands certain actions. To follow the negative ethic is to be decent, to have clean hands. But to follow the positive ethic, to be one's brother's keeper, is to be more than decent—it is to be active, even aggressive. If the negative ethic is one of decency, the positive one is the ethic of riskful, strenuous nobility.

In my early studies of particularized ethical terms, I found myself dwelling upon negative ethics, upon prohibitions. And among the most conspicuous prohibitions I found embodied in history was the prohibition against deliberate harmdoing, against cruelty. "Thou shalt not be cruel" had as much to do with the nightmare of history as did the prohibitions against murder and betrayal. In fact, many of the Ten Commandments—especially those against murder, adultery, stealing, and betrayal—were ways of prohibiting cruelty.

Early in my research it became clear that there are various approaches to cruelty, as the different commandments suggest. For instance, there is the way reflected in the origins of the word "cruel." The Latin *crudus* is related to still older words standing for bloodshed, or raw flesh. According to the etymology of the word, cruelty involves the spilling of blood.

But modern dictionaries give the word a different meaning. They define it as "disposed to giving pain." They emphasize awareness, not simply bloodshed. After all, they seem to say, you cannot be cruel to a dead body. There is no cruelty without consciousness.

And so I found myself studying the kinds of awareness associated with the hurting of human beings. It is certainly true that for millennia in history and literature people have been torturing each other not only with hard weapons but also with hard words.

Still, the word "pain" seemed to be a simplistic and superficial way of describing the many different sorts of cruelty. In Reska Weiss's *Journey Through Hell* (London, 1961) there is a brief passage of one of the deepest cruelties that Nazis perpetrated upon extermination camp inmates. On a march

> Urine and excreta poured down the prisoners' legs, and by nightfall the excrement, which had frozen to our limbs, gave off its stench.

And Weiss goes on to talk not in terms of "pain" or bloodshed, but in other terms:

> . . . We were really no longer human beings in the accepted sense. Not even animals, but putrefying corpses moving on two legs.

There is one factor that the idea of "pain" and the simpler idea of bloodshed do not touch: cruelty, not playful, quotidian teasing or raging, but cruelty (what the anti-cruelty societies usually call "substantial cruelty") involves the maiming of a person's dignity, the crushing of a person's self-respect. Bloodshed, the idea of pain (which is usually something involving a localizable occurrence, localizable in a tooth, in a head, in short, in the body), these are superficial ideas of cruelty. A whip, bleeding flesh, these are what the journalists of cruelty emphasize, following the etymology and dictionary meaning of the word. But the depths of an understanding of cruelty lie in the depths of an understanding of human dignity and of how you can maim it without bloodshed, and often without localizable bodily pain.

In excremental assault, in the process of keeping camp inmates from wiping themselves or from going to the latrine, and in making them drink water from a toilet bowl full of excreta (and the excreta of the guards at that) localizable pain is nothing. Deep humiliation is everything. We human beings believe in hierarchies, whether we are skeptics or not about human value. There is a hierarchical gap between shit and me. We are even above using the word. We are "above" walking around besmirched with feces. Our dignity, whatever the origins of that dignity may be, does not permit it. In order to be able to want to live, in order to be able to walk erect, we must respect ourselves as beings "higher" than our feces. When we feel that we are not "higher" than dirt or filth, then our lives are maimed at the very center, in the very depths, not merely in some localizable portion of our bodies. And when our lives are so maimed we become things, slaves, instruments. From ancient times until this moment, and as long as there will be human beings on this planet, there are those who know this and will use it, just as the Roman slave owners and the Southern American slave owners knew it when—one time a year—they encouraged the slaves to drink all the alcohol they could drink so that they could get bestially drunk and then even more bestially sick afterwards, under the eyes of their generous owners. The self-hatred, the loss of self-respect that the Saturnalia created in ancient Rome, say, made it possible to continue using the slaves as things, since they themselves came to think of themselves as things, as sub-human tools of the owners and the overseers.

Institutionalized cruelty, I learned, is the subtlest kind of cruelty. In episodic cruelty the victim knows he is being hurt, and his victimizer knows it too. But in a persistent pattern of humiliation that endures for years in a community, both the victim and the victimizer find ways of obscuring the harm that is being done. Blacks come to think of themselves as inferior, even esthetically inferior (black is "dirty"); and Jews come to think of themselves as inferior, even esthetically (dark hair and aquiline noses are "ugly"), so that the way they are being treated is justified by their "actual" inferiority, by the inferiority they themselves feel.

A similar process happens in the minds of the victimizers in institutionalized cruelty. They feel that since they are superior, even esthetically ("to be blonde is to be beautiful"), they deserve to do what they wish, deserve to have these lower creatures under their control. The words of Heinrich Himmler, head of the Nazi SS, in Posen in the year 1943 in a speech to his SS subordinates in a closed session, show how institutionalized cruelty can obscure harmdoing:

> . . . the words come so easily. "The Jewish people will be exterminated," says every party member, "of course. It's in our program . . . extermination. We'll take care of it." And then they come, these nice 80 million Germans, and every one of them has his decent Jew. Sure the others are swine, but his one is a fine Jew. . . . Most of you will know what it means to have seen 100 corpses together, or 500 to 1000. To have made one's way through that, and . . . to have remained a decent person throughout, that is what has made us hard. That is a page of glory in our history. . . .

In this speech he was making a sharp distinction between the program of crushing the Jews and the personal sentiments of individual Germans. The program stretched over years; personal sentiments were momentary. He was pleading for the program, for institutionalized destruction.

But one of the most interesting parts of the speech occurs toward the end of it:

> . . . in sum, we can say that we fulfilled the heaviest of tasks [destroying the Jews] in love to our people. And we suffered no harm in our essence, in our soul, in our character. . . .

Commitment that overrides all sentimentality transforms cruelty and destruction into moral nobility, and commitment is the lifeblood of an institution.

CRUELTY AND THE POWER RELATIONSHIPS

But when I studied all these ways that we have used the word "cruelty," I was nagged by the feeling that I had not penetrated into its inner structure. I was classifying, sorting out symptoms; but symptoms are signals, and what were the symptoms signals *of?* I felt like a person who had been studying cancer by sorting out brief pains from persistent pains, pains in the belly from pains in the head. I was being superficial, and I was not asking the question, "What are the forces behind these kinds of cruelty?" I felt that there were such forces, but as yet I had not touched them.

Then one day I was reading in one of the great autobiographies of western civilization, Frederick Douglass's *Life and Times.* The passage I was reading was about Douglass's thoughts on the origins of slavery. He was asking himself: "How could these whites keep us enslaved?" And he suddenly realized:

> My faculties and powers of body and soul are not my own, but are the property of a fellow-mortal in no sense superior to me, except that he has the physical power to compel me to be owned and controlled by him. By the combined physical force of the community I am his slave—a slave for life.

And then I saw that a disparity in power lay at the center of the dynamism of cruelty. If it was institutional cruelty, it was in all likelihood a difference involving both verbal and physical power that kept the cruelty going. The power of the majority and the weakness of a minority were at the center of the institutional cruelty of slavery and of Nazi anti-Semitism. The whites not only outnumbered the blacks in America, but had economic and political ascendancy over them. But just as important as these "physical" powers was the power that words like "nigger" and "slave" gave the white majority. Their language sanctified if it did not create their power ascendancy over the blacks, and one of the most important projects of the slave-holders and their allies was that of seeing to it that the blacks themselves thought of themselves in just these powerless terms. They utilized the language to convince not only the whites but the blacks themselves that blacks were weak in mind, in will power, and in worth. These words were like the excremental assault in the killing camps of the Nazis: they diminished both the respect the victimizers might have for their victims and the respect the victims might have for themselves.

It occurred to me that if a power differential is crucial to the idea of cruelty, then when that power differential is maintained, cruelty will tend to be maintained, and when that power differential is eliminated, cruelty will tend to be eliminated. And this seemed to work. In all kinds of cruelty, violent and polite, episodic and institutional, when the victim arms himself with the appropriate strength, the cruelty diminishes or disappears. When Jews joined the Bush Warriors of France, the Maquis, and became powerful enough to strike at Vichy or the Nazis, they stopped being victims of French and Nazi cruelty. When Frederick Douglass learned to use the language with great skill and expressiveness, and when he learned to use his physical strength against his masters, the power differential between him and his masters diminished, and so did their cruelty to him. In his autobiography he wrote:

> A man without force is without the essential dignity of humanity. Human nature is so constituted that it cannot honor a helpless man, though it can pity him, and even this it cannot do long if signs of power do not arise.

When I looked back at my own childhood in Chicago, I remembered that the physical and mental cruelties that I suffered in the slums of the southwest side when I was about ten years old sharply diminished and finally disappeared when I learned how to defend myself physically and verbally. It is exactly this lesson that Douglass learned while growing up in the cruel institution of slavery.

Cruelty then, whatever else it is, is a kind of power relationship, an imbalance of power wherein the stronger party becomes the victimizer and the weaker becomes the victim. And since many general terms are most swiftly understood in relationship with their opposites (just as "heavy" can be understood most handily in relationship with what we mean by "light") the opposite of cruelty lay in a situation where there is no imbalance of power. The opposite of cruelty, I learned, was freedom from that unbalanced power relationship. Either the victim should get stronger and stand up to the victimizer, and thereby bring about a balance of their powers, or the victim should free himself from the whole relationship by flight.

In pursuing this line of thought, I came to believe that, again, dictionaries are misleading: many of them give "kindness" as the antonym for "cruelty." In studying slavery in America and the concentration camps of central Europe I found that kindness could be the ultimate cruelty, especially when it was given within that unbalanced power relationship. A kind overseer or a kind camp guard can exacerbate cruelty, can remind his victim that there are other relationships than the relationship of cruelty, and can make the victim deeply bitter, especially when he sees the self-satisfied smile of his victimizer. He is being cruelly treated when he is given a penny or a bun after having endured the crushing and grinding of his mental and bodily well-being. As Frederick Douglass put it:

> The kindness of the slave-master only gilded the chain. It detracted nothing from its weight or strength. The thought that men are for other and better uses than slavery throve best under the gentle treatment of a kind master.

No, I learned, the opposite of cruelty is not kindness. The opposite of the cruelty of the overseer in American slavery was not the kindness of that overseer for a moment or for a day. An episodic kindness is not the opposite of an institutionalized cruelty. The opposite of institutionalized cruelty is freedom from the cruel relationship.

It is important to see how perspectival the whole meaning of cruelty is. From the perspective of the SS guard or the southern overseer, a bit of bread, a smile is indeed a diminution of cruelty. But in the relationship of cruelty, the point of view of the victimizer is of only minor importance; it is the point of view of the victim that is authoritative. The victim feels the suffering in his own mind and body, whereas the victimizer, like Himmler's "hard" and "decent" Nazi, can be quite unaware of that suffering. The sword does not feel the pain that it inflicts. Do not ask it about suffering.

GOODNESS PERSONIFIED IN LE CHAMBON

All these considerations drove me to write my book *The Paradox of Cruelty*. But with the book behind me, I felt a deep discontent. I saw cruelty as an embodiment, a particular case of evil. But if cruelty is one of the main evils of human history, why is the opposite of cruelty not one of the key goods of human history? Freedom from the cruel relationship, either by escaping it or by redressing the imbalance of power, was not essential to what western philosophers and theologians have thought of as goodness. Escape is a negative affair. Goodness has something positive in it, something triumphantly affirmative.

Hoping for a hint of goodness in the very center of evil, I started looking closely at the so-called "medical experiments" of the Nazis upon children, usually Jewish and Gypsy children, in the death camps. Here were the weakest of the weak. Not only were they despised minorities, but they were, as individuals, still in their non-age. They were dependents. Here the power imbalance between the cruel experimenters and their victims was at its greatest. But instead of seeing light or finding insight by going down into this hell, into the deepest depth of cruelty, I found myself unwillingly becoming part of the world I was studying. I found myself either yearning to be viciously cruel to the victimizers of the children, or I found myself feeling compassion for the children, feeling their despair and pain as they looked up at the men and women in white coats cutting off their fingertips one at a time, or breaking their slender bones, or wounding their internal organs. Either I became a would-be victimizer or one more Jewish victim, and in either case I was not achieving insight, only misery, like so many other students of the Holocaust. And when I was trying to be "objective" about my studies, when I was succeeding at being indifferent to both the victimizers and the victims of these cruel relationships, I became cold; I became another monster who could look upon the maiming of a child with an indifferent eye.

To relieve this unending suffering, from time to time I would turn to the literature of the French resistance to the Nazis. I had been trained by the U.S. Army to understand it. The resistance was a way of trying to redress the power imbalance between Hitler's Fortress Europe and Hitler's victims, and so I saw it as an enemy of cruelty. Still, its methods were often cruel like the methods of most power struggles, and I had little hope of finding goodness here. We soldiers violated the negative ethic forbidding killing in order, we thought, to follow the positive ethic of being our brothers' keepers.

And then one gray April afternoon I found a brief article on the French village of Le Chambon-sur-Lignon. I shall not analyze here the tears of amazement and gladness and release from despair—in short, of joy—that I shed when I first read that story. Tears themselves interest me greatly—but not the tears of melancholy hindsight and existential despair; rather the tears of awe you experience when the realization of an ideal suddenly appears before your very eyes or thunders inside your mind; these tears interest me.

And one of the reasons I wept at first reading about Le Chambon in those brief, inaccurate pages was that at last I had discovered an embodiment of goodness in opposition to cruelty. I had discovered in the flesh and blood of history, in people with definite names in a definite place at a definite time in the nightmare of history, what no classical or religious ethicist could deny was goodness.

The French Protestant village of Le Chambon, located in the Cévennes Mountains of southeastern France, and with a population of about 3,500, saved the lives of about 6,000 people, most of them Jewish children whose parents had been murdered in the killing camps of central Europe. Under a national government which was not only collaborating with the Nazi conquerors of France but frequently trying to outdo the Germans in anti-Semitism in order to please their conquerors, and later under the day-to-day threat of destruction by the German Armed SS, they started to save children in the winter of 1940, the winter after the fall of France, and they continued to do so until the war in France was over. They sheltered the refugees in their own homes and in various houses they established especially for them; and they took many of them across the terrible mountains to neutral Geneva, Switzerland, in the teeth of French and German police and military power. The people of Le Chambon are poor, and the Huguenot faith to which they belong is a diminishing faith in Catholic and atheist France; but their spiritual power, their capacity to act in unison against the victimizers who surrounded them, was immense, and more than a match for the military power of those victimizers.

But for me as an ethicist the heart of the matter was not only their special power. What interested me was that they obeyed *both* the negative and the positive injunctions of ethics; they were good not only in the sense of trying to be their brothers' keepers, protecting the victim, "defending the fatherless," to use the language of Isaiah; they were also good in the sense that they obeyed the negative injunctions against killing and betraying. While those around them—including myself—were murdering in order presumably, to help mankind in some way or other, they murdered nobody, and betrayed not a single child in those long and dangerous four years. For me as an ethicist they were the embodiment of unambiguous goodness.

But for me as a student of cruelty they were something more: they were an embodiment of the opposite of cruelty. And so, somehow, at last, I had found goodness in opposition to cruelty. In studying their story, and in telling it in *Lest Innocent Blood Be Shed,* I learned that the opposite of cruelty is not simply freedom from the cruel relationship; it is *hospitality.* It lies not only in something negative, an absence of cruelty or of imbalance; it lies in unsentimental, efficacious love. The opposite of the cruelties of the camps was not the liberation of the camps, the cleaning out of the barracks and the cessation of the horrors. All of this was the *end* of the cruelty relationship, not the opposite of that relationship. And it was not even the end of it, because the victims would never forget and would remain in agony as long as they remembered their humiliation and suffering. No, the opposite of cruelty was not the liberation of the camps, not freedom; it was the hospitality of the people of Chambon, and of very few others during the Holocaust. The opposite of cruelty was the kind of goodness that happened in Chambon.

Let me explain the difference between liberation and hospitality by telling you about a letter I received a year ago from a woman who had been saved by the people of Le Chambon when she was a young girl. She wrote:

> Never was there a question that the Chambonnais would not share all they had with us, meager as it was. One Chambonnais once told me that even if there was less, they still would want more for us.

And she goes on:

> It was indeed a very different attitude from the one in Switzerland, which while saving us also resented us so much.
>
> If today we are not bitter people like most survivors it can only be due to the fact that we met people like the people of Le Chambon, who showed to us simply that life can be different, that there are people who care, that people can live together and even risk their own lives for their fellow man.

The Swiss liberated refugees and removed them from the cruel relationship; the people of Le Chambon did more. They taught them that goodness could conquer cruelty, that loving hospitality could remove them from the cruel relationship. And they taught me this, too.

It is important to emphasize that cruelty is not simply an episodic, momentary matter, especially institutional cruelty like that of Nazism or slavery. As we have seen throughout this essay, not only does it persist while it is being exerted upon the weak; *it can persist in the survivors* after they have escaped the power relationship. The survivors torture themselves, continue to suffer, continue to maim their own lives long after the actual torture is finished. The self-hatred and rage of the blacks and the despair of the native Americans and the Jews who have suffered under institutional crushing and maiming are continuations of original cruelties. And these continuations exist because only a superficial liberation from torture has occurred. The sword has stopped falling on their flesh in the old obvious ways, but the wounds still bleed. I am not saying that the village of Chambon healed these wounds—they go too deep. What I am saying is that the people I have talked to who were once children in Le Chambon have more hope for their species and more respect for themselves as human beings than most other survivors I have met. The enduring hospitality they met in Le Chambon helped them find realistic hope in a world of persisting cruelty.

What was the nature of this hospitality that saved and deeply changed so many lives? It is hard to summarize briefly what the Chambonnais did, and above all how they did it. The morning after a new refugee family came to town they would find on their front door a wreath with "*Bienvenue!*" "Welcome!" painted on a piece of cardboard attached to the wreath. Nobody knew who had brought the wreath; in effect, the whole town had brought it.

It was mainly the women of Chambon who gave so much more than shelter to these, the most hated enemies of the Nazis. There was Madame Barraud, a tiny Alsatian, who cared for the refugee boys in her house with all the love such a tiny body could hold, and who cared for the way they felt day and night. And there were others.

But there was one person without whom Le Chambon could not have become the safest place in Europe for Jews: the Huguenot minister of the village, André Trocmé. Trocmé was a passionately religious man. He was massive, more than six feet tall, blonde, with a quick temper. Once long after the war, while he was lecturing on the main project of his life, the promotion of the idea of nonviolence in international relations, one of the members of his audience started to whisper a few words to his neighbor. Trocmé let this go on for a few moments, then interrupted his speech, walked up to the astonished whisperer, raised his massive arm, pointed toward the door, and yelled, "Out! Out! Get out!" And the lecture was on nonviolence.

The center of his thought was the belief that God showed how important man was by becoming Himself a human being, and by becoming a particular sort of human being who was the embodiment of sacrificially generous love. For Trocmé, every human being was like Jesus, had God in him or her, and was just as precious as God Himself. And when Trocmé with the help of the Quakers and others organized his village into the most efficient rescue machine in Europe, he did so not only to save the Jews, but also to save the Nazis and their collaborators. He wanted to keep them from blackening their souls with more evil—he wanted to save them, the victimizers, from evil.

One of the reasons he was successful was that the Huguenots had been themselves persecuted for hundreds of years by the kings of France, and they knew what persecution was. In fact, when the people of Chambon took Jewish children and whole families across the mountains of southeastern France into neutral Switzerland, they often followed pathways that had been taken by Huguenots in their flight from the Dragoons of the French kings.

A particular incident from the story of Le Chambon during the Nazi occupation of France will explain succinctly why he was successful in making the village a village of refuge. But before I relate the story, I must point out that the people of the village did not think of themselves as "successful," let alone as "good." From their point of view, they did not do anything that required elaborate explanation. When I asked them why they helped these dangerous guests, they invariably answered, "What do you mean, 'Why'? Where else could they go? How could you turn them away? What is so special about being ready to help (*prête à servir*)? There was nothing else to do." And some of them laughed in amazement when I told them that I thought they were "good people." They saw no alternative to their actions and to the way they acted, and therefore they saw what they did as necessary, not something to be picked out for praise. Helping these guests was for them as natural as breathing or eating—one does not think of alternatives to these functions; they did not think of alternatives to sheltering people who were endangering not only the lives of their hosts but the lives of all the people of the village.

And now the story. One afternoon a refugee woman knocked on the door of a farmhouse outside the village. The farmers around the village proper were Protestants like most of the others in Chambon, but with one difference: they were mostly "Darbystes," followers of a strange Scot named Darby, who taught their ancestors in the nineteenth century to believe every word of the Bible, and indeed, who had them memorize the Bible. They were literal fundamentalists. The farm-woman opened the door to the refugee and invited her into the kitchen where it was warm. Standing in the middle of the floor the refugee, in heavily accented French, asked for eggs for her children. In those days of very short supplies, people with children often went to the farmers in the "gray market" (neither black nor exactly legal) to get necessary food. This was early in 1941, and the farmers were not yet accustomed to the refugees. The farm-woman looked into the eyes of the shawled refugee and asked, "Are you Jewish?" The woman started to tremble, but she could not lie, even though that question was usually the beginning of the end of life for Jews in Hitler's Fortress Europe. She answered, "Yes."

The woman ran from the kitchen to the staircase nearby, and while the refugee trembled with terror in the kitchen, she called up the stairs, "Husband, children, come down, come down! We have in our house at this very moment a representative of the Chosen People!"

Not all the Protestants in Chambon were Darbyste fundamentalists; but almost all were convinced that people are the children of God, and are as precious as God Himself. Their leaders were Huguenot preachers and their following of the negative and positive commandments of the Bible came in part from their personal generosity and courage, but also in part from the depths of their religious conviction that we are all children of God, and we must take care of each other lovingly. This combined with the ancient and deep historical ties between the Huguenots and the Jews of France and their own centuries of persecution by the Dragoons and Kings of France helped make them what they were, "always ready to help," as the Chambonnais saying goes.

A CHOICE OF PERSPECTIVES

We have come a long way from cruelty to the people of Chambon, just as I have come a long way in my research from concrete evil to concrete goodness. Let me conclude with a point that has been alternately hinted at and stressed in the course of this essay.

A few months after *Lest Innocent Blood Be Shed* was published I received a letter from Massachusetts that opened as follows:

> I have read your book, and I believe that you mushy-minded moralists should be awakened to the facts. Nothing happened in Le Chambon, nothing of any importance whatsoever.
>
> The Holocaust, dear Professor, was like a geological event, like an earthquake. No person could start it; no person could change it; and no person could end it. And no small group of persons could do so either. It was the armies and the nations that performed actions that counted. Individuals did nothing. You sentimentalists have got to learn that the great masses and big political ideas make the difference. Your people and the people they saved simply do not exist.

Now between this position and mine there is an abyss that no amount of shouted arguments or facts can cross. And so I shall not answer this letter with a tightly organized reply. I shall answer it only by telling you that one of the reasons institutional cruelty exists and persists is that people believe that individuals can do nothing, that only vast ideologies and armies can act meaningfully. Every act of institutional cruelty—Nazism, slavery, and all the others—lives not with people in the concrete, but with abstractions that blind people to individuals. Himmler's speech to the SS leadership in 1943 is full of phrases like "exterminating a bacillus," and "The Jewish people will be exterminated." And in that speech he attacks any German who believes in "his decent Jew." Institutional cruelty, like other misleading approaches to ethics, blinds us to the victim's point of view; and when we are blind to that point of view we can countenance and perpetrate cruelty with impunity.

I have told you that I cannot and will not try to refute the letter from Massachusetts. I shall only summarize the point of view of this essay with another story.

I was lecturing a few months ago in Minneapolis, and when I finished talking about the Holocaust and the village of Le Chambon, a woman stood up and asked me if the village of Le Chambon was in the Department of Haute-Loire, the high sources of the Loire River. Obviously she was French, with her accent; and all French people know that there are many villages called "Le Chambon" in France, just as any American knows that there are many "Main Streets" in the United States. I said that Le Chambon was indeed in the Haute-Loire.

She said, "Then you have been speaking about the village that saved all three of my children. I want to thank you for writing this book, not only because the story will now be permanent, but also because I shall be able to talk about those terrible days with Americans now, for they will understand those days better than they have. You see, you Americans, though you sometimes cross the oceans, live on an island here as far as war is concerned. . . . "

Then she asked to come up and say one sentence. There was not a sound, not even breathing, to be heard in the room. She came to the front of the room and said, "The Holocaust was storm, lightning, thunder, wind, rain, yes. And Le Chambon was the rainbow."

Only from her perspective can you understand the cruelty and the goodness I have been talking about, not from the point of view of the gentleman from Massachusetts. You must choose which perspective is best, and your choice will have much to do with your feelings about the preciousness of life, and not only the preciousness of other people's lives. If the lives of others are precious to you, your life will become more precious to you.

For Further Reflection

1. What does Hallie mean when he says that "philosophy is personal; it is closer to literature and history than it is to the exact sciences"?
2. How does Hallie characterize cruelty? Why does he think that institutionalized cruelty is the worst kind of cruelty?
3. Explain Hallie's notion of power relations and how they bear on the reality of cruelty.
4. Reflect on the story of the people of Le Chambon, who saved thousands of Jews. What were their motives? What lessons can we learn from them?
5. How does Hallie use this story to illustrate the antidote to cruelty? Compare the letter from Massachusetts with the statement of the woman in Minneapolis: "The Holocaust was storm, lightning, thunder, wind, rain, yes. And Le Chambon was the rainbow."

Natural Goodness

PHILIPPA FOOT

Philippa Foot (1920–2010) was a British moral philosopher who championed a form of naturalistic ethics and did influential work in virtue theory. In this article (excerpted from her book *Natural Goodness*) she contends that moral norms can be derived from what she calls "natural norms." Natural norms, which define what ought to be the case regarding plants, animals, and humans, can be derived from a study of the nature of these things. Inherent in a deer's nature is the capacity to run fast to escape predators, and this capacity constitutes a natural norm for deer. By this norm, we would have to judge a deer unfit if it could not run fast. Likewise, Foot argues, natural norms for humans—standards that tell humans how to live—can be derived from their nature. The nature of humans includes the "need to be industrious and tenacious of purpose not only so as to be able to house, clothe, and feed themselves, but also to pursue human ends having to do with love and friendship."

NATURAL NORMS

Judgements of goodness and badness can have, it seems, a special "grammar" when the subject belongs to a living thing, whether plant, animal, or human being. This, at least, is what I argue in this book. I think that this special category of goodness is easily overlooked; perhaps because we make so many evaluations of other kinds, as when we assess non-living things in the natural world, such as soil or weather, or again assess artefacts either made by humans as are houses and bridges, or made by animals as are the nests of birds or beavers' dams. But the goodness predicated in these latter cases, like goodness predicated to living things when they are evaluated in a relationship to members of species other than their own, is what I should like to call secondary goodness. It is in this derivative way that we can speak of the goodness of, for example, soil or weather, as such things are related to plants, to animals, or to us. And we also ascribe this secondary goodness to living things, as, for instance, to specimens of plants that grow as we want them to grow, or to horses that carry us as we want to be carried, while artefacts are often named and evaluated by the need or interest that they chiefly serve. By contrast, "natural" goodness, as I define it, which is attributable only to living things themselves and to their parts, characteristics, and operations, is intrinsic or "autonomous" goodness in that it depends directly on the relation of an individual to the "life form" of its species. On barren Mars there is no natural goodness, and even secondary goodness can be attributed to things on that planet only by relating them to our own lives, or to living things existing elsewhere. . . .

My belief is that for all the differences that there are, as we shall see, between the evaluation of plants and animals and their parts and characteristics on the one hand, and the moral evaluation of humans on the other, we shall find that these evaluations share a basic logical structure and status. I want to suggest that moral defect is a form of natural defect not as different as is generally supposed from defect in sub-rational living things. So this is what I shall go on to argue, after a discussion of "natural goodness" as it is found in sub-rational living things.

Firstly, therefore, I shall explore natural goodness in plants and in animals other than human beings. For help I shall turn to a paper published by Michael Thompson: a paper I admire very much.

Michael Thompson's subject in this paper, which is called "The Representation of Life," is the description of living things. His thesis is that to understand certain distinctive ways in which we describe individual organisms, we must recognize the logical dependence of these descriptions on the nature of the species to which the individual belongs. Species-dependence is his leitmotif. For this reason he concerns himself with propositions of the form "S's are F" or "The S is F," where "S" holds a place for the name of a species (or "life form" as he is ready to say for the sake of those who want to give "species" a technical definition) and "F" a place for a predicate; so that a representative sentence would be "Rabbits are herbivores" or "The rabbit is a herbivore." He contrasts the logical form of the sentences

S's are F	(Rabbits are herbivores)
S's do V	(Rabbits eat grass)

with

N.N. is F	(Mrs. Muff is a rabbit)
N.N. is doing V	(Mrs. Muff is eating grass).

He points out, referring back to an early article by Elizabeth Anscombe, a peculiarity of the *logical form* of the first pair of sentences: that they are logically unquantifiable.[1] They do not speak of an individual rabbit, though the same verbal form can of course be used with that reference, as when the conjurer says to his wife "The rabbit does not look well." Nor, of course, do the propositions that interest Michael Thompson predicate something of every member of the species: "Cats are four-legged but Tibbles may have only three." Elizabeth Anscombe's original example concerned the number of teeth that human beings have—which is 32, though most human beings have lost quite a few and some never had the full complement. It is arguable that if "The S is F" (understood in this way) is true then at least some S's must be F. But even if this is so, "Some S's are F" is clearly not the whole of what such a proposition asserts. Thompson speaks in this context of a "natural-history account" of the life form or species: of how creatures of this kind live. And he points out, as part of his insistence on the way in which descriptions of individuals depend on the species to which they belong, that without this reference, "life activities" such as eating or reproducing cannot even be identified in an individual. Eating, for instance, is essentially, conceptually, related to nourishment, and could not be conclusively identified by a story about the taking in, crushing, transforming, and spewing out of substances since, for all that, its purpose might be not the maintenance of tissue but, say, skunk-like defence. Mitosis occurs in amoebae and human beings, and is given a uniform description in textbooks: in the first, however, it is reproduction of an individual organism, but in the second not.[2]

Thompson also points out peculiarities of the time references found within such propositions. It is said for instance that certain animals mate at a certain

[1]Anscombe, "Modern Moral Philosophy," in *Collected Philosophical Papers*, pp. 111, 38.
[2]Thompson, "The Representation of Life," pp. 272–273.

time of the year, and give birth, or lay eggs, so many weeks or months later; but this is "typically a matter of before and after—'in the spring,' 'in the fall' . . . and not of now and then . . . and when I was young and so forth."[3] Natural-history sentences, which Thompson also calls "Aristotelian categoricals," speak of the life cycle of individuals of a given species.[4] In one way, therefore, this is the time-span with which they have to do. In another way, however, a longer time reference is needed, since we must speak of *reproduction,* and the characteristics of a single individual cannot determine what will count as *another of the same.*

It will no doubt be objected here that reproduction is in fact not fixed, since species themselves are subject to change. This is of course important, and it means that Aristotelian categoricals must take account of sub-species adapted to local conditions. The history of a species is not, however, the subject with which Aristotelian categoricals deal. Their truth is truth about a species at a given historical time, and it is only the relative stability of at least the most general features of the different species of living things that makes these propositions possible at all. They tell how a kind of plant or animal, considered at a particular time and in its natural habitat, develops, sustains itself, defends itself, and reproduces. It is only in so far as "stills" can be made from the moving picture of the evolution of species that we can have a natural history account of the life of a particular kind of living thing. And it is only in so far as we have a "natural history account" that we can have a "vital description" of individuals here and now.

Let us now ask how all this is relevant to the normative judgements that we make about plants and animals when we say, for instance, that a plant in our garden is diseased, or not growing properly, or that a certain lioness is a neglectful parent, or a particular rabbit not as reproductive as a rabbit should be. Thompson suggests that the relation between the Aristotelian categorical and the evaluative assessment is very close indeed. In fact, he says that if we have a true natural-history proposition to the effect that S's are F, then if a certain individual S—the individual here and now or then and there—is not F it is therefore not as it should be, but rather weak, diseased, or in some other way defective.[5] The evaluative assessment is the product of propositions of the two logically different kinds.

Essentially, I think that Thompson is right about this, although I seem to see a gap in his account of Aristotelian categoricals that has to be filled in here. For I think he has not said enough to isolate the kind of proposition that will

[3]Ibid., p. 282.
[4]Ibid., p. 267.
[5]Ibid., p. 295.

yield evaluations of individual organisms. His talk of "natural-history propositions" was perhaps misleading in that it did not explicitly separate out what I would like to call the teleological from the non-teleological attachment of predicates to a subject term that is the name of a species. Consider, for instance, a sentence such as "The blue tit has a round blue patch on its head" This is superficially like "The male peacock has a brightly coloured tail," but in a way of course it is not. For, on the assumption that colour of head plays no part in the life of the blue tit, it is in this respect quite unlike the colour of the male peacock's tail: there would be nothing wrong with the blue tit in my garden *in that* it had a drab-coloured head; and the peculiarity might or might not accompany a defect. So how are we to distinguish these two types of propositions? Or how, again, are we to distinguish the case of leaves rustling when it is windy from that of flowers opening when the sun comes out? It is natural to say that the rustling of its leaves plays no part in the life of a tree, whereas pollination is gained by a display of scent and colours in sunshine. But then we must ask what we mean by "playing a part in the life" of a living thing. What counts as "its life" in this context? And what is "playing a part"?

There emerges here the special link, mentioned but not explored by Thompson, between his "Aristotelian categoricals" and teleology in living things. Aristotelian categoricals are propositions having to do with the way that certain features appear or that certain things are done in organisms of a given species either by the whole organism or by their characteristics or parts. But, speaking now for myself rather than for Thompson, I should say that to obtain the connection between Aristotelian categoricals and evaluation another move must be made. I should say that in plants and non-human animals these things all have to do, directly or indirectly, with self-maintenance, as by defence and the obtaining of nourishment, or with the reproduction of the individual, as by the building of nests. This is "the life" characteristic of the kind of animal with which the categoricals here have to do. What "plays a part" in this life is that which is causally and teleologically related to it, as putting out roots is related to obtaining nourishment, and attracting insects is related to reproduction in plants.

We start from the fact that there is a basis for the Aristotelian categorical that does not come from the counting of heads. What is this basis? In what was said about the blue tits and the peacocks it was suggested that some but not all general propositions about a species have to do with the teleology of living things of this kind. There is an Aristotelian categorical about the species *peacock* to the effect that the male peacock displays his brilliant tail *in order to* attract a female during the mating season. The display serves this purpose. Let us call such language, purposive language. But be careful here! Where something that S's do is, in this sense, purposive we should beware of slipping over into saying of an individual S that it *has* this purpose when it does this thing. Plants grow upwards in order to get to the light, but it is fanciful to say that that is what my honeysuckle is trying to do or that that is "its end." Migrating birds flying off in order to reach the southern insects do not *have* this as their end or purpose even though it could be said to be the end or purpose of the operation. What is crucial to all teleological propositions is the expectation of an answer to the question "What part does it play in the life cycle of things of the species S?" In other words, "What is its function? " or "What good does it do?" . . .

Thus, evaluation of an individual living thing in its own right, with no reference to our interests or desires, is possible where there is intersection of two types of propositions: on the one hand, Aristotelian categoricals (life-form descriptions relating to the species), and on the other, propositions about particular individuals that are the subject of evaluation.

It will be useful to remind ourselves at this point of the elements that came to light in the earlier discussion of "good" and "bad" as applied to characteristics and operations of plants and animals.

(a) There was the life cycle, which in those cases consisted roughly of self-maintenance and reproduction.
(b) There was the set of propositions saying *how* for a certain species this was achieved: how nourishment was obtained, how development took place, what defences were available, and how reproduction was secured.
(c) From all this, *norms* were derived, requiring, for instance, a certain degree of swiftness in the deer, night vision in the owl, and cooperative hunting in the wolf.
(d) By the application of these norms to an individual member of the relevant species it (this individual) was judged to be as it should be or by contrast, to a lesser or greater degree defective in a certain respect.

There are here many details that are not germane to the aim of this book. But something more must be said about the way in which Aristotelian categoricals about the "how and what" of the life cycle determine normative assessments of individual living things in the here and now or there and then of historical place and time.

As illustration let us consider the Aristotelian categorical stating that the deer is an animal whose form of defence is flight. From this we know that it is a defect, a weakness, in an individual deer if it is slow of foot. Swiftness, as opposed to fierceness or camouflage, is what fits it to escape from its predators. But two remarks must be added about this. In the first place, swiftness does no more than *fit* it to survive: in some circumstances even the greatest speed possible for this type of animal would not be enough. Moreover, by chance it may sometimes be that the fastest deer fleeing from one predator is the very one that gets caught in a trap.[6] Secondly, what is excellence, and what defect, is relative to the natural habitat of the species. Even in a zoo a fleeing animal like a deer that cannot run well is so far forth defective and not as it should be, in spite of the fact that, as this particular individual is by chance placed, this may be no disadvantage for defence or feeding or mating or rearing the young. . . .

TRANSITION TO HUMAN BEINGS

The idea that any features and operations of humans could be evaluated in the same way as those of plants and animals may provoke instant opposition. For to say that this is possible is to imply that some at least of our judgements of goodness and badness in human beings are given truth or falsity by the conditions of human life. And even if it is allowed that certain evaluations of this kind are possible—those vaguely thought of perhaps as "merely biological"—there is bound to be scepticism about the possibility that "moral evaluation" could be like this. Surely, it will be urged, we must start afresh when thinking about the subject of moral philosophy. I believe, however, that this is only partly true.

The question remains, however, as to whether once we have made the transition from sub-rational to rational beings we may not need a new theory of evaluation. Surely, my critics will say, it must be so, given the part that the life cycle of a plant or animal rightly played in Michael Thompson's account of the conceptual structure within which the evaluation of properties and operations of individual organisms had a place. For such an evaluation is based on the general relation of this kind of feature to the pattern of life that is the *good of* creatures of this species. But how could we possibly see human good in the same terms? The life cycle of a plant or animal ultimately has to do with what is involved in development, self-sustenance, and reproduction. Are we really going to suggest that human strengths and weaknesses, and even virtues and vices, are to be identified by reference to such "biological" cycles?

This challenge, ill-conceived as it is in suggesting that the natural-history account of human beings could be explained in terms of a merely animal life, raises a most important and difficult topic. For it is true that to the course of describing "natural goodness" in plants and animals we have implicitly adverted to the idea of the good of a living thing as well as its goodness in various respects, and the two ideas, though related, are distinct. That this is

[6]As it may be the skillful archer who fails to hit a target in the presence of a freak gust of wind.

so can be seen if we think about what it means to benefit a plant or an animal. Very often, to be sure, a living thing is benefited by itself being made better, and there must be a systematic connection between natural goodness and benefit—whether reflexive or other-related as in the case of the stinging bees. But it does not follow that benefit of either kind follows goodness whatever circumstance an individual happens to be in. In our earlier example it was the swiftest deer, ahead of the others, that fell into the hunter's trap; and the properly acting bee that stings a gardener may well bring about the destruction of the nest.

Whether an individual plant or animal actually succeeds in living the life that it is its good to live depends on chance as well as on its own qualities. But its own goodness or defect is conceptually determined by the interaction of natural habitat and natural (species-general) "strategies" for survival and reproduction. What conceptually determines goodness in a feature or operation is the relation, for the species, of that feature or operation to survival and reproduction, because it is in that that good lies in the botanical and zoological worlds. At that point questions of "How?" and "Why?" and "What for?" come to an end. But clearly this is not true when we come to human beings.

Take reproduction, for instance. Lack of capacity to reproduce is a defect in a human being. But choice of childlessness and even celibacy is not thereby shown to be defective choice, because human good is not the same as plant or animal good. The bearing and rearing of children is not an ultimate good in human life, because other elements of good such as the demands of work to be done may give a man or woman reason to renounce family life. And the great (if often troubling) good of having children has to do with the love and ambition of parents for children, the special role of grandparents, and many other things that simply do not belong to animal life.

Moreover, the good of survival itself is something more complex for human beings than for animals; even for the animals closest to us. The human desire to live is, of course, instinctual, but it often also has to do with a desperate hope that something may yet turn out well in the future. And it seems that the preciousness of the unique memories that each person has is part of what he or she may cling to even in the most terrible of circumstances. In other words, the teleological story goes beyond a reference to survival itself.

The idea of human good is deeply problematic. One may be inclined to think of it as happiness, but much would have to be said before that could be so understood as to be true, and I shall discuss this in a later chapter. Here I want only to recall that Wittgenstein famously said on his deathbed, "Tell them I have had a wonderful life." The example should teach us not to be too ready to speak of every good life as "a happy life:" Wittgenstein surely did not have a happy life, being too tormented and self-critical for that.

Thus the idea of a good life for a human being, and the question of its relation to happiness, is each deeply problematic. And, moreover, there is so much diversity in human beings and human cultures that the schema of natural normativity may seem to be inapplicable from the start. Nevertheless, for all the diversities of human life, it is possible to give some quite general account of human necessities, that is, of what is quite generally needed for human good, if only by starting from the negative idea of human deprivation. For then we see at once that human good depends on many characteristics and capacities that are not needed even by animals, never mind by plants. There are, for instance, physical properties such as the kind of larynx that allows of the myriad sounds that make up human language, as well as the kind of hearing that can distinguish them. Moreover, human beings need the mental capacity for learning language; they also need powers of imagination that allow them to understand stories, to join in songs and dances—and to laugh at jokes. Without such things human beings may survive and reproduce themselves, but they are deprived. And what could be more natural than to say on this account that we have introduced the subject of possible human defects; calling them "natural defects" as we used these terms in the discussion of plant and animal life?

We can see, moreover, that, as with animals, some defects have as we might say "a reflexive role," in that the deprivation comes primarily to the defective individual; but that there are some that chiefly or at least most directly affect other people. We might think here, for instance, of the failure of maternal affection, or of (non-iterated) "prisoner's dilemma" cases where each person gains from the action of others but loses through his own. The way of solving the dilemma, however we should understand its details, depends on our human way of thinking. We act within a language that allows us to say "I owe it to him" or "I suppose I should play my part" (as we nowadays think, for instance, of taking a bus rather than a car, to reduce traffic on the road, knowing that we ourselves may need to get somewhere urgently by car some other time). There are also human enjoyments such as songs and ceremonials that need cooperative participation. And, further, human societies depend on especially talented individuals playing special roles in a society's life. As some species of animals need a lookout, or as herds of elephants need an old she-elephant to lead them to a watering hole, so human societies need leaders, explorers, and artists. Failure to perform a special role can here be a defect in a man or woman who is not ready to contribute what he or she alone—or best—can give. There is also something wrong with the rest of us if we do not support those of genius, or even special talent, in their work.

In spite of the diversity of human goods—the elements that can make up good human lives—it is therefore possible that the concept of a good human life plays the same part in determining goodness of human characteristics and operations that the concept of flourishing plays in the determination of goodness in plants and animals. So far the conceptual structure seems to be intact. Nor is there any reason to think that it could not be in place even in the evaluations that are nowadays spoken of as the special domain of morality. This special domain—and more generally that of goodness of the will—will be discussed in detail in the next two chapters. But if we ask whether Geach was right to say that human beings need virtues as bees need stings . . ., the answer is surely that he was. Men and women need to be industrious and tenacious of purpose not only so as to be able to house, clothe, and feed themselves, but also to pursue human ends having to do with love and friendship. They need the ability to form family ties, friendships, and special relations with neighbours, They also need codes of conduct. And how could they have all these things without virtues such as loyalty, fairness, kindness, and in certain circumstances obedience? . . .

Thus the structure of the derivation is the same whether we derive an evaluation of the roots of a particular tree or the action of a particular human being. The meaning of the words "good" and "bad" is not different when used of features of plants on the one hand and humans on the other, but is rather the same as applied, in judgements of natural goodness and defect, in the case of all living things.

For Further Reflection

1. Foot argues that judgments of goodness and badness have a "special grammar" when they apply to living things, including humans. What does she mean by this?
2. What is Foot's argument for her view that it is possible to derive standards of goodness and badness from an account of the basic needs of human beings? Explain.
3. How does Foot use Wittgenstein in her argument that a good life is not necessarily a happy one?

On the Origin of Good and Evil

RICHARD TAYLOR

Richard Taylor taught philosophy at Brown University, Rochester University, and Union College. In this essay he argues that morality, especially the concepts of good and evil, is not a transcendental but a naturalistic reality, something that originates in the fact that we are *conative* beings (having desires and felt needs). If we had no desires, no values would exist—no good and evil, which are functional terms, referring to our goals and interests. Right and wrong emerge in social situations, as rules for behavior. They are based on common goals and interests. The rules and practices that either promote cooperation toward meeting our desires or resolve interpersonal conflict are *right* rules and practices, and those rules and practices that hinder cooperation and conflict resolution are wrong ones.

It has, as we have seen, been fairly characteristic of moral philosophers to begin with an assumed dichotomy between what *is* and what *ought* to be. Having turned their backs on the former as having little relevance to philosophical ethics, they have proclaimed the content of the latter as the unique realm of ethics. Some, in fact, have declared it a fallacy even to attempt to derive any philosophy of what ought to be from what in fact is, which pretty much amounts to declaring that facts can have little bearing upon ethics. One result of this is that moral philosophy has all too often resembled declamation. The advocates for the various and conflicting programs have had little to appeal to other than their own intuitions of things, these being sometimes baptized as the deliverances of "practical reason" and the like.

I am now going to remove this distinction between *is* and *ought*. More precisely, I shall show that all moral distinctions, beginning with the basic distinction between good and evil, are based entirely on certain facts and, in particular, on facts concerning human nature. It is because men are the kind of beings they are—namely, what I have called conative beings—that the distinction between good and evil arises in the first place. Once this has been seen, we can see what good and evil in fact are. This basic distinction then having been made clear—and having been based not on intuitions and sentiments or abstract reasoning but on a certain conception of human nature—we can derive the further distinctions between moral right and wrong and give a fairly clear content to the idea of the common good.

Reprinted from Richard Taylor, *Good and Evil: A New Direction* (Amherst, NY: Prometheus Books, 1984), pp. 119–133.

MEN AS CONATIVE BEINGS

Men are rational or cognitive beings, but to say this is very far from stating the whole truth about them. So far as ethics is concerned, it leaves entirely out of account the most important fact about men, that they are desiderative or conative beings as well. I have already explained what this means, but it needs to be briefly reiterated here, as it is crucial to establishing the distinction between good and evil.

To describe men as conative is not to say anything at all abstruse or metaphysical, as this bit of terminology might suggest. It is only to call attention to a fact of human nature with which everyone is perfectly familiar: men have needs, desires, and goals; they pursue ends; they have certain wants and generally go about trying to satisfy them in various ways. Psychologists, metaphysicians, and others might have conflicting theories concerning how this fact is to be understood and explained, but the fact itself is hardly open to any question. It is more obvious that men are, in the sense just explained, conative beings, than that they are rational ones. There are men whom one might genuinely doubt to be rational, but it is doubtful whether anyone has ever seen a living man whom he suspected had no needs, desires, or wants. Such a man would be totally inactive and resemble a statue more than a man.

Thus, when a man is seen doing anything, it can generally be asked why he is doing it, what he is doing it for, or what he is trying to accomplish. This need not suggest that his behavior is not caused in the usual ways, although some might want to maintain this. What it does mean is that there is some point to what he is doing, some outcome that he intends. It implies nothing more.

For example, a man is seen operating a typewriter. Why is he doing that? Perhaps he is writing a letter, or an editorial, or something of that sort. In short, he has some purpose, and his typewriting activity is his means to fulfilling it. Or a man is seen running. What for? Perhaps to get to a store before it closes, or to catch a bus. Again, he has some purpose and is trying to fulfill it by running. Or once more, a man is seen walking toward a pump with an empty bucket. What for? Presumably, to fill the bucket (a goal) to enable himself to drink, wash, and so on (further purposes or goals).

I have used these exceedingly commonplace examples of human activity to illustrate three points. The first is that voluntary or deliberate human activity is generally interpreted as goal-directed. When we ask why a man is doing whatever it is that he is doing, we are usually seeking some explanation in terms of what he is trying to accomplish by that activity. This presupposes something about men that is universally taken for granted: men have goals and purposes and wants and desires, and they generally act in ways they consider appropriate to fulfilling them. It presupposes, in fact, that they are conative beings or, as I shall sometimes express it, that they are beings having desires and wants.

The second point is that, in speaking of a man's goals or purposes, one need not be referring to some *ultimate* goal, or even to any that is very important. The goal of one's activity might be exceedingly trivial and of only momentary significance, as in the foregoing examples. It could hardly be one's ultimate goal, or the goal of one's lifetime, to fill a bucket with water or to catch a bus. Yet, that might be precisely what his goal is then and there. Of course most men do have larger, more long-range goals. A man will spend years struggling, for example, in pursuit of some objective important to him, such as a degree in medicine, or perhaps fame as an author. Some men do devote the better part of their lives to ends having that kind of personal importance. In speaking of human behavior as goal-directed, however, I do not have this sort of thing primarily in mind, even though I include it. What I am calling attention to is much simpler and more commonplace. The conative aspect of human nature is as well exhibited by a man munching an apple or swatting a fly as it is by someone devoting his lifetime to a great ambition.

And the third point is that reason appears to enter into men's purposeful activity primarily to devise the means to attain the ends and has little to do with ends themselves. Thus, if a man wants to fill a bucket with water, it is in the clearest sense rational that he should carry it to the pump, as the most elementary reason or intelligence indicates that this is the appropriate means to that end. Merely wishing that pail might become filled, or trying to find some way to bring the pump to the pail, would be unreasonable, precisely in the sense that these are not means that give much promise of working. There is not, however, any reason for filling the pail in the first place. There is, to be sure, some further purpose that can thus be fulfilled—the purpose of drinking, for example, or of washing—but this only indicates that filling the pail, which is his immediate purpose, is in turn a means to still some further purpose. It is, for example, neither rational nor irrational that one should want to drink; it is merely an expression of fact that he is thirsty. In the same sense, it is neither rational nor irrational that a man should want to swat a fly, or catch a bus, or become a physician, or attain fame as an author. These are simply statements of this or that man's aims or goals, both trivial and great, and they have nothing to do with reason. How they are to be reached, on the other hand, has a great deal to do with reason, for in general, one can set about trying to accomplish whatever it is he wants to accomplish in either an intelligent and rational way or otherwise. To say he is pursuing his goals in an intelligent way is only to say, as an inference from experience, that the means he adopts has some promise of succeeding.

CONATION AS THE PRECONDITION OF GOOD AND EVIL

With these rather commonplace observations in mind, let us now ask what conditions are necessary in order that any distinction between good and evil and between right and wrong can be made. That is, what must be presupposed in saying of something that it is good, or that it is bad, or in saying of an action that it is morally right or morally wrong?

Unthinking men have a tendency to assume that some things are just naturally good and others bad, and some actions right and some wrong, and that we need only to discover which are which. Even some of the most thoughtful philosophers, as we have seen, have started out with the same assumption. Thus, it is supposed that men are born into a world in which these distinctions already hold. Many have insisted that these distinctions cannot either have been contrived by men, or have awaited man's invention of laws, conventions, and customs. Ever so many things are man-made, including laws and moral customs; however, it is often thought that we cannot suppose the ultimate distinctions between good and evil or right and wrong to be such, for this would render all ethics, all justice, and all morality entirely relative. Indeed, most philosophers have thought that the problem of the moralist is simply to discover the true nature of goodness and rightness; they have disagreed not on whether such things exist independently of men, but on what *is* truly good, and what is truly right.

But now let us note that the basic distinction between good and evil could not even theoretically be drawn in a world that we imagined to be devoid of all life. That is, if we suppose the world to be exactly as it is, except that it contains not one living thing, it seems clear that nothing in it would be good and nothing bad. It would just be a dead world, turning through space with a lifeless atmosphere. Having deprived our imagined world of all life, we can modify it in numberless ways, but by no such modification can we ever produce the slightest hint of good or evil in it until we introduce at least one living being capable of reacting in one way or another to the world as that being finds it. Thus, we can imagine on the one hand that it is filled with things satisfying, lovely, and beautiful—with sunrises and sunsets, pleasing sights and sounds and fragrant odors, and with all things that beings like ourselves would find necessary and agreeable to life. Or we can imagine the opposite—a world that is dark and cold, filled with nauseous smells and barren of anything that would redeem such bleak aspects. But so long as we suppose that neither of these worlds does contain any being like ourselves, or any sentient being whatever, then neither world is *better* or *worse* than the other. Each is simply a world of facts, neutral with respect to good or evil, and destined to remain so until we suppose at least one onlooker capable of some sort of reaction to such facts.

Next we note that, if we begin to add inhabitants to this world who are, like ourselves, more or less rational, intelligent, and capable of perception but who, unlike ourselves, have no needs, purposes, or desires, the distinction between good and evil still does not arise. Imagine, for example, a whole colony of machinelike beings, living together and interacting in various ways. These beings, we can suppose, can perceive what is going on around them, distinguish between true and false, and make various inferences; but they are machinelike in that nothing matters to them, nothing makes any difference so far as their needs and purposes are concerned, because they have no needs or purposes, they do not care about anything. If it is raining, they observe that it is raining, but they seek no shelter, for they have no interest in being dry. If it is bitterly cold, then again they note this fact, but make no attempt to warm themselves because they care not whether they are warm or cold. If one of these beings observes another moving with great speed and force toward itself, it infers that a collision is impending, but makes no attempt to step aside, because it has no purpose that would be frustrated by such a collision. It has not even the desire to perpetuate its own existence, because it has no desires whatever. Having then been run down and broken by the onrushing being, losing a few limbs perhaps, it simply notes that this has happened, but it does not retaliate, because it had no interest in preserving any of its limbs or other parts anyway; and so on.

Such beings are, to be sure, difficult to imagine, for if we suppose them to be capable of perceiving, then we seem to imagine them to be living things, and it is difficult to imagine *any* living thing having no interests or purposes whatever, not even an interest in self-preservation. But of course we need not imagine that they are living things; we can instead suppose that they are enormously complicated machines, if that makes it easier. And then we need only suppose that they share with certain living things, such as ourselves, the capacity to perceive what is going on and to draw certain conclusions from what they perceive, but that they do *not* share with other living things, such as ourselves, any interest in what is going on. They are, in short, possessed of some degree of intelligence, but of no will whatever.

Now I think it is clear that a world inhabited by such beings would still be a world devoid of any good or evil. Like the first world we imagined, which did not even contain any beings of the most elementary intelligence, this one might contain anything we care to put into it without there arising the least semblance of good or of evil—until we imagine it to contain at least one being having some need, interest, or purpose. It would not matter to the beings just described whether their world was one filled with sunlight, warmth, and beauty, or dark and cold and filled with nauseous smells, because nothing would matter to them. They could tell the difference between sunlight and darkness, between warmth and cold, but they could in no way tell the difference between good and bad. Such a distinction would in fact have no meaning to them, and if they found their world dark, smelly, and cold they would have no basis for pronouncing it bad, simply because they would have no preference for any other kind of world.

THE EMERGENCE OF GOOD AND EVIL

Thus far, then, there is no good and no evil; there is nothing but bare facts of this kind or that.

But now let us suppose a world, much like our own, except that it contains throughout its vastness just one sentient being, a being who, like ourselves, cannot only perceive what is contained in the world around him and make certain inferences, but one to whom what he finds makes a difference. Suddenly, with the introduction of just one such being, certain things in the world do acquire the aspect of good and evil. Those things are good that this one being finds satisfying to his needs and desires, and those bad to which he reacts in the opposite way. Things in the world are not merely perceived by this being, but perceived as holding promise or threat to whatever interests him. Thus, the things that nourish and give warmth and enhance life are deemed good, and those that frustrate and threaten are deemed bad. The distinction between good and evil in a world containing only one living being possessed of needs and wants arises, then, only in relation to those needs and wants, and in no way existed in their absence. In the most general terms, those things are good that satisfy this being's actual wants, those that frustrate them are bad.

Now, with this picture still before us, let us note two things that are highly significant for the problems before us. The first is that the judgments of this solitary being concerning good and evil are as *absolute* as any judgment can be. Such a being is, indeed, the measure of all things: of good things as good and of bad things as bad. Whatever this being finds and declares to be good *is* good, and what he similarly finds to be evil, *is* evil. No distinction can be made, in terms of this being, between what is merely good *for him* and what is good *absolutely*. Whatever is good for him is good absolutely; there is no higher standard of goodness. For what could it be? If good and evil in this world arise only in relation to this being's wants and needs, then what could it possibly mean to say that something satisfies these but is nevertheless bad, or that something frustrates them but is nevertheless good? There simply is nothing else, apart from these wants and needs, in terms of which good and evil can possibly be measured, or even exist.

The second thing to note is that, even though good and evil have emerged with the appearance in this world of a single living being having wants and needs, no moral obligation has similarly arisen. The distinction between moral *right* and *wrong* has not yet come into the picture at all. That such a being should find something useful and agreeable and subsequently seize it, or find something threatening and shun it, is neither right nor wrong. Whatever he finds and wants is his for the taking, by a kind of natural right that is nothing but the absence of any natural wrong, and he cannot possibly have an obligation to undertake what would injure him, or even so much as make him the least uncomfortable. Although he can in this moral solitude create good and evil for himself, merely by his own declaration of what he finds things to be, he can in no way inflict them. For who could be his beneficiary or victim, besides himself? To whom could he owe any obligation to do anything? And by what standard, other than good and evil themselves, over which he is the sole judge, could any action of his be deemed right or wrong? He could, to be sure, fail to act in his own best interest, or even injure himself through neglect or stupidity, for which he would be accountable to no one. It would be as inappropriate to ascribe any moral responsibility to this solitary being as to the merest insect crawling through the grass.

Our next step, then, is to add another being like ourselves, another conative being with his own feelings, wants, and interests, and to suppose that the two who now inhabit our world have some interaction with each other. No new distinction between good and evil is introduced with the introduction of this new inhabitant, for that distinction emerged, complete and perfect, as soon as we assumed the existence of but one such inhabitant. With this small plurality of beings, it remains just what it was before. The first inhabitant deemed those things good that he found agreeable to his needs and purposes, and those things bad that threatened the opposite, and in this judgment he was absolutely correct. For him, the good and evil of things consisted of precisely such promise and threat to his interests. Such, accordingly, will it also be for our second sentient and goal-directed inhabitant. Those things will be good for him that promise fulfillment of his aims, whether grand or trifling, and those that threaten the opposite will be bad. In this judgment he, too, cannot err. For this will be precisely what the distinction between good and evil will mean to him, as it is what it means to the first; it will be the condition, and the only condition, of such a distinction being drawn by either of them. And we are not, it should be noted, here supposing any power of reasoning in either of our two beings. We do not suppose them to be appraising the various features of their common environment in terms of what they promise or threaten, and then *inferring* from such features that they have the moral qualities of good or evil. We do not even assume these two beings to be rational, though the picture is not altered in case they are. We only assume them to be sentient beings with needs, or in other words, beings who desire and shun, and can feel it when their needs are fulfilled, and when they are not.

THE EMERGENCE OF RIGHT AND WRONG

There was, we noted, no place for such ethical notions as right and wrong or for moral obligation, so long as we imagined a world containing only one purposeful and sentient being, although the presence of such a being was enough to produce good and evil. With the introduction of a multiplicity of such beings, however, we have supplied the foundation for these additional notions, for they are based on the fact that the aims or purposes of such beings can conflict. Thus, two or more such beings can covet the same thing. In that case each will deem it a good, but it can easily arise that not both can possess it, that its possession by one will mean deprivation for the other. The result is a conflict of wills, which can lead to a mutual aggression in which each stands to lose more than the thing for which they are contending is worth to either of them. Such a situation can produce a threat to life itself, for example, and without life all good and evil are reduced to zero.

There is, moreover, another side to the coin. For just as the wills of two purposeful beings can conflict, in the manner just suggested, so also can they coincide in a very significant way. That is, situations can arise in which each of two such beings needs the help of the other in order to attain what it wants, or to ward off some evil. They may, for example, be threatened by some force, animate or inanimate, that the strength of neither is sufficient to overcome, but from which their combined strength offers some hope of safety. Or again, each may find that he possesses in excess of his own needs something that the other requires. One, for example, may possess an excess of food, of which the other has none, while the latter one possesses an excess of the requirements for shelter, entirely lacking to the former. The possibility of mutual giving and taking thus presents itself, wherein each can benefit greatly at small cost to himself. Or again, two such beings may have some common end, such as the begetting of children, for which some sort of cooperation is needed by the very nature of things, and so on.

The supposition of a multiplicity of beings, each with its own needs and purposes, presents, in short, numberless possibilities for (1) conflict, and (2) cooperation. Possibilities of the first kind are loaded with the threat of evil, and those of the second kind with the promise of good, still thinking of good and evil in the sense already adduced—namely, as that which satisfies or fulfills, and that which frustrates felt needs and goals.

RIGHT AND WRONG AS RELATIVE TO RULES

If needs are to be satisfied and goals fulfilled, however, then situations of conflict and, particularly, situations of cooperation must be resolved in the context of *rules,* using the notion of rules in an extremely broad sense that encompasses any regular and predictable behavior. Thus, it becomes a "rule" that two or more such beings, faced with a common threat, shall abstain from attacking each other until that threat is overcome. It becomes another rule that they shall meet the threat together by combining their resources, inasmuch as acting in accordance with such rules will enable each to avoid what appears as an evil. When two such beings each covet the same thing, and not both can possess it, it may become a rule that it remains with him who first possessed it. The underlying basis for such a rule is that, if it is disregarded, the coveted thing may end up in the hands of neither, and that evils even greater than this, such as mutual injury or even death, may follow instead. When each of two such beings possesses an excess of what is sought by the other, a rule of trading becomes obviously advantageous to both. Through such behavior, the good of each is enhanced at no significant cost. The alternative is combat, in which each would be faced with the possibility of total loss.

Now it should be clear from this that by rules I do not mean rational principles of conduct, in the sense that it would require any powers of reason to discover them, much less do I mean principles that are set forth in any coherent writing or speech. They need not be things that are formulated at all. Rules, in the sense that I am now considering them, are nothing but practices or ways of behaving that are more or less regular and that can, therefore, be expected. They are, on the other hand, rational in this sense: such behavior offers promise, to those who behave in the manner in question, of avoiding evil and attaining good. Mutual aggression, for example, always presents the threat of great and unpredictable evil to each aggressor, and the possibility of such evil is almost certain to outweigh any possibility of good. To the extent, therefore, that some good can be ensured by a certain mode of behavior or, as I am using the term, by action in accordance with a rule, and that such behavior will remove the threat of evil contained in any situation of combat, then action in accordance with the rule is better than combat. In that sense, but only in that sense, it is more rational.

Suppose, for example, that among a certain people the practice arises that men, on approaching one another, extend a forearm with the palm of the hand open and exposed to view, each thus indicating that he is unarmed. The gesture is recognized and acknowledged by each then grasping the other's open hand, that is, by shaking hands. Now here, clearly, is a rule, as I am using the term, even though it does not need to be formulated or embodied in any code. It is simply a regular mode of behavior. It has as its obvious purpose the avoidance of evil and the advancement of good and is in that sense, but that sense only, rational. It would be most treacherously violated by one who, extending his open hand of friendship, assaulted his greeter with a weapon concealed in his other hand. The treachery of this would consist in using the rule to promote the very evil the rule was meant to avoid.

THE WORLD AS IT IS

We have been imagining, then, a world, at first lifeless and barren, that gradually becomes occupied with beings having needs, feelings, and purposes. Until the appearance of the first such being, that world contains no hint of good or evil, but both arise the moment he comes into the picture. With the multiplication of such beings, the possibilities of further goods and evils arise with the appearance of situations of cooperation and conflict. Good is increased and enhanced by the former and evil by the latter. Cooperation, however, and the safe resolution of conflict obviously require certain regular modes of behavior, or what I have called rules. These notions having been made tolerably clear, we can now refine and elaborate on the imaginary picture with which we began until it begins to resemble the world of men in which we actually live.

Thus, we can suppose that the multiplicity of sentient and purposeful beings by which our imaginary world is inhabited are men like ourselves, for we, too, are sentient and purposeful beings. We can suppose that those modes of behavior required for cooperation and the resolution of conflict situations become actual precepts, conveyed by one generation to the next, and that the most important of them come to be rules embodied in traditional literature for which men have a certain awe. They are, thus, passed from generation to generation, like the Ten Commandments of scripture. Others come to assume the form of written laws, and various practical means are hit on for securing, as nearly as possible, the adherence to them on the part of all. Groupings of men are formed for the attainment of the maximum of good for some or all and the minimization of evil. Thus do societies arise, by their common adherence to rules that become more elaborate as the societies themselves become larger and more complex. The behavior required by such rules rises, by some degree or other, to that level we call civilized conduct; but the basic principle of those rules remains exactly what it was from the outset: the minimization of conflict and its consequent evil, and the maximization of cooperation and its consequent good.

All this is, of course, but a sketch, and a very superficial one, but no more is really needed for our present purpose, which is to explain good and evil and moral right and wrong.

How, then, do moral right and wrong arise? The answer is fairly obvious in the light of what has been said. Right is simply the adherence to rule, and wrong is violation of it. The notions of right and wrong absolutely presuppose the existence of rules, at least in the broad sense of rule with which we began. That two beings should fight and injure each other in their contest for something that each covets, and thereby, perhaps, each lose the good he wanted to seize, is clearly an evil to both. But in the absence of a rule of behavior—that is, some anticipated behavior to the contrary—no wrong has been done; only an evil has been produced. Given such a rule, however—for example, given the simple and rudimentary expectation that the thing in question shall be his who first took it—then a wrong is committed by the one who attempts to divest the holder of that good. The wrong comes into being with the violation of the rule, and in no way existed ahead of the rule. The same is, of course, true of right. If, for example, we presuppose no expectation that a good may be enjoyed in peace by whoever first seizes it, then, if another nevertheless, in the absence of any such rule, abstains from seizing that good from its first possessor, this potential aggressor has clearly fostered a good, simply by eschewing an evil. But he has in no way done "the right thing," for the notion of *right* conduct can have no meaning in the absence of some sort of rule. If one is tempted to say that this would-be aggressor has done something morally right, then one will find that all he means is that he has produced an effect that was good. That is something entirely different. One also may be reading into a situation, in which, by hypothesis, there is no rule to which to adhere, certain rules of right and wrong that one has learned to respect.

For Further Reflection

1. Examine Taylor's theory of good and evil and right and wrong. First, note that he claims that humans are basically conative beings—moved by will and desire—rather than rational beings. Do you agree with this? What role does he think reason plays in life?
2. Outline the four stages in the thought process, from a world with no conscious beings to his final stage. Where do good and evil enter the picture? Where do right and wrong enter it? How are the two categories related to each other? Do you agree with Taylor's analysis? Explain your answer.
3. What, according to Taylor, is the purpose of rules? Give an example of a rule to illustrate his point. Do you find his analysis convincing? Explain your answer.
4. Are some rules better than others?

Further Readings for Chapter 2

Hallie, Philip P. *Cruelty.* Middletown, Conn.: Wesleyan University Press, 1982.

Kekes, John. "The Reflexivity of Evil." *Social Philosophy and Policy* 15, no. 1 (1998).

Midgley, Mary. *Wickedness: A Philosophical Essay.* Boston: Routledge and Kegan Paul, 1984.

Milo, Ronald. *Immorality.* Princeton, N.J.: Princeton University Press, 1984.

———. "Virtue, Knowledge and Wickedness." *Social Philosophy and Policy* 15, no. 1 (1998).

Nietzsche, Frederich. *Beyond Good and Evil.* Translated by R. J. Hollingdale. New York: Penguin, 1990.

Taylor, Richard. *Good and Evil.* Buffalo, N.Y.: Prometheus, 1970.

CHAPTER 3

Is Everything Relative?

Is morality essentially relative, or are there objective moral truths? This question haunts contemporary society. On the one hand, anthropologists have uncovered a multitudinous array of variegated cultural codes and moral practices. Who are we to judge another culture? Tolerance would seem to require that we allow for a plethora of practices and ways of expressing morality. We've been taught that multicultural diversity is a good in its own right, so we should be accepting of difference. On the other hand, some actions seem wrong in principle (torturing or killing the innocent, breaking promises, lying, and destroying other people's property), and some actions seem morally good (helping people who are in need, keeping contracts, cooperating for mutual benefit, and promoting justice). How do we reconcile these opposing insights?

The readings in this chapter inquire into the strengths and weaknesses of moral relativism, the theory that the validity of moral principles is dependent on cultural or subjective acceptance. Our first reading is an ancient observation of the Greek historian Herodotus on how different cultures project their customs onto the heavens, identifying them with eternal verities. Our second reading is a defense of relativism by the cultural anthropologist Ruth Benedict, who develops the theme set forth by Herodotus. Cultural norms are the colored glasses through which we view all our world. In our third reading, David Enoch arques for an objective ethics that he says we are all committed to. James Rachels in our fourth reading critiques the main argument for cultural relativism and finds it seriously defective. In our fifth reading, "Judge Not?" Jean Bethke Elshtain questions the dictum that is at the heart of relativism. In our fifth reading, "Trying Out One's New Sword," Mary Midgley uses a compelling example from Japanese history to argue that understanding and judging other cultures are not only possible but inescapable. And, finally, Henrik Ibsen illustrates the philosophy of moral objectivism in the person of Dr. Stockmann, who defies his culture in the name of truth.

Custom Is King

HERODOTUS

Herodotus (485–430 B.C.), a Greek and the first Western historian, in this brief passage from his *Histories* illustrates cultural relativism and may suggest that ethical relativism is the correct view ("culture is king").

Thus it appears certain to me, by a great variety of proofs, that Cambyses was raving mad; he would not else have set himself to make a mock of holy rites and long-established usages. For if one were to offer men to choose out of all the customs in the world such as seemed to them the best, they would examine the whole number, and end by preferring their own; so convinced are they that their own usages far surpass those of all others. Unless, therefore, a man was mad, it is not likely that he would make sport of such matters. That people have this feeling about their laws may be seen by very many proofs: among others, by the following. Darius, after he had got the kingdom, called into his presence certain Greeks who were at hand, and asked—"What he should pay them to eat the bodies of their fathers when they died?" To which they answered, that there was no sum that would tempt them to do such a thing. He then sent for certain Indians, of the race called Callatians, men who eat their fathers, and asked them, while the Greeks stood by, and knew by the help of an interpreter all that was said—"What he should give them to burn the bodies of their fathers at their decease?" The Indians exclaimed aloud, and bade him forbear such language. Such is men's wont herein; and Pindar was right, in my judgment, when he said, "Custom is the king o'er all."

From Herodotus, *The Histories of Herodotus,* translated by George Rawlinson (New York: Appleton, 1859).

The Case for Moral Relativism

RUTH BENEDICT

Ruth Benedict (1887–1948), an American anthropologist, taught at Columbia University and is best known for her book *Patterns of Culture* (1934). Benedict sets forth a theory of moral relativism in which moral principles are based on the common beliefs and practices of social systems. Since these systems or cultures can vary, so can morality. Like a work of art, the social system chooses which theme of its repertoire of basic tendencies to emphasize and then goes about to create a more or less comprehensive system of mores to support those tendencies. What is considered normal or abnormal behavior will depend on the choices of these social systems, or what Benedict calls the "idea-practice pattern of the culture."

In this selection Benedict assembles a varied array of cultural data from her research on tribal behavior on an island in northwest Melanesia, from which she draws her conclusions that moral relativism is the correct view of morality.

Modern social anthropology has become more and more a study of the varieties and common elements of cultural environment and the consequences of these in human behavior. For such a study of diverse social orders primitive peoples fortunately provide a laboratory not yet entirely vitiated by the spread of a standardized worldwide civilization. Dyaks and Hopis, Fijians and Yakuts are significant for psychological and sociological study because only among these simpler peoples has there been sufficient isolation to give opportunity for the development of localized social forms. In the higher cultures the standardization of custom and belief over a couple of continents has given a false sense of the inevitability of the particular forms that have gained currency, and we need to turn to a wider survey in order to check the conclusions we hastily base upon this near-universality of familiar customs. Most of the simpler cultures did not gain the wide currency of the one which, out of our experience, we identify with human nature, but this was for various historical reasons, and certainly not for any that gives us as its carriers a monopoly of social good or of social sanity. Modern civilization, from this point of view, becomes not a necessary pinnacle of human achievement but one entry in a long series of possible adjustments.

From "Anthropology and the Abnormal," in *The Journal of General Psychology* 10 (1934): 59–82, Helen Dwight Reid Educational Foundation.

These adjustments, whether they are in mannerisms like the ways of showing anger, or joy, or grief in any society, or in major human drives like those of sex, prove to be far more variable than experience in any one culture would suggest. In certain fields, such as that of religion or of formal marriage arrangements, these wide limits of variability are well known and can be fairly described. In others it is not yet possible to give a generalized account, but that does not absolve us of the task of indicating the significance of the work that has been done and of the problems that have arisen.

One of these problems relates to the customary modern normal-abnormal categories and our conclusions regarding them. In how far are such categories culturally determined, or in how far can we with assurance regard them as absolute? In how far can we regard inability to function socially as diagnostic of abnormality, or in how far is it necessary to regard this as a function of the culture?

As a matter of fact, one of the most striking facts that emerge from a study of widely varying cultures is the ease with which our abnormals function in other cultures. It does not matter what kind of "abnormality" we choose for illustration, those which indicate extreme instability, or those which are more in the nature of character traits like sadism or delusions of grandeur or of persecution, there are well-described cultures in which these abnormals function at ease and with honor, and apparently without danger or difficulty to the society. . . .

The most notorious of these is trance and catalepsy. Even a very mild mystic is aberrant in our culture. But most peoples have regarded even extreme psychic manifestations not only as normal and desirable, but even as characteristic of highly valued and gifted individuals. This was true even in our own cultural background in that period when Catholicism made the ecstatic experience the mark of sainthood. It is hard for us, born and brought up in a culture that makes no use of the experience, to realize how important a role it may play and how many individuals are capable of it, once it has been given an honorable place in any society. . . .

Cataleptic and trance phenomena are, of course, only one illustration of the fact that those whom we regard as abnormals may function adequately in other cultures. Many of our culturally discarded traits are selected for elaboration in different societies. Homosexuality is an excellent example, for in this case our attention is not constantly diverted, as in the consideration of trance, to the interruption of routine activity which it implies. Homosexuality poses the problem very simply. A tendency toward this trait in our culture exposes an individual to all the conflicts to which all aberrants are always exposed, and we tend to identify the consequences of this conflict with homosexuality. But these consequences are obviously local and cultural. Homosexuals in many societies are not incompetent, but they may be such if the culture asks adjustments of them that would strain any man's vitality. Wherever homosexuality has been given an honorable place in any society, those to whom it is congenial have filled adequately the honorable roles society assigns to them. Plato's *Republic* is, of course, the most convincing statement of such a reading of homosexuality. It is presented as one of the major means to the good life, and it was generally so regarded in Greece at that time.

The cultural attitude toward homosexuals has not always been on such a high ethical plane, but it has been very varied. Among many American Indian tribes there exists the institution of the berdache, as the French called them. These men-women were men who at puberty or thereafter took the dress and the occupations of women. Sometimes they married other men and lived with them. Sometimes they were men with no inversion, persons of weak sexual endowment who chose this role to avoid the jeers of the women. The berdaches were never regarded as of first-rate supernatural power, as similar men-women were in Siberia, but rather as leaders in women's occupations, good healers in certain diseases, or, among certain tribes, as the genial organizers of social affairs. In any case, they were socially placed. They were not left exposed to the conflicts that visit the deviant who is excluded from participation in the recognized patterns of his society.

The most spectacular illustrations of the extent to which normality may be culturally defined are those cultures where an abnormality of our culture is the cornerstone of their social structure. It is not possible to do justice to these possibilities in a short discussion. A recent study of an island of northwest Melanesia by Fortune describes a society built upon traits which we regard as beyond the border of paranoia. In this tribe the exogamic groups look upon each other as prime manipulators of black magic, so that one marries always into an enemy group which remains for life one's deadly and unappeasable foes. They look upon a good garden crop as a confession of theft, for everyone is engaged in making magic to induce into his garden the productiveness of his neighbors'; therefore no secrecy in the island is so rigidly insisted upon as the secrecy of a man's harvesting of his yams. Their polite phrase at the acceptance of a gift is, "And if you now poison me, how shall I repay you this present?" Their preoccupation with poisoning is constant; no woman ever leaves her cooking pot for a moment untended. Even the great affinal economic exchanges that are characteristic of this Melanesian culture area are quite altered in Dobu since they are incompatible with this fear and distrust that pervades the culture. They go farther and people the whole world outside their own quarters with such malignant spirits that all-night feasts and ceremonials simply do not occur here. They have even rigorous religiously enforced customs that forbid the sharing of seed even in one family group. Anyone else's food is deadly poison to you, so that communality of stores is out of the question. For some months before harvest the whole society is on the verge of starvation, but if one falls to the temptation and eats up one's seed yams, one is an outcast and a beachcomber for life. There is no coming back. It involves, as a matter of course, divorce and the breaking of all social ties.

Now in this society where no one may work with another and no one may share with another, Fortune describes the individual who was regarded by all his fellows as crazy. He was not one of those who periodically ran amok and, beside himself and frothing at the mouth, fell with a knife upon anyone he could reach. Such behavior they did not regard as putting anyone outside the pale. They did not even put the individuals who were known to be liable to these attacks under any kind of control. They merely fled when they saw the attack coming on and kept out of the way. "He would be all right tomorrow." But there was one man of sunny, kindly disposition who liked work and liked to be helpful. The compulsion was too strong for him to repress it in favor of the opposite tendencies of his culture. Men and women never spoke of him without laughing; he was silly and simple and definitely crazy. Nevertheless, to the ethnologist used to a culture that has, in Christianity, made his type the model of all virtue, he seemed a pleasant fellow. . . .

. . . Among the Kwakiutl it did not matter whether a relative had died in bed of disease, or by the hand of an enemy, in either case death was an affront to be wiped out by the death of another person. The fact that one had been caused to mourn was proof that one had been put upon. A chief's sister and her daughter had gone up to Victoria, and either because they drank bad whiskey or because their boat capsized they never came back. The chief called together his warriors, "Now I ask you, tribes, who shall wail? Shall I do it or shall another?" The spokesman answered, of course, "Not you, Chief. Let some other of the tribes." Immediately they set up the war pole to announce their intention of wiping out the injury, and gathered a war party. They set out, and found seven men and two children asleep and killed them. "Then they felt good when they arrived at Sebaa in the evening."

The point which is of interest to us is that in our society those who on that occasion would feel good when they arrived at Sebaa that evening would be the definitely abnormal. There would be some, even in our society, but it is not a recognized and approved mood under the circumstances. On the Northwest Coast those are favored and fortunate to whom that mood under those circumstances is congenial, and those to whom it is repugnant are unlucky. This latter minority can register in their own culture only by doing violence to their congenial responses and acquiring others that are difficult for them. The person, for instance, who, like a Plains Indian whose wife has been taken from him, is too proud to fight, can deal with the Northwest Coast civilization only by ignoring its strongest bents. If he cannot achieve it, he is the deviant in that culture, their instance of abnormality.

This head-hunting that takes place on the Northwest Coast after a death is no matter of blood revenge or of organized vengeance. There is no effort to tie up the subsequent killing with any responsibility on the part of the victim for the death of the person who is being mourned. A chief whose son has died goes visiting wherever his fancy dictates, and he says to his host, "My prince has died today, and you go with him." Then he kills him. In this, according to their interpretation, he acts nobly because he has not been downed. He has thrust back in return. The whole procedure is meaningless without the fundamental paranoid reading of bereavement. Death, like all the other untoward accidents of existence, confounds man's pride and can only be handled in the category of insults.

Behavior honored upon the Northwest Coast is one which is recognized as abnormal in our civilization, and yet it is sufficiently close to the attitudes of our own culture to be intelligible to us and to have a definite vocabulary with which we may discuss it. The megalomaniac paranoid trend is a definite danger in our society. It is encouraged by some of our major preoccupations, and it confronts us with a choice of two possible attitudes. One is to brand it as abnormal and reprehensible, and is the attitude we have chosen in our civilization. The other is to make it an essential attribute of ideal man, and this is the solution in the culture of the Northwest Coast.

These illustrations, which it has been possible to indicate only in the briefest manner, force upon us the fact that normality is culturally defined. An adult shaped to the drives and standards of either of these cultures, if he were transported into our civilization, would fall into our categories of abnormality. He would be faced with the psychic dilemmas of the socially unavailable. In his own culture, however, he is the pillar of society, the end result of socially inculcated mores, and the problem of personal instability in his case simply does not arise.

No one civilization can possibly utilize in its mores the whole potential range of human behavior. Just as there are great numbers of possible phonetic articulations, and the possibility of language depends on a selection and standardization of a few of these in order that speech communication may be possible at all, so the possibility of organized behavior of every sort, from the fashions of local dress and houses to the dicta of a people's ethics and religion, depends upon a similar selection among the possible behavior traits. In the field of recognized economic obligations or sex taboos this selection is as nonrational and subconscious a process as it is in the field of phonetics. It is a process which goes on in the group for long periods of time and is historically conditioned by innumerable accidents of isolation or of contact of peoples.

In any comprehensive study of psychology, the selection that different cultures have made in the course of history within the great circumference of potential behavior is of great significance.

Every society, beginning with some slight inclination in one direction or another, carries its preference farther and farther, integrating itself more and more completely upon its chosen basis, and discarding those types of behavior that are uncongenial. Most of those organizations of personality that seem to us most uncontrovertibly abnormal have been used by different civilizations in the very foundations of their institutional life. Conversely the most valued traits of our normal individuals have been looked on in differently organized cultures as aberrant. Normality, in short, within a very wide range, is culturally defined. It is primarily a term for the socially elaborated segment of human behavior in any culture; and abnormality, a term for the segment that that particular civilization does not use. The very eyes with which we see the problem are conditioned by the long traditional habits of our own society.

It is a point that has been made more often in relation to ethics than in relation to psychiatry. We do not any longer make the mistake of deriving the morality of our locality and decade directly from the inevitable constitution of human nature. We do not elevate it to the dignity of a first principle. We recognize that morality differs in every society, and is a convenient term for socially approved habits. Mankind has always preferred to say, "It is morally good," rather than "It is habitual," and the fact of this preference is matter enough for a critical science of ethics. But historically the two phrases are synonymous.

The concept of the normal is properly a variant of the concept of the good. It is that which society has approved. A normal action is one which falls well within the limits of expected behavior for a particular society. Its variability among different peoples is essentially a function of the variability of the behavior patterns that different societies have created for themselves, and can never be wholly divorced from a consideration of culturally institutionalized types of behavior.

Each culture is a more or less elaborate working-out of the potentialities of the segment it has chosen. In so far as a civilization is well integrated and consistent within itself, it will tend to carry farther and farther, according to its nature, its initial impulse toward a particular type of action, and from the point of view of any other culture those elaborations will include more and more extreme and aberrant traits.

Each of these traits, in proportion as it reinforces the chosen behavior patterns of that culture, is for that culture normal. Those individuals to whom it is congenial either congenitally, or as the result of childhood sets, are accorded prestige in that culture, and are not visited with the social contempt or disapproval which their traits would call down upon them in a society that was differently organized. On the other hand, those individuals whose characteristics are not congenial to the selected type of human behavior in that community are the deviants, no matter how valued their personality traits may be in a contrasted civilization.

The Dobuan who is not easily susceptible to fear of treachery, who enjoys work and likes to be helpful, is their neurotic and regarded as silly. On the Northwest Coast the person who finds it difficult to read life in terms of an insult contest will be the person upon whom fall all the difficulties of the culturally unprovided for. The person who does not find it easy to humiliate a neighbor, nor to see humiliation in his own experience, who is genial and loving, may, of course, find some unstandardized way of achieving satisfactions in his society, but not in the major patterned responses that his culture requires of him. If he is born to play an important role in a family with many hereditary privileges, he can succeed only by doing violence to his whole personality. If he does not succeed, he has betrayed his culture; that is, he is abnormal.

I have spoken of individuals as having sets toward certain types of behavior, and of these sets as running sometimes counter to the types of behavior which are institutionalized in the culture to which they belong. From all that we know of contrasting cultures it seems clear that differences of temperament occur in every society. The matter has never been made the subject of investigation, but from the available material it would appear that these temperament types are very likely of universal recurrence. That is, there is an ascertainable range of human behavior that is found wherever a sufficiently large series of individuals is observed. But the proportion in which behavior types stand to one another in different societies is not universal. The vast majority of individuals in any group are shaped to the fashion of that culture. In other words, most individuals are plastic to the moulding force of the society into which they are born. In a society that values trance, as in India, they will have supernormal experience. In a society that institutionalizes homosexuality, they will be homosexual. In a society that sets the gathering of possessions as the chief human objective, they will amass property. The deviants, whatever the type of behavior the culture has institutionalized, will remain few in number, and there seems no more difficulty in moulding the vast malleable majority to the "normality" of what we consider an aberrant trait, such as delusions of reference, than to the normality of such accepted behavior patterns as acquisitiveness. The small proportion of the number of the deviants in any culture is not a function of the sure instinct with which that society has built itself upon the fundamental sanities, but of the universal fact that, happily, the majority of mankind quite readily take any shape that is presented to them. . . .

For Further Reflection

1. Is Benedict correct in saying that our culture is "but one entry in a long series of possible adjustments"? What are the implications of this statement?
2. Can we separate the descriptive (or fact-stating) aspect of anthropological study from the prescriptive (evaluative) aspect of evaluating cultures? Are there some independent criteria by which we can say that some cultures are better than others? Can you think how this project might begin?
3. What are the implications of Benedict's claim that morality is simply whatever a culture deems normal behavior? Is this a satisfactory equation? Can you apply it to the institution of slavery or the Nazi policy of anti-Semitism?
4. What is the significance of Benedict's statement, "The very eyes with which we see the problem are conditioned by the long traditional habits of our own society"? Can we apply the conceptual relativism embodied in this statement to her own position?

Why I Am an Objectivist about Ethics (And Why You Are, Too)

DAVID ENOCH

David Enoch is a philosopher in the Faculty of Humanities, Hebrew University of Jerusalem. In this article he argues that almost everyone assumes the objectivity of ethics. He offers three tests he thinks suggest that we do indeed have such a commitment. Then he examines and critiques arguments that seem to undercut claims of moral objectivity. He concludes, "Until we get . . . a conclusive argument against moral objectivity, then, objectivism should be the view to beat."

You may think that you're a moral relativist or subjectivist—many people today seem to. But I don't think you are. In fact, when we start doing metaethics—when we start, that is, thinking philosophically about our moral

From *The Ethical Life*, 3rd ed., edited by Shafer-Landau (2015). Chp."Why I Am an Objectivist about Ethics (And Why You Are, Too)" by Enoch pp.192–205. By permission of Oxford University Press, USA.

discourse and practice—thoughts about morality's objectivity become almost irresistible. Now, as is always the case in philosophy, that some thoughts seem irresistible is only the starting point for the discussion, and under argumentative pressure we may need to revise our relevant beliefs. Still, it's important to get the starting points right. So it's important to understand the deep ways in which rejecting morality's objectivity is unappealing. What I want to do, then, is to highlight the ways in which accepting morality's objectivity is appealing, and to briefly address some common worries about it, worries that may lead some to reject—or to think they reject—such objectivity. In the final section, I comment on the (not obvious) relation between the underlying concerns about morality's objectivity and the directions in which current discussion in metaethics are developing. As it will emerge, things are not (even) as simple as the discussion below seems to suggest. This is just one reason why metaethics is so worth doing.

WHY OBJECTIVITY? THREE (RELATED) REASONS

In the next section we're going to have to say a little more about what objectivity is. But sometimes it's helpful to start by engaging the underlying concerns, and return to more abstract, perhaps conceptual, issues later on.

The Spinach Test

Consider the following joke (which I borrow from Christine Korsgaard): A child hates spinach. He then reports that he's glad he hates spinach. To the question "Why?" he responds: "Because if I liked it, I would have eaten it, and it's yucky!"

In a minute we're going to have to annoyingly ask why the joke is funny. For now, though, I want to highlight the fact that similar jokes are not always similarly funny. Consider, for instance, someone who grew up in the twentieth-century West and who believes that the earth revolves around the sun. Also, she reports to be happy she wasn't born in the Middle Ages, "because had I grown up in the Middle Ages, I would have believed that the earth is in the center of the universe, and that belief is false!"

To my ears, the joke doesn't work in this latter version (try it on your friends!). The response in the earth-revolves-around-the-sun case sounds perfectly sensible, precisely in a way in which the analogous response does not sound sensible in the spinach case.

We need one last case. Suppose someone grew up in the United States in the late twentieth century and rejects any manifestation of racism as morally wrong. He then reports that he's happy that that's when and where he grew up, "because had I grown up in the eighteenth century, I would have accepted slavery and racism. And these things are wrong!" How funny is this third, last version of the joke? To my ears, it's about as (un) funny as the second one, and nowhere nearly as amusing as the first. The response to the question in this last case (why he is happy that he grew up in the twentieth century) seems to me to make perfect sense, and I suspect it makes sense to you too. And this is why there's nothing funny about it.

OK, then, why is the spinach version funny and the others are not? Usually, our attitude towards our own likings and dislikings (when it comes to food, for instance) is that it's all about us. If you don't like spinach, the reason you shouldn't have it is precisely that you don't like it. So if we're imagining a hypothetical scenario in which you do like it, then you no longer have any reason not to eat it. This is what the child in the first example gets wrong: he's holding fixed his dislike for spinach, even in thinking about the hypothetical case in which he likes spinach. But because these issues are all about him and what he likes and dislikes, this makes no sense.

But physics is different: What we want, believe or do—none of this affects the earth's orbit. The fact that the earth revolves around the sun is just not about us at all. So it makes sense to hold this truth fixed even when thinking about hypothetical cases in which you don't believe it. And so it makes sense to be happy that you aren't in the Middle Ages, since you'd then be in a situation in which your beliefs about the earth's orbit would be false (even if you couldn't know that they were). And because this makes sense, the joke isn't funny.

And so we have the spinach test: About any relevant subject matter, formulate an analogue of the spinach joke. If the joke works, this seems to indicate that the subject matter is all about us and our responses, our likings and dislikings, our preferences, and so on. If the joke doesn't work, the subject matter is much more objective than that, as in the astronomy case. And when we apply the spinach test to a moral issue (like the moral status of racism), it seems to fall squarely on the objective side.

(Exercise: Think about your taste in music, and formulate the spinach test for it. Is the joke funny?)

Disagreement and Deliberation

We sometimes engage in all sorts of disagreements. Sometimes, for instance, we may engage in a disagreement about even such silly things as whether bitter chocolate is better than milk chocolate. Sometimes we disagree about such things as whether human actions influence global warming. But these two kinds of disagreement are very different. One way of seeing this is thinking about what it feels like from the inside to engage in such disagreements. In the chocolate case, it feels like stating one's own preference, and perhaps trying to influence the listener into getting his own preferences in line. In the global warming case, though, it feels like trying to get at an objective truth, one that is there anyway, independently of our beliefs and preferences. (Either human actions contribute to global warming, or they don't, right?)

And so another test suggests itself, a test having to do with what it *feels like* to engage in disagreement (or, as we sometimes say, with the *phenomenology* of disagreement).

But now think of some serious moral disagreement—about the moral status of abortion, say. Suppose, then, that you are engaged in such disagreement. (It's important to imagine this from the inside, as it were. Don't imagine looking from the outside at two people arguing over abortion; think what it's like to be engaged in such argument yourself—if not about abortion, then about some other issue you care deeply about.) Perhaps you think that there is nothing wrong with abortion, and you're arguing with someone who thinks that abortion is morally wrong. What does such disagreement feel like? In particular, does it feel more like disagreeing over which chocolate is better, or like disagreeing over factual matters (such as whether human actions contribute to global warming)?

Because this question is a phenomenological one (that is, it's about what something feels like from the inside), I can't answer this question for you. You have to think about what it feels like for you when you are engaged in moral disagreement. But I can say that in my case such moral disagreement feels exactly like the one about global warming—it's about an objective matter of fact, that exists independently of us and our disagreement. It is in no way like disagreeing over the merits of different kinds of chocolate. And I think I can rather safely predict that this is how it feels for you too.

So on the phenomenology-of-disagreement test as well, morality seems to fall on the objective side.

In fact, we may be able to take disagreement out of the picture entirely. Suppose there is no disagreement—perhaps because you're all by yourself trying to make up your mind about what to do next. In one case, you're thinking about what kind of chocolate to get. In another, you're choosing between buying a standard car and a somewhat more expensive hybrid car (whose effect on global warming, if human actions contribute to global warming, is less destructive). Here, too, there's a difference. In the first case, you seem to be asking questions about yourself and what you like more (in general, or right now). In the second case, you need to make up your mind about your own action, of course, but you're asking yourself questions about objective matters of fact that do not depend on you at all—in particular, about whether human actions affect global warming.

Now consider a third case, in which you're trying to make up your mind about having an abortion, or advising a friend who is considering an abortion. So you're wondering whether abortion is wrong. Does it feel like asking about your own preferences or like an objective matter of fact? Is it more like the chocolate case or like the hybrid car case? If, like me, you answer that it's much more like the hybrid car case, then you think, like me, that the phenomenology of deliberation too indicates that morality is objective.

(Exercise: think about your taste in music again. In terms of the phenomenology of disagreement and deliberation, is it on the objective side?)

Would It Still Have Been Wrong If . . . ?

Top hats are out of fashion. This may be an interesting, perhaps even practically relevant, fact—it may, for instance, give you reason to wear a top hat (if you want to be special) or not to (if not). But think about the following question: Had our fashion practices been very different—had we all worn top hats, thought they were cool, and so on—would it still have been true that top hats are out of fashion? The answer, it seems safe to assume, is "no."

Smoking causes cancer. This is an interesting, practically relevant, fact—it most certainly gives you a reason not to smoke, or perhaps to stop smoking. Now, had our relevant practices and beliefs regarding smoking been different—had we been OK with it, had we not banned it, had we thought smoking was actually quite harmless—would it still have been true that smoking causes cancer? I take it to be uncontroversial that the answer is "yes." The effects of smoking on our health do not depend on our beliefs and practices in anything like the way in which the fashionability of top hats does. Rather, it is an objective matter of fact.

And so we have a third objectivity test, one in terms of the relevant "what if" sentences (or *counterfactuals*, as they are often called), such as "Had our beliefs and practices been very different, would it still have been true that so-and-so?" Let's apply this test to morality.

Gender-based discrimination is wrong. I hope you agree with me on this (if you don't, replace this with a moral judgment you're rather confident in). Would it still have been wrong had our relevant practices and beliefs been different? Had we been all for gender-based discrimination, would that have made gender-based discrimination morally acceptable? Of course, in such a case we would have *believed* that there's nothing wrong with gender-based discrimination. But would it *be* wrong? To me it seems very clear that the answer is "Yes!" Gender-based discrimination is just as wrong in a society where everyone believes it's morally permissible. (This, after all, is why we would want such a society to change, and why, if we are members, we would fight for reform.) The problem in such a society is precisely that its members miss something so important—namely, the wrongness of gender-based discrimination. Had we thought gender-based discrimination was okay, we would have been mistaken. The morality of such discrimination does not depend on our opinion of it. The people in that hypothetical society may accept gender-based discrimination, but that doesn't make such discrimination acceptable.

In this respect too, then, morality falls on the objective side. When it comes to the counterfactual test, moral truths behave more like objective, factual truths (like whether smoking causes cancer) than like purely subjective, perhaps conventional claims (say, that top hats are unfashionable).

(Exercises: Can you see how the counterfactual test relates to the spinach test? And think about your favorite music, the kind of music that you don't just like, but that you think is *good*. Had you not liked it, would it still have been good?)

WHAT'S AT ISSUE?

We have, then, three tests for objectivity—the spinach test, the phenomenology-of-disagreement-and-deliberation test, and the counterfactual test. And though we haven't yet said much about what objectivity comes to, these tests test for something that is recognizably in the vicinity of what we're after with our term "objectivity."

Objectivity, like many interesting philosophical terms, can be understood in more than one way. As a result, when philosophers affirm or deny the objectivity of some subject matter, it's not to be taken for granted that they're asserting or denying the same thing. But we don't have to go through a long list of what may be meant by morality's objectivity. It will be more productive, I think, to go about things in a different way. We can start by asking, why does it matter whether morality is objective? If we have a good enough feel for the answer to this question, we can then use it to find the sense of objectivity that we care about.

I suggest that we care about the objectivity of morality for roughly the reasons specified in the previous section. We want morality's objectivity to support our responses in those cases. We want morality's objectivity to vindicate the phenomenology of deliberation and disagreement, and our relevant counterfactual judgments. We want morality's objectivity to explain why the moral analogue of the spinach test isn't funny.

Very well, then, in what sense must morality be objective in order for the phenomenology of disagreement and deliberation and our counterfactual judgments to be justified? The answer, it seems to me, is that a subject matter is objective if the truths or facts in it exist independently of what we think or feel about them.

This notion of objectivity nicely supports the counterfactual test. If a certain truth (say, that smoking causes cancer) doesn't depend on our views about it, then it would have been true even had we not believed it. Not so for truths that do depend on our beliefs, practices, or emotions (such as the truth that top hats are unfashionable). And if moral truths are similarly independent of our beliefs, desires, preferences, emotions, points of view, and so on—if, as is sometimes said, moral truths are *response-independent*—then it's clear why gender-based discrimination would have been wrong even had we approved of it.

Similarly, if it's our responses that make moral claims true, then in a case of disagreement, it seems natural to suppose that both sides may be right. Perhaps, in other words, your responses make it the case that abortion is morally permissible ("for you," in some sense of this very weird phrase?), and your friend's responses make it the case that abortion is morally wrong ("for her"?). But if the moral status of abortion is response-*in*dependent, we understand why moral disagreement feels like factual disagreement—only one of you is right, and it's important to find out who. And of course, the whole point of the spinach test was to distinguish between caring about things just because we care about them (such as not eating spinach, if you find it yucky) and caring about things that seem to us important independently of us caring about them (such as the wrongness of racism).

Another way of making the same point is as follows: Objective facts are those we seek to discover, not those we make true. And in this respect too, when it comes to moral truths, we are in a position more like that of the scientist who tries to discover the laws of nature (which exist independently of her investigations) than that of the legislator (who creates laws).

Now, in insisting that morality is objective in this sense—for instance, by relying on the reasons given in the previous section—it's important to see what has and what has not been established. In order to see this, it may help to draw an analogy with religious discourse. So think of your deeply held religious beliefs, if you have any. (If, like me, you do not, try to think what it's like to be deeply committed to a religious belief, or perhaps think of your commitment to atheism.) And try to run our tests—does it make sense to be happy that you were brought up under the religion in which you deeply believe, even assuming that with a different education you would have believed another religion, or no religion at all? What do you think of the phenomenology of religious deliberation and disagreement? And had you stopped believing, would the doctrines of your faith still have been true?

Now, perhaps things are not obvious here, but it seems to me that for many religious people, religious discourse passes all these objectivity tests. But from this it does not follow that atheism is false, much less that a specific religion is true. When they are applied to some specific religious discourse, the objectivity tests show that such discourse *aspires* to objectivity. In other words, the tests show what the world must be like for the commitments of the discourse to be vindicated: if (say) a Catholic's religious beliefs are to be true, what must be the case is that the doctrines of the Catholic Church hold objectively, that is, response-independently. This leaves entirely open the question whether these doctrines do in fact hold.

Back to morality, then. Here too, what the discussion of objectivity (tentatively) establishes is just something about the *aspirations* of moral discourse: namely, that it aspires to objectivity. If our moral judgments are to be true, it must be the case that things have value, that people have rights and duties, that there are better and worse ways to live our lives—and all of this must hold objectively, that is, response-independently. But establishing that moral discourse *aspires* to objectivity is one thing. Whether *there actually are* objective moral truths is quite another.

And now you may be worried. Why does it matter, you may wonder, what morality's aspirations are, if (for all I've said so far) they may not be met? I want to offer two replies here. First, precisely in order to check whether morality's aspirations are in fact fulfilled, we should understand them better. If you are trying to decide, for instance, whether the commitments of Catholicism are true, you had better understand them first. Second, and more importantly, one of the things we are trying to do here is to gain a better understanding of what we are already committed to. You may recall that I started with the hypothesis that you may think you're a relativist or a subjectivist. But if the discussion so far gets things right (if, that is, morality aspires to this kind of objectivity), and if you have any moral beliefs at all (don't you think that some things are wrong? do we really need to give gruesome examples?), then it follows that you yourself are already committed to morality's objectivity. And this is already an interesting result, at least for you.

That morality aspires in this way to objectivity also has the implication that any full metaethical theory—any theory, that is, that offers a full description and explanation of moral discourse and practice—has to take this aspiration into account. Most likely, it has to accommodate it. Less likely, but still possibly, such a theory may tell us that this aspiration is futile, explaining why even though morality is not objective, we tend to think that it is, why it manifests the marks of objectivity that the tests above catch on, and so on. What no metaethical theory can do, however, is ignore the very strong appearance that morality is objective. I get back to this in the final section, below.

WHY NOT?

As I already mentioned, we cannot rule out the possibility that under argumentative pressure we're going to have to revise even some of our most deeply held beliefs. Philosophy, in other words, is hard. And as you can imagine, claims about morality's objectivity have not escaped criticism. Indeed, perhaps some such objections have already occurred to you. In this section, I quickly mention some of them, and hint at the ways in which I think they can be coped with. But let me note how incomplete the discussion here is. There are, of course, other objections, objections that I don't discuss here. More importantly, there are many more things to say—on both sides—regarding the objections that I do discuss. The discussion here is meant as an introduction to these further discussions, no more than that. (Have I mentioned that philosophy is hard?)

Disagreement

I have been emphasizing ways in which moral disagreement may motivate the thought that morality is objective. But it's very common to think that something about moral disagreement actually goes the other way. For if there are perfectly objective moral truths, why is there so much disagreement about them? Wouldn't we expect, if there are such objective truths, to see everyone converging on them? Perhaps such convergence cannot be expected to be perfect and quick, but still—why is there so much persistent, apparently irreconcilable disagreement in morality, but not in subject matters whose objectivity is less controversial? If there is no answer to this question, doesn't this count heavily against morality's objectivity?

It is not easy to see exactly what this objection comes to. (Exercise: Can you try and formulate a precise argument here?) It may be necessary to distinguish between several possible arguments. Naturally, different ways of understanding the objection will call for different responses. But there are some things that can be said in general here. First, the objection seems to underrate the extent of disagreement in subject matters whose objectivity is pretty much uncontroversial (think of the causes and effects of global warming again). It may also overrate the extent of disagreement in morality. Still, the requirement to explain the scope and nature of moral disagreements seems legitimate. But objectivity-friendly explanations seem possible.

Perhaps, for instance, moral disagreement is sometimes best explained by noting that people tend to accept the moral judgments that it's in their interest to accept, or that tend to show their lives and practices in good light. Perhaps this is why the poor tend to believe in the welfare state, and the rich tend to believe in property rights.

Perhaps the most important general lesson here is that not all disagreements count against the objectivity of the relevant discourse. So what we need is a criterion to distinguish between objectivity-undermining and non-objectivity-undermining disagreements. And then we need an argument showing that moral disagreement is of the former kind. I don't know of a fully successful way of filling in these details here.

Notice, by the way, that such attempts are going to have to overcome a natural worry about *self-defeat*. Some theories defeat themselves, that is, roughly, fail even by their own lights. Consider, for instance, the theory "All theories are false," or the belief "No belief is justified." (Exercise: Can you think of other self-defeating theories?) Now, disagreement in philosophy has many of the features that moral disagreement seems to have. In particular, so does metaethical disagreement. Even more in particular, so does disagreement about *whether disagreement undermines objectivity*. If moral disagreement undermines the objectivity of moral conclusions, metaethical disagreement seems to undermine the objectivity of metaethical conclusions, including the conclusion that disagreement of this kind undermines objectivity. And this starts to look like self-defeat. So if some disagreement-objection to the objectivity of morality is going to succeed, it must show how moral disagreement undermines the objectivity of morality, but metaethical disagreement does *not* undermine the objectivity of metaethical claims. Perhaps it's possible to do so. But it's not going to be easy.

But How Do We Know?

Even if there are these objective moral truths—for instance, the kind of objective moral truth that both sides to a moral disagreement typically lay a claim to—how can we ever come to know them? In the astronomical case of disagreement about the relative position and motion of the earth and the sun, there are things we can say in response to a similar question—we can talk about perception, and scientific methodology, and progress. Similarly in other subject matters where we are very confident that objective truths await our discovery. Can anything at all be said in the moral case? We do not, after all, seem to possess something worth calling moral perception, a direct perception of the moral status of things. And in the moral case it's hard to argue that we have an established, much less uncontroversial, methodology either. (Whether there is moral progress is, I'm sure you've already realized, highly controversial.)

In other words, what we need is a moral epistemology, an account of how moral knowledge is possible, of how moral beliefs can be more or less justified, and the like. And I do not want to belittle the need for a moral epistemology, in particular an epistemology that fits well with an objectivist understanding of moral judgments. But the objectivist is not without resources here. After all, morality is not the only subject matter where perception and empirical methodology do not seem to be relevant. Think, for instance, of mathematics, and indeed of philosophy. But we do not often doubt the reality of mathematical knowledge. (Philosophical knowledge is a harder case, perhaps. Exercise: Can you see how claiming that we do not have philosophical knowledge may again give rise to a worry about self-defeat?)

Perhaps, then, what is really needed is a general epistemology of the a priori—of those areas, roughly, where the empirical method seems out of place. And perhaps it's not overly optimistic to think that any plausible epistemology of the a priori will vindicate moral knowledge as well.

Also, to say that there is no methodology of doing ethics is at the very least an exaggeration. Typically, when facing a moral question, we do not just stare at it helplessly. Perhaps we're not always very good at morality. But this doesn't mean that we never are. And perhaps at our best, when we employ our best ways of moral reasoning, we manage to attain moral knowledge.

(Exercise: There is no *uncontroversial* method of doing ethics. What, if anything, follows from this?)

Who Decides?

Still, even if moral knowledge is not especially problematic, even if moral disagreement can be explained in objectivity-friendly ways, and even if there are perfectly objective moral truths, what should we do in cases of disagreement and conflict? Who gets to decide what the right way of proceeding is? Especially in the case of intercultural disagreement and conflict, isn't saying something like "We're right and you're wrong about what is objectively morally required" objectionably dogmatic, intolerant, perhaps an invitation to fanaticism?

Well, in a sense, no one decides. In another sense, everyone does. The situation here is precisely as it is everywhere else: no one gets to decide whether smoking causes cancer, whether human actions contribute to global warming, whether the earth revolves around the sun. Our decisions do not make these claims true or false. But everyone gets (roughly speaking) to decide what they are going to believe about these matters. And this is so for moral claims as well.

How about intolerance and fanaticism? If the worry is that people are likely to become dangerously intolerant if they believe in objective morality, then first, such a prediction would have to be established. After all, many social reformers (think, for instance, of Martin Luther King, Jr.) who fought *against* intolerance and bigotry seem to have been inspired by the thought that their vision of equality and justice was objectively correct. Further, even if it's very dangerous for people to believe in the objectivity of their moral convictions, this doesn't mean that morality isn't objective. Such danger would give us reasons not to let people know about morality's objectivity. It would not give us a reason to believe that morality is not objective. (Compare: even if it were the case that things would go rapidly downhill if atheism were widely believed, this wouldn't prove that atheism is false.)

More importantly, though, it's one thing to believe in the objectivity of morality, it's quite another to decide what to do about it. And it's quite possible that the right thing to do, given morality's objectivity, is hardly ever to respond with "I am simply right and you are simply wrong!" or to be intolerant. In fact, if you think that it's wrong to be intolerant, aren't you committed to the objectivity of this very claim? (Want to run the three tests again?) So it seems as if the only way of accommodating the importance of toleration is actually to *accept* morality's objectivity, not to *reject* it.

CONCLUSION

As already noted, much more can be said—about what objectivity is, about the reasons to think that morality is objective, and about these (and many other) objections to morality's objectivity. Much more work remains to be done.

And one of the ways in which current literature addresses some of these issues may sound surprising, for a major part of the debate *assumes* something like morality's aspiration to objectivity in the sense above, but refuses to infer from such observations quick conclusions about the nature of moral truths and facts. In other words, many metaethicists today deny the most straightforward objectivist view of morality, according to which moral facts are a part of response-independent reality, much like mathematical and physical facts. But they do not deny morality's objectivity—they care, for instance, about passing the three tests above. And so they attempt to show how even on other metaethical views, morality's objectivity can be accommodated. As you can imagine, philosophers disagree about the success (actual and potential) of such accommodation projects.

Naturally, such controversies also lead to attempts to better understand what the objectivity at stake exactly is, and why it matters (if it matters) whether morality is objective. As is often the case, attempts to evaluate answers to a question make us better understand—or wonder about—the question itself.

Nothing here, then, is simple. But I hope that you now see how you are probably a moral objectivist, at least in your intuitive starting point. Perhaps further philosophical reflection will require that you abandon this starting point. But this will be an *abandoning,* and a very strong reason is needed to justify it. Until we get such a conclusive argument against moral objectivity, then, objectivism should be the view to beat.

For Further Reflection

1. What is Enoch's spinach test? What does it reveal about moral objectivity?
2. How is the disagreement test relevant to the question of moral objectivity? What happens when you engage in this test? What do the results mean?
3. What is the moral disagreement argument? Does it undermine moral objectivity? Explain.
4. What does Enoch say about how we come to know objective moral truths? Do you agree? Why or why not?

Why Morality Is Not Relative

JAMES RACHELS

James Rachels (1941–2003) analyzes the structure of ethical relativism, which he calls "cultural relativism," to show that the claims made by its proponents go beyond what the facts or arguments can establish. He contends that the central argument, "the cultural differences argument," is invalid, for even if there is broad cultural disagreement over morality, it does not prove that there is no truth in the matter, any more than the fact that flat-earthers disagree with round-earthers proves that there is no independent truth of that matter. Rachels goes on to point out three unfavorable consequences of cultural relativism that make it implausible. Finally, he reviews two virtues of the doctrine.

To many thinkers, this observation—"Different cultures have different moral codes"—has seemed to be the key to understanding morality. The idea of universal truth in ethics, they say, is a myth. The customs of different societies

From James Rachels, *The Elements of Moral Philosophy* (McGraw-Hill, 1999), 20–36.

are all that exist. These customs cannot be said to be "correct" or "incorrect," for that implies we have an independent standard of right and wrong by which they may be judged. But there is no such independent standard; every standard is culture-bound. The great pioneering sociologist William Graham Sumner, writing in 1906, put it like this:

> The "right" way is the way which the ancestors used and which has been handed down. The tradition is its own warrant. It is not held subject to verification by experience. The notion of right is in the folkways. It is not outside of them, of independent origin, and brought to test them. In the folkways, whatever is, is right. This is because they are traditional, and therefore contain in themselves the authority of the ancestral ghosts. When we come to the folkways we are at the end of our analysis.

This line of thought has probably persuaded more people to be skeptical about ethics than any other single thing. Cultural Relativism, as it has been called, challenges our ordinary belief in the objectivity and universality of moral truth. It says, in effect, that there is no such thing as universal truth in ethics; there are only the various cultural codes, and nothing more. Moreover, our own code has no special status; it is merely one among many. As we shall see, this basic idea is really a compound of several different thoughts. It is important to separate the various elements of the theory because, on analysis, some parts turn out to be correct, while others seem to be mistaken. As a beginning, we may distinguish the following claims, all of which have been made by cultural relativists:

1. Different societies have different moral codes.
2. The moral code of a society determines what is right within that society; that is, if the moral code of a society says that a certain action is right, then that action *is* right, at least within that society.
3. There is no objective standard that can be used to judge one society's code better than another's.
4. The moral code of our own society has no special status; it is merely one among many.
5. There is no "universal truth" in ethics; that is, there are no moral truths that hold for all peoples at all times.
6. It is mere arrogance for us to try to judge the conduct of other peoples. We should adopt an attitude of tolerance toward the practices of other cultures.

Although it may seem that these six propositions go naturally together, they are independent of one another, in the sense that some of them might be false even if others are true. In what follows, we will try to identify what is correct in Cultural Relativism, but we will also be concerned to expose what is mistaken about it.

THE CULTURAL DIFFERENCES ARGUMENT

Cultural Relativism is a theory about the nature of morality. At first blush it seems quite plausible. However, like all such theories, it may be evaluated by subjecting it to rational analysis; and when we analyze Cultural Relativism, we find that it is not so plausible as it first appears to be.

The first thing we need to notice is that at the heart of Cultural Relativism there is a certain *form of argument*. The strategy used by cultural relativists is to argue from facts about the differences between cultural outlooks to a conclusion about the status of morality. Thus we are invited to accept this reasoning:

(1) The Greeks believed it was wrong to eat the dead, whereas the Callatians believed it was right to eat the dead.
(2) Therefore, eating the dead is neither objectively right nor objectively wrong. It is merely a matter of opinion that varies from culture to culture.

Or, alternatively:

(1) The Eskimos see nothing wrong with infanticide, whereas Americans believe infanticide is immoral.
(2) Therefore, infanticide is neither objectively right nor objectively wrong. It is merely a matter of opinion, which varies from culture to culture.

Clearly, these arguments are variations of one fundamental idea. They are both special cases of a more general argument, which says:

(1) Different cultures have different moral codes.
(2) Therefore, there is no objective "truth" in morality. Right and wrong are only matters of opinion, and opinions vary from culture to culture.

We may call this the Cultural Differences Argument. To many people, it is persuasive. But from a logical point of view, is it sound?

It is not sound. The trouble is that the conclusion does not follow from the premise—that is, even if the premise is true, the conclusion still might be false. The premise concerns what people *believe*—in some societies, people believe one thing; in other societies, people believe differently. The conclusion, however, concerns what *really is the case.* The trouble is that this sort of conclusion does not follow logically from this sort of premise.

Consider again the example of the Greeks and Callatians. The Greeks believed it was wrong to eat the dead; the Callatians believed it was right. Does it follow, *from the mere fact that they disagreed*, that there is no objective truth in the matter? No, it does not follow; for it could be that the practice was objectively right (or wrong) and that one or the other of them was simply mistaken.

To make the point clearer, consider a different matter. In some societies, people believe the earth is flat. In other societies, such as our own, people believe the earth is (roughly) spherical. Does it follow, from the mere fact that people disagree, that there is no "objective truth" in geography? Of course not; we would never draw such a conclusion because we realize that, in their beliefs about the world, the members of some societies might simply be wrong. There is no reason to think that if the world is round everyone must know it. Similarly, there is no reason to think that if there is moral truth everyone must know it. The fundamental mistake in the Cultural Differences Argument is that it attempts to derive a substantive conclusion about a subject from the mere fact that people disagree about it.

This is a simple point of logic, and it is important not to misunderstand it. We are not saying (not yet, anyway) that the conclusion of the argument is false. That is still an open question. The logical point is just that the conclusion does not *follow from* the premise. This is important, because in order to determine whether the conclusion is true, we need arguments in its support. Cultural Relativism proposes this argument, but unfortunately the argument turns out to be fallacious. So it proves nothing.

THE CONSEQUENCES OF TAKING CULTURAL RELATIVISM SERIOUSLY

Even if the Cultural Differences Argument is invalid, Cultural Relativism might still be true. What would it be like if it were true?

In the passage quoted above, William Graham Sumner summarizes the essence of Cultural Relativism. He says that there is no measure of right and wrong other than the standards of one's society: "The notion of right is in the folkways. It is not outside of them, of independent origin, and brought to test them. In the folkways, whatever is, is right." Suppose we took this seriously. What would be some of the consequences?

1. *We could no longer say that the customs of other societies are morally inferior to our own.* This, of course, is one of the main points stressed by Cultural

Relativism. We would have to stop condemning other societies merely because they are "different." So long as we concentrate on certain examples, such as the funerary practices of the Greeks and Callatians, this may seem to be a sophisticated, enlightened attitude.

However, we would also be stopped from criticizing other, less benign practices. Suppose a society waged war on its neighbors for the purpose of taking slaves. Or suppose a society was violently anti-Semitic and its leaders set out to destroy the Jews. Cultural Relativism would preclude us from saying that either of these practices was wrong. (We would not even be able to say that a society tolerant of Jews is *better* than the anti-Semitic society, for that would imply some sort of transcultural standard of comparison.) The failure to condemn *these* practices does not seem enlightened; on the contrary, slavery and anti-Semitism seem wrong wherever they occur. Nevertheless, if we took Cultural Relativism seriously, we would have to regard these social practices as immune from criticism.

2. *We could decide whether actions are right or wrong just by consulting the standards of our society.* Cultural Relativism suggests a simple test for determining what is right and what is wrong: All one need do is ask whether the action is in accordance with the code of one's society. Suppose in 1975 a resident of South Africa was wondering whether his country's policy of apartheid—a rigidly racist system—was morally correct. All he has to do is ask whether this policy conformed to his society's moral code. If it did, there would have been nothing to worry about, at least from a moral point of view.

This implication of Cultural Relativism is disturbing because few of us think that our society's code is perfect—we can think of all sorts of ways in which it might be improved. Yet Cultural Relativism not only forbids us from criticizing the codes of *other* societies; it also stops us from criticizing our own. After all, if right and wrong are relative to culture, this must be true for our own culture just as much as for other cultures.

3. *The idea of moral progress is called into doubt.* Usually, we think that at least some social changes are for the better. (Although, of course, other changes may be for the worse.) Throughout most of Western history the place of women in society was narrowly circumscribed. They could not own property; they could not vote or hold political office; and generally they were under the almost absolute control of their husbands. Recently much of this has changed, and most people think of it as progress.

But if Cultural Relativism is correct, can we legitimately think of this as progress? Progress means replacing a way of doing things with a better way. But by what standard do we judge the new ways as better? If the old ways were in accordance with the social standards of their time, then Cultural Relativism would say it is a mistake to judge them by the standards of a different time.

Eighteenth-century society was a different society from the one we have now. To say that we have made progress implies a judgment that present-day society is better, and that is just the sort of transcultural judgment that, according to Cultural Relativism, is impossible.

Our idea of social *reform* will also have to be reconsidered. Reformers such as Martin Luther King, Jr., have sought to change their societies for the better. Within the constraints imposed by Cultural Relativism, there is one way this might be done. If a society is not living up to its own ideals, the reformer may be regarded as acting for the best; the ideals of the society are the standard by which we judge his or her proposals as worthwhile. But no one may challenge the ideals themselves, for those ideals are by definition correct. According to Cultural Relativism, then, the idea of social reform makes sense only in this limited way.

These three consequences of Cultural Relativism have led many thinkers to reject it as implausible on its face. It does make sense, they say, to condemn some practices, such as slavery and anti-Semitism, wherever they occur. It makes sense to think that our own society has made some moral progress, while admitting that it is still imperfect and in need of reform. Because Cultural Relativism implies that these judgments make no sense, the argument goes, it cannot be right.

WHY THERE IS LESS DISAGREEMENT THAN IT SEEMS

The original impetus for Cultural Relativism comes from the observation that cultures differ dramatically in their views of right and wrong. But just how much do they differ? It is true that there are differences. However, it is easy to overestimate the extent of those differences. Often, when we examine what seems to be a dramatic difference, we find that the cultures do not differ nearly as much as it appears.

Consider a culture in which people believe it is wrong to eat cows. This may even be a poor culture, in which there is not enough food; still, the cows are not to be touched. Such a society would appear to have values very different from our own. But does it? We have not yet asked *why* these people will not eat cows. Suppose it is because they believe that after death the souls of humans inhabit the bodies of animals, especially cows, so that a cow may be someone's grandmother. Now shall we say that their values are different from ours? No; the difference lies elsewhere. The difference is in our belief systems, not in our values. We agree that we shouldn't eat Grandma; we simply disagree about whether the cow is (or could be) Grandma.

The point is that many factors work together to produce the customs of a society. The society's values are only one of them. Other matters, such as the religious and factual beliefs held by its members, and the physical circumstances in which they must live, are also important. We cannot conclude, then, merely because customs differ, that there is a disagreement about values. The difference in customs may be attributable to some other aspect of social life. Thus there may be less disagreement about values than there appears to be.

Consider again the Eskimos, who often kill perfectly normal infants, especially girls. We do not approve of such things; in our society, a parent who killed a baby would be locked up. Thus there appears to be a great difference in the values of our two cultures. But suppose we ask why the Eskimos do this. The explanation is not that they have less affection for their children or less respect for human life. An Eskimo family will always protect its babies if conditions permit. But they live in a harsh environment, where food is in short supply. A fundamental postulate of Eskimo thought is: "Life is hard, and the margin of safety small." A family may want to nourish its babies but be unable to do so.

As in many "primitive" societies, Eskimo mothers will nurse their infants over a much longer period of time than mothers in our culture. The child will take nourishment from its mother's breast for four years, perhaps even longer. So even in the best of times there are limits to the number of infants that one mother can sustain. Moreover, the Eskimos are a nomadic people—unable to farm, they must move about in search of food. Infants must be carried, and a mother can carry only one baby in her parka as she travels and goes about her outdoor work. Other family members help however they can.

Infant girls are more readily disposed of because, first, in this society the males are the primary food providers—they are the hunters, following the traditional division of labor—and it is obviously important to maintain a sufficient number of food providers. But there is an important second reason as well. Because the hunters suffer a high casualty rate, the adult men who die prematurely far outnumber the women who die early. Thus if male and female infants survived in equal numbers, the female adult population would greatly outnumber the male adult population. Examining the available statistics, one writer concluded that "were it not for female infanticide . . . there would be approximately one-and-a-half times as many females in the average Eskimo local group as there are food-producing males."

So among the Eskimos, infanticide does not signal a fundamentally different attitude toward children. Instead, it is a recognition that drastic measures are sometimes needed to ensure the family's survival. Even then, however, killing the baby is not the first option considered. Adoption is common; childless couples are especially happy to take a more fertile couple's "surplus." Killing is only the last resort. I emphasize this in order to show that the raw data of the anthropologists can be misleading; it can make the differences in values between cultures appear greater than they are. The Eskimos' values are not all that different from our values. It is only that life forces upon them choices that we do not have to make.

HOW ALL CULTURES HAVE SOME VALUES IN COMMON

It should not be surprising that, despite appearances, the Eskimos are protective of their children. How could it be otherwise? How could a group survive that did not value its young? It is easy to see that, in fact, all cultural groups must protect their infants. Babies are helpless and cannot survive if they are not given extensive care for a period of years. Therefore, if a group did not care for its young, the young would not survive, and the older members of the group would not be replaced. After a while the group would die out. This means that any cultural group that continues to exist must care for its young. Infants that are not cared for must be the exception rather than the rule.

Similar reasoning shows that other values must be more or less universal. Imagine what it would be like for a society to place no value at all on truth telling. When one person spoke to another, there would be no presumption that she was telling the truth, for she could just as easily be speaking falsely. Within that society, there would be no reason to pay attention to what anyone says. (I ask you what time it is, and you say "Four o'clock." But there is no presumption that you are speaking truly; you could just as easily have said the first thing that came into your head. So I have no reason to pay attention to your answer. In fact, there was no point in my asking you in the first place.) Communication would then be extremely difficult, if not impossible. And because complex societies cannot exist without communication among their members, society would become impossible. It follows that in any complex society there must be a presumption in favor of truthfulness. There may of course be exceptions to this rule: There may be situations in which it is thought to be permissible to lie. Nevertheless, these will be exceptions to a rule that *is* in force in the society.

Here is one further example of the same type. Could a society exist in which there was no prohibition on murder? What would this be like? Suppose people were free to kill other people at will, and no one thought there was anything wrong with it. In such a "society," no one could feel safe. Everyone would have to be constantly on guard. People who wanted to survive would have to avoid other people as much as possible. This would inevitably result in individuals trying to become as self-sufficient as possible—after all, associating with others would be dangerous. Society on any large scale would collapse. Of course, people might band together in smaller groups with others that they could trust not to harm them. But notice what this means: They would be forming smaller societies that did acknowledge a rule against murder. The prohibition of murder, then, is a necessary feature of all societies.

There is a general theoretical point here, namely, that *there are some moral rules that all societies must have in common, because those rules are necessary for society to exist.* The rules against lying and murder are two examples. And in fact, we do find these rules in force in all viable cultures. Cultures may differ in what they regard as legitimate exceptions to the rules, but this disagreement exists against a background of agreement on the larger issues. Therefore, it is a mistake to overestimate the amount of difference between cultures. Not every moral rule can vary from society to society.

JUDGING A CULTURAL PRACTICE TO BE UNDESIRABLE

In 1996, a 17-year-old girl named Fauziya Kassindja arrived at Newark International Airport and asked for asylum. She had fled her native country of Togo, a small west African nation, to escape what people there call "excision." Excision is a permanently disfiguring procedure that is sometimes called "female circumcision," although it bears little resemblance to the Jewish practice. More commonly, at least in Western newspapers, it is referred to as "female genital mutilation."

According to the World Health Organization, the practice is widespread in 26 African nations, and two million girls each year are "excised." In some instances, excision is part of an elaborate tribal ritual, performed in small traditional villages, and girls look forward to it because it signals their acceptance into the adult world. In other instances, the practice is carried out by families living in cities on young women who desperately resist.

Fauziya Kassindja was the youngest of five daughters in a devoutly Muslim family. Her father, who owned a successful trucking business, was opposed to excision, and he was able to defy the tradition because of his wealth. His first four daughters were married without being mutilated. But when Fauziya was 16, he suddenly died. Fauziya then came under the authority of his father, who arranged a marriage for her and prepared to have her excised. Fauziya was terrified, and her mother and oldest sister helped her to escape. Her mother, left without resources, eventually had to formally apologize and submit to the authority of the patriarch she had offended.

Meanwhile, in America, Fauziya was imprisoned for two years while the authorities decided what to do with her. She was finally granted asylum, but not before she became the center of a controversy about how we should regard the cultural practices of other peoples. A series of articles in the *New York Times* encouraged the idea that excision is a barbaric practice that should be condemned. Other observers were reluctant to be so judgmental—live and let live, they said; after all, our culture probably seems just as strange to them.

Suppose we are inclined to say that excision is bad. Would we merely be imposing the standards of our own culture? If Cultural Relativism is correct, that is all we can do, for there is no culture-neutral moral standard to which we may appeal. But is that true?

Is There a Culture-Neutral Standard of Right and Wrong?

There is, of course, a lot that can be said against excision. Excision is painful and it results in the permanent loss of sexual pleasure. Its short-term effects include hemorrhage, tetanus, and septicemia. Sometimes the woman dies. Long-term effects include chronic infection, scars that hinder walking, and continuing pain.

Why, then, has it become a widespread social practice? It is not easy to say. Excision has no apparent social benefits. Unlike Eskimo infanticide, it is not necessary for the group's survival. Nor is it a matter of religion. Excision is practiced by groups with various religions, including Islam and Christianity, neither of which commend it.

Nevertheless, a number of reasons are given in its defense. Women who are incapable of sexual pleasure are said to be less likely to be promiscuous; thus there will be fewer unwanted pregnancies in unmarried women. Moreover, wives for whom sex is only a duty are less likely to be unfaithful to their husbands; and because they will not be thinking about sex, they will be more attentive to the needs of their husbands and children. Husbands, for their part, are said to enjoy sex more with wives who have been excised. (The women's own lack of enjoyment is said to be unimportant.) Men will not want unexcised women, as they are unclean and immature. And above all, it has been done since antiquity, and we may not change the ancient ways.

It would be easy, and perhaps a bit arrogant, to ridicule these arguments. But we may notice an important feature of this whole line of reasoning: It attempts to justify excision by showing that excision is beneficial—men, women, and their families are said to be better off when women are excised. Thus we might approach this reasoning, and excision, itself, by asking whether this is true: Is excision, on the whole, helpful or harmful?

In fact, this is a standard that might reasonably be used in thinking about any social practice whatever: We may ask *whether the practice promotes or hinders the welfare of the people whose lives are affected by it*. And, as a corollary, we may ask if there is an alternative set of social arrangements that would do a better job of promoting their welfare. If so, we may conclude that the existing practice is deficient.

But this looks like just the sort of independent moral standard that Cultural Relativism says cannot exist. It is a single standard that may be brought to bear in judging the practices of any culture, at any time, including our own. Of course, people will not usually see this principle as being "brought in from the outside" to judge them, because, like the rules against lying and homicide, the welfare of its members is a value internal to all viable cultures.

Why, Despite All This, Thoughtful People May Nevertheless Be Reluctant to Criticize Other Cultures

Although they are personally horrified by excision, many thoughtful people are reluctant to say it is wrong, for at least three reasons.

First, there, is an understandable nervousness about "interfering in the social customs of other peoples." Europeans and their cultural descendents in America have a shabby history of destroying native cultures in the name of Christianity and Enlightenment. Recoiling from this record, some people refuse to make any negative judgments about other cultures, especially cultures that resemble those that have been wronged in the past. We should notice, however, that there is a difference between (a) judging a cultural practice to be deficient, and (b) thinking that we should announce the fact, conduct a campaign, apply diplomatic pressure, or send in the army. The first is just a matter of trying to see the world clearly, from a moral point of view. The second is another matter altogether. Sometimes it may be right to "do something about it," but often it will not be.

People also feel, rightly enough, that they should be tolerant of other cultures. Tolerance is, no doubt, a virtue—a tolerant person is willing to live in peaceful cooperation with those who see things differently. But there is nothing in the nature of tolerance that requires you to say that all beliefs, all religions, and all social practices are equally admirable. On the contrary, if you did not think that some were better than others, there would be nothing for you to tolerate.

Finally, people may be reluctant to judge because they do not want to express contempt for the society being criticized. But again, this is misguided: To condemn a particular practice is not to say that the culture is on the whole contemptible or that it is generally inferior to any other culture, including one's own. It could have many admirable features. In fact, we should expect this to be true of most human societies—they are mixes of good and bad practices. Excision happens to be one of the bad ones.

WHAT CAN BE LEARNED FROM CULTURAL RELATIVISM

At the outset, I said that we were going to identify both what is right and what is wrong in Cultural Relativism. But I have dwelled on its mistakes: I have said that it rests on an invalid argument, that it has consequences that make it implausible on its face, and that the extent of moral disagreement is far less than it implies. This all adds up to a pretty thorough repudiation of the theory. Nevertheless, it is still a very appealing idea, and the reader may have the feeling that all this is a little unfair. The theory must have something going for it, or else why has it been so influential? In fact, I think there is something right about Cultural Relativism, and now I want to say what that is. There are two lessons we should learn from the theory, even if we ultimately reject it.

First, Cultural Relativism warns us, quite rightly, about the danger of assuming that all our preferences are based on some absolute rational standard. They are not. Many (but not all) of our practices are merely peculiar to our society, and it is easy to lose sight of that fact. In reminding us of it, the theory does a service.

Funerary practices are one example. The Callatians, according to Herodotus, were "men who eat their fathers"—a shocking idea, to us at least. But eating the flesh of the dead could be understood as a sign of respect. It could be taken as a symbolic act that says: we wish this person's spirit to dwell within us. Perhaps this was the understanding of the Callatians. On such a way of thinking, burying the dead could be seen as an act of rejection, and burning the corpse as positively scornful. If this is hard to imagine, then we may need to have our imaginations stretched. Of course we may feel a visceral repugnance at the idea of eating human flesh in any circumstances. But what of it? This repugnance may be, as the relativists say, only a matter of what is customary in our particular society.

There are many other matters that we tend to think of in terms of objective right and wrong that are really nothing more than social conventions. We could make a long list. Should women cover their breasts? A publicly exposed breast is scandalous in our society, whereas in other cultures it is unremarkable. Objectively speaking, it is neither right nor wrong—there is no objective reason why either custom is better. Cultural Relativism begins with the valuable insight that many of our practices are like this; they are only cultural products. Then it goes wrong by inferring that, because some practices are like this, all must be.

The second lesson has to do with keeping an open mind. In the course of growing up, each of us has acquired some strong feelings: We have learned to think of some types of conduct as acceptable, and others we have learned to reject. Occasionally, we may find those feelings challenged. For example, we may have been taught that homosexuality is immoral, and we may feel quite uncomfortable around gay people and see them as alien and "different." Now someone suggests that this may be a mere prejudice; that there is nothing evil about homosexuality; that gay people are just people, like anyone else, who happen, through no choice of their own, to be attracted to others of the same sex. But because we feel so strongly about the matter, we may find it hard to take this seriously. Even after we listen to the arguments, we may still have the unshakable feeling that homosexuals must, somehow, be an unsavory lot.

Cultural Relativism, by stressing that our moral views can reflect the prejudices of our society, provides an antidote for this kind of dogmatism. When he tells the story of the Greeks and Callatians, Herodotus adds:

> For if anyone, no matter who, were given the opportunity of choosing from amongst all the nations of the world the set of beliefs which he thought best, he would inevitably, after careful consideration of their relative merits, choose that of his own country. Everyone without exception believes his own native customs, and the religion he was brought up in, to be the best.

Realizing this can result in our having more open minds. We can come to understand that our feelings are not necessarily perceptions of the truth—they may be nothing more than the result of cultural conditioning. Thus when we hear it suggested that some element of our social code is *not* really the best, and we find ourselves instinctively resisting the suggestion, we might stop and remember this. Then we may be more open to discovering the truth, whatever that might be.

We can understand the appeal of Cultural Relativism, then, even though the theory has serious shortcomings. It is an attractive theory because it is based on a genuine insight, that many of the practices and attitudes we think so natural are really only cultural products. Moreover, keeping this thought firmly in view is important if we want to avoid arrogance and have open minds. These are important points, not to be taken lightly. But we can accept these points without going on to accept the whole theory.

For Further Reflection

1. Do you agree with Rachels's analysis of the cultural differences argument? Why or why not?
2. What, according to Rachels, are the consequences of taking cultural relativism seriously? Are his arguments sound? Explain.

Judge Not?

JEAN BETHKE ELSHTAIN

Jean Bethke Elshtain (1941–2013) was the Laura Spelman Rockfeller Professor of Social and Political Ethics at the University of Chicago. She authored several works in social ethics, including *Democracy on Trial.* In this essay she examines the platitude that we should not judge other people and gives reasons for thinking that we are not only permitted to make moral judgments but have an obligation to do so.

We are a society awash in exculpatory strategies. We've devised lots of fascinating ways to let ourselves or others off the hook: all one need do is think of recent, well-publicized trials to appreciate the truth of this. We Americans are at present being bombarded with sensationalistic tales of victimization and equally sensationalistic proclamations of immunity from responsibility. Alternately bemused and troubled by the Oprah Winfreyization of American life, I sometimes think of my grandmother.

Dear Grandma (may she rest in peace) knew how to judge. She was tough as nails on people she found despicable or merely wanting. She chewed them out in her low German dialect (being a Volga German, *hochdeutsch* was not her tongue), and we grandchildren could figure out a thing or two. We knew when she was describing someone as "swinish" or "dirty," these being ways to characterize those who stole from others, beat their wives or their livestock, or abused their children. (Women, of course, could be abusers, too.) We missed a good bit of her assessments, though, as it was the policy of my grandmother, my mother, and Aunts Mary and Martha not to teach us *plattdeutsch.* When Grandma was really on a roll and wanted nothing less than to condemn someone to perdition, her favorite judging word was "Russki." Hearing it sent a frisson through our tender flesh and bones. The last time I heard her say this I was forty-three or forty-four years old and it still frightened me, not quite out of my wits, but I remained convinced, as I had been since the age of five or six when I had acquired some inkling of what was at stake, that that person was doomed, no two ways about it.

"Russki" was her shorthand judgment on the garden-variety cheat, the ordinary bum, the farmer who shortchanged his hired hands, or the mother who kept her kids in dirty clothes, let their noses run, and never washed their hair. Why "Russki" as a term of judgment? That was historic

---

Reprinted from Jean Bethke Elshtain, "Judge Not?" *First Things* (October 1994) with permission of the Institute on Religion & Public Life, New York, N.Y.

overdetermination. It was the Russians who had begun to undermine the historic immunities of the Volga German communities. Under Tsar Nicholas, on the throne when my grandparents' families emigrated to the New Country from what my grandmother always called the Old Country, their sons were being drafted into the Russian Army; and they were so fearful that they hid their Bibles (Luther's German translation) in secret places.

I suppose my grandmother would be a good candidate for sensitivity training. She is beyond the reach of the enthusiasts of pop psychology with its quivering "non-judgmentalism," having died at the age of ninety-four two years ago, but it gives me a shiver of another sort (one of delight) to imagine a confrontation between Grandma and a "facilitator," eyes agleam with programmed goodness, saying things like, "Now, Mrs. Lind, *why* do you feel that way?" Or: "Don't you think that's a little harsh? Have you considered how hurtful such words can be?" Probably the facilitator would want to take a good look at my mother, and, in addition to Aunts Mary and Martha, Uncle Bill and Uncle Ted, too, no doubt damaged beyond repair, having been reared by such a no-nonsense judger. Good luck! I doubt they would have the slightest inkling of what she was going on about. There was no room in the family idiom for evasions of responsibility and you would find yourself the subject of an assessment of a rather decisive sort if you tried one.

No doubt from time to time my grandmother and her children rushed to judgment. I know my sisters and brothers and I sometimes wished Mom wouldn't embarrass us in public by being so, well, *decisive* in her assessment of things—more than once delivered up in front of those being assessed, too. I recall wanting to seek the nearest exit on more than one occasion. But then I thought, even at the time, better this than someone agreeable and eternally smiling, like my nemesis, the mother of Judy Belcher (not her real name), who was a "pal" to her daughter. They "talked about everything," especially "boyfriends" and "fashion," and they liked to "have fun together." I found this pretty disgusting. I still do. Judging seems to run in the family.

But to say this is not to say much. For what is at stake is the capacity to make judgments as an ethical issue of the gravest sort, and along with it, the discernment of what it means to judge well. In other words, we need a clear sense of why judging is important and what is involved in the activity of judging, and we need a way to distinguish between rash judging—not judging well—and the kind of judging that lies at the heart of what it means to be a self-respecting human subject in a community of other equally self-respecting subjects.

Judging has been in bad odor for quite some time in American culture. It is equated with being punitive, or with insensitivity, or with various "phobias" and "isms." It is the mark of antiquated ways of thinking, feeling, and willing.

Better, no doubt, to be something called "open-minded," a trait thought to be characteristic of sensitive and supportive persons. A young woman well known to me reports that she and her fellow teachers at one of the elite New York public high schools were enjoined not to make students "feel bad" by being too decisive in their assessments of student work and effort. I breathed a sigh of recognition when she told me this; it is the sort of thing one hears in the higher reaches of the academy, too. In fact, this attitude is everywhere, even on bumper stickers. At least some of the readers of this essay will have sighted a bumper sticker that reads: "A Mind Is Like a Parachute. It Works Best When It Is Open." Yes, indeed, one wants to counter, the more open—meaning the more porous and thin—the better. A rather more convenient way of being in the world than being called upon to discriminate in the old—best—sense of the word. An open mind of the sort celebrated by the bumper sticker may signify an empty head, a person incapable of those acts of discernment we call "judging," one who is, in fact, driven to see in such acts mere prejudice.

But prejudice and judgment are two very different human possibilities; indeed, the more we proliferate prejudices, free from the scrutiny of that discernment we aim to evade, the less capable we are, over time, of making judgments. An example or two, in line with Kant's insistence that "Examples are the go-cart of judgments," may suffice. When I first began university teaching, in 1973, I taught a course called "Feminist Politics and Theory." I taught it for several years until I decided the tumult was too much to put up with semester after semester. One problem I encountered went like this. I had designed the course as a sustained exercise in assessing, and critically contrasting, competing feminist accounts of culture and politics. I asked my students to engage certain questions that presupposed their capacity for judgment: What sort of picture of the human condition is presented by this theorist? Could her prescription for change be implemented? How? What would the world look like if it were? And so on. But I ran into trouble straight-off for, in the eyes of many of my students, what I was supposed to be doing was condemning that big booming abstraction, Patriarchy, for fifty minutes three times a week. I was supposed to embrace, not criticize, feminist doctrines—all of them—even though the ideas of the radical separatist feminists scarcely comported with those of liberal feminists on many issues. Needless to say, the Marxist feminists and the eco-feminists didn't see eye-to-eye on lots of things either.

Students sometimes showed up in my office bereft and troubled. One told me she had been a feminist since she was fourteen and didn't need to hear feminism criticized. Another told me she was so "upset" by my criticism of the text of a feminist who proposed test-tube reproduction and a world run by beneficent cyber-engineers, and so "shocked" at my insistence that she respond to a series of questions asking her to sift, discriminate, and assess this text and others, that she had complained to, and sought refuge in, a support group at the women's center. Yet another refused to write a paper contrasting Freud's essays on female development with what the psychoanalytic feminists were doing with Freud because "Freud was a cancer-ridden, cigar-smoking misogynist." This expression of prejudice was not an authentic moment of judging, of course, not least because the student had refused to read the assigned texts. She was repeating a prejudice, not forming a judgment.

A teacher quickly wearies of this sort of thing because it undermines the presuppositions that guide and help to constitute the pedagogical enterprise, one of the most important of these suppositions being that students are capable of weighing alternatives with a generosity of spirit and quality of discernment that makes their subsequent judgments at least plausible if not unassailable. I have always been fond of a pithy sentence in a letter Freud wrote to his fiancee, Martha: "A human being must be able to pull himself together to form a judgment, otherwise he turns into what we Viennese call a *guten Potschen* [doormat]." Apart from being stepped on, what is the problem with persons as doormats? Precisely this: they have sloughed off that which is theirs to do—to enter a community of judging, meaning that one can see error and try to put it right, one can distinguish the more from the less important, one can appropriately name phenomena and act accordingly. As an example of the latter, think of the distinction to be marked between "misfortune" and an "injustice" and what we are enjoined to do whether we confront one or the other. Now Freud was not urging Martha to be cruel or incapable of compassion or forgiveness; rather, he was urging her to stiffen her spine a bit, to stand up for herself, and not to shrink from acts of assessment and discernment.

Judging involves calling things by their real names, embracing the difficult recognition that what Hannah Arendt called "an enormously enlarged empathy" does not in itself suffice to sustain the capacity for that critical thinking we call judging. Arendt had little use for those who treated adults as if they were children by spoon-feeding them palatable "truths" rather than the harder truths of life and politics. If we over-assimilate our situation to that of others, and pretend that we are "at one" with them, we may lose the point at which we leave off and they begin. We are then in danger of losing the faculty of judgment that, for Arendt, consists in "thinking the particular" and through this concrete act reaching for more general conclusions and truths.

Why is judging—what Arendt called the preeminent political faculty—at a nadir among us? Surely much of the explanation lies in the triumph of the ideology of victimization coupled with self-esteem mania. The two are, of course, closely linked. Examples are so numerous it is hard to pick and choose. Take one from the public schools. By now most discerning citizens are familiar with the study showing that American schoolchildren scored much lower on math accomplishment tests than did their counterparts from several other societies—even while these same Americans were the ones who "felt best" about their math ability. Here the emphasis on "feeling good" by contrast to concrete accomplishment results in students being incapable of an accurate discernment of where they really stand on their math ability. Here is a second story, this from the literary front. My son is an aspiring poet and he finds increasingly depressing the many moments, whether in class or out, when a poem that is weak in execution and flat in evocative power is embraced as something "real" and important because it speaks about the poet's own undigested experiences, which by definition can never be assessed and criticized. In other words, the self-referential prejudices of our time swamp a cooler set of criticisms and judgments, and wind up making a triumph of something rather petty. In the process, the work of those young men and women who really struggle with form and language and getting it right is trivialized, their accomplishments discounted. In some circles, if you carefully and precisely criticize a weak poem, you may face censure because the poem and its author's psyche or identity are at one; thus, you find yourself in the position of criticizing her (or his) life, given the utter collapse of one into the other, when what you really want to do is to explain why you think this isn't a very good poem.

The culture of victimization, then, and the triumph of pop-psych notions of "self-esteem," in contrast to a self capable of discernment and judging well, seems a pretty clear source of our discontents in this matter. Of course, any decent person is concerned about victims, and there are *real* victims in our less than perfect world. But that is not the issue. An ideology of victimization (of the feminist sort) casts women as victims of male oppression from the very beginning of time; indeed, female victimization has taken on foundational status. But this victim ideology diverts attention from concrete and specific instances of female victimization in favor of pushing a relentless worldview structured around such dichotomies as victim/victimizer, guilty/innocent, tainted/pure. The female victim, construed as innocent, remains somehow free from sin. Remember Arendt's insistence, following Kant, that judging "is the faculty of thinking the particular." An ideology of victimization—with its harsh and exaggerated polemicism—actually hurts the cause of women's rights, for it provides grounds for callous or sexist individuals to deprecate the claims of actual victims.

Victimization ideology is little more than a politics of resentment, given the growing body of evidence demonstrating that women, though they often have been victims of injustice, have played a variety of active roles throughout history and in every culture. Of course, who didn't know that? It is quite incredible that one must make this point against those who, in the name of feminism, promote the generic prejudice that women are victims *simpliciter.* Our world is filled with noisy forces urging us to refrain from judging precisely in the name of justice. This dangerous nonsense is in evidence in every issue of any daily newspaper anywhere. The jurors in the Reginald Denny beating case decided not to convict because the thugs who smashed a man's face to an unrecognizable pulp and exulted for the cameras as if they had just made the winning touchdown at a Superbowl Game were in the grip of a "mob psychology" and could not, therefore, be judged for their specific acts of wanton, and repeated, violence. The Menendez brothers were "victims" who, although they blasted their parents numerous times with a shotgun, were not to be held accountable. We cannot judge them given what they "went through," as one juror put it.

Take another case, one worth looking at in some detail. A woman in Nashville, Tennessee, starved her infant son to death. Turned into a robot, so it was claimed, she was unable to feed the infant even though the husband was away at work all day. Her defense was based on her having been abused by this husband even though when he got home from work, the two of them would dress up and go out on the town, frequenting sleazy bars, looking for men and women for three-way sex. Meanwhile, a baby is starving to death. Of this terrible story, victimization doctrine holds that as a victim of abuse herself, the woman, by definition, could not in turn be victimizing another. We cannot judge her actions because she is oppressed. According to her lawyers, who are now mounting an appeal, the jury that found her guilty has victimized her twice. But one who looks at victimization as a concrete and specific act would argue that, although it is terrible to be abused, for a twenty-three-year old woman with a range of options open to her (she might have given the infant to her mother to care for, as she had done with an older child) to starve an infant to death is more terrible yet. Surely, to make that assessment is not an act prompted by a harsh desire for revenge. It flows, rather, from a recognition that we are able to distinguish real victims from rhetorical ones, evil acts and crimes from less serious misdeeds.

As the lawyers for this woman said, the woman cannot be "held accountable," and to do so is a "male deal . . . or a society deal, but some people just don't get it." Now, we are told, the perpetrator is a victim twice or even thrice—of that amorphous entity, society, of her husband, and of the jury that found her guilty. The woman's mother has stepped in, proclaiming that she, too, is a "victim" for she "lost a grandson." Notice the language: she "lost" the grandson, as if he had been misplaced, not knowingly, over a six-week period, starved to death as he lay, immobile, listless, no longer able to cry, in his own waste in a filthy crib in a locked room as his parents played out their fantasies with male and female prostitutes. This is nigh unbelievable, but there it is. Even if this awful case gets turned back on appeal, we—all of us—are in danger of being worn down by arguments of this sort; hence, the more likely it is that, at some future point, we will have forgotten what it means to hold *this* person accountable in *this* situation for *this* particular horrible deed.

Let's pursue this just a bit further, depressing as it is, because the elimination of the possibility of judgment, the evacuation of the very capacity of judging would spell the end of the human subject as a self-respecting accountable being. Judging is a sign, a mark, of our respect for the dignity of others and ourselves. We are surrounded by various strategies of exculpation—ways to evade responsibility for a situation or an outcome should one happen to be a member of an "oppressed" or "victimized" group. In a recent book, *The Alchemy of Race and Rights,* the author, Patricia Williams, plays the victim card to achieve both ends simultaneously. Acknowledging that the Tawana Brawley accusations in the now-notorious 1988 scandal were part of a hoax, Williams suggests that that doesn't really matter. For Brawley was a victim of "some unspeakable crime." "No matter how she got there. No matter who did it to her—and even if she did it to herself." That is, even if Brawley injured herself, "her condition was clearly the expression of some crime against her, some tremendous violence, some great violation that challenges comprehension." Brawley was the victim of a "meta-rape," and this secures both her victim status and legitimates the power plays of those who cynically manipulated the situation. These latter escape judgment; and Brawley cannot be judged either. But the "society" that somehow "did" this to her on a "meta" level becomes responsible given the prejudice that in a "racist" society all African Americans are victims of the dominant "metanarrative." Consider the alternative view of black possibility and responsibility noted by Stephen Carter:

> We must never lose the capacity for judgment, especially the capacity to judge ourselves and our people. . . . Standards of morality matter no less than standards of excellence. There are black people who commit heinous crimes, and not all of them are driven by hunger and neglect. . . . We are not automatons. To understand all may indeed be to forgive all, but no civilization can survive when the capacity for understanding is allowed to supersede the capacity for judgment. Otherwise, at the end of the line lies a pile of garbage: Hitler wasn't evil, just insane.

"When the capacity for understanding is allowed to supersede the capacity for judgment"—let the words linger for a moment. Then conjure with the teaching of Jesus: "Judge not that ye be not judged," this, of course, from the Sermon on the Mount. These, too, are words I grew up with. And I pondered them, wondering if my mother's "judgmental" attitude was compatible with Jesus' injunction. We were also told: "There but for the grace of God go I."

We were told to "walk around in the other guy's shoes" before we judged severely or before we judged at all. Squaring this with Grandma's dismissive "Russki" was no easy matter. I sometimes repaired to Lincoln, one of my childhood heroes. I especially loved the magnificent Second Inaugural, "With malice toward none, with charity for all. . . ." Those words I could square with judgment. Malice and judgment: the punitive and the fair are not the same. Lincoln had, after all, insisted that the nations were under God's judgment, and our terrible Civil War, the war he was prosecuting in terms of "unconditional surrender," was our punishment for chattel slavery. Lincoln was no value-free, laid-back kind of guy: compassion with judgment, this framed his life and work. "Judge not" is, then, not an injunction to spineless acceptance but a caution against peremptory legalisms that leave no space for acts of compassion and witness.

I have also found helpful the discussion of the lively British philosopher, Mary Midgley. In her book *Can't We Make Moral Judgments?* Midgley notes our contemporary search for a nonjudgmental politics and quotes all those people who cry, in effect, "But surely it's always wrong to make moral judgments." We are not permitted to make anyone uncomfortable, to be "insensitive." Yet moral judgment of "some kind," says Midgley, "is a necessary element to our thinking." Judging involves our whole nature—it isn't just icing on the cake of self-identity. Judging makes it possible for us to "find our way through a whole forest of possibilities."

Midgley argues that Jesus was taking aim at sweeping condemnations and vindictiveness: he was not trashing the "whole faculty of judgment." Indeed, Jesus is making the "subtle point that while we cannot possibly avoid judging, we can see to it that we judge fairly, as we would expect others to do to us." This is part and parcel, then, of justice as fairness, as a discernment about a particular case and person and deed. Subjectivism in such matters—of the "I'm okay, you're okay," variety—is a cop-out, a way to stop forming and expressing moral judgments altogether. This strange suspension of specific moments of judgment goes hand-in-glove, of course, with an often violent rhetoric of condemnation of whole categories of persons, past and present—that all-purpose villain, the Dead White European Male, comes to mind.

Perhaps this is the point at which we might recall Tocqueville's warnings about "What Sort of Despotism Democratic Nations Have to Fear," for Tocqueville's worst-case scenario has quite a bit to do with judging or, better put, no longer being able to distinguish the better from the worse, the excellent from the mediocre, slavishness from self-responsibility. Democratic despotism, according to Tocqueville, would have a "different character" from the tyranny of the Old World. "It would be more widespread and milder; it would degrade men rather than torment them." Thus, Tocqueville sees citizens withdrawing into themselves, circling around one another in pursuit of "the petty and banal pleasures with which they glut their souls." The exercise of genuine free choice becomes rarer, the activity of free will occurs "within a narrower compass, and little by little robs each citizen of the proper use of his own faculties." The words Tocqueville uses to describe this state of things are "hinder . . . restrain . . . enervate . . . stultify." Losing over time the "faculty of thinking, feeling, and acting for themselves," these citizens "slowly fall below the level of humanity." Tocqueville nowhere talks about collapse of the faculty of judgment in a specific sense but that, surely, is much of what is at stake. Judging is central to, indeed constitutive of, both our self-identity *and* our sociality: it helps us to disentangle, analyze, separate, discern and, in so doing, puts us smack dab in a world of others—not apart, not above, not below, but *among*.

Told that, if we are "powerful" we cannot judge others but can only be judged, and on the other hand that if we are "powerless" we can judge totally but cannot be judged—since the "powerful" by definition "don't get it"—we fall into an intellectual laziness that is itself ethically corrupt and corrupting. As Midgley notes, Jesus' message was: do not stone people, do not cast them out, do not write them off. His target was punitive self-righteousness. With such self-righteousness now a major cottage industry, are we in the danger zone imagined by Tocqueville? That is the question to which sober reflection on judging leads us—or at least where it should.

For Further Reflection

1. Why does judging have a bad odor in American culture?
2. Examine Elshtain's reasons for being judgmental and for thinking non-judgmentalism is "dangerous nonsense." Are they convincing? Explain your answer.

Trying Out One's New Sword

MARY MIDGLEY

Mary Midgley is a British moral philosopher known for her provocative writings on religion and science. Her books include *Heart and Mind: The Varieties of Moral Experience* (1981), *Evolution as a Religion* (1985), and *Myths We Live By* (2003). In this selection, Midgley criticizes what she calls "moral isolationism," the notion that cultures are isolated entities that can neither understand nor legitimately make moral judgments about each other.

All of us are, more or less, in trouble today about trying to understand cultures strange to us. We hear constantly of alien customs. We see changes in our lifetime which would have astonished our parents. I want to discuss here one very short way of dealing with this difficulty, a drastic way which many people now theoretically favour. It consists in simply denying that we can ever understand any culture except our own well enough to make judgements about it. Those who recommend this hold that the world is sharply divided into separate societies, scaled units, each with its own system of thought. They feel that the respect and tolerance due from one system to another forbid us ever to take up a critical position to any other culture. Moral judgement, they suggest, is a kind of coinage valid only in its country of origin.

I shall call this position "moral isolationism." I shall suggest that it is certainly not forced upon us, and indeed that it makes no sense at all. People usually take it up because they think it is a respectful attitude to other cultures. In fact, however, it is not respectful. Nobody can respect what is entirely unintelligible to them. To respect someone, we have to know enough about him to make a *favourable* judgement, however general and tentative. And we do understand people in other cultures to this extent. Otherwise a great mass of our most valuable thinking would be paralysed.

To show this, I shall take a remote example, because we shall probably find it easier to think calmly about it than we should with a contemporary one, such as female circumcision in Africa or the Chinese Cultural Revolution. The principles involved will still be the same. My example is this. There is, it seems, a verb in classical Japanese which means "to try out one's new sword on a chance wayfarer." (The word is *tsujigiri,* literally "crossroads-cut.") A samurai sword had to be tried out because, if it was to work properly, it had to slice

From *Heart and Mind: The Varieties of Moral Experience* by Mary Midgley, pp. 69–75, 2003, David Higham Associates.

through someone at a single blow, from the shoulder to the opposite flank. Otherwise, the warrior bungled his stroke. This could injure his honour, offend his ancestors, and even let down his emperor. So tests were needed, and wayfarers had to be expended. Any wayfarer would do—provided, of course, that he was not another Samurai. Scientists will recognize a familiar problem about the rights of experimental subjects.

Now when we hear of a custom like this, we may well reflect that we simply do not understand it; and therefore are not qualified to criticize it at all, because we are not members of that culture. But we are not members of any other culture either, except our own. So we extend the principle to cover all extraneous cultures, and we seem therefore to be moral isolationists. But this is, as we shall see, an impossible position. Let us ask what it would involve.

We must ask first: Does the isolating barrier work both ways? Are people in other cultures equally unable to criticize *us?* This question struck me sharply when I read a remark in *The Guardian* by an anthropologist about a South American Indian who had been taken into a Brazilian town for an operation, which saved his life. When he came back to his village, he made several highly critical remarks about the white Brazilians' way of life. They may very well have been justified. But the interesting point was that the anthropologist called these remarks "a damning indictment of Western civilization." Now the Indian had been in that town about two weeks. Was he in a position to deliver a damning indictment? Would we ourselves be qualified to deliver such an indictment on the Samurai, provided we could spend two weeks in ancient Japan? What do we really think about this?

My own impression is that we believe that outsiders can, in principle, deliver perfectly good indictments—only, it usually takes more than two weeks to make them damning. Understanding has degrees. It is not a slapdash yes-or-no matter. Intelligent outsiders can progress in it, and in some ways will be at an advantage over the locals. But if this is so, it must clearly apply to ourselves as much as anybody else.

Our next question is this: Does the isolating barrier between cultures block praise as well as blame? If I want to say that the Samurai culture has many virtues, or to praise the South American Indians, am I prevented from doing *that* by my outside status? Now, we certainly do need to praise other societies in this way. But it is hardly possible that we could praise them effectively if we could not, in principle, criticize them. Our praise would be worthless if it rested on no definite grounds, if it did not flow from some understanding. Certainly we may need to praise things which we do not *fully* understand. We say "there's something very good here, but I can't quite make out what it is yet." This happens when we want to learn from strangers. And we can learn from strangers. But to do this we have to distinguish between those strangers who are worth learning from and those who are not. Can we then judge which is which?

This brings us to our third question: What is involved in judging? Now plainly there is no question here of sitting on a bench in a red robe and sentencing people. Judging simply means forming an opinion, and expressing it if it is called for. Is there anything wrong about this? Naturally, we ought to avoid forming—and expressing—*crude* opinions, like that of a simple-minded missionary, who might dismiss the whole Samurai culture as entirely bad, because non-Christian. But this is a different objection. The trouble with crude opinions is that they are crude, whoever forms them, not that they are formed by the wrong people. Anthropologists, after all, are outsiders quite as much as missionaries. Moral isolationism forbids us to form *any* opinions on these matters. Its ground for doing so is that we don't understand them. But there is much that we don't understand in our own culture too. This brings us to our last question: If we can't judge other cultures, can we really judge our own? Our efforts to do so will be much damaged if we are really deprived of our opinions about other societies, because these provide the range of comparison, the spectrum of alternatives against which we set what we want to understand. We would have to stop using the mirror which anthropology so helpfully holds up to us.

In short, moral isolationism would lay down a general ban on moral reasoning. Essentially, this is the programme of immoralism, and it carries a distressing logical difficulty. Immoralists like Nietzsche are actually just a rather specialized sect of moralists. They can no more afford to put moralizing out of business than smugglers can afford to abolish customs regulations. The power of moral judgement is, in fact, not a luxury, not a perverse indulgence of the self-righteous. It is a necessity. When we judge something to be bad or good, better or worse than something else, we are taking it as an example to aim at or avoid. Without opinions of this sort, we would have no framework of comparison for our own policy, no chance of profiting by other people's insights or mistakes. In this vacuum, we could form no judgements on our own actions.

Now it would be odd if Homo sapiens had really got himself into a position as bad as this—a position where his main evolutionary asset, his brain, was so little use to him. None of us is going to accept this sceptical diagnosis. We cannot do so, because our involvement in moral isolationism does not flow from apathy, but from a rather acute concern about human hypocrisy and other forms of wickedness. But we polarize that concern around a few selected moral truths. We are rightly angry with those who despise, oppress or steamroll other cultures. We think that doing these things is actually *wrong*. But this is itself a moral judgement. We could not condemn oppression and insolence if we thought that all our condemnations were just a trivial local quirk of our own culture. We could still less do it if we tried to stop judging altogether.

Real moral scepticism, in fact, could lead only to inaction, to our losing all interest in moral questions, most of all in those which concern other societies. When we discuss these things, it becomes instantly clear how far we are from doing this. Suppose, for instance, that I criticize the bisecting Samurai, that I say his behaviour is brutal. What will usually happen next is that someone will protest, will say that I have no right to make criticisms like that of another culture. But it is most unlikely that he will use this move to end the discussion of the subject. Instead, he will justify the Samurai. He will try to fill in the background, to make me understand the custom, by explaining the exalted ideals of discipline and devotion which produced it. He will probably talk of the lower value which the ancient Japanese placed on individual life generally. He may well suggest that this is a healthier attitude than our own obsession with security. He may add, too, that the wayfarers did not seriously mind being bisected, that in principle they accepted the whole arrangement.

Now an objector who talks like this is implying that it *is* possible to understand alien customs. That is just what he is trying to make me do. And he implies, too, that if I do succeed in understanding them, I shall do something better than giving up judging them. He expects me to change my present judgement to a truer one—namely, one that is favourable. And the standards I must use to do this cannot just be Samurai standards. They have to be ones current in my own culture. Ideals like discipline and devotion will not move anybody unless he himself accepts them. As it happens, neither discipline nor devotion is very popular in the West at present. Anyone who appeals to them may well have to do some more arguing to make *them* acceptable, before he can use them to explain the Samurai. But if he does succeed here, he will have persuaded us, not just that there was something to be said for them in ancient Japan, but that there would be here as well.

Isolating barriers simply cannot arise here. If we accept something as a serious moral truth about one culture, we can't refuse to apply it—in however different an outward form—to other cultures as well, wherever circumstance admits it. If we refuse to do this, we just are not taking the other culture seriously. This becomes clear if we look at the last argument used by my objector—that of justification by consent of the victim. It is suggested that sudden bisection is quite in order, *provided* that it takes place between consenting adults. I cannot now discuss how conclusive this justification is. What I am pointing out is simply that it can only work if we believe that *consent* can make such a transaction respectable—and this is a thoroughly modern and Western idea. It would probably never occur to a Samurai; if it did, it would surprise him very much. It is *our* standard. In applying it, too, we are likely to make another typically Western demand. We shall ask for good factual evidence that the wayfarers actually do have this rather surprising taste—that they are really willing to be bisected. In applying Western standards in this way, we are not being confused or irrelevant. We are asking the questions which arise *from where we stand,* questions which we can see the sense of. We do this because asking questions which you can't see the sense of is humbug. Certainly we can extend our questioning by imaginative effort. We can come to understand other societies better. By doing so, we may make their questions our own, or we may see that they are really forms of the questions which we are asking already. This is not impossible. It is just very hard work. The obstacles which often prevent it are simply those of ordinary ignorance, laziness and prejudice.

If there were really an isolating barrier, of course, our own culture could never have been formed. It is no sealed box, but a fertile jungle of different influences—Greek, Jewish, Roman, Norse, Celtic and so forth, into which further influences are still pouring—American, Indian, Japanese, Jamaican, you name it. The moral isolationist's picture of separate, unmixable cultures is quite unreal. People who talk about British history usually stress the value of this fertilizing mix, no doubt rightly. But this is not just an odd fact about Britain. Except for the very smallest and most remote, all cultures are formed out of many streams. All have the problem of digesting and assimilating things which, at the start, they do not understand. All have the choice of learning something from this challenge, or, alternatively, of refusing to learn, and fighting it mindlessly instead.

This universal predicament has been obscured by the fact that anthropologists used to concentrate largely on very small and remote cultures, which did not seem to have this problem. These tiny societies, which had often forgotten their own history, made neat, self-contained subjects for study. No doubt it was valuable to emphasize their remoteness, their extreme strangeness, their independence of our cultural tradition. This emphasis was, I think, the root of moral isolationism. But, as the tribal studies themselves showed, even there the anthropologists were able to interpret what they saw and make judgements—often favorable—about the tribesmen. And the tribesmen, too, were quite equal to making judgements about the anthropologists—and about the tourists and Coca-Cola salesmen who followed them. Both sets of judgements, no doubt, were somewhat hasty, both have been refined in the light of further experience. A similar transaction between us and the Samurai might take even longer. But that is no reason at all for deeming it impossible. Morally as well as physically, there is only one world, and we all have to live in it.

For Further Reflection

1. What are Midgley's arguments against moral isolationism?
2. Why does Midgley say that moral isolationism is an impossible position?

3. If we can praise other cultures, can't we also blame them? Why or why not?
4. Do you believe that the behavior of the "bisecting Samurai" is brutal? If so, do you believe that you understand enough about the behavior to make such a judgment? Are you a moral isolationist?
5. Suppose someone accuses you of misunderstanding the true nature of the samurai's actions. What would this response imply about your accuser's views toward other cultures?

The Enemy of the People

HENRIK IBSEN

Henrik Ibsen (1828–1906), a Norwegian, is considered one of the greatest dramatists of all time. He was influenced by the Danish existentialist Søren Kierkegaard, who held that truth is unpopular and lonely. Kierkegaard wanted inscribed on his tombstone the epitaph the individual, signifying the idea of individual integrity in the face of the corrupt masses. Several of Ibsen's plays convey this idea, including the one excerpted here.

Our story takes place in a small Norwegian town that has become prosperous thanks to its baths, which bring people from miles around to seek their healing powers. Dr. Thomas Stockmann, the medical officer in charge of overseeing the baths, is also credited with founding them. His brother Peter is the mayor of the town. Noticing that during the previous summer visitors to the baths contracted typhus, Stockmann sends water samples to the university. He has just received the university report stating that the water is dangerously polluted. Dr. Stockmann prepares an article on the problem, which the liberal editor Hovstad is delighted to print in the progressive newspaper the *People's Messenger*. Aslaksen, the printer and leader of the skilled workers' guild, is also strongly behind Stockmann in his endeavor to reveal the truth, seeing it as a means to undermine the power of the old guard and capitalists. However, when these established powers get wind of Stockmann's news, they exert their influence by informing the town that in order to redesign the piping system, the town will have to tax the people for some twenty thousand pounds and the baths will have to be

From *The Best Known Works of Henrik Ibsen* (New York: Blue Ribbon Books, 1928).

closed for two years. The message is clear: cleaning up the polluted baths will have a severe economic cost.

Suddenly, the liberals switch sides. Peter, the mayor, warns his brother against publishing the article. Hovstad squirms and reneges on his promise to publish the exposé. Aslaksen pleads for moderation. Even Stockmann's wife Katherine pleads with him to drop the matter. Only his daughter Petra stands squarely behind him. We enter with Peter discussing the report with Stockmann.

PETER. Was it necessary to make all these investigations behind my back?

DR. STO. Yes, because until I was absolutely certain about it—

PETER. Then you mean that you are absolutely certain now?

DR. STO. Surely you are convinced of that.

PETER. Is it your intention to bring this document before the Baths Committee as a sort of official communication?

DR. STO. Certainly. Something must be done in the matter—and that quickly.

PETER. As usual, you employ violent expressions in your report. You say, amongst other things, that what we offer visitors in our Baths is a permanent supply of poison.

DR. STO. Well, can you describe it any other way, Peter? Just think—water that is poisonous, whether you drink it or bathe in it! And this we offer to the poor sick folk who come to us trustfully and pay us at an exorbitant rate to be made well again!

PETER. And your reasoning leads you to this conclusion, that we must build a sewer to draw off the alleged impurities from Mölledal and must relay the water-conduits.

DR. STO. Yes. Do you see any other way out of it? I don't.

PETER. I made a pretext this morning to go and see the town engineer, and, as if only half seriously, broached the subject of these proposals as a thing we might perhaps have to take under consideration some time later on.

DR. STO. Some time later on!

PETER. He smiled at what he considered to be my extravagance, naturally. Have you taken the trouble to consider what your proposed alterations would cost? According to the information I obtained, the expenses would probably mount up to fifteen or twenty thousand pounds.

DR. STO. Would it cost so much?

PETER. Yes; and the worst part of it would be that the work would take at least two years.

DR. STO. Two years? Two whole years?

PETER. At least. And what are we to do with the Baths in the meantime? Close them? Indeed we should be obliged to. And do you suppose any one would come near the place after it had got about that the water was dangerous?

DR. STO. Yes, but, Peter, that is what it is.

PETER. And all this at this juncture—just as the Baths are beginning to be known. There are other towns in the neighborhood with qualifications to attract visitors for bathing purposes. Don't you suppose they would immediately strain every nerve to divert the entire stream of strangers to themselves? Unquestionably they would; and then where should we be? We should probably have to abandon the whole thing, which has cost us so much money—and then you would have ruined your native town.

DR. STO. I—should have ruined—!

PETER. It is simply and solely through the Baths that the town has before it any future worth mentioning. You know that just as well as I.

DR. STO. But what do you think ought to be done, then?

PETER. Your report has not convinced me that the condition of the water at the Baths is as bad as you represent it to be.

DR. STO. I tell you it is even worse!—or at all events it will be in summer, when the warm weather comes.

PETER. As I said, I believe you exaggerate the matter considerably. A capable physician ought to know what measures to take—he ought to be capable of preventing injurious influences or of remedying them if they become obviously persistent.

DR. STO. Well? What more?

PETER. The water supply for the Baths is now an established fact, and in consequence must be treated as such. But probably the Committee, at its discretion, will not be disinclined to consider the question of how far it might be possible to introduce certain improvements consistently with a reasonable expenditure.

DR. STO. And do you suppose that I will have anything to do with such a piece of trickery as that?

PETER. Trickery!!

DR. STO. Yes, it would be a trick—a fraud, a lie, a downright crime towards the public, towards the whole community!

PETER. I have not, as I remarked before, been able to convince myself that there is actually any imminent danger.

DR. STO. You have! It is impossible that you should not be convinced. I know I have represented the facts absolutely truthfully and fairly. And you know it very well, Peter, only you won't acknowledge it. It was owing to your action that both the Baths and the water-conduits were built where they are; and that is what you won't acknowledge—that damnable blunder of yours. Pooh!—do you suppose I don't see through you?

PETER. And even if that were true? If I perhaps guard my reputation somewhat anxiously, it is in the interests of the town. Without moral authority I am powerless to direct public affairs as seems, to my judgment, to be best for the common good. And on that account—and for various other reasons too—it appears to me to be a matter of importance that your report should not be delivered to the Committee. In the interests of the public, you must withhold it. Then, later on, I will raise the question and we will do our best, privately; but nothing of this unfortunate affair—not a single word of it—must come to the ears of the public.

DR. STO. I am afraid you will not be able to prevent that now, my dear Peter.

PETER. It must and shall be prevented.

DR. STO. It is no use, I tell you. There are too many people that know about it.

PETER. That know about it? Who? Surely you don't mean those fellows on the "People's Messenger"?

DR. STO. Yes, they know. The liberal-minded independent press is going to see that you do your duty.

PETER [*after a short pause*]. You are an extraordinarily independent man, Thomas. Have you given no thought to the consequences this may have for yourself?

DR. STO. Consequences?—for me?

PETER. For you and yours, yes.

DR. STO. What the deuce do you mean?

PETER. I believe I have always behaved in a brotherly way to you—have always been ready to oblige or to help you?

DR. STO. Yes, you have, and I am grateful to you for it.

PETER. There is no need. Indeed, to some extent I was forced to do so—for my own sake. I always hoped that, if I helped to improve your financial position, I should be able to keep some check on you.

DR. STO. What!! Then it was only for your own sake—!

PETER. Up to a certain point, yes. It is painful for a man in an official position to have his nearest relative compromising himself time after time.

DR. STO. And do you consider that I do that?

PETER. Yes, unfortunately, you do, without even being aware of it. You have a restless, pugnacious, rebellious disposition. And then there is that disastrous propensity of yours to want to write about every sort of possible and impossible thing. The moment an idea comes into your head, you must needs go and write a newspaper article or a whole pamphlet about it.

DR. STO. Well, but is it not the duty of a citizen to let the public share in any new ideas he may have?

PETER. Oh, the public doesn't require any new ideas. The public is best served by the good, old-established ideas it already has.

DR. STO. And that is your honest opinion?

PETER. Yes, and for once I must talk frankly to you. Hitherto I have tried to avoid doing so, because I know how irritable you are; but now I must tell you the truth, Thomas. You have no conception what an amount of harm you do yourself by your impetuosity. You complain of the authorities, you even complain of the government—you are always pulling them to pieces; you insist that you have been neglected and persecuted. But what else can such a cantankerous man as you expect?

DR. STO. What next? Cantankerous, am I?

PETER. Yes, Thomas, you are an extremely cantankerous man to work with—I know that to my cost. You disregard everything that you ought to have consideration for. You seem completely to forget that it is me you have to thank for your appointment here as medical officer to the Baths.—

DR. STO. I was entitled to it as a matter of course!—I and nobody else! I was the first person to see that the town could be made into a flourishing watering place, and I was the only one who saw it at that time. I had to fight single-handed in support of the idea for many years; and I wrote and wrote—

PETER. Undoubtedly. But things were not ripe for the scheme then—though, of course, you could not judge of that in your out-of-the-way corner up north. But as soon as the opportune moment came I—and the others—took the matter into our hands—

DR. STO. Yes, and made this mess of all my beautiful plan. It is pretty obvious now what clever fellows you were!

PETER. To my mind the whole thing only seems to mean that you are seeking another outlet for your combativeness. You want to pick a quarrel with your superiors—an old habit of yours. You cannot put up with any authority over you. You look askance at anyone who occupies a superior official position; you regard him as a personal enemy, and then any stick is good enough to beat him with. But now I have called your attention to the fact that the town's interests are at stake—and, incidentally, my own too. And therefore I must tell you, Thomas, that you will find me inexorable with regard to what I am about to require you to do.

DR. STO. And what is that?

PETER. As you have been so indiscreet as to speak of this delicate matter to outsiders, despite the fact that you ought to have treated it as entirely official and confidential, it is obviously impossible to hush it up now. All sorts of rumours will get about directly, and everybody who has a grudge against us will take care to embellish these rumours. So it will be necessary for you to refute them publicly.

DR. STO. I! How? I don't understand.

PETER. What we shall expect is that, after making further investigations, you will come to the conclusion that the matter is not by any means as dangerous or as critical as you imagined in the first instance.

DR. STO. Oho!—so that is what you expect!

PETER. And, what is more, we shall expect you to make public profession of your confidence in the Committee and in their readiness to consider fully and conscientiously what steps may be necessary to remedy any possible defects.

DR. STO. But you will never be able to do that by patching and tinkering at it—never! Take my word for it, Peter; I mean what I say, as deliberately and emphatically as possible.

PETER. As an officer under the Committee, you have no right to any individual opinion.

DR. STO. [*amazed*]. No right?

PETER. In your official capacity, no. As a private person, it is quite another matter. But as a subordinate member of the staff of the Baths, you have no right to express any opinion which runs contrary to that of your superiors.

DR. STO. This is too much! I, a doctor, a man of science, have no right to—!

PETER. The matter in hand is not simply a scientific one. It is a complicated matter, and has its economic as well as its technical side.

DR. STO. I don't care what it is! I intend to be free to express my opinion on any subject under the sun.

PETER. As you please—but not on any subject concerning the Baths. That we forbid.

DR. STO. [*shouting*]. You forbid—! You! A pack of—

PETER. *I* forbid it—I, your chief; and if I forbid it, you have to obey.

DR. STO. [*controlling himself*]. Peter—if you were not my brother—

PETRA. [*throwing open the door*]. Father, you shan't stand this!

MRS. STO. [*coming in after her*]. Petra, Petra!

PETER. Oh, so you have been eavesdropping.

MRS. STO. You were talking so loud, we couldn't help—

PETRA. Yes, I was listening.

PETER. Well, after all, I am very glad—

DR. STO. [*going up to him*]. You were saying something about forbidding and obeying?

PETER. You obliged me to take that tone with you.

DR. STO. And so I am to give myself the lie, publicly?

PETER. We consider it absolutely necessary that you should make some public statement as I have asked for.

DR. STO. And if I do not—obey?

PETER. Then we shall publish a statement ourselves to reassure the public.

DR. STO. Very well; but in that case I shall use my pen against you. I stick to what I have said; I will show that I am right and that you are wrong. And what will you do then?

PETER. Then I shall not be able to prevent your being dismissed.

DR. STO. What—?

PETRA. Father—dismissed!

MRS. STO. Dismissed!

PETER. Dismissed from the staff of the Baths. I shall be obliged to propose that you shall immediately be given notice, and shall not be allowed any further participation in the Baths' affairs.

DR. STO. You would dare to do that!

PETER. It is you that are playing the daring game.

PETRA. Uncle, that is a shameful way to treat a man like father!

MRS. STO. Do hold your tongue, Petra!

PETER [*looking at* PETRA]. Oh, so we volunteer our opinions already, do we? Of course. [*To* MRS. STOCKMANN.] Katherine, I imagine you are the most sensible person in this house. Use any influence you may have over your husband, and make him see what this will entail for his family as well as—

DR. STO. My family is my own concern and nobody else's!

PETER. —for his own family, as I was saying, as well as for the town he lives in.

DR. STO. It is I who have the real good of the town at heart! I want to lay bare the defects that sooner or later must come to the light of day. I will show whether I love my native town.

PETER. You, who in your blind obstinacy want to cut off the most important source of the town's welfare?

DR. STO. The source is poisoned, man! Are you mad? We are making our living by retailing filth and corruption! The whole of our flourishing municipal life derives its sustenance from a lie!

PETER. All imagination—or something even worse. The man who can throw out such offensive insinuations about his native town must be an enemy to our community.

DR. STO. [*going up to him*]. Do you dare to—!

MRS. STO. [*throwing herself between them*]. Thomas!

PETRA. [*catching her father by the arm*]. Don't lose your temper, father!

PETER. I will not expose myself to violence. Now you have had a warning; so reflect on what you owe to yourself and your family. Good-bye. [*Goes out.*]

DR. STO. [*walking up and down*]. Am I to put up with such treatment as this? In my own house, Katherine! What do you think of that!

MRS. STO. Indeed it is both shameful and absurd Thomas—

PETRA. If only I could give uncle a piece of my mind—

DR. STO. It is my own fault. I ought to have flown out at him long ago!—shown my teeth!—bitten! To hear him call me an enemy to our community! Me! I shall not take that lying down, upon my soul!

MRS. STO. But, dear Thomas, your brother has power on his side—

DR. STO. Yes, but I have right on mine, I tell you.

MRS. STO. Oh! yes, right—right. What is the use of having right on your side if you have not got might?

PETRA. Oh, mother!—how can you say such a thing!

DR. STO. Do you imagine that in a free country it is no use having right on your side? You are absurd, Katherine. Besides, haven't I got the liberal-minded, independent press to lead the way, and the compact majority behind me? That is might enough, I should think!

MRS. STO. But, good heavens, Thomas, you don't mean to—?

DR. STO. Don't mean to what?

MRS. STO. To set yourself up in opposition to your brother.

DR. STO. In God's name, what else do you suppose I should do but take my stand on right and truth?

PETRA. Yes, I was just going to say that.

MRS. STO. But it won't do you any earthly good. If they won't do it, they won't.

DR. STO. Oho, Katherine! Just give me time, and you will see how I will carry the war into their camp.

MRS. STO. Yes, you carry the war into their camp, and you get your dismissal—that is what you will do.

DR. STO. In any case I shall have done my duty towards the public—towards the community. I, who am called its enemy!

MRS. STO. But towards your family, Thomas? Towards your own home! Do you think that is doing your duty towards those you have to provide for?

PETRA. Ah, don't think always first of us, mother.

MRS. STO. Oh, it is easy for you to talk; you are able to shift for yourself, if need be. But remember the boys, Thomas; and think a little too of yourself, and of me—

DR. STO. I think you are out of your senses, Katherine! If I were to be such a miserable coward as to go on my knees to Peter and his damned crew, do you suppose I should ever know an hour's peace of mind all my life afterwards?

MRS. STO. I don't know anything about that; but God preserve us from the peace of mind we shall have, all the same, if you go on defying him! You will find yourself again without the means of subsistence, with no income to count upon. I should think we had had enough of that in the old days. Remember that, Thomas; think what that means.

DR. STO. [*collecting himself with a struggle and clenching his fists*]. And this is what this slavery can bring upon a free, honourable man! Isn't it horrible, Katherine?

MRS. STO. Yes, it is sinful to treat you so, it is perfectly true. But, good heavens, one has to put up with so much injustice in this world.—There are the boys, Thomas! Look at them! What is to become of them? Oh, no, no, you can never have the heart—. [EJLIF and MORTEN *have come in while she was speaking, with their school books in their hands*].

DR. STO. The boys—! [*Recovers himself suddenly.*] No, even if the whole world goes to pieces, I will never bow my neck to this yoke! [*Goes towards his room.*]

MRS. STO. [*following him*]. Thomas—what are you going to do!

DR. STO. [*at his door*]. I mean to have the right to look my sons in the face when they are grown men. [*Goes into his room.*]

MRS. STO. [*bursting into tears*]. God help us all!

PETRA. Father is splendid! He will not give in.

[*The boys look on in amazement;* PETRA *signs to them not to speak!* . . .

> [Stockmann is outraged at the moral cowardice of the "progressives." Leaving the Baths polluted in this way will put the unwitting visitors, seeking health, in grave danger. He tries to rent a hall, but the town leaders are united against him. Finally, an old sea captain, Horster, opens his hall to him to reveal his findings. A crowd gathers, including Hovstad and his brother Peter. After an attempt to muzzle him fails, Dr. Stockmann speaks.]

ASL. [*ringing his bell*]. Dr. Stockmann will address the meeting.

DR. STO. I should like to have seen anyone, a few days ago, dare to attempt to silence me as has been done to-night! I would have defended my sacred rights as a man, like a lion! But now it is all one to me; I have something of even weightier importance to say to you.

[*The crowd presses nearer to him,* MORTEN KIIL *conspicuous among them.*]

DR. STO. [*continuing*]. I have thought and pondered a great deal, these last few days—pondered over such a variety of things that in the end my head seemed too full to hold them—

PETER. [*with a cough*]. Ahem!

DR. STO. —but I got them clear in my mind at last, and then I saw the whole situation lucidly. And that is why I am standing here to-night. I have a great revelation to make to you, my fellow-citizens! I will impart to you a discovery of a far wider scope than the trifling matter that our water-supply is poisoned and our medicinal Baths are standing on pestiferous soil.

A NUMBER OF VOICES [*shouting*]. Don't talk about the Baths! We won't hear you! None of that!

DR. STO. I have already told you that what I want to speak about is the great discovery I have made lately—the discovery that all the sources of our moral life are poisoned and that the whole fabric of our civic community is founded on the pestiferous soil of falsehood.

VOICES OF DISCONCERTED CITIZENS. What is that he says?

PETER. Such an insinuation—!

ASL. [*with his hand on his bell*]. I call upon the speaker to moderate his language.

DR. STO. I have always loved my native town as a man only can love the home of his youthful days. I was not old when I went away from here; and exile, longing and memories cast as it were an additional halo over both the town and its inhabitants. [*Some clapping and applause.*] And there I stayed, for many years, in a horrible hole far away up north. When I came into contact with some of the people that lived scattered about among the rocks, I often thought it would of been more service to the poor half-starved creatures if a veterinary doctor had been sent up there, instead of a man like me. [*Murmurs among* the *crowd.*]

BILL. [*laying down his pen*]. I'm damned if I have ever heard—!

HOV. It is an insult to a respectable population!

DR. STO. Wait a bit! I do not think anyone will charge me with having forgotten my native town up there. I was like one of the eider-ducks brooding on its nest, and what I hatched was—the plans for these Baths. [*Applause and protests.*] And then when fate at last decreed for me the great happiness of coming home again—I assure you, gentlemen, I thought I had nothing more in the world to wish for. Or rather, there was one thing I wished for—eagerly, untiringly, ardently—and that was to be able to be of service to my native town and the good of the community.

PETER [*looking at the ceiling*]. You chose a strange way of doing it—ahem!

DR. STO. And so, with my eyes blinded to the real facts, I revelled in happiness. But yesterday morning—no, to be precise, it was yesterday afternoon—the eyes of my mind were opened wide, and the first thing I realised was the colossal stupidity of the authorities—. [*Uproar, shouts and laughter.* MRS. STOCKMANN *coughs persistently.*]

PETER. Mr. Chairman!

ASL. [*ringing his bell*]. By virtue of my authority—!

DR. STO. It is a petty thing to catch me up on a word, Mr. Aslasken. What I mean is only that I got scent of the unbelievable piggishness our leading men had been responsible for down at the Baths. I can't stand leading men at any price!—I have had enough of such people in my time. They are like billy-goats in a young plantation; they do mischief everywhere. They stand in a free man's way, whichever way he turns, and what

I should like best would be to see them exterminated like any other vermin—. [*Uproar.*]

PETER. Mr. Chairman, can we allow such expressions to pass?

ASL. [*with his hand on his bell*]. Doctor—!

DR. STO. I cannot understand how it is that I have only now acquired a clear conception of what these gentry are, when I had almost daily before my eyes in this town such an excellent specimen of them—my brother Peter—slow-witted and hide-bound in prejudice—. [*Laughter, uproar and hisses.* MRS. STOCKMANN *sits coughing assiduously.* ASLAKSEN *rings his bell violently.*]

THE DRUNKEN MAN [*who has got in again*]. Is it me he is talking about? My name's Petersen, all right—but devil take me if I—

ANGRY VOICES. Turn out that drunken man! Turn him out. [*He is turned out again.*]

PETER. Who was that person?

1ST CITIZEN. I don't know who he is, Mr. Mayor.

2ND CITIZEN. He doesn't belong here.

3RD CITIZEN. I expect he is a navvy from over at [*the rest is inaudible*].

ASL. He had obviously had too much beer.—Proceed, Doctor, but please strive to be moderate in your language.

DR. STO. Very well, gentlemen, I will say no more about our leading men. And if anyone imagines, from what I have just said, that my object is to attack these people this evening, he is wrong—absolutely wide of the mark. For I cherish the comforting conviction that these parasites—all these venerable relics of a dying school of thought—are most admirably paving the way for their own extinction; they need no doctor's help to hasten their end. Nor is it folk of that kind who constitute the most pressing danger to the community. It is not they who are most instrumental in poisoning the sources of our moral life and directing the ground on which we stand. It is not they who are the most dangerous enemies of truth and freedom amongst us.

SHOUTS FROM ALL SIDES. Who then? Who is it? Name! Name!

DR. STO. You may depend upon it I shall name them! That is precisely the great discovery I made yesterday. [*Raises his voice.*] The most dangerous enemy to truth and freedom amongst us is the compact majority—yes, the damned compact Liberal majority—that is it! Now you know; [*Tremendous uproar. Most of the crowd are shouting, stamping and hissing. Some of the older men among them exchange stolen glances and seem to be enjoying themselves.* MRS. STOCKMANN *gets up, looking anxious.* EJLIF *and* MORTEN *advance threateningly upon some schoolboys who are playing pranks.* ASLAKSEN *rings his bell and begs for silence.* HOVSTAD *and* BILLING *both talk at once, but are inaudible. At last quiet is restored.*]

ASL. As chairman, I call upon the speaker to withdraw the ill-considered expressions he has just used.

DR. STO. Never, Mr. Aslaksen! It is the majority in our community that denies me my freedom and seeks to prevent my speaking the truth.

HOV. The majority always has right on its side.

BILL. And truth too, by God!

DR. STO. The majority *never* has right on its side. Never, I say! That is one of these social lies against which an independent, intelligent man must wage war. Who is it that constitute the majority of the population in a country? Is it the clever folk or the stupid? I don't imagine you will dispute the fact that at present the stupid people are in an absolutely overwhelming majority all the world over. But, good Lord!—you can never pretend that it is right that the stupid folk should govern the clever ones! [*Up-roar and cries.*] Oh, yes—you can shout me down, I know! but you cannot answer me. The majority has *might* on its side—unfortunately; but *right* it has *not.* I am in the right—I and a few other scattered individuals. The minority is always in the right. [*Renewed uproar.*]

HOV. Aha!—so Dr. Stockmann has become an aristocrat since the day before yesterday!

DR. STO. I have already said that I don't intend to waste a word on the puny, narrow-chested, short-winded crew whom we are leaving astern. Pulsating life no longer concerns itself with them. I am thinking of the few, the scattered few amongst us, who have absorbed new and vigorous truths. Such men stand, as it were, at the outposts, so far ahead that the compact majority has not yet been able to come up with them; and there they are fighting for truths that are too newly-born into the world of consciousness to have any considerable number of people on their side as yet.

HOV. So the Doctor is a revolutionary now!

DR. STO. Good heavens—of course I am, Mr. Hovstad! I propose to raise a revolution against the lie that the majority has the monopoly of the truth. What sort of truths are they that the majority usually supports? They are truths that are of such advanced age that they are beginning to break up. And if a truth is as old as that, it is also in a fair way to become a lie, gentlemen. [*Laughter and mocking cries.*] Yes, believe me or not, as you like; but truths are by no means as long-lived as Methuselah—as some folk imagine. A normally constituted truth lives, let us say, as a rule seventeen or eighteen, or at most twenty years; seldom longer. But truths as aged as that are always worn frightfully thin, and nevertheless it is only then that the majority recognises them and recommends them to the community as wholesome moral nourishment. There is no great nutritive value in that sort of fare, I can assure you; and, as a doctor, I ought to know.

These "majority truths" are like last year's cured meat—like rancid, tainted ham; and they are the origin of the moral scurvy that is rampant in our communities.

ASL. It appears to me that the speaker is wandering a long way from his subject.

PETER. I quite agree with the Chairman.

DR. STO. Have you gone clean out of your senses, Peter? I am sticking as closely to my subject as I can; for my subject is precisely this, that it is the masses, the majority—this infernal compact majority—that poisons the sources of our moral life and infects the ground we stand on.

HOV. And all this because the great, broad-minded majority of the people is prudent enough to show deference only to well-ascertained and well-approved truths?

DR. STO. Ah, my good Mr. Hovstad, don't talk nonsense about well-ascertained truths! The truths of which the masses now approve are the very truths that the fighters at the outposts held to in the days of our grandfathers. We fighters at the outposts nowadays no longer approve of them; and I do not believe there is any other well-ascertained truth except this, that no community can live a healthy life if it is nourished only on such old marrowless truths.

HOV. But instead of standing there using vague generalities, it would be interesting if you would tell us what these old marrowless truths are, that we are nourished on.

[*Applause from many quarters.*]

DR. STO. Oh, I could give you a whole string of such abominations; but to begin with I will confine myself to one well-approved truth, which at bottom is a foul lie, but upon which nevertheless Mr. Hovstad and the "People's Messenger" and all the "Messenger's" supporters are nourished.

HOV. And that is—?

DR. STO. That is, the doctrine you have inherited from your forefathers and proclaim thoughtlessly far and wide—the doctrine that the public, the crowd, the masses, are the essential part of the population—that they constitute the People—that the common folk, the ignorant and incomplete element in the community, have the same right to pronounce judgment and to approve, to direct and to govern, as the isolated, intellectually superior personalities in it.

BILL. Well, damn me if ever I—

HOV. [*at the same time, shouting out*]. Fellow-citizens, take good note of that!

A NUMBER OF VOICES [*angrily*]. Oho!—we are not the People! Only the superior folk are to govern, are they!

A WORKMAN. Turn the fellow out, for talking such rubbish!

ANOTHER. Out with him!

ANOTHER [*calling out*]. Blow your horn, Evensen!

[*A horn is blown loudly, amidst hisses and an angry uproar.*]

DR. STO. [*when the noise has somewhat abated*]. Be reasonable! Can't you stand hearing the voice of truth for once? I don't in the least expect you to agree with me all at once; but I must say I did expect Mr. Hovstad to admit I was right, when he had recovered his composure a little. He claims to be a freethinker—

VOICES [*in murmurs of astonishment*]. Freethinker, did he say? Is Hovstad a freethinker?

HOV. [*shouting*]. Prove it, Dr. Stockmann! When have I said so in print?

DR. STO. [*reflecting*]. No, confound it, you are right!—you have never had the courage to. Well, I won't put you in a hole, Mr. Hovstad. Let us say it is I that am the freethinker, then. I am going to prove to you, scientifically, that the "People's Messenger" leads you by the nose in a shameful manner when it tells you that you—that the common people, the crowd, the masses, are the real essence of the People. That is only a newspaper lie, I tell you! The common people are nothing more than the raw material of which a People is made. [*Groans, laughter and uproar.*] Well, isn't that the case? Isn't there an enormous difference between a well-bred and an ill-bred strain of animals? Take, for instance, a common barn-door hen. What sort of eating do you get from a shrivelled up old scrag of a fowl like that? Not much, do you! And what sort of eggs does it lay? A fairly good crow or a raven can lay pretty nearly as good an egg. But take a well-bred Spanish or Japanese hen, or a good pheasant or a turkey—then you will see the difference. Or take the case of dogs, with whom we humans are on such intimate terms. Think first of an ordinary common cur—I mean one of the horrible, coarse-haired, low-bred curs that do nothing but run about the streets and befoul the walls of the houses. Compare one of these curs with a poodle whose sires for many generations have been bred in a gentleman's house, where they have had the best of food and had the opportunity of hearing soft voices and music. Do you not think that the poodle's brain is developed to quite a different degree from that of the cur? Of course it is. It is puppies of well-bred poodles like that, that showmen train to do incredibly clever tricks—things that a common cur could never learn to do even if it stood on its head. [*Uproar and mocking cries.*]

A CITIZEN [*calls out*]. Are you going to make out we are dogs, now?

ANOTHER CITIZEN. We are not animals, Doctor!

DR. STO. Yes, but, bless my soul, we *are*, my friend! It is true we are the finest animals anyone could wish for; but, even amongst us, exceptionally fine animals are rare. There is a tremendous difference between poodle-men and cur-men. And the amusing part of it is, that Mr. Hovstad quite agrees with me as long as it is a question of four-footed animals—

HOV. Yes, it is true enough as far as they are concerned.

DR. STO. Very well. But as soon as I extend the principle and apply it to two-legged animals, Mr. Hovstad stops short. He no longer dares to think independently, or to pursue his ideas to their logical conclusion; so he turns the whole theory upside down and proclaims in the "People's Messenger" that it is the barn-door hens and street curs that are the finest specimens in the menagerie. But that is always the way, as long as a man retains the traces of common origin and has not worked his way up to intellectual distinction.

HOV. I lay no claim to any sort of distinction. I am the son of humble countryfolk, and I am proud that the stock I come from is rooted deep among the common people he insults.

VOICES. Bravo, Hovstad! Bravo! Bravo!

DR. STO. The kind of common people I mean are not only to be found low down in the social scale; they crawl and swarm all around us—even in the highest social positions. You have only to look at your own fine, distinguished Mayor! My brother Peter is every bit as plebeian as anyone that walks in two shoes—[*laughter and hisses*].

PETER. I protest against personal allusions of this kind.

DR. STO. [*imperturbably*]. —and that, not because he is, like myself, descended from some old rascal of a pirate from Pomerania or thereabouts—because that is who we are descended from—

PETER. An absurd legend. I deny it!

DR. STO. —but because he thinks what his superiors think and holds the same opinions as they. People who do that are, intellectually speaking, common people; and that is why my magnificent brother Peter is in reality so very far from any distinction—and consequently also so far from being liberal-minded.

PETER. Mr. Chairman—!

HOV. So it is only the distinguished men that are liberal-minded in this country? We are learning something quite new! [*Laughter.*]

DR. STO. Yes, that is part of my new discovery too. And another part of it is that broad-mindedness is almost precisely the same thing as morality. That is why I maintain that it is absolutely inexcusable in the "People's Messenger" to proclaim, day in and day out, the false doctrine that it is the masses, the crowd, the compact majority, that have the monopoly of broad-mindedness and morality—and that vice and corruption and every kind of intellectual depravity are the result of culture, just as the filth that is draining into our Baths is the result of the tanneries up at Mölledal! [*Uproar and interruptions.* DR. STOCKMANN *is undisturbed, and goes on, carried away by his ardour, with a smile.*] And yet this same "People's Messenger" can go on preaching that the masses ought to be elevated to higher conditions of life! But, bless my soul, if the "Messenger's" teaching is to be depended upon, this very raising up the masses would mean nothing more or less than setting them straightway upon the paths of depravity! Happily the theory that culture demoralises is only an old falsehood that our forefathers believed in and we have inherited. No, it is ignorance, poverty, ugly conditions of life, that do the devil's work! In a house which does not get aired and swept every day—my wife Katherine maintains that the floor ought to be scrubbed as well, but that is a debatable question—in such a house, let me tell you, people will lose within two or three years the power of thinking or acting in a moral manner. Lack of oxygen weakens the conscience. And there must be a plentiful lack of oxygen in very many houses in this town, I should think, judging from the fact that the whole compact majority can be unconscientious enough to wish to build the town's prosperity on a quagmire of falsehood and deceit.

ASL. We cannot allow such a grave accusation to be flung at a citizen community.

A CITIZEN. I move that the Chairman direct the speaker to sit down.

VOICES [*angrily*]. Hear, hear! Quite right! Make him sit down!

DR. STO. [*losing his self-control*]. Then I will go and shout the truth at every street corner! I will write it in other towns' newspapers! The whole country shall know what is going on here.

HOV. It almost seems as if Dr. Stockmann's intentions were to ruin the town.

DR. STO. Yes, my native town is so dear to me that I would rather ruin it than see it flourishing upon a lie.

ASL. This is really serious. [*Uproar and cat-calls.* MRS. STOCKMANN *coughs, but to no purpose; her husband does not listen to her any longer.*]

HOV. [*shouting above the din.*] A man must be a public enemy to wish to ruin a whole community!

DR. STO. [*with growing fervour*]. What does the destruction of a community matter, I tell you! All who live by lies ought to be exterminated like vermin! You will end by infecting the whole country; you will bring about such a state of things that the whole country will deserve to be ruined. And if things come to that pass, I shall say from the bottom of my heart: Let the whole country perish, let all these people be exterminated!

VOICES FROM THE CROWD. That is talking like an out-and-out enemy of the people!

BILL. There sounded the voice of the people, by all that's holy!

THE WHOLE CROWD [*shouting*]. Yes, yes! He is an enemy of the people! He hates his country! He hates his own people!

ASL. Both as a citizen and as an individual, I am profoundly disturbed by what we have had to listen to. Dr. Stockmann has shown himself in a light I should never have dreamed of. I am unhappily obliged to subscribe to the opinion which I have just heard my estimable fellow-citizens utter; and I propose that we should give expression to that opinion in a resolution. I propose a resolution as follows: "This meeting declares that it considers Dr. Thomas Stockmann, Medical Officer of the Baths, to be an enemy of the people." [*A storm of cheers and applause. A number of men surround the* DOCTOR *and hiss him.* MRS. STOCKMANN *and* PETRA *have got up from their seats.* MORTEN *and* EJLIF *are fighting the other schoolboys for hissing; some of their elders separate them.*]

DR. STO. [*to the men who are hissing him*]. Oh, you fools! I tell you that—

ASL. [*ringing his bell*]. We cannot hear you now, Doctor. A formal vote is about to be taken; but, out of regard for personal feelings, it shall be by ballot and not verbal. Have you any clean paper, Mr. Billing?

BILL. I have both blue and white here.

ASL. [*going to him*]. That will do nicely; we shall get on more quickly that way. Cut it up into small strips—yes, that's it. [*To the meeting.*] Blue means no; white means yes. I will come round myself and collect votes. [PETER STOCKMANN *leaves the hall.* ASLAKSEN *and one or two others go around the room with the slips of paper in their hats.*]

1ST CITIZEN [*to* HOVSTAD]. I say, what has come to the Doctor? What are we to think of it?

HOV. Oh, you know how headstrong he is.

2ND CITIZEN [*to* BILLING]. Billing, you go to their house—have you ever noticed if the fellow drinks?

BILL. Well I'm hanged if I know what to say. There are always spirits on the table when you go.

3RD CITIZEN. I rather think he goes quite off his head sometimes.

1ST CITIZEN. I wonder if there is any madness in his family?

BILL. I shouldn't wonder if there were.

4TH CITIZEN. No, it is nothing more than sheer malice; he wants to get even with somebody for something or other.

BILL. Well certainly he suggested a rise in his salary on one occasion lately, and did not get it.

THE CITIZENS [*together*]. Ah!—then it is easy to understand how it is!

THE DRUNKEN MAN [*who has got amongst the audience again*]. I want a blue one, I do! And I want a white one too!

VOICES. It's that drunken chap again! Turn him out!

MORTEN KIIL [*going up to* DR. STOCKMANN.] Well, Stockmann, do you see what these monkey tricks of yours lead to?

DR. STO. I have done my duty.

MORTEN KIIL. What was that you said about the tanneries at Mölledal?

DR. STO. You heard well enough. I said they were the source of all the filth.

MORTEN KIIL. My tannery too?

DR. STO. Unfortunately your tannery is by far the worst.

MORTEN KIIL. Are you going to put that in the papers?

DR. STO. I shall conceal nothing.

MORTEN KIIL. That may cost you dear, Stockmann. [*Goes out.*]

A STOUT MAN [*going up to* CAPTAIN HORSTER, *without taking any notice of the ladies.*] Well, Captain, so you lend your house to enemies of the people?

HORS. I imagine I can do what I like with my own possessions, Mr. Vik.

THE STOUT MAN. Then you can have no objection to my doing the same with mine.

HORS. What do you mean, sir?

THE STOUT MAN. You shall hear from me in the morning. [*Turns his back on him and moves off.*]

PETRA. Was that not your owner, Captain Horster?

HORS. Yes, that was Mr. Vik the ship-owner.

ASL. [*with the voting-papers in his hands, gets up on to the platform and rings his bell.*] Gentlemen, allow me to announce the result. By the votes of every one here except one person—

A YOUNG MAN. That is the drunk chap!

ASL. By the votes of every one here except a tipsy man, this meeting of citizens declares Dr. Thomas Stockmann to be an enemy of the people. [*Shouts and applause.*] Three cheers for our ancient and honourable citizen community! [*Renewed applause.*] Three cheers for our able and energetic Mayor, who has so loyally suppressed the promptings of family feeling! [*Cheers.*] The meeting is dissolved. [*Gets down.*]

BILL. Three cheers for the Chairman!

THE WHOLE CROWD. Three cheers for Aslaksen! Hurrah!

DR. STO. My hat and coat, Petra! Captain, have you room on your ship for passengers to the New World?

HORS. For you and yours we will make room, Doctor. . . .

[*Horn-blowing, hisses, and wild cries.* DR. STOCKMANN *goes out through the hall with his family,* HORSTER *elbowing a way for them.*]

THE WHOLE CROWD [*howling after as they go.*] Enemy of the People! Enemy of the People!

BILL. [*as he puts his papers together*]. Well, I'm damned if I go and drink toddy with the Stockmanns tonight!

[*The crowd press towards the exit. The uproar continues outside; shouts of* "Enemy of the People!" *are heard from without.*] . . .

> [Dr. Stockmann is declared an enemy of the people and is ostracized by the community. He tells Katherine, "You should never wear your best trousers when you go out to fight for freedom and truth. It is not that I care so much about the trousers, you know; you can always sew them up again for me. But that the common herd should dare to make this attack on me, as if they were my equals—that is what I cannot, for the life of me, swallow!"
>
> He is fired from his post and informed that his patients have been instructed to boycott him. His two sons are attacked at school and Petra is fired from her teaching position. His wife wants the family to move away from this town, and his brother, Peter, agrees. But Dr. Stockmann refuses to leave. He will open up a school and serve the poor. He will fight the battle to its finish.]

For Further Reflection

1. What is the key conflict in this play? How well does Dr. Stockmann deal with it?
2. What virtues and vices are exemplified in this play? Assess the various characters, especially Dr. Stockmann. Do you agree with Aslaksen that he should be more moderate? Or is Stockmann a man of rare courage and integrity?
3. What would you do in this situation? Would you leave town as Stockmann's wife and brother advise?
4. What are the implications of Dr. Stockmann's actions for the issue of moral relativism?
5. Is the problem portrayed in this play relevant today? If so, what are we doing about it? Explain your answer.
6. How important is it to proclaim the truth even when it may have social repercussions?

Further Readings for Chapter 3

Brink, David. *Moral Realism and the Foundation of Ethics.* Cambridge: Cambridge University Press, 1989.

Fishkin, James. *Beyond Subjective Morality.* New Haven, Conn.: Yale University Press, 1984.

Harman, Gilbert. "Moral Relativism Defended." *Philosophical Review* 84 (1975).

Ladd, John, ed. *Ethical Relativism.* Belmont, Calif.: Wadsworth, 1973. A good collection of basic readings.

Shafer-Landau, Russ. *Whatever Happened to Good and Evil*? New York: Oxford University Press, 2004.

Westermarck, Edward. *Ethical Relativity.* Atlantic Highlands, N.J.: Humanities Press, 1960.

Williams, Bernard. *Morality.* New York: Harper Torchbooks, 1972.

Wong, David. *Moral Relativity.* Berkeley and Los Angeles: University of California Press, 1985.

PART II

Moral Theories and Moral Character

Suppose you are on an island with a dying millionaire. As he lies dying, he entreats you for one final favor: "I've dedicated my whole life to baseball and have gotten endless pleasure, and some pain, rooting for the New York Yankees for fifty years. Now that I am dying, I want to give all my assets, $6 million, to the Yankees. Would you take this money [indicating a box containing the money in large bills] back to New York and give it to the New York Yankees' owner, George Steinbrenner, so that he can buy better players?" You agree to carry out his wish, at which point a huge smile of relief and gratitude breaks out on his face as he expires in your arms. After returning to New York, you see a newspaper advertisement placed by the World Hunger Relief Organization (whose integrity you do not doubt) pleading for $6 million to be used to save 100,000 people dying of starvation in East Africa. Not only will the $6 million save their lives, but it will be used to purchase small technology and the kinds of fertilizers necessary to build a sustainable economy. You reconsider your promise to the dying Yankees fan in the light of this consideration. What should you do with the money?

What is the right thing to do in this kind of situation? Consider some traditional moral principles and see if they help you come to a decision. One principle often given to guide action is "Let your conscience be your guide." But does it help here? No.

Since conscience is primarily a function of our upbringing, people's consciences will speak to them in different ways according to how they were brought up. Depending on their upbringing, some people feel no qualms about terrorist acts, whereas others feel the torments of conscience over stepping on a gnat. Suppose your conscience tells you to give the money to the Yankees and my conscience tells me to give the money to the World Hunger Relief Organization. How can we ever discuss the matter? If conscience is the end of the matter, we're left mute.

Another principle urged on us is "Do whatever is most loving." St. Augustine (354–430) said, "Love God and do whatever you want." Love is surely a wonderful value, but is it enough to guide our actions when there is a conflict of interest? "Love is blind," it has been said, "but reason, like marriage, is an eye opener." Whom should I love in the case of the disbursement of the millionaire's money? The millionaire or the starving people? It's not clear how love alone will settle anything. In fact, it is not obvious that we must always do what is most loving. Should we always treat our enemies in loving ways? Or is it morally acceptable to hate those who have purposefully and unjustly harmed us, our loved ones, and other innocent people? Should the survivors of Auschwitz love Adolf Hitler? We will deal with these questions later. Here we must be content to notice that love alone does not solve difficult moral issues.

A third principle often given to guide us in moral actions is the Golden Rule: "Do unto others as you would have them do unto you." We will look more closely at this principle in Chapter 5, but for the moment we should note that it has problems. First of all, it cannot be taken literally. Suppose John loves to hear loud rock music. John would love you to play it loud for him, so he reasons that he should play it loud for you—even though he knows that you hate it. So the rule must be modified: "Do unto others as you would have them do unto you if you were in their shoes." But this still has problems. If John were in the shoes of Sirhan Sirhan (the assassin of Robert Kennedy), he'd want to be released from the penitentiary, but it's not clear that Sirhan should be. If John puts himself in a sex-starved person's shoes, he'd want the next available person to have sex with him, but it's not obvious that he needs to comply with that want. Similarly, the Golden Rule doesn't tell us to whom we should give the millionaire's money.

Conscience, love, and the Golden Rule are all worthy tools to help us through life. They work for most of us most of the time in ordinary moral situations. But in more complicated cases, especially when there are legitimate conflicts of interest, their usefulness is limited.

A more promising strategy for solving dilemmas is that of following definite moral rules. Suppose you decide to give the millionaire's money to the Yankees in order to keep your promise or because to do otherwise would be stealing. The principle you followed would be "Always keep your promise" and/or "Thou shalt not steal" (the Eighth Commandment). Principles are important in life. All learning involves understanding a set of rules. As Oxford University philosopher R. M. Hare says,

> To learn to do anything is never to learn to do an individual act; it is always to learn to do acts of a certain kind in a certain kind of situation; and this is to learn a principle. . . . Without principles we could not learn anything whatever from our elders. . . . Every generation would have to start from scratch and teach itself. But . . . self-teaching, like all other teaching, is the teaching of principles.[1]

If you decide to act on the principle of promise-keeping or not stealing in the case of the millionaire's money, then you adhere to a type of moral theory called *deontology.*

If, on the other hand, you decide to give the money to the World Hunger Relief Organization in order to save an enormous number of lives and restore economic solvency to the region, you side with a type of theory called *teleology* or *teleological ethics.*

Traditionally, two major types of ethical systems have dominated the field. In one, the locus of value is the act or kind of act, and in the other, the locus of value is the outcome or consequences of the act. The former type of theory is called deontological (from the Greek *deon,* meaning "duty," and *logos* meaning "logic"), and the latter is called teleological (from the Greek *teleos,* meaning "having reached one's end" or "finished"). Whereas teleological systems see the ultimate criterion of morality in some nonmoral value that results from acts, deontological systems see certain features in the act itself as having intrinsic value. For example, a teleologist would judge whether lying was morally right

[1]R. M. Hare, *The Language of Morals* (Oxford University Press, 1952), p. 60.

or wrong by the consequences it produced, but a deontologist would see something intrinsically wrong in the very act of lying. In the next chapter we will consider the dominant version of teleological ethics, utilitarianism. In Chapter 5, we'll examine Immanuel Kant's ethics as the major form of deontological ethics. Then in Chapter 6, we shall examine a third theory, virtue ethics, that holds that what is important is moral character—virtue, not (primarily) rules. Virtue ethics rejects the emphasis on rules set forth in these first two theories. Finally, Chapter 7 brings us to two moral perspectives that are very different from the views offered by the major theories explained here: feminist ethics and the ethics of care.

CHAPTER 4

Utilitarianism

The leading consequentialist theory is utilitarianism, the view that right actions are those that result in the most beneficial balance of good over bad consequences for everyone involved. This theory says we should maximize the nonmoral good (the *utility*) of everyone who is affected, regardless of the contrary urgings of moral rules or unbending moral principles. Various forms of utilitarianism differ in how they define utility, with some equating it with happiness or pleasure (the hedonistic view) and others equating it with satisfaction of preferences or desires or some other intrinsically valuable things or states, such as knowledge or perfection.

In applying the utilitarian moral standard (the greatest good, everyone considered), some moral philosophers concentrate on specific acts and some on rules covering kinds of acts. The former approach is called *act-utilitarianism*, the idea that the rightness of actions depends solely on the relative good produced by *individual actions.* An act is right if, in a particular situation, it produces a greater balance of good over bad than any alternative acts; determining rightness is a matter of weighing the effects of each possible act. The latter approach, known as *rule-utilitarianism*, avoids judging rightness by specific acts and focuses instead on *rules governing categories of acts.* It says a right action is one that conforms to a rule that, if followed consistently, would create for everyone involved the most beneficial balance of good over bad. We are to adhere to the rules because they maximize the good for everyone considered—even though a given act may produce bad effects in a particular situation.

The classic, or traditional, version of utilitarianism was devised by English philosopher Jeremy Bentham (1748–1832) and given more detail and plausibility by another English philosopher, John Stuart Mill (1806–1873). Classic utilitarianism is hedonistic in that the utility to be maximized is pleasure, broadly termed happiness, the only intrinsic good. A right action produces more net happiness (amounts of happiness minus unhappiness) than any alternative action, everyone considered.

Bentham and Mill, however, had different ideas about what happiness entailed, as do many philosophers today. Bentham thought that happiness is one-dimensional: it is pleasure, pure and simple, something that varies only in the amount that an agent can experience. In this scheme, it seems that the moral ideal would be to experience maximum amounts of pleasure, as does the glutton or the debauchee. But Mill thought that pleasures can vary in quality as well as quantity. For him, there are lower and higher pleasures—the lower and inferior ones indulged in by the glutton and his ilk and the higher and more satisfying ones found in such experiences as the search for knowledge and the appreciation of art and music. Mill famously summed up this contrast by saying, "It is better to be a human being dissatisfied than a pig satisfied; better to be Socrates dissatisfied than a fool satisfied."

Like all forms of utilitarianism, the classic formulation demands a strong sense of impartiality. When promoting happiness, we must not only take into account the happiness of everyone affected, but also give everyone's needs or interests equal weight.

In classic utilitarianism, the emphasis is on maximizing the total quantity of net happiness, not ensuring that it is rationed in any particular amounts among the people who are involved. This means that an action resulting in one thousand units of happiness for ten people is better than an action yielding only nine hundred units of happiness for the same ten people—regardless of how the units of happiness are distributed among them. Classic utilitarians want to allocate the total amount of happiness among as many people as possible (thus their motto, "the greatest happiness for the greatest number"). But maximizing total happiness is the fundamental concern whether everyone gets an equal portion or one person gets the lion's share.

A common criticism of utilitarianism is that it fails to take human rights seriously. Bentham thought all rights were legal rather than moral. He said that human rights were nonsense and inalienable rights "nonsense on stilts." What is important is responsibility, not rights. We are to take responsibility both for what we do and for what we allow to happen. A discussion of utilitarianism and justice will occur in some of our selections.

We turn first to a famous incident that occurred on the open seas in which Seaman Holmes was confronted with a dilemma of having his longboat sink or throwing passengers overboard. After this, we consider Bentham's classical exposition of utilitarianism, Mill's further development of the doctrine, and then Kai Nielsen's modern defense. Then we examine Bernard Williams's critique of utilitarianism and Ursula Le Guin's short story about a town whose utilitarian happiness was predicated on the suffering of a child.

Seaman Holmes and the Longboat of William Brown, *Reported by John William Wallace*

The American ship *William Brown* left Liverpool on March 13, 1841, bound for Philadelphia. She had on board (besides a heavy cargo) a crew of seventeen and sixty-five passengers. About ten o'clock on the night of April 19, when distant 250 miles southwest of Cape Race, Newfoundland, the vessel struck an iceberg and began to sink rapidly. The long-boat and the jolly-boat were cleared away and lowered. The captain, the second mate, seven of the crew, and one passenger got into the jolly-boat. The first-mate, eight seamen (including Holmes), and thirty-two passengers (forty-one in all) got into the long-boat. This was about twice as many passengers as the boat was made to hold. The remaining thirty-one passengers were forced to stay with the sinking ship and soon perished. On the following morning (Tuesday), the captain, being about to part company with the long-boat, gave its crew several directions and, among other counsel, advised them to obey all the orders of the first-mate, as they would obey his, the captain's. The crew promised that they would do so.

The long-boat was believed to be in generally good condition, but it turned out that she had a leak. The passengers had buckets and bailed so that the vessel remained afloat. However, the captain and mate reported that "a very little irregularity in the stowage would have capsized the long-boat" and "if she had struck any piece of ice she would inevitably have gone down. There was great peril of ice for any boat."

Having survived for 24 hours, on Tuesday night heavy rain fell, and the boat began to sink lower into the sea. The first-mate concluded that the men must be thrown overboard to save the boat. He ordered the crew to throw the male passengers overboard. They hesitated. The first-mate repeated the order. "Men, you must go to work, or we shall all perish." They then went to work; and threw out 14 male passengers. Two sisters of one of the men voluntarily dove into the sea. Two married men and a boy were spared, as well as the women. The long-boat stayed afloat. The next morning Holmes discovered a ship in the distance and drew its attention to the long-boat, so that everyone on board was saved.

United States v. Holmes (case no. 15,383), Circuit Court E. d. Pennsylvania, April 22, 1842. Reported by John William Wallace.

After the ship reached Philadelphia, the first-mate and most of the seamen, aware of the impending trial, disappeared. Holmes alone was present to be tried for manslaughter. The judge instructed the jury that the law of the sea required that passengers must always be saved in preference to seamen except those indispensable for operating the boat. If, after sacrificing the lives of the expendable sailors, passengers still must be sacrificed, lots must be drawn, assuming there is time to do so.

The survivors testified that Holmes acquitted himself heroically and compassionately during this ordeal. As the boat was about to pull away from the wreck, Holmes, hearing the desperate cry of a mother for her little daughter, who had been left behind, dashed back at the risk of his life, found the girl, and carried her in his arms to the long-boat.

The jury found Holmes guilty of manslaughter but recommended mercy. He was sentenced to six months' imprisonment at hard labor, in addition to the nine months he had already served in prison while waiting for the trial.

For Further Reflection

1. Discuss the various aspects of this case. What are the salient features? What should the first mate have done? What should Holmes have done? What would you have done in Holmes's place? Do you agree with the law that passengers' lives should be preferred to seamen's? Why or why not?

Classical Utilitarianism

JEREMY BENTHAM

Jeremy Bentham (1748–1832) was a British utilitarian and legal reformer. In this essay from *An Introduction to the Principles of Morals and Legislation*, he argues that pleasure is the only intrinsic value and pain the only intrinsic evil. All other goods and evils are derived from these two qualities. Moral rightness and wrongness are defined in his hedonistic utilitarian approach according to their consequences in producing pleasure and pain.

Excerpted from *An Introduction to the Principles of Morals and Legislation* (1789).

OF THE PRINCIPLE OF UTILITY

I. Nature has placed mankind under the governance of two sovereign masters, *pain* and *pleasure*. It is for them alone to point out what we ought to do, as well as to determine what we shall do. On the one hand the standard of right and wrong, on the other the chain of causes and effects, are fastened to their throne. They govern us in all we do, in all we say, in all we think: every effort we can make to throw off our subjection, will serve but to demonstrate and confirm it. In words a man may pretend to abjure their empire: but in reality he will remain subject to it all the while. The *principle of utility* recognizes this subjection, and assumes it for the foundation of that system, the object of which is to rear the fabric of felicity by the hands of reason and of law. Systems which attempt to question it, deal in sounds instead of sense, in caprice instead of reason, in darkness instead of light.

But enough of metaphor and declamation: it is not by such means that moral science is to be improved.

II. The principle of utility is the foundation of the present work: it will be proper therefore at the outset to give an explicit and determinate account of what is meant by it. By the principle of utility is meant that principle which approves or disapproves of every action whatsoever, according to the tendency which it appears to have to augment or diminish the happiness of the party whose interest is in question: or, what is the same thing in other words, to promote or to oppose that happiness. I say of every action whatsoever; and therefore not only of every action of a private individual, but of every measure of government.

III. By utility is meant that property in any object, whereby it tends to produce benefit, advantage, pleasure, good, or happiness, (all this in the present case comes to the same thing) or (what comes again to the same thing) to prevent the happening of mischief, pain, evil, or unhappiness to the party whose interest is considered: if that party be the community in general, then the happiness of the community: if a particular individual, then the happiness of that individual.

VALUE OF A LOT OF PLEASURE OR PAIN, HOW TO BE MEASURED

I. Pleasures then, and the avoidance of pains, are the ends which the legislator has in view: it behoves him therefore to understand their *value*. Pleasures and pains are the *instruments* he has to work with; it behoves him therefore to understand their force, which is again, in other words, their value.

II. To a person considered *by himself,* the value of a pleasure or pain considered *by itself,* will be greater or less, according to the four following circumstances:

1. Its *intensity.*
2. Its *duration.*
3. Its *certainty* or *uncertainty.*
4. Its *propinquity* or *remoteness.*

III. These are the circumstances which are to be considered in estimating a pleasure or a pain considered each of them by itself. But when the value of any pleasure or pain is considered for the purpose of estimating the tendency of any *act* by which it is produced, there are two other circumstances to be taken into the account; these are,

5. Its *fecundity,* or the chance it has of being followed by sensations of the *same* kind: that is, pleasures, if it be a pleasure: pains, if it be a pain.
6. Its *purity,* or the chance it has of *not* being followed by sensations of the *opposite* kind: that is, pains, if it be a pleasure: pleasures, if it be a pain.

These two last, however, are in strictness scarcely to be deemed properties of the pleasure or the pain itself; they are not, therefore, in strictness to be taken into the account of the value of that pleasure or that pain. They are in strictness to be deemed properties only of the act, or other event, by which such pleasure or pain has been produced; and accordingly are only to be taken into the account of the tendency of such act or such event.

IV. To a *number* of persons, with reference of each of whom the value of a pleasure or a pain is considered, it will be greater or less, according to seven circumstances: to wit, the six preceding ones; *viz.*

1. Its *intensity.*
2. Its *duration.*
3. Its *certainty* or *uncertainty.*
4. Its *propinquity* or *remoteness.*
5. Its *fecundity.*
6. Its *purity.*

And one other; to wit:

7. Its *extent;* that is, the number of persons to whom it *extends;* or (in other words) who are affected by it.

V. To take an exact account then of the general tendency of any act, by which the interests of a community are affected, proceed as follows. Begin with any one person of those whose interests seem most immediately to be affected by it: and take an account,

1. Of the value of each distinguishable pleasure which appears to be produced by it in the first instance.

2. Of the value of each *pain* which appears to be produced by it in the *first* instance.

3. Of the value of each pleasure which appears to be produced by it *after* the first. This constitutes the *fecundity* of the first *pleasure* and the *impurity* of the first *pain.*

4. Of the value of each *pain* which appears to be produced by it after the first. This constitutes the *fecundity* of the first *pain,* and the *impurity* of the first pleasure.

5. Sum up all the values of all the *pleasures* on the one side, and those of all the pains on the other. The balance, if it be on the side of pleasure, will give the *good* tendency of the act upon the whole, with respect to the interests of that *individual* person; if on the side of pain, the *bad* tendency of it upon the whole.

6. Take an account of the *number* of persons whose interests appear to be concerned; and repeat the above process with respect to each. *Sum up* the numbers expressive of the degrees of *good* tendency, which the act has, with respect to each individual, in regard to whom the tendency of it is *good* upon the whole: do this again with respect to each individual, in regard to whom the tendency of it is *bad* upon the whole. Take the *balance*; which, if on the side of *pleasure,* will give the general *good tendency* of the act, with respect to the total number or community of individuals concerned; if on the side of pain, the general *evil tendency,* with respect to the same community.

VI. It is not to be expected that this process should be strictly pursued previously to every moral judgment, or to every legislative or judicial operation. It may, however, be always kept in view: and as near as the process actually pursued on these occasions approaches to it, so near will such process approach to the character of an exact one.

VII. The same process is alike applicable to pleasure and pain, in whatever shape they appear: and by whatever denomination they are distinguished: to pleasure, whether it be called *good* (which is properly the cause or instrument of pleasure) or *profit* (which is distant pleasure, or the cause or instrument of distant pleasure), or *convenience,* or *advantage, benefit, emolument, happiness,* and so forth: to pain, whether it be called *evil* (which corresponds to *good*) or *mischief*, or *inconvenience*, or *disadvantage*, or *loss*, or *unhappiness*, and so forth.

VIII. Nor is this a novel and unwarranted, any more than it is a useless, theory. In all this there is nothing but what the practice of mankind, wheresoever they have a clear view of their own interest, is perfectly conformable to. An article of property, an estate in land, for instance, is valuable, on what account? On account of the pleasures of all kinds which it enables a man to produce, and what comes to the same thing the pains of all kinds which it enables him to avert. But the value of such an article of property is universally understood to rise or fall according to the length or shortness of the time which a man had in it: the certainty or uncertainty of its coming into possession: and the nearness or remoteness of the time at which, if at all, it is to come into possession. As to the *intensity* of the pleasures which a man may derive from it, this is never thought of, because it depends upon the use which each particular person may come to make of it; which cannot be estimated till the particular pleasures he may come to derive from it, or the particular pains he may come to exclude by means of it, are brought to view. For the same reason, neither does he think of the *fecundity* or *purity* of those pleasures.

Thus much for pleasure and pain, happiness and unhappiness, in *general*. . . .

XVII. Under the Gentoo and Mahometan religions, the interests of the rest of the animal creation seem to have met with some attention. Why have they not, universally, with as much as those of human creatures, allowance made for the difference in point of sensibility? Because the laws that are have been the work of mutual fear; a sentiment which the less rational animals have not had the same means as man has of turning to account. Why *ought* they not? No reason can be given. If the being eaten were all, there is very good reason why we should be suffered to eat such of them as we like to eat: we are the better for it, and they are never the worse. They have none of those long-protracted anticipations of future misery which we have. The death they suffer in our hands commonly is, and always may be, a speedier, and by that means a less painful one, than that which would await them in the inevitable course of nature. If the being killed were all, there is very good reason why we should be suffered to kill such as molest us: we should be the worse for their living, and they are never the worse for being dead. But is there any reason why we should be suffered to torment them? Not any that I can see. Are there any why we should *not* be suffered to torment them? Yes, several. The day has been, I grieve to say in many places it is not yet past, in which the greater part of the species, under the denomination of slaves, have been treated by the law exactly upon the same footing, as, in England for example, the inferior races of animals are still. The day may come, when the rest of the animal creation may acquire those rights which never could have been withholden from them but by the hand of tyranny. The French have already discovered that the blackness of the skin is no reason why a human being should be abandoned without redress to the caprice of a tormentor. It may come one day to be recognized, that the number of the legs, the villosity of the skin, or the termination of the *os sacrum,* are reasons equally insufficient for abandoning a sensitive being to the same fate. What else is it that should trace the insuperable line? Is it the faculty of reason, or, perhaps, the faculty of discourse? But a full-grown horse or dog is beyond comparison a more rational, as well as a more conversable animal, than an infant of a day, or a week, or even a month, old. But suppose the case were otherwise, what would it avail? The question is not, Can they *reason*? nor, Can they *talk?* but, Can they *suffer*?

For Further Reflection

1. Analyze Bentham's utilitarianism. Do you agree with Bentham that "pain and pleasure" are our "two sovereign masters"? What does he mean by *pain* and *pleasure*? Note that *pleasure* is an ambiguous word. It can mean "sensuous titillation" or "satisfaction." Which does Bentham mean? Which concept does he need for his theory?
2. In his own time Bentham was criticized for setting forth a "pig philosophy," since his "simplistic" notions of motivation by pain and pleasure are more suited to pigs than to humans. Do you agree with this judgment?
3. Bentham's utilitarianism requires that we perform a hedonic calculus, summing up all the prospective pleasures that are likely to result from an act and subtracting the pains. Go over his process and note the difficulties of doing this.
4. Reread the last paragraph regarding the criterion of suffering as the basis for moral consideration. What are the implications of this principle for ethics? For our relations with animals?

Utilitarianism Refined

JOHN STUART MILL

English philosopher John Stuart Mill (1806–1873) has earned a prestigious place in the pantheon of respected philosophers for his work in epistemology (the study of knowledge), deductive and inductive logic, political thought, and ethics. The centerpiece of the latter is, of course, his *Utilitarianism* (1861), in which he articulates a more sophisticated version of Jeremy Bentham's views. In this excerpt from the book, Mill tries to improve on Bentham's one-dimensional concept of happiness.

. . . The creed which accepts as the foundation of morals, Utility, or the Greatest Happiness Principle, holds that actions are right in proportion as they tend to promote happiness, wrong as they tend to produce the reverse of happiness. By happiness is intended pleasure, and the absence of pain; by unhappiness, pain, and the privation of pleasure. To give a clear view of the moral standard set up by the theory, much more requires to be said; in particular, what things it includes in the ideas of pain and pleasure; and to what extent this is left an open question. But these supplementary explanations do not affect the theory of life on which this theory of morality is grounded—namely, that pleasure, and freedom from pain, are the only things desirable as ends; and that all desirable things (which are as numerous in the utilitarian as in any other scheme) are desirable either for the pleasure inherent in themselves, or as means to the promotion of pleasure and the prevention of pain.

Now, such a theory of life excites in many minds, and among them in some of the most estimable in feeling and purpose, inveterate dislike. To suppose that life has (as they express it) no higher end than pleasure—no better and nobler object of desire and pursuit—they designate as utterly mean and grovelling; as a doctrine worthy only of swine, to whom the followers of Epicurus were, at a very early period, contemptuously likened; and modern holders of the doctrine are occasionally made the subject of equally polite comparisons by its German, French, and English assailants.

When thus attacked, the Epicureans have always answered, that it is not they, but their accusers, who represent human nature in a degrading light; since the accusation supposes human beings to be capable of no pleasures except those of which swine are capable. If this supposition were true, the charge could not be gainsaid, but would then be no longer an imputation; for

From *Utilitarianism,* 7th ed. (London: Longmans, Green, and Co., 1879).

if the sources of pleasure were precisely the same to human beings and to swine, the rule of life which is good enough for the one would be good enough for the other. The comparison of the Epicurean life to that of beasts is felt as degrading, precisely because a beast's pleasures do not satisfy a human being's conceptions of happiness. Human beings have faculties more elevated than the animal appetites, and when once made conscious of them, do not regard anything as happiness which does not include their gratification. I do not, indeed, consider the Epicureans to have been by any means faultless in drawing out their scheme of consequences from the utilitarian principle. To do this in any sufficient manner, many Stoic, as well as Christian elements require to be included. But there is no known Epicurean theory of life which does not assign to the pleasures of the intellect; of the feelings and imagination, and of the moral sentiments, a much higher value as pleasures than to those of mere sensation. It must be admitted, however, that utilitarian writers in general have placed the superiority of mental over bodily pleasures chiefly in the greater permanency, safety, uncostliness, &c., of the former—that is, in their circumstantial advantages rather than in their intrinsic nature. And on all these points utilitarians have fully proved their case; but they might have taken the other, and, as it may be called, higher ground, with entire consistency. It is quite compatible with the principle of utility to recognise the fact, that some *kinds* of pleasure are more desirable and more valuable than others. It would be absurd that while, in estimating all other things, quality is considered as well as quantity, the estimation of pleasures should be supposed to depend on quantity alone.

If I am asked, what I mean by difference of quality in pleasures, or what makes one pleasure more valuable than another, merely as a pleasure, except its being greater in amount, there is but one possible answer. Of two pleasures, if there be one to which all or almost all who have experience of both give a decided preference, irrespective of any feeling of moral obligation to prefer it, that is the more desirable pleasure. If one of the two is, by those who are competently acquainted with both, placed so far above the other that they prefer it, even though knowing it to be attended with a greater amount of discontent, and would not resign it for any quantity of the other pleasure which their nature is capable of, we are justified in ascribing to the preferred enjoyment a superiority in quality, so far outweighing quantity as to render it, in comparison, of small account.

Now it is an unquestionable fact that those who are equally acquainted with, and equally capable of appreciating and enjoying, both, do give a most marked preference to the manner of existence which employs their higher faculties. Few human creatures would consent to be changed into any of the lower animals, for a promise of the fullest allowance of a beast's pleasures; no intelligent human being would consent to be a fool, no instructed person would be an ignoramus, no person of feeling and conscience would be selfish and base, even though they should be persuaded that the fool, the dunce, or the rascal is better satisfied with his lot than they are with theirs. They would not resign what they possess more than he, for the most complete satisfaction of all the desires which they have in common with him. If they ever fancy they would, it is only in cases of unhappiness so extreme, that to escape from it they would exchange their lot for almost any other, however undesirable in their own eyes. A being of higher faculties requires more to make him happy, is capable probably of more acute suffering, and is certainly accessible to it at more points, than one of an inferior type; but in spite of these liabilities, he can never really wish to sink into what he feels to be a lower grade of existence. We may give what explanation we please of this unwillingness; we may attribute it to pride, a name which is given indiscriminately to some of the most and to some of the least estimable feelings of which mankind are capable; we may refer it to the love of liberty and personal independence, an appeal to which was with the Stoics one of the most effective means for the inculcation of it; to the love of power, or to the love of excitement, both of which do really enter into and contribute to it: but its most appropriate appellation is a sense of dignity, which all human beings possess in one form or other, and in some, though by no means in exact, proportion to their higher faculties, and which is so essential a part of the happiness of those in whom it is strong, that nothing which conflicts with it could be, otherwise than momentarily, an object of desire to them. Whoever supposes that this preference takes place at a sacrifice of happiness—that the superior being, in anything like equal circumstances, is not happier than the inferior—confounds the two very different ideas, of happiness, and content. It is indisputable that the being whose capacities of enjoyment are low, has the greatest chance of having them fully satisfied; and a highly-endowed being will always feel that any happiness which he can look for, as the world is constituted, is imperfect. But he can learn to bear its imperfections, if they are at all bearable; and they will not make him envy the being who is indeed unconscious of the imperfections, but only because he feels not at all the good which those imperfections qualify. It is better to be a human being dissatisfied than a pig satisfied; better to be Socrates dissatisfied than a fool satisfied. And if the fool, or the pig, is of a different opinion, it is because they only know their own side of the question. The other party to the comparison knows both sides.

It may be objected, that many who are capable of the higher pleasures, occasionally, under the influence of temptation, postpone them to the lower. But this is quite compatible with a full appreciation of the intrinsic superiority of the higher. Men often, from infirmity of character, make their election for the nearer good, though they know it to be the less valuable; and this no less when the choice is between two bodily pleasures, than when it is between bodily and mental. They pursue sensual indulgences to the injury of health, though perfectly aware that health is the greater good. It may be further objected, that many who begin with youthful enthusiasm for everything noble, as they advance in years sink into indolence and selfishness. But I do not believe that those who undergo this very common change, voluntarily choose the lower description of pleasures in preference to the higher. I believe that before they devote themselves exclusively to the one, they have already become incapable of the other. Capacity for the nobler feelings is in most natures a very tender plant, easily killed, not only by hostile influences, but by mere want of sustenance; and in the majority of young persons it speedily dies away if the occupations to which their position in life has devoted them, and the society into which it has thrown them, are not favourable to keeping that higher capacity in exercise. Men lose their high aspirations as they lose their intellectual tastes, because they have not time or opportunity for indulging them; and they addict themselves to inferior pleasures, not because they deliberately prefer them, but because they are either the only ones to which they have access, or the only ones which they are any longer capable of enjoying. It may be questioned whether any one who has remained equally susceptible to both classes of pleasures, ever knowingly and calmly preferred the lower; though many, in all ages, have broken down in an ineffectual attempt to combine both.

From this verdict of the only competent judges, I apprehend there can be no appeal. On a question which is the best worth having of two pleasures, or which of two modes of existence is the most grateful to the feelings, apart from its moral attributes and from its consequences, the judgment of those who are qualified by knowledge of both, or, if they differ, that of the majority among them, must be admitted as final. And there needs be the less hesitation to accept this judgment respecting the quality of pleasures, since there is no other tribunal to be referred to even on the question of quantity. What means are there of determining which is the acutest of two pains, or the intensest of two pleasurable sensations, except the general suffrage of those who are familiar with both? Neither pains nor pleasures are homogeneous, and pain is always heterogeneous with pleasure. What is there to decide whether a particular pleasure is worth purchasing at the cost of a particular pain, except the feelings and judgment of the experienced? When, therefore, those feelings and judgment declare the pleasures derived from the higher faculties to be preferable *in kind,* apart from the question of intensity, to those of which the animal nature, disjoined from the higher faculties, is susceptible, they are entitled on this subject to the same regard. . . .

For Further Reflection

1. According to Mill, in what ways can the experience of happiness vary? Do you agree?
2. What does Mill mean by "It is better to be a human being dissatisfied than a pig satisfied; better to be Socrates dissatisfied than a fool satisfied"?
3. In Mill's view, who is to be the judge of the desirability of different forms of pleasure?
4. Do you believe that the quantity of happiness is more important than its quality? Why or why not?

A Defense of Utilitarianism

KAI NIELSEN

Kai Nielsen, until his retirement, was a professor of philosophy at Calgary University. He has written important works in the philosophy of religion and political theory, as well as in ethics. This essay is a clear example of act-utilitarianism, the doctrine that we ought to evaluate each act on its own merits, those merits consisting in whether the act maximizes utility. Nielsen sets forth his theory as a credible alternative to moral conservativism or deontological ethics, which maintain that there are "moral principles, prescribing determinate actions, with which it would always be wrong not to act in accordance no matter what the consequences." He argues, to the contrary, that it is the consequences that determine the moral worth of an action.

Nielsen's arguments in favor of utilitarianism partly depend on the notion of negative responsibility. That is, we are responsible not only for the consequences of our actions but also for the consequences of our *nonactions.*

I

It is sometimes claimed that any consequentialist view of ethics has monstrous implications which make such a conception of morality untenable.

From *Ethics* 82 (1972), "Against Moral Conserativism" by Kai Nielsen. The University of Chicago Press. pp. 219–231.

What we must do—so the claim goes—is reject all forms of consequentialism and accept what has been labeled "conservatism" or "moral absolutism." By "conservatism" is meant, here, a normative ethical theory which maintains that there is a privileged moral principle or cluster of moral principles, prescribing determinate actions, with which it would always be wrong not to act in accordance no matter what the consequences. A key example of such a principle is the claim that it is always wrong to kill an innocent human, whatever the consequences of not doing so.

I will argue that such moral conservatism is itself unjustified and, indeed, has morally unacceptable consequences, while consequentialism does not have implications which are morally monstrous and does not contain evident moral mistakes.

A consequentialist maintains that actions, rules, policies, practices, and moral principles are ultimately to be judged by certain consequences: to wit (for a very influential kind of consequentialism), by whether doing them more than, or at least as much as doing anything else, or acting in accordance with them more than or at least as much as acting in accordance with alternative policies, practices, rules or principles, tends, on the whole, and for *everyone* involved, to maximize satisfaction and minimize dissatisfaction. The states of affairs to be sought are those which maximize these things to the greatest extent possible for all mankind. But while this all sounds very humane and humanitarian, when its implications are thought through, it has been forcefully argued, it will be seen actually to have inhumane and morally intolerable implications. Circumstances could arise in which one holding such a view would have to assert that one was justified in punishing, killing, torturing, or deliberately harming the innocent, and such a consequence is, morally speaking, unacceptable.[1] As Anscombe has put it, anyone who "really thinks, *in advance*, that it is open to question whether such an action as procuring the judicial execution of the innocent should be quite excluded from consideration—I do not want to argue with him; he shows a corrupt mind."[2]

At the risk of being thought to exhibit a corrupt mind and a shallow consequentialist morality, I should like to argue that things are not as simple and straightforward as Anscombe seems to believe.

Surely, every moral man must be appalled at the judicial execution of the innocent or at the punishment, torture, and killing of the innocent. Indeed, being appalled by such behavior partially defines what it is to be a moral

[1]Alan Donagan, "Is There a Credible Form of Utilitarianism?," and H. J. McCloskey, "A Non-Utilitarian Approach to Punishment," both in Michael D. Bayles, ed., *Contemporary Utilitarianism* (Garden City, N.Y.: Doubleday, 1968).
[2]Elizabeth Anscombe, "Modern Moral Philosophy," *Philosophy 23* (January 1957): 16–17.

agent. And a consequentialist has very good utilitarian grounds for being so appalled, namely, that it is always wrong to inflict pain for its own sake. But this does not get to the core considerations which divide a conservative position such as Anscombe's from a consequentialist view. There are a series of tough cases that need to be taken to heart and their implications thought through by any reflective person, be he a conservative or a consequentialist. By doing this, we can get to the heart of the issue between conservatism and consequentialism. Consider this clash between conservatism and consequentialism arising over the problem of a "just war."

> If we deliberately bomb civilian targets, we do not pretend that civilians are combatants in any simple fashion, but argue that this bombing will terminate hostilities more quickly, and will minimize all around suffering. It is hard to see how any brand of utilitarian will escape Miss Anscombe's objections. We are certainly killing the innocent. . . . We are not killing them for the sake of killing them, but to save the lives of other innocent persons. Utilitarians, I think, grit their teeth and put up with this as part of the logic of total war; Miss Anscombe and anyone who thinks like her surely has to either redescribe the situation to ascribe guilt to the civilians or else she has to refuse to accept this sort of military tactics as simply wrong.[3]

It is indeed true that we cannot but feel the force of Anscombe's objections here. But is it the case that anyone shows a corrupt mind if he defends such bombing when, horrible as it is, it will quite definitely lessen appreciably the total amount of suffering and death in the long run, and if he is sufficiently nonevasive not to rationalize such a bombing of civilians into a situation in which all the putatively innocent people—children and all—are somehow in some measure judged guilty? Must such a man exhibit a corrupt moral sense if he refuses to hold that such military tactics are never morally justified? Must this be the monstrous view of a fanatical man devoid of any proper moral awareness? It is difficult for me to believe that this must be so.

Consider the quite parallel actions of guerrilla fighters and terrorists in wars of national liberation. In certain almost unavoidable circumstances, they must deliberately kill the innocent. We need to see some cases in detail here to get the necessary contextual background, and for this reason the motion picture *The Battle of Algiers* can be taken as a convenient point of reference. There we saw Algerian women—gentle, kindly women with children of their own and plainly people of moral sensitivity—with evident

[3]Alan Ryan, "Review of Jan Narveson's *Morality and Utility,*" *Philosophical Books* 9, no. 3 (October 1958): 14.

heaviness of heart, plant bombs which they had every good reason to believe would kill innocent people, including children; and we also saw a French general, also a human being of moral fiber and integrity, order the torture of Arab terrorists and threaten the bombing of houses in which terrorists were concealed but which also contained innocent people, including children. There are indeed many people involved in such activities who are cruel, sadistic beasts, or simply morally indifferent or, in important ways, morally uncomprehending. But the characters I have referred to from *The Battle of Algiers* were not of that stamp. They were plainly moral agents of a high degree of sensitivity, and yet they deliberately killed or were prepared to kill the innocent. And, with inessential variations, this is a recurrent phenomenon of human living in extreme situations. Such cases are by no means desert-island or esoteric cases.

It is indeed arguable whether such actions are always morally wrong—whether anyone should ever act as the Arab women or French general acted. But what could not be reasonably maintained, *pace* Anscombe, by any stretch of the imagination, is that the characters I described from *The Battle of Algiers* exhibited corrupt minds. Possibly morally mistaken, yes; guilty of moral corruption, no.

Dropping the charge of moral corruption but sticking with the moral issue about what actions are right, is it not the case that my consequentialist position logically forces me to conclude that under some circumstances—where the good to be achieved is great enough—I must not only countenance but actually advocate such violence toward the innocent? But is it not always, no matter what the circumstances or consequences, wrong to countenance, advocate, or engage in such violence? To answer such a question affirmatively is to commit oneself to the kind of moral absolutism or conservatism which Anscombe advocates. But, given the alternatives, should not one be such a conservative or at least hold that certain deontological principles must never be overridden?

I will take, so to speak, the papal bull by the horns and answer that there are circumstances when such violence must be reluctantly assented to or even taken to be something that one, morally speaking, must do. But, *pace* Anscombe, this very much needs arguing, and I shall argue it; but first I would like to set out some further but simpler cases which have a similar bearing. They are, by contrast, artificial cases. I use them because, in their greater simplicity, by contrast with my above examples, there are fewer variables to control and I can more conveniently make the essential conceptual and moral points. But, if my argument is correct for these simpler cases, the line of reasoning employed is intended to be applicable to those more complex cases as well.

II

Consider the following cases embedded in their exemplary tales:

1. *The Case of the Innocent Fat Man*

Consider the story (well known to philosophers) of the fat man stuck in the mouth of a cave on a coast. He was leading a group of people out of the cave when he got stuck in the mouth of the cave and in a very short time high tide will be upon them, and unless he is promptly unstuck, they all will be drowned except the fat man, whose head is out of the cave. But, fortunately or unfortunately, someone has with him a stick of dynamite. The short of the matter is, either they use the dynamite and blast the poor innocent fat man out of the mouth of the cave or everyone else drowns. Either one life or many lives. Our conservative presumably would take the attitude that it is all in God's hands and say that he ought never to blast the fat man out, for it is always wrong to kill the innocent. Must or should a moral man come to that conclusion? I shall argue that he should not.

My first exemplary tale was designed to show that our normal, immediate, rather absolutistic, moral reactions need to be questioned along with such principles as "The direct intention of the death of an innocent person is never justifiable." I have hinted (and later shall argue) that we should *beware* of our moral outrage here—our naturally conservative and unreflective moral reactions—for here the consequentialist has a strong case for what I shall call "moral radicalism." But, before turning to a defense of that, I want to tell another story taken from Philippa Foot but used for my own purposes.[4] This tale, I shall argue, has a different import than our previous tale. Here our unrehearsed, commonsense moral reactions will stand up under moral scrutiny. But, I shall also argue when I consider them in Section III, that our commonsense moral reactions here, initial expectations to the contrary notwithstanding, can be shown to be justified on consequentialist grounds. The thrust of my argument for this case is that we are not justified in opting for a theistic and/or deontological absolutism or in rejecting consequentialism.

2. *The Magistrate and the Threatening Mob*

A magistrate or judge is faced with a very real threat from a large and uncontrollable mob of rioters demanding a culprit for a crime. Unless the criminal is produced, promptly tried, and executed, they will take their own bloody revenge on a much smaller and quite vulnerable section of the community

[4]Philippa Foot, "The Problem of Abortion and the Doctrine of the Double Effect," *Oxford Review*, no. 5 (1967): 5–15.

(a kind of frenzied pogrom). The judge knows that the real culprit is unknown and that the authorities do not even have a good clue as to who he may be. But he also knows that there is within easy reach a disreputable, thoroughly disliked, and useless man, who, though innocent, could easily be blamed so that the mob would be quite convinced that he was guilty and would be pacified if he were promptly executed. Recognizing that he can prevent the occurrence of extensive carnage only by framing some innocent person, the magistrate has him framed, goes through the mockery of a trial, and has him executed. Most of us regard such a framing and execution of such a man in such circumstances as totally unacceptable.[5] There are some who would say that it is categorically wrong—morally inexcusable—*whatever the circumstances.* Indeed, such a case remains a problem for the consequentialist, but here again, I shall argue, one can consistently remain a consequentialist and continue to accept commonsense moral convictions about such matters.

My storytelling is at an end. The job is to see what the stories imply. We must try to determine whether thinking through their implications should lead a clear-headed and morally sensitive man to abandon consequentialism and to adopt some form of theistic absolutism and/or deontological absolutism. I shall argue that it does not.

III

I shall consider the last case first because there are good reasons why the consequentialist should stick with commonsense moral convictions for such cases. I shall start by giving my rationale for that claim. If the magistrate were a tough-minded but morally conscientious consequentialist, he could still, on straightforward consequentialist grounds, refuse to frame and execute the innocent man, even knowing that this would unleash the mob and cause much suffering and many deaths. The rationale for his particular moral stand would be that, by so framing and then executing such an innocent man, he would, in the long run, cause still more suffering through the resultant corrupting effect on the institution of justice. That is, in a case involving such extensive general interest in the issue—without that, there would be no problem about preventing the carnage or call for such extreme measures—knowledge that the man was framed, that the law had prostituted itself, would, surely, eventually leak out. This would encourage mob action in other circumstances, would

[5]Later, I shall show that there are desert-island circumstances—i.e., highly improbable situations—in which such judicial railroading might be a moral necessity. But I also show what little force desert-island cases have in the articulation and defense of a normative ethical theory.

lead to an increased skepticism about the incorruptibility or even the reliability of the judicial process, and would set a dangerous precedent for less clearheaded or less scrupulously humane magistrates. Given such a potential for the corruption of justice, a utilitarian or consequentialist judge or magistrate could, on good utilitarian or consequentialist grounds, argue that it was morally wrong to frame an innocent man. If the mob must rampage if such a sacrificial lamb is not provided, then the mob must rampage.

Must a utilitarian or consequentialist come to such a conclusion? The answer is no. It is the conclusion which is, as things stand, the most reasonable conclusion, but that he *must* come to it is far too strong a claim. A consequentialist could *consistently*—I did not say successfully—argue that, in taking the above tough-minded utilitarian position, we have overestimated the corrupting effects of such judicial railroading. His circumstance was an extreme one: a situation not often to be repeated even if, instead of acting as he did, he had set a precedent by such an act of judicial murder. A utilitarian rather more skeptical than most utilitarians about the claims of commonsense morality might reason that the lesser evil here is the judicial murder of an innocent man, vile as it is. He would persist in his moral iconoclasm by standing on the consequentialist rock that the lesser evil is always to be preferred to the greater evil.

The short of it is that utilitarians could disagree, as other consequentialists could disagree, about what is morally required of us in that case. The disagreement here between utilitarians or consequentialists of the same type is not one concerning fundamental moral principles but a disagreement about the empirical facts, about what course of action would in the long run produce the least suffering and the most happiness for *everyone* involved.[6]

However, considering the effect advocating the deliberate judicial killing of an innocent man would have on the reliance people put on commonsense moral beliefs of such a ubiquitous sort as the belief that the innocent must not be harmed, a utilitarian who defended the centrality of commonsense moral beliefs would indeed have a strong utilitarian case here. But the most crucial thing to recognize is that, to regard such judicial bowing to such a threatening mob as unqualifiedly wrong, as morally intolerable, one need not reject utilitarianism and accept some form of theistic or deontological absolutism.

It has been argued, however, that, in taking such a stance, I still have not squarely faced the moral conservative's central objection to the judicial

[6]"Everyone" here is used distributively, i.e., I am talking about the interests of each and every one. In that sense, everyone's interests need to be considered.

railroading of the innocent. I allow, as a consequentialist, that there could be circumstances, at least as far as logical possibilities are concerned, in which such a railroading would be justified but that, as things actually go, it is not and probably never in fact will be justified. But the conservative's point is that in *no circumstances, either actual or conceivable, would it be justified.* No matter what the consequences, it is unqualifiedly unjustified. To say, as I do, that the situations in which it might be justified are desert-island, esoteric cases which do not occur in life, is not to the point, for, as Alan Donagan argues, "Moral theory is *a priori,* as clear-headed utilitarians like Henry Sidgwick recognized. It is, as Leibniz would say, 'true of all possible worlds.'"[7] Thus, to argue as I have and as others have that the counterexamples directed against the consequentialists appeal to conditions which are never in fact fulfilled or are unlikely to be fulfilled is beside the point.[8] Whether "a moral theory is true or false depends on whether its implications for all possible worlds are true. Hence, whether utilitarianism (or consequentialism) is true or false cannot depend on how the actual world is."[9] It is possible to specify logically conceivable situations in which consequentialism would have implications which are monstrous—for example, certain beneficial judicial murders of the innocent (whether they are even remotely likely to obtain is irrelevant)—hence consequentialism must be false.

We should not take such a short way with consequentialists, for what is true in Donagan's claim about moral theory's being a priori will not refute or even render implausible consequentialism, and what would undermine it in such a claim about the a priori nature of moral theory and presumably moral claims is not true.

To say that moral theory is a priori is probably correct if that means that categorical moral claims—fundamental moral statements—cannot be deduced from empirical statements or nonmoral theological statements, such that it is a contradiction to assert the empirical and/or nonmoral theological statements and deny the categorical moral claims or vice versa.[10] In that fundamental sense, it is reasonable and, I believe, justifiable to maintain that moral theory is autonomous and a priori. It is also a priori in the sense that moral statements are not themselves a kind of empirical statement. That is, if I assert "One ought never to torture any sentient creature" or "One ought never to kill an innocent

[7]Donagan, op. cit., p. 189.

[8]T. L. S. Sprigge argues in such a manner in his "A Utilitarian Reply to Dr. McCloskey" in Michael D. Bayles, ed., *Contemporary Utilitarianism* (Garden City, N.Y.: Doubleday, 1968).

[9]Donagan, op. cit., p. 194.

[10]There is considerable recent literature about whether it is possible to derive moral claims from nonmoral claims. See W. D. Hudson, ed., *The Is-Ought Question: A Collection of Papers on the Central Problem in Moral Philosophy* (New York: St. Martin's Press, 1969).

man," I am not trying to predict or describe what people do or are likely to do but am asserting what they are *to do*. It is also true that, if a moral statement is true, it holds for all possible worlds *in which situations are exactly the sort characterized in the statement*. If it is true for one, it is true for all. You cannot consistently say that *A* ought to do *B* in situation Y and deny that someone exactly like *A* in a situation exactly like Y ought to do *B*.

In these ways, moral claims and indeed moral theory are a priori. But it is also evident that none of these ways will touch the consequentialist or utilitarian arguments. After all, the consequentialist need not be, and typically has not been, an ethical naturalist—he need not think moral claims are derivable from factual claims or that moral claims are a subspecies of empirical statement and he could accept—indeed, he must accept—what is an important truism anyway, that you cannot consistently say that *A* ought to do *B* in situation Y and deny that someone exactly like *A* in a situation exactly like Y ought to do *B*. But he could and should deny that moral claims are a priori in the sense that rational men must or even will make them without regard for the context, the situation, in which they are made. We say people ought not to drive way over the speed limit, or speed on icy roads, or throw knives at each other. But, if human beings had a kind of metallic exoskeleton and would not be hurt, disfigured, or seriously inconvenienced by knives sticking in them or by automobile crashes, we would not—so evidently at least—have good grounds for saying such speeding or knife throwing is wrong. It would not be so obvious that it was unreasonable and immoral to do these things if these conditions obtained.

In the very way we choose to describe the situation when we make ethical remarks, it is important in making this choice that we know what the world is like and what human beings are like. Our understanding of the situation, our understanding of human nature and motivation cannot but affect our structuring of the moral case. The consequentialist is saying that, as the world goes, there are good grounds for holding that judicial killings are morally intolerable, though he would have to admit that if the world (including human beings) were very different, such killings could be something that ought to be done. But, in holding this, he is not committed to denying the universalizability of moral judgments, for, where he would reverse or qualify the moral judgment, the situation must be different. He is only committed to claiming that, where the situation is the same or relevantly similar and the persons are relevantly similar, they must, if they are to act morally, do the same thing. However, he is claiming both (1) that, as things stand, judicial killing of the innocent is always wrong and (2) that it is an irrational moral judgment to assert of reasonably determinate actions (e.g., killing an innocent man) that they are unjustifiable and morally unacceptable on all *possible* worlds, whatever the situation and whatever the consequences.

Donagan's claims about the a priori nature of moral theories do not show such a consequentialist claim to be mistaken or even give us the slightest reason for thinking that it is mistaken. What is brutal and vile, for example, throwing a knife at a human being just for the fun of it, would not be so, if human beings were invulnerable to harm from such a direction because they had a metallic exoskeleton. Similarly, what is, as things are, morally intolerable, for example, the judicial killing of the innocent, need not be morally intolerable in all conceivable circumstances.

Such considerations support the utilitarian or consequentialist skeptical of simply taking the claims of our commonsense morality as a rock-bottom ground of appeal for moral theorizing. Yet it may also well be the case—given our extensive cruelty any way—that, if we ever start sanctioning such behavior, an even greater callousness toward life than the very extensive callousness extant now will, as a matter of fact, develop. Given a normative ethical theory which sanctions, *under certain circumstances,* such judicial murders, there may occur an undermining of our moral disapproval of killing and our absolutely essential moral principle that all human beings, great and small, are deserving of respect. This is surely enough, together with the not unimportant weight of even our unrehearsed moral feelings, to give strong utilitarian weight *here* to the dictates of our commonsense morality. Yet, I think I have also said enough to show that someone who questions their "unquestionableness" in such a context does not thereby exhibit a "corrupt mind" and that it is an open question whether he must be conceptually confused or morally mistaken over this matter.

IV

So far, I have tried to show with reference to the case of the magistrate and the threatening mob how consequentialists can reasonably square their normative ethical theories with an important range of commonsense moral convictions. Now, I wish by reference to the case of the innocent fat man to establish that there is at least a serious question concerning whether such fundamental commonsense moral convictions should always function as "moral facts" or a kind of moral ground to test the adequacy of normative ethical theories or positions. I want to establish that careful attention to such cases shows that we are not justified in taking the principles embodied in our commonsense moral reasoning about such cases as normative for all moral decisions. That a normative ethical theory is incompatible with some of our "moral intuitions" (moral feelings or convictions) does not refute the normative ethical theory.

What I will try to do here is to establish that this case, no more than the case examined in Section III, gives us adequate grounds for abandoning consequentialism and for adopting moral conservativism.

Forget the levity of the example and consider the case of the innocent fat man. If there really is no other way of unsticking our fat man and if plainly, without blasting him out, everyone in the cave will drown, then, innocent or not, he should be blasted out. This indeed overrides the principle that the innocent should never be deliberately killed, but it does not reveal a callousness toward life, for the people involved are caught in a desperate situation in which, if such extreme action is not taken, many lives will be lost and far greater misery will obtain. Moreover, the people who do such a horrible thing or acquiesce in the doing of it are not likely to be rendered more callous about human life and human suffering as a result. Its occurrence will haunt them for the rest of their lives and is as likely as not to make them more rather than less morally sensitive. It is not even correct to say that such a desperate act shows a lack of respect for persons. We are not treating the fat man merely as a means. The fat man's person—his interests and rights—are not ignored. Killing him is something which is undertaken with the greatest reluctance. It is only when it is quite certain that there is no other way to save the lives of the others that such a violent course of action is justifiably undertaken.

Alan Donagan, arguing rather as Anscombe argues, maintains that "to use any innocent man ill for the sake of some public good is directly to degrade him to being a mere means" and to do this is of course to violate a principle essential to morality, that is, that human beings should never merely be treated as means but should be treated as ends in themselves (as persons worthy of respect).[11] But, as my above remarks show, it need not be the case, and in the above situation it is not the case, that in killing such an innocent man we are treating him *merely* as a means. The action is universalizable, all alternative actions which would save his life are duly considered, the blasting out is done only as a last and desperate resort with the minimum of harshness and indifference to his suffering and the like. It indeed sounds ironical to talk this way, given what is done to him. But if such a terrible situation were to arise, there would always be more or less humane ways of going about one's grim task. And in acting in the more humane ways toward the fat man, as we do what we must do and would have done to ourselves were the roles reversed, we show a respect for his person.[12]

[11]Donagan, op. cit., pp. 199–200.

[12]Again, I am not asserting that we would have enough fortitude to assent to it were the roles actually reversed. I am making a conceptual remark about what as moral beings we must try to do and not a psychological observation about what we can do.

In so treating the fat man—not just to further the public good but to prevent the certain death of a whole group of people (that is, to prevent an even greater evil than his being killed in this way)—the claims of justice are not overridden either, for each individual involved, if he is reasoning correctly, should realize that if he were so stuck rather than the fat man, he should in such situations be blasted out. Thus, there is no question of being unfair. Surely we must choose between evils here, but is there anything more reasonable, more morally appropriate, than choosing the lesser evil when doing or allowing some evil cannot be avoided? That is, where there is no avoiding both and where our actions can determine whether a greater or lesser evil obtains, should we not plainly always opt for the lesser evil? And is it not obviously a greater evil that all those other innocent people should suffer and die than that the fat man should suffer and die? Blowing up the fat man is indeed monstrous. But letting him remain stuck while the whole group drowns is still more monstrous.

The consequentialist is on strong moral ground here, and, if his reflective moral convictions do not square either with certain unrehearsed or with certain reflective particular moral convictions of human beings, so much the worse for such commonsense moral convictions. One could even usefully and relevantly adapt here—though for a quite different purpose—an argument of Donagan's. Consequentialism of the kind I have been arguing for provides so persuasive "a theoretical basis for common morality that when it contradicts some moral intuition, it is natural to suspect that intuition, not theory, is corrupt."[13] Given the comprehensiveness, plausibility, and overall rationality of consequentialism, it is not unreasonable to override even a deeply felt moral conviction if it does not square with such a theory, though, if it made no sense or overrode the bulk of or even a great many of our considered moral convictions, that would be another matter indeed.

Anticonsequentialists often point to the inhumanity of people who will sanction such killing of the innocent, but cannot the compliment be returned by speaking of the even greater inhumanity, conjoined with evasiveness, of those who will allow even more death and far greater misery and then excuse themselves on the ground that they did not intend the death and misery but merely forbore to prevent it? In such a context, such reasoning and such forbearing to prevent seems to me to constitute a moral evasion. I say it is evasive because rather than steeling himself to do what in normal circumstances would be a horrible and vile act but in this circumstance is a harsh moral necessity, he allows, when he has the power to prevent it, a situation which is still many times worse. He tries to keep his "moral purity" and

[13]Donagan, op. cit., p. 198.

avoid "dirty hands" at the price of utter moral failure and what Kierkegaard called "doublemindedness." It is understandable that people should act in this morally evasive way but this does not make it right.

My consequentialist reasoning about such cases as the case of the innocent fat man is very often resisted on the grounds that it starts a very dangerous precedent. People rationalize wildly and irrationally in their own favor in such situations. To avoid such rationalization, we must stubbornly stick to our deontological principles and recognize as well that very frequently, if people will put their wits to work or just endure, such admittedly monstrous actions done to prevent still greater evils will turn out to be unnecessary.

The general moral principles surrounding bans on killing the innocent are strong and play such a crucial role in the ever-floundering effort to humanize the savage mind—savage as a primitive and savage again as a contemporary in industrial society—that it is of the utmost social utility, it can be argued, that such bans against killing the innocent not be called into question in any practical manner by consequentialist reasoning.

However, in arguing in this way, the moral conservative has plainly shifted his ground, and he is himself arguing on consequentialist grounds that we must treat certain nonconsequentialist moral principles as absolute (as principles which can never *in fact*, from a reasonable moral point of view, be overridden, for it would be just too disastrous to do so).[14] But now he is on my home court, and my reply is that there is no good evidence at all that in the circumstances I characterized, overriding these deontological principles would have this disastrous effect. I am aware that a bad precedent could be set. Such judgments must not be made for more doubtful cases. But my telling my two stories in some detail, and my contrasting them, was done in order to make evident the type of situation, with its attendant rationale, in which the overriding of those deontological principles can be seen clearly to be justified and the situations in which this does obtain and why. My point was to specify the situations in which we ought to override our commonsense moral convictions about those matters, and the contexts in which we are not so justified or at least in which it is not clear which course of action is justified.[15]

If people are able to be sufficiently clear-headed about these matters, they can see that there are relevant differences between the two sorts of cases.

[14]Jonathan Bennett, "Whatever the Consequences," *Analysis* 26 (1966), has shown that this is a very common equivocation for the conservative and makes, when unnoticed, his position seem more plausible than it actually is.

[15]I have spoken, conceding this to the Christian absolutist for the sake of the discussion, as if (1) it is fairly evident what our commonsense moral convictions are here and (2) that they are deontological principles taken to hold no matter what the consequences. But that either (1) or (2) is clearly so seems to me very much open to question.

But I was also carefully guarding against extending such "moral radicalism"—if such it should be called—to other and more doubtful cases. Unless solid empirical evidence can be given that such a "moral radicalism" would—if it were to gain a toehold in the community—overflow destructively and inhumanely into the other doubtful and positively unjustifiable situations, nothing has been said to undermine the correctness of my consequentialist defense of "moral radicalism" in the contexts in which I defended it.

For Further Reflection

1. Analyze Nielsen's arguments for utilitarianism. What are their strengths and weaknesses?
2. Does it make sense to use utilitarian reasoning in deciding how to fight a war? How would a deontologist and a utilitarian differ in deciding on the morality of dropping the A-bomb on Hiroshima during World War II?
3. Consider the two examples given in this article: the fat man in the cave and the judge and the threatening mob. What is the morally right thing to do in these cases? Does utilitarianism have a better answer to this question than deontological ethics?
4. What is negative responsibility? What are its implications? What are some problems with it?

Against Utilitarianism

BERNARD WILLIAMS

Bernard Williams (1929–2003) held a joint appointment as a professor of philosophy at both Oxford University and the University of California at Berkeley. In this selection he argues that utilitarianism is a bad moral theory because it violates moral integrity, itself a deep moral ideal. That is, utilitarians frequently require us to reject conscience and our personal ideals in favor of the "lesser of evils." It is the concept of *negative responsibility* (discussed in Nielsen's article) that is the prime culprit in this degenerate process. Because, according to utilitarianism, we are responsible for evil if

From *Utilitarianism: For and Against,* edited by J. J. C. Smart and Bernard Williams (Cambridge University Press, 1973), pp. 97–99, 101–103, 108–109.

we knowingly let it happen when we could do something about it, the utilitarian requires us to do lesser evils—even when they require us to violate moral principles and do great harm. Williams offers two examples of how utilitarianism infringes on our integrity.

It is because consequentialism attaches value ultimately to states of affairs, and its concern is with what states of affairs the world contains, that it essentially involves the notion of *negative responsibility*: that if I am ever responsible for anything, then I must be just as much responsible for things that I allow or fail to prevent, as I am for things that I myself, in the more everyday restricted sense, bring about. Those things also must enter my deliberations, as a responsible moral agent, on the same footing. What matters is what states of affairs the world contains, and so what matters with respect to a given action is what comes about if it is done, and what comes about if it is not done, and those are questions not intrinsically affected by the nature of the causal linkage, in particular by whether the outcome is partly produced by other agents.

The strong doctrine of negative responsibility flows directly from consequentialism's assignment of ultimate value to states of affairs. Looked at from another point of view, it can be seen also as a special application of something that is favoured in many moral outlooks not themselves consequentialist—something which, indeed, some thinkers have been disposed to regard as the essence of morality itself: a principle of impartiality. Such a principle will claim that there can be no relevant difference from a moral point of view which consists just in the fact, not further explicable in general terms, that benefits or harms accrue to one person rather than to another—"it's me" can never in itself be a morally comprehensible reason. [By] this principle, familiar with regard to the reception of harms and benefits, we can see consequentialism as extending to their production: from the moral point of view, there is no comprehensible difference which consists just in my bringing about a certain outcome rather than someone else's producing it. That the doctrine of negative responsibility represents in this way the extreme of impartiality, and abstracts from the identity of the agent, leaving just a locus of causal intervention in the world—that fact is not merely a surface paradox. It helps to explain why consequentialism can seem to some to express a more serious attitude than nonconsequentialist views, why part of its appeal is to a certain kind of high-mindedness. Indeed, that is part of what is wrong with it.

Let us look more concretely at two examples, to see what utilitarianism might say about them, what we might say about utilitarianism and, most importantly of all, what would be implied by certain ways of thinking about the situations. . . .

(1) George, who has just taken his Ph.D. in chemistry, finds it extremely difficult to get a job. He is not very robust in health, which cuts down the number of jobs he might be able to do satisfactorily. His wife has to go out to work to keep them, which itself causes a great deal of strain, since they have small children and there are severe problems about looking after them. The results of all this, especially on the children, are damaging. An older chemist, who knows about this situation, says that he can get George a decently paid job in a certain laboratory, which pursues research into chemical and biological warfare. George says that he cannot accept this, since he is opposed to chemical and biological warfare. The older man replies that he is not too keen on it himself, come to that, but after all George's refusal is not going to make the job or the laboratory go away; what is more, he happens to know that if George refuses the job, it will certainly go to a contemporary of George's who is not inhibited by any such scruples and is likely if appointed to push along the research with greater zeal than George would. Indeed, it is not merely concern for George and his family, but (to speak frankly and in confidence) some alarm about this other man's excess of zeal, which has led the older man to offer to use his influence to get George the job. . . . George's wife, to whom he is deeply attached, has views (the details of which need not concern us) from which it follows that at least there is nothing particularly wrong with research into CBW. What should he do?

(2) Jim finds himself in the central square of a small South American town. Tied up against the wall are a row of twenty Indians, most terrified, a few defiant, in front of them several armed men in uniform. A heavy man in a sweat-stained khaki shirt turns out to be the captain in charge and, after a good deal of questioning of Jim which establishes that he got there by accident while on a botanical expedition, explains that the Indians are a random group of the inhabitants who, after recent acts of protest against the government, are just about to be killed to remind other possible protestors of the advantages of not protesting. However, since Jim is an honoured visitor from another land, the captain is happy to offer him a guest's privilege of killing one of the Indians himself. If Jim accepts, then as a special mark of the occasion, the other Indians will be let off. Of course, if Jim refuses, then there is no special occasion, and Pedro here will do what he was about to do when Jim arrived, and kill them all. Jim, with some desperate recollection of schoolboy fiction, wonders whether if he got hold of a gun, he could hold the captain, Pedro and the rest of the soldiers to threat, but it is quite clear from the set-up that nothing of that kind is going to work: any attempt at that sort of thing will mean that all the Indians will be killed, and himself. The men against the wall, and the other villagers, understand the situation, and are obviously begging him to accept. What should he do?

To these dilemmas, it seems to me that utilitarianism replies, in the first case, that George should accept the job, and in the second, that Jim should kill the Indian. Not only does utilitarianism give these answers but, if the situations are essentially as described and there are no further special factors, it regards them, it seems to me, as *obviously* the right answers. But many of us would certainly wonder whether, in (1), that could possibly be the right answer at all; and in the case of (2), even one who came to think that perhaps that was the answer, might well wonder whether it was obviously the answer. Nor is it just a question of the rightness or obviousness of these answers. It is also a question of what sort of considerations come into finding the answer. A feature of utilitarianism is that it cuts out a kind of consideration which for some others makes a difference to what they feel about such cases: a consideration involving the idea, as we might first and very simply put it, that each of us is specially responsible for what *he* does, rather than for what other people do. This is an idea closely connected with the value of integrity. It is often suspected that utilitarianism, at least in its direct forms, makes integrity as a value more or less unintelligible. I shall try to show that this suspicion is correct. Of course, even if that is correct, it would not necessarily follow that we should reject utilitarianism; perhaps, as utilitarians sometimes suggest, we should just forget about integrity, in favour of such things as a concern for the general good. However, if I am right, we cannot merely do that, since the reason why utilitarianism cannot understand integrity is that it cannot coherently describe the relations between a man's projects and his actions.

TWO KINDS OF REMOTER EFFECT

A lot of what we have to say about this question will be about the relations between my projects and other people's projects. But before we get on to that, we should first ask whether we are assuming too hastily what the utilitarian answers to the dilemmas will be. In terms of more dire effects of the possible decisions, there does not indeed seem much doubt about the answer in either case; but it might be said that in terms of more remote or less evident effects counterweights might be found to enter the utilitarian scales. Thus the effect on George of a decision to take the job might be invoked, or its effect on others who might know of his decision. The possibility of there being more beneficent labours in the future from which he might be barred or disqualified, might be mentioned; and so forth. Such effects—in particular, possible effects on the agent's character, and effects on the public at large—are often invoked by utilitarian writers dealing with problems about lying or promise-breaking, and some similar considerations might be invoked here.

There is one very general remark that is worth making about arguments of this sort. The certainty that attaches to these hypotheses about possible effects is usually pretty low; in some cases, indeed, the hypothesis invoked is so implausible that it would scarcely pass if it were not being used to deliver the respectable moral answer, as in the standard fantasy that one of the effects of one's telling a particular lie is to weaken the disposition of the world at large to tell the truth. The demands on the certainty or probability of these beliefs as beliefs about particular actions are much milder than they would be on beliefs favouring the unconventional course. It may be said that this is as it should be, since the presumption must be in favour of the conventional course: but that scarcely seems a *utilitarian* answer, unless utilitarianism has already taken off in the direction of not applying the consequences to the particular act at all.

Leaving aside that very general point, I want to consider now two types of effect that are often invoked by utilitarians, and which might be invoked in connection with these imaginary cases. The attitude or tone involved in invoking these effects may sometimes seem peculiar; but that sort of peculiarity soon becomes familiar in utilitarian discussions, and indeed it can be something of an achievement to retain a sense of it.

First, there is the psychological effect on the agent. Our descriptions of these situations have not so far taken account of how George or Jim will be after they have taken the one course or the other; and it might be said that if they take the course which seemed at first the utilitarian one, the effects on them will be in fact bad enough and extensive enough to cancel out the initial utilitarian advantages of that course. Now there is one version of this effect in which, for a utilitarian, some confusion must be involved, namely that in which the agent feels bad, his subsequent conduct and relations are crippled and so on, *because he thinks that he has done the wrong thing*—for if the balance of outcomes was as it appeared to be *before* invoking this effect, then he has not (from the utilitarian point of view) done the wrong thing. So that version of the effect, for a rational and utilitarian agent, could not possibly make any difference to the assessment of right and wrong. However, perhaps he is not a thoroughly rational agent, and is disposed to have bad feelings, whichever he decided to do. Now such feelings, which are from a strictly utilitarian point of view irrational—nothing, a utilitarian can point out, is advanced by having them—cannot, consistently, have any great weight in a utilitarian calculation. I shall consider in a moment an argument to suggest that they should have no weight at all in it. But short of that, the utilitarian could reasonably say that such feelings should not be encouraged, even if we accept their existence, and that to give them a lot of weight is to encourage them. Or, at the very best, even if they are straightforwardly and without any discount to be put into the calculation, their weight must be small: they are after all (and at best) one man's feelings.

That consideration might seem to have particular force in Jim's case. In George's case, his feelings represent a larger proportion of what is to be weighed, and are more commensurate in character with other items in the calculation. In Jim's case, however, his feelings might seem to be of very little weight compared with other things that are at stake. There is a powerful and recognizable appeal that can be made on this point: as that a refusal by Jim to do what he has been invited to do would be a kind of self-indulgent squeamishness. That is an appeal which can be made by other than utilitarians—indeed, there are some uses of it which cannot be consistently made by utilitarians, as when it essentially involves the idea that there is something dishonourable about such self-indulgence. But in some versions it is a familiar, and it must be said a powerful, weapon of utilitarianism. One must be clear, though, about what it can and cannot accomplish. The most it can do, so far as I can see, is to invite one to consider how seriously, and for what reasons, one feels that what one is invited to do is (in these circumstances) wrong, and in particular, to consider that question from the utilitarian point of view. When the agent is not seeing the situation from a utilitarian point of view, the appeal cannot force him to do so; and if he does come round to seeing it from a utilitarian point of view, there is virtually nothing left for the appeal to do. If he does not see it from a utilitarian point of view, he will not see his resistance to the invitation, and the unpleasant feelings he associates with accepting it, *just* as disagreeable experiences of his; they figure rather as emotional expressions of a thought that to accept would be wrong. He may be asked, as by the appeal, to consider whether he is right, and indeed whether he is fully serious, in thinking that. But the assertion of the appeal, that he is being self-indulgently squeamish, will not itself answer that question, or even help to answer it, since it essentially tells him to regard his feelings just as unpleasant experiences of his, and he cannot, by doing that, answer the question they pose when they are precisely not so regarded, but are regarded as indications of what he thinks is right and wrong. If he does come round fully to the utilitarian point of view then of course he will regard these feelings just as unpleasant experiences of his. And once Jim—at least—has come to see them in that light, there is nothing left for the appeal to do, since *of course* his feelings, so regarded, are of virtually no weight at all in relation to the other things at stake. The "squeamishness" appeal is not an argument which adds in a hitherto neglected consideration. Rather, it is an invitation to consider the situation, and one's own feelings, from a utilitarian point of view.

The reason why the squeamishness appeal can be very unsettling, and one can be unnerved by the suggestion of self-indulgence in going against utilitarian considerations, is not that we are utilitarians who are uncertain what utilitarian value to attach to our moral feelings, but that we are partially at least not utilitarians, and cannot regard our moral feelings merely as objects of utilitarian value. Because our moral relation to the world is partly given by such feelings, and by a sense of what we can or cannot "live with," to come to regard those feelings from a purely utilitarian point of view, that is to say, as happenings outside one's moral self, is to lose a sense of one's moral identity; to lose, in the most literal way, one's integrity. At this point utilitarianism alienates one from one's moral feelings; we shall see a little later how, more basically, it alienates one from one's actions as well. . . .

INTEGRITY

The [two] situations have in common that if the agent does not do a certain disagreeable thing, someone else will, and in Jim's situation at least the result, the state of affairs after the other man has acted, if he does, will be worse than after Jim has acted, if Jim does. The same, on a smaller scale, is true of George's case. I have already suggested that it is inherent in consequentialism that it offers a strong doctrine of negative responsibility. If I know that if I do X, O_1 will eventuate, and if I refrain from doing X, O_2 will, and that O_2 is worse than O_1, then I am responsible for O_2 if I refrain voluntarily from doing X. "You could have prevented it," as will be said, and truly, to Jim, if he refuses, by the relatives of the other Indians.

In the present cases, the situation of O_2 includes another agent bringing about results worse than O_1. So far as O_2 has been identified up to this point—merely as the worse outcome which will eventuate if I refrain from doing X—we might equally have said that what that other brings about is O_2; but that would be to underdescribe the situation. For what occurs if Jim refrains from action is not solely twenty Indians dead, but *Pedro's killing twenty Indians,* and that is not a result which Pedro brings about, though the death of the Indians is. We can say: what one does is not included in the outcome of what one does, while what another does can be included in the outcome of what one does. For that to be so, as the terms are now being used, only a very weak condition has to be satisfied: for Pedro's killing the Indians to be the outcome of Jim's refusal, it only has to be causally true that if Jim had not refused, Pedro would not have done it.

That may be enough for us to speak, in some sense, of Jim's responsibility for that outcome, if it occurs; but it is certainly not enough, it is worth noticing, for us to speak of Jim's *making* those things happen. For granted this way of their coming about, he could have made them happen only by making Pedro shoot, and there is no acceptable sense in which his refusal makes Pedro shoot. If the captain had said on Jim's refusal, "you leave me with no alternative," he would have been lying, like most who use that phrase. While the deaths, and the killing, may be the outcome of Jim's refusal, it is misleading to think, in such a case, of Jim having an *effect* on the world through the medium (as it happens) of Pedro's acts; for this is to leave Pedro out of the picture in his essential role of one who has intentions and projects, projects for realizing which Jim's refusal would leave an opportunity. Instead of thinking in terms of supposed effects of Jim's projects on Pedro, it is more revealing to think in terms of the effects of Pedro's projects on Jim's decision.

Utilitarianism would do well then to acknowledge the evident fact that among the things that make people happy is not only making other people happy, but being taken up or involved in any of a vast range of projects, or—if we waive the evangelical and moralizing associations of the word—commitments. One can be committed to such things as a person, a cause, an institution, a career, one's own genius, or the pursuit of danger.

Now none of these is itself the *pursuit of happiness:* by an exceedingly ancient platitude, it is not at all clear that there could be anything which was just that, or at least anything that had the slightest chance of being successful. Happiness, rather, requires being involved in, or at least content with, something else. It is not impossible for utilitarianism to accept that point: it does not have to be saddled with a naive and absurd philosophy of mind about the relation between desire and happiness. What it does have to say is that if such commitments are worthwhile, then pursuing the projects that flow from them, and realizing some of those projects, will make the person for whom they are worthwhile, happy. It may be that to claim that is still wrong: it may well be that a commitment can make sense to a man (can make sense of his life) without his supposing that it will make him *happy*. But that is not the present point; let us grant to utilitarianism that all worthwhile human projects must conduce, one way or another, to happiness. The point is that even if that is true, it does not follow, nor could it possibly be true, that those projects are themselves projects of pursuing happiness. One has to believe in, or at least want, or quite minimally, be content with, other things, for there to be anywhere that happiness can come from.

Utilitarianism, then, should be willing to agree that its general aim of maximizing happiness does not imply that what everyone is doing is just pursuing happiness. On the contrary, people have to be pursuing other things. What those other things may be, utilitarianism, sticking to its professed empirical stance, should be prepared just to find out. No doubt some possible projects it will want to discourage, on the grounds that their being pursued involves a negative balance of happiness to others: though even there, the unblinking accountant's eye of the strict utilitarian will have something to put in the positive column, the satisfactions of the destructive agent. Beyond that, there will be a vast variety of generally beneficent or at least harmless projects; and some no doubt, will take the form not just of tastes or fancies, but of what I have called "commitments." It may even be that the utilitarian researcher will find that many of those with commitments, who have really identified themselves with objects outside themselves, who are thoroughly involved with other persons, or institutions, or activities or causes, are actually happier than those whose projects and wants are not like that. If so, that is an important piece of utilitarian empirical lore.

When I say "happier" here, I have in mind the sort of consideration which any utilitarian would be committed to accepting: as for instance that such people are less likely to have a breakdown or commit suicide. Of course that is not all that is actually involved, but the point in this argument is to use to the maximum degree utilitarian notions, in order to locate a breaking point in utilitarian thought. In appealing to this strictly utilitarian notion, I am being more consistent with utilitarianism than [J. J. C.] Smart is. In his struggles with the problem of the brain-electrode man, Smart commends the idea that "happy" is a partly evaluative term, in the sense that we call "happiness" those kinds of satisfaction which, as things are, we approve of. But *by what standard* is this surplus element of approval supposed, from a utilitarian point of view, to be allocated? There is no source for it, on a strictly utilitarian view, except further degrees of satisfaction, but there are none of those available, or the problem would not arise. Nor does it help to appeal to the fact that we dislike in prospect things which we like when we get there, for from a utilitarian point of view it would seem that the original dislike was merely irrational or based on an error. Smart's argument at this point seems to be embarrassed by a well-known utilitarian uneasiness, which comes from a feeling that it is not respectable to ignore the "deep," while not having anywhere left in human life to locate it.

Let us now go back to the agent as utilitarian, and his higher-order project of maximizing desirable outcomes. At this level, he is committed only to that: what the outcome will actually consist of will depend entirely on the facts, on what persons with what projects and what potential satisfactions there are within calculable reach of the causal levers near which he finds himself. His own substantial projects and commitments come into it, but only as one lot among others—they potentially provide one set of satisfactions among those which he may be able to assist from where he happens to be. He is the agent of the satisfaction system who happens to be at a particular point at a particular time: in Jim's case, our man in South America. His own decisions as a utilitarian agent are a function of all the satisfactions which he can effect from where he is: and this means that the projects of others, to an indeterminately great extent, determine his decision.

This may be so either positively or negatively. It will be so positively if agents within the causal field of his decision have projects which are at any rate harmless and so should be assisted. It will equally be so, but negatively, if there is an agent within the causal field whose projects are harmful, and have to be frustrated to maximize desirable outcomes. So it is with Jim and the soldier Pedro. On the utilitarian view, the undesirable projects of other people as much determine, in this negative way, one's decisions as the desirable ones do positively: if those people were not there, or had different projects, the causal nexus would be different, and it is the actual state of the causal nexus which determines the decision. The determination to an indefinite degree of my decisions by other people's projects is just another aspect of my unlimited responsibility to act for the best in a causal framework formed to a considerable extent by their projects.

The decision so determined is, for utilitarianism, the right decision. But what if it conflicts with some project of mine? This, the utilitarian will say, has already been dealt with: the satisfaction to you of fulfilling your project, and any satisfactions to others of your so doing, have already been through the calculating device and have been found inadequate. Now in the case of many sorts of projects, that is a perfectly reasonable sort of answer. But in the case of projects of the sort I have called "commitments," those with which one is more deeply and extensively involved and identified, this cannot just by itself be an adequate answer, and there may be no adequate answer at all. For, to take the extreme sort of case, how can a man, as a utilitarian agent, come to regard as one satisfaction among others, and a dispensable one, a project or attitude round which he has built his life, just because someone else's projects have so structured the causal scene that that is how the utilitarian sum comes out?

The point here is not, as utilitarians may hasten to say, that if the project or attitude is that central to his life, then to abandon it will be very disagreeable to him and great loss of utility will be involved. I have already argued in section 4 that it is not like that; on the contrary, once he is prepared to look at it like that, the argument in any serious case is over anyway. The point is that he is identified with his actions as flowing from projects and attitudes which in some cases he takes seriously at the deepest level, as what his life is about (or, in some cases, this section of his life—seriousness is not necessarily the same as persistence). It is absurd to demand of such a man, when the sums come in from the utility network which the projects of others have in part determined, that he should just step aside from his own project and decision and acknowledge the decision which utilitarian calculation requires. It is to alienate him in a real sense from his actions and the source of his action in his own convictions. It is to make him into a channel between the input of everyone's projects, including his own, and an output of optimistic decision; but this is to neglect the extent to which *his* actions and *his* decisions have to be seen as the actions and decisions which flow from the projects and attitudes with which he is most closely identified. It is thus, in the most literal sense, an attack on his integrity.

These sorts of considerations do not in themselves give solutions to practical dilemmas such as those provided by our examples; but I hope they help to provide other ways of thinking about them. In fact, it is not hard to see that in George's case, viewed from this perspective, the utilitarian solution would be wrong. Jim's case is different, and harder. But if (as I suppose) the utilitarian is probably right in this case, that is not to be found out just by asking the utilitarian's questions. Discussions of it—and I am not going to try to carry it further here—will have to take seriously the distinction between my killing someone, and its coming about because of what I do that someone else kills them: a distinction based, not so much on the distinction between action and inaction, as on the distinction between my projects and someone else's projects. At least it will have to start by taking that seriously, as utilitarianism does not; but then it will have to build out from there by asking why that distinction seems to have less, or a different, force in this case than it has in George's. One question here would be how far one's powerful objection to killing people just is, in fact, an application of a powerful objection to their being killed. Another dimension of that is the issue of how much it matters that the people at risk are actual, and there, as opposed to hypothetical, or future, or merely elsewhere.

There are many other considerations that could come into such a question, but the immediate point of all this is to draw one particular contrast with utilitarianism: that to reach a grounded decision in such a case should not be regarded as a matter of just discounting one's reactions, impulses and deeply held projects in the face of the pattern of utilities, nor yet merely adding them in—but in the first instance of trying to understand them.

Of course, time and circumstances are unlikely to make a grounded decision, in Jim's case at least, possible. It might not even be decent. Instead of thinking in a rational and systematic way either about utilities or about the value of human life, the relevance of the people at risk being present, and so forth, the presence of the people at risk may just have its effect. The significance of the immediate should not be underestimated. Philosophers, not only utilitarian ones, repeatedly urge one to view the world *sub specie aeternitatis*, but for most human purposes that is not a good *species* to view it under. If we are not agents of the universal satisfaction system, we are not primarily janitors of any system of values, even our own: very often, we just act, as a possibly confused result of the situation in which we are engaged. That, I suspect, is very often an exceedingly good thing.

For Further Reflection

1. Why does Williams reject the utilitarian notion of negative responsibility?
2. What is Williams's main objection to *consequentialism* (his term for utilitarianism)? Examine the cases of George and Jim. What do you think is the right thing to do in each of these cases? What are Williams's answers? Do you agree with his reasoning?
3. What does Williams mean by *integrity?* What role does this notion play in his argument? Some have criticized Williams for unjustifiably exalting integrity too highly. They say, if my feelings of integrity conflict with making hard but rationally supported choices, I ought to overcome those feelings and do what is right. Here is an illustration. I have given my whole life to support political party X, which had admirable goals and did much good. But the party has been irremediably morally corrupted and now is harming people. Still, my sense of integrity is tied up in all the good the party once stood for. I reason that it would be a good thing to destroy the party for the good of humanity, and I have the opportunity to do so. But my sense of integrity prevents me from easily doing this. I deeply identify with party X. Although this may be a hard decision, many ethicists would argue that I must overcome my squeamishness and do the right thing: destroy party X so that its present evil will be ineffectual. How would Williams deal with this case? How would you?

The Ones Who Walk Away from Omelas

URSULA LE GUIN

Ursula Le Guin is the author of many novels and short story collections, including *The Wind's Twelve Quarters,* from which this short story is taken. The story is about an ideal utilitarian, utopian society that is dependent on one individual's significant suffering. Le Guin credits a passage from the philosopher William James as the point of departure for this story. James wrote:

> Or if the hypothesis were offered us of a world in which Messr. Fourier's and Bellamy's and Morris's utopias should all be outdone, and millions kept permanently happy on the one simple condition that a certain lost soul on the far-off edge of things should lead a life of lonely torment, what except a special and independent sort of emotion can it be which would make us immediately feel, even though an impulse arose within us to clutch at the happiness so offered, how hideous a thing would be its enjoyment when deliberately accepted as the fruit of such a bargain?

With a clamor of bells that set the swallows soaring, the Festival of Summer came to the city Omelas, bright-towered by the sea. The rigging of the boats in harbor sparkled with flags. In the streets between houses with red roofs and painted walls, between old moss-grown gardens and under avenues of trees, past great parks and public buildings, processions moved. Some were decorous: old people in long stiff robes of mauve and grey, grave master workmen, quiet, merry women carrying their babies and chatting as they walked. In other streets the music beat faster, a shimmering of gong and tambourine, and the people went dancing, the procession was a dance. Children dodged in and out, their high calls rising like the swallows' crossing flights over the music and the singing. All the processions wound towards the north side of the city, where on the great water-meadow called the Green Fields boys and girls, naked in the bright air, with mud-stained feet and ankles and long, lithe arms, exercised their restive horses before the race. The horses wore no gear at all but a halter without bit. Their manes were braided with streamers of silver, gold, and green. They flared their nostrils and pranced and boasted to one another; they were vastly excited, the horse being the only animal who has adopted our ceremonies as his own. Far off to the north and west the mountains stood up half encircling Omelas on her bay. The air of morning was so clear that the snow still crowning the Eighteen Peaks burned with white-gold fire across the miles of sunlit air, under the dark blue of the sky. There was just enough wind to make the banners that marked the racecourse snap and flutter now and then. In the silence of the broad green meadows one could hear the music winding through the city streets, farther and nearer and ever approaching, a cheerful faint sweetness of the air that from time to time trembled and gathered together and broke out into the great joyous clanging of the bells.

Joyous! How is one to tell about joy? How describe the citizens of Omelas?

They were not simple folk, you see, though they were happy. But we do not say the words of cheer much any more. All smiles have become archaic. Given a description such as this one tends to make certain assumptions. Given a description such as this one tends to look next for the King, mounted on a splendid stallion and surrounded by his noble knights, or perhaps in a golden litter borne by great-muscled slaves. But there was no king. They did not use swords, or keep slaves. They were not barbarians. I do not know the rules and laws of their society, but I suspect that they were singularly few. As they did without monarchy and slavery, so they also got on without the stock exchange, the advertisement, the secret police, and the bomb. Yet I repeat that these were not simple folk, not dulcet shepherds, noble savages, bland utopians. They were not less complex than us. The trouble is that we have a bad habit, encouraged by pedants and sophisticates, of considering happiness as something rather stupid. Only pain is intellectual, only evil interesting. This is the treason of the artist: a refusal to admit the banality of evil and the terrible boredom of pain. If you can't lick 'em, join 'em. If it hurts, repeat it. But to praise despair is to condemn delight, to embrace violence is to lose hold of everything else. We have almost lost hold; we can no longer describe a happy man, nor make any celebration of joy. How can I tell you about the people of Omelas? They were not naïve and happy children—though their children were, in fact, happy. They were mature, intelligent, passionate adults whose lives were not wretched. O miracle! but I wish I could describe it better. I wish I could convince you. Omelas sounds in my words like a city in a fairy tale, long ago and far away, once upon a time. Perhaps it would be best if you imagined it as your own fancy bids, assuming it will rise to the occasion, for certainly I cannot suit you all. For instance, how about technology? I think that there would be no cars or helicopters in and above the streets; this follows from the fact that the people of Omelas are happy people. Happiness is based on a just discrimination of what is necessary, what is neither necessary nor destructive, and what is destructive. In the middle category, however—that of the unnecessary but undestructive, that of comfort, luxury, exuberance, etc.—they could perfectly well have central heating, subway trains, washing machines, and all kinds of marvelous devices not yet invented here, floating light-sources, fuelless power, a cure for the common cold. Or they could have none of that: it doesn't matter. As you like it. I incline to think that people from towns up and down the coast have been coming in to Omelas during the last days before the Festival on very fast little trains and double-decked trams, and that the train station of Omelas is actually the handsomest building in town, though plainer than the magnificent Farmers' Market. But even granted trains, I fear that Omelas so far strikes some of you as goody-goody. Smiles, bells, parades, horses, blah. If so, please add an orgy. If an orgy would help, don't hesitate. Let us not, however, have temples from which issue beautiful nude priests and priestesses already half in ecstasy and ready to copulate with any man or woman, lover or stranger, who desires union with the deep godhead of the blood, although that was my first idea. But really it would be better not to have any temples in Omelas—at least, not manned temples. Religion yes, clergy no. Surely the beautiful nudes can just wander about, offering themselves like divine soufflés to the hunger of the needy and the rapture of the flesh. Let them join the processions. Let tambourines be struck above the copulations, and the glory of desire be proclaimed upon the gongs, and (a not unimportant point) let the offspring of these delightful rituals be beloved and looked after by all. One thing I know there is none of in Omelas is guilt. But what else should there be? I thought at first there were no drugs, but that is puritanical. For those who like it, the faint insistent sweetness of *drooz* may perfume the ways of the city, *drooz* which first brings a great lightness and brilliance to the mind and limbs, and then after some hours a dreamy languor, and wonderful visions at last of the very arcana and inmost secrets of the Universe, as well as exciting the pleasure of sex beyond all belief; and it is not habit-forming. For more modest tastes I think there ought to be beer. What else, what else belongs in the joyous city? The sense of victory, surely, the celebration of courage. But as we did without clergy, let us do without soldiers. The joy built upon successful slaughter is not the right kind of joy; it will not do; it is fearful and it is trivial. A boundless and generous contentment, a magnanimous triumph felt not against some outer enemy but in communion with the finest and fairest in the souls of all men everywhere and the splendor of the world's summer: this is what swells the hearts of the people of Omelas, and the victory they celebrate is that of life. I really don't think many of them need to take *drooz*.

Most of the processions have reached the Green Fields by now. A marvelous smell of cooking goes forth from the red and blue tents of the provisioners. The faces of small children are amiably sticky; in the benign grey beard of a man a couple of crumbs of rich pastry are entangled. The youths and girls have mounted their horses and are beginning to group around the starting line of the course. An old woman, small, fat, and laughing, is passing out flowers from a basket, and tall young men wear her flowers in their shining hair. A child of nine or ten sits at the edge of the crowd, alone, playing on a wooden flute. People pause to listen, and they smile, but they do not speak to him, for he never ceases playing and never sees them, his dark eyes wholly rapt in the sweet, thin magic of the tune.

He finishes, and slowly lowers his hands holding the wooden flute.

As if that little private silence were the signal, all at once a trumpet sounds from the pavilion near the starting line: imperious, melancholy, piercing. The horses rear on their slender legs, and some of them neigh in answer. Sober-faced, the young riders stroke the horses' necks and soothe them, whispering, "Quiet, quiet, there my beauty, my hope. . . ." They begin to form in rank along the starting line. The crowds along the racecourse are like a field of grass and flowers in the wind. The Festival of Summer has begun.

Do you believe? Do you accept the festival, the city, the joy? No? Then let me describe one more thing.

In a basement under one of the beautiful public buildings of Omelas, or perhaps in the cellar of one of its spacious private homes, there is a room. It has one locked door, and no window. A little light seeps in dustily between cracks in the boards, secondhand from a cobwebbed window somewhere across the cellar. In one corner of the little room a couple of mops, with stiff, clotted, foul-smelling heads, stand near a rusty bucket. The floor is dirt, a little damp to the touch, as cellar dirt usually is. The room is about three paces long and two wide: a mere broom closet or disused tool room. In the room a child is sitting. It could be a boy or a girl. It looks about six, but actually is nearly ten. It is feeble-minded. Perhaps it was born defective, or perhaps it has become imbecile through fear, malnutrition, and neglect. It picks its nose and occasionally fumbles vaguely with its toes or genitals, as it sits hunched in the corner farthest from the bucket and the two mops. It is afraid of the mops. It finds them horrible. It shuts its eyes, but it knows the mops are still standing there; and the door is locked; and nobody will come. The door is always locked; and nobody ever comes, except that sometimes—the child has no understanding of time or interval—sometimes the door rattles terribly and opens, and a person, or several people, are there. One of them may come in and kick the child to make it stand up. The others never come close, but peer in at it with frightened, disgusted eyes. The food bowl and the water jug are hastily filled, the door is locked, the eyes disappear. The people at the door never say anything, but the child, who has not always lived in the tool room, and can remember sunlight and its mother's voice, sometimes speaks. "I will be good," it says. "Please let me out. I will be good!" They never answer. The child used to scream for help at night, and cry a good deal, but now it only makes a kind of whining, "eh-haa, eh-haa," and it speaks less and less often. It is so thin there are no calves to its legs; its belly protrudes; it lives on a half-bowl of corn meal and grease a day. It is naked. Its buttocks and thighs are a mass of festered sores, as it sits in its own excrement continually.

They all know it is there, all the people of Omelas. Some of them have come to see it, others are content merely to know it is there. They all know that it has to be there. Some of them understand why, and some do not, but they all understand that their happiness, the beauty of their city, the tenderness of their friendships, the health of their children, the wisdom of their scholars, the skill of their makers, even the abundance of their harvest and the kindly weathers of their skies, depend wholly on this child's abominable misery.

This is usually explained to children when they are between eight and twelve, whenever they seem capable of understanding; and most of those who come to see the child are young people, though often enough an adult comes, or comes back, to see the child. No matter how well the matter has been explained to them, these young spectators are always shocked and sickened at the sight. They feel disgust, which they had thought themselves superior to. They feel anger, outrage, impotence, despite all the explanations. They would like to do something for the child. But there is nothing they can do. If the child were brought up into the sunlight out of that vile place, if it were cleaned and fed and comforted, that would be a good thing, indeed; but if it were done, in that day and hour all the prosperity and beauty and delight of Omelas would wither and be destroyed. Those are the terms. To exchange all the goodness and grace of every life in Omelas for that single, small improvement: to throw away the happiness of thousands for the chance of the happiness of one: that would be to let guilt within the walls indeed.

The terms are strict and absolute; there may not even be a kind word spoken to the child.

Often the young people go home in tears, or in a tearless rage, when they have seen the child and faced this terrible paradox. They may brood over it for weeks or years. But as time goes on they begin to realize that even if the child could be released, it would not get much good of its freedom: a little vague pleasure of warmth and food, no doubt, but little more. It is too degraded and imbecile to know any real joy. It has been afraid too long ever to be free of fear. Its habits are too uncouth for it to respond to humane treatment. Indeed, after so long it would probably be wretched without walls about it to protect it, and darkness for its eyes, and its own excrement to sit in. Their tears at the bitter injustice dry when they begin to perceive the terrible justice of reality, and to accept it. Yet it is their tears and anger, the trying of their generosity and the acceptance of their helplessness, which are perhaps the true source of the splendor of their lives. Theirs is no vapid, irresponsible happiness. They know that they, like the child, are not free. They know compassion. It is the existence of the child, and their knowledge of its existence, that makes possible the nobility of their architecture, the poignancy of their music, the profundity of their science. It is because of the child that they are so gentle with children. They know that if the wretched one were not there snivelling in the dark, the other one, the flute-player, could make no joyful music as the young riders line up in their beauty for the race in the sunlight of the first morning of summer.

Now do you believe in them? Are they not more credible? But there is one more thing to tell, and this is quite incredible.

At times one of the adolescent girls or boys who go to see the child does not go home to weep or rage, does not, in fact, go home at all. Sometimes also a man or woman much older falls silent for a day or two, and then leaves home. These people go out into the street, and walk down the street alone. They keep walking, and walk straight out of the city of Omelas, through the beautiful gates. They keep walking across the farmlands of Omelas. Each one goes alone, youth or girl, man or woman. Night falls; the traveler must pass down village streets, between the houses with yellow-lit windows, and on out into the darkness of the fields. Each alone, they go west or north, towards the mountains. They go on. They leave Omelas, they walk ahead into the darkness, and they do not come back. The place they go towards is a place even less imaginable to most of us than the city of happiness. I cannot describe it at all. It is possible that it does not exist. But they seem to know where they are going, the ones who walk away from Omelas.

For Further Reflection

1. Discuss how this short story applies to the debate over utilitarianism. Would you walk away from Omelas (Salem spelled backward plus O for Oregon)? Explain your answer.
2. Do we already live in a world like Omelas, only not a utopia? Is our happiness predicated on the suffering of poorer nations from whom we get cheap goods?

Further Readings for Chapter 4

Bentham, Jeremy. *Introduction to the Principles of Morals and Legislation.* Edited by W. Harrison. Oxford: Oxford University Press, 1948.

Hardin, Russell. *Morality within the Limits of Reason.* Chicago: University of Chicago Press, 1988. A cogent contemporary defense of utilitarianism.

Hare, R. M. *Moral Thinking.* Oxford: Oxford University Press, 1981.

Mill, John Stuart. *Utilitarianism.* Indianapolis: Bobbs-Merrill, 1957.

Quinton, Anthony. *Utilitarian Ethics.* New York: Macmillan, 1973. A clear exposition of classical utilitarianism.

Smart, J. J. C., and Bernard Williams. *Utilitarianism For and Against.* Cambridge: Cambridge University Press, 1973. A classic debate on the subject.

CHAPTER 5

Deontological Ethics

We have already outlined the basic ideas of deontological ethics in the introduction to this part. Deontologists distinguish themselves from consequentialists, like utilitarians, by holding that rightness and wrongness of acts are determined by the intrinsic quality of the act itself or the kind of act it is, not by its consequences. So, recurring to the example in the last chapter, a deontologist would tend to give the millionaire's money to the owner of the New York Yankees, according to the millionaire's request, not to the world hunger organization. There are two classic versions of deontological ethics: Kant's categorical imperative and Ross's intuitionism. Both are featured in this chapter. As you will see from the first reading, Immanuel Kant, the great eighteenth-century German philosopher, held that we may test the moral status of our acts by asking whether we could will the maxim (or principle) of that act to be a universal law of nature. If we can so universalize the principle, the act passes the test of what is morally permissible. If we cannot, then the act is immoral. Kant argued that we cannot will that lying or promise-breaking be universal laws, so they must be seen as immoral. For Kant, such moral principles are absolute. They have no exceptions. Kant's notion of the categorical imperative is critiqued in the second reading by William Frankena.

The second kind of deontological ethics is that of W. D. Ross, the Oxford philosopher, who in our third reading sets forth an intuitionist morality. If we consult our conscience, we will hit upon obvious moral principles. W. D. Ross, unlike Kant, is not an absolutist. Moral principles have prima facie or conditional bindingness. They are valid principles, having universal application, but they may not always win out in the end. Another, more stringent, duty may override the normal duty. So, while we should generally tell the truth, we may be obligated to lie, if by so doing we may save an innocent person's life.

We then examine Ambrose Bierce's Civil War short story "A Horseman in the Sky," which is followed by Charles Fried's discourse on the evil of lying. After this, we encounter Plato's classic Euthyphro problem, which asks whether religion is the basis of morality or vice versa. Next we study James Rachels's article on that same topic—"The Divine Command Theory." We end with Carl Dennis's poem and Thomas Nagel's provocative essay—both about moral luck.

The Moral Law

IMMANUEL KANT

Immanuel Kant (1724–1804) was born into a deeply pietistic Lutheran family in Königsberg, Germany, and lived in that town his entire life. At sixteen he entered the University of Königsberg, where he later taught philosophy. He is considered the greatest philosopher of the Enlightenment. Among his works are *Critique of Pure Reason* (1781), *Prolegomena to Any Future Metaphysic* (1785), and *Foundations of the Metaphysic of Morals* (1785), from which the present selection is taken.

In this classic work Kant rejects such ethical theories as the theory of moral sentiments, set forth by the eighteenth-century Scottish moralists Francis Hutcheson and David Hume, in which morality is naturalistic, contingent, and hypothetical. The moral sentiment view is contingent in that it is based on human nature and, in particular, on our feelings or sentiments. Had we been created differently, we would have a different nature and hence different moral duties. Morality in this view consists of hypothetical imperatives, in that they depend on our desires for their realization. For example, we should obey the law because we want a peaceful, orderly society. We should seek peace because it is necessary for personal happiness. The naturalistic ethicists were typically utilitarians who sought to maximize human happiness.

Kant rejects this naturalistic, utilitarian account of ethics. Ethics is not *contingent* but *absolute*, and its duties or imperatives are not *hypothetical* but *categorical* (nonconditional). Ethics is based not on feeling but on reason. It is because we are rational beings that we are valuable and capable of discovering moral laws binding on all persons at all times. As such, our moral duties are not dependent on feelings but on reason. They are unconditional, universally valid, and necessary, regardless of the possible consequences or opposition to our inclinations.

This is Kant's first formulation of his *categorical imperative:* "Act only on that maxim whereby you can at the same time will that it would become a universal law." This imperative is given as the criterion (or second-order principle) by which to judge all other principles. If we can consistently will that everyone do some type of action, then the categorical imperative enjoins that type of action. If we cannot consistently will that everyone do some type of action, then that type of action is morally wrong. Kant argues, for example, that we cannot consistently will that everyone make false promises, for the very institution of promising entails or depends on general adherence to keeping the promise or intending to do so.

Reprinted from *The Foundations of the Metaphysic of Morals,* translated by T. K. Abbott (this translation first published in 1873).

Kant offers a second formulation of the categorical imperative: "So act as to treat humanity, whether in your own person or in that of any other, in every case as an end and never as merely a means only." Each person by virtue of his or her reason has dignity and profound worth, which entail that he or she must never be exploited, manipulated, or merely used as a means to our idea of what is for the general good.

PREFACE

As my concern here is with moral philosophy, I limit the question suggested to this: Whether it is not of the utmost necessity to construct a pure moral philosophy, perfectly cleared of everything which is only empirical, and which belongs to anthropology? for that such a philosophy must be possible is evident from the common idea of duty and of the moral laws. Everyone must admit that if a law is to have moral force, *i.e.*, to be the basis of an obligation, it must carry with it absolute necessity; that, for example, the precept, "Thou shall not lie," is not valid for men alone, as if other rational beings had no need to observe it; and so with all the other moral laws properly so called; that, therefore, the basis of obligation must not be sought in the nature of man, or in the circumstances in the world in which he is placed, but *a priori* simply in the conception of pure reason; and although any other precept which is founded on principles of mere experience may be in certain respects universal, yet in as far as it rests even in the least degree on an empirical basis, perhaps only as to a motive, such a precept, while it may be a practical rule, can never be called a moral law. . . .

THE GOOD WILL

Nothing can possibly be conceived in the world, or even out of it, which can be called good, without qualification, except a Good Will. Intelligence, wit, judgment, and the other *talents* of the mind, however they may be named, or courage, resolution, perseverance, as qualities of temperament, are undoubtedly good and desirable in many respects; but these gifts of nature may also become extremely bad and mischievous if the will which is to make use of them, and which, therefore, constitutes what is called *character,* is not good. It is the same with the *gifts of fortune.* Power, riches, honour, even health, and the general well-being and contentment with one's conditions which is called *happiness,* inspire pride, and often presumption, if there is not a good will to correct the influence of these on the mind, and with this also to rectify the whole principle of acting, and adapt it to its end. The sight of a being who is not adorned with a single feature of a pure and good will, enjoying unbroken prosperity, can never give pleasure to an impartial rational spectator. Thus a good will appears to constitute the indispensable condition even of being worthy of happiness.

There are even some qualities which are of service to this good will itself, and may facilitate its action, yet which have no intrinsic unconditional value, but always presuppose a good will, and this qualifies the esteem that we justly have for them, and does not permit us to regard them as absolutely good. Moderation in the affections and passions, self-control, and calm deliberation are not only good in many respects, but even seem to constitute part of the intrinsic worth of the person; but they are far from deserving to be called good without qualification, although they have been so unconditionally praised by the ancients. For without the principles of a good will, they may become extremely bad; and the coolness of a villain not only makes him far more dangerous, but also directly makes him more abominable in our eyes than he would have been without it.

A good will is good not because of what it performs or effects, not by its aptness for the attainment of some proposed end, but simply by virtue of the volition, that is, it is good in itself, and considered by itself to be esteemed much higher than all that can be brought about by it in favour of any inclination, nay, even of the sum-total of all inclinations. Even if it should happen that, owing to special disfavour of fortune, or the niggardly provision of a step-motherly nature, this will should wholly lack power to accomplish its purpose, if with its greatest efforts it should yet achieve nothing, and there should remain only the good will (not, to be sure, a mere wish, but the summoning of all means in our power), then, like a jewel, it would still shine by its own light, as a thing which has its whole value in itself. Its usefulness or fruitlessness can neither add to nor take away anything from this value. It would be, as it were, only the setting to enable us to handle it the more conveniently in common commerce, or to attract to it the attention of those who are not yet connoisseurs, but not to recommend it to true connoisseurs, or to determine its value.

WHY REASON WAS MADE TO GUIDE THE WILL

There is, however, something so strange in this idea of the absolute value of the mere will, in which no account is taken of its utility, that notwithstanding the thorough assent of even common reason to the idea, yet a suspicion must arise that it may perhaps really be the product of mere high-blown fancy, and that we may have misunderstood the purpose of nature in assigning reason as the governor of our will. Therefore we will examine this idea from this point of view.

In the physical constitution of an organized being, that is, a being adapted suitably to the purposes of life, we assume it as a fundamental principle that no organ for any purpose will be found but what is also the fittest and best adapted for that purpose. Now in a being which has reason and a will, if the proper object of nature were its *conservatism,* its *welfare,* in a word, its *happiness,* then nature would have hit upon a very bad arrangement in selecting the reason of the creature to carry out this purpose. For all the actions which the creature has to perform with a view to this purpose, and the whole rule of its conduct, would be far more surely prescribed to it by instinct, and that end would have been attained thereby much more certainly than it ever can be by reason. Should reason have been communicated to this favoured creature over and above, it must only have served it to contemplate the happy constitution of its nature, to admire it, to congratulate itself thereon, and to feel thankful for it to the beneficent cause, but not that it should subject its desires to that weak and delusive guidance, and meddle bunglingly with the purpose of nature. In a word, nature would have taken care that reason should not break forth into *practical exercise,* nor have the presumption, with its weak insight, to think out for itself the plan of happiness, and of the means of attaining it. Nature would not only have taken on herself the choice of the ends, but also of the means, and with wise foresight would have entrusted both to instinct.

And, in fact, we find that the more a cultivated reason applies itself with deliberate purpose to the enjoyment of life and happiness, so much the more does the man fail of true satisfaction. And from this circumstance there arises in many, if they are candid enough to confess it, a certain degree of *misology,* that is, hatred of reason, especially in the case of those who are most experienced in the use of it, because after calculating all the advantages they derive, I do not say from the invention of all the arts of common luxury, but even from the sciences (which seem to them to be after all only a luxury of the understanding), they find that they have, in fact, only brought more trouble on their shoulders, rather than gained in happiness; and they end by envying, rather than despising, the more common stamp of men who keep closer to the guidance of mere instinct, and do not allow their reason much influence on their conduct. And this we must admit, that the judgment of those who would very much lower the lofty eulogies of the advantages which reason gives us in regard to the happiness and satisfaction of life, or who would even reduce them below zero, is by no means morose or ungrateful to the goodness with which the world is governed, but that there lies at the root of these judgments the idea that our existence has a different and far nobler end, for which, and not for happiness, reason is properly intended, and which must, therefore, be regarded as the supreme condition to which the private ends of man must, for the most part, be postponed.

For as reason is not competent to guide the will with certainty in regard to its objects and the satisfaction of all our wants (which it to some extent even multiplies), this being an end to which an implanted instinct would have led with much greater certainty; and since, nevertheless, reason is imparted to us as a practical faculty, *i.e.*, as one which is to have influence on the *will*, therefore, admitting that nature generally in the distribution of her capacities has adapted the means to the end, its true destination must be to produce a *will*, not merely good as a *means* to something else, but *good in itself*, for which reason was absolutely necessary. This will then, though not indeed the sole and complete good, must be the supreme good and the condition of every other, even of the desire of happiness. Under these circumstances, there is nothing inconsistent with the wisdom of nature in the fact that the cultivation of the reason, which is requisite for the first and unconditional purpose, does in many ways interfere, at least in this life, with the attainment of the second, which is always conditional, namely, happiness. Nay, it may even reduce it to nothing, without nature thereby failing in her purpose. For reason recognizes the establishment of a good will as its highest practical destination, and in attaining this purpose is capable only of a satisfaction of its own proper kind, namely, that from the attainment of an end, which end again is determined by reason only, notwithstanding that this may involve many a disappointment to the ends of inclination.

THE FIRST PROPOSITION OF MORALITY

[An action must be done from a sense of duty, if it is to have moral worth]

We have then to develop the notion of a will which deserves to be highly esteemed for itself, and is good without a view to anything further, a notion which exists already in the sound natural understanding, requiring rather to be cleared up than to be taught, and which in estimating the value of our actions always takes the first place, and constitutes the condition of all the rest. In order to do this, we will take the notion of duty, which includes that of a good will, although implying certain subjective restrictions and hindrances. These, however, far from concealing it, or rendering it unrecognizable, rather bring it out by contrast, and make it shine forth so much the brighter.

I omit here all actions which are already recognized as inconsistent with duty although they may be useful for this or that purpose, for with these the question whether they are done *from duty* cannot arise at all, since they even conflict with it. I also set aside those actions which really conform to duty, but to which men have *no* direct *inclination*, performing them because they are impelled thereto by some other inclination. For in this case we can readily distinguish whether the action which agrees with duty is done *from duty*, or from a selfish view. It is much harder to make this distinction when the action accords with duty, and the subject has besides a *direct* inclination to it. For example, it is always a matter of duty that a dealer should not overcharge an inexperienced purchaser; and wherever there is much commerce the prudent tradesman does not overcharge, but keeps a fixed price for everyone, so that a child buys of him as well as any other. Men are thus *honestly* served; but this is not enough to make us believe that the tradesman has so acted from duty and from principles of honesty: his own advantage required it; it is out of the question in this case to suppose that he might besides have a direct inclination in favour of the buyers, so that, as it were, from love he should give no advantage to one over another. Accordingly the action was done neither from duty nor from direct inclination, but merely with a selfish view.

On the other hand, it is a duty to maintain one's life; and, in addition, everyone has also a direct inclination to do so. But on this account the often anxious care which most men take for it has no intrinsic worth, and their maxim has no moral import. They preserve their life *as duty requires,* no doubt, but not *because duty requires.* On the other hand, if adversity and hopeless sorrow have completely taken away the relish for life; if the unfortunate one, strong in mind, indignant at his fate rather than desponding or dejected, wishes for death, and yet preserves his life without loving it—not from inclination or fear, but from duty—then his maxim has a moral worth.

To be beneficent when we can is a duty; and besides this, there are many minds so sympathetically constituted that, without any other motive of vanity or self-interest, they find a pleasure in spreading joy around them, and can take delight in the satisfaction of others so far as it is their own work. But I maintain that in such a case an action of this kind, however proper, however amiable it may be, has nevertheless no true moral worth, but is on a level with other inclinations, *e.g.*, the inclination to honour, which, if it is happily directed to that which is in fact of public utility and accordant with duty, and consequently honourable, deserves praise and encouragement, but not esteem. For the maxim lacks the moral import, namely, that such actions be done *from duty,* not from inclination. Put the case that the mind of that philanthropist was clouded by sorrow of his own, extinguishing all sympathy with the lot of others, and that while he still has the power to benefit others in distress, he is not touched by their trouble because he is absorbed with his own; and now suppose that he tears himself out of this dead insensibility, and performs the action without any inclination to it, but simply from duty, then first has his action its genuine moral worth. Further still; if nature has put little sympathy in the heart of this or that man; if he, supposed to be an upright man, is by temperament cold and indifferent to the sufferings of others, perhaps because in respect of his own he is provided with the special gift of patience and fortitude, and supposes, or even requires, that others should have the same—and such a man would certainly not be the meanest product of nature—but if nature had not specially framed him for a philanthropist, would he not still find in himself a source from whence to give himself a far higher worth than that of a good-natured temperament could be? Unquestionably. It is just in this that the moral worth of the character is brought out which is incomparably the highest of all, namely, that he is beneficent, not from inclination, but from duty.

To secure one's own happiness is a duty, at least indirectly; for discontent with one's condition, under a pressure of many anxieties and amidst unsatisfied wants, might easily become a great *temptation to transgression of duty*. But here again, without looking to duty, all men have already the strongest and most intimate inclination to happiness, because it is just in this idea that all inclinations are combined in one total. But the precept of happiness is often of such a sort that it greatly interferes with some inclinations, and yet a man cannot form any definite and certain conception of the sum of satisfaction of all of them which is called happiness. It is not then to be wondered at that a single inclination, definite both as to what it promises and as to the time within which it can be gratified, is often able to overcome such a fluctuating idea, and that a gouty patient, for instance, can choose to enjoy what he likes, and to suffer what he may, since, according to his calculation, on this occasion at least, he has [only] not sacrificed the enjoyment of the present moment to a possibly mistaken expectation of a happiness which is supposed to be found in health. But even in this case, if the general desire for happiness did not influence his will, and supposing that in his particular case health was not a necessary element in this calculation, there yet remains in this, as in all other cases, this law, namely, that he should promote his happiness not from inclination but from duty, and by this would his conduct first acquire true moral worth.

It is in this manner, undoubtedly, that we are to understand those passages of Scripture also in which we are commanded to love our neighbour, even our enemy. For love, as an affection, cannot be commanded, but beneficence for duty's sake may; even though we are not impelled to it by any inclination—nay, are even repelled by a natural and unconquerable aversion. This is *practical* love, and not *pathological*[1]—a love which is seated in the will, and not in the propensions of sense—in principles of action and not of tender sympathy; and it is this love alone which can be commanded.

THE SECOND PROPOSITION OF MORALITY

The second proposition is: That an action done from duty derives its moral worth, *not from the purpose* which is to be attained by it, but from the maxim

[1]Passional or emotional.

by which it is determined, and therefore does not depend on the realization of the object of the action, but merely on the *principle of volition* by which the action has taken place, without regard to any object of desire. It is clear from what precedes that the purposes which we may have in view in our actions, or their effects regarded as ends and springs of the will, cannot give to actions any unconditional or moral worth. In what, then, can their worth lie, if it is not to consist in the will and in reference to its expected effect? It cannot lie anywhere but in the *principle of the will* without regard to the ends which can be attained by the action. For the will stands between its *a priori principle*, which is formal, and its *a posteriori* spring, which is material, as between two roads, and as it must be determined by something, it follows that it must be determined by the formal principle of volition when an action is done from duty, in which case every material principle has been withdrawn from it.

THE THIRD PROPOSITION OF MORALITY

The third proposition, which is a consequence of the two preceding, I would express thus: *Duty is the necessity of acting from respect for the law.* I may have *inclination* for an object as the effect of my proposed action, but I cannot have *respect* for it, just for this reason, that it is an effect and not an energy of will. Similarly, I cannot have respect for inclination, whether my own or another's; I can at most, if my own, approve it; if another's, sometimes even love it; *i.e.*, look on it as favourable to my own interest. It is only what is connected with my will as a principle, by no means as an effect—what does not subserve my inclination, but overpowers it, or at least in case of choice excludes it from its calculation—in other words, simply the law of itself, which can be an object of respect, and hence a command. Now an action done from duty must wholly exclude the influence of inclination, and with it every object of the will, so that nothing remains which can determine the will except objectively the *law*, and subjectively *pure respect* for this practical law, and consequently the maxim that I should follow this law even to the thwarting of all my inclinations.

Thus the moral worth of an action does not lie in the effect expected from it, nor in any principle of action which requires to borrow its motive from this expected effect. For all these effects—agreeableness of one's condition, and even the promotion of the happiness of others—could have been also brought about by other causes, so that for this there would have been no need of the will of a rational being; whereas it is in this alone that the supreme and unconditional good can be found. The pre-eminent good which we call moral can therefore consist in nothing else than *the conception of law* in itself, *which certainly is only possible in a rational being,* in so far as this conception, and not the expected effect, determines the will. This is a good which is already present in the person who acts accordingly, and we have not to wait for it to appear first in the result.

THE SUPREME PRINCIPLE OF MORALITY: THE CATEGORICAL IMPERATIVE

But what sort of law can that be, the conception of which must determine the will, even without paying any regard to the effect expected from it, in order that this will may be called good absolutely and without qualification? As I have deprived the will of every impulse which could arise to it from obedience to any law, there remains nothing but the universal conformity of its actions to law in general, which alone is to serve the will as a principle, *i.e.*, I am never to act otherwise than so *that I could also will that my maxim should become a universal law.* Here, now, it is the simple conformity to law in general, without assuming any particular law applicable to certain actions, that serves the will as its principle, and must so serve it, if duty is not to be a vain delusion and a chimerical notion. The common reason of men in its practical judgments perfectly coincides with this, and always has in view the principle here suggested. Let the question be, for example: May I when in distress make a promise with the intention not to keep it? I readily distinguish here between the two significations which the question may have: Whether it is prudent, or whether it is right, to make a false promise? The former may undoubtedly often be the case. I see clearly indeed that it is not enough to extricate myself from a present difficulty by means of this subterfuge, but it must be well considered whether there may not hereafter spring from this lie much greater inconvenience than that from which I now free myself, and as, with all my supposed *cunning,* the consequences cannot be so easily foreseen but that credit once lost may be much more injurious to me than any mischief which I seek to avoid at present, it should be considered whether it would not be more *prudent* to act herein according to a universal maxim, and to make it a habit to promise nothing except with the intention of keeping it. But it is soon clear to me that such a maxim will still only be based on the fear of consequences. Now it is a wholly different thing to be truthful from duty, and to be so from apprehension of injurious consequences. In the first case, the very notion of the action already implies a law for me; in the second case, I must first look about elsewhere to see what results may be combined with it which would affect myself. For to deviate from the principle of duty is beyond all doubt wicked; but to be unfaithful to my maxim of prudence may often be very advantageous to me, although to abide by it is certainly safer. The shortest way, however, and an unerring one, to discover the answer to this question whether a lying promise is consistent with duty, is to ask myself, Should I be content that my maxim (to extricate myself from difficulty by a false promise) should hold good as a universal law, for myself as well as for others? and should I be able to say to myself, "Every one may make a deceitful promise when he finds himself in a difficulty from which he cannot otherwise extricate himself"? Then I presently become aware that while I can will the lie, I can by no means will that lying should be a universal law. For with such a law there would be no promises at all, since it would be in vain to allege my intention in regard to my future actions to those who would not believe this allegation, or if they over-hastily did so, would pay me back in my own coin. Hence my maxim, as soon as it should be made a universal law, would necessarily destroy itself.

I do not, therefore, need any far-reaching penetration to discern what I have to do in order that my will may be morally good. Inexperienced in the course of the world, incapable of being prepared for all its contingencies, I only ask myself: Canst thou also will that thy maxim should be a universal law? If not, then it must be rejected, and that not because of a disadvantage accruing from myself or even to others, but because it cannot enter as a principle into a possible universal legislation, and reason extorts from me immediate respect for such legislation. I do not indeed as yet *discern* on what this respect is based (this the philosopher may inquire), but at least I understand this, that it is an estimation of the worth which far outweighs all worth of what is recommended by inclination, and that the necessity of acting from *pure* respect for the practical law is what constitutes duty, to which every other motive must give place, because it is the condition of a will being good *in itself*, and the worth of such a will is above everything.

Thus, then, without quitting the moral knowledge of common human reason, we have arrived at its principle. And although, no doubt, common men do not conceive it in such an abstract and universal form, yet they always have it really before their eyes, and use it as the standard of their decision. . . .

Nor could anything be more fatal to morality than that we should wish to derive it from examples. For every example of it that is set before me must be first itself tested by principles of morality, whether it is worthy to serve as an original example, *i.e.*, as a pattern, but by no means can it authoritatively furnish the conception of morality. Even the Holy One of the Gospels must first be compared with our ideal of moral perfection before we can recognize Him as such; and so He says of Himself, "Why call ye Me [whom you see] good; none is good [the model of good] but God only [whom ye do not see]." But whence have we the conception of God as the supreme good? Simply from the *idea* of moral perfection, which reason frames *a priori*, and connects inseparably with the notion of a free will. Imitation finds no place at all in morality, and examples serve only for encouragement, *i.e.*, they put beyond doubt the feasibility of what the law commands, they make visible that which the practical rule expresses more generally, but they can never authorize us to set aside the true original which lies in reason, and to guide ourselves by examples.

From what has been said, it is clear that all moral conceptions have their seat and origin completely *a priori* in the reason, and that, moreover, in the commonest reason just as truly as in that which is in the highest degree speculative; that they cannot be obtained by abstraction from any empirical, and therefore merely contingent knowledge; that it is just this purity of their origin that makes them worthy to serve as our supreme practical principle, and that just in proportion as we add anything empirical, we detract from their genuine influence, and from the absolute value of actions; that it is not only of the greatest necessity, in a purely speculative point of view, but is also of the greatest practical importance, to derive these notions and laws from pure reason, to present them pure and unmixed, and even to determine the compass of this practical or pure rational knowledge, *i.e.* to determine the whole faculty of pure practical reason; and, in doing so, we must not make its principles dependent on the particular nature of human reason, though in speculative philosophy this may be permitted, or may even at times be necessary; but since moral laws ought to hold good for every rational creature, we must derive them from the general concept of a rational being. In this way, although for its *application* to man morality has need of anthropology, yet, in the first instance, we must treat it independently as pure philosophy, *i.e.*, as metaphysic, complete in itself (a thing which in such distinct branches of science is easily done); knowing well that unless we are in possession of this, it would not only be vain to determine the moral element of duty in right actions for purposes of speculative criticism, but it would be impossible to base morals on their genuine principles, even for common practical purposes, especially of moral instruction, so as to produce pure moral dispositions, and to engraft them on men's minds to the promotion of the greatest possible good in the world. . . .

THE RATIONAL GROUND OF THE CATEGORICAL IMPERATIVE

. . . [T]he question, how the imperative of *morality* is possible, is undoubtedly one, the only one, demanding a solution, as this is not at all hypothetical, and the objective necessity which it presents cannot rest on any hypothesis, as is the case with the hypothetical imperatives. Only here we must never leave out of consideration that we *cannot* make out *by any example,* in other words empirically, whether there is such an imperative at all; but it is rather to be feared that all those which seem to be categorical may yet be at bottom hypothetical. For instance, when the precept is: Thou shalt not promise deceitfully; and it is assumed that the necessity of this is not a mere counsel to avoid some other evil, so that it should mean: Thou shalt not make a lying promise, lest if it become known thou shouldst destroy thy credit, but that an action of this kind must be regarded as evil in itself, so that the imperative of the prohibition is categorical; then we cannot show with certainty in any example that the will was determined merely by the law, without any other spring of action, although it may appear to be so. For it is always possible that fear of disgrace, perhaps also obscure dread of other dangers, may have a secret influence on the will. Who can prove by experience the nonexistence of a cause when all that experience tells us is that we do not perceive it? But in such a case the so-called moral imperative, which as such appears to be categorical and unconditional, would in reality be only a pragmatic precept, drawing our attention to our own interests, and merely teaching us to take these into consideration.

We shall therefore have to investigate *a priori* the possibility of a categorical imperative, as we have not in this case the advantage of its reality being given in experience, so that [the elucidation of] its possibility should be requisite only for its explanation, not for its establishment. In the meantime it may be discerned beforehand that the categorical imperative alone has the purport of a practical law: all the rest may indeed be called *principles* of the will but not laws, since whatever is only necessary for the attainment of some arbitrary purpose may be considered as in itself contingent, and we can at any time be free from the precept if we give up the purpose: on the contrary, the unconditional command leaves the will no liberty to choose the opposite; consequently it alone carries with it that necessity which we require in a law.

Secondly, in the case of this categorical imperative or law of morality, the difficulty (of discerning its possibility) is a very profound one. It is an *a priori* synthetical practical proposition; and as there is so much difficulty in discerning the possibility of speculative propositions of this kind, it may readily be supposed that the difficulty will be no less with the practical.

FIRST FORMULATION OF THE CATEGORICAL IMPERATIVE: UNIVERSAL LAW

In this problem we will first inquire whether the mere conception of a categorical imperative may not perhaps supply us also with the formula of it, containing the proposition which alone can be a categorical imperative; for even if we know the tenor of such an absolute command, yet how it is possible will require further special and laborious study, which we postpone to the last section.

When I conceive a hypothetical imperative, in general I do not know beforehand what it will contain until I am given the condition. But when I conceive a categorical imperative, I know at once what it contains. For as the imperative contains besides the law only the necessity that the maxims shall conform to this law, while the law contains no conditions restricting it, there remains nothing but the general statement that the maxim of the action should conform to a universal law, and it is this conformity alone that the imperative properly represents as necessary.

There is therefore but one categorical imperative, namely, this: *Act only on that maxim whereby thou canst at the same time will that it should become a universal law.*

Now if all imperatives of duty can be deduced from this one imperative as from their principle, then, although it should remain undecided whether what is called duty is not merely a vain notion, yet at least we shall be able to show what we understand by it and what this notion means.

Since the universality of the law according to which effects are produced constitutes what is properly called *nature* in the most general sense (as to form), that is the existence of things so far as it is determined by general laws, the imperative of duty may be expressed thus: *Act as if the maxim of thy action were to become by thy will a universal law of nature.*

FOUR ILLUSTRATIONS

We will now enumerate a few duties, adopting the usual division of them into duties to ourselves and to others, and into perfect and imperfect duties.

1. A man reduced to despair by a series of misfortunes feels wearied of life, but is still so far in possession of his reason that he can ask himself whether it would not be contrary to his duty to himself to take his own life. Now he inquires whether the maxim of his action could become a universal law of nature. His maxim is: From self-love I adopt it as a principle to shorten my life when its longer duration is likely to bring more evil than satisfaction. It is asked then simply whether this principle founded on self-love can become a universal law of nature. Now we see at once that a system of nature of which it should be a law to destroy life by means of the very feeling whose special nature it is to impel to the improvement of life would contradict itself, and therefore could not exist as a system of nature; hence that maxim cannot possibly exist as a universal law of nature, and consequently would be wholly inconsistent with the supreme principle of all duty.

2. Another finds himself forced by necessity to borrow money. He knows that he will not be able to repay it, but sees also that nothing will be lent to him, unless he promises stoutly to repay it in a definite time. He desires to make this promise, but he has still so much conscience as to ask himself: Is it not unlawful and inconsistent with duty to get out of a difficulty in this way? Suppose, however, that he resolves to do so, then the maxim of his action would be expressed thus: When I think myself in want of money, I will borrow money and promise to repay it, although I know that I never can do so. Now this principle of self-love or of one's own advantage may perhaps be consistent with my whole future welfare; but the question is, Is it right? I change then the suggestion of self-love into a universal law, and state the question thus: How would it be if my maxim were a universal law? Then I see at once that it could never hold as a universal law of nature, but would necessarily contradict itself. For supposing it to be a universal law that everyone when he thinks himself in a difficulty should be able to promise whatever he pleases, with the purpose of not keeping his promise, the promise itself would become impossible, as well as the end that one might have in view in it, since no one would consider that anything was promised to him, but would ridicule all such statements as vain pretenses.

3. A third finds in himself a talent which with the help of some culture might make him a useful man in many respects. But he finds himself in comfortable circumstances, and prefers to indulge in pleasure rather than to take pains in enlarging and improving his happy natural capacities. He asks, however, whether his maxim of neglect of his natural gifts, besides agreeing with his inclination to indulgence, agrees also with what is called duty. He sees then that a system of nature could indeed subsist with such a universal law although men (like the South Sea islanders) should let their talents rest, and resolve to devote their lives merely to idleness, amusement, and propagation of their species—in a word, to enjoyment; but he cannot possibly *will* that this should be a universal law of nature, or be implanted in us as such by a natural instinct. For, as a rational being, he necessarily wills that his faculties be developed, since they serve him, and have been given him, for all sorts of possible purposes.

4. A fourth, who is in prosperity, while he sees that others have to contend with great wretchedness and that he could help them, thinks: What concern is it of mine? Let everyone be as happy as Heaven pleases, or as he can make himself; I will take nothing from him nor even envy him, only I do not wish to contribute anything to his welfare or to his assistance in distress! Now no doubt if such a mode of thinking were a universal law, the human race might very well subsist, and doubtless even better than in a state in which everyone talks of sympathy and good-will, or even takes care

occasionally to put it into practice, but, on the other side, also cheats when he can, betrays the rights of men, or otherwise violates them. But although it is possible that a universal law of nature might exist in accordance with that maxim, it is impossible to *will* that such a principle should have the universal validity of a law of nature. For a will which resolved this would contradict itself, inasmuch as many cases might occur in which one would have need of the love and sympathy of others, and in which, by such a law of nature, sprung from his own will, he would deprive himself of all hope of the aid he desires.

These are a few of the many actual duties, or at least what we regard as such, which obviously fall into two classes on the one principle that we have laid down. We must be *able to will* that a maxim of our action should be a universal law. This is the canon of the moral appreciation of the action generally. Some actions are of such a character that their maxim cannot without contradiction be even *conceived* as a universal law of nature, far from it being possible that we should *will* that it *should* be so. In others this intrinsic impossibility is not found, but still it is impossible to *will* that their maxim should be raised to the universality of a law of nature, since such a will would contradict itself. It is easily seen that the former violate strict or rigorous (inflexible) duty; the latter only laxer (meritorious) duty. Thus it has been completely shown by these examples how all duties depend as regards the nature of the obligation (not the object of the action) on the same principle.

SECOND FORMULATION OF THE CATEGORICAL IMPERATIVE: HUMANITY AS AN END IN ITSELF

. . . Now I say: man and generally any rational being *exists* as an end in himself, *not merely as a means* to be arbitrarily used by this or that will, but in all his actions, whether they concern himself or other rational beings, must be always regarded at the same time as an end. All objects of the inclinations have only a conditional worth; for if the inclinations and the wants founded on them did not exist, then their object would be without value. But the inclinations themselves being sources of want are so far from having an absolute worth for which they should be desired, that, on the contrary, it must be the universal wish of every rational being to be wholly free from them. Thus the worth of any object which is *to be acquired* by our action is always conditional. Beings whose existence depends not on our will but on nature's, have nevertheless, if they are nonrational beings, only a relative value as means, and are therefore called *things*; rational beings, on the contrary, are called *persons,* because their very nature points them out as ends in themselves, that is as something which must not be used merely as means, and so far therefore restricts freedom of action (and is an object of respect). These, therefore, are not merely subjective ends whose existence has a worth *for us* as an effect of our action, but *objective ends,* that is things whose existence is an end in itself: an end moreover for which no other can be substituted, which they should subserve *merely* as means, for otherwise nothing whatever would possess *absolute worth*; but if all worth were conditioned and therefore contingent, then there would be no supreme practical principle of reason whatever.

If then there is a supreme practical principle or, in respect of the human will, a categorical imperative, it must be one which, being drawn from the conception of that which is necessarily an end for everyone because it is *an end in itself,* constitutes an *objective* principle of will, and can therefore serve as a universal practical law. The foundation of this principle is: *rational nature exists as an end in itself.* Man necessarily conceives his own existence as being so: so far then this is a *subjective* principle of human actions. But every other rational being regards its existence similarly, just on the same rational principle that holds for me: so that it is at the same time an objective principle, from which as a supreme practical law all laws of the will must be capable of being deduced. Accordingly the practical imperative will be as follows: *So act as to treat humanity, whether in thine own person or in that of any other, in every case as an end withal, never as means only. . . .*

. . . Looking back now on all previous attempts to discover the principle of morality, we need not wonder why they all failed. It was seen that man was bound to laws by duty, but it was not observed that the laws to which he is subject are *only those of his own giving,* though at the same time they are *universal,* and that he is only bound to act in conformity with his own will; a will, however, which is designed by nature to give universal laws. For when one has conceived man only as subject to a law (no matter what), then this law required some interest, either by way of attraction or constraint, since it did not originate as a law from *his own* will, but his will was according to a law obliged by *something else* to act in a certain manner. Now by this necessary consequence all the labour spent in finding a supreme principle of *duty* was irrevocably lost. For men never elicited duty, but only a necessity of acting from a certain interest. Whether this interest was private or otherwise, in any case the imperative must be conditional, and could not by any means be capable of being a moral command. I will therefore call this the principle of *Autonomy* of the will, in contrast with every other which I accordingly reckon as *Heteronomy.*

THE KINGDOM OF ENDS

The conception of every rational being as one which must consider itself as giving in all the maxims of its will universal laws, so as to judge itself and its actions from this point of view—this conception leads to another which depends on it and is very fruitful, that of a *kingdom of ends.*

By a *kingdom* I understand the union of different rational beings in a system by common laws. Now since it is by laws that ends are determined as regards their universal validity, hence, if we abstract from the personal differences of rational beings, and likewise from all the content of their private ends, we shall be able to conceive all ends combined in a systematic whole (including both rational beings as ends in themselves, and also the special ends which each may propose to himself), that is to say, we can conceive a kingdom of ends, which on the preceding principles is possible.

For all rational beings come under the *law* that each of them must treat itself and all others *never merely as means,* but in every case *at the same time as ends in themselves.* Hence results a systematic union of rational beings by common objective laws, *i.e.,* a kingdom which may be called a kingdom of ends, since what these laws have in view is just the relation of these beings to one another as ends and means. . . .

For Further Reflection

1. Is Kant's philosophy merely a development of the Golden Rule: "Do unto others what you would have them do unto you"? If it is equivalent, does it make Kant's system more intuitively plausible? But does it also lead to problems with what Kant thought to be the implications of his system? For example, on the basis of the Golden Rule, one might endorse certain instances of euthanasia, but Kant's discussion of suicide seems to rule this out.
2. Kant's ethics is called deontological (from the Greek word for "duty") because Kant believes that the value of an act is in the act itself rather than in its consequences (as teleologists hold). Deontological ethics has been criticized as being too rigid. Do you think that this is true? Should the notion of consequences be taken into consideration?
3. How would Kant deal with moral conflicts? When two universal principles conflict, how would Kant resolve the dilemma?
4. Kant's categorical imperative has also been criticized for being more wide open than he realized, for it doesn't limit what could be universalized. How would Kant respond to these counterexamples? (1) Everyone should tie his right shoe before his left shoe. (2) All retarded or senile people

should be executed by the government (adding, if I should become retarded or senile, I should also undergo this fate).

Kant's Theory

WILLIAM K. FRANKENA

William Frankena (1908–1994) earned an international reputation for his writings on moral theory and the history of ethics, including numerous papers and his much-lauded textbook *Ethics*. For more than four decades he was a highly regarded teacher of philosophy at the University of Michigan. In this selection taken from his famous text, Frankena argues that Kant's categorical imperative has several defects that Kant and his followers have failed to appreciate.

. . . Another example of a monistic kind of rule deontology is presented by Immanuel Kant. We must confine our discussion to what he calls the first form of the categorical imperative, "Act only on that maxim which you can at the same time will to be a universal law." In this dictum, Kant is taking a principle, very similar to those quoted from Sidgwick and Rashdall, and offering it as the necessary and sufficient criterion for determining what more concrete maxims or rules we should live by. We have, in effect, already accepted the principle as *necessary*, the question is whether it is *sufficient*. If so, our search for a normative ethics is ended.

There are problems about the interpretation of Kant, but we may take him as saying, first, that when one acts voluntarily one always acts on a formulizable maxim or rule; second, that one is choosing and judging from the moral point of view if and only if one is or would be willing to universalize one's maxim, that is, if he is or would be willing to see his rule acted on by everyone who is in a situation of a similar kind, even if he himself turns out to be on the receiving end on occasion; and, third, that an action is morally right and/or obligatory if and only if one can consistently will that the maxim or rule involved be acted on by everyone in similar circumstances, and an action is morally wrong if and only if one cannot consistently will this. Here we are concerned primarily with the last contention, though we will also have a word to say about the second. Is Kant's criterion sufficient as well as necessary for determining what is morally right or obligatory?

Let us first take an example of how he applies it. In one of his illustrations he supposes that A makes a promise but is ready to break it if this suits his purposes. A's maxim then may be expressed thus, "When it suits my purposes I will make promises, intending also to break them if this suits my purposes." But A cannot consistently will this maxim to be universally acted on, says Kant.

> . . . could I say to myself that everyone make a false promise when he is in difficulty from which he otherwise cannot escape? I immediately see that I could will the lie but not a universal law to lie. For with such a law [i.e., with such a maxim universally acted on] there would be no promises at all. . . . Thus my maxim would necessarily destroy itself as soon as it was made a universal law.[1]

Kant concludes, therefore, that it is wrong to make deceitful promises. By somewhat similar arguments, he believes he can also show, for example, that it is wrong to commit suicide, that we ought to cultivate our natural gifts or talents, and that we ought to help others who are in trouble.

It is often alleged that Kant is being a utilitarian in these arguments, not a deontologist as he purports to be. This is a mistake. He is not arguing that one must keep one's promises because the results of everyone's breaking them when convenient or advantageous to themselves would be so bad as to be intolerable. This is how a rule-utilitarian would run the argument. Kant, however, is contending that one cannot even will such a maxim to be universally acted on, because in so doing, one would be involved in a contradiction of will; one would be willing both that it be possible to make promises and have them credited (else why make them?) and that everyone be free to break promises to suit his own purposes. In other words, he is arguing, not that the results of everyone's always acting on the deceitful promise maxim are bad, but that the results are self-defeating, since if that maxim were universally acted on, we could not even have the institution of promise making which that maxim presupposes.

It must be admitted that Kant's arguments are not always as convincing as the one against deceitful promising. It must also be pointed out that he is not free from the difficulties due to conflicts between duties; it seems possible, at

[1]Immanuel Kant, *Foundations of the Metaphysic of Morals,* tr. L. W. Beck (New York: The Liberal Arts Press, 1959), p. 19. See selections in Frankena and Granrose, eds., *Introductory Readings in Ethics* (Englewood Cliffs, N.J.: Prentice-Hall, Inc., 1974), Chap. II.

any rate, that keeping a promise might on occasion prevent one from helping someone in trouble. Possibly Kant could argue in this case that it would be right to break the promise and help the person in trouble, since one can will the maxim, "When breaking a promise is required in order to help someone I will break it," to be universally acted on in the situations specified, especially if it is also specified in the maxim that the promise is not crucially important and that the help is. Kant, however, does not take this line, and talks as if he can show that promises ought never to be broken. But this his argument does not suffice to show. As was just indicated, one may be able to will a specific rule that permits promises to be broken in a certain kind of situation to be universally acted on, even though one cannot will a more blanket one to become a universal law.

Thus Kant's arguments, even if good, do not prove as much as he thinks; and in the case just presented, this is just as well, since he thought he could prove too much. Even if we admit that his criterion rules out certain sorts of action as immoral (for example, deceitful promising which does not enable one to help another), must we agree that all of our duties can be established by his test? Take the duty to help others. It is true that if one adopts the maxim of not helping others in need and wills this to be a universal law, he is likely to find himself willing inconsistently to abrogate this rule, since he is likely himself to be in need sometime. Still, it is not hard to imagine a man whose fortune is fairly sure or one who is willing to be consistent and to take the consequences of his maxim's being universally acted on; if there are such people, Kant's test will not suffice to establish benevolence as a duty. Of course, one might conclude that it is not a duty just because it does not pass this test; but this seems a drastic conclusion, and, deontological as he was, even Kant could not draw it.

Is every maxim that does pass Kant's test a duty, as he sometimes seems to think? "When alone in the dark, whistle"—this seems to be a maxim one can will to be a universal law. If not, "Tie your left shoestring first" clearly is. Yet, surely, neither of these rules can be regarded as a duty. One might reply here that such questions about whistling and tying shoestrings are not moral ones, and this is correct, but Kant does not tell us how to determine whether they are moral or not. It might also be argued that Kant was not regarding all maxims one *can* will to be universal laws as *duties,* but only holding that maxims one *cannot* will to be universal laws are *immoral* or *wrong* to act on. That is, Kant meant to say (a) that it is *permissible* to act on a maxim if and only if one can will it to be a universal law, (b) that it is *wrong* to act on a maxim if and only if one cannot will it to be a universal law, and (c) that it is a *duty* to act on a maxim if and only if one cannot will its *opposite* to be a universal law. I am, in fact, inclined to think this is what Kant meant and should have said. But even then his criterion of right and wrong is not sufficient, for it does not actually rule out all immoral maxims, e.g., the maxim of never helping anyone.

In any event, it seems to me that in order for one's maxims to be considered moral duties, it is not enough that one be able consistently to will one's maxims to be universally acted on. Much depends on the point of view from which one wills one's rules to be universally followed. One might do this from the aesthetic point of view or, more probably, from a prudential one. One might, for example, will honesty to be universally practiced because one regards everyone's being honest, including oneself (else one is not universalizing, but making an exception of oneself, which Kant is right in putting out of moral bounds), as being advantageous to oneself. "Everyone's being honest is the best policy from my point of view." If one uses such reasoning, one can hardly claim to be taking the moral point of view. There is more to the moral point of view than being willing to universalize one's rules; Kant and his followers fail to see this fact, although they are right in thinking such a willingness is part of it.

For Further Reflection

1. According to Frankena, what difficulty exists in Kant's theory "due to conflicts between duties"?
2. Why does Frankena suggest that Kant's universalization test may not be enough to establish benevolence as a duty?
3. What does Frankena mean by "There is more to the moral point of view than being willing to universalize one's rules"?
4. Do you agree with Frankena's criticisms of Kant's theory? Explain.

Intuitionism

W. D. ROSS

Sir William D. Ross (1877–1971) was provost of Oriel College, Oxford University. His book *The Right and the Good* (1930), from which the present selection is taken, is a classic treatise in ethical intuitionism. Ross argues against utilitarianism (both hedonistic utilitarianism and Moore's ideal

---

From *The Right and the Good*, 2nd ed. by Ross (2002). 5,000w from "Intuitionism." Introduction and other editorial material © Philip Stratton-Lake 2002. By permission of Oxford University Press.

> utilitarianism), asserting that optimal consequences have nothing to do with moral rightness or wrongness. We have intuitive knowledge of rightness and wrongness in terms of action-guiding principles, such as to keep promises made, to promote justice, to show gratitude for benefits rendered, and to refrain from harming others. Unlike Kant's principles, however, these principles are not absolutes, that is, duties that must never be overridden by more binding moral duties. Moral principles are prima facie duties. That is, while their intrinsic value is not dependent on circumstances, their application is. They can be overridden by other prima facie duties. Essentially, these principles are the outcomes of generations of reflection on our duty, and their holistic schema has been internalized within us, so that ultimately, as Aristotle said, the "decision lies in the perception."

. . . A . . . theory has been put forward by Professor Moore that what makes actions right is that they are productive of more *good* than could have been produced by any other action open to the agent.

This theory is in fact the culmination of all the attempts to base rightness on productivity of some sort of result. The first form this attempt takes is the attempt to base rightness on conduciveness to the advantage or pleasure of the agent. This theory comes to grief over the fact, which stares us in the face, that a great part of duty consists in an observance of the rights and a furtherance of the interests of others, whatever the cost to ourselves may be. Plato and others may be right in holding that a regard for the rights of others never in the long run involves a loss of happiness for the agent, that "the just life profits a man." But this, even if true, is irrelevant to the rightness of the act. As soon as a man does an action *because* he thinks he will promote his own interests thereby, he is acting not from a sense of its rightness but from self-interest.

To the egoistic theory hedonistic utilitarianism supplies a much-needed amendment. It points out correctly that the fact that a certain pleasure will be enjoyed by the agent is no reason why he *ought* to bring it into being, rather than an equal or greater pleasure to be enjoyed by another, though, human nature being what it is, it makes it not unlikely that he *will* try to bring it into being. But hedonistic utilitarianism in its turn needs a correction. On reflection it seems clear that pleasure is not the only thing in life that we think good in itself, that for instance we think the possession of a good character, or an intelligent understanding of the world, as good or better. A great advance is made by the substitution of "productive of the greatest good" for "productive of the greatest pleasure."

Not only is this theory more attractive than hedonistic utilitarianism, but its logical relation to that theory is such that the latter could not be true unless *it* were true, while it might be true though hedonistic utilitarianism were not. It is in fact one of the logical bases of hedonistic utilitarianism. For the view that what produces the maximum pleasure is right has for its bases the views (1) that what produces the maximum good is right, and (2) that pleasure is the only thing good in itself. If they were not assuming that what produces the maximum *good* is right, the utilitarians' attempt to show that pleasure is the only thing good in itself, which is in fact the point they take most pains to establish, would have been quite irrelevant to their attempt to prove that only what produces the maximum *pleasure* is right. If, therefore, it can be shown that productivity of the maximum good is not what makes all right actions right, we shall *a fortiori* have refuted hedonistic utilitarianism.

When a plain man fulfills a promise because he thinks he ought to do so, it seems clear that he does so with no thought of its total consequences, still less with any opinion that these are likely to be the best possible. He thinks in fact much more of the past than of the future. What makes him think it right to act in a certain way is the fact that he has promised to do so—that and, usually, nothing more. That his act will produce the best possible consequences is not his reason for calling it right. What lends colour to the theory we are examining, then, is not the actions (which form probably a great majority of our actions) in which some such reflection as "I have promised" is the only reason we give ourselves for thinking a certain action right, but the exceptional cases in which the consequences of fulfilling a promise (for instance) would be so disastrous to others that we judge it right not to do so. It must of course be admitted that such cases exist. If I have promised to meet a friend at a particular time for some trivial purpose, I should certainly think myself justified in breaking my engagement if by doing so I could prevent a serious accident or bring relief to the victims of one. And the supporters of the view we are examining hold that my thinking so is due to my thinking that I shall bring more good into existence by the one action than by the other. A different account may, however, be given of the matter, an account which will, I believe, show itself to be the true one. It may be said that besides the duty of fulfilling promises, I have and recognize a duty of relieving distress, and that when I think it right to do the latter at the cost of not doing the former, it is not because I think I shall produce more good thereby but because I think it the duty which is in the circumstances more of a duty. This account surely corresponds much more closely with what we really think in such a situation. If, so far as I can see, I could bring equal amounts of good into being by fulfilling my promise and by helping someone to whom I had made no promise, I should not hesitate to regard the former as my duty. Yet on the view that what is right is right because it is productive of the most good I should not so regard it.

There are two theories, each in its way simple, that offer a solution of such cases of conscience. One is the view of Kant, that there are certain duties of perfect obligation, such as those of fulfilling promises, of paying debts, of telling the truth, which admit of no exception whatever in favour of duties of imperfect obligation, such as that of relieving distress. The other is the view of, for instance, Professor Moore and Dr. Rashdall, that there is only the duty of producing good, and that all "conflicts of duties" should be resolved by asking "By which action will most good be produced?" But it is more important that our theory fit the facts than that it be simple, and the account we have given above corresponds (it seems to me) better than either of the simpler theories with what we really think, viz. that normally promise-keeping, for example, should come before benevolence, but that when and only when the good to be produced by the benevolent act is very great and the promise comparatively trivial, the act of benevolence becomes our duty.

In fact the theory of "ideal utilitarianism" if I may for brevity refer so to the theory of Professor Moore, seems to simplify unduly our relations to our fellows. It says, in effect, that the only morally significant relation in which my neighbours stand to me is that of being possible beneficiaries by my action. They do stand in this relation to me, and this relation is morally significant. But they may also stand to me in the relation of promisee to promiser, of creditor to debtor, of wife to husband, of child to parent, of friend to friend, of fellow countryman to fellow countryman, and the like; and each of these relations is the foundation of a *prima facie* duty which is more or less incumbent on me according to the circumstances of the case. When I am in a situation, as perhaps I always am, in which more than one of these *prima facie* duties is incumbent on me, what I have to do is to study the situation as fully as I can until I form the considered opinion (it is never more) that in the circumstances one of them is more incumbent than any other; then I am bound to think that to do this *prima facie* duty is my duty *sans phrase* in the situation.

I suggest "*prima facie* duty" or "conditional duty" as a brief way of referring to the characteristic (quite distinct from that of being a duty proper) which an act has, in virtue of being of a certain kind (e.g., the keeping of a promise), of being an act which would be a duty proper if it were not at the same time of another kind which is morally significant. Whether an act is a duty proper or actual duty depends on *all* the morally significant kinds it is an instance of. The phrase "*prima facie* duty" must be apologized for, since (1) it suggests that what we are speaking of is a certain kind of duty, whereas it is in fact not a duty but something related in a special way to duty. Strictly speaking, we want not a phrase in which duty is qualified by an adjective, but a separate noun. (2) *"Prima" facie* suggests that one is speaking only of an appearance which a moral situation presents at first sight, and which may turn out to be illusory; whereas what I am speaking of is an objective fact involved in the nature of the situation, or more strictly in an element of its nature, though not, as duty proper does, arising from its *whole* nature. I can, however, think of no term which fully meets the case. "Claim" has been suggested by Professor Prichard. The word "claim" has the advantage of being quite a familiar one in this connexion, and it seems to cover much of the ground. It would be quite natural to say, "a person to whom I have made a promise has a claim on me," and also, "a person whose distress I could relieve (at the cost of breaking the promise) has a claim on me." But (1) while "claim" is appropriate from *their* point of view, we want a word to express the corresponding fact from the agent's point of view—the fact of his being subject to claims that can be made against him; and ordinary language provides us with no such correlative to "claim." And (2) (what is more important) "claim" seems inevitably to suggest two persons, one of whom might make a claim on the other; and while this covers the ground of social duty, it is inappropriate in the case of that important part of duty which is the duty of cultivating a certain kind of character in oneself. It would be artificial, I think, and at any rate metaphorical, to say that one's character has a claim on oneself.

There is nothing arbitrary about these *prima facie* duties. Each rests on a definite circumstance which cannot seriously be held to be without moral significance. Of *prima facie* duties I suggest, without claiming completeness or finality for it, the following division.

(1) Some duties rest on previous acts of my own. These duties seem to include two kinds, (*a*) those resting on a promise or what may fairly be called an implicit promise, such as the implicit undertaking not to tell lies which seems to be implied in the act of entering into conversation (at any rate by civilized men), or of writing books that purport to be history and not fiction. These may be called the duties of fidelity. (*b*) Those resting on a previous wrongful act. These may be called the duties of reparation. (2) Some rest on previous acts of other men, i.e., services done by them to me. These may be loosely described as the duties of gratitude. (3) Some rest on the fact or possibility of a distribution of pleasure or happiness (or of the means thereto) which is not in accordance with the merit of the persons concerned; in such cases there arises a duty to upset or prevent such a distribution. These are the duties of justice. (4) Some rest on the mere fact that there are other beings in the world whose condition we can make better in respect of virtue, or of intelligence, or of pleasure. These are the duties of beneficence. (5) Some rest on the fact that we can improve our own condition in respect of virtue

or of intelligence. These are the duties of self-improvement. (6) I think that we should distinguish from (4) the duties that may be summed up under the title of "not injuring others." No doubt to injure others is incidentally to fail to do them good; but it seems to me clear that non-maleficence is apprehended as a duty distinct from that of beneficence, and as a duty of a more stringent character. It will be noticed that this alone among the types of duty has been stated in a negative way. An attempt might no doubt be made to state this duty, like the others, in a positive way. It might be said that it is really the duty to prevent ourselves from acting either from an inclination to harm others or from an inclination to seek our own pleasure, in doing which we should incidentally harm them. But on reflection it seems clear that the primary duty here is the duty not to harm others, this being a duty whether or not we have an inclination that if followed would lead to our harming them; and that when we have such an inclination the primary duty not to harm others gives rise to a consequential duty to resist the inclination. The recognition of this duty of non-maleficence is the first step on the way to the recognition of the duty of beneficence; and that accounts for the prominence of the commands "thou shalt not kill," "thou shalt not commit adultery," "thou shalt not steal," "thou shalt not bear false witness," in so early a code as the Decalogue. But even when we have come to recognize the duty of beneficence, it appears to me that the duty of non-maleficence is recognized as a distinct one, and as *prima facie* more binding. We should not in general consider it justifiable to kill one person in order to keep another alive, or to steal from one in order to give alms to another.

The essential defect of the "ideal utilitarian" theory is that it ignores, or at least does not do full justice to, the highly personal character of duty. If the only duty is to produce the maximum of good, the question who is to have the good—whether it is myself, or my benefactor, or a person to whom I have made a promise to confer that good on him, or a mere fellow man to whom I stand in no such special relation—should make no difference to my having a duty to produce that good. But we are all in fact sure that it makes a vast difference.

One or two other comments must be made on this provisional list of the divisions of duty. (1) The nomenclature is not strictly correct. For by "fidelity" or "gratitude" we mean, strictly, certain states of motivation; and, as I have urged, it is not our duty to have certain motives, but to do certain acts. By "fidelity," for instance, is meant, strictly, the disposition to fulfil promises and implicit promises *because we have made them*. We have no general word to cover the actual fulfilment of promises and implicit promises *irrespective of motive*; and I use "fidelity," loosely but perhaps conveniently, to fill this gap. So too I use "gratitude" for the returning of services, irrespective of motive.

The term "justice" is not so much confined, in ordinary usage, to a certain state of motivation, for we should often talk of a man as acting justly even when we did not think his motive was the wish to do what was just simply for the sake of doing so. Less apology is therefore needed for our use of "justice" in this sense. And I have used the word "beneficence" rather than "benevolence," in order to emphasize the fact that it is our duty to do certain things, and not to do them from certain motives.

(2) If the objection be made that this catalogue of the main types of duty is an unsystematic one resting on no logical principle, it may be replied, first, that it makes no claim to being ultimate. It is a *prima facie* classification of the duties which reflection on our moral convictions seems actually to reveal. And if these convictions are, as I would claim that they are, of the nature of knowledge, and if I have not misstated them, the list will be a list of authentic conditional duties, correct as far as it goes though not necessarily complete. The list of *goods* put forward by the rival theory is reached by exactly the same method—the only sound one in the circumstances—viz. that of direct reflection on what we really think. Loyalty to the facts is worth more than a symmetrical architectonic or a hastily reached simplicity. If further reflection discovers a perfect logical basis for this or for a better classification, so much the better.

(3) It may, again, be objected that our theory that there are these various and often conflicting types of *prima facie* duty leaves us with no principle upon which to discern what is our actual duty in particular circumstances. But this objection is not one which the rival theory is in a position to bring forward. For when we have to choose between the production of two heterogeneous goods, say knowledge and pleasure, the "ideal utilitarian" theory can only fall back on an opinion, for which no logical basis can be offered, that one of the goods is the greater; and this is no better than a similar opinion that one of two duties is the more urgent. And again, when we consider the infinite variety of the effects of our actions in a way of pleasure, it must surely be admitted that the claim which *hedonism* sometimes makes, that it offers a readily applicable criterion of right conduct, is quite illusory.

I am unwilling, however, to content myself with an *argumentum ad hominem*, and I would contend that in principle there is no reason to anticipate that every act that is our duty is so for one and the same reason. Why should two sets of circumstances, or one set of circumstances, *not* possess different characteristics, any one of which makes a certain act our *prima facie* duty? When I ask what it is that makes me in certain cases sure that I have a *prima facie* duty to do so and so, I find that it lies in the fact that I have made a promise; when I ask the same question in another case, I find the answer lies in the fact that I have done a wrong. And if on reflection I find (as I think I do) that neither of these reasons is reducible to the other, I must not on any *a priori* ground assume that such a reduction is possible.

It is necessary to say something by way of clearing up the relation between *prima facie* duties and the actual or absolute duty to do one particular act in particular circumstances. If, as almost all moralists except Kant are agreed and as most plain men think, it is sometimes right to tell a lie or to break a promise, it must be maintained that there is a difference between *prima facie* duty and actual or absolute duty. When we think ourselves justified in breaking, and indeed morally obliged to break, a promise in order to relieve someone's distress, we do not for a moment cease to recognize a *prima facie* duty to keep our promise, and this leads us to feel, not indeed shame or repentance, but certainly compunction, for behaving as we do; we recognize, further, that it is our duty to make up somehow to the promisee for the breaking of the promise. We have to distinguish from the characteristic of being our duty that of tending to be our duty. Any act that we do contains various elements in virtue of which it falls under various categories. In virtue of being the breaking of a promise, for instance, it tends to be wrong; in virtue of being an instance of relieving distress it tends to be right. Tendency to be one's duty may be called a parti-resultant attribute, i.e., one which belongs to an act in virtue of some one component in its nature. *Being* one's duty is a toti-resultant attribute, one which belongs to an act in virtue of its whole nature and of nothing less than this.

Something should be said of the relation between our apprehension of the *prima facie* rightness of certain types of acts and our mental attitude toward particular acts. It is proper to use the word "apprehension" in the former case and not in the latter. That an act, *qua* fulfilling a promise, or *qua* effecting a just distribution of good, or *qua* returning services rendered, or *qua* promoting the good of others, or *qua* promoting the virtue or insight of the agent, is *prima facie* right, is self-evident; not in the sense that it is evident from the beginning of our lives, or as soon as we attend to the proposition for the first time, but in the sense that when we have reached sufficient mental maturity and have given sufficient attention to the proposition it is evident without any need of proof, or of evidence beyond itself. It is self-evident, just as a mathematical axiom, or the validity of a form of inference, is evident. The moral order expressed in these propositions is just as much part of the fundamental nature of the universe (and, we may add, of any possible universe in which there were moral agents at all) as is the spatial or numerical structure expressed in the axioms of geometry or arithmetic. In our confidence that these propositions are true there is involved the same trust in our reason that is involved in our confidence in mathematics; and we should have no justification for trusting it in the latter sphere and distrusting it in the former. In both cases we are dealing with propositions that cannot be proved, but that just as certainly need no proof.

Supposing it to be agreed, as I think on reflection it must, that no one *means* by "right" just "productive of the best possible consequences," or "optimific," the attributes "right" and "optimific" might stand in either of two kinds of relation to each other. (1) They might be so related that we could apprehend *a priori,* either immediately or deductively, that any act that is optimific is right and any act that is right is optimific, as we can apprehend that any triangle that is equilateral is equiangular and *vice versa.* Professor Moore's view is, I think, that the coextensiveness of "right" and "optimific" is apprehended immediately. He rejects the possibility of any proof of it. Or (2) the two attributes might be such that the question whether they are invariably connected had to be answered by means of an inductive inquiry. Now at first sight it might seem as if the constant connexion of the two attributes could be immediately apprehended. It might seem absurd to suggest that it could be right for anyone to do an act which would produce consequences less good than those which would be produced by some other act in his power. Yet a little thought will convince us that this is not absurd. The type of case in which it is easiest to see that this is so is, perhaps, that in which one has made a promise. In such a case we all think that *prima facie* it is our duty to fulfil the promise irrespective of the precise goodness of the total consequences. And though we do not think it is necessarily our actual or absolute duty to do so, we are far from thinking that any, even the slightest, gain in the value of the total consequences will necessarily justify us in doing something else instead. Suppose, to simplify the case by abstraction, that the fulfilment of a promise to *A* would produce 1,000 units of good for him, but that by doing some other act I could produce 1,001 units of good for *B,* to whom I have made no promise, the other consequences of the two acts being of equal value; should we really think it self-evident that it was our duty to do the second act and not the first? I think not. We should, I fancy, hold that only a much greater disparity of value between the total consequences would justify us in failing to discharge our *prima facie* duty to *A.* After all, a promise is a promise, and is not to be treated so lightly as the theory we are examining would imply. What, exactly, a promise is, is not so easy to determine, but we are surely agreed that it constitutes a serious moral limitation to our freedom of action. To produce the 1,001 units of good for *B* rather than fulfil our promise to *A* would be to take, not perhaps our duty as philanthropists too seriously, but certainly our duty as makers of promises too lightly.

Or consider another phase of the same problem. If I have promised to confer on *A* a particular benefit containing 1,000 units of good, is it self-evident that if by doing some different act I could produce 1,001 units of good for *A* himself (the other consequences of the two acts being supposed equal in value), it would be right for me to do so? Again, I think not. Apart from my general *prima facie* duty to do *A* what goal I can, I have another *prima facie* duty to do him the particular service I have promised to do him, and this is not to be set aside in consequence of a disparity of good of the order of 1,001 to 1,000, though a much greater disparity might justify me in so doing.

Or again, suppose that *A* is a very good and *B* a very bad man, should I then, even when I have made no promise, think it self-evidently right to produce 1,001 units of good for *B* rather than 1,000 for *A*? Surely not. I should be sensible of a *prima facie* duty of justice, i.e. of producing a distribution of goods in proportion to merit, which is not outweighed by such a slight disparity in the total goods to be produced.

Such instances—and they might easily be added to—make it clear that there is no self-evident connexion between the attributes "right" and "optimific." The theory we are examining has a certain attractiveness when applied to our decision that a particular act is our duty (though I have tried to show that it does not agree with our actual moral judgements even here). But it is not even plausible when applied to our recognition of *prima facie* duty. For if it were self-evident that the right coincides with the optimific, it should be self-evident that what is *prima facie* right is *prima facie* optimific. But whereas we are certain that keeping a promise is *prima facie* right, we are not certain that it is *prima facie* optimific (though we are perhaps certain that it is *prima facie* bonific). Our certainty that it is *prima facie* right depends not on its consequences but on its being the fulfilment of a promise. The theory we are examining involves too much difference between the evident ground of our conviction about *prima facie* duty and the alleged ground of our conviction about actual duty.

The coextensiveness of the right and the optimific is, then, not self-evident. And I can see no way of proving it deductively; nor, so far as I know, has anyone tried to do so. There remains the question whether it can be established inductively. Such an inquiry, to be conclusive, would have to be very thorough and extensive. We should have to take a large variety of the acts which we, to the best of our ability, judge to be right. We should have to trace as far as possible their consequences, not only for the persons directly affected but also for those indirectly affected, and to these no limit can be set. To make our inquiry thoroughly conclusive, we should have to do what we cannot do, viz. trace these consequences into an unending future. And even to make it reasonably conclusive, we should have to trace them far into the future. It is clear that the most we could possibly say is that a large variety of typical acts that are judged right appear, so far as we can trace their consequences, to produce more good than any other acts possible to the agents in the circumstances. And such a result falls far short of proving the constant connexion of the two attributes. But it is surely clear that no inductive inquiry justifying even this result has ever been carried through. The advocates of utilitarian systems have been so much persuaded either of the identity or of the self-evident connexion of the attributes "right" and "optimific" (or "felicific") that they have not attempted even such an inductive inquiry as is possible. And in view of the enormous complexity of the task and the inevitable inconclusiveness of the result, it is worth no one's while to make the attempt. What, after all, would be gained by it? If, as I have tried to show, for an act to be right and to be optimific are not the same thing, and an act's being optimific is not even the ground of its being right, then if we could ask ourselves (though the question is really unmeaning) which we ought to do, right acts because they are right or optimific acts because they are optimific, our answer must be "the former." If they are optimific as well as right, that is interesting but not morally important; if not, we still ought to do them (which is only another way of saying that they *are* the right acts), and the question whether they are optimific has no importance for moral theory.

There is one direction in which a fairly serious attempt has been made to show the connexion of the attributes "right" and "optimific." One of the most evident facts of our moral consciousness is the sense which we have of the sanctity of promises, a sense which does not, on the face of it, involve the thought that one will be bringing more good into existence by fulfilling the promise than by breaking it. It is plain, I think, that in our normal thought we consider that the fact that we have made a promise is in itself sufficient to create a duty of keeping it, the sense of duty resting on remembrance of the past promise and not on thoughts of the future consequences of its fulfilment. Utilitarianism tries to show that this is not so, that the sanctity of promises rests on the good consequences of the fulfilment of them and the bad consequences of their nonfulfilment. It does so in this way: it points out that when you break a promise you not only fail to confer a certain advantage on your promisee but you diminish his confidence, and indirectly the confidence of others, in the fulfilment of promises. You thus strike a blow at one of the devices that have been found most useful in the relations between man and man—the device on which, for example, the whole system of commercial credit rests—and you tend to bring about a state of things wherein each man, being entirely unable to rely on the keeping of promises by others, will have to do everything for himself, to the enormous impoverishment of human well-being.

To put the matter otherwise, utilitarians say that when a promise ought to be kept it is because the total good to be produced by keeping it is greater than the total good to be produced by breaking it, the former including as its main element the maintenance and strengthening of general mutual confidence, and the latter being greatly diminished by a weakening of this confidence. They say, in fact, that the case I put some pages back never arises—the case in which by fulfilling a promise I shall bring into being 1,000 units of good for my promisee, and by breaking it 1,001 units of good for someone else, the other effects of the two acts being of equal value. The other effects, they say, never are of equal value. By keeping my promise I am helping to strengthen the system of mutual confidence; by breaking it I am helping to weaken this; so that really the first act produces $1{,}000 + x$ units of good, and the second $1{,}001 - y$ units, and the difference between $+x$ and $-y$ is enough to outweigh the slight superiority in the immediate effects of the second act. In answer to this it may be pointed out that there must be *some* amount of good that exceeds the difference between $+x$ and $-y$ (i.e. exceeds $x + y$); say, $x + y + z$. Let us suppose the *immediate* good effects of the second act to be assessed not at 1,001 but at $1{,}000 + x + y + z$. Then its *net* good effects are $1{,}000 + x + z$, i.e. greater than those of the fulfilment of the promise; and the utilitarian is bound to say forthwith that the promise should be broken. Now, we may ask whether that is really the way we think about promises. Do we really think that the production of the slightest balance of good, no matter who will enjoy it, by the breach of a promise frees us from the obligation to keep our promise? We need not doubt that a system by which promises are made and kept is one that has great advantages for the general well-being. But that is not the whole truth. To make a promise is not merely to adapt an ingenious device for promoting the general well-being; it is to put oneself in a new relation to one person in particular, a relation which creates a specifically new *prima facie* duty to him, not reducible to the duty of promoting the general well-being of society. By all means let us try to foresee the net good effects of keeping one's promise and the net good effects of breaking it, but even if we assess the first at $1{,}000 + x$ and the second at $1{,}000 + x + z$, the question still remains whether it is not our duty to fulfil the promise. It may be suspected, too, that the effect of a single keeping or breaking of a promise in strengthening or weakening the fabric of mutual confidence is greatly exaggerated by the theory we are examining. And if we suppose two men dying together alone, do we think that the duty of one to fulfil before he dies a promise he has made to the other would be extinguished by the fact that neither act would have any effect on the general confidence? Anyone who holds this may be suspected of not having reflected on what a promise is.

I conclude that the attributes "right" and "optimific" are not identical, and that we do not know either by intuition, by deduction, or by induction that they coincide in their application, still less that the latter is the foundation of the former. It must be added, however, that if we are ever under no special obligation such as that of fidelity to a promisee or of gratitude to a benefactor, we ought to do what will produce most good; and that even when we are under a special obligation the tendency of acts to promote general good is one of the main factors in determining whether they are right.

In what has preceded, a good deal of use has been made of "what we really think" about moral questions; a certain theory has been rejected because it does not agree with what we really think. It might be said that this is in principle wrong; that we should not be content to expound what our present moral consciousness tells us but should aim at a criticism of our existing moral consciousness in the light of theory. Now I do not doubt that the moral consciousness of men has in detail undergone a good deal of modification as regards the things we think right, at the hands of moral theory. But if we are told, for instance, that we should give up our view that there is a special obligatoriness attaching to the keeping of promises because it is self-evident that the only duty is to produce as much good as possible, we have to ask ourselves whether we really, when we reflect, *are* convinced that this is self-evident, and whether we really *can* get rid of our view that promise-keeping has a bindingness independent of productiveness of maximum good. In my own experience I find that I cannot, in spite of a very genuine attempt to do so; and I venture to think that most people will find the same, and that just because they cannot lose the sense of special obligation, they cannot accept as self-evident, or even as true, the theory which would require them to do so. In fact it seems, on reflection, self-evident that a promise, simply as such, is something that *prima facie* ought to be kept, and it does *not,* on reflection, seem self-evident that production of maximum good is the only thing that makes an act obligatory. And to ask us to give up at the bidding of a theory our actual apprehension of what is right and what is wrong seems like asking people to repudiate their actual experience of beauty, at the bidding of a theory which says "only that which satisfies such and such conditions can be beautiful." If what I have called our actual apprehension is (as I would maintain that it is) truly an apprehension, i.e. an instance of knowledge, the request is nothing less than absurd.

I would maintain, in fact, that what we are apt to describe as "what we think" about moral questions contains a considerable amount that we do not think but know, and that this forms the standard by reference to which the truth of any moral theory has to be tested, instead of having itself to be tested by reference to any theory. I hope that I have in what precedes indicated what in my view these elements of knowledge are that are involved in our ordinary moral consciousness.

It would be a mistake to found a natural science on "what we really think," i.e., on what reasonably thoughtful and well-educated people think about the subjects of the science before they have studied them scientifically. For such opinions are interpretations, and often misinterpretations, of sense-experience; and the man of science must appeal from these to sense-experience itself, which furnishes his real data. In ethics no such appeal is possible. We have no more direct way of access to the facts about rightness and goodness and about what things are right or good, than by thinking about them; the moral convictions of thoughtful and well-educated people are the data of ethics just as sense-perceptions are the data of a natural science. Just as some of the latter have to be rejected as illusory, so have some of the former; but as the latter are rejected only when they are in conflict with other more accurate sense-perceptions, the former are rejected only when they are in conflict with other convictions which stand better the test of reflection. The existing body of moral convictions of the best people is the cumulative product of the moral reflection of many generations, which has developed an extremely delicate power of appreciation of moral distinctions; and this the theorist cannot afford to treat with anything other than the greatest respect. The verdicts of the moral consciousness of the best people are the foundation on which he must build; though he must first compare them with one another and eliminate any contradictions they may contain.

For Further Reflection

1. What is Ross's argument against all types of utilitarianism?
2. Ross is both an intuitionist and a pluralist. He thinks we can acquire knowledge of the correct moral principles by consulting our deepest intuitions, and he thinks that by so doing, we will discover a plurality of principles that are not reducible to a single principle, as utilitarians claim. First of all, do you agree with Ross that we can discover the true principles by consulting our intuitions? And second, do you agree that the principles are, in the last analysis, irreducible to one overarching principle? What are the objections to these positions? Suppose you and I consult our intuitions and come to different conclusions. How can we adjudicate the conflict?
3. What does Ross mean by *prima facie* duty? How does this notion separate his theory from Kant's?

A Horseman in the Sky

AMBROSE BIERCE

Ambrose Bierce (1842–1914?) was a journalist who fought in the Civil War. He was famous for his sardonically humorous essays, including *The Devil's Dictionary* (1906). He disappeared into Mexico in 1913 and was presumed dead shortly thereafter.

In this Civil War story, Carter Druse, a young Virginian, decides to join the Union Army. He announces this decision to his father, who, though disappointed, instructs him to do what he conceives to be his duty, whatever happens. The story begins with Carter asleep at his post.

I

One sunny afternoon in the autumn of the year 1861 a soldier lay in a clump of laurel by the side of a road in western Virginia. He lay at full length upon his stomach, his feet resting upon the toes, his head upon the left forearm. His extended right hand loosely grasped his rifle. But for the somewhat methodical disposition of his limbs and a slight rhythmic movement of the cartridge-box at the back of his belt he might have been thought to be dead. He was asleep at his post of duty. But if detected he would be dead shortly afterward, death being the just and legal penalty of his crime.

The clump of laurel in which the criminal lay was in the angle of a road which after ascending southward a steep acclivity to that point turned sharply to the west, running along the summit for perhaps one hundred yards. There it turned southward again and went zigzagging downward through the forest. At the salient of that second angle was a large flat rock, jutting out northward, overlooking the deep valley from which the road ascended. The rock capped a high cliff; a stone dropped from its outer edge would have fallen sheer downward one thousand feet to the tops of the pines. The angle where the soldier lay was on another spur of the same cliff. Had he been awake he would have commanded a view, not only of the short arm of the road and the jutting rock, but of the entire profile of the cliff below it. It might well have made him giddy to look.

The country was wooded everywhere except at the bottom of the valley to the northward, where there was a small natural meadow, through which flowed a stream scarcely visible from the valley's rim. This open ground looked hardly larger than an ordinary door-yard, but was really several acres in extent. Its green was more vivid than that of the inclosing forest. Away

---

Reprinted from Ambrose Bierce, *Civil War Stories.*

beyond it rose a line of giant cliffs similar to those upon which we are supposed to stand in our survey of the savage scene, and through which the road had somehow made its climb to the summit. The configuration of the valley, indeed, was such that from this point of observation it seemed entirely shut in, and one could but have wondered how the road which found a way out of it had found a way into it, and whence came and whither went the waters of the stream that parted the meadow more than a thousand feet below.

No country is so wild and difficult but men will make it a theatre of war; concealed in the forest at the bottom of that military rat-trap, in which half a hundred men in possession of the exits might have starved an army to submission, lay five regiments of Federal infantry. They had marched all the previous day and night and were resting. At nightfall they would take to the road again, climb to the place where their unfaithful sentinel now slept, and descending the other slope of the ridge fall upon a camp of the enemy at about midnight. Their hope was to surprise it, for the road led to the rear of it. In case of failure, their position would be perilous in the extreme; and fail they surely would should accident or vigilance apprise the enemy of the movement.

II

The sleeping sentinel in the clump of laurel was a young Virginian named Carter Druse. He was the son of wealthy parents, an only child, and had known such ease and cultivation and high living as wealth and taste were able to command in the mountain country of western Virginia. His home was but a few miles from where he now lay. One morning he had risen from the breakfast-table and said, quietly but gravely: "Father, a Union regiment has arrived at Grafton. I am going to join it."

The father lifted his leonine head, looked at the son a moment in silence, and replied: "Well, go, sir, and whatever may occur do what you conceive to be your duty. Virginia, to which you are a traitor, must get on without you. Should we both live to the end of the war, we will speak further of the matter. Your mother, as the physician has informed you, is in a most critical condition; at the best she cannot be with us longer than a few weeks, but that time is precious. It would be better not to disturb her."

So Carter Druse, bowing reverently to his father, who returned the salute with a stately courtesy that masked a breaking heart, left the home of his childhood to go soldiering. By conscience and courage, by deeds of devotion and daring, he soon commended himself to his fellows and his officers; and it was to these qualities and to some knowledge of the country that he owed his selection for his present perilous duty at the extreme outpost. Nevertheless, fatigue had been stronger than resolution and he had fallen asleep. What good or bad angel came in a dream to rouse him from his state of crime, who shall say? Without a movement, without a sound, in the profound silence and the languor of the late afternoon, some invisible messenger of fate touched with unsealing finger the eyes of his consciousness—whispered into the ear of his spirit the mysterious awakening word which no human lips ever have spoken, no human memory ever has recalled. He quietly raised his forehead from his arm and looked between the masking stems of the laurels, instinctively closing his right hand about the stock of his rifle.

His first feeling was a keen artistic delight. On a colossal pedestal, the cliff—motionless at the extreme edge of the capping rock and sharply outlined against the sky—was an equestrian statue of impressive dignity. The figure of the man sat on the figure of the horse, straight and soldierly, but with the repose of a Grecian god carved in the marble which limits the suggestion of activity. The gray costume harmonized with its aërial background; the metal of accoutrement and caparison was softened and subdued by the shadow; the animal's skin had no points of high light. A carbine strikingly foreshortened lay across the pommel of the saddle, kept in place by the right hand grasping it at the "grip"; the left hand, holding the bridle rein, was invisible. In silhouette against the sky the profile of the horse was cut with the sharpness of a cameo; it looked across the heights of air to the confronting cliffs beyond. The face of the rider, turned slightly away, showed only an outline of temple and beard; he was looking downward to the bottom of the valley. Magnified by its lift against the sky and by the soldier's testifying sense of the formidableness of a near enemy the group appeared of heroic, almost colossal, size.

For an instant Druse had a strange, half-defined feeling that he had slept to the end of the war and was looking upon a noble work of art reared upon that eminence to commemorate the deeds of an heroic past of which he had been an inglorious part. The feeling was dispelled by a slight movement of the group: the horse, without moving its feet, had drawn its body slightly backward from the verge; the man remained immobile as before. Broad awake and keenly alive to the significance of the situation, Druse now brought the butt of his rifle against his cheek by cautiously pushing the barrel forward through the bushes, cocked the piece, and glancing through the sights covered a vital spot of the horseman's breast. A touch upon the trigger and all would have been well with Carter Druse. At that instant the horseman turned his head and looked in the direction of his concealed foeman—seemed to look into his very face, into his eyes, into his brave, compassionate heart.

Is it then so terrible to kill an enemy in war—an enemy who has surprised a secret vital to the safety of one's self and comrades—an enemy more formidable for his knowledge than all his army for its numbers? Carter Druse grew pale; he shook in every limb, turned faint, and saw the statuesque group before him as black figures, rising, falling, moving unsteadily in arcs of circles in a fiery sky. His hand fell away from his weapon, his head slowly dropped until his face rested on the leaves in which he lay. This courageous gentleman and hardy soldier was near swooning from intensity of emotion.

It was not for long; in another moment his face was raised from earth, his hands resumed their places on the rifle, his forefinger sought the trigger; mind, heart, and eyes were clear, conscience and reason sound. He could not hope to capture that enemy; to alarm him would but send him dashing to his camp with his fatal news. The duty of the soldier was plain: the man must be shot dead from ambush—without warning, without a moment's spiritual preparation, with never so much as an unspoken prayer, he must be sent to his account. But no—there is a hope; he may have discovered nothing—perhaps he is but admiring the sublimity of the landscape. If permitted, he may turn and ride carelessly away in the direction whence he came. Surely it will be possible to judge at the instant of his withdrawing whether he knows. It may well be that his fixity of attention—Druse turned his head and looked through the deeps of air downward, as from the surface to the bottom of a translucent sea. He saw creeping across the green meadow a sinuous line of figures of men and horses—some foolish commander was permitting the soldiers of his escort to water their beasts in the open, in plain view from a dozen summits!

Druse withdrew his eyes from the valley and fixed them again upon the group of man and horse in the sky, and again it was through the sights of his rifle. But this time his aim was at the horse. In his memory, as if they were a divine mandate, rang the words of his father at their parting: "Whatever may occur, do what you conceive to be your duty." He was calm now. His teeth were firmly but not rigidly closed; his nerves were as tranquil as a sleeping babe's—not a tremor affected any muscle of his body; his breathing, until suspended in the act of taking aim, was regular and slow. Duty had conquered; the spirit had said to the body: "Peace, be still." He fired.

III

An officer of the Federal force, who in a spirit of adventure or in quest of knowledge had left the hidden *bivouac* in the valley, and with aimless feet had made his way to the lower edge of a small open space near the foot of the cliff, was considering what he had to gain by pushing his exploration further. At a distance of a quarter-mile before him, but apparently at a stone's throw, rose from its fringe of pines the gigantic face of rock, towering to so great a height above him that it made him giddy to look up to where its edge cut a sharp, rugged line against the sky. It presented a clean, vertical profile against a background of blue sky to a point half the way down, and of distant hills, hardly less blue, thence to the tops of the trees at its base. Lifting his eyes to the dizzy altitude of its summit the officer saw an astonishing sight—a man on horseback riding down into the valley through the air!

Straight upright sat the rider, in military fashion, with a firm seat in the saddle, a strong clutch upon the rein to hold his charger from too impetuous a plunge. From his bare head his long hair streamed upward, waving like a plume. His hands were concealed in the cloud of the horse's lifted mane. The animal's body was as level as if every hoofstroke encountered the resistant earth. Its motions were those of a wild gallop, but even as the officer looked they ceased, with all the legs thrown sharply forward as in the act of alighting from a leap. But this was a flight!

Filled with amazement and terror by this apparition of a horseman in the sky—half believing himself the chosen scribe of some new Apocalypse, the officer was overcome by the intensity of his emotions; his legs failed him and he fell. Almost the same instant he heard a crashing sound in the trees—a sound that died without an echo—and all was still.

The officer rose to his feet, trembling. The familiar sensation of an abraded shin recalled his dazed faculties. Pulling himself together he ran rapidly obliquely away from the cliff to a point distant from its foot; thereabout he expected to find his man; and thereabout he naturally failed. In the fleeting instant of his vision his imagination had been so wrought upon by the apparent grace and ease and intention of the marvelous performance that it did not occur to him that the line of march of aërial cavalry is directly downward, and that he could find the objects of his search at the very foot of the cliff. A half-hour later he returned to camp.

This officer was a wise man; he knew better than to tell an incredible truth. He said nothing of what he had seen. But when the commander asked him if in his scout he had learned anything of advantage to the expedition he answered:

"Yes, sir; there is no road leading down into this valley from the southward."

The commander, knowing better, smiled.

IV

After firing his shot, Private Carter Druse reloaded his rifle and resumed his watch. Ten minutes had hardly passed when a Federal sergeant crept cautiously to him on hands and knees. Druse neither turned his head nor looked at him, but lay without motion or sign of recognition.

"Did you fire?" the sergeant whispered.

"Yes."

"At what?"

"A horse. It was standing on yonder rock—pretty far out. You see it is no longer there. It went over the cliff."

The man's face was white, but he showed no other sign of emotion. Having answered, he turned away his eyes and said no more. The sergeant did not understand.

"See here, Druse," he said, after a moment's silence, "it's no use making a mystery. I order you to report. Was there anybody on the horse?"

"Yes."

"Well?"

"My father."

The sergeant rose to his feet and walked away. "Good God!" he said.

For Further Reflection

1. What was Carter Druse's duty in this situation? Was it different from what he thought it to be? What should he have done? What would you have done?
2. How does this story bear upon deontological ethics? How would a Kantian evaluate Carter Druse's action?
3. What would a utilitarian have done in these circumstances?

The Evil of Lying

CHARLES FRIED

Charles Fried is a professor of law at Harvard University. In this selection from his book *Right and Wrong*, he argues that lying is wrong even if it sometimes has good results. However, all things considered, sometimes other special duties override our duty not to lie. Fried defines lying earlier in the book this way: "A person lies when he asserts a proposition he believes to be false." It could turn out that the lie is in fact true, such as when Mary wants to deceive you and tells you that your friend has betrayed you—and it turns out, unbeknownst to Mary, that he really has. Lying is intentional and bad because it fails to respect truth. But it is not only bad, it is morally wrong, since it violates respect for persons.

The evil of lying is as hard to pin down as it is strongly felt. Is lying wrong or is it merely something bad? If it is bad, why is it bad—is it bad in itself or because of some tendency associated with it? Compare lying to physical harm. Harm is a state of the world and so it can only be classified as bad; the wrong I argued for was the *intentional doing* of harm. Lying, on the other hand, can be wrong, since it is an action. But the fact that lying is an action does not mean that it *must* be wrong rather than bad. It might be that the action of lying should be judged as just another state of the world—a time-extended state, to be sure, but there is no problem about that—and as such it would count as a negative element in any set of circumstances in which it occurred. Furthermore, if lying is judged to be bad it can be bad in itself, like something ugly or painful, or it can be bad only because of its tendency to produce results that are bad in themselves.

If lying were bad, not wrong, this would mean only that, other things being equal, we should avoid lies. And if lying were bad not in itself but merely because of its tendencies, we would have to avoid lies only when those tendencies were in fact likely to be realized. In either case lying would be permissible to produce a net benefit, including the prevention of more or worse lies. By contrast the categorical norm "Do not lie" does not evaluate states of affairs but is addressed to moral agents, forbidding lies. Now if lying is wrong it is also bad in itself, for the category of the intrinsically bad is weaker and more inclusive than the category of the wrong. And accordingly, many states of the world are intrinsically bad (such as destruction of valuable property) but intentional acts bringing them about are not necessarily wrong.

Bentham plainly believed that lying is neither wrong nor even intrinsically bad: "Falsehood, take it by itself, consider it as not being accompanied by any other material circumstances, nor therefore productive of any material effects, can never, upon the principle of utility, constitute any offense at all." By contrast, Kant and Augustine argued at length that lying is wrong. Indeed, they held that lying is not only wrong *unless* excused or justified in defined ways (which is my view) but that lying is always wrong. Augustine sees lying as a kind of defilement, the liar being tainted by the lie, quite apart from any consequences of the lie. Kant's views are more complex. He argues at one point that lying undermines confidence and trust among men generally: "Although by making a false statement I do no wrong to him who unjustly compels me to speak, yet I do wrong to men in general. . . . I cause that declarations in general find no credit, and hence all rights founded on contract should lose their force; and this is a wrong to mankind." This would seem to be a consequentialist argument, according to which lying is bad only insofar as it produces these bad results. But elsewhere he makes plain that he believes these bad consequences to be necessarily, perhaps even conceptually linked to lying. In this more rigoristic vein, he asserts that lying is a perversion of one's uniquely human capacities irrespective of any consequences of the lie, and thus lying is not only intrinsically bad but wrong.

Finally, a number of writers have taken what looks like an intermediate position: the evil of lying is indeed identified with its consequences, but the connection between lying and those consequences, while not a necessary connection, is close and persistent, and the consequences themselves are pervasive and profound. Consider this passage from a recent work by G. J. Warnock:

> I do not necessarily do you any harm at all by deed or word if I induce you to believe what is not in fact the case; I may even do you good, possibly by way, for example, of consolation or flattery. Nevertheless, though deception is not thus necessarily directly damaging it is easy to see how crucially important it is that the natural inclination to have recourse to it should be counteracted. It is, one might say, not the implanting of false beliefs that is damaging, but rather the generation of the suspicion that they may be being implanted. For this undermines trust; and, to the extent that trust is undermined, all cooperative undertakings, in which what one person can do or has reason to do is dependent on what others have done, are doing, or are going to do, must tend to break down. . . . There is no sense in my asking you for your opinion on some point, if I do not suppose that your answer will actually express your opinion (verbal communication is doubtless the most important of all our co-operative undertakings). (*The Object of Morality* [London: Methuen, 1971], p. 84)

Warnock does not quite say that truth-telling is good in itself or that lying is wrong, yet the moral quality of truth-telling and lying is not so simply instrumental as it is, for instance, for Bentham. Rather, truth-telling seems to bear a fundamental, pervasive relation to the human enterprise, just as lying appears to be fundamentally subversive of that enterprise. What exactly is the nature of this relation? How does truth-telling bear to human goods a relation which is more than instrumental but less than necessary?

The very definition of lying makes plain that consequences are crucial, for lying is intentional and the intent is an intent to produce a consequence: false belief. But how can I then resist the consequentialist analysis of lying? Lying is an attempt to produce a certain effect on another, and if that effect (consequence) is not bad, how can lying be wrong? I shall have to argue, therefore, that to lie is to intend to produce an effect which always has something bad about it, an effect moreover of the special sort that it is wrong to produce it intentionally. To lay that groundwork for my argument about lying, I must consider first the moral value of truth.

TRUTH AND RATIONALITY

A statement is true when the world is the way the statement says it is. Utilitarians insist (as in the quotation from Bentham above) that truth, like everything else, has value just exactly as it produces value—pleasure, pain, the satisfaction or frustration of desire. And of course it is easy to show that truth (like keeping faith, not harming the innocent, respecting rights) does not always lead to the net satisfactions of desire, to the production of utility. It may *tend* to do so, but that tendency explains only why we should discriminate between occasions when truth does and when it does not have value—an old story. It is an old story, for truth—like justice, respect, and self-respect—has a value which consequentialist analyses (utilitarian or any other) do not capture. Truth, like respect, is a foundational value.

The morality of right and wrong does not count the satisfaction of desire as the overriding value. Rather, the integrity of persons, as agents and as the objects of the intentional agency of others, has priority over the attainment of the goals which agents choose to attain. I have sought to show how respect for physical integrity is related to respect for the person. The person, I argued, is not just a locus of potential pleasure and pain but an entity with determinate characteristics. The person is, among other things, necessarily an incorporated, a physical, not an abstract entity. In relation to truth we touch another necessary aspect of moral personality: the capacity for judgment, and thus for choice. It is that aspect which Kant used to ground his moral theory, arguing that freedom and rationality are the basis for moral personality. John Rawls makes the same point, arguing that "moral personality and not the capacity for pleasure and pain . . . [is] the fundamental aspect of the self. . . . The essential unity of the self is . . . provided by the concept of right." The concept of the self is prior to the goods which the self chooses, and these goods gather their moral significance from the fact that they have been chosen by moral beings—beings capable of understanding and acting on moral principles.

In this view freedom and rationality are complementary capacities, or aspects of the same capacity, which is moral capacity. A man is free insofar as he is able to act on a judgment because he perceives it to be correct; he is free insofar as he may be moved to action by the judgments his reason offers to him. This is the very opposite of the Humean conception of reason as the slave of the passions. There is no slavery here. The man who follows the steps of a mathematical argument to its conclusion because he judges them to be correct is free indeed. To the extent that we choose our ends we are free; and as to objectively valuable ends which we choose because we see their value, we are still free.

Now, rational judgment is true judgment, and so the moral capacity for rational choice implies the capacity to recognize the matter on which choice is to act and to recognize the kind of result our choices will produce. This applies to judgments about other selves and to judgments in which one locates himself as a person among persons, a self among selves. These judgments are not just arbitrary suppositions: *they are judged to be true of the world.* For consider what the self would be like if these judgments were not supposed to be true. Maybe one might be content to be happy in the manner of the fool of Athens who believed all the ships in the harbor to be his. But what of our perceptions of other people? Would we be content to have those whom we love and trust the mere figments of our imaginations? The foundational values of freedom and rationality imply the foundational value of truth, for the rational man is the one who judges aright, that is, truly. Truth is not the same as judgment, as rationality; it is rather the proper subject of judgment. If we did not seek to judge truly, and if we did not believe we could judge truly, the act of judgment would not be what we know it to be at all.

Judgment and thus truth are *part* of a structure which as a whole makes up the concept of self. A person's relation to his body and the fact of being an incorporated self are another part of that structure. These two parts are related. The bodily senses provide matter for judgments of truth, and the body includes the physical organs of judgment.

THE WRONG OF LYING

So our capacity for judgment is foundational and truth is the proper object of that capacity, but how do we get to the badness of lying, much less its categorical wrongness? The crucial step to be supplied has to do not with the value of truth but with the evil of lying. We must show that to lie to someone is to injure him in a way that particularly touches his moral personality. From that, the passage is indeed easy to the conclusion that to inflict such injury intentionally (remember that all lying is by hypothesis intentional) is not only bad but wrong. It is this first, crucial step which is difficult. After all, a person's capacity for true judgment is not necessarily impaired by inducing in him a particular false belief. Nor would it seem that a person suffers a greater injury in respect to that capacity when he is induced to believe a falsity than when we intentionally prevent him from discovering the truth, yet only in the first case do we lie. Do we really do injury to a person's moral personality when we persuade him falsely that it rained yesterday in Bangkok—a fact in which he has no interest?

And do we do him more injury than when we fail to answer his request for yesterday's football scores, in which he is mildly interested? Must we not calculate the injury by the *other* harm it does: disappointed expectations, lost property, missed opportunities, physical harm? In this view, lying would be a way of injuring a person in his various substantive interests—a way of stealing from him, hurting his feelings, perhaps poisoning him—but then the evil of lying would be purely instrumental, not wrong at all.

All truth, however irrelevant or trivial, has value, even though we may cheerfully ignore most truths, forget them, erase them as encumbrances from our memories. The value of every truth is shown just in the judgment that the only thing we must not do is falsify truth. Truths are like other people's property, which we can care nothing about but may not use for our own purposes. It is as if the truth were not ours (even truth we have discovered and which is known only to us), and so we may not exercise an unlimited dominion over it. Our relations to other people have a similar structure: we may perhaps have no duty to them, we may be free to put them out of our minds to make room for others whom we care about more, but we may not harm them. And so we may not falsify truth. But enough of metaphors—what does it mean to say that the truth is not ours?

The capacity for true judgment is the capacity to arrive at judgments which are in fact true of the world as it exists apart from our desires, our choices, our values. It is the world presented to us by true judgments—including true judgments about ourselves—which we then make the subject of our choices, our valuation. Now, if we treat the truth as our own, it must be according to desire or valuation. But for rational beings these activities are supposed to depend on truth; we are supposed to desire and choose according to the world as it is. To choose that something not be the case when it is in fact the case is very nearly self-contradictory—for choice is not *of* truth but *on the basis of* truth. To deliberate about whether to believe a truth (not whether it is indeed true—another story altogether) is like deciding whether to cheat at solitaire. All this is obvious. In fact I suppose one cannot even coherently talk about choosing to believe something one believes to be false. And this holds equally for all truths—big and little, useful, and downright inconvenient. But we do and must calculate *about* (and not just *with*) truths all the time as we decide what truths to acquire, what to forget. We decide all the time not to pursue some inquiry because it is not worth it. Such calculations surely must go forward on the basis of what truths are useful, given one's plans and desires. Even when we pursue truth for its own sake, we distinguish between interesting and boring truths.

Considering what truth to acquire or retain differs, however, from deliberately acquiring false beliefs. All truths are acquired as propositions correctly (truly) corresponding to the world, and in this respect, all truths are equal.

A lie, however, has the form and occupies the role of truth in that it too purports to be a proposition about the world; only the world does not correspond to it. So the choice of a lie is not like a choice among truths, for the choice of a lie is a choice to affirm as the basis for judgment a proposition which does not correspond to the world. So, when I say that truth is foundational, that truth precedes choice, what I mean is *not* that this or that truth is foundational but that judging according to the facts is foundational to judging at all. A scientist may deliberate about which subject to study and, having chosen his subject, about the data worth acquiring, but he cannot even deliberate as a scientist about whether to acquire false data. Clearly, then, there is something funny (wrong?) about lying to oneself, but how do we go from there to the proposition that it is wrong to lie to someone else? After all, much of the peculiarity about lying to oneself consists in the fact that it seems not so much bad as downright self-contradictory, logically impossible, but that does not support the judgment that it is wrong to lie to another. I cannot marry myself, but that hardly makes it wrong to marry someone else.

Let us imagine a case in which you come as close as you can to lying to yourself: You arrange some operation, some fiddling with your brain that has no effect other than to cause you to believe a proposition you know to be false and also to forget entirely the prior history of how you came to believe that proposition. It seems to me that you do indeed harm yourself in such an operation. This is because a free and rational person wishes to have a certain relation to reality: as nearly perfect as possible. He wishes to build his conception of himself and the world and his conception of the good on the basis of truth. Now if he affirms that the truth is available for fiddling in order to accommodate either his picture of the world or his conception of the good, then this affirms that reality is dependent on what one wants, rather than what one wants being fundamentally constrained by what there is. Rationality is the respect for this fundamental constraint of truth. This is just another way of saying that the truth is prior to our plans and prospects and must be respected whatever our plans might be. What if the truth we "destroy" by this operation is a very trivial and irrelevant truth—the state of the weather in Bangkok on some particular day? There is still an injury to self, because the fiddler must have some purpose in his fiddling. If it is a substantive purpose, then the truth is in fact relevant to that purpose, and my argument holds. If it is just to show it can be done, then he is only trying to show he can do violence to his rationality—a kind of moral blasphemy. Well, what if it is a very *little* truth? Why, then, it is a very little injury he does himself—but that does not undermine my point.

Now, when I lie to you, I do to you what you cannot actually do to yourself—brain-fiddling being only an approximation. The nature of the injury I would do to myself, if I could, explains why lying to you is to do you harm, indeed why it is wrong. The lie is an injury because it produces an effect (or seeks to) which a person as a moral agent should not wish to have produced in him, and thus it is as much an injury as any other effect which a moral agent would not wish to have produced upon his person. To be sure, some people may want to be lied to. That is a special problem; they are like people who want to suffer (not just are willing to risk) physical injury. In general, then, I do not want you to lie to me in the same way that as a rational man I would not lie to myself if I could. But why does this make lying wrong and not merely bad?

Lying is wrong because when I lie I set up a relation which is essentially exploitative. It violates the principle of respect, for I must affirm that the mind of another person is available to me in a way in which I cannot agree my mind would be available to him—for if I do so agree, then I would not expect my lie to be believed. When I lie, I am like a counterfeiter: I do not want the market flooded with counterfeit currency; I do not want to get back my own counterfeit bill. Moreover, in lying to you, I affirm such an unfairly unilateral principle in respect to an interest and capacity which is crucial, as crucial as physical integrity: your freedom and your rationality. When I do intentional physical harm, I say that your body, your person, is available for my purposes. When I lie, I lay claim to your mind.

Lying violates respect and is wrong, as is any breach of trust. Every lie is a broken promise, and the only reason this seems strained is that in lying the promise is made and broken at the same moment. Every lie necessarily implies—as does every assertion—an assurance, a warranty of its truth. The fact that the breach accompanies the making should, however, only strengthen the conclusion that this is wrong. If promise-breaking is wrong, then a lie must be wrong, since there cannot be the supervening factor of changed circumstances which may excuse breaches of promises to perform in the future.

The final one of the convergent strands that make up the wrong of lying is the shared, communal nature of language. This is what I think Kant had in mind when he argued that a lie does wrong "to men in general." If whether people stood behind their statements depended wholly on the particular circumstances of the utterance, then the whole point of communication would be undermined. For every utterance would simply be the occasion for an analysis of the total circumstances (speaker's and hearer's) in order to determine what, if anything, to make of the utterance. And though we do often wonder and calculate whether a person is telling the truth, we do so from a baseline, a presumption that people do stand behind their statements. After all, the speaker surely depends on such a baseline. He wants us to think that he is telling the truth. Speech is a paradigm of communication, and all human relations are based on some form of communication. Our very ability to think, to conceptualize, is related to speech. Speech allows the social to penetrate the intimately personal. Perhaps that is why Kant's dicta seem to vacillate between two positions: lying as a social offense, and lying as an offense against oneself; the requirement of an intent to deceive another, and the insistence that the essence of the wrong is not injury to another but to humanity. Every lie violates the basic commitment to truth which stands behind the social fact of language.

I have already argued that bodily integrity bears a necessary relation to moral integrity, so that an attack upon bodily integrity is wrong, not just bad. The intimate *and* social nature of truth make the argument about lying stronger. For not only is the target aspect of the victim crucial to him as a moral agent but, by lying, we attack that target by a means which itself offends his moral nature; the means of attack are social means which can be said to belong as much to the victim as to his assailant. There is not only the attack at his moral vitals, but an attack with a weapon which belongs to him. Lying is, thus, a kind of treachery. (*Kind of* treachery? Why not treachery pure and simple?) It is as if we not only robbed a man of his treasure but in doing so used his own servants or family as our agents. That speech is our *common* property, that it belongs to the liar, his victim and all of us makes the matter if anything far worse.

So this is why lying is not only bad (a hurt), but wrong, why lying is wrong apart from or in addition to any other injury it does, and why lying seems at once an offense against the victim and against mankind in general, an offense against the liar himself, and against the abstract entity, truth. Whom do you injure when you pass a counterfeit bill?

What about little pointless lies? Do I really mean they are wrong? Well, yes, even a little lie is wrong, *if* it is a true piece of communication, an assertion of its own truth and not just a conventional way of asserting nothing at all or something else (as in the case of polite or diplomatic formulas). A little lie is a little wrong, but it is still something you must not do.

For Further Reflection

1. Evaluate Fried's argument against lying. Why is lying always wrong—even if only a little wrong? Is his argument sound? Explain.
2. Fried makes several comparisons of lying with other acts: stealing, injuring, counterfeiting, promise-breaking, and violating the social fact of language. Are these good analogies?
3. Fried says lying is exploitative. Is this always the case? Can you think of cases in which one lies not to exploit but to help another?

Does Morality Depend on Religion?

PLATO

Plato (427–347 B.C.) is one of the greatest philosophers who ever lived and the first philosopher to write systematically about metaphysics and ethics. Here we see his mentor, Socrates, engaged in a dialogue with the self-righteously religious Euthyphro, who is going to court to report his father for having killed a slave. In the course of the discussion, Socrates raises the question that is known as the question of the divine command theory of ethics: Is the good good because God loves it, or does God love the good because it is good? The doctrine that morality depends on religion is called the divine command theory, since God's commands determine what is right and what is wrong.

SOCRATES. But shall we . . . say that whatever all the gods hate is unholy, and whatever they all love is holy: while whatever some of them love, and others hate, is either both or neither? Do you wish us now to define holiness and unholiness in this manner?

EUTHYPHRO. Why not, Socrates?

SOCR. There is no reason why I should not, Euthyphro. It is for you to consider whether that definition will help you to instruct me as you promised.

EUTH. Well, I should say that holiness is what all the gods love, and that unholiness is what they all hate.

SOCR. Are we to examine this definition, Euthyphro, and see if it is a good one? Or are we to be content to accept the bare assertions of other men, or of ourselves, without asking any questions? Or must we examine the assertions?

EUTH. We must examine them. But for my part I think that the definition is right this time.

SOCR. We shall know that better in a little while, my good friend. Now consider this question. Do the gods love holiness because it is holy, or is it holy because they love it?

EUTH. I do not understand you, Socrates.

SOCR. I will try to explain myself: we speak of a thing being carried and carrying, and being led and leading, and being seen and seeing; and you

---

Reprinted from the *Euthyphro,* translated by William Jowett (New York: Charles Scribner's Sons, 1889).

understand that all such expressions mean different things, and what the difference is.

EUTH. Yes, I think I understand.

SOCR. And we talk of a thing being loved, and, which is different, of a thing loving?

EUTH. Of course.

SOCR. Now tell me: is a thing which is being carried in a state of being carried, because it is carried, or for some other reason?

EUTH. No, because it is carried.

SOCR. And a thing is in a state of being led, because it is led, and of being seen, because it is seen?

EUTH. Certainly.

SOCR. Then a thing is not seen because it is in a state of being seen; it is in a state of being seen because it is seen; and a thing is not led because it is in a state of being led; it is in a state of being led because it is led; and a thing is not carried because it is in a state of being carried; it is in a state of being carried because it is carried. Is my meaning clear now, Euthyphro? I mean this: if anything becomes, or is affected, it does not become because it is in a state of becoming; it is in a state of becoming because it becomes; and it is not affected because it is in a state of being affected; it is in a state of being affected because it is affected. Do you not agree?

EUTH. I do.

SOCR. Is not that which is being loved in a state, either of becoming, or of being affected in some way by something?

EUTH. Certainly.

SOCR. Then the same is true here as in the former cases. A thing is not loved by those who love it because it is in a state of being loved. It is in a state of being loved because they love it.

EUTH. Necessarily.

SOCR. Well, then, Euthyphro, what do we say about holiness? Is it not loved by all the gods, according to your definition?

EUTH. Yes.

SOCR. Because it is holy, or for some other reason?

EUTH. No, because it is holy.

SOCR. Then it is loved by the gods because it is holy; it is not holy because it is loved by them?

EUTH. It seems so.

SOCR. But then what is pleasing to the gods is pleasing to them, and is in a state of being loved by them, because they love it?

EUTH. Of course.

SOCR. Then holiness is not what is pleasing to the gods, and what is pleasing to the gods is not holy, as you say, Euthyphro. They are different things.

EUTH. And why, Socrates?

SOCR. Because we are agreed that the gods love holiness because it is holy; and that it is not holy because they love it. Is not this so?

EUTH. Yes.

SOCR. And that what is pleasing to the gods because they love it, is pleasing to them by reason of this same love; and that they do not love it because it is pleasing to them.

EUTH. True.

SOCR. Then, my dear Euthyphro, holiness, and what is pleasing to the gods, are different things. If the gods had loved holiness because it is holy, they would also have loved what is pleasing to them because it is pleasing to them; but if what is pleasing to them had been pleasing to them because they loved it, then holiness too would have been holiness, because they loved it. But now you see that they are opposite things, and wholly different from each other. For the one is of a sort to be loved because it is loved: while the other is loved, because it is of a sort to be loved. My question, Euthyphro, was, What is holiness? But it turns out that you have not explained to me the essence of holiness; you have been content to mention an attribute which belongs to it, namely, that all the gods love it. You have not yet told me what is its essence. Do not, if you please, keep from me what holiness is; begin again and tell me that. Never mind whether the gods love it, or whether it has other attributes: we shall not differ on that point. Do your best to make it clear to me what is holiness and what is unholiness.

For Further Reflection

1. Does morality depend on religion for its validity, or does it have independent validity? In other words, is the divine command theory true? What does Socrates seem to believe? What do you believe? Why?
2. What are the implications of holding that ethics depends on religion? Could God make rape and murder morally right actions today? How do you know that he hasn't (and has kept it a secret)? If it turns out that no God exists, does that mean that morality is an illusion?
3. If "goodness" means simply "what God commands," what do we mean when we say that "God is good"?
4. If the divine command theory is true, how is God different from the devil? Is he simply more powerful?

The Divine Command Theory

JAMES RACHELS

Is the divine command theory a good moral theory? In this reading, James Rachels argues that this conception of morality is false and that neither the theist nor nontheist should accept it.

In the major theistic traditions, including Judaism, Christianity, and Islam, God is conceived as a lawgiver who has laid down rules that we are to obey. He does not compel us to obey them. We were created as free agents, so we may choose to accept or to reject his commandments. But if we are to live as we should live, we must follow God's laws. This conception has been elaborated by some theologians into a theory about the nature of right and wrong known as the Divine Command Theory. Essentially, this theory says that "morally right" means "commanded by God" and "morally wrong" means "forbidden by God."

This theory has a number of attractive features. It immediately solves the old problem about the objectivity of ethics. Ethics is not merely a matter of personal feeling or social custom. Whether something is right or wrong is perfectly objective: It is right if God commands it, wrong if God forbids it. Moreover, the Divine Command Theory suggests an answer to the perennial question of why anyone should bother with morality. Why not forget about "ethics" and just look out for oneself? If immorality is the violation of God's commandments, there is an easy answer: On the day of final reckoning, you will be held accountable.

There are, however, serious problems for the theory. Of course, atheists would not accept it, because they do not believe that God exists. But there are difficulties even for believers. The main problem was first noted by Plato, the Greek philosopher who lived 400 years before the birth of Jesus.

Plato's writings were in the form of dialogues, usually between Socrates and one or more interlocutors. In one of these dialogues, the *Euthyphro*, there is a discussion concerning whether "right" can be defined as "that which the gods command." Socrates is skeptical and asks: Is conduct right because the gods command it, or do the gods command it because it is right? This is one of the most famous questions in the history of philosophy. The British philosopher Antony Flew suggests that "one good test of a person's aptitude for philosophy is to discover whether he can grasp its force and point."

From James Rachels, *The Elements of Moral Philosophy* (McGraw-Hill, 1999), pp. 55–59.

The point is that if we accept the theological conception of right and wrong, we are caught in a dilemma. Socrates's question asks us to clarify what we mean. There are two things we might mean, and both lead to trouble.

1. First, we might mean that *right conduct is right because God commands it*. For example, according to Exodus 20:16, God commands us to be truthful. On this option, the reason we should be truthful is simply that God requires it. Apart from the divine command, truth telling is neither good nor bad. It is God's command that *makes* truthfulness right.

But this leads to trouble, for it represents God's commands as arbitrary. It means that God could have given different commands just as easily. He could have commanded us to be liars, and then lying, and not truthfulness, would be right. (You may be tempted to reply: "But God would never command us to lie." But why not? If he did endorse lying, God would not be commanding us to do wrong, because his command would make it right.) Remember that on this view, honesty was not right before God commanded it. Therefore, he could have had no more reason to command it than its opposite; and so, from a moral point of view, his command is arbitrary.

Another problem is that, on this view, the doctrine of the goodness of God is reduced to nonsense. It is important to religious believers that God is not only all-powerful and all-knowing, but that he is also good; yet if we accept the idea that good and bad are defined by reference to God's will, this notion is deprived of any meaning. What could it mean to say that God's commands are good? If "X is good" means "X is commanded by God," then "God's commands are good" would mean only "God's commands are commanded by God," an empty truism. In 1686, Leibniz observed in his *Discourse on Metaphysics:*

> So in saying that things are not good by any rule of goodness, but sheerly by the will of God, it seems to me that one destroys, without realizing it, all the love of God and all his glory. For why praise him for what he has done if he would be equally praiseworthy in doing exactly the contrary?

Thus if we choose the first of Socrates's two options, we seem to be stuck with consequences that even the most religious people would find unacceptable.

2. There is a way to avoid these troublesome consequences. We can take the second of Socrates's options. We need not say that right conduct is right because God commands it. Instead, we may say that God commands us to do certain things because they are right. God, who is infinitely wise, realizes that truthfulness is better than deceitfulness, and so he commands us to be truthful; he sees that killing is wrong, and so he commands us not to kill; and so on for all the moral rules.

If we take this option, we avoid the troublesome consequences that spoiled the first alternative. God's commands are not arbitrary; they are the result of his wisdom in knowing what is best. And the doctrine of the goodness of God is preserved: To say that his commands are good means that he commands only what, in perfect wisdom, he sees to be best.

Unfortunately, however, this second option leads to a different problem, which is equally troublesome. In taking this option, we have abandoned the theological conception of right and wrong—when we say that God commands us to be truthful because truthfulness is right, we are acknowledging a standard of right and wrong that is independent of God's will. The rightness exists prior to and independent of God's command, and it is the reason for the command. Thus, if we want to know why we should be truthful, the reply "Because God commands it" does not really tell us, for we may still ask "But why does God command it?" and the answer to *that* question will provide the underlying reason why truthfulness is a good thing.

All this may be summarized in the following argument:

(1) Suppose God commands us to do what is right. Then either (a) the right actions are right because he commands them or (b) he commands them because they are right.
(2) If we take option (a), then God's commands are, from a moral point of view, arbitrary; moreover, the doctrine of the goodness of God is rendered meaningless.
(3) If we take option (b), then we will have acknowledged a standard of right and wrong that is independent of God's will. We will have, in effect, given up the theological conception of right and wrong.
(4) Therefore, we must either regard God's commands as arbitrary, and give up the doctrine of the goodness of God, or admit that there is a standard of right and wrong that is independent of his will, and give up the theological conception of right and wrong.
(5) From a religious point of view, it is unacceptable to regard God's commands as arbitrary or to give up the doctrine of the goodness of God.
(6) Therefore, even from a religious point of view, a standard of right and wrong that is independent of God's will must be accepted.

Many religious people believe that they must accept a theological conception of right and wrong because it would be impious not to do so. They feel, somehow, that if they believe in God, they should say that right and wrong are to be defined in terms of his will. But this argument suggests otherwise: It suggests that, on the contrary, the Divine Command Theory itself leads to impious results, so that a devout person should not accept it. And in fact, some of the greatest theologians, such as St. Thomas Aquinas (1225–1274), rejected the theory for just this reason. Thinkers such as Aquinas connect morality with religion in a different way.

For Further Reflection

1. What would Rachels likely say to this objection to his argument: "The arbitrariness claim has no force because God would never command us to do wrong—to murder the innocent or to torture babies, for example—because God is all-good."
2. Why does Leibniz say that the divine command theory, if true, would destroy any reasons we might have for praising God?
3. Do you think Rachels's argument sound? Why or why not?
4. Would it be impious to reject the divine command theory? to accept it? Explain.

Moral Luck

THOMAS NAGEL

Thomas Nagel is a professor of philosophy at New York University and the author of several works in moral and political philosophy. In this selection Nagel challenges the Kantian way of viewing morality, which assumes that we are all equal rational participants in the moral enterprise, each having the same opportunity to be moral. Nagel suggests that this view is simplistic and fails to take into account the manner in which external factors impinge upon us. These factors introduce the idea of moral luck, which he defines thus: "Where a significant aspect of what someone does depends on factors beyond his control, yet we continue to treat him in that respect as an object of moral judgment, it can be called moral luck."

Four types of moral luck are considered: constitutive luck, which has to do with the qualities of temperament and personality that one has; circumstantial luck, which refers to luck inherent in the circumstances of an action; resultant luck, which is "luck in the way one's actions and projects turn out"; and casual luck, which is luck in being determined by antecedent causes.

From *Mortal Questions* by Thomas Nagel (1979), pp. 24–38, Cambridge University Press.

Kant believed that good or bad luck should influence neither our moral judgment of a person and his actions, nor his moral assessment of himself.

> The good will is not good because of what it effects or accomplishes or because of its adequacy to achieve some proposed end; it is good only because of its willing, i.e., it is good of itself. And, regarded for itself, it is to be esteemed incomparably higher than anything which could be brought about by it in favor of any inclination or even of the sum total of all inclinations. Even if it should happen that, by a particular unfortunate fate or by the niggardly provision of a stepmotherly nature, this will should be wholly lacking in power to accomplish its purpose, and if even the greatest effort should not avail it to achieve anything of its end, and if there remained only the good will (not as a mere wish but as the summoning of all the means in our power), it would sparkle like a jewel in its own light, as something that had its full worth in itself. Usefulness or fruitlessness can neither diminish nor augment this worth.

He would presumably have said the same thing about a bad will: whether it accomplishes its evil purposes is morally irrelevant. And a course of action that would be condemned if it had a bad outcome cannot be vindicated if by luck it turns out well. There cannot be moral risk. This view seems to be wrong, but it arises in response to a fundamental problem about moral responsibility to which we possess no satisfactory solution.

The problem develops out of the ordinary conditions of moral judgment. Prior to reflection it is intuitively plausible that people cannot be morally assessed for what is not their fault, or for what is due to factors beyond their control. Such judgment is different from the evaluation of something as a good or bad thing, or state of affairs. The latter may be present in addition to moral judgment, but when we blame someone for his actions we are not merely saying it is bad that they happened, or bad that he exists: we are judging *him,* saying he is bad, which is different from his being a bad thing. This kind of judgment takes only a certain kind of object. Without being able to explain exactly why, we feel that the appropriateness of moral assessment is easily undermined by the discovery that the act or attribute, no matter how good or bad, is not under the person's control. While other evaluations remain, this one seems to lose its footing. So a clear absence of control, produced by involuntary movement, physical force, or ignorance of the circumstances, excuses what is done from moral judgment. But what we do depends in many more ways than these on what is not under our control—what is not produced by a good or a bad will in Kant's phrase. And external influences in this broader range are not usually thought to excuse what is done from moral judgment, positive or negative.

Let me give a few examples, beginning with the type of case Kant has in mind. Whether we succeed or fail in what we try to do nearly always depends to some extent on factors beyond our control. This is true of murder, altruism, revolution, the sacrifice of certain interests for the sake of others—almost any morally important act. What has been done, and what is morally judged, is partly determined by external factors. However jewel-like the good will may be in its own right, there is a morally significant difference between rescuing someone from a burning building and dropping him from a twelfth-story window while trying to rescue him. Similarly, there is a morally significant difference between reckless driving and manslaughter. But whether a reckless driver hits a pedestrian depends on the presence of the pedestrian at the point where he recklessly passes a red light. What we do is also limited by the opportunities and choices with which we are faced, and these are largely determined by factors beyond our control. Someone who was an officer in a concentration camp might have led a quiet and harmless life if the Nazis had never come to power in Germany. And someone who led a quiet and harmless life in Argentina might have become an officer in a concentration camp if he had not left Germany for business reasons in 1930.

I shall say more later about these and other examples. I introduce them here to illustrate a general point. Where a significant aspect of what someone does depends on factors beyond his control, yet we continue to treat him in that respect as an object of moral judgment, it can be called moral luck. Such luck can be good or bad. And the problem posed by this phenomenon, which led Kant to deny its possibility, is that the broad range of external influences here identified seems on close examination to undermine moral assessment as surely as does the narrower range of familiar excusing conditions. If the condition of control is consistently applied, it threatens to erode most of the moral assessments we find it natural to make. The things for which people are morally judged are determined in more ways than we at first realize by what is beyond their control. And when the seemingly natural requirement of fault or responsibility is applied in light of these facts, it leaves few pre-reflective moral judgments intact. Ultimately, nothing or almost nothing about what a person does seems to be under his control.

Why not conclude, then, that the condition of control is false—that it is an initially plausible hypothesis refuted by clear counter-examples? One could in that case look instead for a more refined condition which picked out the *kinds* of lack of control that really undermine certain moral judgments, without yielding the unacceptable conclusion derived from the broader condition, that most or all ordinary moral judgments are illegitimate.

What rules out this escape is that we are dealing not with a theoretical conjecture but with a philosophical problem. The condition of control does not suggest itself merely as a generalization from certain clear cases. It seems *correct* in the further cases to which it is extended beyond the original set. When we undermine moral assessment by considering new ways in which control is absent, we are not just discovering what *would* follow given the general hypothesis, but are actually being persuaded that in itself the absence of control is relevant in these cases too. The erosion of moral judgment emerges not as the absurd consequence of an over-simple theory, but as a natural consequence of the ordinary idea of moral assessment, when it is applied in view of a more complete and precise account of the facts. It would therefore be a mistake to argue from the unacceptability of the conclusions to the need for a different account of the conditions of moral responsibility. The view that moral luck is paradoxical is not a *mistake,* ethical or logical, but a perception of one of the ways in which the intuitively acceptable conditions of moral judgment threaten to undermine it all. . . .

[Here Nagel begins his discussion of the four types of moral luck:

1. Luck in the way one's actions and projects turn out.
2. Luck in how one is determined by antecedent circumstances.
3. Constitutive luck—"the kind of person you are, where this is not just a question of what you deliberately do, but of your inclinations, capacities, and temperament."
4. Circumstantial luck—if circumstances had been different, the judgment of your act would have been assessed differently.]

Let us first consider luck, good and bad, in the way things turn out. Kant, in the above-quoted passage, has one example of this in mind, but the category covers a wide range. It includes the truck driver who accidentally runs over a child, the artist who abandons his wife and five children to devote himself to painting, and other cases in which the possibilities of success and failure are even greater. The driver, if he is entirely without fault, will feel terrible about his role in the event, but will not have to reproach himself. Therefore this example of agent-regent is not yet a case of *moral* bad luck. However, if the driver was guilty of even a minor degree of negligence—failing to have his brakes checked recently, for example—then if that negligence contributes to the death of the child, he will not merely feel terrible. He will blame himself for the death. And what makes this an example of moral luck is that he would have to blame himself only slightly for the negligence itself if no situation arose which required him to brake suddenly and violently to avoid hitting a child. Yet the *negligence* is the same in both cases, and the driver has no control over whether a child will run into his path.

The same is true at higher levels of negligence. If someone has had too much to drink and his car swerves onto the sidewalk, he can count himself morally lucky if there are no pedestrians in his path. If there were, he would be to blame for their deaths, and would probably be prosecuted for manslaughter. But if he hurts no one, although his recklessness is exactly the same, he is guilty of a far less serious legal offense and will certainly reproach himself and be reproached by others much less severely. To take another legal example, the penalty for attempted murder is less than that for successful murder—however similar the intentions and motives of the assailant may be in the two cases. His degree of culpability can depend, it would seem, on whether the victim happened to be wearing a bullet-proof vest, or whether a bird flew into the path of the bullet—matters beyond his control.

Finally, there are cases of decision under uncertainty—common in public and in private life. Anna Karenina goes off with Vronsky, Gauguin leaves his family, Chamberlain signs the Munich Agreement, the Decembrists persuade the troops under their command to revolt against the czar, the American colonies declare their independence from Britain, you introduce two people in an attempt at matchmaking. It is tempting in all such cases to feel that some decision must be possible, in the light of what is known at the time, which will make reproach unsuitable no matter how things turn out. But this is not true; when someone acts in such ways he takes his life, or his moral position, into his hands, because how things turn out determines what he has done. It is possible *also* to assess the decision from the point of view of what could be known at the time, but this is not the end of the story. If the Decembrists had succeeded in overthrowing Nicholas I in 1825 and establishing a constitutional regime, they would be heroes. As it is, not only did they fail and pay for it, but they bore some responsibility for the terrible punishments meted out to the troops who had been persuaded to follow them. If the American Revolution had been a bloody failure resulting in greater repression, then Jefferson, Franklin, and Washington would still have made a noble attempt, and might not even have regretted it on their way to the scaffold, but they would also have had to blame themselves for what they had helped to bring on their compatriots. (Perhaps peaceful efforts at reform would eventually have succeeded.) If Hitler had not overrun Europe and exterminated millions, but instead had died of a heart attack after occupying the Sudetenland, Chamberlain's action at Munich would still have utterly betrayed the Czechs, but it would not be the great moral disaster that has made his name a household word.

In many cases of difficult choice the outcome cannot be foreseen with certainty. One kind of assessment of the choice is possible in advance, but another kind must await the outcome, because the outcome determines what has been done. The same degree of culpability or estimability in intention, motive, or concern is compatible with a wide range of judgments, positive or negative, depending on what happened beyond the point of decision. The *mens rea* which could have existed in the absence of any consequences does not exhaust the grounds of moral judgment. Actual results influence culpability or esteem in a large class of unquestionably ethical cases ranging from negligence through political choice.

That these are genuine moral judgments rather than expressions of temporary attitude is evident from the fact that one can say *in advance* how the moral verdict will depend on the results. If one negligently leaves the bath running with the baby in it, one will realize, as one bounds up the stairs toward the bathroom, that if the baby has drowned one has done something awful, whereas if it has not one has merely been careless. Someone who launches a violent revolution against an authoritarian regime knows that if he fails he will be responsible for much suffering that is in vain, but if he succeeds he will be justified by the outcome. I do not mean that *any* action can be retroactively justified by history. Certain things are so bad in themselves, or so risky, that no results can make them all right. Nevertheless, when moral judgment does depend on the outcome, it is objective and timeless and not dependent on a change of standpoint produced by success or failure. The judgment after the fact follows from an hypothetical judgment that can be made beforehand, and it can be made as easily by someone else as by the agent.

From the point of view which makes responsibility dependent on control, all this seems absurd. How is it possible to be more or less culpable depending on whether a child gets into the path of one's car, or a bird into the path of one's bullet? Perhaps it is true that what is done depends on more than the agent's state of mind or intention. The problem then is, why is it not irrational to base moral assessment on what people do, in this broad sense? It amounts to holding them responsible for the contributions of fate as well as for their own—provided they have made some contribution to begin with. If we look at cases of negligence or attempt, the pattern seems to be that overall culpability corresponds to the product of mental or intentional fault and the seriousness of the outcome. Cases of decision under uncertainty are less easily explained in this way, for it seems that the overall judgment can even shift from positive to negative depending on the outcome. But here too it seems rational to subtract the effects of occurrences subsequent to the choice, that were merely possible at the time, and concentrate moral assessment on the actual decision in light of the probabilities. If the object of moral judgment is the *person*, then to hold him accountable for what he has done in the broader sense is akin to strict liability, which may have its legal uses but seems irrational as a moral position.

The result of such a line of thought is to pare down each act to its morally essential core, an inner act of pure will assessed by motive and intention.

Adam Smith advocates such a position in *The Theory of Moral Sentiments,* but notes that it runs contrary to our actual judgments.

> But how well soever we may seem to be persuaded of the truth of this equitable maxim, when we consider it after this manner, in abstract, yet when we come to particular cases, the actual consequences which happen to proceed from any action, have a very great effect upon our sentiments concerning its merit or demerit, and almost always either enhance or diminish our sense of both. Scarce, in any one instance, perhaps, will our sentiments be found, after examination, to be entirely regulated by this rule, which we all acknowledge ought entirely to regulate them.

Joel Feinberg points out further that restricting the domain of moral responsibility to the inner world will not immunize it to luck. Factors beyond the agent's control, like a coughing fit, can interfere with his decisions as surely as they can with the path of a bullet from his gun. Nevertheless the tendency to cut down the scope of moral assessment is pervasive, and does not limit itself to the influence of effects. It attempts to isolate the will from the other direction, so to speak, by separating out constitutive luck. Let us consider that next.

Kant was particularly insistent on the moral irrelevance of qualities of temperament and personality that are not under the control of the will. Such qualities as sympathy or coldness might provide the background against which obedience to moral requirements is more or less difficult, but they could not be objects of moral assessment themselves, and might well interfere with confident assessment of its proper object—the determination of the will by the motive of duty. This rules out moral judgment of many of the virtues and vices, which are states of character that influence choice but are certainly not exhausted by dispositions to act deliberately in certain ways. A person may be greedy, envious, cowardly, cold, ungenerous, unkind, vain, or conceited, but *behave* perfectly by a monumental effort of will. To possess these vices is to be unable to help having certain feelings under certain circumstances, and to have strong spontaneous impulses to act badly. Even if one controls the impulses, one still has the vice. An envious person hates the greater success of others. He can be morally condemned as envious even if he congratulates them cordially and does nothing to denigrate or spoil their success. Conceit, likewise, need not be displayed. It is fully present in someone who cannot help dwelling with secret satisfaction on the superiority of his own achievements, talents, beauty, intelligence, or virtue. To some extent such a quality may be the product of earlier choices; to some extent it may be amenable to change by current actions. But it is largely a matter of constitutive bad fortune. Yet people are morally condemned for such qualities, and esteemed for others equally beyond control of the will: they are assessed for what they are *like.*

To Kant this seems incoherent because virtue is enjoined on everyone and therefore must in principle be possible for everyone. It may be easier for some than for others, but it must be possible to achieve it by making the right choices, against whatever temperamental background. One may want to have a generous spirit, or regret not having one, but it makes no sense to condemn oneself or anyone else for a quality which is not within the control of the will. Condemnation implies that you should not be like that, not that it is unfortunate that you are.

Nevertheless, Kant's conclusion remains intuitively unacceptable. We may be persuaded that these moral judgments are irrational, but they reappear involuntarily as soon as the argument is over. This is the pattern throughout the subject.

The third category to consider is luck in one's circumstances, and I shall mention it briefly. The things we are called upon to do, the moral tests we face, are importantly determined by factors beyond our control. It may be true of someone that in a dangerous situation he would behave in a cowardly or heroic fashion, but if the situation never arises, he will never have the chance to distinguish or disgrace himself in this way, and his moral record will be different.

A conspicuous example of this is political. Ordinary citizens of Nazi Germany had an opportunity to behave heroically by opposing the regime. They also had an opportunity to behave badly, and most of them are culpable for having failed this test. But it is a test to which the citizens of other countries were not subjected, with the result that even if they, or some of them, would have behaved as badly as the Germans in like circumstances, they simply did not and therefore are not similarly culpable. Here again one is morally at the mercy of fate, and it may seem irrational upon reflection, but our ordinary moral attitudes would be unrecognizable without it. We judge people for what they actually do or fail to do, not just for what they would have done if circumstances had been different.

This form of moral determination by the actual is also paradoxical, but we can begin to see how deep in the concept of responsibility the paradox is embedded. A person can be morally responsible only for what he does; but what he does results from a great deal that he does not do; therefore he is not morally responsible for what he is and is not responsible for. (This is not a contradiction, but it is a paradox.)

It should be obvious that there is a connection between these problems about responsibility and control and an even more familiar problem, that of freedom of the will. That is the last type of moral luck I want to take up, though I can do no more within the scope of this essay than indicate its connection with the other types.

If one cannot be responsible for consequences of one's acts due to factors beyond one's control, or for antecedents of one's acts that are properties of temperament not subject to one's will, or for the circumstances that pose one's moral choices, then how can one be responsible even for the stripped-down acts of the will itself, if *they* are the product of antecedent circumstances outside of the will's control?

The area of genuine agency, and therefore of legitimate moral judgment, seems to shrink under this scrutiny to an extensionless point. Everything seems to result from the combined influence of factors, antecedent and posterior to action, that are not within the agent's control. Since he cannot be responsible for them, he cannot be responsible for their results—though it may remain possible to take up the aesthetic or other evaluative analogues of the moral attitudes that are thus displaced.

It is also possible, of course, to brazen it out and refuse to accept the results, which indeed seem unacceptable as soon as we stop thinking about the arguments. Admittedly, if certain surrounding circumstances had been different, then no unfortunate consequences would have followed from a wicked intention, and no seriously culpable act would have been performed; but since the circumstances were *not* different, and the agent *in fact* succeeded in perpetrating a particularly cruel murder, *that* is what he did, and that is what he is responsible for. Similarly, we may admit that if certain antecedent circumstances had been different, the agent would never have developed into the sort of person who would do such a thing; but since he *did* develop (as the inevitable result of those antecedent circumstances) into the sort of swine he is, and into the person who committed such a murder, *that* is what he is blamable for. In both cases one is responsible for what one actually does—even if what one actually does depends in important ways on what is not within one's control. This [compatibilist] account of our moral judgments would leave room for the ordinary conditions of responsibility—the absence of coercion, ignorance, or involuntary movement—as part of the determination of what someone has done—but it is understood not to exclude the influence of a great deal that he has not done.

The only thing wrong with this solution is its failure to explain how skeptical problems arise. For they arise not from the imposition of an arbitrary external requirement, but from the nature of moral judgment itself. Something in the ordinary idea of what someone does must explain how it can seem necessary to subtract from it anything that merely happens—even though the ultimate consequence of such subtraction is that nothing remains. And something in the ordinary idea of knowledge must explain why it seems to be undermined by any influences on belief not within the control of the subject—so that knowledge seems impossible without an impossible foundation in autonomous reason. But let us leave epistemology aside and concentrate on action, character, and moral assessment.

The problem arises, I believe, because the self which acts and is the object of moral judgment is threatened with dissolution by the absorption of its acts and impulses into the class of events. Moral judgment of a person is judgment not of what happens to him, but of him. It does not say merely that a certain event or state of affairs is fortunate or unfortunate or even terrible. It is not an evaluation of a state of the world, or of an individual as part of the world. We are not thinking just that it would be better if he were different, or did not exist, or had not done some of the things he has done. We are judging *him*, rather than his existence or characteristics. The effect of concentrating on the influence of what is not under his control is to make this responsible self seem to disappear, swallowed up by the order of mere events.

What, however, do we have in mind that a person must *be* to be the object of these moral attitudes? While the concept of agency is easily undermined, it is very difficult to give it a positive characterization. That is familiar from the literature on Free Will.

I believe that in a sense the problem has no solution, because something in the idea of agency is incompatible with actions being events, or people being things. But as the external determinants of what someone has done are gradually exposed, in their effect on consequences, character, and choice itself, it becomes gradually clear that actions are events and people things. Eventually nothing remains which can be ascribed to the responsible self, and we are left with nothing but a portion of the larger sequences of events, which can be deplored or celebrated, but not blamed or praised.

Though I cannot define the idea of the active self that is thus undermined, it is possible to say something about its sources. There is a close connection between our feelings about ourselves and our feelings about others. Guilt and indignation, shame and contempt, pride and admiration are internal and external sides of the same moral attitudes. We are unable to view ourselves simply as portions of the world, and from inside we have a rough idea of the boundary between what is us and what is not, what we do and what happens to us, what is our personality and what is an accidental handicap. We apply the same essentially internal conception of the self to others. About ourselves we feel pride, shame, guilt, remorse—and agent-regret. We do not regard our actions and our characters merely as fortunate or unfortunate episodes—though they may also be that. We cannot *simply* take an external evaluative view of ourselves—of what we most essentially are and what we do. And this remains true even when we have seen that we are not responsible for our own existence, or our nature, or the choices we have to make, or the circumstances that give our acts the consequences they have. Those acts remain ours and we remain ourselves, despite the persuasiveness of the reasons that seem to argue us out of existence.

It is this internal view that we extend to others in moral judgment—when we judge *them* rather than their desirability or utility. We extend to others the refusal to limit ourselves to external evaluation, and we accord to them selves like our own. But in both cases this comes up against the brutal inclusion of humans and everything about them in a world from which they cannot be separated and of which they are nothing but contents. The external view forces itself on us at the same time that we resist it. One way this occurs is through the gradual erosion of what we do by the subtraction of what happens.

The inclusion of consequences in the conception of what we have done is an acknowledgment that we are parts of the world, but the paradoxical character of moral luck which emerges from this acknowledgment shows that we are unable to operate with such a view, for it leaves us with no one to be. The same thing is revealed in the appearance that determinism obliterates responsibility. Once we see an aspect of what we or someone else does as something that happens, we lose our grip on the idea that it has been done and that we can judge the doer and not just the happening. This explains why the absence of determinism is no more hospitable to the concept of agency than is its presence—a point that has been noticed often. Either way the act is viewed externally, as part of the course of events.

The problem of moral luck cannot be understood without an account of the internal conception of agency and its special connection with the moral attitudes as opposed to other types of value. I do not have such an account. The degree to which the problem has a solution can be determined only by seeing whether in some degree the incompatibility between this conception and the various ways in which we do not control what we do is only apparent. I have nothing to offer on that topic either. But it is not enough to say merely that our basic moral attitudes toward ourselves and others are determined by what is actual; for they are also threatened by the sources of that actuality, and by the external view of action which forces itself on us when we see how everything we do belongs to a world that we have not created.

For Further Reflection

1. What is Nagel's criticism of Kant? Why does he think that Kant's notion of the good will as the sole determinant of moral goodness is simplistic?
2. Go over the types of moral luck that Nagel discusses. Are his arguments cogent and persuasive? It might help to examine the main examples. Take the German who becomes a Nazi officer and does great evil, but who in different, more peaceful circumstances would have been an average

citizen with no great moral culpability. Is Nagel correct to say that the officer just has bad moral luck? Or can more be said about this assessment that would make sense of the Kantian idea of moral goodness?

3. Why does Nagel think that our notion of moral responsibility is deeply problematic, even incoherent?
4. Nagel believes that the free will determinist debate is paradoxical. If we are determined by antecedent circumstances, then we are not responsible for what we do; but if we are not determined by these conditions, then everything seems arbitrary—free will seems to presuppose the very causal structure that it attacks. Does this make sense? Do you believe that you have free will? Explain your answer.
5. Do you believe there is moral luck, or can we, in principle, make genuine moral judgments about people and their actions?

New Year's Eve

CARL DENNIS

Carl Dennis is an American poet and a professor of English at the State University of New York–Buffalo. His many books of poetry include *Meetings with Time* (1992) and *Practical Gods* (2001), for which he won the Pulitzer Prize.

However busy you are, you should still reserve
One evening a year for thinking about your double,
The man who took the curve on Conway Road
Too fast, given the icy patches that night,
But no faster than you did; the man whose car
When it slid through the shoulder
Happened to strike a girl walking alone
From a neighbor's party to her parents' farm,
While your car struck nothing more notable
Than a snowbank.

First published in *The New Yorker*, 2011. Reprinted with permission of the author.

One evening for recalling how soon you transformed
Your accident into a comic tale
Told first at a body shop, for comparing
That hour of pleasure with his hour of pain
At the house of the stricken parents, and his many
Long afternoons at the Lutheran graveyard.

If nobody blames you for assuming your luck
Has something to do with your character,
Don't blame him for assuming that his misfortune
Is somehow deserved, that justice would be undone
If his extra grief was balanced later
By a portion of extra joy.

Lucky you, whose personal faith has widened
To include an angel assigned to protect you
From the usual outcome of heedless moments.
But this evening consider the angel he lives with,
The stern enforcer who drives the sinners
Out of the Garden with a flaming sword
And locks the gate.

For Further Reflection

1. What is Dennis saying about moral luck? Does he think that luck plays an important role in the moral life? Or does he consider it a negligible factor best ignored? Explain.
2. According to Dennis, should good fortune be viewed as a reward for having good character? Should misfortune be seen as deserved punishment? Why or why not?
3. What is Dennis's point about protective and stern angels?

Further Readings for Chapter 5

Acton, Harry. *Kant's Moral Philosophy.* New York: Macmillan, 1970.

Broad, C. D. *Five Types of Ethical Theory.* London: Routledge and Kegan Paul, 1930.

Donagan, Alan. *The Theory of Morality.* Chicago: University of Chicago Press, 1977.

Feldman, Fred. *Introductory Ethics.* Englewood Cliffs, N.J.: Prentice-Hall, 1978. Chapters 7 and 8 offer a clear and critical exposition.

Harris, C. E. *Applying Moral Theories.* Belmont, Calif.: Wadsworth, 1986. Chapter 7 offers an excellent exposition of contemporary deontological theories, especially of Gewirth's work.

Kant, Immanuel. *Critique of Practical Reason.* Translated by Lewis White Beck. Indianapolis: Bobbs-Merrill, 1956.

———. *Grounding for the Metaphysics of Morals.* Translated by James Ellington. Indianapolis: Hackett, 1981.

———. *Lectures on Ethics.* Translated by Louis Infield. Indianapolis: Hackett, 1963.

Raphael, D. D. *Moral Philosophy.* Oxford: Oxford University Press, 1981. See Chapter 6 in particular.

Ross, W. D. *Kant's Ethical Theory.* Oxford: Clarendon Press, 1954.

———. *The Right and the Good.* Oxford: Oxford University Press, 1930.

Ward, Keith. *The Development of Kant's Views of Ethics.* Oxford: Blackwell's, 1972.

Wolff, Robert P. *The Autonomy of Reason: A Commentary on Kant's Groundwork of the Metaphysics of Morals.* New York: Harper & Row, 1973.

CHAPTER 6

Virtue Ethics

John hears that 100,000 people are starving in Ethiopia. He feels deep sorrow about this and sends $100 of his hard-earned money to a famine relief project in that country. Joan hears the same news but doesn't feel anything. However, out of a sense of duty, she also sends $100 of her hard-earned money to the relief project.

Jack and Jill each have the opportunity to embezzle a million dollars from the bank at which they work. Jill never even considers embezzling; the possibility is not even an option for her. Jack wrestles valiantly with the temptation, almost succumbs to it, but through a grand effort of the will finally succeeds in resisting the temptation.

Who in each case is more moral?

Whereas most ethical theories have been either duty-oriented or action-oriented, that is, either deontological or teleological (utilitarian), there is a third tradition that goes back to Plato and especially Aristotle, and that receives support in the writings of the Epicureans, the Stoics, Jesus, and the early Christian church. We refer to *virtue ethics* (sometimes called *aretaic ethics* after the Greek word *arete,* meaning "excellence" or "virtue"). Rather than seeing the heart of ethics in action or duties, virtue ethics centers in the heart and personality of the agent—in his or her character. Whereas an action-based ethics emphasizes *doing,* virtue ethics emphasizes *being*—being a certain kind of person who will no doubt manifest his or her being in actions or nonactions. For traditional duty-based ethics, the question is "What should I do?" For the virtue ethicist, the question is "What sort of person should I become?"

Virtue ethics seeks to produce excellent persons, who act well out of spontaneous goodness and serve as examples to inspire others. It seeks to create people like Moses, Confucius, Socrates, Jesus, Buddha, Albert Schweitzer, Mohandas Gandhi, and Rosa Parks—people who light up our moral landscape as jewels who shine in their own light.

We begin our study with a classic passage on the virtues by Aristotle. Then we contemplate modern interpretations of virtues by Alasdair MacIntyre, Susan Wolf, and Bernard Mayo. Next comes Nathaniel Hawthorne's short story "The Great Stone Face," and William K. Frankena's argument that whatever is valid about virtue ethics should be subordinate to a deontological system. We round out the chapter with several literary and philosophical meditations on specific virtues and vices.

Virtue Ethics

ARISTOTLE

Aristotle (384–322 B.C.) was born in Stagira in Macedon, the son of a physician. He was a student of Plato at the Academy in Athens and tutor of Alexander the Great. Aristotle saw ethics as the branch of political philosophy concerned with the good life. He thus views ethics as a practical rather than a purely theoretical science. In this selection from *Nicomachean Ethics*, Aristotle considers the nature of ethics in relation to human nature. From this same perspective he discusses the nature of virtue, which he defines as traits that enable us to live well in communities. To achieve a state of well-being or happiness, proper social institutions are necessary. Thus, the moral person cannot exist in isolation from a flourishing political community that enables the person to develop the necessary virtues for the good life.

Aristotle goes on to show the difference between moral and intellectual virtues. While the intellectual virtues may be taught directly, the moral ones must be lived in order to be learned. By living well, we acquire the best guarantee to the happy life. But again, happiness requires that one be lucky enough to live in a flourishing state. By considering luck as part of morality, Aristotle distinguishes his position from deontological ones like those of the Bible and Kant and so defends a point noted in Nagel's article—the importance of luck to morality. In the last analysis, the moral life consists in moderation, living in accordance with the "golden mean," a middle ground between extremes.

BOOK I

All Human Activities Aim at Some Good

Chapter 1. Every art and every scientific inquiry, and similarly every action and purpose, may be said to aim at some good. Hence the good has been well defined as that at which all things aim. But it is clear that there is a difference in ends; for the ends are sometimes activities, and sometimes results beyond the mere activities. Where there are ends beyond the action, the results are naturally superior to the action.

As there are various actions, arts, and sciences, it follows that the ends are also various. Thus health is the end of the medical art, a ship of shipbuilding,

---

Reprinted from *Aristotle's Nichomachean Ethics,* translated by James E. C. Weldon (Macmillan, 1897).

victory of strategy, and wealth of economics. It often happens that a number of such arts or sciences combine for a single enterprise, as the art of making bridles and all such other arts as furnish the implements of horsemanship combine for horsemanship, and horsemanship and every military action for strategy; and in the same way, other arts or sciences combine for others. In all these cases, the ends of the master arts or sciences, whatever they may be, are more desirable than those of the subordinate arts or sciences, as it is for the sake of the former that the latter are pursued. It makes no difference to the argument whether the activities themselves are the ends of the action, or something beyond the activities, as in the above-mentioned sciences.

If it is true that in the sphere of action there is some end which we wish for its own sake, and for the sake of which we wish everything else, and if we do not desire everything for the sake of something else (for, if that is so, the process will go on *ad infinitum,* and our desire will be idle and futile), clearly this end will be good and the supreme good. Does it not follow then that the knowledge of this good is of great importance for the conduct of life? Like archers who have a mark at which to aim, shall we not have a better chance of attaining what we want? If this is so, we must endeavor to comprehend, at least in outline, what this good is, and what science or faculty makes it its object.

It would seem that this is the most authoritative science. Such a kind is evidently the political, for it is that which determines what sciences are necessary in states, and what kinds should be studied, and how far they should be studied by each class of inhabitant. We see too that even the faculties held in highest esteem, such as strategy, economics, and rhetoric, are subordinate to it. Then since politics makes use of the other sciences and also rules what people may do and what they may not do, it follows that its end will comprehend the ends of the other sciences, and will therefore be the good of mankind. For even if the good of an individual is identical with the good of a state, yet the good of the state is evidently greater and more perfect to attain or to preserve. For though the good of an individual by himself is something worth working for, to ensure the good of a nation or a state is nobler and more divine.

These then are the objects at which the present inquiry aims, and it is in a sense a political inquiry. . . .

The Science of the Good for Man Is Politics

Chapter 2. As every science and undertaking aims at some good, what is in our view the good at which political science aims, and what is the highest of all practical goods? As to its name there is, I may say, a general agreement. The masses and the cultured classes agree in calling it happiness, and conceive that "to live well" or "to do well" is the same thing as "to be happy." But as to what happiness is they do not agree, nor do the masses give the same account of it as the philosophers. The former take it to be something visible and palpable, such as pleasure, wealth, or honor; different people, however, give different definitions of it, and often even the same man gives different definitions at different times. When he is ill, it is health, when he is poor, it is wealth; if he is conscious of his own ignorance, he envies people who use grand language above his own comprehension. Some philosophers, on the other hand, have held that, besides these various goods, there is an absolute good which is the cause of goodness in them all.[1] It would perhaps be a waste of time to examine all these opinions; it will be enough to examine such as are most popular or as seem to be more or less reasonable.

Chapter 3. Men's conception of the good or of happiness may be read in the lives they lead. Ordinary or vulgar people conceive it to be a pleasure, and accordingly choose a life of enjoyment. For there are, we may say, three conspicuous types of life, the sensual, the political, and, thirdly, the life of thought. Now the mass of men present an absolutely slavish appearance, choosing the life of brute beasts, but they have ground for so doing because so many persons in authority share the tastes of Sardanapalus.[2] Cultivated and energetic people, on the other hand, identify happiness with honor, as honor is the general end of political life. But this seems too superficial an idea for our present purpose; for honor depends more upon the people who pay it than upon the person to whom it is paid, and the good we feel is something which is proper to a man himself and cannot be easily taken away from him. Men too appear to seek honor in order to be assured of their own goodness. Accordingly, they seek it at the hands of the sage and of those who know them well, and they seek it on the ground of their virtue; clearly then, in their judgment at any rate, virtue is better than honor. Perhaps then we might look on virtue rather than honor as the end of political life. Yet even this idea appears not quite complete; for a man may possess virtue and yet be asleep or inactive throughout life, and not only so, but he may experience the greatest calamities and misfortunes. Yet no one would call such a life a life of happiness, unless he were maintaining a paradox. But we need not dwell further on this subject, since it is sufficiently discussed in popular philosophical treatises. The third life is the life of thought, which we will discuss later.

The life of money making is a life of constraint; and wealth is obviously not the good of which we are in quest; for it is useful merely as a means to

[1]Plato.

[2]A half-legendary ruler whose name to the Greeks stood for extreme mental luxury and extravagance.

something else. It would be more reasonable to take the things mentioned before—sensual pleasure, honor, and virtue—as ends than wealth, since they are things desired on their own account. Yet these too are evidently not ends, although much argument has been employed to show that they are. . . .

Characteristics of the Good

Chapter 5. But leaving this subject for the present, let us revert to the good of which we are in quest and consider what it may be. For it seems different in different activities or arts; it is one thing in medicine, another in strategy, and so on. What is the good in each of these instances? It is presumably that for the sake of which all else is done. In medicine this is health, in strategy victory, in architecture a house, and so on. In every activity and undertaking it is the end, since it is for the sake of the end that all people do whatever else they do. If then there is an end for all our activity, this will be the good to be accomplished; and if there are several such ends, it will be these.

Our argument has arrived by a different path at the same point as before; but we must endeavor to make it still plainer. Since there are more ends than one, and some of these ends—for example, wealth, flutes, and instruments generally—we desire as means to something else, it is evident that not all are final ends. But the highest good is clearly something final. Hence if there is only one final end, this will be the object of which we are in search; and if there are more than one, it will be the most final. We call that which is sought after for its own sake more final than that which is sought after as a means to something else; we call that which is never desired as a means to something else more final than things that are desired both for themselves and as means to something else. Therefore, we call absolutely final that which is always desired for itself and never as a means to something else. Now happiness more than anything else answers to this description. For happiness we always desire for its own sake and never as a means to something else, whereas honor, pleasure, intelligence, and every virtue we desire partly for their own sakes (for we should desire them independently of what might result from them), but partly also as means to happiness, because we suppose they will prove instruments of happiness. Happiness, on the other hand, nobody desires for the sake of these things, nor indeed as a means to anything else at all.

If we start from the point of view of self-sufficiency, we reach the same conclusion; for we assume that the final good is self-sufficient. By self-sufficiency we do not mean that a person leads a solitary life all by himself, but that he has parents, children, wife and friends and fellow citizens in general, as man is naturally a social being. Yet here it is necessary to set some limit; for if the circle must be extended to include ancestors, descendants, and friends'

friends, it will go on indefinitely. Leaving this point, however, for future investigation, we call the self-sufficient that which, taken even by itself, makes life desirable and wanting nothing at all; and this is what we mean by happiness.

Again, we think happiness the most desirable of all things, and that not merely as one good thing among others. If it were only that, the addition of the smallest more good would increase its desirableness; for the addition would make an increase of goods, and the greater of two goods is always the more desirable. Happiness is something final and self-sufficient and the end of all action.

Chapter 6. Perhaps, however, it seems a commonplace to say that happiness is the supreme good; what is wanted is to define its nature a little more clearly. The best way of arriving at such a definition will probably be to ascertain the function of man. For, as with a flute player, a sculptor, or any artist, or in fact anybody who has a special function or activity, his goodness and excellence seem to lie in his function, so it would seem to be with man, if indeed he has a special function. Can it be said that, while a carpenter and a cobbler have special functions and activities, man, unlike them, is naturally functionless? Or, as the eye, the hand, the foot, and similarly each part of the body has a special function, so may man be regarded as having a special function apart from all these? What, then, can this function be? It is not life; for life is apparently something that man shares with plants; and we are looking for something peculiar to him. We must exclude therefore the life of nutrition and growth. There is next what may be called the life of sensation. But this too, apparently, is shared by man with horses, cattle, and all other animals. There remains what I may call the active life of the rational part of man's being. Now this rational part is twofold; one part is rational in the sense of being obedient to reason, and the other in the sense of possessing and exercising reason and intelligence. The active life too may be conceived of in two ways, either as a state of character, or as an activity; but we mean by it the life of activity, as this seems to be the truer form of the conception.

The function of man then is activity of soul in accordance with reason, or not apart from reason. Now, the function of a man of a certain kind, and of a man who is good of that kind—for example, of a harpist and a good harpist—are in our view the same in kind. This is true of all people of all kinds without exception, the superior excellence being only an addition to the function; for it is the function of a harpist to play the harp, and of a good harpist to play the harp well. This being so, if we define the function of man as a kind of life, and this life as an activity of the soul or a course of action in accordance with reason, and if the function of a good man is such activity of a good and noble kind, and if everything is well done when it is done in accordance with its proper excellence, it follows that the good of man is activity of soul in accordance with virtue, or, if there are more virtues than one, in accordance with the best and most complete virtue. But we must add the words "in a complete life." For as one swallow or one day does not make a spring, so one day or a short time does not make a man blessed or happy. . . .

Inasmuch as happiness is an activity of soul in accordance with perfect virtue, we must now consider virtue, as this will perhaps be the best way of studying happiness. . . . Clearly it is human virtue we have to consider; for the good of which we are in search is, as we said, human good, and the happiness, human happiness. By human virtue or excellence we mean not that of the body, but that of the soul, and by happiness we mean an activity of the soul. . . .

BOOK II

Moral virtues can best be acquired by practice and habit. They imply a right attitude toward pleasures and pains. A good man deliberately chooses to do what is noble and right for its own sake. What is right in matters of moral conduct is usually a mean between two extremes.

Chapter 1. Virtue then is twofold, partly intellectual and partly moral, and intellectual virtue is originated and fostered mainly by teaching; it demands therefore experience and time. Moral virtue on the other hand is the outcome of habit, and accordingly its name, *ethike,* is derived by a slight variation from *ethos,* habit. From this fact it is clear that moral virtue is not implanted in us by nature; for nothing that exists by nature can be transformed by habit. Thus a stone, that naturally tends to fall downwards, cannot be habituated or trained to rise upwards, even if we tried to train it by throwing it up ten thousand times. Nor again can fire be trained to sink downwards, nor anything else that follows one natural law be habituated or trained to follow another. It is neither by nature then nor in defiance of nature that virtues grow in us. Nature gives us the capacity to receive them, and that capacity is perfected by habit.

Again, if we take the various natural powers which belong to us, we first possess the proper faculties and afterwards display the activities. It is obviously so with the senses. Not by seeing frequently or hearing frequently do we acquire the sense of seeing or hearing; on the contrary, because we have the senses we make use of them; we do not get them by making use of them. But the virtues we get by first practicing them, as we do in the arts. For it is by doing what we ought to do when we study the arts that we learn the arts themselves; we become builders by building and harpists by playing the harp. Similarly, it is by doing just acts that we become just, by doing temperate acts that we become temperate, by doing brave acts that we become brave. The experience of states confirms this statement, for it is by training in good habits that lawmakers make the citizens good. This is the object all lawmakers have at heart; if they do not succeed in it, they fail of their purpose; and it makes the distinction between a good constitution and a bad one.

Again, the causes and means by which any virtue is produced and destroyed are the same; and equally so in any part. For it is by playing the harp that both good and bad harpists are produced; and the case of builders and others is similar, for it is by building well that they become good builders and by building badly that they become bad builders. If it were not so, there would be no need of anybody to teach them; they would all be born good or bad in their several crafts. The case of the virtues is the same. It is by our actions in dealings between man and man that we become either just or unjust. It is by our actions in the face of danger and by our training ourselves to fear or to courage that we become either cowardly or courageous. It is much the same with our appetites and angry passions. People become temperate and gentle, others licentious and passionate, by behaving in one or the other way in particular circumstances. In a word, moral states are the results of activities like the states themselves. It is our duty therefore to keep a certain character in our activities, since our moral states depend on the differences in our activities. So the difference between one and another training in habits in our childhood is not a light matter, but important, or rather, all-important.

Chapter 2. Our present study is not, like other studies, purely theoretical in intention; for the object of our inquiry is not to know what virtue is but how to become good, and that is the sole benefit of it. We must, therefore, consider the right way of performing actions, for it is acts, as we have said, that determine the character of the resulting moral states.

That we should act in accordance with right reason is a common general principle, which may here be taken for granted. The nature of right reason, and its relation to the virtues generally, will be discussed later. But first of all it must be admitted that all reasoning on matters of conduct must be like a sketch in outline; it cannot be scientifically exact. We began by laying down the principle that the kind of reasoning demanded in any subject must be such as the subject matter itself allows; and questions of conduct and expediency no more admit of hard and fast rules than questions of health.

If this is true of general reasoning on ethics, still more true is it that scientific exactitude is impossible in treating of particular ethical cases. They do not fall under any art or law, but the actors themselves have always to take account of circumstances, as much as in medicine or navigation. Still, although such is the nature of our present argument, we must try to make the best of it.

The first point to be observed is that in the matters we are now considering deficiency and excess are both fatal. It is so, we see, in questions of health and strength. (We must judge of what we cannot see by the evidence of what we do see.) Too much or too little gymnastic exercise is fatal to strength. Similarly, too much or too little meat and drink is fatal to health, whereas a suitable amount produces, increases, and sustains it. It is the same with temperance, courage, and other moral virtues. A person who avoids and is afraid of everything and faces nothing becomes a coward; a person who is not afraid of anything but is ready to face everything becomes foolhardy. Similarly, he who enjoys every pleasure and abstains from none is licentious; he who refuses all pleasures, like a boor, is an insensible sort of person. For temperance and courage are destroyed by excess and deficiency but preserved by the mean.

Again, not only are the causes and agencies of production, increase, and destruction in moral states the same, but the field of their activity is the same also. It is so in other more obvious instances, as, for example, strength; for strength is produced by taking a great deal of food and undergoing a great deal of exertion, and it is the strong man who is able to take most food and undergo most exertion. So too with the virtues. By abstaining from pleasures we become temperate, and, when we have become temperate, we are best able to abstain from them. So again with courage; it is by training ourselves to despise and face terrifying things that we become brave, and when we have become brave, we shall be best able to face them.

The pleasure or pain which accompanies actions may be regarded as a test of a person's moral state. He who abstains from physical pleasures and feels pleasure in so doing is temperate; but he who feels pain at so doing is licentious. He who faces dangers with pleasure, or at least without pain, is brave; but he who feels pain at facing them is a coward. For moral virtue is concerned with pleasures and pains. It is pleasure which makes us do what is base, and pain which makes us abstain from doing what is noble. Hence the importance of having a certain training from very early days, as Plato says, so that we may feel pleasure and pain at the right objects; for this is true education. . . .

Chapter 3. But we may be asked what we mean by saying that people must become just by doing what is just and temperate by doing what is temperate. For, it will be said, if they do what is just and temperate they are already just and temperate themselves, in the same way as, if they practice grammar and music, they are grammarians and musicians.

But is this true even in the case of the arts? For a person may speak grammatically either by chance or at the suggestion of somebody else; hence he will not be a grammarian unless he not only speaks grammatically but does so in a grammatical manner, that is, because of the grammatical knowledge which he possesses.

There is a point of difference too between the arts and the virtues. The productions of art have their excellence in themselves. It is enough then that, when they are produced, they themselves should possess a certain character. But acts in accordance with virtue are not justly or temperately performed simply because they are in themselves just or temperate. The doer at the time of performing them must satisfy certain conditions; in the first place, he must know what he is doing; secondly, he must deliberately choose to do it and do it for its own sake; and thirdly, he must do it as part of his own firm and immutable character. If it be a question of art, these conditions, except only the condition of knowledge, are not raised; but if it be a question of virtue, mere knowledge is of little or no avail; it is the other conditions, which are the results of frequently performing just and temperate acts, that are not slightly but all-important. Accordingly, deeds are called just and temperate when they are such as a just and temperate person would do; and a just and temperate person is not merely one who does these deeds but one who does them in the spirit of the just and the temperate.

It may fairly be said that a just man becomes just by doing what is just, and a temperate man becomes temperate by doing what is temperate, and if a man did not so act, he would not have much chance of becoming good. But most people, instead of acting, take refuge in theorizing; they imagine that they are philosophers and that philosophy will make them virtuous; in fact, they behave like people who listen attentively to their doctors but never do anything that their doctors tell them. But a healthy state of the soul will no more be produced by this kind of philosophizing than a healthy state of the body by this kind of medical treatment.

Chapter 4. We have next to consider the nature of virtue. Now, as the properties of the soul are three, namely, emotions, faculties, and moral states, it follows that virtue must be one of the three. By emotions I mean desire, anger, fear, pride, envy, joy, love, hatred, regret, ambition, pity—in a word, whatever feeling is attended by pleasure or pain. I call those faculties through which we are said to be capable of experiencing these emotions, for instance, capable of getting angry or being pained or feeling pity. And I call those moral states through which we are well or ill disposed in our emotions, ill disposed, for instance, in anger, if our anger be too violent or too feeble, and well disposed, if it be rightly moderate; and similarly in our other emotions.

Now neither the virtues nor the vices are emotions; for we are not called good or bad for our emotions but for our virtues or vices. We are not praised or blamed simply for being angry, but only for being angry in a certain way; but we are praised or blamed for our virtues or vices. Again, whereas we are angry or afraid without deliberate purpose, the virtues are matters of deliberate purpose, or require deliberate purpose. Moreover, we are said to be moved by our emotions, but by our virtues or vices we are not said to be moved but to have a certain disposition.

For these reasons the virtues are not faculties. For we are not called either good or bad, nor are we praised or blamed for having simple capacity for emotion. Also while Nature gives us our faculties, it is not Nature that makes us good or bad; but this point we have already discussed. If then the virtues are neither emotions nor faculties, all that remains is that they must be moral states.

Chapter 5. The nature of virtue has been now described in kind. But it is not enough to say merely that virtue is a moral state; we must also describe the character of that moral state.

We may assert then that every virtue or excellence puts into good condition that of which it is a virtue or excellence, and enables it to perform its work well. Thus excellence in the eye makes the eye good and its function good, for by excellence in the eye we see well. Similarly, excellence of the horse makes a horse excellent himself and good at racing, at carrying its rider and at facing the enemy. If then this rule is universally true, the virtue or excellence of a man will be such a moral state as makes a man good and able to perform his proper function well. How this will be the case we have already explained, but another way of making it clear will be to study the nature or character of virtue.

Now of everything, whether it be continuous or divisible, it is possible to take a greater, a smaller, or an equal amount, and this either in terms of the thing itself or in relation to ourselves, the equal being a mean between too much and too little. By the mean in terms of the thing itself, I understand that which is equally distinct from both its extremes, which is one and the same for every man. By the mean relatively to ourselves, I understand that which is neither too much nor too little for us; but this is not one nor the same for everybody. Thus if 10 be too much and 2 too little, we take 6 as a mean in terms of the thing itself; for 6 is as much greater than 2 as it is less than 10, and this is a mean in arithmetical proportion. But the mean considered relatively to ourselves may not be ascertained in that way. It does not follow that if 10 pounds of meat is too much and 2 too little for a man to eat, the trainer will order him 6 pounds, since this also may be too much or too little for him who is to take it; it will be too little, for example, for Milo but too much for a beginner in gymnastics. The same with running and wrestling; the right amount will vary with the individual. This being so, the skillful in any art avoids alike excess and deficiency; he seeks and chooses the mean, not the absolute mean, but the mean considered relatively to himself.

Every art then does its work well, if it regards the mean and judges the works it produces by the mean. For this reason we often say of successful works of art that it is impossible to take anything from them or to add anything to them, which implies that excess or deficiency is fatal to excellence but that the mean state ensures it. Good artists too, as we say, have an eye to the mean in their works. Now virtue, like Nature herself, is more accurate and better than any art; virtue, therefore, will aim at the mean. I speak of moral virtue, since it is moral virtue which is concerned with emotions and actions, and it is in these we have excess and deficiency and the mean. Thus it is possible to go too far, or not far enough in fear, pride, desire, anger, pity, and pleasure and pain generally, and the excess and the deficiency are alike wrong; but to feel these emotions at the right times, for the right objects, towards the right persons, for the right motives, and in the right manner, is the mean or the best good, which signifies virtue. Similarly, there may be excess, deficiency, or the mean, in acts. Virtue is concerned with both emotions and actions, wherein excess is an error and deficiency a fault, while the mean is successful and praised, and success and praise are both characteristics of virtue.

It appears then that virtue is a kind of mean because it aims at the mean.

On the other hand, there are many different ways of going wrong; for evil is in its nature infinite, to use the Pythagorean phrase, but good is finite and there is only one possible way of going right. So the former is easy and the latter is difficult; it is easy to miss the mark but difficult to hit it. And so by our reasoning excess and deficiency are characteristics of vice and the mean is a characteristic of virtue.

For good is simple, evil manifold.

Chapter 6. Virtue then is a state of deliberate moral purpose, consisting in a mean relative to ourselves, the mean being determined by reason, or as a prudent man would determine it. It is a mean, firstly, as lying between two vices, the vice of excess on the one hand, the vice of deficiency on the other, and, secondly, because, whereas the vices either fall short of or go beyond what is right in emotion and action, virtue discovers and chooses the mean. Accordingly, virtue, if regarded in its essence or theoretical definition, is a mean, though, if regarded from the point of view of what is best and most excellent, it is an extreme.

But not every action or every emotion admits of a mean. There are some whose very name implies wickedness, as, for example, malice, shamelessness, and envy among the emotions, and adultery, theft, and murder among the actions. All these and others like them are marked as intrinsically wicked, not merely the excesses or deficiencies of them. It is never possible then to be right in them; they are always sinful. Right or wrong in such acts as adultery does not depend on our committing it with the right woman, at the right time, or in the right manner; on the contrary, it is wrong to do it at all. It would be equally false to suppose that there can be a mean or an excess or deficiency in unjust, cowardly or licentious conduct; for, if that were so, it would be a mean of excess and deficiency, an excess of excess and a deficiency of deficiency. But as in temperance and courage there can be no excess or deficiency, because the mean there is in a sense an extreme, so too in these other cases there cannot be a mean or an excess or a deficiency, but however the acts are done, they are wrong. For in general an excess or deficiency does not have a mean, nor a mean an excess or deficiency. . . .

Chapter 8. There are then three dispositions, two being vices, namely, excess and deficiency, and one virtue, which is the mean between them; and they are all in a sense mutually opposed. The extremes are opposed both to the mean and to each other, and the mean is opposed to the extremes. For as the equal if compared with the less is greater, but if compared with the greater is less, so the mean state, whether in emotion or action, if compared with deficiency is excessive, but if compared with excess is deficient. Thus the brave man appears foolhardy compared with the coward, but cowardly compared with the foolhardy. Similarly, the temperate man appears licentious compared with the insensible man but insensible compared with the licentious; and the liberal man appears extravagant compared with the stingy man but stingy compared with the spendthrift. The result is that the extremes each denounce the mean as belonging to the other extreme; the coward calls the brave man foolhardy, and the foolhardy man calls him cowardly; and so on in other cases.

But while there is mutual opposition between the extremes and the mean, there is greater opposition between the two extremes than between extreme and the mean; for they are further removed from each other than from the mean, as the great is further from the small and the small from the great than either from the equal. Again, while some extremes show some likeness to the mean, as foolhardiness to courage and extravagance to liberality, there is the greatest possible dissimilarity between extremes. But things furthest removed from each other are called opposites; hence the further things are removed, the greater is the opposition between them.

In some cases it is deficiency and in others excess which is more opposed to the mean. Thus it is not foolhardiness, an excess, but cowardice, a deficiency, which is more opposed to courage, nor is it insensibility, a deficiency, but licentiousness, an excess, which is more opposed to temperance. There are two reasons why this should be so. One lies in the nature of the matter itself; for when one of two extremes is nearer and more like the mean, it is not this extreme but its opposite that we chiefly contrast with the mean. For instance, as foolhardiness seems more like and nearer to courage than cowardice, it is cowardice that we chiefly contrast with courage; for things further removed from the mean seem to be more opposite to it. This reason lies in the nature of the matter itself; there is a second which lies in our own nature. The things to which we ourselves are naturally more inclined we think more opposed to the mean. Thus we are ourselves naturally more inclined to pleasures than to their opposites, and are more prone therefore to self-indulgence than to moderation. Accordingly we speak of those things in which we are more likely to run to great lengths as more opposed to the mean. Hence licentiousness, which is an excess, seems more opposed to temperance than insensibility.

Chapter 9. We have now sufficiently shown that moral virtue is a mean, and in what sense it is so; that it is a mean as lying between two vices, a vice of excess on the one side and a vice of deficiency on the other, and as aiming at the mean in emotion and action.

That is why it is so hard to be good; for it is always hard to find the mean in anything; it is not everyone but only a man of science who can find the mean or center of a circle. So too anybody can get angry—that is easy—and anybody can give or spend money, but to give it to the right person, to give the right amount of it, at the right time, for the right cause and in the right way, this is not what anybody can do, nor is it easy. That is why goodness is rare and praise worthy and noble. One then who aims at a mean must begin by departing from the extreme that is more contrary to the mean; he must act in the spirit of Calypso's advice,

> Far from this spray and swell hold thou thy ship,

for of the two extremes one is more wrong than the other. As it is difficult to hit the mean exactly, we should take the second best course, as the saying is, and choose the lesser of two evils. This we shall best do in the way described, that is, steering clear of the evil which is further from the mean. We must also note the weaknesses to which we are ourselves particularly prone, since different natures tend in different ways; and we may ascertain what our tendency is by observing our feelings of pleasure and pain. Then we must drag ourselves away towards the opposite extreme; for by pulling ourselves as far as possible from what is wrong we shall arrive at the mean, as we do when we pull a crooked stick straight.

In all cases we must especially be on our guard against the pleasant, or pleasure, for we are not impartial judges of pleasure. Hence our attitude towards pleasure must be like that of the elders of the people in the *Iliad* towards Helen, and we must constantly apply the words they use; for if we dismiss pleasure as they dismissed Helen, we shall be less likely to go wrong. By action of this kind, to put it summarily, we shall best succeed in hitting the mean.

Undoubtedly this is a difficult task, especially in individual cases. It is not easy to determine the right manner, objects, occasion and duration of anger. Sometimes we praise people who are deficient in anger, and call them gentle, and at other times we praise people who exhibit a fierce temper as high spirited. It is not however a man who deviates a little from goodness, but one who deviates a great deal, whether on the side of excess or of deficiency, that is blamed; for he is sure to call attention to himself. It is not easy to decide in theory how far and to what extent a man may go before he becomes blameworthy, but neither is it easy to define in theory anything else in the region of the senses; such things depend on circumstances, and our judgment of them depends on our perception.

So much then is plain, that the mean is everywhere praiseworthy, but that we ought to aim at one time towards an excess and at another towards a deficiency; for thus we shall most easily hit the mean, or in other words reach excellence.

For Further Reflection

1. Is Aristotle's concept of happiness clear? Is it a subjective or objective notion? That is, is it subjective, in the mind of the beholder, so one is just as happy as one feels oneself to be; or is it objective, defined by a state of being and having certain characteristics regardless of how one feels? According to Aristotle, could a criminal be happy?
2. Is Aristotle's ethics sufficiently action-guiding? Does it help us make decisions? If I ask what should I do in situation *X*, Aristotle would seem to say, "Do what the virtuous person would do." But if I ask how I am to recognize the virtuous person, he would seem to say, "He is one who acts justly." Is there something circular about this reasoning? Does virtue ethics need supplementation from other ethical systems, or can it solve this problem?

The Virtues

ALASDAIR MACINTYRE

In this selection Alasdair MacIntyre reviews major accounts of virtues in history—those of Homer, Aristotle, and the New Testament—and asks whether there exists a core concept of virtue that is common to these diverse views. His answer is that virtues arise from and are defined by a coherent social practice, which in turn is derived from a particular cultural tradition. A virtue, then, is "an acquired human quality the possession and exercise of which tends to enable us to achieve those goods which are internal to practices and the lack of which effectively prevents us from achieving any such goods." For MacIntyre, virtues are relative to traditions.

One response to the history which I have narrated so far might well be to suggest that even within the relatively coherent tradition of thought which I have sketched there are just too many different and incompatible conceptions of a virtue for there to be any real unity to the concept or indeed to the history. Homer, Sophocles, Aristotle, the New Testament and medieval thinkers differ from each other in too many ways. They offer us different and incompatible lists of the virtues; they give a different rank order of importance to different virtues; and they have different and incompatible theories of the virtues. If we were to consider later Western writers on the virtues, the list of differences and incompatibilities would be enlarged still further; and if we extended our enquiry to Japanese, say, or American Indian cultures, the differences would become greater still. It would be all too easy to conclude that there are a number of rival and alternative conceptions of the virtues, but, even within the tradition which I have been delineating, no single core conception.

The case for such a conclusion could not be better constructed than by beginning from a consideration of the very different lists of items which different authors in different times and places have included in their catalogues of virtues. Some of these catalogues—Homer's, Aristotle's and the New Testament's—I have already noticed at greater or lesser length. Let me at the risk of some repetition recall some of their key features and then introduce

From *After Virtue: A Study In Moral Theory*, 3rd ed. (2007) by Alasdair Macintyre. Published by the University of Notre Dame Press.

for further comparison the catalogues of two later Western writers, Benjamin Franklin and Jane Austen.

The first example is that of Homer. At least some of the items in a Homeric list of the *aretai* would clearly not be counted by most of us nowadays as virtues at all, physical strength being the most obvious example. To this it might be replied that perhaps we ought not to translate the word *aretê* in Homer by our word "virtue" but instead by our word "excellence"; and perhaps, if we were so to translate it, the apparently surprising difference between Homer and ourselves would at first sight have been removed. For we could allow without any kind of oddity that the possession of physical strength is the possession of an excellence. But in fact we would not have removed, but instead would merely have relocated, the difference between Homer and ourselves. For we would now seem to be saying that Homer's concept of an *aretê*, an excellence, is one thing and that our concept of a virtue is quite another since a particular quality can be an excellence in Homer's eyes, but not a virtue in ours and vice versa.

But of course it is not that Homer's list of virtues differs only from our own; it also notably differs from Aristotle's. And Aristotle's of course also differs from our own. For one thing, as I noticed earlier, some Greek virtue-words are not easily translated into English or rather out of Greek. Moreover consider the importance of friendship as a virtue in Aristotle's list—how different from us! Or the place of *phronêsis*—how different from Homer and from us! The mind receives from Aristotle the kind of tribute which the body receives from Homer. But it is not just the case that the difference between Aristotle and Homer lies in the inclusion of some items and the omission of others in their respective catalogues. It turns out also in the way in which those catalogues are ordered, in which items are ranked as relatively central to human excellence and which marginal.

Moreover the relationship of virtues to the social order has changed. For Homer the paradigm of human excellence is the warrior; for Aristotle it is the Athenian gentleman. Indeed according to Aristotle certain virtues are only available to those of great riches and of high social status; there are virtues which are unavailable to the poor man, even if he is a free man. And those virtues are on Aristotle's view ones central to human life; magnanimity—and once again, any translation of *megalopsuchia* is unsatisfactory—and munificence are not just virtues, but important virtues within the Aristotelian scheme.

At once it is impossible to delay the remark that the most striking contrast with Aristotle's catalogue is to be found neither in Homer's nor in our own, but in the New Testament's. For the New Testament not only praises virtues of which Aristotle knows nothing—faith, hope and love—and says nothing about virtues such as *phronêsis* which are crucial for Aristotle, but it praises at least one quality as a virtue which Aristotle seems to count as one of the vices relative to magnanimity, namely humility. Moreover since the New Testament quite clearly sees the rich as destined for the pains of Hell, it is clear that the key virtues cannot be available to them; yet they *are* available to slaves. And the New Testament of course differs from both Homer and Aristotle not only in the items included in its catalogue, but once again in its rank ordering of the virtues.

Turn now to compare all three lists of virtues considered so far—the Homeric, the Aristotelian, and the New Testament's—with two much later lists, one which can be compiled from Jane Austen's novels and the other which Benjamin Franklin constructed for himself. Two features stand out in Jane Austen's list. The first is the importance that she allots to the virtue which she calls "constancy," a virtue about which I shall say more in a later chapter. In some ways constancy plays a role in Jane Austen analogous to that of *phronêsis* in Aristotle; it is a virtue the possession of which is a prerequisite for the possession of other virtues. The second is the fact that what Aristotle treats as the virtue of agreeableness (a virtue for which he says there is no name) she treats as only the simulacrum of a genuine virtue—the genuine virtue in question is the one she calls amiability. For the man who practices agreeableness does so from considerations of honor and expediency, according to Aristotle; whereas Jane Austen thought it possible and necessary for the possessor of that virtue to have a certain real affection for people as such. (It matters here that Jane Austen is a Christian.) Remember that Aristotle himself had treated military courage as a simulacrum of true courage. Thus we find here yet another type of disagreement over the virtues; namely, one as to which human qualities are genuine virtues and which mere simulacra.

In Benjamin Franklin's list we find almost all the types of difference from at least one of the catalogues we have considered and one more. Franklin includes virtues which are new to our consideration such as cleanliness, silence and industry; he clearly considers the drive to acquire itself a part of virtue, whereas for most ancient Greeks this is the vice of *pleonexia*; he treats some virtues which earlier ages had considered minor as major; but he also redefines some familiar virtues. In the list of thirteen virtues which Franklin compiled as part of his system of private moral accounting, he elucidates each virtue by citing a maxim, obedience to which *is* the virtue in question. In the case of chastity the maxim is "Rarely use venery but for health or offspring—never to dullness, weakness or the injury of your own or another's peace or reputation." This is clearly not what earlier writers had meant by "chastity."

We have therefore accumulated a startling number of differences and incompatibilities in the five stated and implied accounts of the virtues. So the question which I raised at the outset becomes more urgent. If different writers in different times and places, but all within the history of Western culture, include such different sets and types of items in their lists, what grounds have we for supposing that they do indeed aspire to list items of one and the same kind, that there is any shared concept at all? A second kind of consideration reinforces the presumption of a negative answer to this question. It is not just that each of these five writers lists different and differing kinds of items; it is also that each of these lists embodies the expression of a different theory about what a virtue is.

In the Homeric poems a virtue is a quality the manifestation of which enables someone to do exactly what their well-defined social role requires. The primary role is that of the warrior king and that Homer lists those virtues which he does becomes intelligible at once when we recognize that the key virtues therefore must be those which enable a man to excel in combat and in the games. It follows that we cannot identify the Homeric virtues until we have first identified the key social roles in Homeric society and the requirements of each of them. The concept *of what anyone filling such-and-such a role ought to do* is prior to the concept of a virtue; the latter concept has application only via the former.

On Aristotle's account matters are very different. Even though some virtues are available only to certain types of people, nonetheless virtues attach not to men as inhabiting social roles, but to man as such. It is the *telos* of man as a species which determines what human qualities are virtues. We need to remember however that although Aristotle treats the acquisition and exercise of the virtues as means to an end, the relationship of means to end is internal and not external. I call a means internal to a given end when the end cannot be adequately characterized independently of a characterization of the means. So it is with the virtues and the *telos* which is the good life for man on Aristotle's account. The exercise of the virtues is itself a crucial component of the good life for man. This distinction between internal and external means to an end is not drawn by Aristotle himself in the *Nicomachean Ethics,* as I noticed earlier, but it is an essential distinction to be drawn if we are to understand what Aristotle intended. The distinction *is* drawn explicitly by Aquinas in the course of his defence of St. Augustine's definition of a virtue, and it is clear that Aquinas understood that in drawing it he was maintaining an Aristotelian point of view.

The New Testament's account of the virtues, even if it differs as much as it does in content from Aristotle's—Aristotle would certainly not have admired Jesus Christ and he would have been horrified by St. Paul—does have the same logical and conceptual structure as Aristotle's account. A virtue is, as with Aristotle, a quality the exercise of which leads to the achievement of the human *telos. The* good for man is of course a supernatural and not only a natural good, but supernature redeems and completes nature. Moreover the relationship of virtues as means to the end which is human incorporation in the divine kingdom of the age to come is internal and not external, just as it is in Aristotle. It is of course this parallelism which allows Aquinas to synthesize Aristotle and the New Testament. A key feature of this parallelism is the way in which the concept of *the good life for man* is prior to the concept of a virtue in just the way in which on the Homeric account the concept of a social role was prior. Once again it is the way in which the former concept is applied which determines how the latter is to be applied. In both case the concept of a virtue is a secondary concept.

The intent of Jane Austen's theory of the virtues is of another kind. C. S. Lewis has rightly emphasized how profoundly Christian her moral vision is and Gilbert Ryle has equally rightly emphasized her inheritance from Shaftesbury and from Aristotle. In fact her views combine elements from Homer as well, since she is concerned with social roles in a way that neither the New Testament nor Aristotle are. She is therefore important for the way in which she finds it possible to combine what are at first sight disparate theorectical accounts of the virtues. But for the moment any attempt to assess the significance of Jane Austen's systhesis must be delayed. Instead we must notice the quite different style of theory articulated in Benjamin Franklin's account of the virtues.

Franklin's account, like Aristotle's, is teleological; but unlike Aristotle's, it is utilitarian. According to Franklin in his *Autobiography* the virtues are means to an end, but he envisages the means-ends relationship as external rather than internal. The end to which the cultivation of the virtues ministers is happiness, but happiness understood as success, prosperity in Philadelphia and ultimately in heaven. The virtues are to be useful and Franklin's account continuously stresses utility as a criterion in individual cases: "Make no expence but to do good to others or yourself; i.e. waste nothing," "Speak not but what may benefit others or yourself. Avoid trifling conversation" and, as we have already seen, "Rarely use venery but for health or offspring. . . . " When Franklin was in Paris he was horrified by Parisian architecture: "Marble, porcelain and gilt are squandered without utility."

We thus have at least three very different conceptions of a virtue to confront: a virtue is a quality which enables an individual to discharge his or her social role (Homer); a virtue is a quality which enables an individual to move towards the achievement of the specifically human *telos*, whether natural or supernatural (Aristotle, the New Testament and Aquinas); a virtue is a quality which has utility in achieving earthly and heavenly success (Franklin). Are we to take these as three different rival accounts of the same thing? Or are they instead accounts of three different things? Perhaps the moral structures in archaic Greece, in fourth-century Greece, and in eighteenth-century Pennsylvania were so different from each other that we should treat them as embodying quite different concepts, whose difference is initially disguised from us by the historical accident of an inherited vocabulary which misleads us by linguistic resemblance long after conceptual identity and similarity have failed. Our initial question has come back to us with redoubled force.

Yet although I have dwelt upon the *prima facie* case for holding that the differences and incompatibilities between different accounts at least suggest that there is no single, central, core conception of the virtues which might make a claim for universal allegiance, I ought also to point out that each of the five moral accounts which I have sketched so summarily does embody just such a claim. It is indeed just this feature of those accounts that makes them of more than sociological or antiquarian interest. Every one of these accounts claims not only theoretical, but also an institutional hegemony. For Odysseus the Cyclopes stand condemned because they lack agriculture, an *agora* and *themis*. For Aristotle the barbarians stand condemned because they lack the *polis* and are therefore incapable of politics. For New Testament Christians there is no salvation outside the apostolic church. And we know that Benjamin Franklin found the virtues more at home in Philadelphia than in Paris and that for Jane Austen the touchstone of the virtues is a certain kind of marriage and indeed a certain kind of naval officer (that is, a certain kind of *English* naval officer).

The question can therefore now be posed directly: are we or are we not able to disentangle from these rival and various claims a unitary core concept of the virtues of which we can give a more compelling account than any of the other accounts so far? I am going to argue that we can in fact discover such a core concept and that it turns out to provide the tradition of which I have written the history with its conceptual unity. It will indeed enable us to distinguish in a clear way those beliefs about the virtues which genuinely belong to the tradition from those which do not. Unsurprisingly perhaps it is a complex concept, different parts of which derive from different stages in the development of the tradition. Thus the concept itself in some sense embodies the history of which it is the outcome.

One of the features of the concept of a virtue which has emerged with some clarity from the argument so far is that it always requires for its application the acceptance for some prior account of certain features of social and moral life in terms of which it has to be defined and explained. So in the Homeric account the concept of a virtue is secondary to that of *a social role*, in Aristotle's account it is secondary to that of *the good life for man* conceived as the *telos* of human action and in Franklin's much later account it is secondary to that of utility. What is it in the account which I am about to give which provides in a similar way the necessary background against which the concept of a virtue has to be made intelligible? It is in answering this question that the complex, historical, multi-layered character of the core concept of virtue becomes clear. For there are no less than three stages in the logical development of the concept which have to be identified in order, if the core conception of a virtue is to be understood, and each of these stages has its own conceptual background. The first stage requires a background account of what I shall call a practice, the second an account of what I have already characterized as the narrative order of a single human life and the third an account a good deal fuller than I have given up to now of what constitutes a moral tradition. Each later stage presupposes the earlier, but not *vice versa*. Each earlier stage is both modified by and reinterpreted in the light of, but also provides an essential constituent of each later stage. The progress in the development of the concept is closely related to, although it does not recapitulate in any straightforward way, the history of the tradition of which it forms the core.

In the Homeric account of the virtues—and in heroic societies more generally—the exercise of a virtue exhibits qualities which are required for sustaining a social role and for exhibiting excellence in some well-marked area of social practice: to excel is to excel at war or in the games, as Achilles does, in sustaining a household, as Penelope does, in giving counsel in the assembly, as Nestor does, in the telling of a tale, as Homer himself does. When Aristotle speaks of excellence in human activity, he sometimes though not always, refers to some well-defined type of human practice: flute-playing, or war, or geometry. I am going to suggest that this notion of a particular type of practice as providing the arena in which the virtues are exhibited and in terms of which they are to receive their primary, if incomplete, definition is crucial to the whole enterprise of identifying a core concept of the virtues. I hasten to add two *caveats* however.

The first is to point out that my argument will not in any way imply that virtues are *only* exercised in the course of what I am calling practices. The second is to warn that I shall be using the word "practice" in a specially defined way which does not completely agree with current ordinary usage, including my own previous use of that word. What am I going to mean by it?

By a "practice" I am going to mean any coherent and complex form of socially established cooperative human activity through which goods internal to that form of activity are realized in the course of trying to achieve those standards of excellence which are appropriate to, and partially definitive of, that form of activity, with the result that human powers to achieve excellence, and human conceptions of the ends and goods involved, are systematically extended. Tic-tac-toe is not an example of a practice in this sense, nor is throwing a football with skill; but the game of football is, and so is chess. Bricklaying is not a practice; architecture is. Planting turnips is not a practice; farming is. So are the enquiries of physics, chemistry and biology, and so is the work of the historian, and so are painting and music. In the ancient and medieval worlds the creation and sustaining of human communities—of households, cities, nations—is generally taken to be a practice in the sense in which I have defined it. Thus the range of practices is wide: arts, sciences, games, politics in the Aristotelian sense, the making and sustaining of family life, all fall under the concept. But the question of the precise range of practices is not at this stage of the first importance. Instead let me explain some of the key terms involved in my definition, beginning with the notion of goods internal to practice.

Consider the example of a highly intelligent seven-year-old child whom I wish to teach to play chess, although the child has no particular desire to learn the game. The child does however have a very strong desire for candy and little chance of obtaining it. I therefore tell the child that if the child will play chess with me once a week I will give the child 50 cents worth of candy; moreover I tell the child that I will always play in such a way that it will be difficult, but not impossible, for the child to win and that, if the child wins, the child will receive an extra 50 cents worth of candy. Thus motivated the child plays and plays to win. Notice however that, so long as it is the candy alone which provides the child with a good reason for playing chess, the child has no reason not to cheat and every reason to cheat, provided he or she can do so successfully. But, so we may hope, there will come a time when the child will find in those goods specific to chess, in the achievement of a certain highly particular kind of analytical skill, strategic imagination and competitive intensity, a new set of reasons, reasons now not just for winning on a particular occasion, but for trying to excel in whatever way the game of chess demands. Now if the child cheats, he or she will be defeating not me, but himself or herself.

There are thus two kinds of good possibly to be gained by playing chess. On the one hand there are those goods externally and contingently attached to chess-playing and to other practices by the accidents of social circumstance—in the case of the imaginary child candy, in the case of real adults such goods as prestige, status and money. There are always alternative ways for achieving such goods, and their achievement is never to be had *only* by engaging in some particular kind of practice. On the other hand there are the goods internal to the practice of chess which cannot be had in any way but by playing chess or some other game of that specific kind. We call them internal for two reasons: first, as I have already suggested, because we can only specify them in terms of chess or some other game of that specific kind and by means of examples from such games (otherwise the meagerness of our vocabulary for speaking of such goods forces us into such devices as my own resort to writing of "a certain highly particular kind of"); and secondly because they can only be identified and recognized by the experience of participating in the practice in question. Those who lack the relevant experience are incompetent thereby as judges of internal goods.

This is clearly the case with all the major examples of practices: consider for example—even if briefly and inadequately—the practice of portrait painting as it developed in Western Europe from the late middle ages to the eighteenth century. The successful portrait painter is able to achieve many goods which are in the sense just defined external to the practice of portrait painting—fame, wealth, social status, even a measure of power and influence at courts upon occasion. But those external goods are not to be confused with the goods which are internal to the practice. The internal goods are those which result from an extended attempt to show how Wittgenstein's dictum "The human body is the best picture of the human soul" (*Investigations,* p. 178e) might be made to become true by teaching us "to regard . . . the picture on our wall as the object itself (the men, landscape and so on) depicted there" (p. 205e) in a quite new way. What is misleading about Wittgenstein's dictum as it stands is its neglect of the truth in George Orwell's thesis "At fifty everyone has the face he deserves." What painters from Giotto to Rembrandt learnt to show was how the face at any age may be revealed as the face that the subject of a portrait deserves.

Originally in medieval paintings of the saints the face was an icon; the question of a resemblance between the depicted face of Christ or St. Peter and the face that Jesus or Peter actually possessed at some particular age did not even arise. The antithesis to this iconography was the relative naturalism of certain fifteenth-century Flemish and German painting. The heavy eyelids, the coifed hair, the lines around the mouth undeniably represent some particular woman, either actual or envisaged. Resemblance has usurped the iconic relationship. But with Rembrandt there is, so to speak, synthesis: the naturalistic portrait is now rendered as an icon but an icon of a new and hitherto inconceivable kind. Similarly in a very different kind of sequence mythological faces in a certain kind of seventeenth-century French painting become aristocratic faces in the eighteenth century. Within each of these sequences at least two different kinds of good internal to the painting of human faces and bodies are achieved.

There is first of all the excellence of the products, both the excellence in performance by the painters and that of each portrait itself. This excellence—the very verb "excel" suggests it—has to be understood historically. The sequences of development find their point and purpose in a progress towards and beyond a variety of types and modes of excellence. There are of course sequences of decline as well as of progress, and progress is rarely to be understood as straightforwardly linear. But it is in participation in the attempts to sustain progress and to respond creatively to problems that the second kind of good internal to the practices of portrait painting is to be found. For what the artist discovers within the pursuit of excellence in portrait painting—and what is true of portrait painting is true of the practice of the fine arts in general—is the good of a certain kind of life. That life may not constitute the whole of life for someone who is a painter by a very long way or it may at least for a period, Gauguin-like, absorb him or her at the expense of almost everything else. But it is the painter's living out of a greater or lesser part of his or her life *as a painter* that is the second kind of good internal to painting. And judgment upon these goods requires at the very least the kind of competence that is only to be acquired either as a painter or as someone willing to learn systematically what the portrait painter has to teach.

A practice involves standards of excellence and obedience to rules as well as the achievement of goods. To enter into a practice is to accept the authority of those standards and the inadequacy of my own performance as judged by them. It is to subject my own attitudes, choices, preferences and tastes to the standards which currently and partially define the practice. Practices of course, as I have just noticed, have a history: games, sciences and arts all have histories. Thus the standards are not themselves immune from criticism, but nonetheless we cannot be initiated into a practice without accepting the authority of the best standards realized so far. If, on starting to listen to music, I do not accept my own incapacity to judge correctly, I will never learn to hear, let alone to appreciate, Bartok's last quartets. If, on starting to play baseball, I do not accept that others know better than I when to throw a fast ball and when not, I will never learn to appreciate good pitching let alone to pitch. In the realm of practices the authority of both goods and standards operates in such a way as to rule out all subjectivist and emotivist analyses of judgment. De gustibus *est* disputandum.

We are now in a position to notice an important difference between what I have called internal and what I have called external goods. It is characteristic of what I have called external goods that when achieved they are always some individual's property and possession. Moreover characteristically they are such that the more someone has of them, the less there is for other people. This is sometimes necessarily the case, as with power and fame, and sometimes the case by reason of contingent circumstance as with money. External goods are therefore characteristically objects of competition in which there must be losers as well as winners. Internal goods are indeed the outcome of competition to excel, but it is characteristic of them that their achievement is a good for the whole community who participate in the practice. So when Turner transformed the seascape in painting or W. G. Grace advanced the art of batting in cricket in a quite new way their achievement enriched the whole relevant community.

But what does all or any of this have to do with the concept of the virtues? It turns out that we are now in a position to formulate a first, even if partial and tentative definition of a virtue: *A virtue is an acquired human quality the possession and exercise of which tends to enable us to achieve those goods which are internal to practices and the lack of which effectively prevents us from achieving any such goods.* Later this definition will need amplification and amendment. But as a first approximation to an adequate definition it already illuminates the place of the virtues in human life. For it is not difficult to show for a whole range of key virtues that without them the goods internal to practices are barred to us, but not just barred to us generally, barred in a very particular way.

It belongs to the concept of a practice as I have outlined it—and as we are all familiar with it already in our actual lives, whether we are painters or physicists or quarterbacks or indeed just lovers of good painting or first-rate experiments or a well-thrown pass—that its goods can only be achieved by subordinating ourselves within the practice in our relationship to other practitioners. We have to learn to recognize what is due to whom; we have to be prepared to take whatever self-endangering risks are demanded along the way; and we have to listen carefully to what we are told about our own inadequacies and to reply with the same carefulness for the facts. In other words we have to accept as necessary components of any practice with internal goods and standards of excellence the virtues of justice, courage and honesty. For not to accept these, to be willing to cheat as our imagined child was willing to cheat in his or her early days at chess, so far bars us from achieving the standards of excellence or the goods internal to the practice that it renders the practice pointless except as a device for achieving external goods.

We can put the same point in another way. Every practice requires a certain kind of relationship between those who participate in it. Now the virtues are those goods by reference to which, whether we like it or not, we define our relationships to those other people with whom we share the kind of purposes and standards which inform practices. Consider an example of how reference to the virtues has to be made in certain kinds of human relationship.

A, B, C, and D are friends in that sense of friendship which Aristotle takes to be primary: they share in the pursuit of certain goods. In my terms they share in a practice. D dies in obscure circumstances, A discovers how D died and tells the truth about it to B while lying to C. C discovers the lie. What A cannot then intelligibly claim is that he stands in the same relationship of friendship to both B and C. By telling the truth to one and lying to the other he has partially defined a difference in the relationship. Of course it is open to A to explain this difference in a number of ways; perhaps he was trying to spare C pain or perhaps he is simply cheating C. But some difference in the relationship now exists as a result of the lie. For their allegiance to each other in the pursuit of common goods has been put in question.

Just as, so long as we share the standards and purposes characteristic of practices, we define our relationship to each other, whether we acknowledge it or not, by reference to standards of truthfulness and trust, so we define them too by reference to standards of justice and of courage. If A, a professor, gives B and C the grades that their papers deserve, but grades D because he is attracted by D's blue eyes or is repelled by D's dandruff, he has defined his relationship to D differently from his relationship to the other members of the class, whether he wishes it or not. Justice requires that we treat others in respect of merit or desert according to uniform and impersonal standards; to depart from the standards of justice in some particular instance defines our relationship with the relevant person as in some way special or distinctive.

The case with courage is a little different. We hold courage to be a virtue because the care and concern for individuals, communities and causes which is so crucial to so much in practices requires the existence of such a virtue. If someone says that he cares for some individual, community or cause, but is unwilling to risk harm or danger on his, her or its own behalf, he puts in question the genuineness of his care and concern. Courage, the capacity to risk harm or danger to oneself, has its role in human life because of this connection with care and concern. This is not to say that a man cannot genuinely care and also be a coward. It is in part to say that a man who genuinely cares and has not the capacity for risking harm or danger has to define himself, both to himself and to others, as a coward.

I take it then that from the standpoint of those types of relationship without which practices cannot be sustained truthfulness, justice and courage—and perhaps some others—are genuine excellences, are virtues in the light of which we have to characterize ourselves and others, whatever our private moral standpoint or our society's particular codes may be. For this recognition that we cannot escape the definition of our relationships in terms of such goods is perfectly compatible with the acknowledgment that different societies have and have had different codes of truthfulness, justice and courage. Lutheran pietists brought up their children to believe that one ought to tell the truth to everybody at all times, whatever the circumstances or consequences, and Kant was one of their children. Traditional Bantu parents brought up their children not to tell the truth to unknown strangers, since they believed that this could render the family vulnerable to witchcraft. In our culture many of us have been brought up not to tell the truth to elderly great-aunts who invite us to admire their new hats. But each of these codes embodies an acknowledgment of the virtue of truthfulness. So it is also with varying codes of justice and of courage.

Practices then might flourish in societies with very different codes; what they could not do is flourish in societies in which the virtues were not valued, although institutions and technical skills serving unified purposes might well continue to flourish. (I shall have more to say about the contrast between institutions and technical skills mobilized for a unified end, on the one hand, and practices on the other, in a moment.) For the kind of cooperation, the kind of recognition of authority and of achievement, the kind of respect for standards and the kind of risk-taking which are characteristically involved in practices demand for example fairness in judging oneself and others—the kind of fairness absent in my example of the professor, a ruthless truthfulness without which fairness cannot find application—the kind of truthfulness absent in my example of A, B, C, and D—and willingness to trust the judgments of those whose achievement in the practice give them an authority to judge which presupposes fairness and truthfulness in those judgments, and from time to time the taking of self-endangering and even achievement-endangering risks. It is no part of my thesis that great violinists cannot be vicious or great chess-players mean-spirited. Where the virtues are required, the vices also may flourish. It is just that the vicious and mean-spirited necessarily rely on the virtues of others for the practices in which they engage to flourish and also deny themselves the experience of achieving those internal goods which may reward even not very good chess-players and violinists.

To situate the virtues any further within practices it is necessary now to clarify a little further the nature of a practice by drawing two important contrasts. The discussion so far I hope makes it clear that a practice, in the sense intended, is never just a set of technical skills, even when directed towards some unified purpose and even if the exercise of those skills can on occasion be valued or enjoyed for their own sake. What is distinctive in a practice is in part the way in which conceptions of the relevant goods and ends which the technical skills serve—and every practice does require the exercise of technical skills—are transformed and enriched by these extensions of human powers and by that regard for its own internal goods which are partially definitive of each particular practice or type of practice. Practices never have a goal or goals fixed for all time—painting has no such goal nor has physics—but the goals themselves are transmuted by the history of the activity. It therefore turns out not to be accidental that every practice has its own history and a history which is more and other than that of the improvement of the relevant technical skills. This historical dimension is crucial in relation to the virtues.

To enter into a practice is to enter into a relationship not only with its contemporary practitioners, but also with those who have preceded us in the practice, particularly those whose achievements extended the reach of the practice to its present point. It is thus the achievement, and *a fortiori* the authority, of a tradition which I then confront and from which I have to learn. And for this learning and the relationship to the past which it embodies the virtues of justice, courage and truthfulness are prerequisite in precisely the same way and for precisely the same reasons as they are in sustaining present relationships within practices.

It is not only of course with sets of technical skills that practices ought to be contrasted. Practices must not be confused with institutions. Chess, physics and medicine are practices; chess clubs, laboratories, universities and hospitals are institutions. Institutions are characteristically and necessarily concerned with what I have called external goods. They are involved in acquiring money and other material goods; they are structured in terms of power and status, and they distribute money, power and status as rewards. Nor could they do otherwise if they are to sustain not only themselves, but also the practices of which they are the bearers. For no practices can survive for any length of time unsustained by institutions. Indeed so intimate is the relationship of practices to institutions—and consequently of the goods external to the goods internal to the practices in question—that institutions and practices characteristically form a single causal order in which the ideals and the creativity of the practice are always vulnerable to the acquisitiveness of the institution, in which the cooperative care for common goods of the practice is always vulnerable to the competitiveness of the institution. In this context the essential function of the virtues is clear. Without them, without justice, courage and truthfulness, practices could not resist the corrupting power of institutions.

Yet if institutions do have corrupting power, the making and sustaining of forms of human community—and therefore of institutions—itself has all the characteristics of a practice, and moreover of a practice which stands in a peculiarly close relationship to the exercise of the virtues in two important ways. The exercise of the virtues is itself apt to require a highly determinate attitude to social and political issues; and it is always within some particular community with its own specific institutional forms that we learn or fail to learn to exercise the virtues. There is of course a crucial difference between the way in which the relationship between moral character and political community is envisaged from the standpoint of liberal individualist modernity and the way in which that relationship was envisaged from the standpoint of the type of ancient and medieval tradition of the virtues which I have sketched. For liberal individualism a community is simply an arena in which individuals each pursue their own self-chosen conception of the good life, and political institutions exist to provide that degree of order which makes such self-determined activity possible. Government and law are, or ought to be, neutral between rival conceptions of the good life for man, and hence, although it is the task of government to promote law-abidingness, it is on the liberal view no part of the legitimate function of government to inculcate any one moral outlook.

By contrast, on the particular ancient and medieval view which I have sketched political community not only requires the exercise of the virtues for its own sustenance, but it is one of the tasks of parental authority to make children grow up so as to be virtuous adults. The classical statement of this analog is by Socrates in the *Crito*. It does not of course follow from an acceptance of the Socratic view of political community and political authority that we ought to assign to the modern state the moral function which Socrates assigned to the city and its laws. Indeed the power of the liberal individualist standpoint partly derives from the evident fact that the modern state is indeed totally unfitted to act as moral educator of any community. But the history of how the modern state emerged is of course itself a moral history. If my account of the complex relationship of virtues to practices and to institutions is correct, it follows that we shall be unable to write a true history of practices and institutions unless that history is also one of the virtues and vices. For the ability of a practice to retain its integrity will depend on the way in which the virtues can be and are exercised in sustaining the institutional forms which are the social bearers of the practice. The integrity of a practice causally requires the exercise of the virtues by at least some of the individuals who embody it in their activities; and conversely the corruption of institutions is always in part at least an effect of the vices.

The virtues are of course themselves in turn fostered by certain types of social institution and endangered by others. Thomas Jefferson thought that only in a society of small farmers could the virtues flourish; and Adam Ferguson with a good deal more sophistication saw the institutions of modern commercial society as endangering at least some traditional virtues. It is Ferguson's type of sociology which is the empirical counterpart of the conceptual account of the virtues which I have given, a sociology which aspires to lay bare the empirical, causal connection between virtues, practices and institutions. For this kind of conceptual account has strong empirical implications; it provides an explanatory scheme which can be tested in particular cases. Moreover my thesis has empirical content in another way; it does entail that without the virtues there could be a recognition only of what I have called external goods and not at all of internal goods in the context of practices. And in any society which recognized only external goods competitiveness would be the dominant and even exclusive feature. We have a brilliant portrait of such a society in Hobbes's account of the state of nature; and Professor Turnbull's report of the fate of the Ik suggests that social reality does in the most horrifying way confirm both my thesis and Hobbes's.

Virtues then stand in a different relationship to external and to internal goods. The possession of the virtues—and not only of their semblance and simulacra—is necessary to achieve the latter; yet the possession of the virtues may perfectly well hinder us in achieving external goods. I need to emphasize at this point that external goods genuinely are goods. Not only are they characteristic objects of human desire, whose allocation is what gives point to the virtues of justice and of generosity, but no one can despise them altogether without a certain hypocrisy. Yet notoriously the cultivation of truthfulness, justice and courage will often, the world being what it contingently is, bar us from being rich or famous or powerful. Thus although we may hope that we can not only achieve the standards of excellence and the internal goods of certain practices by possessing the virtues *and* become rich, famous and powerful, the virtues are always a potential stumbling block to this comfortable ambition. We should therefore expect that, if in a particular society the pursuit of external goods were to become dominant, the concept of the virtues might suffer first attrition and then perhaps something near total effacement, although simulacra might abound. . . .

For Further Reflection

1. What is MacIntyre's concept of virtues? Do you agree with MacIntyre's view? Why or why not?
2. Some have charged MacIntyre's ethical theory with being a form of tradition relativism, the notion that morality is relative to particular traditions. Is this criticism accurate? Could the typical criticisms of cultural relativism also apply to tradition relativism? Explain.

Moral Saints

SUSAN WOLF

Susan Wolf is a professor of philosophy at the University of North Carolina, Chapel Hill, working mostly in ethics and the related areas of philosophy of mind, philosophy of action, political philosophy, and aesthetics. In this selection, she examines the idea of moral saints, exploring the implications of moral sainthood for utilitarianism, Kantian ethics, and moral philosophy generally.

I don't know whether there are any moral saints. But if there are, I am glad that neither I nor those about whom I care most are among them. By *moral saint* I mean a person whose every action is as morally good as possible, a person, that is, who is as morally worthy as can be. Though I shall in a moment acknowledge the variety of types of person that might be thought to satisfy this description, it seems to me that none of these types serve as unequivocally compelling personal ideals. In other words, I believe that moral perfection, in the sense of moral saintliness, does not constitute a model of personal well-being toward which it would be particularly rational or good or desirable for a human being to strive.

Outside the context of moral discussion, this will strike many as an obvious point. But, within that context, the point, if it be granted, will be granted with some discomfort. For within that context it is generally assumed that one ought to be as morally good as possible and that what limits there are to morality's hold on us are set by features of human nature of which we ought not to be proud. If, as I believe, the ideals that are derivable from common sense and philosophically popular moral theories do not support these assumptions, then something has to change. Either we must change our moral theories in ways that will make them yield more palatable ideals, or, as I shall argue, we must change our conception of what is involved in affirming a moral theory.

In this paper, I wish to examine the notion of a moral saint, first, to understand what a moral saint would be like and why such a being would be unattractive, and, second, to raise some questions about the significance of this paradoxical figure for moral philosophy. I shall look first at the model(s) of moral sainthood that might be extrapolated from the morality or moralities of common sense. Then I shall consider what relations these have to

Susan Wolf, "Moral Saints," *Journal of Philosophy*, vol. LXXIX, no. 8, 1982, 419–439.

conclusions that can be drawn from utilitarian and Kantian moral theories. Finally, I shall speculate on the implications of these considerations for moral philosophy.

MORAL SAINTS AND COMMON SENSE

Consider first what, pretheoretically, would count for us—contemporary members of Western culture—as a moral saint. A necessary condition of moral sainthood would be that one's life be dominated by a commitment to improving the welfare of others or of society as a whole. As to what role this commitment must play in the individual's motivational system, two contrasting accounts suggest themselves to me which might equally be thought to qualify a person for moral sainthood.

First, a moral saint might be someone whose concern for others plays the role that is played in most of our lives by more selfish, or, at any rate, less morally worthy concerns. For the moral saint, the promotion of the welfare of others might play the role that is played for most of us by the enjoyment of material comforts, the opportunity to engage in the intellectual and physical activities of our choice, and the love, respect, and companionship of people whom we love, respect, and enjoy. The happiness of the moral saint, then, would truly lie in the happiness of others, and so he would devote himself to others gladly, and with a whole and open heart.

On the other hand, a moral saint might be someone for whom the basic ingredients of happiness are not unlike those of most of the rest of us. What makes him a moral saint is rather that he pays little or no attention to his own happiness in light of the overriding importance he gives to the wider concerns of morality. In other words, this person sacrifices his own interests to the interests of others, and feels the sacrifice as such.

Roughly, these two models may be distinguished according to whether one thinks of the moral saint as being a saint out of love or one thinks of the moral saint as being a saint out of duty (or some other intellectual appreciation and recognition of moral principles). We may refer to the first model as the model of the Loving Saint; to the second, as the model of the Rational Saint.

The two models differ considerably with respect to the qualities of the motives of the individuals who conform to them. But this difference would have limited effect on the saints' respective public personalities. The shared content of what these individuals are motivated to be—namely, as morally good as possible—would play the dominant role in the determination of their characters. Of course, just as a variety of large-scale projects, from tending the sick to political campaigning, may be equally and maximally morally worthy, so a variety of characters are compatible with the ideal of moral sainthood.

One moral saint may be more or less jovial, more or less garrulous, more or less athletic than another. But, above all, a moral saint must have and cultivate those qualities which are apt to allow him to treat others as justly and kindly as possible. He will have the standard moral virtues to a nonstandard degree. He will be patient, considerate, even-tempered, hospitable, charitable in thought as well as in deed. He will be very reluctant to make negative judgments of other people. He will be careful not to favor some people over others on the basis of properties they could not help but have.

Perhaps what I have already said is enough to make some people begin to regard the absence of moral saints in their lives as a blessing. For there comes a point in the listing of virtues that a moral saint is likely to have where one might naturally begin to wonder whether the moral saint isn't, after all, too good—if not too good for his own good, at least too good for his own well-being. For the moral virtues, given that they are, by hypothesis, *all* present in the same individual, and to an extreme degree, are apt to crowd out the nonmoral virtues, as well as many of the interests and personal characteristics that we generally think contribute to a healthy, well-rounded, richly developed character.

In other words, if the moral saint is devoting all his time to feeding the hungry or healing the sick or raising money for Oxfam, then necessarily he is not reading Victorian novels, playing the oboe, or improving his backhand. Although no one of the interests or tastes in the category containing these latter activities could be claimed to be a necessary element in a life well lived, a life in which *none* of these possible aspects of character are developed may seem to be a life strangely barren.

The reasons why a moral saint cannot, in general, encourage the discovery and development of significant nonmoral interests and skills are not logical but practical reasons. There are, in addition, a class of nonmoral characteristics that a moral saint cannot encourage in himself for reasons that are not just practical. There is a more substantial tension between having any of these qualities unashamedly and being a moral saint. These qualities might be described as going against the moral grain. For example, a cynical or sarcastic wit, or a sense of humor that appreciates this kind of wit in others, requires that one take an attitude of resignation and pessimism toward the flaws and vices to be found in the world. A moral saint, on the other hand, has reason to take an attitude in opposition to this—he should try to look for the best in people, give them the benefit of the doubt as long as possible, try to improve regrettable situations as long as there is any hope of success. This suggests that, although a moral saint might well enjoy a good episode of *Father Knows Best,* he may not in good conscience be able to laugh at a Marx Brothers movie or enjoy a play by George Bernard Shaw.

An interest in something like gourmet cooking will be, for different reasons, difficult for a moral saint to rest easy with. For it seems to me that no plausible argument can justify the use of human resources involved in producing a *paté de canard en croute* against possible alternative beneficent ends to which these resources might be put. If there is a justification for the institution of haute cuisine, it is one which rests on the decision *not* to justify every activity against morally beneficial alternatives, and this is a decision a moral saint will never make. Presumably, an interest in high fashion or interior design will fare much the same, as will, very possibly, a cultivation of the finer arts as well.

A moral saint will have to be very, very nice. It is important that he not be offensive. The worry is that, as a result, he will have to be dull-witted or humorless or bland.

This worry is confirmed when we consider what sorts of characters, taken and refined both from life and from fiction, typically form our ideals. One would hope they would be figures who are morally good—and by this I mean more than just not morally bad—but one would hope, too, that they are not *just* morally good, but talented or accomplished or attractive in nonmoral ways as well. We may make ideals out of athletes, scholars, artists—more frivolously, out of cowboys, private eyes, and rock stars. We may strive for Katharine Hepburn's grace, Paul Newman's "cool"; we are attracted to the high-spirited passionate nature of Natasha Rostov; we admire the keen perceptiveness of Lambert Strether. Though there is certainly nothing immoral about the ideal characters or traits I have in mind, they cannot be superimposed upon the ideal of a moral saint. For although it is a part of many of these ideals that the characters set high, and not merely acceptable, moral standards for themselves, it is also essential to their power and attractiveness that the moral strengths go, so to speak, alongside of specific, independently admirable, nonmoral ground projects and dominant personal traits.

When one does finally turn one's eyes toward lives that are dominated by explicitly moral commitments, moreover, one finds oneself relieved at the discovery of idiosyncrasies or eccentricities not quite in line with the picture of moral perfection. One prefers the blunt, tactless, and opinionated Betsy Trotwood to the unfailingly kind and patient Agnes Copperfield; one prefers the mischievousness and the sense of irony in Chesterton's Father Brown to the innocence and undiscriminating love of St. Francis.

It seems that, as we look in our ideals for people who achieve nonmoral varieties of personal excellence in conjunction with or colored by some version of high moral tone, we look in our paragons of moral excellence for people whose moral achievements occur in conjunction with or colored by some interests or traits that have low moral tone. In other words, there seems to be a limit to how much morality we can stand. . . .

Moreover, there is something odd about the idea of morality itself, or moral goodness, serving as the object of a dominant passion in the way that a more concrete and specific vision of a goal (even a concrete *moral* goal) might be imagined to serve. Morality itself does not seem to be a suitable object of passion. Thus, when one reflects, for example, on the Loving Saint easily and gladly giving up his fishing trip or his stereo or his hot fudge sundae at the drop of the moral hat, one is apt to wonder not at how much he loves morality, but at how little he loves these other things. One thinks that, if he can give these up so easily, he does not know what it is to truly love them. There seems, in other words, to be a kind of joy which the Loving Saint, either by nature or by practice, is incapable of experiencing. The Rational Saint, on the other hand, might retain strong nonmoral and concrete desires—he simply denies himself the opportunity to act on them. But this is no less troubling. The Loving Saint one might suspect of missing a piece of perceptual machinery, of being blind to some of what the world has to offer. The Rational Saint, who sees it but foregoes it, one suspects of having a different problem—a pathological fear of damnation, perhaps, or an extreme form of self-hatred that interferes with his ability to enjoy the enjoyable in life.

In other words, the ideal of a life of moral sainthood disturbs not simply because it is an ideal of a life in which morality unduly dominates. The normal person's direct and specific desires for objects, activities, and events that conflict with the attainment of moral perfection are not simply sacrificed but removed, suppressed, or subsumed. The way in which morality, unlike other possible goals, is apt to dominate is particularly disturbing, for it seems to require either the lack or the denial of the existence of an identifiable, personal self. . . .

It must be remembered that from the fact that there is a tension between having any of these qualities and being a moral saint it does not follow that having any of these qualities is immoral. For it is not part of common-sense morality that one ought to be a moral saint. Still, if someone just happened to want to be a moral saint, he or she would not have or encourage these qualities, and, on the basis of our common-sense values, this counts as a reason *not* to want to be a moral saint. . . .

MORAL SAINTS AND MORAL THEORIES

I have tried so far to paint a picture—or, rather, two pictures—of what a moral saint might be like, drawing on what I take to be the attitudes and beliefs about morality prevalent in contemporary, common-sense thought. To my suggestion that common-sense morality generates conceptions of moral saints that are unattractive or otherwise unacceptable, it is open to someone to reply, "so much the worse for common-sense morality." After all, it is often claimed that the goal of moral philosophy is to correct and improve upon common-sense morality, and I have as yet given no attention to the question of what conceptions of moral sainthood, if any, are generated from the leading moral theories of our time.

A quick, breezy reading of utilitarian and Kantian writings will suggest the images, respectively, of the Loving Saint and the Rational Saint. A utilitarian, with his emphasis on happiness, will certainly prefer the Loving Saint to the Rational one, since the Loving Saint will himself be a happier person than the Rational Saint. A Kantian, with his emphasis on reason, on the other hand, will find at least as much to praise in the latter as in the former. Still, both models, drawn as they are from common sense, appeal to an impure mixture of utilitarian and Kantian intuitions. A more careful examination of these moral theories raises questions about whether either model of moral sainthood would really be advocated by a believer in the explicit doctrines associated with either of these views.

Certainly, the utilitarian in no way denies the value of self-realization. He in no way disparages the development of interests, talents, and other personally attractive traits that I have claimed the moral saint would be without. Indeed, since just these features enhance the happiness both of the individuals who possess them and of those with whom they associate, the ability to promote these features both in oneself and in others will have considerable positive weight in utilitarian calculations.

This implies that the utilitarian would not support moral sainthood as a universal ideal. A world in which everyone, or even a large number of people, achieved moral sainthood—even a world in which they *strove* to achieve it—would probably contain less happiness than a world in which people realized a diversity of ideals involving a variety of personal and perfectionist values. More pragmatic considerations also suggest that, if the utilitarian wants to influence more people to achieve more good, then he would do better to encourage them to pursue happiness-producing goals that are more attractive and more within a normal person's reach.

These considerations still leave open, however, the question of what kind of an ideal the committed utilitarian should privately aspire to himself. Utilitarianism requires him to want to achieve the greatest general happiness, and this would seem to commit him to the ideal of the moral saint.

One might try to use the claims I made earlier as a basis for an argument that a utilitarian should choose to give up utilitarianism. If, as I have said, a moral saint would be a less happy person both to be and to be around than many other possible ideals, perhaps one could create more total happiness by not trying too hard to promote the total happiness. But this argument is simply unconvincing in light of the empirical circumstances of our world. The gain in happiness that would accrue to oneself and one's neighbors by a more well-rounded, richer life than that of the moral saint would be pathetically small in comparison to the amount by which one could increase the general happiness if one devoted oneself explicitly to the care of the sick, the downtrodden, the starving, and the homeless. Of course, there may be psychological limits to the extent to which a person can devote himself to such things without going crazy. But the utilitarian's individual limitations would not thereby become a positive feature of his personal ideals.

The unattractiveness of the moral saint, then, ought not rationally convince the utilitarian to abandon his utilitarianism. It may, however, convince him to take efforts not to wear his saintly moral aspirations on his sleeve. If it is not too difficult, the utilitarian will try not to make those around him uncomfortable. He will not want to appear "holier than thou"; he will not want to inhibit others' ability to enjoy themselves. In practice, this might make the perfect utilitarian a less nauseating companion than the moral saint I earlier portrayed. But insofar as this kind of reasoning produces a more bearable public personality, it is at the cost of giving him a personality that must be evaluated as hypocritical and condescending when his private thoughts and attitudes are taken into account.

Still, the criticisms I have raised against the saint of common-sense morality should make some difference to the utilitarian's conception of an ideal which neither requires him to abandon his utilitarian principles nor forces him to fake an interest he does not have or a judgment he does not make. For it may be that a limited and carefully monitored allotment of time and energy to be devoted to the pursuit of some nonmoral interests or to the development of some nonmoral talents would make a person a better contributor to the general welfare than he would be if he allowed himself no indulgences of this sort. The enjoyment of such activities in no way compromises a commitment to utilitarian principles as long as the involvement with these activities is conditioned by a willingness to give them up whenever it is recognized that they cease to be in the general interest.

This will go some way in mitigating the picture of the loving saint that an understanding of utilitarianism will on first impression suggest. But I think it will not go very far. For the limitations on time and energy will have to be rather severe, and the need to monitor will restrict not only the extent but also the quality of one's attachment to these interests and traits. They are only weak and somewhat peculiar sorts of passions to which one can consciously remain so conditionally committed. Moreover, the way in which the utilitarian can enjoy these "extracurricular" aspects of his life is simply not the way in which these aspects are to be enjoyed insofar as they figure into our less saintly ideals.

The problem is not exactly that the utilitarian values these aspects of his life only as a means to an end, for the enjoyment he and others get from these aspects are not a means to, but a part of, the general happiness. Nonetheless, he values these things only because of and insofar as they *are* a part of the general happiness. He values them, as it were, under the description "a contribution to the general happiness." This is to be contrasted with the various ways in which these aspects of life may be valued by nonutilitarians. A person might love literature because of the insights into human nature literature affords. Another might love the cultivation of roses because roses are things of great beauty and delicacy. It may be true that these features of the respective activities also explain why these activities are happiness-producing. But, to the nonutilitarian, this may not be to the point. For if one values these activities in these more direct ways, one may not be willing to exchange them for others that produce an equal, or even a greater amount of happiness. From that point of view, it is not because they produce happiness that these activities are valuable; it is because these activities are valuable in more direct and specific ways that they produce happiness. . . .

The Kantian believes that being morally worthy consists in always acting from maxims that one could will to be universal law, and doing this not out of any pathological desire but out of reverence for the moral law as such, Or, to take a different formulation of the categorical imperative, the Kantian believes that moral action consists in treating other persons always as ends and never as means only. Presumably, and according to Kant himself, the Kantian thereby commits himself to some degree of benevolence as well as to the rules of fair play. But we surely would not will that *every* person become a moral saint, and treating others as ends hardly requires bending over backwards to protect and promote their interests. On one interpretation of Kantian doctrine, then, moral perfection would be achieved simply by unerring obedience to a limited set of side-constraints. On this interpretation, Kantian theory simply does not yield an ideal conception of a person of any fullness comparable to that of the moral saints I have so far been portraying.

On the other hand, Kant does say explicitly that we have a duty of benevolence, a duty not only to allow others to pursue their ends, but to take up their ends as our own. In addition, we have positive duties to ourselves, duties to increase our natural as well as our moral perfection. These duties are unlimited in the degree to which they *may* dominate a life. If action in accordance with and motivated by the thought of these duties is considered virtuous, it is natural to assume that the more one performs such actions, the more virtuous one is. Moreover, of virtue in general Kant says, "it is an ideal which is unattainable while yet our duty is constantly to approximate to it."[1] On this interpretation, then, the Kantian moral saint, like the other moral saints I have been considering, is dominated by the motivation to be moral.

[1]Immanuel Kant, *The Doctrine of Virtue,* Mary J. Gregor, trans. (New York: Harper & Row, 1964), p. 71.

Which of these interpretations of Kant one prefers will depend on the interpretation and the importance one gives to the role of the imperfect duties in Kant's over-all system. Rather than choose between them here, I shall consider each briefly in turn.

On the second interpretation of Kant, the Kantian moral saint is, not surprisingly, subject to many of the same objections I have been raising against other versions of moral sainthood. Though the Kantian saint may differ from the utilitarian saint as to *which* actions he is bound to perform and which he is bound to refrain from performing, I suspect that the range of activities acceptable to the Kantian saint will remain objectionably restrictive. Moreover, the manner in which the Kantian saint must think about and justify the activities he pursues and the character traits he develops will strike us, as it did with the utilitarian saint, as containing "one thought too many." As the utilitarian could value his activities and character traits only insofar as they fell under the description of "contributions to the general happiness," the Kantian would have to value his activities and character traits insofar as they were manifestations of respect for the moral law. If the development of our powers to achieve physical, intellectual, or artistic excellence, or the activities directed toward making others happy are to have any moral worth, they must arise from a reverence for the dignity that members of our species have as a result of being endowed with pure practical reason. This is a good and noble motivation, to be sure. But it is hardly what one expects to be dominantly behind a person's aspirations to dance as well as Fred Astaire, to paint as well as Picasso, or to solve some outstanding problem in abstract algebra, and it is hardly what one hopes to find lying dominantly behind a father's action on behalf of his son or a lover's on behalf of her beloved. . . .

MORAL SAINTS AND MORAL PHILOSOPHY

In pointing out the regrettable features and the necessary absence of some desirable features in a moral saint, I have not meant to condemn the moral saint or the person who aspires to become one. Rather, I have meant to insist that the ideal of moral sainthood should not be held as a standard against which any other ideal must be judged or justified, and that the posture we take in response to the recognition that our lives are not as morally good as they might be need not be defensive.[2] It is misleading to insist that one is *permitted*

[2]George Orwell makes a similar point in "Reflections on Gandhi," in *A Collection of Essays by George Orwell* (New York: Harcourt Brace Jovanovich, 1945), p. 176: "sainthood is . . . a thing that human beings must avoid. . . It is too readily assumed that . . . the ordinary man only rejects it because it is too difficult; in other words, that the average human being is a failed saint. It is doubtful whether this is true. Many people genuinely do not wish to be saints, and it is probable that some who achieve or aspire to sainthood have never felt much temptation to be human beings."

to live a life in which the goals, relationships, activities, and interests that one pursues are not maximally morally good. For our lives are not so comprehensively subject to the requirement that we apply for permission, and our nonmoral reasons for the goals we set ourselves are not excuses, but may rather be positive, good reasons which do not exist *despite* any reasons that might threaten to outweigh them. In other words, a person may be *perfectly wonderful* without being *perfectly moral.*

Recognizing this requires a perspective which contemporary moral philosophy has generally ignored. This perspective yields judgments of a type that is neither moral nor egoistic. Like moral judgments, judgments about what it would be good for a person to be are made from a point of view outside the limits set by the values, interests, and desires that the person might actually have. And, like moral judgments, these judgments claim for themselves a kind of objectivity or a grounding in a perspective which any rational and perceptive being can take up. Unlike moral judgments, however, the good with which these judgments are concerned is not the good of anyone or any group other than the individual himself.

Nonetheless, it would be equally misleading to say that these judgments are made for the sake of the individual himself. For these judgments are not concerned with what kind of life it is in a person's interest to lead, but with what kind of interests it would be good for a person to have, and it need not be in a person's interest that he acquire or maintain objectively good interests. Indeed, the model of the Loving Saint, whose interests are identified with the interests of morality, is a model of a person for whom the dictates of rational self-interest and the dictates of morality coincide. Yet, I have urged that we have reason not to aspire to this ideal and that some of us would have reason to be sorry if our children aspired to and achieved it.

The moral point of view, we might say, is the point of view one takes up insofar as one takes the recognition of the fact that one is just one person among others equally real and deserving of the good things in life as a fact with practical consequences, a fact the recognition of which demands expression in one's actions and in the form of one's practical deliberations. Competing moral theories offer alternative answers to the question of what the most correct or the best way to express this fact is. In doing so, they offer alternative ways to evaluate and to compare the variety of actions, states of affairs, and so on that appear good and bad to agents from other, nonmoral points of view. But it seems that alternative interpretations of the moral point of view do not exhaust the ways in which our actions, characters, and their consequences can be comprehensively and objectively evaluated. Let us call the point of view from which we consider what kinds of lives are good lives, and what kinds of persons it would be good for ourselves and others to be, the *point of view of individual perfection.*

Since either point of view provides a way of comprehensively evaluating a person's life, each point of view takes account of, and, in a sense, subsumes the other. From the moral point of view, the perfection of an individual life will have some, but limited, value—for each individual remains, after all, just one person among others. From the perfectionist point of view, the moral worth of an individual's relation to his world will likewise have some, but limited, value—for, as I have argued, the (perfectionist) goodness of an individual's life does not vary proportionally with the degree to which it exemplifies moral goodness.

It may not be the case that the perfectionist point of view is like the moral point of view in being a point of view we are ever *obliged* to take up and express in our actions. Nonetheless, it provides us with reasons that are independent of moral reasons for wanting ourselves and others to develop our characters and live our lives in certain ways. When we take up this point of view and ask how much it would be good for an individual to act from the moral point of view, we do not find an obvious answer.[3]

The considerations of this paper suggest, at any rate, that the answer is not "as much as possible." This has implications both for the continued development of moral theories and for the development of metamoral views and for our conception of moral philosophy more generally. From the moral point of view, we have reasons to want people to live lives that seem good from outside that point of view. If, as I have argued, this means that we have reason to want people to live lives that are not morally perfect, then any plausible moral theory must make use of some conception of supererogation.[4]

If moral philosophers are to address themselves at the most basic level to the question of how people should live, however, they must do more than

[3]A similar view, which has strongly influenced mine, is expressed by Thomas Nagel) in "The Fragmentation of Value," in *Mortal Questions* (New York: Cambridge, 1979), pp. 128–141. Nagel focuses on the difficulties such apparently incommensurable points of view create for specific, isolable practical decisions that must be made both by individuals and by societies. In focusing on the way in which these points of view figure into the development of individual personal ideals, the questions with which I am concerned are more likely to lurk in the background of any individual's life.

[4]The variety of forms that a conception of supererogation might take, however, has not generally been noticed. Moral theories that make use of this notion typically do so by identifying some specific set of principles as universal moral requirements and supplement this list with a further set of directives which it is morally praiseworthy but not required for an agent to follow. [See, e.g., Charles Fried, *Right and Wrong* (Cambridge, Mass.: Harvard, 1979).] But it is possible that the ability to live a morally blameless life cannot be so easily or definitely secured as this type of theory would suggest. The fact that there are some situations in which an agent is morally required to do something and other situations in which it would be good but not required for an agent to do something does not imply that there are specific principles such that, in any situation, an agent is required to act in accordance with these principles and other specific principles such that, in any situation, it would be good but not required for an agent to act in accordance with those principles.

adjust the content of their moral theories in ways that leave room for the affirmation of nonmoral values. They must examine explicitly the range and nature of these nonmoral values, and, in light of this examination, they must ask how the acceptance of a moral theory is to be understood and acted upon. For the claims of this paper do not so much conflict with the content of any particular currently popular moral theory as they call into question a metamoral assumption that implicitly surrounds discussions of moral theory more generally. Specifically, they call into question the assumption that it is always better to be morally better.

The role morality plays in the development of our characters and the shape of our practical deliberations need be neither that of a universal medium into which all other values must be translated nor that of an ever-present filter through which all other values must pass. This is not to say that moral value should not be an important, even the most important, kind of value we attend to in evaluating and improving ourselves and our world. It is to say that our values cannot be fully comprehended on the model of a hierarchical system with morality at the top.

The philosophical temperament will naturally incline, at this point, toward asking, "What, then, *is* at the top—or, if there is no top, how *are* we to decide when and how much to be moral?" In other words, there is a temptation to seek a metamoral—though not, in the standard sense, metaethical—theory that will give us principles, or, at least, informal directives on the basis of which we can develop and evaluate more comprehensive personal ideals. Perhaps a theory that distinguishes among the various roles a person is expected to play within a life—as professional, as citizen, as friend, and so on—might give us some rules that would offer us, if nothing else, a better framework in which to think about and discuss these questions. I am pessimistic, however, about the chances of such a theory to yield substantial and satisfying results. For I do not see how a metamoral theory could be constructed which would not be subject to considerations parallel to those which seem inherently to limit the appropriateness of regarding moral theories as ultimate comprehensive guides for action.

This suggests that, at some point, both in our philosophizing and in our lives, we must be willing to raise normative questions from a perspective that is unattached to a commitment to any particular well-ordered system of values. It must be admitted that, in doing so, we run the risk of finding normative answers that diverge from the answers given by whatever moral theory one accepts. This, I take it, is the grain of truth in G. E. Moore's "open question" argument. In the background of this paper, then, there lurks a commitment to what seems to me to be a healthy form of intuitionism. It is a form of intuitionism which is not intended to take the place of more rigorous, systematically developed, moral theories—rather, it is intended to put these more rigorous and systematic moral theories in their place.

For Further Reflection

1. According to Wolf, what kind of person would count as a moral saint in the contemporary Western view?
2. Why does Wolf think that moral perfection does not constitute a good model of personal well-being?
3. Why does Wolf say that some people might "regard the absence of moral saints in their lives as a blessing"?

The Great Stone Face

NATHANIEL HAWTHORNE

Nathaniel Hawthorne (1804–1864) was born in Salem, Massachusetts, and educated at Bowdoin College. He is one of America's greatest novelists, best known for *The Scarlet Letter* (1850). In this less-known short story, Hawthorne deals with such themes as moral imagination, insight, and the virtues. The Great Stone Face that dominates the story may be based on the rock formation in the White Mountains of New Hampshire known as Franconia Notch. The people in the valley are waiting for a great person to appear, modeled on the Great Stone Face, who will lead them. The main character, Ernest, is powerfully influenced, even educated, by what he sees in that face.

One afternoon, when the sun was going down, a mother and her little boy sat at the door of their cottage, talking about the Great Stone Face. They had but to lift their eyes, and there it was plainly to be seen, though miles away, with the sunshine brightening all its features.

And what was the Great Stone Face?

Embosomed amongst a family of lofty mountains, there was a valley so spacious that it contained many thousand inhabitants. Some of these good

---

Reprinted from the *Complete Works of Nathaniel Hawthorne* (Modern Library, 1937).

people dwelt in log-huts, with the black forest all around them, on the steep and difficult hill-sides. Others had their homes in comfortable farm-houses, and cultivated the rich soil on the gentle slopes or level surfaces of the valley. Others, again, were congregated into populous villages, where some wild, highland rivulet, tumbling down from its birthplace in the upper mountain region, had been caught and tamed by human cunning, and compelled to turn the machinery of cotton-factories. The inhabitants of this valley, in short, were numerous, and of many modes of life. But all of them, grown people and children, had a kind of familiarity with the Great Stone Face, although some possessed the gift of distinguishing this grand natural phenomenon more perfectly than many of their neighbors.

The Great Stone Face, then, was a work of Nature in her mood of majestic playfulness, formed on the perpendicular side of a mountain by some immense rocks, which had been thrown together in such a position as, when viewed at a proper distance, precisely to resemble the features of the human countenance. It seemed as if an enormous giant, or a Titan, had sculptured his own likeness on the precipice. There was the broad arch of the forehead, a hundred feet in height; the nose, with its long bridge; and the vast lips, which, if they could have spoken, would have rolled their thunder accents from one end of the valley to the other. True it is, that if the spectator approached too near, he lost the outline of the gigantic visage, and could discern only a heap of ponderous and gigantic rocks, piled in chaotic ruin one upon another. Retracing his steps, however, the wondrous features would again be seen; and the farther he withdrew from them, the more like a human face, with all its original divinity intact, did they appear; until, as it grew dim in the distance, with the clouds and glorified vapor of the mountains clustering about it, the Great Stone Face seemed positively to be alive.

It was a happy lot for children to grow up to manhood or womanhood with the Great Stone Face before their eyes, for all the features were noble, and the expression was at once grand and sweet, as if it were the glow of a vast, warm heart, that embraced all mankind in its affections, and had room for more. It was an education only to look at it. According to the belief of many people, the valley owed much of its fertility to this benign aspect that was continually beaming over it, illuminating the clouds, and infusing its tenderness into the sunshine.

As we began with saying, a mother and her little boy sat at their cottage-door, gazing at the Great Stone Face, and talking about it. The child's name was Ernest.

"Mother," said he, while the Titanic visage smiled on him, "I wish that it could speak, for it looks so very kindly that its voice must needs be pleasant. If I were to see a man with such a face. I should love him dearly."

"If an old prophecy should come to pass," answered his mother, "we may see a man, some time or other, with exactly such a face as that."

"What prophecy do you mean, dear mother?" eagerly inquired Ernest. "Pray tell me about it!"

So his mother told him a story that her own mother had told to her, when she herself was younger than little Ernest; a story, not of things that were past, but of what was yet to come; a story, nevertheless, so very old, that even the Indians, who formerly inhabited this valley, had heard it from their forefathers, to whom, as they affirmed, it had been murmured by the mountain streams, and whispered by the wind among the tree-tops. The purport was, that, at some future day, a child should be born hereabouts, who was destined to become the greatest and noblest personage of his time, and whose countenance, in manhood, should bear an exact resemblance to the Great Stone Face. Not a few old-fashioned people, and young ones likewise, in the ardor of their hopes, still cherished an enduring faith in this old prophecy. But others, who had seen more of the world, had watched and waited till they were weary, and had beheld no man with such a face, nor any man that proved to be much greater or nobler than his neighbors, concluded it to be nothing but an idle tale. At all events, the great man of the prophecy had not yet appeared.

"O mother, dear mother!" cried Ernest, clapping his hands above his head, "I do hope that I shall live to see him!"

His mother was an affectionate and thoughtful woman, and felt that it was wisest not to discourage the generous hopes of her little boy. So she only said to him, "Perhaps you may."

And Ernest never forgot the story that his mother told him. It was always in his mind, whenever he looked upon the Great Stone Face. He spent his childhood in the log-cottage where he was born, and was dutiful to his mother, and helpful to her in many things, assisting her much with his little hands, and more with his loving heart. In this manner, from a happy yet often pensive child, he grew up to be a mild, quiet, unobtrusive boy, and sun-browned with labor in the fields, but with more intelligence brightening his aspect than is seen in many lads who have been taught at famous schools. Yet Ernest had had no teacher, save only that the Great Stone Face became one to him. When the toil of the day was over, he would gaze at it for hours, until he began to imagine that those vast features recognized him, and gave him a smile of kindness and encouragement, responsive to his own look of veneration. We must not take upon us to affirm that this was a mistake, although the Face may have looked no more kindly at Ernest than at all the world besides. But the secret was that the boy's tender and confiding simplicity discerned what other people could not see; and thus the love, which was meant for all, became his peculiar portion.

About this time there went a rumor throughout the valley, that the great man, foretold from ages long ago, who was to bear a resemblance to the Great Stone Face, had appeared at last. It seems that, many years before, a young man had migrated from the valley and settled at a distant seaport, where, after getting together a little money, he had set up as a shopkeeper. His name—but I could never learn whether it was his real one, or a nickname that had grown out of his habits and success in life—was Gathergold. Being shrewd and active, and endowed by Providence with that inscrutable faculty which develops itself in what the world calls luck, he became an exceedingly rich merchant, and owner of a whole fleet of bulky-bottomed ships. All the countries of the globe appeared to join hands for the mere purpose of adding heap after heap to the mountainous accumulation of this one man's wealth. The cold regions of the north, almost within the gloom and shadow of the Arctic Circle, sent him their tribute in the shape of furs; hot Africa sifted for him the golden sands of her rivers, and gathered up the ivory tusks of her great elephants out of the forests; the East came bringing him the rich shawls, and spices, and teas, and the effulgence of diamonds, and the gleaming purity of large pearls. The ocean, not to be behind-hand with the earth, yielded up her mighty whales, that Mr. Gathergold might sell their oil, and make a profit of it. Be the original commodity what it might, it was gold within his grasp. It might be said of him, as of Midas in the fable, that whatever he touched with his finger immediately glistened, and grew yellow, and was changed at once into sterling metal, or, which suited him still better, into piles of coin. And, when Mr. Gathergold had become so very rich that it would have taken him a hundred years only to count his wealth, he bethought himself of his native valley, and resolved to go back thither, and end his days where he was born. With this purpose in view, he sent a skilful architect to build him such a palace as should be fit for a man of his vast wealth to live in.

As I have said above, it had already been rumored in the valley that Mr. Gathergold had turned out to be the prophetic personage so long and vainly looked for, and that his visage was the perfect and undeniable similitude of the Great Stone Face. People were the more ready to believe that this must needs be the fact, when they beheld the splendid edifice that rose, as if by enchantment, on the site of his father's old weatherbeaten farm-house. The exterior was of marble, so dazzlingly white that it seemed as though the whole structure might melt away in the sunshine, like those humbler ones which Mr. Gathergold, in his young play-days, before his fingers were gifted with the touch of transmutation, had been accustomed to build of snow. It had a richly ornamented portico, supported by tall pillars, beneath which was a lofty door, studded with silver knobs, and made of a kind of variegated wood that had been brought from beyond the sea. The windows, from the floor to the ceiling of each stately apartment, were composed, respectively, of but one enormous pane of glass, so transparently pure that it was said to be a finer medium than even the vacant atmosphere. Hardly anybody had been permitted to see the interior of this palace; but it was reported, and with good semblance of truth, to be far more gorgeous than the outside, insomuch that whatever was iron or brass in other houses was silver or gold in this; and Mr. Gathergold's bedchamber, especially, made such a glittering appearance that no ordinary man would have been able to close his eyes there. But, on the other hand, Mr. Gathergold was now so inured to wealth, that perhaps he could not have closed his eyes unless where the gleam of it was certain to find its way beneath his eyelids.

In due time, the mansion was finished; next came the upholsterers, with magnificent furniture; then, a whole troop of black and white servants, the harbingers of Mr. Gathergold, who, in his own majestic person, was expected to arrive at sunset. Our friend Ernest, meanwhile, had been deeply stirred by the idea that the great man, the noble man, the man of prophecy, after so many ages of delay, was at length to be made manifest to his native valley. He knew, boy as he was, that there were a thousand ways in which Mr. Gathergold, with his vast wealth, might transform himself into an angel of beneficence, and assume a control over human affairs as wide and benignant as the smile of the Great Stone Face. Full of faith and hope, Ernest doubted not that what the people said was true, and that now he was to behold the living likeness of those wondrous features on the mountain-side. While the boy was still gazing up the valley, and fancying, as he always did, that the Great Stone Face returned his gaze and looked kindly at him, the rumbling of wheels was heard, approaching swiftly along the winding road.

"Here he comes!" cried a group of people who were assembled to witness the arrival. "Here comes the great Mr. Gathergold!"

A carriage, drawn by four horses, dashed round the turn of the road. Within it, thrust partly out of the window, appeared the physiognomy of the old man, with a skin as yellow as if his own Midas-hand had transmuted it. He had a low forehead, small, sharp eyes, puckered about with innumerable wrinkles, and very thin lips, which he made still thinner by pressing them forcibly together.

"The very image of the Great Stone Face!" shouted the people. "Sure enough, the old prophecy is true; and here we have the great man come, at last!"

And, what greatly perplexed Ernest, they seemed actually to believe that here was the likeness which they spoke of. By the roadside there chanced to be an old beggar-woman and two little beggar-children, stragglers from some far-off region, who, as the carriage rolled onward, held out their hands and lifted up their doleful voices, most piteously beseeching charity. A yellow claw—the very same that had clawed together so much wealth—poked itself out of the coach-window, and dropt some copper coins upon the ground; so that, though the great man's name seems to have been Gathergold, he might just as suitably have been nicknamed Scattercopper. Still, nevertheless, with an earnest shout, and evidently with as much good faith as ever, the people bellowed,

"He is the very image of the Great Stone Face!"

But Ernest turned sadly from the wrinkled shrewdness of that sordid visage, and gazed up the valley, where, amid a gathering mist, gilded by the last sunbeams, he could still distinguish those glorious features which had impressed themselves into his soul. Their aspect cheered him. What did the benign lips seem to say?

"He will come! Fear not, Ernest; the man will come!"

The years went on, and Ernest ceased to be a boy. He had grown to be a young man now. He attracted little notice from the other inhabitants of the valley; for they saw nothing remarkable in his way of life, save that, when the labor of the day was over, he still loved to go apart and gaze and meditate upon the Great Stone Face. According to their idea of the matter, it was a folly, indeed, but pardonable, inasmuch as Ernest was industrious, kind, and neighborly, and neglected no duty for the sake of indulging this idle habit. They knew not that the Great Stone Face had become a teacher to him, and that the sentiment which was expressed in it would enlarge the young man's heart, and fill it with wider and deeper sympathies than other hearts. They knew not that thence would come a better wisdom than could be learned from books, and a better life than could be moulded on the defaced example of other human lives. Neither did Ernest know that the thoughts and affections which came to him so naturally, in the fields and at the fireside, and wherever he communed with himself, were of a higher tone than those which all men shared with him. A simple soul—simple as when his mother first taught him the old prophecy—he beheld the marvellous features beaming adown the valley, and still wondered that their human counterpart was so long in making his appearance.

By this time poor Mr. Gathergold was dead and buried; and the oddest part of the matter was, that his wealth, which was the body and spirit of his existence, had disappeared before his death, leaving nothing of him but a living skeleton, covered over with a wrinkled yellow skin. Since the melting away of his gold, it had been very generally conceded that there was no such striking resemblance, after all, betwixt the ignoble features of the ruined merchant and that majestic face upon the mountain-side. So the people ceased to honor him during his lifetime, and quietly consigned him to forgetfulness after his decease. Once in a while, it is true, his memory was brought up in connection with the magnificent palace which he had built, and which had long ago been turned into a hotel for the accommodation of strangers, multitudes of whom came, every summer, to visit that famous natural curiosity, the Great Stone Face. Thus, Mr. Gathergold being discredited and thrown into the shade, the man of prophecy was yet to come.

It so happened that a native-born son of the valley, many years before, had enlisted as a soldier, and, after a great deal of hard fighting, had now become an illustrious commander. Whatever he may be called in history, he was known in camps and on the battle-field under the nickname of Old Blood-and-Thunder. This war-worn veteran being now infirm with age and wounds, and weary of the turmoil of a military life, and of the roll of the drum and the clangor of the trumpet, that had so long been ringing in his ears, had lately signified a purpose of returning to his native valley, hoping to find repose where he remembered to have left it. The inhabitants, his old neighbors and their grown-up children, were resolved to welcome the renowned warrior with a salute of cannon and a public dinner; and all the more enthusiastically, it being affirmed that now, at last, the likeness of the Great Stone Face had actually appeared. An aid-de-camp of Old Blood-and-Thunder, travelling through the valley, was said to have been struck with the resemblance. Moreover the schoolmates and early acquaintances of the general were ready to testify, on oath, that, to the best of their recollection, the aforesaid general had been exceedingly like the majestic image, even when a boy, only the idea had never occurred to them at that period. Great, therefore, was the excitement throughout the valley; and many people, who had never once thought of glancing at the Great Stone Face for years before, now spent their time in gazing at it, for the sake of knowing exactly how General Blood-and-Thunder looked.

On the day of the great festival, Ernest, with all the other people of the valley, left their work, and proceeded to the spot where the sylvan banquet was prepared. As he approached, the loud voice of the Rev. Dr. Battleblast was heard, beseeching a blessing on the good things set before them, and on the distinguished friend of peace in whose honor they were assembled. The tables were arranged in a cleared space of the woods, shut in by the surrounding trees, except where a vista opened eastward, and afforded a distant view of the Great Stone Face. Over the general's chair, which was a relic from the home of Washington, there was an arch of verdant boughs, with the laurel profusely intermixed, and surmounted by his country's banner, beneath which he had won his victories. Our friend Ernest raised himself on his tiptoes, in hopes to get a glimpse of the celebrated guest; but there was a mighty crowd about the tables anxious to hear the toasts and speeches, and to catch any word that might fall from the general in reply; and a volunteer company, doing duty as a guard, pricked ruthlessly with their bayonets at any particularly quiet person among the throng. So Ernest, being of an unobtrusive character, was thrust quite into the background, where he could see no more of Old Blood-and-Thunder's physiognomy than if it had been still blazing on the battle-field. To console himself, he turned towards the Great Stone Face, which, like a faithful and long-remembered friend, looked back and smiled upon him through the vista of the forest. Meantime, however, he could overhear the remarks of various individuals, who were comparing the features of the hero with the face on the distant mountain-side.

"'Tis the same face, to a hair!" cried one man, cutting a caper for joy.

"Wonderfully like, that's a fact!" responded another.

"Like! why, I call it Old Blood-and-Thunder himself, in a monstrous looking-glass!" cried a third. "And why not? He's the greatest man of this or any other age, beyond a doubt."

And then all three of the speakers gave a great shout, which communicated electricity to the crowd, and called forth a roar from a thousand voices, that went reverberating for miles among the mountains, until you might have supposed that the Great Stone Face had poured its thunder-breath into the cry. All these comments, and this vast enthusiasm, served the more to interest our friend; nor did he think of questioning that now, at length, the mountain-visage had found its human counterpart. It is true, Ernest had imagined that this long-looked-for personage would appear in the character of a man of peace, uttering wisdom, and doing good, and making people happy. But, taking an habitual breadth of view, with all his simplicity, he contended that Providence should choose its own method of blessing mankind, and could conceive that this great end might be effected even by a warrior and a bloody sword, should inscrutable wisdom see fit to order matters so.

"The general! the general!" was now the cry. "Hush! silence! Old Blood-and-Thunder's going to make a speech."

Even so; for, the cloth being removed, the general's health had been drunk, amid shouts of applause, and he now stood upon his feet to thank the company. Ernest saw him. There he was, over the shoulders of the crowd, from the two glittering epaulets and embroidered collar upward, beneath the arch of green boughs with intertwined laurel, and the banner drooping as if to shade his brow! And there, too, visible in the same glance, through the vista of the forest, appeared the Great Stone Face! And was there, indeed, such a resemblance as the crowd had testified? Alas, Ernest could not recognize it! He beheld a war-worn and weather-beaten countenance, full of energy, and expressive of an iron will; but the gentle wisdom, the deep, broad, tender sympathies, were altogether wanting in Old Blood-and-Thunder's visage; and even if the Great Stone Face had assumed his look of stern command, the milder traits would still have tempered it.

"This is not the man of prophecy," sighed Ernest to himself, as he made his way out of the throng. "And must the world wait longer yet?"

The mists had congregated about the distant mountain-side, and there were seen the grand and awful features of the Great Stone Face, awful but benignant, as if a mighty angel were sitting among the hills, and enrobing himself in a cloud-vesture of gold and purple. As he looked, Ernest could hardly believe but that a smile beamed over the whole visage, with a radiance still brightening, although without motion of the lips. It was probably the effect of the western sunshine, melting through the thinly diffused vapors that had swept between him and the object that he gazed at. But—as it always did—the aspect of his marvellous friend made Ernest as hopeful as if he had never hoped in vain.

"Fear not, Ernest," said his heart, even as if the Great Face were whispering to him, "—fear not, Ernest; he will come."

More years sped swiftly and tranquilly away. Ernest still dwelt in his native valley, and was now a man of middle age. By imperceptible degrees, he had become known among the people. Now, as heretofore, he labored for his bread, and was the same simple-hearted man that he had always been. But he had thought and felt so much, he had given so many of the best hours of his life to unworldly hopes for some great good to mankind, that it seemed as though he had been talking with the angels, and had imbibed a portion of their wisdom unawares. It was visible in the calm and well-considered beneficence of his daily life, the quiet stream of which had made a wide green margin all along its course. Not a day passed by, that the world was not the better because this man, humble as he was, had lived. He never stepped aside from his own path, yet would always reach a blessing to his neighbor. Almost involuntarily, too, he had become a preacher. The pure and high simplicity of his thought, which, as one of its manifestations, took shape in the good deeds that dropped silently from his hand, flowed also forth in speech. He uttered truths that wrought upon and moulded the lives of those who heard him. His auditors, it may be, never suspected that Ernest, their own neighbor and familiar friend, was more than an ordinary man; least of all did Ernest himself suspect it; but, inevitably as the murmur of a rivulet, came thoughts out of his mouth that no other human lips had spoken.

When the people's minds had had a little time to cool, they were ready enough to acknowledge their mistake in imagining a similarity between General Blood-and-Thunder's truculent physiognomy and the benign visage on the mountain-side. But now, again, there were reports and many paragraphs in the newspapers, affirming that the likeness of the Great Stone Face had appeared upon the broad shoulders of a certain eminent statesman. He, like Mr. Gathergold and Old Blood-and-Thunder, was a native of the valley, but had left it in his early days, and taken up the trades of law and politics. Instead of the rich man's wealth and the warrior's sword, he had but a tongue, and it was mightier than both together. So wonderfully eloquent was he, that whatever he might choose to say, his auditors had no choice but to believe him; wrong looked like right, and right like wrong; for when it pleased him, he could make a kind of illuminated fog with his mere breath, and obscure the natural daylight with it. His tongue, indeed, was a magic instrument: sometimes it rumbled like the thunder; sometimes it warbled like the sweetest music. It was the blast of war, the song of peace; and it seemed to have a heart in it, when there was no such matter. In good truth, he was a wondrous man; and when his tongue had acquired him all other imaginable success—when it had been heard in halls of state, and in the courts of princes and potentates—after it had made him known all over the world, even as a voice crying from shore to shore—it finally persuaded his countrymen to select him for the Presidency. Before this time—indeed, as soon as he began to grow celebrated—his admirers had found out the resemblance between him and the Great Stone Face; and so much were they struck by it, that throughout the country this distinguished gentleman was known by the name of Old Stony Phiz. The phrase was considered as giving a highly favorable aspect to his political prospects; for, as is likewise the case with the Popedom, nobody ever becomes President without taking a name other than his own.

While his friends were doing their best to make him President, Old Stony Phiz, as he was called, set out on a visit to the valley where he was born. Of course, he had no other object than to shake hands with his fellow-citizens and neither thought nor cared about any effect which his progress through the country might have upon the election. Magnificent preparations were made to receive the illustrious statesman; a cavalcade of horsemen set forth to meet him at the boundary line of the State, and all the people left their business and gathered along the wayside to see him pass. Among these was Ernest. Though more than once disappointed, as we have seen, he had such a hopeful and confiding nature, that he was always ready to believe in whatever seemed beautiful and good. He kept his heart continually open, and thus was sure to catch the blessing from on high when it should come. So now again, as buoyantly as ever, he went forth to behold the likeness of the Great Stone Face.

The cavalcade came prancing along the road, with a great clattering of hoofs and a mighty cloud of dust, which rose up so dense and high that the visage of the mountain-side was completely hidden from Ernest's eyes. All the great men of the neighborhood were there on horseback; militia officers, in uniform; the member of Congress; the sheriff of the county; the editors of newspapers; and many a farmer, too, had mounted his patient steed, with his Sunday coat upon his back. It really was a very brilliant spectacle, especially as there were numerous banners flaunting over the cavalcade, on some of which were gorgeous portraits of the illustrious statesman and the Great Stone Face, smiling familiarly at one another, like two brothers. If the pictures were to be trusted, the mutual resemblance, it must be confessed, was marvellous. We must not forget to mention that there was a band of music, which made the echoes of the mountains ring and reverberate with the loud triumph of its strains; so that airy and soul-thrilling melodies broke out among all the heights and hollows, as if every nook of his native valley had found a voice, to welcome the distinguished guest. But the grandest effect was when the far-off mountain precipice flung back the music; for then the Great Stone Face itself seemed to be swelling the triumphant chorus, in acknowledgment that, at length, the man of prophecy was come.

All this while the people were throwing up their hats and shouting, with enthusiasm so contagious that the heart of Ernest kindled up, and he likewise threw up his hat, and shouted, as loudly as the loudest, "Huzza for the great man! Huzza for Old Stony Phiz!" But as yet he had not seen him.

"Here he is, now!" cried those who stood near Ernest. "There! There! Look at Old Stony Phiz and then at the Old Man of the Mountain, and see if they are not as like as two twin-brothers!"

In the midst of all this gallant array came an open barouche, drawn by four white horses; and in the barouche, with his massive head uncovered, sat the illustrious statesman, Old Stony Phiz himself.

"Confess it," said one of Ernest's neighbors to him, "the Great Stone Face has met its match at last!"

Now, it must be owned that, at his first glimpse of the countenance which was bowing and smiling from the barouche, Ernest did fancy that there was a resemblance between it and the old familiar face upon the mountain-side. The brow, with its massive depth and loftiness, and all the other features, indeed, were boldly and strongly hewn, as if in emulation of a more than heroic, of a Titanic model. But the sublimity and stateliness, the grand ex-presson of a divine sympathy, that illuminated the mountain visage and etherealized its ponderous granite substance into spirit, might here be sought in vain. Something had been originally left out, or had departed. And therefore the marvellously gifted statesman had always a weary gloom in the deep caverns of his eyes, as of a child that has outgrown its playthings or a man of mighty faculties and little aims, whose life, with all its high performances, was vague and empty, because no high purpose had endowed it with reality.

Still, Ernest's neighbor was thrusting his elbow into his side, and pressing him for an answer.

"Confess! confess! Is not he the very picture of your Old Man of the Mountain?"

"No!" said Ernest bluntly, "I see little or no likeness."

"Then so much the worse for the Great Stone Face!" answered his neighbor; and again he set up a shout for Old Stony Phiz.

But Ernest turned away, melancholy, and almost despondent: for this was the saddest of his disappointments, to behold a man who might have fulfilled the prophecy, and had not willed to do so. Meantime, the cavalcade, the banners, the music, and the barouches swept past him, with the vociferous crowd in the rear, leaving the dust to settle down, and the Great Stone Face to be revealed again, with the grandeur that it had worn for untold centuries.

"Lo, here I am, Ernest!" the benign lips seemed to say. "I have waited longer than thou, and am not yet weary. Fear not; the man will come."

The years hurried onward, treading in their haste on one another's heels. And now they began to bring white hairs, and scatter them over the head of Ernest; they made reverend wrinkles across his forehead, and furrows in his cheeks. He was an aged man. But not in vain had he grown old: more than the white hairs on his head were the sage thoughts in his mind; his wrinkles and furrows were inscriptions that Time had graved, and in which he had written legends of wisdom that had been tested by the tenor of a life. And Ernest had ceased to be obscure. Unsought for, undesired, had come the fame which so many seek, and made him known in the great world, beyond the limits of the valley in which he had dwelt so quietly. College professors, and even the active men of cities, came from far to see and converse with Ernest; for the report had gone abroad that this simple husbandman had ideas unlike those of other men, not gained from books, but of a higher tone—a tranquil and familiar majesty, as if he had been talking with the angels as his daily friends. Whether it were sage, statesman, or philanthropist, Ernest received these visitors with the gentle sincerity that had characterized him from boyhood, and spoke freely with them of whatever came uppermost, or lay deepest in his heart or their own. While they talked together, his face would kindle, unawares, and shine upon them, as with a mild evening light. Pensive with the fulness of such discourse, his guests took leave and went their way; and passing up the valley, paused to look at the Great Stone Face, imagining that they had seen its likeness in a human countenance, but could not remember where.

While Ernest had been growing up and growing old, a bountiful Providence had granted a new poet to this earth. He likewise, was a native of the valley, but had spent the greater part of his life at a distance from that romantic region, pouring out his sweet music amid the bustle and din of cities. Often, however, did the mountains which had been familiar to him in his childhood lift their snowy peaks into the clear atmosphere of his poetry. Neither was the Great Stone Face forgotten, for the poet had celebrated it in an ode, which was grand enough to have been uttered by its own majestic lips. This man of genius, we may say, had come down from heaven with wonderful endowments. If he sang of a mountain, the eyes of all mankind beheld a mightier grandeur reposing on its breast, or soaring to its summit, than had before been seen there. If his theme were a lovely lake, a celestial smile had now been thrown over it, to gleam forever on its surface. If it were the vast old sea, even the deep immensity of its dread bosom seemed to swell the higher, as if moved by the emotions of the song. Thus the world assumed another and a better aspect from the hour that the poet blessed it with his happy eyes. The Creator had bestowed him, as the last best touch to his own handiwork. Creation was not finished till the poet came to interpret, and so complete it.

The effect was no less high and beautiful, when his human brethren were the subject of his verse. The man or woman, sordid with the common dust of life, who crossed his daily path, and the little child who played in it, were glorified if he beheld them in his mood of poetic faith. He showed the golden links of the great chain that intertwined them with an angelic kindred; he brought out the hidden traits of a celestial birth that made them worthy of such kin. Some, indeed, there were, who thought to show the soundness of their judgment by affirming that all the beauty and dignity of the natural world existed only in the poet's fancy. Let such men speak for themselves, who undoubtedly appear to have been spawned forth by Nature with a contemptuous bitterness; she having plastered them up out of her refuse stuff, after all the swine were made. As respects all things else, the poet's ideal was the truest truth.

The songs of this poet found their way to Ernest. He read them after his customary toil, seated on the bench before his cottage-door, where for such a length of time he had filled his repose with thought, by gazing at the Great Stone Face. And now as he read stanzas that caused the soul to thrill within him, he lifted his eyes to the vast countenance beaming on him so benignantly.

"O majestic friend," he murmured, addressing the Great Stone Face, "is not this man worthy to resemble thee?"

The Face seemed to smile, but answered not a word.

Now it happened that the poet, though he dwelt so far away, had not only heard of Ernest, but had meditated much upon his character, until he deemed nothing so desirable as to meet this man, whose untaught wisdom walked hand in hand with the noble simplicity of his life. One summer morning, therefore, he took passage by the railroad, and, in the decline of the afternoon, alighted from the cars at no great distance from Ernest's cottage. The great hotel, which had formerly been the palace of Mr. Gathergold, was close at hand, but the poet, with his carpet-bag on his arm, inquired at once where Ernest dwelt, and was resolved to be accepted as his guest.

Approaching the door, he there found the good old man, holding a volume in his hand, which alternately he read, and then, with a finger between the leaves, looked lovingly at the Great Stone Face.

"Good evening," said the poet. "Can you give a traveller a night's lodging?"

"Willingly," answered Ernest; and then he added, smiling, "Methinks I never saw the Great Stone Face look so hospitably at a stranger."

The poet sat down on the bench beside him, and he and Ernest talked together. Often had the poet held intercourse with the wittiest and the wisest, but never before with a man like Ernest, whose thoughts and feelings gushed up with such a natural freedom, and who made great truths so familiar by his simple utterance of them. Angels, as had been so often said, seemed to have wrought with him at his labor in the fields; angels seemed to have sat with him by the fireside; and, dwelling with angels as friend with friends, he had imbibed the sublimity of their ideas, and imbued it with the sweet and lowly charm of household words. So thought the poet. And Ernest, on the other hand, was moved and agitated by the living images which the poet flung out of his mind, and which peopled all the air about the cottage-door with shapes of beauty, both gay and pensive. The sympathies of these two men instructed them with a profounder sense than either could have attained alone. Their minds accorded into one strain, and made delightful music which neither of them could have claimed as all his own, nor distinguished his own share from the other's. They led one another, as it were, into a high pavilion of their thoughts, so remote, and hitherto so dim, that they had never entered it before, and so beautiful that they desired to be there always.

As Ernest listened to the poet, he imagined that the Great Stone Face was bending forward to listen too. He gazed earnestly into the poet's glowing eyes.

"Who are you, my strangely gifted guest?" he said.

The poet laid his finger on the volume that Ernest had been reading.

"You have read these poems," said he. "You know me, then—for I wrote them."

Again, and still more earnestly than before, Ernest examined the poet's features; then turned towards the Great Stone Face; then back, with an uncertain aspect, to his guest. But his countenance fell; he shook his head, and sighed.

"Wherefore are you sad?" inquired the poet.

"Because," replied Ernest, "all through life I have awaited the fulfilment of a prophecy; and, when I read these poems, I hoped that it might be fulfilled in you."

"You hoped," answered the poet, faintly smiling, "to find in me the likeness of the Great Stone Face. And you are disappointed, as formerly with Mr. Gathergold, and Old Blood-and-Thunder, and Old Stony Phiz. Yes, Ernest, it is my doom. You must add my name to the illustrious three, and record another failure of your hopes. For—in shame and sadness do I speak it, Ernest—I am not worthy to be typified by yonder benign and majestic image."

"And why?" asked Ernest. He pointed to the volume. "Are not those thoughts divine?"

"They have a strain of the Divinity," replied the poet. "You can hear in them the far-off echo of a heavenly song. But my life, dear Ernest, has not corresponded with my thought. I have had grand dreams, but they have been only dreams, because I have lived—and that, too, by my own choice—among poor and mean realities. Sometimes even—shall I dare to say it?—I lack faith in the grandeur, the beauty, and the goodness, which my own words are said to have made more evident in nature and in human life. Why, then, pure seeker of the good and true, shouldst thou hope to find me, in yonder image of the divine?"

The poet spoke sadly, and his eyes were dim with tears. So, likewise, were those of Ernest.

At the hour of sunset, as had long been his frequent custom, Ernest was to discourse to an assemblage of the neighboring inhabitants in the open air. He and the poet, arm in arm, still talking together as they went along, proceeded to the spot. It was a small nook among the hills, with a gray precipice behind, the stern front of which was relieved by the pleasant foliage of many creeping plants that made a tapestry for the naked rock, by hanging their festoons from all its rugged angles. At a small elevation above the ground, set in a rich framework of verdure, there appeared a niche, spacious enough to admit a human figure, with freedom for such gestures as spontaneously accompany earnest thought and genuine emotion. Into this natural pulpit Ernest ascended, and threw a look of familiar kindness around upon his audience. They stood, or sat, or reclined upon the grass, as seemed good to each, with the departing sunshine falling obliquely over them, and mingling its subdued cheerfulness with the solemnity of a grove of ancient trees, beneath and amid the boughs of which the golden rays were constrained to pass. In another direction was seen the Great Stone Face, with the same cheer, combined with the same solemnity, in its benignant aspect.

Ernest began to speak, giving to the people of what was in his heart and mind. His words had power, because they accorded with his thoughts; and his thoughts had reality and depth, because they harmonized with the life which he had always lived. It was not mere breath that this preacher uttered; they were the words of life, because a life of good deeds and holy love was melted into them. Pearls, pure and rich, had been dissolved into this precious draught. The poet, as he listened, felt that the being and character of Ernest were a nobler strain of poetry than he had ever written. His eyes glistening with tears, he gazed reverentially at the venerable man, and said within himself that never was there an aspect so worthy of a prophet and a sage as that mild, sweet, thoughtful countenance, with the glory of white hair diffused about it. At a distance, but distinctly to be seen, high up in the golden light of the setting sun, appeared the Great Stone Face, with hoary mists around it, like the white hairs around the brow of Ernest. Its look of grand beneficence seemed to embrace the world.

At that moment, in sympathy with a thought which he was about to utter, the face of Ernest assumed a grandeur of expression, so imbued with benevolence, that the poet, by an irresistible impulse, threw his arms aloft and shouted,

"Behold! Behold! Ernest is himself the likeness of the Great Stone Face!"

Then all the people looked, and saw that what the deep-sighted poet said was true. The prophecy was fulfilled. But Ernest, having finished what he had to say, took the poet's arm, and walked slowly homeward, still hoping that some wiser and better man than himself would by and by appear, bearing a resemblance to the GREAT STONE FACE.

For Further Reflection

1. What is the significance of the Great Stone Face in this story? Many people think that we must have good role models in order to develop into good people, but this story suggests that we need not have great people but simply great ideas and ideals. Is this plausible?
2. Explain how the Great Stone Face affects the values and virtues of the people of the valley, especially Ernest. What virtues does Ernest manifest?

A Critique of Virtue-Based Ethical Systems

WILLIAM K. FRANKENA

William Frankena (1908–1994) was a professor of philosophy at the University of Michigan and the author of several works in ethical theory, including *Ethics* (1973), from which this selection is taken. Frankena, a defender of a deontological duty-based ethic, agrees with the virtue ethicist on the importance of traits (virtues) but argues that all of the virtues can be derived from principles: "Traits without principles are blind." For every virtue there must be some possible action to which the virtue corresponds and from which it derives its virtuousness. For example, the virtue of truthfulness corresponds to the principle "Tell the truth," and the virtue of being benevolent derives from the general principle to act beneficently. There is a close corresponding relationship between all of the virtues and all of the principles.

MORALITY AND CULTIVATION OF TRAITS

Our present interest, then, is not in moral principles nor in nonmoral values, but in moral values, in what is morally good or bad. Throughout its history morality has been concerned about the cultivation of certain dispositions, or traits, among which are "character" and such "virtues" (an old-fashioned but still useful term) as honesty, kindness, and conscientiousness. Virtues are dispositions or traits that are not wholly innate; they must all be acquired, at least in part, by teaching and practice, or, perhaps, by grace. They are also traits of "character," rather than traits of "personality" like charm or shyness, and they all involve a tendency to do certain kinds of action in certain kinds of situations, not just to think or feel in certain ways. They are not just abilities or skills, like intelligence or carpentry, which one may have without using.

In fact, it has been suggested that morality is or should be conceived as primarily concerned, not with rules or principles as we have been supposing so far, but with the cultivation of such dispositions or traits of character. Plato and Aristotle seem to conceive of morality in this way, for they talk mainly in terms of virtues and the virtuous, rather than in terms of what is right or obligatory. Hume uses similar terms, although he mixes in some nonmoral traits like cheerfulness and wit along with moral ones like benevolence and justice. More recently, Leslie Stephen stated the view in these words:

> . . . morality is internal. The moral law . . . has to be expressed in the form, "be this," not in the form, "do this." . . . The true moral law says "hate not," instead of "kill not." . . . The only mode of stating the moral law must be as a rule of character.[1]

ETHICS OF VIRTUE

Those who hold this view are advocating an *ethics of virtue* or being, in opposition to an ethics of duty, principle, or doing. . . . The notion of an ethics of virtue is worth looking at here, not only because it has a long history but also because some spokesmen of "the new morality" seem to espouse it. What would an ethics of virtue be like? It would, of course, not take deontic judgments or principles as basic in morality, as we have been doing; instead, it would take as basic aretaic judgments like "That was a courageous deed," "His action was virtuous," or "Courage is a virtue," and it would insist that deontic judgments are either derivative from such aretaic ones or can be dispensed with entirely. Moreover, it would regard aretaic judgments about actions as secondary and as based on aretaic judgments about agents and their motives or traits, as Hume does when he writes:

> . . . when we praise any actions, we regard only the motives that produced them. . . . The external performance has no merit. . . . All virtuous actions derive their merit only from virtuous motives.[2]

For an ethics of virtue, then, what is basic in morality is judgments like "Benevolence is a good motive," "Courage is a virtue," "The morally good man is kind to everyone" or, more simply and less accurately, "Be loving!"— not judgments or principles about what our duty is or what we ought to do. But, of course, it thinks that its basic instructions will guide us, not only about what to be, but also about what to do.

It looks as if there would be three kinds of ethics of virtue, corresponding to the three kinds of ethics of duty covered earlier. The question to be answered is: What dispositions or traits are moral virtues? *Trait-egoism* replies that the virtues are the dispositions that are most conducive to one's own good or welfare, or, alternatively, that prudence or a careful concern for one's own good is

[1]Leslie Stephen, *The Science of Ethics* (New York: G. P. Putnam's Sons, 1882), pp. 155, 158.
[2]David Hume, *Treatise of Human Nature* (1739), Book III, Part II, opening of Sec. I.

the cardinal or basic moral virtue, other virtues being derivative from it. *Trait-utilitarianism* asserts that the virtues are those traits that most promote the general good, or, alternatively, that benevolence is the basic or cardinal moral virtue. These views may be called *trait-teleological,* but, of course, there are also *trait-deontological theories,* which will hold that certain traits are morally good or virtuous simply as such, and not just because of the nonmoral value they may have or promote, or, alternatively, that there are other cardinal or basic virtues besides prudence or benevolence, for example, obedience to God, honesty, or justice. If they add that there is only one such cardinal virtue, they are monistic, otherwise pluralistic.

To avoid confusion, it is necessary to notice here that we must distinguish between *virtues* and *principles of duty* like "We ought to promote the good" and "We ought to treat people equally." A virtue is not a principle of this kind; it is a disposition, habit, quality, or trait of the person or soul, which an individual either has or seeks to have. Hence, I speak of the principle of *beneficence* and the virtue of *benevolence,* since we have two words with which to mark the difference. In the case of justice, we do not have different words, but still we must not confuse the principle of equal treatment with the disposition to treat people equally.

On the basis of our earlier discussions, we may assume at this point that views of the first two kinds are unsatisfactory, and that the most adequate ethics of virtue would be one of the third sort, one that would posit two cardinal virtues, namely, benevolence and justice, considered now as dispositions or traits of character rather than as principles of duty. By a set of cardinal virtues is meant a set of virtues that (1) cannot be derived from one another and (2) all other moral virtues can be derived from or shown to be forms of them. Plato and other Greeks thought there were four cardinal virtues in this sense: wisdom, courage, temperance, and justice. Christianity is traditionally regarded as having seven cardinal virtues: three "theological" virtues—faith, hope, and love; and four "human" virtues—prudence, fortitude, temperance, and justice. This was essentially St. Thomas Aquinas's view; since St. Augustine regarded the last four as forms of love, only the first three were really cardinal for him. However, many moralists, among them Schopenhauer, have taken benevolence and justice to be the cardinal moral virtues, as I would. It seems to me that all of the usual virtues (such as love, courage, temperance, honesty, gratitude, and considerateness), at least insofar as they are *moral* virtues, can be derived from these two. Insofar as a disposition cannot be derived from benevolence and justice, I should try to argue either that it is not a *moral* virtue (e.g., I take faith, hope, and wisdom to be religious or intellectual, not moral, virtues) or that it is not a virtue at all.

ON BEING AND DOING: MORALITY OF TRAITS VS. MORALITY OF PRINCIPLES

We may now return to the issue posed by the quotation from Stephen, though we cannot debate it as fully as we should. To be or to do, that is the question. Should we construe morality as primarily a following of certain principles or as primarily a cultivation of certain dispositions and traits? Must we choose? It is hard to see how a morality of principles can get off the ground except through the development of dispositions to act in accordance with its principles, else all motivation to act on them must be of an *ad hoc* kind, either prudential or impulsively altruistic. Moreover, morality can hardly be content with a mere conformity to rules, however willing and self-conscious it may be, unless it has no interest in the spirit of its law but only in the letter. On the other hand, one cannot conceive of traits of character except as including dispositions and tendencies to act in certain ways in certain circumstances. Hating involves being disposed to kill or harm, being just involves tending to do just acts (acts that conform to the principle of justice) when the occasion calls. Again, it is hard to see how we could know what traits to encourage or inculcate if we did not subscribe to principles, for example, to the principle of utility, or to those of benevolence and justice.

I propose therefore that we regard the morality of duty and principles and the morality of virtues or traits of character not as rival kinds of morality between which we must choose, but as two complementary aspects of the same morality. Then, for every principle there will be a morally good trait, often going by the same name, consisting of a disposition or tendency to act according to it; and for every morally good trait there will be a principle defining the kind of action in which it is to express itself. To parody a famous dictum of Kant's, I am inclined to think that principles without traits are impotent and traits without principles are blind.

Even if we adopt this double-aspect conception of morality, in which principles are basic, we may still agree that morality does and must put a premium on *being* honest, conscientious, and so forth. If its sanctions or sources of motivation are not to be entirely external (for example, the prospect of being praised, blamed, rewarded, or punished by others) or adventitious (for example, a purely instinctive love of others), if it is to have adequate "internal sanctions," as Mill called them, then morality must foster the development of such dispositions and habits as have been mentioned. It could hardly be satisfied with a mere conformity to its principles even if it could provide us with fixed principles of actual duty. For such a conformity might be motivated entirely by extrinsic or nonmoral considerations, and would then be at the mercy of these other considerations. It could not be counted on in a moment of trial. Besides, since morality cannot provide us with fixed principles of actual duty but only with principles of prima facie duty, it cannot be content with the letter of its law, but must foster in us the dispositions that will sustain us in the hour of decision when we are choosing between conflicting principles of prima facie duty or trying to revise our working rules of right and wrong.

There is another reason why we must cultivate certain traits of character in ourselves and others, or why we must be certain sorts of persons. Although morality is concerned that we act in certain ways, it cannot take the hard line of insisting that we act in precisely those ways, even if those ways could be more clearly defined. We cannot praise and blame or apply other sanctions to an agent simply on the ground that he has or has not acted in conformity with certain principles. It would not be right. Through no fault of his own, the agent may not have known all the relevant facts. What action the principles of morality called for in the situation may not have been clear to him, again through no fault of his own, and he may have been honestly mistaken about his duty. Or his doing what he ought to have done might have carried with it an intolerable sacrifice on his part. He may even have been simply incapable of doing it. Morality must therefore recognize various sorts of excuses and extenuating circumstances. All it can really insist on, then, except in certain critical cases, is that we develop and manifest fixed dispositions to find out what the right thing is and to do it if possible. In this sense a person must "be this" rather than "do this." But it must be remembered that "being" involves at least *trying* to "do." Being without doing, like faith without works, is dead.

At least it will be clear from this discussion that an ethics of duty or principles also has an important place for the virtues and must put a premium on their cultivation as a part of moral education and development. The place it has for virtue and/or the virtues is, however, different from that accorded them by an ethics of virtue. Talking in terms of . . . an ethics of duty, we may say that, if we ask for *guidance* about what to do or not do, then the answer is contained, at least primarily, in two deontic principles and their corollaries, namely, the principles of beneficence and equal treatment. Given these two deontic principles, plus the necessary clarity of thought and factual knowledge, we can know what we morally ought to do or not do, except perhaps in cases of conflict between them. We also know that we should cultivate two virtues, a disposition to be beneficial (i.e., benevolence) and a disposition to treat people equally (justice as a trait). But the point of acquiring these virtues is not further guidance or instruction; the function of the virtues in an ethics of duty is not to tell us what to do but to ensure that we will do it willingly in whatever situations we may face. In an ethics of virtue, on the other hand, the virtues play a dual role—they must not only move us to do what we do, they must also tell us what to do. To parody Alfred Lord Tennyson:

> Theirs not (only) to do or die,
> Theirs (also) to reason why.

MORAL IDEALS

This is the place to mention ideals again, which are among what we called the ingredients of morality. One may, perhaps, identify moral ideals with moral principles, but, more properly speaking, moral ideals are ways of being rather than of doing. Having a moral ideal is wanting to be a person of a certain sort, wanting to have a certain trait of character rather than others, for example, moral courage or perfect integrity. That is why the use of exemplary persons like Socrates, Jesus, or Martin Luther King has been such an important part of moral education and self-development, and it is one of the reasons for the writing and reading of biographies or of novels and epics in which types of moral personality are portrayed, even if they are not all heroes or saints. Often such moral ideals of personality go beyond what can be demanded or regarded as obligatory, belonging among the things to be praised rather than required, except as one may require them of oneself. It should be remembered, however, that not all personal ideals are moral ones. Achilles, Hercules, Napoleon, and Prince Charming may all be taken as ideals, but the ideals they represent are not moral ones, even though they may not be immoral ones either. Some ideals, e.g., those of chivalry, may be partly moral and partly nonmoral. There is every reason why one should pursue nonmoral as well as moral ideals, but there is no good reason for confusing them.

When one has a moral ideal, wanting to be a certain sort of moral person, one has at least some motivation to live in a certain way, but one also has something to guide him in living. Here the idea of an ethics of virtue may have a point. One may, of course, take as one's ideal that of being a good man who always does his duty from a sense of duty, perhaps gladly, and perhaps even going a second mile on occasion. Then one's guidance clearly comes entirely from one's rules and principles of duty. However, one may also have an ideal that goes beyond anything that can be regarded by others or even oneself as strict duty or obligation, a form or style of personal being that may be morally good or virtuous, but is not morally required of one. An ethics of virtue seems to provide for such an aspiration more naturally than an ethics of duty or principle, and perhaps an adequate morality should at least contain a region in which we can follow such an idea, over and beyond the region in which we are to listen to the call of duty. There certainly should be moral heroes and saints who go beyond the merely good man, if only to serve as an inspiration to others to be better and do more than they would otherwise be or do. Granted all this, however, it still seems to me that, if one's ideal is truly a moral one, there will be nothing in it that is not covered by the principles of beneficence and justice conceived as principles of what we ought to do in the wider sense referred to earlier.

DISPOSITIONS TO BE CULTIVATED

Are there any other moral virtues to be cultivated besides benevolence and justice? No cardinal ones, of course. In this sense our answer to Socrates' question whether virtue is one or many is that it is two. We saw, however, that the principles of beneficence and equality have corollaries like telling the truth, keeping promises, etc. It follows that character traits like honesty and fidelity are virtues, though subordinate ones, and should be acquired and fostered. There will then be other such virtues corresponding to other corollaries of our main principles. Let us call all of these virtues, cardinal and noncardinal, first-order moral virtues. Besides first-order virtues like these, there are certain other moral virtues that ought also to be cultivated, which are in a way more abstract and general and may be called second-order virtues. Conscientiousness is one such virtue; it is not limited to a certain sector of the moral life, as gratitude and honesty are, but is a virtue covering the whole of the moral life. Moral courage, or courage when moral issues are at stake, is another such second-order virtue; it belongs to all sectors of the moral life. Others that overlap with these are integrity and good-will, understanding good-will in Kant's sense of respect for the moral law.

In view of what was said in a previous chapter, we must list two other second-order traits: a disposition to find out and respect the relevant facts and a disposition to think clearly. These are not just abilities but character traits; one might have the ability to think intelligently without having a disposition to use it. They are therefore virtues, though they are intellectual virtues, not moral ones. Still, though their role is not limited to the moral life, they are necessary to it. More generally speaking, we should cultivate the virtue Plato called wisdom and Aristotle practical wisdom, which they thought of as including all of the intellectual abilities and virtues essential to the moral life.

Still other second-order qualities, which may be abilities rather than virtues, but which must be cultivated for moral living, and so may, perhaps, best be mentioned here, are moral autonomy, the ability to make moral decisions and to revise one's principles if necessary, and the ability to realize vividly, in imagination and feeling, the "inner lives" of others. Of these second-order qualities, the first two have been referred to on occasion and will be again, but something should be said about the last.

If our morality is to be more than a conformity to internalized rules and principles, if it is to include and rest on an understanding of the point of these rules and principles, and certainly if it is to involve *being* a certain kind of person and not merely *doing* certain kinds of things, then we must somehow attain and develop an ability to be aware of others as persons, as important to themselves as we are to ourselves, and to have a lively and sympathetic representation in imagination of their interests and of the effects of our actions on their lives. The need for this is particularly stressed by Josiah Royce and William James. Both men point out how we usually go our own busy and self-concerned ways, with only an external awareness of the presence of others, much as if they were things, and without any realization of their inner and peculiar worlds of personal experience; and both emphasize the need and the possibility of a "higher vision of an inner significance" which pierces this "certain blindness in human beings" and enables us to realize the existence of others in a wholly different way, as we do our own.

> What then is thy neighbor? He too is a mass of states, of experiences, thoughts and desires, just as concrete, as thou art. . . . Dost thou believe this? Art thou sure what it means? This is for thee the turning-point of thy whole conduct towards him.

These are Royce's quaint old-fashioned words. Here are James's more modern ones.

> This higher vision of an inner significance in what, until then, we had realized only in the dead external way, often comes over a person suddenly; and, when it does so, it makes an epoch in his history.

Royce calls this more perfect recognition of our neighbors "the moral insight" and James says that its practical consequence is "the well-known democratic respect for the sacredness of individuality." It is hard to see how either a benevolent (loving) or a just (equalitarian) disposition could come to fruition without it. To quote James again,

> We ought, all of us, to realize each other in this intense, pathetic, and important way.

Doing this is part of what is involved in fully taking the moral point of view.

TWO QUESTIONS

We can now deal with the question, sometimes raised, whether an action is to be judged right or wrong because of its results, because of the principle it exemplifies, or because the motive, intention, or trait of character involved is morally good or bad. The answer . . . is that an action is to be judged *right* or *wrong* by reference to a principle or set of principles. Even if we say it is right or wrong because of its effects, this means that it is right or wrong by the principle of utility or some other teleological principle. But an act may also be said to be *good* or *bad,* praiseworthy or blameworthy, noble or despicable, and so on, and then the moral quality ascribed to it will depend on the agent's motive, intention, or disposition in doing it.

Another important question here is: What is moral goodness? When is a person morally good and when are his actions, dispositions, motives, or intentions morally good? Not just when he does what is actually right, for he may do what is right from bad motives, in which case he is not morally good, or he may fail to do what is right though sincerely trying to do it, in which case he is not morally bad. Whether he and his actions are morally good or not depends, not on the rightness of what he does or on its consequences, but on his character or motives; so far the statement quoted from Hume is certainly correct. But when are his motives and dispositions morally good? Some answer that a person and his actions are morally good if and only if they are motivated wholly by a sense of duty or a desire to do what is right; the Stoics and Kant sometimes seem to take this extreme view. Others hold that a man and his actions are morally good if and only if they are motivated primarily by a sense of duty or desire to do what is right, though other motives may be present too; still others contend, with Aristotle, that they are at any rate not morally good unless they are motivated at least in part by such a sense or desire. A more reasonable view, to my mind, is that a man and his actions are morally good if it is at least true that, whatever his actual motives in acting are, his sense of duty or desire to do the right is so strong in him that it would keep him trying to do his duty anyway.

Actually, I find it hard to believe that no dispositions or motivations are good or virtuous from the moral point of view except those that include a will to do the right as such. It is more plausible to distinguish two kinds of morally good dispositions or traits of character, first, those that are usually called moral virtues and do include a will to do the right, and second, others like purely natural kindliness or gratefulness, which, while they are nonmoral, are still morality-supporting, since they dispose us to do such actions as morality requires and even to perform deeds, for example, in the case of motherly love, which are well beyond the call of duty.

It has even been alleged that conscientiousness or moral goodness in the sense of a disposition to act from a sense of duty alone is not a good thing or not a virtue—that it is more desirable to have people acting from motives like friendship, gratitude, honor, love, and the like, than from a dry or driven sense of obligation. There is something to be said for this view, though it ignores the nobility of great moral courage and of the higher reaches of moral idealism. But even if conscientiousness or good will is not the only thing that is unconditionally good, as Kant believed, or the greatest of intrinsically good things, as Ross thought, it is surely a good thing from the moral point of view. For an ethics of duty, at any rate, it must be desirable that people do what is right for its own sake, especially if they do it gladly, as a gymnast may gladly make the right move just because it is right.

For Further Reflection

1. What are Frankena's main criticisms of virtue ethics? Are you convinced by them?
2. What does he propose in place of contrasting the ethics of *doing* with the ethics of *being*? How cogent are his arguments?
3. What does Frankena think the two cardinal virtues are?
4. Do you agree with Frankena that a moral person must want to do the right thing just because it is right? What if I think that I must have a self-interested reason for being moral? We will look at this issue more fully in Chapter 8, but you should start thinking about it now.

The Sermon on the Mount; The Good Samaritan

JESUS OF NAZARETH

Jesus of Nazareth (died c. A.D. 30) is the founder of the Christian religion and is believed by Christians to have risen from the dead. He is considered by them to be the son of God and savior of the world. In this famous sermon given on a mountain near Capernaum in modern Israel, Jesus sets forth a

New Testament: Matthew 5; Luke 10.

radical ethic of nonviolence and love. This is followed by his parable of the Good Samaritan. The Samaritans were a despised ethnic group with whom the Jews would have no relations. Jesus broke with his culture in his fellowship with the Samaritans.

THE SERMON ON THE MOUNT

Jesus saw the crowds and went up a hill, where he sat down. His disciples gathered around him, and he began to teach them:

"Happy are those who know they are spiritually poor;
the Kingdom of heaven belongs to them!
"Happy are those who mourn;
God will comfort them!
"Happy are the meek;
they will receive what God has promised!
"Happy are those whose greatest desire is to do what God requires;
God will satisfy them fully!
"Happy are those who are merciful to others;
God will be merciful to them!
"Happy are the pure in heart;
they will see God!
"Happy are those who work for peace among men;
God will call them his sons!
"Happy are those who are persecuted because they do what
God requires;
the Kingdom of heaven belongs to them!
"Happy are you when men insult you, and persecute you, and tell all kinds of evil lies against you because you are my followers. Be glad and happy, because a great reward is kept for you in heaven. This is how men persecuted the prophets who lived before you."

"You are like salt for all mankind. But if salt loses its taste, there is no way to make it salty again. It has become worthless, so it is thrown away and people walk on it.

"You are like light for the whole world. A city built on a hill cannot be hid. No one lights a lamp to put it under a bowl; instead he puts it on the lampstand, where it gives light for everyone in the house. In the same way your light must shine before people, so that they will see the good things you do and give praise to your Father in heaven.

"Do not think that I have come to do away with the Law of Moses and the teachings of the prophets. I have not come to do away with them, but to make their teachings come true. Remember this! As long as heaven and earth last, the least point or the smallest detail of the Law will not be done away with—not until the end of all things. So then, whoever disobeys even the smallest of the commandments, and teaches others to do the same, will be least in the Kingdom of heaven. On the other hand, whoever obeys the Law, and teaches others to do the same, will be great in the Kingdom of heaven. I tell you, then, that you will be able to enter the Kingdom of heaven only if you are more faithful than the teachers of the Law and the Pharisees in doing what God requires.

"You have heard that men were told in the past, 'Do not murder; anyone who commits murder will be brought before the judge.' But now I tell you: whoever is angry with his brother will be brought before the judge; whoever calls his brother 'You good-for-nothing!' will be brought before the Council; and whoever calls his brother a worthless fool will be in danger of going to the fire of hell. So if you are about to offer your gift to God at the altar and there you remember that your brother has something against you, leave your gift there in front of the altar and go at once to make peace with your brother; then come back and offer your gift to God.

"If a man brings a lawsuit against you and takes you to court, be friendly with him while there is time, before you get to court; once you are there he will turn you over to the judge, who will hand you over to the police, and you will be put in jail. There you will stay, I tell you, until you pay the last penny of your fine.

"You have heard that it was said, 'Do not commit adultery.' But now I tell you: anyone who looks at a woman and wants to possess her is guilty of committing adultery with her in his heart. So if your right eye causes you to sin, take it out and throw it away! It is much better for you to lose a part of your body than to have your whole body thrown into hell. If your right hand causes you to sin, cut it off and throw it away! It is much better for you to lose one of your limbs than to have your whole body go off to hell.

"It was also said, 'Anyone who divorces his wife must give her a written notice of divorce.' But now I tell you: if a man divorces his wife, and she has not been unfaithful, then he is guilty of making her commit adultery if she marries again; and the man who marries her also commits adultery.

"You have also heard that men were told in the past, 'Do not break your promise, but do what you have sworn to the Lord to do.' But now I tell you: do not use any vow when you make a promise; do not swear by heaven, because it is God's throne; nor by earth, because it is the resting place for his feet; nor by Jerusalem, because it is the city of the great King. Do not even swear by your head, because you cannot make a single hair white or black. Just say 'Yes' or 'No'—anything else you have to say comes from the Evil One.

"You have heard that it was said, 'An eye for an eye, and a tooth for a tooth.' But now I tell you: do not take revenge on someone who does you wrong. If anyone slaps you on the right cheek, let him slap your left cheek too. And if someone takes you to court to sue you for your shirt, let him have your coat as well. And if one of the occupation troops forces you to carry his pack one mile, carry it another mile. When someone asks you for something, give it to him; when someone wants to borrow something, lend it to him.

"You have heard that it was said, 'Love your friends, hate your enemies.' But now I tell you: love your enemies, and pray for those who persecute you, so that you will become the sons of your Father in heaven. For he makes his sun to shine on bad and good people alike, and gives rain to those who do good and those who do evil. Why should God reward you if you love only the people who love you? Even the tax collectors do that! And if you speak only to your friends, have you done anything out of the ordinary? Even the pagans do that! You must be perfect—just as your Father in heaven is perfect."

THE GOOD SAMARITAN

A certain teacher of the Law came up and tried to trap Jesus. "Teacher," he asked, "what must I do to receive eternal life?" Jesus answered him, "What do the Scriptures say? How do you interpret them?" The man answered, "'You must love the Lord your God with all your heart, with all your soul, with all your strength, and with all your mind'; and, 'You must love your fellow-man as yourself.'" "Your answer is correct," replied Jesus; "do this and you will live."

But the teacher of the Law wanted to put himself in the right, so he asked Jesus, "Who is my fellow-man?" Jesus answered, "There was a man who was going down from Jerusalem to Jericho, when robbers attacked him, stripped him, and beat him up, leaving him half dead. It so happened that a priest was going down that road; when he saw the man he walked on by, on the other side. In the same way a Levite also came there, went over and looked at the man, and then walked on by, on the other side. But a certain Samaritan who was traveling that way came upon him, and when he saw the man his heart was filled with pity. He went over to him, poured oil and wine on his wounds and bandaged them; then he put the man on his own animal and took him to an inn, where he took care of him. The next day he took out two silver coins and gave them to the innkeeper. 'Take care of him,' he told the innkeeper, 'and when I come back this way I will pay you back whatever you spend on him.'" And Jesus concluded, "In your opinion, which one of these three acted like a fellow-man toward the man attacked by the robbers?" The teacher of the Law answered, "The one who was kind to him." Jesus replied, "You go, then, and do the same."

For Further Reflection

1. Can you detect a pattern of virtue in these teachings of Jesus? Compare and contrast these virtues with contemporary virtues of acquisitiveness and good business sense or with the Greek virtues of wisdom, courage, pride, and self-control.
2. Evaluate these teachings, for example, "If your right eye causes you to sin, take it out and throw it away." How should we interpret them? What are their implications?
3. What does the parable of the Good Samaritan teach us? If moral relativism is correct, isn't the Good Samaritan really immoral, since his culture forbids helping its enemies, the Jews? So if the Good Samaritan is really virtuous, does that indicate that moral objectivism is true?

How Much Land Does a Man Need?

Greed

LEO TOLSTOY

Leo Nicolayevich Tolstoy (1828–1910) was born to a Russian noble family and became one of the greatest Russian writers of all time. Among his most famous works are *War and Peace* and *Anna Karenina.* He was a deeply spiritual Christian anarchist, whose works were considered heretical by the Russian Orthodox Church, which banned his book *What I Believe* (1899) and finally excommunicated him in 1901. During the last years of his life, he liberated his peasants, gave them most of his possessions, and lived a frugal, ascetic life like a peasant. We get a powerful glimpse of his philosophy of life in this parable on greed.

Translated from Leo Tolstoy, "How Much Land Does a Man Need?"

1

An elder sister came to visit her younger sister in the country. The elder was married to a merchant in town, the younger to a peasant in the village. As the sisters sat drinking their tea and talking, the elder began to talk proudly of the advantages of town life, saying in what comfort they lived there, how well they dressed, what fine clothes her children wore, what good things they ate and drank, and how she went to the theatre and other amusements.

The younger sister did not like this at all, and in turn spoke ill of the life of a merchant and praised the life of a peasant.

"I would not change my way of life for yours," said she. "We may live roughly, but at least we have no worries. You may have better food and clothes and more amusements than we have, but though you often earn more than you need, you may easily lose all you have. People who are rich one day are often begging their bread next day. Our way is safer. Though a peasant's life is not a rich one, it is a long one. We shall never have a lot of money, but we shall always have enough to eat."

"Enough!" laughed the older sister. "Yes, if you want to live like the animals! What do you know of fine living and good manners! However hard your husband may work, you will die as you are living—on a waste heap—and your children also!"

"Well, what of that?" replied the younger sister. "Of course our work is rough and hard. But it is also sure, and we need not bow down to anyone. But you, in your towns, have all kinds of trouble; to-day all may be well, but to-morrow the Devil may lead your husband into wrong-doing with cards or wine, and all will be lost. Such things happen often!"

Pahom, the master of the house, was lying on the top of the stove and he listened to the women's talk.

"It is perfectly true," he said. "We peasants are so busy growing food in the fields from the time we are children, that we have no time to let any foolish ideas get into our heads. Our only trouble is that we have not enough land. If I had plenty of land I should not fear even the Devil himself!"

The women finished their tea, talked for a while about dress, and then cleared away the tea-things and lay down to sleep.

But the Devil had been sitting behind the stove and had heard all that was said. He was pleased that the peasant's wife had caused her husband to talk so proudly, and that he had said that if he had plenty of land he would not fear even the Devil himself.

"All right," thought the Devil. "We will have a test. I will give you enough land; and because of that land I will get you into my power."

2

Near the village there lived a lady who owned about three hundred acres of land. The peasants had always liked her until she put an old soldier in charge of her land, and he began to annoy the people by making them pay fines. Although Pahom tried to be very careful, again and again one of his horses went into the lady's corn, a cow of his wandered into her garden, or his oxen got into her fields—and always he had to pay a fine.

Each time Pahom paid the fine unwillingly, and then went home in anger and was rough with his family. All through that summer Pahom was in trouble because of this old soldier, and he was even glad when winter came and the cattle had to be put under cover. Though he disliked having to buy hay for them when they could no longer feed in the fields, at least he was free from worrying about where they were.

In the winter the peasants heard that the lady was going to sell her land and that the keeper of the inn on the main road was making an offer for it. This news troubled them greatly.

"Indeed," they thought, "if the innkeeper gets the land, he will annoy us with fines more than the old soldier does. We all depend upon that land."

So the peasants went, in the name of their Village Society, and asked the lady not to sell the land to the innkeeper, offering her a better price for it themselves. The lady agreed to let them have it. Then the peasants tried to arrange for the Society to buy the whole of it, so that they might all share it. They met twice to discuss the question, but could not reach an agreement. The Devil spread doubt among them, and they would not trust one another. So they decided to buy the land separately, each taking as much as he could afford. And the lady agreed to this plan also.

Soon Pahom heard that a man who lived near him was buying fifty acres, and that the lady had agreed to accept a half of the payment in ready money and wait a year for the other half. Pahom wished that he, too, could buy some land.

"That is bad," he thought. "The land is all being sold, and I shall get none of it." So he spoke to his wife.

"Other people are buying," said he, "and we must also buy forty acres at least. Life is becoming impossible. That fellow's fines are ruining us."

So they considered together how they could manage to buy it. They had saved one hundred roubles. They sold a young horse and one half of their bees, and sent one of their sons out to work and took his pay in advance. They borrowed the rest of the money from a relation, and so collected half the price of the land.

When he had done this, Pahom chose a farm of forty acres, with fine woods, and went to the lady to make her an offer for it. They made a bargain, and he shook hands with her upon it and paid her a sum of money in advance. Then they went to town and signed the agreement. He paid half the price at once and promised to pay the rest before the end of two years.

So now Pahom had his own land. He borrowed seed and sowed it on the land he had bought. The harvest was a good one, and within a year he had managed to pay his debts both to the lady and to his relation. So he became a landowner, ploughing and sowing and making hay on his own land, cutting his own trees and feeding his cattle on his own grass. When he went out to plough his fields or to look at his growing corn, or at his fields of grass, his heart was full of joy. The grass and the flowers that grew there seemed to him unlike any that grew anywhere else. Before, when he had passed by that land, it had appeared the same as any other land, but now it seemed quite different.

3

So Pahom was very happy, and everything would have been right if only the peasants had not wandered on to his cornfields and grassland. He asked them most politely to keep away, but they did not. Sometimes the herdsmen would let the village cows wander into his fields; sometimes horses would get into his corn. Pahom turned them out again and again, and forgave their owners, and for a long time he did not make use of the law. But at last he became impatient and took the matter to the District Court. He knew that the peasants only came on to his land because they had none themselves, and that they did not intend to do wrong, but he thought: "I cannot go on letting it happen or they will destroy all I have. They must be taught a lesson."

So he had them brought to the court, gave them one lesson, and then another, and two or three of the peasants had to pay fines. After a time the men who lived near Pahom began to dislike him because of this, and on some occasions they let their cattle go on to his land on purpose.

One peasant even went into Pahom's wood at night and cut down five beautiful young trees in order to have their bark. As Pahom passed through the wood one day he noticed something white. He came nearer and saw the stripped trees lying on the ground, and nearby stood the roots where the trees had been. Pahom was very angry. "If he had only cut one tree here and there it would have been bad enough," Pahom thought, "but the fellow has actually cut down the whole group. If I could find out who did this I would punish him as he deserves."

He thought hard who it could be. At last he decided: "It must be Simon—no one else could have done it." So he went to Simon's home to have a look round, but he found nothing, and only had an angry quarrel. However, he now felt very certain that Simon had done it, and he reported him. Simon was brought before the court. The case was heard twice, and at the end of it all Simon was let off, for there was no proof against him. Pahom felt still more wronged and turned angrily to the judges.

"You take money from robbers," said he. "If you were honest people yourselves you would not let a robber go free."

So Pahom quarrelled with the judges and with everyone in his district. People began to threaten to burn his buildings. So though Pahom had more land, he was liked in the village much less than before.

About this time the peasants heard that many people were leaving this part of Russia to go to other parts.

"There is no need for me to leave my land," Pahom thought. "But some of the others may leave our village and then there will be more room for us. I will take their land myself and make my farm bigger. I can then live in greater comfort. At present I am shut in too much to be comfortable."

One day Pahom was sitting at home when a peasant who was passing through the village happened to come in. Pahom allowed him to stay for the night and gave him supper. He had a talk with this peasant and asked him where he came from. The stranger answered that he came from beyond the river Volga, where he had been working. One word led to another, and the man went on to say that many people were going to live in those lands. He told how some people from his village had settled there. They had joined a Society, and each of them had received twenty-five acres of land. This land was so good that the corn sown on it grew as high as a horse and was very thick. The stranger said that one peasant had brought nothing with him but his hands, and now he had six horses and two cows of his own.

Pahom's heart was filled with desire. He thought: "Why should I suffer in this narrow hole, if men can live so well in other places? I will sell my land and my home here, and with the money I will make a fresh start there and get everything new. We are always having trouble in this crowded place. But I must first go and find out all about it myself."

When summer was near he got ready and started. He went down the river Volga on a steamer to Samara, and walked another three hundred miles, and at last reached the place. Everything was as the stranger had said. The peasants had plenty of land, for the Society had given every man twenty-five acres of land for his own use, and any one who had money could buy, at a rouble an acre, as much more good land as he wanted.

When Pahom had found out all he wished to know, he returned home in the autumn and began to sell everything he had. He sold his land at a profit, and also his home and all his cattle. He waited only till the spring, and then started with his family to find a new home.

4

As soon as Pahom and his family reached their new home he applied to be admitted into the Society of a large village. The Society allowed him the use of a hundred and twenty-five acres in different fields as well as its own grassland. Pahom bought cattle and put up the buildings he needed in the village. He had three times as much land as he had owned before, and it was good corn-land. He was ten times wealthier than he had been. He had plenty of land for cultivation and for grass, and could keep as many cattle as he wished.

At first, in the excitement of building and living in his new home, Pahom was pleased with everything, but when he became used to it he began to think that even here he had not enough land. In the first year, he sowed wheat on his share of the Society's land, and had a good crop. He wanted to go on sowing wheat, but had not enough land for the purpose, for he could not sow his land again till it had rested and grass had grown over it. Many people wanted such land and there was not enough for all, so that there were quarrels about it. Those who were wealthy wanted to grow wheat and those who were poor wanted to make money out of it through dealers. Pahom wanted to sow more wheat, so he rented land from a dealer for a year. He sowed a lot of wheat and had a fine crop, but the land was too far from the village—the wheat had to be taken more than ten miles. After a time Pahom noticed that some peasant dealers were living on separate farms away from the Society's village and were becoming wealthy; and he thought, "If I were to buy some land of my own and have a separate farm on it, it would be quite a different thing. Then it would all be nice and convenient." The idea of buying land of his own, instead of renting it, came into his mind again and again.

For three years he rented land and sowed wheat. The seasons and the crops were good, and he saved more money. He might have continued to live happily, but he grew tired of renting other people's land every year. Where the land was good the peasants used to rush for it and it was taken immediately, so that unless you were quick you got none. In the third year it happened that Pahom and a dealer together rented a piece of grassland from some peasants. When they had already ploughed it, there was a quarrel and the peasants went to law about it, and the result was that the work of ploughing was all lost.

"If it were my own land," thought Pahom, "I should not have all this trouble."

So Pahom began looking for land which he could buy, and he met a peasant who had bought thirteen hundred acres. This man had got into difficulties and was willing to sell again cheaply. Pahom bargained with him, and at last they decided on the price of 1,500 roubles, partly in ready money and partly to be paid later. When they had almost settled the matter, a passing dealer happened to stop at Pahom's house one day to get a feed for his horses. He drank tea with Pahom and they had a talk. The dealer said that he was just returning from the land of the Bashkirs far away, where he had bought thirteen thousand acres of land, all for 1,000 roubles. Pahom asked him more questions, and the dealer said, "All you need to do is to make friends with the chiefs. I gave away about one hundred roubles' worth of silk dresses and furnishings, besides a case of tea, and I gave wine to those who wished to drink it; and I got the land for eight kopeks an acre." He showed Pahom the papers about the sale, and said, "The land lies near a river. The soil is good; none of it has been cultivated before."

Pahom asked him many questions, and the dealer said, "Even if you walked for a year you could not cover all the land, and it all belongs to the Bashkirs. They are as simple as sheep, and you can get land almost for nothing."

"Well," thought Pahom, "why should I get only thirteen hundred acres in exchange for my one thousand roubles? If I take my money there I can get more than ten times as much for it."

5

Pahom asked how to get to the place, and as soon as the dealer had left him he prepared to go there himself. He left his wife to look after the farm and started on his journey, taking a servant with him. They stopped at a town on their way and bought a case of tea, some wine and other gifts, as the dealer had advised. They went on and on until they had gone more than three hundred miles, and on the seventh day they came to the tents of the Bashkirs. All was as the dealer had said. The people lived on the plains by the river, in their tents. They did not cultivate the land or eat bread. Their herds of cattle and horses fed on the grass of the plains. The young horses were tied up behind the tents, and the mares were driven to them twice a day. The men milked the mares, and the women made kumiss and cheese from the milk. The men only cared about drinking kumiss and tea, eating meat, and playing tunes on their pipes. They were all strong and merry, and all through the summer they never thought of doing any work. They were simple people and could not speak Russian, but were very kind.

As soon as they saw Pahom they came out of their tents and crowded round their visitor. They found an interpreter who explained what was said, and Pahom told them that he had come to see if he could buy some land. The Bashkirs seemed to be very glad; they took Pahom and led him into one of the biggest tents. They made him sit in the best place in comfort while they sat round him. They gave him tea and kumiss and killed a sheep for him and gave him meat to eat. Pahom took gifts out of his cart and gave them to the

Bashkirs, and divided the tea among them. The Bashkirs were filled with delight. They talked among themselves, and then told the interpreter to explain their words to Pahom.

"They wish to tell you," said the interpreter, "that they like you, and that it is their custom to do all they can to please a guest. You have given them gifts. Now tell them which of their possessions you like best, so that they may give them to you."

"The thing which pleases me best here," answered Pahom, "is your land. Our land is crowded and the soil is no longer fruitful. But you have plenty of land, and it is good land. I never saw such land before."

The interpreter explained what Pahom had said. The Bashkirs talked among themselves for a short time. Pahom could not understand what they were saying, but saw that they were much amused and that they shouted and laughed. Then there was silence, and they looked at Pahom while the interpreter said, "They wish me to tell you that in exchange for your gifts they will gladly give you as much land as you want. You need only point it out with your hand and it will be yours."

The Bashkirs talked again for a short time and began to argue. Pahom asked what they were arguing about. The interpreter told him, "Some of them think they ought to ask their Chief about the land and not do anything while he is absent. The others think that there is no need to wait for his return."

6

While the Bashkirs were arguing, a man in a large fur cap arrived. They all stopped talking and stood up. The interpreter said, "This is our Chief himself."

Pahom immediately fetched the finest coat and five pounds of tea, and offered these to the Chief. The Chief accepted them and sat down in the place of honour. The Bashkirs at once began telling him something. The Chief listened for a while, and then made a sign with his head which demanded silence, and speaking Russian he said to Pahom, "Well, let it be so. Choose whatever piece of land you like; we have plenty of it."

"How can I take as much as I like?" thought Pahom. "I must get an official paper to make it certain, or else now they may say, 'It is yours,' and afterwards they may take it away again."

"Thank you for your kind words," he said aloud. "You have a lot of land, and I only want a little. But I should like to be sure which bit is mine. Could it not be measured and officially given to me? Life and death are in God's hands. You good people give it to me, but your children might wish to take it away again."

"You are quite right," said the Chief. "We will give it to you officially."

"I heard that a dealer had been here," Pahom continued, "and that you gave him a little land too, and signed the official papers. I should like to have it done in the same way."

The Chief understood.

"Yes," he replied, "that can be done quite easily. We have a law-writer, and we will go to town with you and have the papers properly signed."

"And what will be the price?" asked Pahom.

"Our price is always the same: one thousand roubles a day."

Pahom did not understand.

"A day? What measure is that? How many acres would that be?"

"We do not know how to measure it," said the Chief. "We sell it by the day. You may have as much as you can go round on your feet in one day, and the price is one thousand roubles a day."

Pahom was surprised.

"But in one day you can get round a large district!" he said.

The chief laughed.

"It will all be yours!" said he. "But there is one condition. If you do not return on the same day to the spot you started from, your money is lost."

"But how am I to mark the way that I have gone?"

"Why, we shall go to any spot you like, and stay there. You must start from that spot and make your round, taking a spade with you. Make a mark wherever you think one is necessary. Each time you make a turn, dig a hole and make a heap of earth. You may make as large a course as you please, but before the sun sets you must return to the place you started from. All the land you cover will be yours."

Pahom was delighted. He decided to start early next morning. They talked for a short time, and after drinking some more kumiss and eating some more meat, they had tea again, and then night came on. They gave Pahom a soft bed to sleep on, and the Bashkirs went away for the night, promising to meet together the next morning at daybreak and ride out before sunrise to the spot they had chosen.

7

Pahom lay on the soft bed, but could not sleep. He thought all the time about the land.

"What a large piece I will mark off!" he thought. "I can easily walk thirty-five miles in a day. The days are long now, and there will be a great deal of land within a course of thirty-five miles. I will sell the poorer land, or the peasants can rent it from me. But I will choose the best and farm it. I will buy two pairs of oxen, and employ two more workers. About a hundred and fifty acres shall be ploughed and I will let cattle feed on the rest."

Pahom lay awake all night and did not sleep until just before daybreak. Immediately, he had a dream. He thought that he was lying in that same tent and heard somebody laughing outside. He wondered who it could be, and he dreamed that he got up and walked out, and saw the Bashkir Chief sitting in front of the tent, holding his sides and laughing so much that he rolled about. Pahom went nearer to the Chief and asked, "What are you laughing at?" But then he saw that it was not the Chief, but the dealer who had recently stopped at his house and told him about the land. Just as Pahom was going to ask, "Have you been here long?" he saw that it was not the dealer, but the peasant who had come up from the Volga, long ago, to Pahom's old home. Then he saw that it was not even the peasant, but the Devil himself, with the body of an animal, who sat there laughing. In front of him a man, wearing only a shirt and trousers, lay flat on the ground. And Pahom dreamed that he looked more carefully to see what kind of man it was that was lying there, and he saw that the man was dead, and that it was himself! He awoke terribly frightened.

"What terrible things one dreams!" he thought, and as he looked round he saw through the open door the first light of day.

"It's time to wake them up," he thought. "We ought to make a start."

He got up, awoke his servant, who was sleeping in his cart, told him to get the horse ready, and went to call the Bashkirs.

"It's time to go to the plain to measure the land," he said.

The Bashkirs got up and met together, and the Chief came too. Then they began drinking kumiss again, and offered Pahom some tea, but he would not wait.

"The time has come," he said. "Let us go."

The Bashkirs got ready, and they all started; some were on horses, and some in carts. Pahom drove in his own small cart with his servant and took a spade with him. When they reached the plain, the red of the morning was beginning to flame. They climbed up a small hill and, getting down from their carts and their horses, they met together in one spot. The Chief came up to Pahom and stretched out his arm towards the plain.

"See," said he, "all this, as far as your eye can reach, is ours. You may have any part of it you like."

Pahom's eyes shone; it was all uncultivated land, flat and black, and different kinds of grass grew in the low-lying parts almost up to a man's shoulders.

The Chief took off his fur cap, placed it on the ground and said, "This will be the mark. Start from here, and return here again. All the land you go round shall be yours."

Pahom took out his money and put it on the cap. Then he took off his overcoat, remaining in his undercoat. He took his belt, tied it tightly round his middle, and put a little bag of bread inside his coat. Then he tied a bottle of water to his belt, fastened up the tops of his high boots, took the spade from his servant, and stood ready to start. He considered for a few moments which way he ought to go. Everywhere seemed good.

"It does not matter," he thought. "I will go towards the rising sun."

He turned his face to the east, stretched himself, and waited for the sun to come up.

"I must lose no time," he thought, "and it is easier walking while it is still cool."

The sun had hardly shone above the skyline, before Pahom, carrying the spade over his shoulder, went down into the plain.

Pahom started walking neither slowly nor quickly. After he had gone a thousand yards he stopped, dug a hole, and placed pieces of earth and grass one on another so that it could be easily seen. Then he went on; and now that he was walking more freely he increased his speed. After a short time he dug another hole.

Pahom looked back. He could see the hill clearly in the sunlight, with the people on it, and the shining metal of the cart-wheels. Pahom made a rough guess that he had walked three miles. It was growing warmer. He took off his under-coat, put it across his shoulder and went on again. It was quite warm now; he looked at the sun. It was time to think of breakfast.

"The first part is done, but there are four parts in a day and it is too soon yet to turn. But I will take off my boots," he said to himself.

He sat down, took off his boots, put them under his belt, and went on. It was easy walking now.

"I will go on for another three miles," he thought, "and then turn to the left. This spot is so fine that it would be a shame to lose it. The farther one goes the better the land seems."

He went straight on for a short time, and when he looked round he could scarcely see the hill. The people on it looked like black ants, and he could just see something shining there in the sun.

"Ah," thought Pahom. "I have gone far enough this way, it is time to turn. Besides, I am very hot and thirsty."

He stopped, dug a hole and made a heap by the side of it. Next he untied his bottle, had a drink and then turned sharply to the left. He went on and on; the grass was high, and it was very hot.

Pahom began to grow tired; he looked at the sun and saw that it was noon.

"Well," he thought, "I must have a rest."

He sat down and ate some bread and drank some water; but he did not lie down, thinking that if he did he might fall asleep. After sitting a little while, he went on again. At first he walked easily, for the food had given him strength; but it had become terribly hot and he felt sleepy. Still he went on, thinking, "An hour to suffer, a lifetime to live."

He went on in this way for a long time also, and was about to turn to his left again when he saw a damp low-lying area. "It would be a shame to leave that out," he thought. "Flax would grow well there." So he went on, past the low-lying ground, and dug a hole on the other side of it before he turned the corner.

Pahom looked towards the hill. The heat made the air misty; it seemed to be shaking and he could scarcely see the people on the hill through the mist.

"Ah," thought Pahom, "I have made the sides too long; I must make this one shorter." And he went along the third side, walking faster. He looked at the sun. It was nearly half-way down to the skyline, and he had not yet done two miles of the third side of the square. He was still ten miles from the hill.

"No," he thought, "though it will make the shape of my land uneven, I must hurry back in a straight line now. I might go too far, and I already have a great deal of land."

So Pahom hurriedly dug a hole, and turned straight towards the hill.

8

Pahom went straight towards the hill, but he now walked with difficulty. He was tired with the heat, his feet were cut and hurt, and his legs were weak. He wished to rest, but it was not possible if he meant to get back before sunset. The sun waits for no man, and it was sinking lower and lower.

"Oh dear," he thought, "if only I had not made a mistake trying for too much! What will happen if I am too late?"

He looked towards the hill and at the sun. He was still far from the place. He began running, threw away his coat, his boots, his bottle, and his cap, and kept only the spade which he used as a support.

"What shall I do?" he thought again. "I have tried to get too much and lost everything. I can't get there before the sun sets."

And this fear made him breathe even harder. Pahom went on running, his soaking shirt and trousers stuck to him, and his mouth was very dry. His breathing was hard, his heart was beating like a hammer, and his legs were weak and felt as if they did not belong to him. Pahom was terribly frightened that he would die from the effort. Though afraid of death, he could not stop. "They will call me a fool if I stop now after I have run all that way," he thought. And he ran on and on, nearer and nearer, and heard the Bashkirs calling and shouting to him. Their cries excited him still more. He gathered his last strength and ran on.

The sun was close to the skyline, and, with mist all around, it looked large and red as blood. It was just about to set. The sun was very low, but he was also quite near the hill. Pahom could already see the people on the hill waving their arms to make him hurry. He could see the fur cap on the ground, and the Chief sitting beside it holding his sides. And Pahom remembered his dream.

"There is plenty of land," he thought, "but will God let me live on it? I have lost my life, I have lost my life! I shall never reach that spot!"

Pahom looked at the sun, which had reached the earth: the bottom of it had already disappeared. With all his remaining strength he rushed on, bending his body forward so that his legs could hardly follow fast enough to keep him from falling. Just as he reached the hill it suddenly grew dark. He looked up—the sun had already set! He gave a cry. "All my efforts have been useless," he thought, and was about to stop, but he heard the Bashkirs still shouting, and remembered that though to him, down below, the sun seemed to have set, those on the hill could still see it. He breathed deeply and ran up the slope of the small hill. It was still light there. He reached the top and saw the cap. The Chief sat in front of it, laughing and holding his sides. Again Pahom remembered his dream, and he gave a loud cry. His legs gave way beneath him, he fell forward and reached the cap with his hands.

"Ah, that's a fine fellow!" said the Chief. "He has gained a lot of land!"

Pahom's servant came running up and tried to raise him, but he saw that blood was flowing from his mouth. Pahom was dead! The Bashkirs looked sad and showed their pity.

His servant picked up the spade and dug a hole long enough for Pahom to lie in, and buried him in it. Six feet from his head to his toes was all the land he needed.

For Further Reflection

1. How applicable is Tolstoy's parable to our day?
2. Write an essay on modern-day greed.

The Stoic Catechism

EPICTETUS AND OTHERS

Stoicism is the view that we can attain happiness and peace of mind if we focus on controlling only what is up to us (attitudes, intentions, perceptions, and feelings) and ignoring what is not up to us (body, reputation, property, and political office), thereby restraining our desires, cultivating virtue, and conforming our lives with Nature (or God). It arose in the fourth century BCE to eventually become one of the great moral systems in philosophy's history. This is how A. A. Long, a Stoicism scholar, describes its significance:

> Stoicism was the most important and influential development in Hellenistic philosophy. For more than four centuries it claimed the allegiance of a large number of educated men in the Graeco-Roman world, and its impact was not confined to Classical antiquity. Many of the Christian fathers were more deeply affected by Stoicism than they themselves recognized, and from the Renaissance up to modern times the effect of Stoic moral teaching on Western culture has been pervasive. Sometimes Stoic doctrines have reappeared in the work of major philosophers. Spinoza, Bishop Butler and Kant were all indebted to the Stoics. . . . Even today, the influence persists at the most mundane level. Not only the words *stoic* (uncapitalized) and *stoical* recall it. In popular language to be "philosophical" means to show that fortitude in the face of adversity recommended by Stoic writers. This is a small, but highly significant example, of Stoicism's influence. [Endnote: A. A. Long, *Hellenistic Philosophers: Stoics, Epicureans, and Sceptics* (Berkeley: University of California Press, 1986), 107.]

In this chapter we concentrate on Stoic moral theory, but we should keep in mind that Stoicism is more than that. The Stoics developed an impressive—and highly coherent—philosophical system comprising logic, epistemology, physics, metaphysics, linguistics, and theology. All these areas of Stoic thinking fit together well, with each one supporting and explaining others. Stoics believed, for example, that the universe is a kind of organizing being, or *logos*—a rational, all-pervading Nature, or God, that structured and directed everything. Human beings have the power of reason because they too have this *logos* within them. They are happiest and wisest when they live according to the *logos,* this inner spark of rationality, which in turn harmonizes their lives with the *logos* of Nature. The result is a good life in the most profound sense.

Stoicism began in Athens with Zeno of Citium (334–262 BCE) discoursing on his philosophy in the marketplace from a porch (a *stoa,* the root word of Stoicism). Stoicism was attractive to many for a variety of reasons. First, it offered itself as an antidote for the miseries of the world: it addressed the question of how people can cope with, even surmount, all the suffering that befalls them. And in Zeno's time, and for hundreds of years after, immeasurable pain and sorrow were extraordinarily common. For the Stoic, the only real harm that can be done to a person is self-inflicted injury to the soul by a lack of virtue. Zeno and the rest of the Stoics, like the Buddhists and other followers of Eastern religions, sought virtue and inner peace through moderation or elimination of desire.

Second, the antidote was available to everyone—high- and low-born, slave and master, rulers and the ruled. The shining philosophies of Plato and Aristotle spoke of wisdom, truth, and virtue—but few non-philosophers could understand what all the fuss was about. Stoicism, however, could be grasped by Everyman. To receive the blessings of Stoicism, the advantages of wealth, status, and birth were not required. Virtue, a condition of the soul, was the only prerequisite, which anyone could acquire.

Third, the Stoics were the first to preach cosmopolitanism, the idea that all men—whether Roman, Athenian, or barbarian—are brothers. We are all, they declared, made of the same stuff, fated to travel the same mortal road, and part of the same universal community composed of humans and benign providence.

The three most widely read Stoics can also claim to have the most interesting life stories. Seneca (after 4 BCE–65 CE) was a distinguished Roman statesman whose suicide (demanded by the emperor Nero) became an exemplar of Stoic indifference to misfortune. Epictetus (c. 55–135 CE) was a former slave, maimed in captivity, who took to heart Socrates's claim that a good man cannot be harmed. Marcus Aurelius (121–180 CE) was a Roman emperor who applied Stoicism to his life in a time of cultural tumult and confusion. The views of these men on Stoicism are in remarkable agreement, despite their separation in time.

So Stoicism holds that people of true Stoic virtue cannot be wounded by things external to their souls. Trouble may swarm around them, yet they cannot be distressed or frightened or coerced or enslaved or injured. This is an astonishing claim, and the Stoics spend a lot of time explaining how it could be true. As Epictetus says, "It is not things that upset people but rather ideas about things."

Consider these two people in identical situations. Bailey's sunglasses have been stolen, and so have Payton's. The sunglasses are alike, and the circumstances surrounding the thefts are the same. But Bailey gets angry and remains upset all day long, while Payton is slightly annoyed but soon forgets about the incident and later buys new sunglasses. The difference between these two reactions cannot be due to anything inherent in the events themselves, because the events are the same. The difference lies in the attitudes and feelings of the persons involved. One woman is unhappy and the other happy, because they *think* about the incident differently. And that means their happiness or unhappiness is *up to them*. The power to be happy is theirs to use or not use. So it goes, says the Stoic, for everything in life. We may not be in charge of events, but we are in charge of our happiness. We may not be able to change the world, but we can change the way we think about it. Epictetus would say, as Shakespeare did, that the problem lies not in our stars but in ourselves.

Epictetus asks us to distinguish between things that are up to us and things that are ultimately not up to us. We must focus on what is in our control and not dedicate all our energies, hopes, and desires to what we cannot control. This idea of distinguishing between what is and is not within our power is a theme that runs throughout the Stoics' writings.

Note that the Stoic ideal is not total impassiveness, a complete lack of emotion or desire in every situation. The Stoics were not, as some ancient critics asserted, "men of stone." The ideal Stoic—the Stoic sage—is not emotionless. But he is selective about what he does and does not feel. He does not give in to excessive and "irrational" feelings—anger, fear, dread, lust, and anxiety. But he does experience "good emotional states"—kindness, generosity, joy, and goodwill. The central Stoic insight is the need to *moderate* our attitudes and feelings through reason: to ask ourselves whether things not in our control are really appropriate objects of our desires, whether our desires are in proportion to the true worth of what we seek, and whether we have attained an evenness of mind and a sense of calm regarding the ups and downs of life.

The Stoic attitude toward suffering and tragedy is not a relic of the third century. Today it's often on display in the aftermath of disasters, although it's not called Stoicism; it's called grace. When a woman's house has been obliterated by a tornado, and she has lost every material possession she has, and she says, "We're lucky; I'm alive, and my children are alive, and we can always rebuild"—that's grace: Stoicism by another name.

The first short selection is from Marcus Aurelius. The second short selection on suicide is from the Seneca. The third, long selection is from Epictetus's teachings.

MARCUS AURELIUS, *DEDICATION TO DUTY*

Hour by hour resolve to do the task of the hour carefully, with unaffected dignity, affectionately, freely, and justly. You can avoid distractions that might interfere with such performance if every act is done as though it were the last act of your life. Free yourself from random aims and curb any tendency to let the passions of emotion, hypocrisy, self-love, and dissatisfaction with your allotted share cause you to ignore the commands of reason.

SENECA, *DEATH AND SUICIDE*

Life has carried some men with the greatest rapidity to the harbor, the harbor they were bound to reach if they tarried on the way, while others it has fretted and harassed. To such a life, as you are aware, one should not always cling. *For mere living is not a good, but living well.* Accordingly, the wise man will live as long as he ought, not as long as he can. He will mark in what place, with whom, and how he is to conduct his existence, and what he is about to do. He always reflects concerning the quality, and not the quantity of his life. As soon as there are many events in his life that give him trouble and disturb his peace of mind, he sets himself free. And this privilege is his, not only when the crisis is upon him, but as soon as Fortune seems to be playing him false; then he looks about carefully and sees whether he ought, or ought not, to end his life on that account. . . . He does not regard death with fear, as if it were a great loss; for no man can lose very much when but a driblet remains. It is not a question of dying earlier or later, but of dying well or ill. And dying well means escape from the danger of living ill.

EPICTETUS, *ENCHIRIDION*

1. Here is a fundamental distinction of which you ought to be aware: *Some things are up to us, some are not up to us.* Up to us are perception, intention, desire, aversion, and in sum, whatever are our own doings; not up to us are body, property, reputation, political office and in sum, whatever are not our own doings. And the things that are up to us are naturally free, unforbidding, unimpeding, while those not up to us are weak, slavish, forbidding, alien. Remember, then, that if you think naturally slavish things are free and that alien things are your own, you will be impeded, grieved, troubled, you will blame gods and men; but if you think that what is yours is yours and what is alien is alien, as it really is, nobody will ever compel you, nobody will forbid you, you will not blame anyone, you will not complain about anything, you will not do a single thing unwillingly,

you will have no enemy, no one will hurt you; for you will not suffer anything harmful.

If you are aiming for such great things, remember that you must not be moderate in exerting yourself to attain them: you must avoid some things altogether and postpone others for the time being. For if you want both to accomplish these aims, and also to achieve eminence and riches, it may come about that you will not get the latter because you were trying for the former, and certainly you will not get the former, which are the only things that produce freedom and well-being.

So take rigorous care to say to every menacing impression, "You are just an impression, not the real thing at all." Then test it and consider it according to your rules—first and foremost this: whether it belongs among the things that are up to us or to those not up to us. And if it is something not up to us, be ready to say "It is nothing to me."

2. Remember that the aim of desire is to get what arouses the desire, the aim of aversion is to avoid that to which you are averse; and he who fails to get what he desires is miserable, and so is he who gets what he is averse to. So then, if you are averse only to things contrary to nature that are up to you, you will not get anything to which you are averse; but if you are averse to sickness or death or poverty, you will be miserable. So take your aversion away from everything that is not up to you and transfer it to things contrary to nature that are up to you. But for the time being, destroy desire altogether; for if you desire something not up to you, necessarily you will be unfortunate; as for things that are up to us, and would be good to desire, none of them is yet within your grasp. But only make use of selection and rejection, and these lightly, discreetly, and tentatively.

3. As for every thing that delights your mind or is useful or beloved, remember to describe it as it really is, starting with the smallest thing. If you are fond of a pot, say "It is a pot that I am fond of." For then, if it breaks, you will not be upset. If you kiss your child or your wife, say that you are kissing a human being. Then if they die you will not be upset. . . .

5. *It is not things that upset people but rather ideas about things.* For example, death is nothing terrible, else it would have seemed so even to Socrates; rather it is the idea that death is terrible that is terrible. So whenever we are frustrated or upset or grieved, let us not blame others, but ourselves—that is, our ideas. It is the act of a philosophically ignorant person to blame others for his own troubles. One who is beginning to learn blames himself. An educated person blames neither anyone else nor himself.

6. Do not pride yourself on superiority that is not your own. If a horse in its pride should say, "I am a fine horse," that could be tolerated. You however, when you boast "I have a fine horse," should realize that you are boasting about the excellence of a horse. What then is your own? The use of impressions. So, make use of your impressions in accord with nature, and then take pride; for your pride will be in a good thing that is your own. . . .

8. Don't seek for things to happen as you wish, but wish for things to happen as they do, and you will get on well.

9. Illness is an impediment of the body, but not of the will, as long as the will itself does not so wish. Lameness is an impediment of the leg, not of the will. And say this to yourself of every accident that befalls you; for you will find it an impediment to something else, not to yourself.

10. Whatever occasion befalls you, remember to turn around and look into yourself to see what power you have to make use of it. If you see a handsome boy or a beautiful girl, you will find the relevant power to be self-control. If labor is heaped on you, endurance is what you need; if abuse, forbearance. And thus habituating yourself, you will not be carried away by impressions.

11. Never say about anything that you have "lost it," but that you have "given it back." Your child has died? It has been given back. Your wife has died? She has been given back. "I have been deprived of my estate." This too has been given back. "But the usurper is wicked." What concern is it of yours, through whom the gift was returned to the giver? For the time it is given to you, treat it as someone else's, as travellers do an inn.

12. If you want to make progress, shun these sorts of reasonings: "If I neglect my affairs, I shall have nothing to live on"; "If I don't punish my slave, he will be good for nothing." For it is better to attain freedom from sorrow and fear and then die of hunger than to live lavishly in vexation. It is better for your slave to be bad than for you to be unhappy. Begin with little things. A little oil has been spilled, a little wine has been swiped: say to yourself, "This is the price of peace, that of serenity." Nothing is free. When you call for your slave, consider that maybe he won't hear you, and even if he does he still won't do what you want him to do. But he is not so well off that your tranquillity should depend on him.

13. If you want to make progress, be content to appear stupid and foolish about externals, and don't wish to seem to know anything. And whenever you seem to be somebody to someone, distrust yourself. For be aware that it is not easy both to have your will in accordance with nature and to be on your guard about externals also, if you are to take care of the one it is absolutely necessary to neglect the other. . . .

15. Remember that you ought to conduct yourself as you do at a banquet. When something passed around reaches you, extend your hand and take it politely. If it is passing you by, don't grab. If it has not yet reached you, don't crave for it, but wait until it gets to you. Thus toward children, thus toward women, thus toward jobs, thus toward riches; and in due time you will be worthy to dine with the gods. But if you do not take even the things set out for you, but despise them, then not only will you be a banquet companion of the gods, you will even be a co-ruler. By thus acting, Diogenes and Heraclitus and like men came to be called divine, and deservedly.

16. Whenever you see someone weeping in grief because his child is going away or he has lost his property, be careful not to be misled by the impression that he is in a bad way because of external things, but be ready to say at once "It is not the circumstances that distress him (for someone else would not be distressed), but the idea he has about them." Don't, of course, hesitate to condole with him in words, and, if there is occasion, even to groan with him; but take care not to groan inwardly.

17. Remember that you are an actor in a drama such as the playwright wishes it to be. If he wants it short, it will be short; if long, long. If he wants you to play a beggar, play even that capably; or a lame man, or a ruler, or a private person. For this is yours, to play the assigned role well. Casting is the business of another. . . .

19. You can be unbeatable if you never enter a contest in which it is not up to you who wins. Beware lest ever, seeing someone else preferred in honor or having great power or otherwise esteemed, you get carried away by impressions and deem him blessed. For since the essence of the good lies in the things up to us, neither jealousy nor envy has a place; and you yourself will not wish to be a praetor or a senator or a consul, but a free man. There is but one way to this: *contempt for things not up to us.*

20. Remember that it is not the man who curses you or the man who hits you that insults you, but the idea you have of them as insulting. So, whenever someone irritates you, realize that it is your own opinion that has irritated you. First of all, try not to be carried away by impressions; if you succeed just once in gaining time and avoiding hastiness, you will easily control yourself.

21. Let death and exile and all dreadful appearances be before your eyes every day, and most of all, death; and you will never deem anything trivial, nor desire anything excessively.

22. If you are eager for philosophy, be prepared from the beginning to be ridiculed and sneered at by the mob, who will say things like "All of a sudden he has come back to us a philosopher!" and "Where did he get that

high brow?" But don't be a highbrow; hold fast to what seems best for you, as one who has been assigned to this territory by the god. And remember this: if you stay with it, the ones who ridicule you at first will admire you afterwards; but if they get the better of you, it will be your lot to be laughed at twice.

23. If ever it happens that you turn to externals because you want to please someone, realize that you have lost your bearings. It suffices to *be* a philosopher in all things; but if you also want to *appear* to be one, appear so to yourself and that will be enough.

24. Don't let reflections like this upset you: "I shall live without honor, a complete nobody." For suppose not being honored is an evil: you cannot be subjected to evil by another, any more than to shamefulness. Is it your business to acquire power or an invitation to a banquet? By no means. How then is this being without honor? How then will you be a complete nobody, when you ought to be somebody only with respect to those things that are up to you—the domain wherein it is given to you to be of the greatest worth? But your friends will get no help from you? What do you mean by help? They won't have a penny from you; nor will you make them Roman citizens. So who told you that these things are up to you, and not the business of others? Who can give to another things that he does not have himself? "Then get them," one says, "so that we can have them." If I can get them while preserving my self-respect and trustworthiness and high-mindedness, show me the way and I'll get them. But if you require me to be one who will lose my proper goods in order to produce worthless things for you—just look, how partial and unfair you are. Which do you want more? Money, or a faithful and upright friend? Then you had better help me to acquire the characteristics of one and not require me to do the things that would ruin them. . . .

26. We can learn the will of nature by considering the matters about which we don't disagree with one another. For instance, when somebody else's miserable servant breaks a cup, you are ready right away to say "So it goes." But realize that when it is yours that gets broken, you ought to behave the same way you did when it was someone else's. Apply this to more important matters as well. Somebody else's child or wife has died; there is no one who would not say "That's life." But when his own child or wife dies, it is "Alas, woe is me!" We ought to remember what we feel when we hear the same thing about other people.

27. As a target is not set up for the purpose of being missed, so nothing in the world is intrinsically evil.

28. If someone were to hand over your body to just whomever happened along, you would be outraged. Why aren't you outraged at the fact that *you* turn over your own mind to whomever happens along—if he insults you and you let it upset and trouble you?

29. . . . Some people, when they have seen a philosopher and have heard someone speaking the way Euphrates speaks (but who can speak like him?), wish to philosophize themselves. Man, consider first what kind of business this is. And then learn what your own nature is; can you bear it? Do you want to be a pentathlete or a wrestler? Look at your arms, your thighs, learn about your hips. One man is naturally fitted for one thing, another for another. Do you suppose you can do these things and keep on eating and drinking and enthusing and sulking just as you do now? You will have to go without sleep, labor, leave home, be despised by a slave, have everyone laugh at you, get the worse in everything, in honors, in jobs, in lawsuits, in every trifle. Look these things over and decide whether you want to exchange them for tranquillity, freedom, and peace; if not, don't go ahead, don't be, like a child, now philosopher, afterwards tax collector, then orator, finally Caesar's procurator. These things do not go together. You ought to be one man, good or evil; you must cultivate either your own guiding principle or externals; that is, apply yourself either to the inner man or to outward things: assume either the role of philosopher or of layman.

30. What is proper for us to do is for the most part defined by our social relationships. He is your father: this means that it is for you to look after him, to defer to him in all things, to put up with his abuse and his beatings. "But he is a bad father." Did nature then assign you to a *good* father? No, just to a father. "My brother is wronging me." Then keep up your relationship toward him; don't look at what he may be doing, but at what you should do to keep your will in accord with nature. No other person will hurt you unless *you* will it; you will be hurt to the extent that you think you are hurt. Thus if you will make a habit of contemplating social relationships, you will discover what it is fitting to do as a neighbor, as a citizen, as a consul. . . .

33. Prescribe a certain character and type for yourself, and guard it both when you are by yourself and when you meet people. And be silent about most things, or chat only when necessary and about few matters. On rare occasions, when the time is ripe and you are called on to talk, talk—but not about banal topics; not about gladiators, or athletes, or horse races, or food and drink, such as you hear everywhere; and above all, not about blaming or praising

or comparing people. If you can, lead the conversation around to something proper. But if you happen to be alone with strange people, be silent.

Laugh seldom and about few things and with restraint.

Totally abstain from taking oaths, if you can; if not, then refuse whenever circumstances allow.

Avoid celebrations, both public and private; but if the occasion calls you, be alert not to lapse into vulgarity. For know that if a companion is defiled, necessarily also one who keeps company with him will be defiled, even if he himself happens to be pure.

Partake of things having to do with the body only as far as bare need goes: such things as food, drink, clothing, housing, slaves. Dispense altogether with whatever has to do with reputation or luxury.

As to sex, be as pure as you can before marriage; but if you are aroused, indulge only to the extent that is customary. Sex is not a game. It can promote salient emotions which foster intimate relations, which enrich life. However, don't by any means be troublesome to those who do indulge, or censorious; and don't keep mentioning that you yourself can get along without it.

If someone tells you that somebody else is saying awful things about you, don't defend yourself against the accusations, but reply, "He must not know about the other faults that I have, if these are the only ones he mentioned."

It isn't necessary to attend shows for the most part. But if there is a proper occasion, do not appear to be more enthusiastic for anyone else than for yourself, that is, wish only that those things should happen that do happen and that only the winner should win; that way you will not be frustrated. Abstain altogether from shouting and ridiculing anyone or getting emotionally involved. And after the performance don't talk much about what happened, if it does not tend toward your improvement. For it would be evident from this that you were dazzled by the spectacle. . . .

Whenever you are going to meet someone, especially one reputed to be important, consider what Socrates or Zeno would have done in the circumstances, and you will not be puzzled about how to use the occasion properly. When you are going to visit a powerful personage, propose to yourself that you will not find him at home, that you will be shut out, that the gates will be slammed in your face, that he will not notice you. And if nevertheless it is your duty to go, when you arrive bear with what happens and by no means say to yourself "It wasn't worth it." For it is unphilosophical to be troubled by externals.

In conversation avoid overmuch talk about your own deeds and dangers. For although it is pleasant for you to recall your own adventures, it may not be so for others to hear about what happened to you.

Also avoid raising laughter; for this is a slippery slope to vulgarity and at the same time sufficient to cancel the respect that others have for you. It is also dangerous to get into dirty talk. Whenever anything of this sort begins, if you get the opportunity, you might rebuke the person who starts it; or if not, make it clear by being silent or blushing and scowling that you are displeased by the talk.

34. When you receive an impression of a certain pleasure, be on your guard, just as you are with other impressions, lest you get carried away by it. Take your time with the thing, wait a while. Next call to mind both times— the time when you will enjoy the pleasure, and the time when, after enjoying it, you will change your mind and scold yourself; and set against these the thought of how, if you abstain, you will rejoice and praise yourself. But if it still seems to you to be the proper occasion to indulge, consider, lest you be overcome by the gentleness and sweetness of it and its seductiveness; set against it, how much better it will be to be conscious of yourself as having won this victory.

35. When you do something because you have recognized that it ought to be done, never go out of your way not to be seen doing it, not even if public opinion takes a different view of it. For if it isn't right for you to do, shun the deed itself; if it is right, why are you afraid of people who would be censuring you wrongly? . . .

37. If you take on a role that is too much for you, you both disgrace yourself in it and neglect the one that you might have filled.

38. Just as in walking you pay attention not to step on a nail or to turn your ankle, pay attention not to hurt your ruling principle. And if we look out for this in all of our activities, we will take them on more securely. . . .

41. It is the sign of a weak mind to spend too much time on things having to do with the body, such as exercising a lot, eating a lot, drinking a lot, excreting, sex. Such things should be done incidentally; let all your attention be concentrated on your mind.

42. Whenever someone treats you badly or says bad things about you, remember that he does it or says it thinking that he is doing the right thing. Now it is not possible for him to adhere to *your* conception of the right, but only his own. Whence it follows that if he has a wrong view of things, he, being deceived, is the one who is hurt. For if someone believes that a true proposition is false, it is not the proposition that suffers but the deceived believer. If you

consider these things you will deal gently with the slanderer. On each occasion just say, "So it seemed to him."

43. Every thing has two handles, one by which it may be borne, one by which it cannot be borne. If your brother has done wrong, don't grasp this by the "wrongdoing" handle—it can't be borne by that one—but by the "brother," the "brought-uptogether" handle, and thereby you will be able to bear it.

44. These sorts of arguments are invalid: "I am richer than you are, therefore I am better than you"; "I am more eloquent than you are, therefore I am better than you." But these are valid: "I am richer than you are, therefore my possessions are better than yours"; "I am more eloquent than you are, therefore my speech is better than yours." *You,* however, are neither your possessions nor your speech. . . .

48. Position and character of a vulgar person: he never expects help or harm from himself, but only from outside. Position and character of a philosopher: he expects all help and harm to come from himself.

Marks of one making progress: he blames nobody, he praises nobody, he complains about nobody, he accuses nobody, he never speaks of himself as if he were anybody or knew anything. If he is impeded or frustrated he blames himself. And if someone praises him, he smiles to himself at the person giving the praise; but if he is blamed, he offers no defense. He comports himself as invalids do, taking care not to move a damaged limb before it has healed. He has purged himself of all desire; he has concentrated aversion solely on things that are against nature but up to us. He takes things as they come. If he appears stupid or ignorant, he doesn't care. In sum, he guards against himself as against an enemy lying in wait. . . .

50. Whatever principles are set before you, follow them as laws, the dishonoring of which would be impious. But don't worry about what anyone says about you; for this is not at all up to you.

51. How much time will you take yet before you judge yourself worthy of the best, and never step over the bounds discriminated by reason? You have been apprised of the philosophical principles to which you ought to subscribe, and you have subscribed. So what sort of teacher are you still waiting for, that you put off your own reformation until he gets here? You are no longer a child, but a grown man. If now you take no care and loaf and always keep putting things off and set one day after another on which to start attending to your own affairs, you will lose yourself, making no progress but going on being a layman in life and in death. Right now, then, deem yourself worthy of living as an adult making progress. And let all that

appears best to you be your inviolable law. And if some task is set for you, whether pleasant or glorious or inglorious, remember, that right now you are the contestant and here are the Olympic games, and there can't be any more delay, and that one day and one deed will determine whether progress is lost or saved. That is how Socrates became what he was: by attending in all things that he encountered to nothing other than reason. But you—even if you are not yet a Socrates, at least you ought to live as someone desiring to be like Socrates.

52. The primary and most essential topic in philosophy is that of the use of philosophical principles, for instance, not to lie. The secondary is that of proofs, for instance why one ought not to lie. Tertiary is of what gives certainty and consequence to the first two, for instance, why is this a proof? what indeed is a proof? implication?

If the room is smoky, if only moderately, I will stay; if there is too much smoke, I will go. Remember this, keep [a] firm hold on it: the door is always open.

For Further Reflection

1. What are the principal ideas of Stoicism, as contained in these readings? Is it really possible to live by this philosophy? Is it an optimistic or pessimistic philosophy?
2. Would you want to have a Stoic for a spouse or a parent or a friend? Why or why not?
3. Examine Seneca's statement on suicide and the last sentence in Epictetus's manual on Stoicism. Do these ideas contradict the Stoic philosophy of accepting what one cannot change? Or do they specify limits about what one should have to endure?

The World of Epictetus

Courage and Endurance

VICE ADMIRAL JAMES STOCKDALE

Vice Admiral James Stockdale (1923–2005) was a combat naval aviator whose plane was shot down over North Vietnam. He spent eight years in a North Vietnam prison, four of them in solitary confinement. He was later a fellow at the Hoover Institute and was a vice presidential candidate in the 1992 election.

The following is Vice Admiral Stockdale's tale of his experience in prison and of what helped him endure deprivation and torture. He refers to the Stoic catechism *Enchiridion* as his inspiration during his ordeal. You may find that work in this chapter.

In 1965 I was a forty-one-year-old commander, the senior pilot of Air Wing 16, flying combat missions in the area just south of Hanoi from the aircraft carrier *Oriskany*. By September of that year I had grown quite accustomed to briefing dozens of pilots and leading them on daily air strikes; I had flown nearly 200 missions myself and knew the countryside of North Vietnam like the back of my hand. On the ninth of that month I led about thirty-five airplanes to the Thanh Hoa Bridge, just west of that city. That bridge was tough; we had been bouncing 500-pounders off it for weeks.

The September 9 raid held special meaning for *Oriskany* pilots because of a special bomb load we had improvised; we were going in with our biggest, the 2000-pounders, hung not only on our attack planes but on our F-8 fighter-bombers as well. This increase in bridge-busting capability came from the innovative brain of a major flying with my Marine fighter squadron. He had figured out how we could jury-rig some switches, hang the big bombs, pump out some of the fuel to stay within takeoff weight limits, and then top off our tanks from our airborne refuelers while en route to the target. Although the pilot had to throw several switches in sequence to get rid of his bombs, a procedure requiring above-average cockpit agility, we routinely operated on the premise that all pilots of Air Wing 16 were above average. I test-flew the new load on a mission, thought it over, and approved it; that's the way we did business.

Our spirit was up. That morning, the *Oriskany* Air Wing was finally going to drop the bridge that was becoming a North Vietnamese symbol of resistance.

This essay by Vice Admiral James Stockdale, USN, "The World of Epictetus" is reprinted from the *Atlantic Monthly* (April 1978) by permission.

You can imagine our dismay when we crossed the coast and the weather scout I had sent on ahead radioed back that ceiling and visibility were zero-zero in the bridge area. In the tiny cockpit of my A-4 at the front of the pack, I pushed the button on the throttle, spoke into the radio mike in my oxygen mask, and told the formation to split up and proceed in pairs to the secondary targets I had specified in my contingency briefing. What a letdown.

The adrenaline stopped flowing as my wingman and I broke left and down and started sauntering along toward our "milk run" target: boxcars on a railroad siding between Vinh and Thanh Hoa, where the flak was light. Descending through 10,000 feet, I unsnapped my oxygen mask and let it dangle, giving my pinched face a rest—no reason to stay uncomfortable on this run.

As I glided toward that easy target, I'm sure I felt totally self-satisfied. I had the top combat job that a Navy commander can hold and I was in tune with my environment. I was confident—I knew airplanes and flying inside out. I was comfortable with the people I worked with and I knew the trade so well that I often improvised variations in accepted procedures and encouraged others to do so under my watchful eye. I was on top. I thought I had found every key to success and had no doubt that my Academy and test-pilot schooling had provided me with everything I needed in life.

I passed down the middle of those boxcars and smiled as I saw the results of my instinctive timing. A neat pattern—perfection. I was just pulling out of my dive low to the ground when I heard a noise I hadn't expected—the *boom boom boom* of a 57-millimeter gun—and then I saw it just behind my wingtip. I was hit—all the red lights came on, my control system was going out—and I could barely keep that plane from flying into the ground while I got that damned oxygen mask up to my mouth so I could tell my wingman that I was about to eject. What rotten luck. And on a "milk run"!

The descent in the chute was quiet except for occasional rifle shots from the streets below. My mind was clear, and I said to myself, "five years." I knew we were making a mess of the war in Southeast Asia, but I didn't think it would last longer than that; I was also naive about the resources I would need in order to survive a lengthy period of captivity.

The Durants have said that culture is a thin and fragile veneer that superimposes itself on mankind. For the first time I was on my own, without the veneer. I was to spend years searching through and refining my bag of memories, looking for useful tools, things of value. The values were there, but they were all mixed up with technology, bureaucracy, and expediency, and had to be brought up into the open.

Education should take care to illuminate values, not bury them amongst the trivia. Are our students getting the message that without personal integrity intellectual skills are worthless?

Integrity is one of those words which many people keep in that desk drawer labeled "too hard." It's not a topic for the dinner table or the cocktail party. You can't buy or sell it. When supported with education, a person's integrity can give him something to rely on when his perspective seems to blur, when rules and principles seem to waver, and when he's faced with hard choices of right or wrong. It's something to keep him on the right track, something to keep him afloat when he's drowning; if only for practical reasons, it is an attribute that should be kept at the very top of a young person's consciousness.

The importance of the latter point is highlighted in prison camps, where everyday human nature, stripped bare, can be studied under a magnifying glass in accelerated time. Lessons spotlighted and absorbed in that laboratory sharpen one's eye for their abstruse but highly relevant applications in the "real time" world of now.

In the five years since I've been out of prison, I've participated several times in the process of selecting senior naval officers for promotion or important command assignments. I doubt that the experience is significantly different from that of executives who sit on "selection boards" in any large hierarchy. The system must be formal, objective, and fair; if you've seen one, you've probably seen them all. Navy selection board proceedings go something like this.

The first time you know the identity of the other members of the board is when you walk into a boardroom at eight o'clock on an appointed morning. The first order of business is to stand, raise your right hand, put your left hand on the Bible, and swear to make the best judgment you can, on the basis of merit, without prejudice. You're sworn to confidentiality regarding all board members' remarks during the proceedings. Board members are chosen for their experience and understanding; they often have knowledge of the particular individuals under consideration. They must feel free to speak their minds. They read and grade dozens of dossiers, and each candidate is discussed extensively. At voting time, a member casts his vote by selecting and pushing a "percent confidence" button, visible only to himself, on a console attached to his chair. When the last member pushes his button, a totalizer displays the numerical average "confidence" of the board. No one knows who voted what.

I'm always impressed by the fact that every effort is made to be fair to the candidate. Some are clearly out, some are clearly in; the borderline cases are the tough ones. You go over and over those in the "middle pile" and usually you vote and revote until late at night. In all the boards I've sat on, no inference or statement in a "jacket" is as sure to portend a low confidence score on the vote as evidence of a lack of directness or rectitude of a candidate in his dealings with others. Any hint of moral turpitude really turns people off. When the crunch comes, they prefer to work with forthright plodders rather than with devious geniuses. I don't believe that this preference is unique to the military. In any hierarchy where people's fates are decided by committees or boards, those who lose credibility with their peers and who cause their superiors to doubt their directness, honesty, or integrity are dead. Recovery isn't possible.

The linkage of men's ethics, reputations, and fates can be studied in even more vivid detail in prison camp. In that brutally controlled environment a perceptive enemy can get his hooks into the slightest chink in a man's ethical armor and accelerate his downfall. Given the right opening, the right moral weakness, a certain susceptibility on the part of the prisoner, a clever extortionist can drive his victim into a downhill slide that will ruin his image, self-respect, and life in a very short time.

There are some uncharted aspects to this, some traits of susceptibility which I don't think psychologists yet have words for. I am thinking of the tragedy that can befall a person who has such a need for love or attention that he will sell his soul for it. I use tragedy with the rigorous definition Aristotle applied to it: the story of a good man with a flaw who comes to an unjustified bad end. This is a rather delicate point and one that I want to emphasize. We had very very few collaborators in prison, and comparatively few Aristotelian tragedies, but the story and fate of one of these good men with a flaw might be instructive.

He was handsome, smart, articulate, and smooth. He was almost sincere. He was obsessed with success. When the going got tough, he decided expediency was preferable to principle.

This man was a classical opportunist. He befriended and worked for the enemy to the detriment of his fellow Americans. He made a tacit deal; moreover, he accepted favors (a violation of the code of conduct). In time, out of fear and shame, he withdrew; we could not get him to communicate with the American prisoner organization.

I couldn't learn what made the man tick. One of my best friends in prison, one of the wisest persons I have ever known, had once been in a squadron with this fellow. In prisoners' code I tapped a question to my philosophical friend: "What in the world is going on with that fink?"

"You're going to be surprised at what I have to say," he meticulously tapped back. "In a squadron he pushes himself forward and dominates the scene.

He's a continual fountain of information. He's the person everybody relies on for inside dope. He works like mad; often flies more hops than others. It drives him crazy if he's not liked. He tends to grovel and ingratiate himself before others. I didn't realize he was really pathetic until I was sitting around with him and his wife one night when he was spinning his yarns of delusions of grandeur, telling of his great successes and his pending ascension to the top. His wife knew him better than anybody else; she shook her head with genuine sympathy and said to him: 'Gee, you're just a phony.'"

In prison, this man had somehow reached the point where he was willing to sell his soul just to satisfy this need, this immaturity. The only way he could get the attention that he demanded from authority was to grovel and ingratiate himself before the enemy. As a soldier he was a miserable failure, but he had not crossed the boundary of willful treason; he was not written off as an irrevocable loss, as were the two patent collaborators with whom the Vietnamese soon arranged that he live.

As we American POWs built our civilization, and wrote our own laws (which we leaders obliged all to memorize), we also codified certain principles which formed the backbone of our policies and attitudes. I codified the principles of compassion, rehabilitation, and forgiveness with the slogan: "It is neither American nor Christian to nag a repentant sinner to his grave." (Some didn't like it, thought it seemed soft on finks.) And so, we really gave this man a chance. Over time, our efforts worked. After five years of self-indulgence he got himself together and started to communicate with the prisoner organization. I sent the message "Are you on the team or not?"; he replied, "Yes," and came back. He told the Vietnamese that he didn't want to play their dirty games anymore. He wanted to get away from those willful collaborators and he came back and he was accepted, after a fashion.

I wish that were the end of the story. Although he came back, joined us, and even became a leader of sorts, he never totally won himself back. No matter how forgiving we were, he was conscious that many resented him—not so much because he was weak but because he had broken what we might call a gentleman's code. In all of those years when he, a senior officer, had willingly participated in making tape recordings of anti-American material, he had deeply offended the sensibilities of the American prisoners who were forced to listen to him. To most of us it wasn't the rhetoric of the war or the goodness or the badness of this or that issue that counted. The object of our highest value was the well-being of our fellow prisoners. He had broken that code and hurt some of those people. Some thought that as an informer he had indirectly hurt them physically. I don't believe that. What indisputably hurt them was his not having the sensitivity to realize the damage his opportunistic conduct would do to the morale of a bunch of Middle American guys with

Middle American attitudes which they naturally cherished. He should have known that in those solitary cells where his tapes were piped were idealistic, direct, patriotic fellows who would be crushed and embarrassed to have him, a senior man in excellent physical shape, so obviously not under torture, telling the world that the war was wrong. Even if he believed what he said, which he did not, he should have had the common decency to keep his mouth shut. You can sit and think anything you want, but when you insensitively cut down those who want to love and help you, you cross a line. He seemed to sense that he could never truly be one of us.

And yet he was likable—particularly back in civilization after release—when tension was off, and making a deal did not seem so important. He exuded charm and "hail fellow" sophistication. He wanted so to be liked by all those men he had once discarded in his search for new friends, new deals, new fields to conquer in Hanoi. The tragedy of his life was obvious to us all. Tears were shed by some of his old prison mates when he was killed in an accident that strongly resembled suicide some months later. The Greek drama had run its course. He was right out of Aristotle's book, a good man with a flaw who had come to an unjustified bad end. The flaw was insecurity: the need to ingratiate himself, the need for love and adulation at any price.

He reminded me of Paul Newman in *The Hustler*. Newman couldn't stand success. He knew how to make a deal. He was handsome, he was smart, he was attractive to everybody; but he had to have adulation, and therein lay the seed of tragedy. Playing high-stakes pool against old Minnesota Fats (Jackie Gleason), Newman was well in the lead, and getting more full of himself by the hour. George C. Scott, the pool bettor, whispered to his partner: "I'm going to keep betting on Minnesota Fats; this other guy [Newman] is a born loser—he's all skill and no character." And he was right, a born loser—I think that's the message.

How can we educate to avoid these casualties? Can we by means of education prevent this kind of tragedy? What we prisoners were in was a one-way leverage game in which the other side had all the mechanical advantage. I suppose you could say that we all live in a leverage world to some degree; we all experience people trying to use us in one way or another. The difference in Hanoi was the degradation of the ends (to be used as propaganda agents of an enemy, or as informers on your fellow Americans), and the power of the means (total environmental control including solitary confinement, restraint by means of leg-irons and handcuffs, and torture). Extortionists always go down the same track: the imposition of guilt and fear for having disobeyed their rules, followed in turn by punishment, apology, confession, and atonement (their payoff). Our captors would go to great lengths to get a man to compromise his own code, even if only slightly, and then they would hold that in their bag, and the next time get him to go a little further.

Some people are psychologically, if not physically, at home in extortion environments. They are tough people who instinctively avoid getting sucked into the undertows. They never kid themselves or their friends; if they miss the mark they admit it. But there's another category of person who gets tripped up. He makes a small compromise, perhaps rationalizes it, and then makes another one; and then he gets depressed, full of shame, lonesome, loses his willpower and self-respect, and comes to a tragic end. Somewhere along the line he realizes that he has turned a corner that he didn't mean to turn. All too late he realizes that he has been worshiping the wrong gods and discovers the wisdom of the ages: life is not fair.

In sorting out the story after our release, we found that most of us had come to combat constant mental and physical pressure in much the same way. We discovered that when a person is alone in a cell and sees the door open only once or twice a day for a bowl of soup, he realizes after a period of weeks in isolation and darkness that he has to build some sort of ritual into his life if he wants to avoid becoming an animal. Ritual fills a need in a hard life and it's easy to see how formal church ritual grew. For almost all of us, this ritual was built around prayer, exercise, and clandestine communication. The prayers I said during those days were prayers of quality with ideas of substance. We found that over the course of time our minds had a tremendous capacity for invention and introspection, but had the weakness of being an integral part of our bodies. I remembered Descartes and how in his philosophy he separated mind and body. One time I cursed my body for the way it decayed my mind. I had decided that I would become a Gandhi. I would have to be carried around on a pallet and in that state I could not be used by my captors for propaganda purposes. After about ten days of fasting, I found that I had become so depressed that soon I would risk going into interrogation ready to spill my guts just looking for a friend. I tapped to the guy next door and I said, "Gosh, how I wish Descartes could have been right, but he's wrong." He was a little slow to reply; I reviewed Descartes's deduction with him and explained how I had discovered that body and mind are inseparable.

On the positive side, I discovered the tremendous file-cabinet volume of the human mind. You can memorize an incredible amount of material and you can draw the past out of your memory with remarkable recall by easing slowly toward the event you seek and not crowding the mind too closely. You'll try to remember who was at your birthday party when you were five years old, and you can get it, but only after months of effort. You can break the locks and find the answers, but you need time and solitude to learn how to use this marvelous device in your head which is the greatest computer on earth.

Of course many of the things we recalled from the past were utterly useless as sources of strength or practicality. For instance, events brought back from cocktail parties or insincere social contacts were almost repugnant because of their emptiness, their utter lack of value. More often than not, the locks worth picking had been on old schoolroom doors. School days can be thought of as a time when one is filling the important stacks of one's memory library. For me, the golden doors were labeled history and the classics. The historical perspective which enabled a man to take himself away from all the agitation, not necessarily to see a rosy lining, but to see the real nature of the situation he faced, was truly a thing of value.

Here's how this historical perspective helped me see the reality of my own situation and thus cope better with it. I learned from a Vietnamese prisoner that the same cells we occupied had in years before been lived in by many of the leaders of the Hanoi government. From my history lessons I recalled that when metropolitan France permitted communists in the government in 1936, the communists who occupied cells in Vietnam were set free. I marveled at the cycle of history, all within my memory, which prompted Hitler's rise in Germany, then led to the rise of the Popular Front in France, and finally vacated this cell of mine halfway around the world ("Perhaps Pham Van Dong lived here"). I came to understand what tough people these were. I was willing to fight them to the death, but I grew to realize that hatred was an indulgence, a very inefficient emotion. I remember thinking, "If you were committed to beating the dealer in a gambling casino, would *hating* him help your game?" In a pidgin English propaganda book the guard gave me, speeches by these old communists about their prison experiences stressed how they learned to beat down the enemy by being united. It seemed comforting to know that we were united against the communist administration of Hoa Lo prison just as the Vietnamese communists had united against the French administration of Hoa Lo in the thirties. Prisoners are prisoners, and there's only one way to beat administrations. We resolved to do it better in the sixties than they had in the thirties. You don't base system-beating on any thought of political idealism; you do it as a competitive thing, as an expression of self-respect.

Education in the classics teaches you that all organizations since the beginning of time have used the power of guilt; that cycles are repetitive; and that this is the way of the world. It's a naive person who comes in and says, "Let's see, what's good and what's bad?" That's a quagmire. You can get out of that quagmire only by recalling how wise men before you accommodated the same dilemmas. And I believe a good classical education and an understanding of history can best determine the rules you should live by. They also give you the power to analyze reasons for these rules and guide you as to how to apply them to your own situation. In a broader sense, all my education helped me. Naval Academy discipline and body contact sports helped me. But the education which I found myself using most was what I got in graduate school. The messages of history and philosophy I used were simple.

The first one is this business about life not being fair. That is a very important lesson and I learned it from a wonderful man named Philip Rhinelander. As a lieutenant commander in the Navy studying political science at Stanford University in 1961, I went over to philosophy corner one day and an older gentleman said, "Can I help you?" I said, "Yes, I'd like to take some courses in philosophy." I told him I'd been in college for six years and had never had a course in philosophy. He couldn't believe it. I told him that I was a naval officer and he said, "Well, I used to be in the Navy. Sit down." Philip Rhinelander became a great influence in my life.

He had been a Harvard lawyer and had pleaded cases before the Supreme Court and then gone to war as a reserve officer. When he came back he took his doctorate at Harvard. He was also a music composer, had been director of general education at Harvard, dean of the School of Humanities and Sciences at Stanford, and by the time I met him had by choice returned to teaching in the classroom. He said, "The course I'm teaching is my personal two-term favorite—The Problem of Good and Evil—and we're starting our second term." He said the message of his course was from the Book of Job. The number one problem in this world is that people are not able to accommodate the lesson in the book.

He recounted the story of Job. It starts out by establishing that Job was the most honorable of men. Then he lost all his goods. He also lost his reputation, which is what really hurt. His wife was badgering him to admit his sins, but he knew he had made no errors. He was not a patient man and demanded to speak to the Lord. When the Lord appeared in the whirlwind, he said, "Now, Job, you have to shape up! Life is not fair." That's my interpretation and that's the way the book ended for hundreds of years. I agree with those of the opinion that the happy ending was spliced on many years later. If you read it, you'll note that the meter changes. People couldn't live with the original message. Here was a good man who came to unexplained grief, and the Lord told him: "That's the way it is. Don't challenge me. This is my world and you either live in it as I designed it or get out."

This was a great comfort to me in prison. It answered the question "Why me?" It cast aside any thoughts of being punished for past actions. Sometimes I shared the message with fellow prisoners as I tapped through the walls to them, but I learned to be selective. It's a strong message which upsets some people.

Rhinelander also passed on to me another piece of classical information which I found of great value. On the day of our last session together he said, "You're a military man, let me give you a book to remember me by. It's a book of military ethics." He handed it to me, and I bade him goodbye with great emotion. I took the book home and that night started to read it. It was the *Enchiridion* of the philosopher Epictetus, his "manual" for the Roman field soldier.

As I began to read, I thought to myself in disbelief, "Does Rhinelander think I'm going to draw lessons for my life from this thing? I'm a fighter pilot. I'm a technical man. I'm a test pilot. I know how to get people to do technical work. I play golf; I drink martinis. I know how to get ahead in my profession. And what does he hand me? A book that says in part, 'It's better to die in hunger, exempt from guilt and fear, than to live in affluence and with perturbation.'" I remembered this later in prison because perturbation was what I was living with. When I ejected from the airplane on that September morn in 1965, I had left the land of technology. I had entered the world of Epictetus, and it's a world that few of us, whether we know it or not, are ever far away from.

In Palo Alto, I had read this book, not with contentment, but with annoyance. Statement after statement: "Men are disturbed not by things, but by the view that they take of them." "Do not be concerned with things which are beyond your power." "Demand not that events should happen as you wish, but wish them to happen as they do happen and you will go on well." This is stoicism. It's not the last word, but it's a viewpoint that comes in handy in many circumstances, and it surely did for me. Particularly this line: "Lameness is an impediment to the body but not to the will." That was significant for me because I wasn't able to stand up and support myself on my badly broken leg for the first couple of years I was in solitary confinement.

Other statements of Epictetus took on added meaning in the light of extortions which often began with our captors' callous pleas: "If you are just reasonable with us we will compensate you. You get your meals, you get to sleep, you won't be pestered, you might even get a cellmate." The catch was that by being "reasonable with us" our enemies meant being their informers, their propagandists. The old stoic had said, "If I can get the things I need with the preservation of my honor and fidelity and self-respect, show me the way and I will get them. But, if you require me to lose my own proper good, that you may gain what is no good, consider how unreasonable and foolish you are." To love our fellow prisoners was within our power. To betray, to propagandize, to disillusion conscientious and patriotic shipmates and destroy their morale so that they in turn would be destroyed was to lose one's proper good.

What attributes serve you well in the extortion environment? We learned there, above all else, that the best defense is to keep your conscience clean.

When we did something we were ashamed of, and our captors realized we were ashamed of it, we were in trouble. A little white lie is where extortion and ultimately blackmail start. In 1965, I was crippled and I was alone. I realized that they had all the power. I couldn't see how I was ever going to get out with my honor and self-respect. The one thing I came to realize was that if you don't lose integrity you can't be had and you can't be hurt. Compromises multiply and build up when you're working against a skilled extortionist or a good manipulator. You can't be had if you don't take that first shortcut, or "meet them halfway," as they say, or look for that tacit "deal," or make that first compromise.

Bob North, a political science professor at Stanford, taught me a course called Comparative Marxist Thought. This was not an anticommunist course. It was the study of dogma and thought patterns. We read no criticisms of Marxism, only primary sources. All year we read the works of Marx and Lenin. In Hanoi, I understood more about Marxist theory than my interrogator did. I was able to say to that interrogator, "That's not what Lenin said; you're a deviationist."

One of the things North talked about was brainwashing. A psychologist who studied the Korean prisoner situation, which somewhat paralleled ours, concluded that three categories of prisoners were involved there. The first was the redneck Marine sergeant from Tennessee who had an eighth-grade education. He would get in that interrogation room and they would say that the Spanish-American War was started by the bomb within the *Maine,* which might be true, and he would answer, "B.S." They would show him something about racial unrest in Detroit. "B.S." There was no way they could get to him; his mind was made up. He was a straight guy, red, white, and blue, and everything else was B.S.! He didn't give it a second thought. Not much of a historian, perhaps, but a good security risk.

In the next category were the sophisticates. They were the fellows who could be told these same things about the horrors of American history and our social problems, but had heard it all before, knew both sides of every story, and thought we were on the right track. They weren't ashamed that we had robber barons at a certain time in our history; they were aware of the skeletons in most civilizations' closets. They could not be emotionally involved and so they were good security risks.

The ones who were in trouble were the high school graduates who had enough sense to pick up the innuendo, and yet not enough education to accommodate it properly. Not many of them fell, but most of the men that got entangled started from that background.

The psychologist's point is possibly oversimplistic, but I think his message has some validity. A little knowledge is a dangerous thing.

Generally speaking, I think education is a tremendous defense; the broader, the better. After I was shot down my wife, Sybil, found a clipping glued in the front of my collegiate dictionary: "Education is an ornament in prosperity and a refuge in adversity." She certainly agrees with me on that. Most of us prisoners found that the so-called practical academic exercises in how to do things, which I'm told are proliferating, were useless. I'm not saying that we should base education on training people to be in prison, but I am saying that in stress situations, the fundamentals, the hardcore classical subjects, are what serve best.

Theatrics also helped sustain me. My mother had been a drama coach when I was young and I was in many of her plays. In prison I learned how to manufacture a personality and live it, crawl into it, and hold that role without deviation. During interrogations, I'd check the responses I got to different kinds of behavior. They'd get worried when I did things irrationally. And so, every so often, I would play that "irrational" role and come completely unglued. When I could tell that pressure to make a public exhibition of me was building, I'd stand up, tip the table over, attempt to throw the chair through the window, and say, "No way, Goddammit! I'm not doing that! Now, come over here and fight!" This was a risky ploy, because if they thought you were acting, they would slam you into the ropes and make you scream in pain like a baby. You could watch their faces and read their minds. They had expected me to behave like a stoic. But a man would be a fool to make their job easy by being conventional and predictable. I could feel the tide turn in my favor at that magic moment when their anger turned to pleading: "Calm down, now calm down." The payoff would come when they decided that the risk of my going haywire in front of some touring American professor on a "fact-finding" mission was too great. More important, they had reason to believe that I would tell the truth—namely, that I had been in solitary confinement for four years and tortured fifteen times—without fear of future consequences. So theatrical training proved helpful to me.

Can you educate for leadership? I think you can, but the communists would probably say no. One day in an argument with an interrogator, I said, "You are so proud of being a party member, what are the criteria?" He said in a flurry of anger, "There are only four: you have to be seventeen years old, you have to be selfless, you have to be smart enough to understand the theory, and you've got to be a person who innately influences others." He stressed that fourth one. I think psychologists would say that leadership is innate, and there is truth in that. But, I also think you can learn some leadership traits that naturally accrue from a good education: compassion is a necessity for leaders, as are spontaneity, bravery, self-discipline, honesty, and above all, integrity.

I remember being disappointed about a month after I was back when one of my young friends, a prison mate, came running up after a reunion at the

Naval Academy. He said with glee, "This is really great, you won't believe how this country has advanced. They've practically done away with plebe year at the Academy, and they've got computers in the basement of Bancroft Hall." I thought, "My God, if there was anything that helped us get through those eight years, it was plebe year, and if anything screwed up that war, it was computers!"

For Further Reflection

1. You may want to read Epictetus's *Enchiridion* (in this chapter) before you answer this question: How did Stoicism help Vice Admiral Stockdale to endure his torture and suffering in prison? Why do you think so many other prisoners failed to maintain their self-respect and loyalty to their country?
2. What other virtues besides courage do you find implicit in this article? Explain.
3. How would you endeavor to maintain your spirits if you were in Stockdale's situation?
4. Stockdale praises his college teacher for introducing him to ideas that were to help him survive later. Should moral education be included as part of public education, including college education?

Further Readings for Chapter 6

Becker, Lawrence. *On Justifying Moral Arguments.* London: Routledge and Kegan Paul, 1973. See Chapter 19.

Cooper, John. *Reason and the Human Good in Aristotle.* Cambridge, Mass.: Harvard University Press, 1975.

Kruschwitz, Robert, and Robert Roberts, eds. *The Virtues.* Belmont, Calif.: Wadsworth, 1987. An excellent up-to-date anthology containing an extensive bibliography.

MacIntyre, Alasdair. *After Virtue.* Notre Dame, Ind.: University of Notre Dame Press, 1981.

Murdoch, Iris. *The Sovereignty of Good.* New York: Schocken Books, 1971.

Pence, Gregory. "Recent Work on Virtues." *American Philosophical Quarterly* 21 (1984).

Pojman, Louis. *Ethics: Discovering Right and Wrong.* 3rd ed. Belmont, Calif.: Wadsworth, 1999. See Chapter 8.

Sommers, Christina Hoff, and Fred Sommers. *Vice and Virtues in Everyday Life.* New York: Harcourt Brace Jovanovich, 1985.

Taylor, Richard. *Ethics, Faith and Reason.* Englewood Cliffs, N.J.: Prentice-Hall, 1985.

Trianosky, Gregory. "Supererogation, Wrongdoing, and Vice: On the Autonomy of the Ethics of Virtue." *Journal of Philosophy* (January 1986).

Wallace, James. *Virtues and Vices.* Ithaca, N.Y.: Cornell University Press, 1978.

CHAPTER 7

Feminist Ethics and the Ethics of Care

In recent decades, an important development has challenged the traditional theories and concepts of moral philosophy: the rise of *feminist ethics*. Feminist ethics is an approach to morality aimed at advancing women's interests, underscoring their distinctive experiences and characteristics, and advancing the obvious truth that women and men are morally equal. It is defined by a distinctive focus on these issues, rather than by a set of doctrines or ideology held in common by feminists, many of whom may disagree on the nature of feminist ethics or on particular moral issues.

Feminist ethics generally downplays the role of moral principles and traditional ethical concepts, insisting instead that moral reflection must take into account the social realities—the relevant social practices, relationships, institutions, and power arrangements. Many feminists think that the familiar principles of Western ethics—autonomy, utility, freedom, equality, and the like—are too broad and abstract to help us make moral judgments about specific persons who are enmeshed in concrete social situations. It is not enough, for example, to respect a woman's decision to have an abortion if she is too poor to have one, or if her culture is so oppressive (or oppressed) as to make abortion impossible to obtain, or if social conditioning leads her to believe that she has no choice or that her views don't count. Theoretical autonomy does not mean much if it is so thoroughly undermined in reality.

Many feminist writers maintain that the values and virtues inherent in most traditional moral theories reflect a typically masculine perspective—and thus offer a one-sided (or wrong-sided) view of the moral life. What's needed, they say, is a moral outlook that takes into account values and experiences that usually have been identified with women. According to the feminist philosopher

Alison Jaggar in our first selection, feminists claim that traditional ethics favors the

> supposedly masculine or male-associated values of independence, autonomy, intellect, will, wariness, hierarchy, domination, culture, transcendence, product, asceticism, war and death over the supposedly feminine or female-associated values of interdependence, community, connection, sharing, emotion, body, trust, absence of hierarchy, nature, immanence, process, joy, peace and life.[1]

Some proponents of feminist ethics also reject the traditional concept of the moral agent. In our second reading, Jan Crosthwaite says the old notion is that of "abstract individuals as fundamentally autonomous agents, aware of their own preferences and values, and motivated by rational self-interest (though not necessarily selfish)."[2] But, she says, many feminists

> present a richer conception of persons as historically and culturally located, socially related and essentially embodied. Individuals are located in and formed by specific relationships (chosen and unchosen) and ties of affection and responsibility. . . . Such a conception of socially embedded selves refocuses thinking about autonomy, shifting the emphasis from independent self-determination towards ideals of integrity within relatedness. . . . Respecting autonomy becomes less a matter of protecting individuals from "coercive" influences than one of positive empowerment, recognizing people's interdependence and supporting individuals' development of their own understanding of their situation and options.[3]

Many of these themes run through the *ethics of care*, a moral perspective that arose out of feminist concerns and grew to challenge core elements of most other moral theories. Generally those theories emphasize abstract principles, general duties, individual rights, justice, utility, impartial judgments, and deliberative reasoning. But the ethics of care shifts the focus to the unique demands of specific situations and the virtues and feelings that are central to close personal relationships—empathy, compassion, love, sympathy, and fidelity. The heart of the moral life is feeling and caring for those with whom you have a special, intimate connection.

[1]Alison Jaggar, "Feminist Ethics," in *Encyclopedia of Ethics*, ed. Lawrence Becker and Charlotte Becker (New York: Garland, 1992), 364.
[2]Jan Crosthwaite, "Gender and Bioethics," in *A Companion to Bioethics*, ed. Helga Kuhse and Peter Singer (Malden, Mass.: Blackwell, 2001), 32–40.
[3]Crosthwaite, "Gender and Bioethics," 37.

Early on, the ethics of care drew inspiration from the notion that men and women have dramatically different styles of moral decision-making, with men seizing on principles, duties, and rights, and women homing in on personal relationships, caring, and empathy. This difference was highlighted in research done by psychologist Carol Gilligan and published in her 1982 book *In a Different Voice*.[4] Typically, men recognize an ethic of justice and rights, she says, and women are guided by an ethic of compassion and care. In her view, the latter is as legitimate as the former, and both have their place in ethics.

Other research has suggested that the differences between men and women in styles of moral thinking may not be as great as Gilligan suggests. But the credibility of the empirical claim does not affect the larger insight that the research seemed to some writers to suggest: caring is an essential part of morality, and the most influential theories have not fully taken it into account.

These points get support along several lines. First, virtue ethics reminds us that virtues are part of the moral life. If caring is viewed as a virtue—in the form of compassion, empathy, or kindness—then caring too must be an element of morality. A moral theory then would be deficient if it made no room for care.

Moreover, many argue that unlike the ethics of care, most moral theories push the principle of impartiality too far. Recall that impartiality in morality requires us to consider everyone as equal, counting everyone's interests the same. The principle applies widely, especially in matters of public justice, but less so in personal relationships of love, family, friendship, and the like. We seem to have special obligations (partiality) to close friends, family members, and others for whom we care, duties that we do not have to strangers or to universal humanity.

Most moral theories emphasize duties and downplay the role of emotions, attitudes, and motivations. Kant, for example, would have us do our duty for duty's sake, whatever our feelings. For him, to be a morally good parent, we need only act from duty. But taking care of our children as a matter of moral obligation alone seems an empty exercise. Surely, being a morally good parent also involves having feelings of love and attitudes of caring. The ethics of care eagerly takes these emotional elements into account. In our fourth reading, the feminist philosopher Virginia Held offers an analysis of the main elements of this perspective.

Many philosophers, including some who favor traditional theories, think the ethics of care is surely right about certain aspects of the moral life. Caring,

[4]Carol Gilligan, *In a Different Voice: Psychological Theory and Women's Development* (Cambridge, Mass.: Harvard University Press, 1982).

they say, is indeed a vital part of morality. Sometimes the most important factor in moral decision-making is not justice, utility, or rights, but compassionate consideration. Impartiality is a basic requirement of morality, an ideal that guides us to fairness and justice and away from prejudice and inequality. But it often does not apply in our relationships with friends and loved ones, for we may have special obligations to those close to us that we do not have toward others. And, contrary to Kant, feelings do matter. They can alert us to important moral issues and give us a deeper understanding of morality's point and purpose. True, reason must hold the reins of our emotions, but there can be no denying that they have a legitimate place in the moral life.

To these concessions many moral philosophers would add a cautionary note: the ethics of care is not the whole of morality, and to view it that way is a mistake. To decide on the right action, we often cannot avoid applying the concepts of justice and rights. Sometimes impartiality is the best (or only) policy, without which our moral decisions would be misguided, even tragic. And abstract principles or rules, though unwieldy in many cases, may be essential to reconciling conflicting obligations or intuitions.

So should plausible moral theories try to accommodate both an ethic of obligation and an ethic of care? Many theorists, including several writing from a feminist perspective, think so. Such a theorist is Annette Baier, the author of our third selection. She asserts that

> [T]he best moral theory has to be a cooperative product of women and men, has to harmonize justice and care. The morality it theorizes about is after all for all persons, for men and for women, and will need their combined insights. As Gilligan said, what we need now is a "marriage" of the old male and the newly articulated female insights.[5]

[5]Annette C. Baier, "The Need for More than Justice," *Canadian Journal of Philosophy* 13, suppl. 1 (1988): 56.

Feminist Ethics

ALISON M. JAGGAR

Jaggar provides an instructive overview of feminist ethics and the issues with which it wrestles. She traces the development of the field in modern times, provides a survey of its main complaints against traditional ethics, rebuts common misconceptions about it, and reviews many of the topics that have recently preoccupied its practitioners.

Feminist approaches to ethics, often known collectively as feminist ethics, are distinguished by an explicit commitment to correcting male biases they perceive in traditional ethics, biases that may be manifest in rationalizations of women's subordination, or in disregard for, or disparagement of, women's moral experience. Feminist ethics, by contrast, begins from the convictions that the subordination of women is morally wrong and that the moral experience of women is as worthy of respect as that of men. The practical goals of feminist ethics, then, are the following: first, to articulate moral critiques of actions and practices that perpetuate women's subordination; second, to prescribe morally justifiable ways of resisting such actions and practices; and, third, to envision morally desirable alternatives that will promote women's emancipation. The meta-ethical goal of feminist ethics is to develop theoretical understandings of the nature of morality that treat women's moral experience respectfully, though never uncritically.

Just as feminist ethics may be identified by its explicit commitment to challenging perceived male bias in ethics, so approaches that do not express such a commitment may be characterized as nonfeminist. Nonfeminist approaches to ethics are not necessarily anti-feminist or male-biased; they may or may not be so.

THE DEVELOPMENT OF CONTEMPORARY FEMINIST ETHICS

The history of western philosophy includes a number of isolated but indisputable instances of moral opposition to women's subordination. Noteworthy examples are Mary Wollstonecraft's (1759–1797) *A Vindication of the Rights of Woman* (1792), John Stuart Mill's (1806–1873) *The Subjection of Women* (1869), Frederick Engels' (1820–1895) *The Origin of the Family, Private Property and the State* (1884), and Simone de Beauvoir's (1908–1986) *The Second Sex* (1949).

From *Encyclopedia of Ethics*, Lawrence C. Becker and Charlotte B. Becker, eds. (New York: Garland Publishing, 1992), 361–370.

In the late 1960s, however, as part of a general resurgence of feminist activism, an unprecedented explosion of feminist ethical debate occurred, first among the general public, soon in academic discourse. Actions and practices whose gendered dimensions hitherto either had been unnoticed or unchallenged now became foci of public and philosophical attention, as feminists subjected them to outspoken moral critique, developed sometimes dramatic strategies for opposing them, and proposed alternatives that nonfeminists often perceived as dangerously radical. First grassroots and soon academic feminist perspectives were articulated on topics such as abortion, equality of opportunity, domestic labor, portrayals of women in the media, and a variety of issues concerning sexuality, such as rape and compulsory heterosexuality. A little later, feminists displayed increasing ethical concern about pornography, reproductive technology, so-called surrogate motherhood, militarism, the environment and the situation of women in developing nations.

Despite the long history of feminist ethical debate, the term "feminist ethics" itself did not come into general use until the late 1970s or early 1980s. At this time, a number of feminists began expressing doubts about the possibility of fruitfully addressing so-called women's issues in terms of the conceptual apparatus supplied by traditional ethical theory. For instance, a rights framework was alleged by some to distort discussions of abortion insofar as it constructed pregnancy and motherhood as adversarial situations. Other feminists charged that certain assumptions widely accepted by traditional ethical theory were incompatible with what was now beginning to be claimed as a distinctively feminine moral experience or sensibility. Contract theory, for instance, was criticized for postulating a conception of human individuals as free, equal, independent and mutually disinterested, a conception claimed by some to be contrary to the moral experience of most women. Even the requirement of impartiality, usually taken as a defining feature of morality, became the object of feminist criticism insofar as it was alleged to generate prescriptions counter to many women's moral intuitions. Some feminists began to speculate that traditional ethics was more deeply male-biased and needed more fundamental rethinking than they had realized hitherto.

Such speculations were fuelled by the much-publicized work of developmental psychologist Carol Gilligan, whose 1982 book, *In a Different Voice: Psychological Theory and Women's Development*, seemed to demonstrate empirically that the moral development of women was significantly different from that of men. Claiming that females tend to fear separation or abandonment while males, by contrast, tend to perceive closeness as dangerous, Gilligan reported that girls and women often construe moral dilemmas as conflicts of responsibilities rather than of rights and seek to resolve those dilemmas in ways that will repair and strengthen webs of relationship. Furthermore, Gilligan described females as supposedly less likely than males to make or justify moral decisions by the application of abstract moral rules; instead, she claimed girls and women were more likely to act on their feelings of love and compassion for particular individuals. Gilligan concluded that whereas men typically adhere to a morality of justice, whose primary values are fairness and equality, women often adhere to a morality of care, whose primary values are inclusion and protection from harm. For this reason, studies of moral development based exclusively on a morality of justice do not provide an appropriate standard for measuring female moral development and may be said to be male-biased.

Many feminists seized on Gilligan's work as offering evidence for the existence of a characteristically feminine approach to morality, an approach assumed to provide the basis for a distinctively feminist ethics. For some, indeed, feminist ethics became and remains synonymous with an ethics of care. Just how an ethics of care should be delineated, however, was far from evident; nor was it clear whether it should supplement or supplant an ethics of justice. Many feminists today are exploring such questions, even though the connection between women and care is challenged by some psychologists who allege Gilligan's samples to be nonrepresentative, her methods of interpreting her data suspect, and her claims impossible to substantiate, especially when the studies are controlled for occupation and class.

Regardless of empirical findings in moral psychology, debate continues over whether the fundamental tenets of western ethics are male biased in some sense: if not in the sense that they express a moral sensibility characteristic of men rather than women, then perhaps in that they promote a culturally masculine image of moral psychology, discourage preoccupation with issues defined culturally as feminine, or in other ways covertly advance men's interests over women's. Since feminism is essentially a normative stance, and since its meaning is continually contested by feminists themselves, all feminists are constantly engaged in ethical reflection. In this sense, feminist ethics is practiced both inside and outside the academy. Within the academy, its main practitioners are scholars in philosophy, religion and jurisprudence. These scholars represent a variety of philosophical traditions, secular and religious, Anglo-American and continental European; in challenging perceived male bias in those traditions, they draw extensively on feminist scholarship in other disciplines, such as literature, history and psychology.

Scholarly work in feminist ethics often is also responsive to the ethical reflections of nonacademic feminists as these occur, for instance, in much feminist fiction and poetry. In addition, a considerable body of nonfiction, written by nonacademics and directed towards a nonacademic audience, presents itself as feminist ethics. Popular feminist books and journals frequently engage in ethical consideration of moral or public policy issues and sometimes also offer more general discussions of supposedly "masculine" and "feminine" value systems. There are even grassroots journals of feminist ethics, such as *Lesbian Ethics*, published in the United States, and *Gossip: A Journal of Lesbian Feminist Ethics*, published in the United Kingdom. *Feminist Ethics,* published in Canada, seeks to combine academic scholarship with accessibility to a general audience. One may note striking parallels between many of the claims made by feminists inside the academy and those on the outside.

Those who currently claim the field of feminist ethics are mainly, though not exclusively, white western women. Nevertheless, a few male philosophers are doing significant work in feminist ethics, and people of color have produced a considerable amount of writing, both fiction and nonfiction, that seems compatible with the moral and theoretical inspiration of feminist ethics. It is predictable that women would be more likely than men to identify themselves as feminists, and both nonwesterners and western people of color are less likely than western whites either to be philosophers or, because of feminism's racist history, to be feminists. "Womanist" is a term that many African American authors currently prefer to "feminist" but they might not object to the description of their work as feminist ethics if feminism could be cleansed of racism and ethnocentrism.

FEMINIST CRITICISMS OF WESTERN ETHICS

Since most feminist ethics is done in a western context, it is western ethics, particularly (though not exclusively) the European Enlightenment tradition, that is the most frequent target of feminist critique. The feminist challenges to this tradition may be grouped conveniently under five main headings.

Lack of Concern for Women's Interests

Many of the major theorists, such as Aristotle (384–322 B.C.) and Rousseau (1712–1778), are accused of having given insufficient consideration to women's interests, a lack of concern expressed theoretically by their prescribing for women allegedly feminine virtues such as obedience, silence, and faithfulness. Some feminists charge that many contemporary ethical discussions continue the tendency to regard women as instrumental to male-dominated institutions, such as the family or the state; in debates on abortion, for instance, the pregnant woman may be portrayed as little more than a container or environment for the fetus, while debates on reproductive technology are alleged to assume frequently that infertility is a problem only for heterosexual married women, i.e., women defined in relationship to men.

Neglect of "Women's Issues"

Issues of special concern to women are said to have been ignored by modern moral philosophers, who have tended to portray the domestic realm as an arena outside the economy and beyond justice, private in the sense of being beyond the scope of legitimate political regulation. Even philosophers like Aristotle or Hegel (1770–1831), who give some ethical importance to the domestic realm, have tended to portray the home as an arena in which the most fully human excellences are incapable of being realized. Feminist philosophers began early to criticize this conceptual bifurcation of social life. They pointed out that the home was precisely that realm to which women historically had been confined, and that it had become symbolically associated with the feminine, despite the fact that heads of households were paradigmatically male. They argued that the philosophical devaluation of the domestic realm made it impossible to raise questions about the justice of the domestic division of labor, because it obscured the far-reaching social significance and creativity of women's work in the home, and concealed, even legitimated, the domestic abuse of women and girls.

Denial of Women's Moral Agency

Women's moral agency is said to have often been denied, not simply by excluding women from moral debate or ignoring their contributions, but through philosophical claims to the effect that women lack moral reason. Such claims were made originally by Aristotle, but they have been elaborated and refined by modern theorists such as Rousseau, Kant (1724–1804), Hegel, and Freud (1856–1939).

Depreciation of "Feminine" Values

Western moral theory is said to embody values that are "masculine," insofar as they are associated, empirically, normatively, or symbolically, with men. For instance, western ethics is alleged to prefer the supposedly masculine or male-associated values of independence, autonomy, intellect, will, wariness, hierarchy, domination, culture, transcendence, product, asceticism, war and death over the supposedly feminine or female-associated values of interdependence, community, connection, sharing, emotion, body, trust, absence of hierarchy, nature, immanence, process, joy, peace and life. Claims like this are common in both popular and academic feminist writings on ethics.

Devaluation of Women's Moral Experience

Finally, prevailing western conceptualizations of the nature of morality, moral problems, and moral reasoning are also charged with being masculine insofar as they too are associated with men, an association that again may be empirical, symbolic or normative. For instance, feminists have accused modern moral theory of being excessively preoccupied with rules, obsessed with impartiality and exclusively focussed on discrete deeds. In addition, feminists have charged modern moral theory with taking the contract as the paradigmatic moral relation and construing moral rationality so narrowly as to exclude emotions of assessment, sometimes called moral emotions. All these characteristics have been asserted to be masculine in some sense. A feminine approach to ethics, by contrast, has been supposed to avoid assuming that individuals ordinarily are free, equal and independent; to take more account of the specificities of particular contexts; and to be more likely to resolve moral dilemmas by relying on empathic feeling rather than by appealing to rules.

Not all feminists endorse all of the above clusters of criticisms—and even where they agree with the general statement, they may well disagree over its applicability in the case of specific philosophers or debates. Despite such differences of relative detail, feminists tend generally to agree on the first three clusters of criticisms, whose correction seems not only attainable in principle within the framework of Enlightenment moral theory but even to be required by that framework. However, there is sharp feminist disagreement on the last two clusters of criticisms, especially the fifth, which obviously contains clear parallels with a number of nonfeminist criticisms of Enlightenment ethics made by proponents of, for example, situation ethics, virtue ethics, communitarianism and postmodernism.

COMMON MISCONSTRUALS OF FEMINIST ETHICS

Feminist ethics has sometimes been construed, both by some of its proponents and some of its critics, as a simple inversion of the criticisms listed above. In other words, it has sometimes been identified with one or more of the following: putting women's interests first; focusing exclusively on so-called women's issues; accepting women (or feminists) as moral experts or authorities; substituting "female" (or feminine) for "male" (or masculine) values; or extrapolating directly from women's moral experience. These characterizations of feminist ethics are sufficiently pervasive that it is worth noting just why they cannot be correct.

1. Putting women's interests first occasionally has been recommended as a way of achieving a "woman-centered" ethics that transcends the covert bias of a supposed humanism grounded in fact on male norms. Whatever might be said for or against this recommendation, however, it cannot be definitive of feminist ethics. This is because the formula, as it stands, raises more questions than it answers insofar as it fails to specify not only which women's interests should be preferred over which men's (or children's) and in what circumstances, but also what should be done about conflicts of interest between women and even how interests should be identified at all. Most obviously, feminist ethics cannot be identified with "putting women's interests first" simply because many feminists would refuse to accept and, indeed, be morally outraged by what they would perceive as blatant partiality and immorality.

2. Feminist ethics certainly is concerned to address issues of special concern to women, issues that have been neglected by modern moral theory, but it cannot be identified with an exclusive focus on such issues. This is partly because nonfeminists as well as feminists have addressed these issues—and, indeed, are doing so increasingly as feminism grows stronger and more articulate. It is also because feminism rejects the notion that moral issues can be divided cleanly into those that are and those that are not of special concern to women. On the one hand, since men's and women's lives are inextricably intertwined, there are no "women's issues" that are not also men's issues; the availability or otherwise of child care and abortion, for instance, has significant consequences for the lives of men as well as women. On the other hand, since men and women typically are not what lawyers call "similarly situated" relative to each other, it is difficult to think of any moral or public policy ("human") issue in which women do not have a special interest. For instance, such "human" issues as war, peace and world starvation have special significance for women because the world's hungry are disproportionately women (and children), because women are primarily those in need of the social services neglected to fund military spending, and because women benefit relatively little from militarism and the weapons industries. For these reasons, it would be a mistake to identify feminist ethics with attention to some explicitly gendered subset of ethical issues. On the contrary, rather than being limited to a restricted ethical domain, feminist ethics has *enlarged* the traditional concerns of ethics, both through identifying previously unrecognized ethical issues and by introducing fresh perspectives on issues already acknowledged as having an ethical dimension.

3. Feminist ethics certainly is being developed by feminists, most of whom are women, but this does not imply, of course, that any women, or even

feminists, therefore should be regarded as moral experts whose moral authority is beyond question. Not only are there deep disagreements among women and even among feminists such that it would be difficult to know whom to select as an expert, but many painful examples of the failure of insight or principle on the part of feminist leaders also demonstrate only too clearly that no women, even feminists, are morally infallible.

4. There are also serious difficulties with thinking of feminist ethics as the substitution of female or feminine for male or masculine values. These difficulties include problems with establishing that *any* values are male or female in the sense of being generally held by men or women, when both women's and men's values vary so much, both within cultures as well as across them. Similar problems confront attempts to establish that certain values are masculine or feminine in the sense of being considered socially appropriate for individuals of one gender or the other. Again, norms of masculinity and femininity vary not only between societies but even within the same society along such axes as class and ethnicity: some social groups, for instance, value physical health, strength or athletic prowess in women; others values physical fragility, weakness or incompetence. But even if certain values could be identified in some sense as male or female, masculine or feminine, the conclusive objection to identifying feminist ethics with the elaboration of female or feminine values is that the femin*ine* is not necessarily the femin*ist*. Indeed, since the feminine typically has been constructed in circumstances of male domination, it is likely to be quite opposed to the feminist. Personal charm, for example, may be valued not only *in* women but also *by* them; even if charm were, in these senses, a feminine value, however, it would seem at least as likely to undermine feminist goals as to promote them.

5. Similar problems apply to defining feminist ethics as the systematic extrapolation of women's moral experience, exclusive of men's. While no approach to morality can be adequate if it ignores the moral experience of women, it seems most unlikely that women generally are similar enough to each other and different enough from men that a single distinctively female or feminine approach to ethics can be identified. Attempts to establish such an identification frequently commit the fallacy of generalizing about the experience of *all* or *most* women from the moral experience of *some* women; this seems to have been one flaw at least in Gilligan's earlier work. Again, even if a distinctively femin*ine* approach to morality could be identified, perhaps in terms of symbolic or normative connections with women rather than empirical ones, there is no reason to suppose that such an approach would be femin*ist*. Indeed, given the feminist commitment to a critical rethinking of cultural constructions of both masculinity and femininity, there is good *prima facie* reason to suppose that it would not.

MINIMUM CONDITIONS OF ADEQUACY FOR FEMINIST ETHICS

Even though feminist ethics is far broader and more open than it appears in the foregoing misconstruals, its goals are sufficiently specific, especially when taken in conjunction with its criticisms of traditional ethics, as to generate certain minimum conditions of adequacy for any approach to ethics that purports to be feminist.

1. First of all, feminist ethics can never begin by assuming that women and men are similarly situated—although it may discover that this is the case in certain respects in specific contexts. In addition, not only does feminist ethics need constant vigilance to detect subtle as well as blatant manifestations of gender privilege, it must also be sensitive to the ways in which gendered norms are different for different groups of women—or in which the same norms, such as a cultural preference for slimness or blondness, affect different groups of women differently. Ultimately feminism's concern for *all* women means that feminist ethics must address not only "domestic" issues of racism or homophobia or class privilege but also such international issues as environmental destruction, war, and access to world resources.

2. In order to offer guides to action that will tend to subvert rather than reinforce the present systematic subordination of women, feminist approaches to ethics must understand individual actions in the context of broader social practices, evaluating the symbolic and cumulative implications of action as well as its immediately observable consequences. They must be equipped to recognize covert as well as overt manifestations of domination, subtle as well as blatant forms of control, and they must develop sophisticated accounts of coercion and consent. Similarly, they must provide the conceptual resources for identifying and evaluating the varieties of resistance and struggle in which women, particularly, have engaged. They must recognize the often unnoticed ways in which women and other members of the underclass have refused cooperation and opposed domination, while acknowledging the inevitability of collusion and the impossibility of totally clean hands. In short, feminist approaches to ethics must be transitional and nonutopian, often extensions of, rather than alternatives to, feminist political theory, exercises in non-ideal rather than ideal theory.

3. Since most of most women's lives have been excluded from that domain conceptualized as public, a third requirement for feminist approaches to ethics is that they should be able to provide guidance on issues of so-called private life: intimate relations, sexuality and childrearing. Thus, they must articulate the moral dimensions of issues that may not hitherto have been recognized as moral. In addition, we have seen that feminist approaches to ethics

must provide appropriate guidance for dealing with national and international issues, strangers and foreigners. In developing the conceptual tools for undertaking these tasks, feminist ethics cannot assume that moral concepts developed originally for application to the so-called public realm, concepts such as impartiality or exploitation, are appropriate for use in the so-called private; neither can it assume that concepts such as care, developed in intimate relationships, will necessarily be helpful in the larger world. Indeed, the whole distinction between public and private life must be examined critically by feminist ethics, with no prior assumptions as to whether the distinction should be retained, redrawn or rejected.

4. Finally, feminist ethics must take the moral experience of all women seriously, though not, of course, uncritically. Though what is *feminist* often will turn out to be very different from what is *feminine*, a basic respect for women's moral experience is necessary to acknowledging women's capacities as moralists and to countering traditional stereotypes of women as less than full moral agents, as childlike or close to nature. Furthermore, empirical claims about differences in the moral sensibility of women and men make it impossible to assume that any approach to ethics will be unanimously accepted if it fails to consult the moral experience of women. Additionally, it seems plausible to suppose that women's distinctive social experience may make them especially perceptive regarding the implications of domination, especially gender domination, and especially well equipped to detect the male bias that feminists believe has pervaded so much of male-authored western moral theory.

Most feminist, and perhaps even many nonfeminist, philosophers might well find the general statement of these conditions quite uncontroversial, but they will inevitably disagree sharply over when the conditions have been met. Not only may feminists disagree with nonfeminists, but they are likely even to differ with each other over, for instance, what are women's interests, what are manifestations of domination and coercion, how resistance should be expressed, and which aspects of women's moral experience are worth developing and in which directions.

Those who practice feminist ethics thus may be seen both as united by a shared project and as diverging widely in their views as to how this project may be accomplished. Their divergences result from a variety of philosophical differences, including differing conceptions of feminism itself, which, as we have seen, is a constantly contested concept. The inevitability of such divergence means that feminist ethics can never be identified in terms of a specific range of topics, methods or orthodoxies. While feminist ethics is distinguished by its explicit commitment to developing approaches to ethics that will respect women's moral experience and avoid rationalizing women's subordination, attempts to define it more precisely or substantively than this are likely to disregard the richness and variety of feminist moral thinking and prematurely foreclose the feminist moral debate.

CURRENT CONCERNS IN FEMINIST ETHICS

Despite the scope and diversity of feminist ethics, certain current preoccupations may be identified. These preoccupations are not definitive of feminist ethics, but they are characteristic of its present stage of development. (They are also, sometimes in different ways, preoccupations of much contemporary nonfeminist ethics.) They include concern with issues of universality and particularity, sociality and individuality, moral emotion and moral rationality. These concerns are not independent of each other and they may be discerned underlying many contemporary feminist approaches to practical issues, such as equality, health care, or the environment, as well as being foci of feminist reflection on such traditional philosophical issues as moral subjectivity and moral epistemology.

Feminist challenges to traditional views of moral subjectivity are not limited to assertions (*contra* Aristotle, Rousseau, Kant and Hegel) that women are as capable as men of moral virtue or rationality. Instead, many feminists have drawn on and extended nonfeminist criticisms of the basic model of the moral self most characteristic of Enlightenment moral theory, a model derived from Descartes (1596–1650) and portraying the self as disembodied, asocial, autonomous, unified, rational and essentially similar to all other selves. This model, of course, has been under attack for over a century from, among others, Marxists, Freudians, contemporary communitarians, and postmodernists. Feminists often share many conclusions with such nonfeminist critics of Enlightenment theory, but they arrive at those conclusions by different routes, and often they add to them the claim that the Cartesian model is male-biased (as well as class- and possibly race-biased), in that it reflects the interests and values of European bourgeois men and either ignores divergent interests and values or portrays them as less than fully human.

One source of feminist challenge to the Cartesian self is a growing philosophical interest in embodiment. This itself springs partly from feminist outrage over the male control and exploitation of women's bodies, partly from the feminist recognition that much of the responsibility for physical reproduction and bodily maintenance traditionally has been assigned to women—both of which reinforce symbolic western associations between women and the body. Philosophical reflection that begins from the body tends to highlight features of human nature very different from those emphasized by Cartesianism: temporality rather than timelessness, growth and decay rather than changelessness, particularity rather than universality, sociality rather than isolation. These features, in turn, tend to generate concerns for ethics different from those that dominated much Enlightenment theory: inequality, dependence and interdependence, specificity, social embeddedness and historical community now must all be recognized as permanent circumstances of moral life, never to be avoided or transcended by focusing on equality, independence, autonomy, generality, isolated individuals, ideal communities or the universal human condition. It does not escape feminist authors that concern with precisely the former circumstances has been claimed by many to be distinctively feminine—preoccupying women in virtue of their social situation, associated symbolically with women or defined culturally as appropriate to women.

Conceiving moral subjects as embodied also has psychological implications: insofar as their identity is significantly constituted by their specific social relationships (relationships determined at least in part by the social meaning attributed to bodily characteristics such as parentage, age or sex), moral subjects conceived in this way are revealed as likely to be moved by considerations of particular attachment as much as abstract concern for duty, care as much as respect, solidarity as much as dignity, responsibility as much as right. Many feminists currently argue that much Enlightenment moral psychology is inadequate insofar as it fails to take adequate account of these propensities, conceiving them at best as morally irrelevant, at worst as morally subversive. In addition, noting the ways in which the psyche is shaped by social practices, especially childrearing and other gendered practices, many feminists criticize the common Enlightenment assumption that people are essentially alike, rational and autarchic. Noting the significance of fantasy in our lives, they deny that consciousness is transparent and unified and that individuals always know their own interests best. In general, they challenge much Enlightenment moral psychology for its failure to recognize that, if autonomy exists at all, it is an achievement with complex material and social preconditions.

That people in fact have certain psychological propensities of course does not entail that those propensities are morally relevant, let alone morally desirable; on the other hand, an adequate moral theory cannot be grounded in a psychology that is descriptively inadequate. Many feminists claim that much Enlightenment moral psychology is so alien to the ways in which people in fact do act and think morally that it cannot serve even as an acceptable reconstruction of moral reasoning. For instance, by failing to appreciate the moral significance of the psychological characteristics noted above, it offers a model of moral rationality that is unduly narrow in disregarding emotion, and likely to generate morally repugnant conclusions that ignore our responsibility for the welfare of others, neglect the claims of conventional morality, and undervalue the moral weight of particular relationships. Some feminists go on to argue that most Enlightenment models of moral rationality are not only empirically and morally inadequate but also serve, insofar as they are culturally accepted, as oppressive norms for those social groups, including perhaps some groups of women, whose moral thinking is stigmatized as amoral or immoral for failing to conform to these models.

Morality on most Enlightenment views is a system of rationally justified rules or principles that guide action in specific cases. Many contemporary feminists, by contrast, deny that morality is reducible to rules and assert the impossibility of justifying the claims of ethics by appeal to a universal, impartial reason. They charge that undue emphasis on the epistemological importance of moral rules obscures the crucial role of moral insight, virtue and character in determining the right course of action. Some give a feminist twist to this essentially Aristotelian criticism by claiming that excessive reliance on rules reflects a juridical-administrative interest that is characteristic of modern masculinity—contemporary women, by contrast, are claimed to be more likely to disregard conventionally accepted moral rules because such rules are insensitive to the specificities of particular situations. Some feminists assert, therefore, that a morality of rule devalues the moral wisdom of women and gives insufficient weight to such supposedly feminine virtues as kindness, generosity, helpfulness and sympathy.

Though many feminists continue to defend various versions of Enlightenment moral theory, many others are concerned not merely to criticize them but also to develop alternatives to them—alternatives that will avoid their perceived shortcomings while meeting the conditions of adequacy identified earlier. Thus, contemporary feminists are exploring ways of thinking about moral subjects that are sensitive both to their concrete particularity and their intrinsic shared value—the ideal expressed in Enlightenment claims about common humanity, equality and impartiality; developing "particularist" epistemologies that recognize the moral validity of immediate, emotion-laden responses to particular others while avoiding subjective relativism; and finding ways of simultaneously acknowledging and criticizing the claims of conventional morality—known colloquially as living with contradictions. They are exploring these approaches in the context of developing feminist perspectives on many of the most pressing moral issues of our time.

For Further Reflection

1. What challenges to Western ethics does Jaggar identify? Do you think these are justified?
2. According to Jaggar, how has feminist ethics been misconstrued by its proponents and its critics?
3. What are Jaggar's four "minimum conditions of adequacy for feminist ethics?" Do you agree with her?

Gender and Bioethics

JAN CROSTHWAITE

Crosthwaite observes that although feminism encompasses diverse viewpoints and even many conceptions of feminism itself, feminism has a unifying theme: "The concern to understand and eliminate the oppression of women in all its guises." She points out that feminists have drawn attention to gender-based inequality and discrimination and long-held but unsupportable assumptions about the proper roles and moral status of women. From these concerns, feminists have formulated critiques of traditional notions of ethical (and bioethical) theorizing, moral deliberation, moral agents, and concepts of justice.

The professions and disciplines from which bioethics emerged—medicine, theology, philosophy and law—have long been male-dominated, male-focused and sometimes misogynist. Early bioethical writings, even when addressing issues of primary concern to women, like abortion, rarely considered women's views specifically or engaged with feminist thinking on these issues. They showed little awareness of the patriarchal character of institutions within which bioethical issues arose, or of the possible impact on bioethical issues of cultural assumptions about differences between women and men. Nor was the possibility of gender bias in ethical theorizing itself considered. That fundamental conceptions of human norms and the processes of ethical deliberation might reflect a particular gendered perspective went largely unremarked. Bioethical debate and the principles underlying it were assumed to be open to all rational minds and uncontaminated by such contingencies as gender.

While women have not been absent from bioethical discussions, it is relatively recently that women's voices have being heard as making a distinctive contribution. This largely reflects the increasing recognition of feminist thinking as an important contribution to critical reflection on intellectual traditions and social institutions. The contributions of women and feminists can be both disturbing and enriching: disturbing because they are often critical of health-care institutions and practices, and also of bioethics and its reflections

From *A Companion to Bioethics*, 2nd edn. Helga Kuhse and Peter Singer, eds. (Malden, MA: Blackwell Publishing, 2001), 36–45.

on these; enriching (and essential) because they are disturbing and because they bring to debates the diverse but often distinctive experiences, interests and values of women.

FEMINISM AND GENDER

It is feminism which allows the significance of women's voices to be understood. Feminism is not a single viewpoint; feminist thinking is informed by different disciplinary backgrounds, different political frameworks, different race, class, cultural and individual experiences, and different understandings of feminism itself. (Tong (1989) provides a helpful introduction to a variety of feminisms.) Indeed, a recurrent issue for feminists is whether there is anything which can be held to unify the different feminist voices without thereby disrespectfully diminishing their differences and effectively silencing some.

I think there is a unifying distinctive theme in feminism: the concern to understand and eliminate the oppression of women in all its guises. This underpins feminist concerns to document women's experiences, preferably in their own voices, and to provide theoretical analyses of these experiences, their origins and implications, as the basis for a critique of social institutions.

Feminist concern with the oppression of women provides the framework for understanding the significance of gender. "Gender" refers to the social elaboration of a biological difference between male and female into two distinct kinds of people, men and women. Feminists have identified both the existence of gender differences and their particular construction in Western civilization as contributing to the oppression of women. Feminist writers in the 1970s distinguished sex, the biological differentiation of male and female, from gender, the social differentiation of masculine and feminine individuals in terms of roles, behaviour and psychological traits. More recent feminists have been critical of the conceptualization and use of any sex/gender distinction. They argue that it presents a false dichotomy, and that accounts of gender often privilege a particular cultural/historical perspective at the expense of recognizing the diversity of ways of understanding differences between men and women to be found across different times, cultures and classes. Emphasis on gender *simpliciter* also obscures the contribution of other factors (including race and class) to the life experiences, social relationships and sense of self of individual women and men.

How to accommodate the multifarious and cross-cutting differences between women (and between social groups in general) is a major issue in contemporary feminist thinking. Recognition of difference complicates feminist social analysis and feminist attempts to eliminate women's oppression, but it also promotes more sophisticated analysis and political theorizing.

Whatever the theoretical standing of the concept of gender, attention to differences between men and women (both assumed and actual) is important to understanding and ethically evaluating any social practice, including health care. It reveals unjust differences in distribution of or access to rights and goods, and it reveals the existence and operation of oppressive relationships and social structures. Attention to gender enriches bioethical understanding and evaluation. It encourages attention more generally to the operation of power relations in health-care institutions and practices, and to the impact of health-related issues on the oppression of social groups. It forces bioethicists to attend more to the political and social contexts of both bioethical issues and the practice of bioethics itself.

GENDER AND HEALTH CARE

Feminists have drawn attention to gender inequality and discrimination within health-care professions, and have pointed out the gendered division of labour and status in health-care institutions (Miles, 1991, chapter 5). Activities of "care" are women's work, while "curing" (and the scientific expertise which backs it) is men's province and more valued. This reflects traditional Western stereotypes of femininity and masculinity. It also reinforces a distorted conception (characteristically expressed in war metaphors) of health care as the (masculine) conquest of disease through technological wizardry and the valiant battles of physicians and surgeons against invading organisms and unruly organs.

Feminists have also documented the exploitation and abuse of women patients, from unnecessary hysterectomies to genital reconstructions performed without women's knowledge (Scully, 1980). Even within the practice of beneficent medicine, there are disturbing ethical failures in the treatment of women. Research suggests that women may receive a lesser quality of health care than men with similar conditions (Muller, 1990). But women's most frequent complaints concern failures of respect: not being taken seriously as authorities on their own experience and preferences; not being properly informed about their condition and treatment options; and generally not being accorded the rights of competent adults to decide about their own health care. Gender stereotypes and behaviour patterns foster these failures and reinforce the inequalities inherent in physician–patient encounters (Todd, 1989). Yet while bioethics has been centrally concerned with issues of patient autonomy and power imbalances between health professionals and their clients, it has had little to say about the impact of gender on these issues.

The protection of research subjects is also a major concern of bioethics, but it is feminists who have primarily drawn attention to unethical experimentation on women, including the therapeutic use of drugs which have not been adequately tested for effects on women. Women have been under-represented in and excluded from studies concerning illnesses which affect them as well as men (Bird, 1994). Sometimes gender differences are explicitly used as a reason for excluding women, because incorporating such factors as women's hormonal cycles and the possibility of pregnancy complicates research and adds to its cost. Therapies and illnesses may affect women differently from men, and their exclusion or under-representation in research is medically, scientifically and ethically problematic.

Feminists have attributed much gender bias in health care and research to the assumption that women's health issues are primarily reproductive, a reflection of a long tradition of identifying women with their reproductive biology. They have discerned also the effects of Western culture's identification of human norms with men and men's experience and values (usually men of a particular race and class). Even in those areas where women's physiology and experience are unique, their reproductive biology, traces of an assumption that women are deviations from the human (i.e., male) norm can be found. Women's normal functioning is seen as medically problematic; menopause becomes an "oestrogen deficiency disease." Prophylactic removal of healthy but supposedly "useless" reproductive organs from older women also suggests a narrowly reproductive focus on women's bodies and lives, particularly when not accompanied by any consideration of other possible functions (e.g., in sexual response) of such organs. Feminists have also argued that research into some diseases in women, such as HIV/AIDS, has been more concerned with the implications of women's illness for men and babies than for women themselves (Faden, Kass and McGraw, 1996). Such attitudes can be seen as reflecting and reinforcing oppressive views of women as fundamentally bearers of men's children.

Feminists have long criticized medicine as an agent of the social control of women. In areas which significantly affect women's reproductive lives, predominantly male medical professionals control information and access to technologies, and dominate individual and social decision-making. In these areas, and in mental health, medicine has sustained women's oppression through control of their bodies and behaviour, and through its articulation and enforcement of gender roles and characteristics. Gynaecological surgery of various kinds has been used to "cure" behaviour deemed inappropriate for women. Psychiatry and access to reproductive technology (both conceptive and contraceptive) have been used to enforce socially acceptable (hetero) sexual and maternal behaviour and roles (Miles, 1991: Scully, 1994).

Such analyses are of course disputed. The motivations of health-care professionals for the therapies they offer or the research they undertake rarely include deliberate harm to or exploitation of women. Hence accusations of oppression can be shocking and painful. Moreover, differential treatment of women and men may be justified in terms of the sex-differentiated distribution and implications of diseases (as Mertz and others, 1996, argue in response to feminist accusations of bias in AIDS research), and treatments such as hysterectomy or hormone replacement may be proper and desirable in individual cases. However, feminist analysis is concerned less with conscious motivations than with discerning underlying assumptions, and patterns of thinking and practices, of which people may be quite unaware. Feminists draw attention to the systemic effects of what may be individually well-motivated actions. Nor do all feminists agree about analyses, implications or acceptability of particular health-care practices or policies.

Feminist criticism of health-care professions, practices and policies provides important data for bioethical reflection. The defence of actions and practices against such criticism is therapeutic in that it requires that feminist concerns be explicitly addressed and the possibility of gender as a category of analysis be considered. Relations of dominance between social groups are ethical concerns and should be part of bioethical deliberation. Feminist analyses provide distinctive ways of understanding and evaluating social practices and institutions, including those concerned with health care, and feminist debates stimulate reflection on issues which might otherwise go unstudied. . . .

GENDER AND ETHICS

As recent work in feminist bioethics makes clear (e.g., Sherwin, 1992: Wolf, 1996), the importance for bioethics of feminist attention to gender goes beyond the critique of specific health-care practices and institutions. It also prompts reflection on the possibility of gender biases in the theoretical frameworks of bioethics, particularly in conceptions of the nature of moral agents and moral deliberation.

Feminist approaches to ethics and consequently to bioethics are varied. Though sometimes mistakenly identified with feminine ethics of care, they reflect a range of theoretical positions. What they share is the fundamental feminist concern with understanding and eliminating women's oppression, and with ensuring proper attention is paid to women's experiences and interests. These concerns underpin feminist critiques of ethical (and bioethical) theorizing. But feminist ethics move beyond critique to articulating alternative theories and approaches to moral deliberation. . . .

Such theories often incorporate elements of the ethic of care described by Carol Gilligan, who claimed to hear a distinctive "ethic of care or responsibility" in women's moral deliberations (Gilligan, 1982). It is characterized by an emphasis on maintaining connection and relationships, on care for others (and self) and on avoiding harm. Care thinkers focus on the particular features and contextual location of moral problems, rather than attempting to abstract features which would allow these to be subsumed under general rules or principles. They seek to resolve problems through communication, appealing to shared understanding of relationships and needs, and prefer the creative exploration of options that might dissipate conflicts to the consistency of universal rules.

Gilligan contrasted this "moral orientation" with the "ethic of justice" she saw as dominant in contemporary moral discourse. She argued that the voices of care and justice are gender-inflected, though neither uniquely nor universally found in women and men respectively. An ethic of justice emphasizes values of fairness and equal respect for individuals (particularly their rights to self-determination). It focuses on the impartial adjudication of conflicting claims or obligations through an appeal to rationally derived and universally applicable principles. While this does not adequately reflect the range or subtlety of Western ethical theorizing, it does capture certain dominant themes, which emerge strongly in bioethical debates.

Both the content of an ethic of care and its presentation as an alternative to dominant moral theorizing throw into question the claims of traditional ethical theories to present universal, impartial and gender-neutral moral thinking. This, together with its resonance with many women's experience and values, makes care ethics of particular interest to feminists. But care's characterization as a feminine ethic is problematic, given feminist concern with gender and oppression. A feminine morality embedded in nurture, close personal attachments and emotional response to others, recalls demeaning characterizations of women as morally inadequate. Ideas of women as emotional, lacking a sense of justice and incapable of objective and impartial rationality, have been used in Western culture to justify their exclusion from public life and their subordination to men. Feminists are also justifiably cautious about any ethic generated within a situation of subordination. The inclusion of women's moral thinking in a feminist ethic must be moderated by critical awareness of gender and of the location of women's experiences and values within (usually patriarchal) social structures and contexts.

Many feminists wish to transcend a justice–care dichotomy. They endorse certain aspects of feminine ethics of care, but also appeal to justice values to ground their critique of oppression. Indeed, feminist analyses of oppression suggest reconceptualizing and extending our understanding of justice beyond the dominant focus on distributive justice (Young, 1990). Care-oriented values also support feminist advocacy of individual empowerment as a means to counteracting unequal and oppressive relationships.

Like care ethics, feminist ethics emphasize the importance of attention to context, particularly social context, and to the unique properties of specific individuals and moral problems. They also argue that human relationships, emotional responses, and individuals' understandings of themselves and their situations are essential components of moral reflection and should not be seen as antithetical to it (Sherwin, 1992). Such emphases favour a different account of the nature of moral deliberation and of human beings as moral agents from those dominant in Western ethical and political thinking.

MORAL PERSONS AND MORAL DELIBERATION

Susan Wolf attributes part of bioethics' failure to engage with feminism to its "early embrace of a liberal individualism largely inattentive to social context" and "its emphasis on deduction from ethical principles rather than induction from concrete cases" (1996: 5). Liberal individualism gives priority to respect for individual self-determination or autonomy. It sees fairness and equality of treatment as requiring the impartial application of universal principles which abstract essential commonalities from the messy specificities of real individuals. This yields a notion of abstract individuals as fundamentally autonomous agents, aware of their own preferences and values, and motivated by rational self-interest (though not necessarily selfish). Their connections to one another are primarily through voluntary contractual relationships mediated by reason-determined codes of rights and obligations. The imposition of any particular conception of what is good or valuable is a failure of respect for the essentially self-determining nature of such individuals. Such a conception has difficulty in recognizing the complex relationships between individuals and social groups, except as these emerge in individual preferences.

Against such abstract ciphers, many feminists present a richer conception of persons as historically and culturally located, socially related and essentially embodied (for example, Diprose, 1994). Individuals are located in and formed by specific relationships (chosen and unchosen) and ties of affection and responsibility. Their preferences and possibilities are affected by membership of social groups with specific concrete and symbolic properties. Such a conception of socially embedded selves refocuses thinking about autonomy, shifting the emphasis from independent self-determination towards ideals of integrity within relatedness. It demands an approach to moral deliberation which does not require detachment from others, nor the idea of a self-transparent "self." Respecting autonomy becomes less a matter of protecting individuals from "coercive" influences than one of positive empowerment, recognizing people's interdependence and supporting individuals' development of their own understanding of their situation and options.

Attention to social groups also shifts ethical emphasis on individual judgement more towards ideals of communicative and collaborative decision-making. The understanding and judgements of concrete individuals are particular rather than universal, and are constrained by personal situation and experience. Many feminists reject the possibility of an unsituated epistemological or moral perspective, arguing that knowledge and morality are products of social negotiation. Current debates in feminist epistemology and feminist ethics address the possibility of recognizing and valuing diverse perspectives without embracing a relativism that would limit the possibility of shared social life and moral standards and undercut the ground from which to condemn oppression.

Against the ideal of objective and impartial moral rationality, many feminists emphasize an engaged moral response. Moral perception and response involve some form of empathic engagement with specific others, rather than detached application of abstract principles. This, together with recognition of the moral significance of emotions and affective relationships, calls into question ideals of impartiality in ethics. While there are clearly contexts in which it is wrong to favour particular others, certain professional and personal relationships may permit or even morally require such preferential treatment. Health professionals are increasingly feeling the tension between obligations to their own patients and the impartiality required of custodians of scarce public resources.

Distinguishing proper responsiveness to the needs of particular others from distorting bias (and harmful self-sacrifice) requires a carefully nuanced understanding of the nature and demands of the variety of interconnected human relationships—personal, professional and political—and a sense of how these fit into a wider social framework. Feminist thinking, with its concern to understand oppression and the many faces of power, both personal and institutional, helps provide such a perspective. . . .

References

Bird, C. E. (1994). Women's representation as subjects in clinical studies: a pilot study of research published in JAMA in 1990 and 1992. In A. Mastroianni, R. Faden, and D. Federman (eds). *Women and Health Research: Ethical and legal issues of including women in clinical studies. Vol. 2. Workshop and commissioned papers*. Washington, DC: National Academy Press, 157–73.

Diprose, R. (1994). *The Bodies of Women: ethics, embodiment and sexual difference*. London and New York: Routledge.

Faden, R., Kass, N. and McGraw. D. (1996). Women as vessels and vectors: lessons from the HIV epidemic. In S. *M. Wolf (ed.), Feminism and Bioethics: Beyond reproduction. New York and Oxford: Oxford* University Press, 252–81.

Gilligan, C. (1982). *In a Different Voice: psychological theory and women's development*. Cambridge, MA: Harvard University Press.

Mertz, D., Sushinsky, M. A. and Schüklenk, U. (1996). Women and AIDS: the ethics of exaggerated harm. *Bioethics*, 10/2, 92–113.

Miles, A. (1991). *Women, Health and Medicine*. Milton Keynes and Philadelphia: Open University Press.

Muller, C. F. (1990). *Health Care and Gender*. New York: Russell Sage Foundation.

Scully, D. (1980). *Men who Control Women's Health: The miseducation of Obstetrician-Gynecologists*. New York and London: Teachers College Press. Teachers College, Columbia University.

Sherwin, S. (1992). *No Longer Patient: Feminist ethics and health care*. Philadelphia: Temple University Press.

Todd, A. D. (1989). *Intimate Adversaries: Cultural conflict between doctors and women patients*. Philadelphia: University of Pennsylvania Press.

Tong, R. (1989). *Feminist Thought: A comprehensive introduction*. Boulder, CO, and San Francisco: Westview Press.

Wolf, S. M. (ed.) (1996). *Feminism and Bioethics: Beyond reproduction*. New York and Oxford: Oxford University Press.

Young, I. M. (1990). *Justice and the Politics of Difference*. Princeton, NJ: Princeton University Press.

For Further Reflection

1. According to Crosthwaite, how have gender inequality and discrimination manifested themselves in health care?
2. Why does Crosthwaite say that the idea of care as a feminine ethic is problematic?
3. What is the difference between the liberal individualist and the feminist concepts of moral persons?

The Need for More than Justice

ANNETTE C. BAIER

Baier makes a case for moral theories that can accommodate both an ethic of justice (thought by some to be the traditional male view) and an ethic of care (the alleged female view). "I think," she says, "that the best moral theory has to be a cooperative product of women and men, has to harmonize justice and care."

In recent decades in North American social and moral philosophy, alongside the development and discussion of widely influential theories of justice, taken as Rawls takes it as the "first virtue of social institutions,"[1] there has been a counter-movement gathering strength, one coming from some interesting sources. For some of the most outspoken of the diverse group who have in a variety of ways been challenging the assumed supremacy of justice among the moral and social virtues are members of those sections of society whom one might have expected to be especially aware of the supreme importance of justice, namely blacks and women. Those who have only recently won recognition of their equal rights, who have only recently seen the correction or partial correction of longstanding racist and sexist injustices to their race and sex, are among the philosophers now suggesting that justice is only one virtue among many, and one that may need the presence of the others in order to deliver its own undenied value. Among these philosophers of the philosophical counterculture, as it were—but an increasingly large counterculture—I include Alasdair MacIntyre,[2] Michael Stocker,[3] Lawrence Blum,[4] Michael Slote,[5] Laurence Thomas,[6] Claudia Card,[7] Alison Jaggar,[8] Susan Wolf[9] and a whole group of

[1]John Rawls, *A Theory of Justice* (Harvard University Press).
[2]Alasdair MacIntyre, *After Virtue* (Notre Dame: Notre Dame University Press).
[3]Michael Stocker, "The Schizophrenia of Modern Ethical Thieories," *Journal of Philosophy* 73, 14, 453–66; and "Agent and Other: Against Ethical Universalism," *Australasian Journal of Philosophy* 54, 206–20.
[4]Lawrence Blum, *Friendship, Altruism and Morality* (London: Routledge & Kegan Paul 1980).
[5]Michael Slote, *Goods and Virtues* (Oxford: Oxford University Press 1983).
[6]Laurence Thomas, "Love and Morality," in *Epistemology and Sociobiology*, James Fetzer, ed. (1985); and "Justice, Happiness and Self Knowledge," *Canadian Journal of Philosophy* (March, 1986). Also "Beliefs and the Motivation to be Just," *American Philosophical Quarterly* 22 (4), 347–52.
[7]Claudia Card, "Mercy," *Philosophical Review* 81, 1; and "Gender and Moral Luck," forthcoming.
[8]Alison Jaggar, *Feminist Politics and Human Nature* (London: Rowman and Allenheld 1983).
[9]Susan Wolf, "Moral Saints," *Journal of Philosophy* 79 (August, 1982), 419–39.

men and women, myself included, who have been influenced by the writings of Harvard educational psychologist Carol Gilligan, whose book *In a Different Voice* (Harvard 1982; hereafter D.V.) caused a considerable stir both in the popular press and, more slowly, in the philosophical journals.[10]

Let me say quite clearly at this early point that there is little disagreement that justice is a social value of very great importance, and injustice an evil. Nor would those who have worked on theories of justice want to deny that other things matter besides justice. Rawls, for example, incorporates the value of freedom into his account of justice, so that denial of basic freedoms counts as injustice. Rawls also leaves room for a wider theory of the right, of which the theory of justice is just a part. Still, he does claim that justice is the "first" virtue of social institutions, and it is only that claim about priority that I think has been challenged. It is easy to exaggerate the differences of view that exist, and I want to avoid that. The differences are as much in emphasis as in substance, or we can say that they are differences in tone of voice. But these differences do tend to make a difference in approaches to a wide range of topics not just in moral theory but in areas like medical ethics, where the discussion used to be conducted in terms of patients' rights, of informed consent, and so on, but now tends to get conducted in an enlarged moral vocabulary, which draws on what Gilligan calls the ethics of *care* as well as that of *justice*.

For "care" is the new buzz-word. It is not, as Shakespeare's Portia demanded, mercy that is to season justice, but a less authoritarian humanitarian supplement, a felt concern for the good of others and for community with them. The "cold jealous virtue of justice" (Hume) is found to be too cold, and it is "warmer" more communitarian virtues and social ideals that are being called into supplement it. One might say that liberty and equality are being found inadequate without fraternity, except that "fraternity" will be quite the wrong word, if as Gilligan initially suggested, it is *women* who perceive this value most easily. ("Sorority" will do no better, since it is too exclusive, and English has no gender-neuter word for the mutual concern of siblings.) She has since modified this claim, allowing that there are two perspectives on moral and social issues that we all tend to alternate between, and which are not always easy to combine, one of them what she called the justice perspective, the other the care perspective. It is increasingly obvious that there are many male philosophical spokespersons for the care perspective (Laurence Thomas, Lawrence Blum, Michael Stocker) so that it cannot be the prerogative of women. Nevertheless Gilligan still wants to claim that women are most unlikely to take *only* the

[10]For a helpful survey article see Owen Flanagan and Kathryn Jackson, "Justice, Care & Gender: The Kohlberg-Gilligan Debate Revisited," *Ethics*.

justice perspective, as some men are claimed to, at least until some mid-life crisis jolts them into "bifocal" moral vision (see D.V., ch. 6).

Gilligan in her book did not offer any explanatory theory of why there should be any difference between female and male moral outlook, but she did tend to link the naturalness to women of the care perspective with their role as primary care-takers of young children, that is with their parental and specifically maternal role. She avoided the question of whether it is their biological or their social role that is relevant, and some of those who dislike her book are worried precisely by this uncertainty. Some find it retrograde to hail as a special sort of moral wisdom an outlook that may be the product of the socially enforced restriction of women to domestic roles (and the reservation of such roles for them alone). For that might seem to play into the hands of those who still favor such restriction. (Marxists, presumably, will not find it so surprising that moral truths might depend for their initial clear voicing on the social oppression, and memory of it, of those who voice the truths.) Gilligan did in the first chapter of D.V. cite the theory of Nancy Chodorow (as presented in *The Reproduction of Mothering* [Berkeley 1978]) which traces what appears as gender differences in personality to early social development, in particular to the effects of the child's primary caretaker being or not being of the same gender as the child. Later, both in "The Conquistador and the Dark Continent: Reflections on the Nature of Love" (*Daedalus* [Summer 1984]), and "The Origins of Morality in Early Childhood" (in press), she develops this explanation. She postulates two evils that any infant may become aware of, the evil of detachment or isolation from others whose love one needs, and the evil of relative powerlessness and weakness. Two dimensions of moral development are thereby set—one aimed at achieving satisfying community with others, the other aiming at autonomy or equality of power. The relative predominance of one over the other development will depend both upon the relative salience of the two evils in early childhood, and on early and later reinforcement or discouragement in attempts made to guard against these two evils. This provides the germs of a theory about *why*, given current customs of childrearing, it should be mainly women who are not content with only the moral outlook that she calls the justice perspective, necessary though that was and is seen by them to have been to their hard won liberation from sexist oppression. They, like the blacks, used the language of rights and justice to change their own social position, but nevertheless see limitations in that language, according to Gilligan's findings as a moral psychologist. She reports their discontent with the individualist more or less Kantian moral framework that dominates Western moral theory and which influenced moral psychologists such as Lawrence Kohlberg, to whose conception of moral maturity she seeks an alternative. Since the target of Gilligan's criticism is the dominant

Kantian tradition, and since that has been the target also of moral philosophers as diverse in their own views as Bernard Williams, Alasdair MacIntyre, Philippa Foot, Susan Wolf, Claudia Card, her book is of interest as much for its attempt to articulate an alternative to the Kantian justice perspective as for its implicit raising of the question of male bias in Western moral theory, especially liberal-democratic theory. For whether the supposed blind spots of that outlook are due to male bias, or to non-parental bias, or to early traumas of powerlessness or to early resignation to "detachment" from others, we need first to be persuaded that they *are* blind spots before we will have any interest in their cause and cure. Is justice blind to important social values, or at least only one-eyed? What is it that comes into view from the "care perspective" that is not seen from the "justice perspective"?

Gilligan's position here is mostly easily described by contrasting it with that of Kohlberg, against which she developed it. Kohlberg, influenced by Piaget and the Kantian philosophical tradition as developed by John Rawls, developed a theory about typical moral development which saw it to progress from a pre-conventional level, where what is seen to matter is pleasing or not offending parental authority-figures, through a conventional level in which the child tries to fit in with a group, such as a school community, and conform to its standards and rules, to a post-conventional critical level, in which such conventional rules are subjected to tests, and where those tests are of a Utilitarian, or, eventually, a Kantian sort—namely ones that require respect for each person's individual rational will, or autonomy, and conformity to any implicit social contract such wills are deemed to have made, or to any hypothetical ones they would make if thinking clearly. What was found when Kohlberg's questionnaires (mostly by verbal response to verbally sketched moral dilemmas) were applied to female as well as male subjects, Gilligan reports, is that the girls and women not only scored generally lower than the boys and men, but tended to *revert* to the lower stage of the conventional level even after briefly (usually in adolescence) attaining the post conventional level; Piaget's finding that girls were deficient in "the legal sense" was confirmed.

These results led Gilligan to wonder if there might not be a quite different pattern of development to be discerned, at least in female subjects. She therefore conducted interviews designed to elicit not just how far advanced the subjects were towards an appreciation of the nature and importance of Kantian autonomy, but also to find out what the subjects themselves saw as progress or lack of it, what conceptions of moral maturity they came to possess by the time they were adults. She found that although the Kohlberg version of moral maturity as respect for fellow persons, and for their rights as equals (rights including that of free association), did seem shared by many young men, the women tended to speak in a different voice about morality itself and about moral maturity. To quote Gilligan, "Since the reality of interconnexion is experienced by women as given rather than freely contracted, they arrive at an understanding of life that reflects the limits of autonomy and control. As a result, women's development delineates the path not only to a less violent life but also to a maturity realized by interdependence and taking care" (D.V., 172). She writes that there is evidence that "women perceive and construe social reality differently from men, and that these differences center around experiences of attachment and separation . . . because women's sense of integrity appears to be intertwined with an ethics of care, so that to see themselves as women is to see themselves in a relationship of connexion, the major changes in women's lives would seem to involve changes in the understanding and activities of care" (D.V., 171). She contrasts this progressive understanding of care, from merely pleasing others to helping and nurturing, with the sort of progression that is involved in Kohlberg's stages, a progression in the understanding, not of mutual care, but of mutual *respect*, where this has its Kantian overtones of distance, even of some fear for the respected, and where personal autonomy and independence, rather than more satisfactory interdependence, are the paramount values.

This contrast, one cannot but feel, is one which Gilligan might have used the Marxist language of alienation to make. For the main complaint about the Kantian version of a society with its first virtue justice, construed as respect for equal rights to formal goods such as having contracts kept, due process, equal opportunity including opportunity to participate in political activities leading to policy and law-making, to basic liberties of speech, free association and assembly, religious worship, is that none of these goods do much to ensure that the people who have and mutually respect such rights will have any other relationships to one another than the minimal relationship needed to keep such a "civil society" going. They may well be lonely, driven to suicide, apathetic about their work and about participation in political processes, find their lives meaningless and have no wish to leave offspring to face the same meaningless existence. Their rights, and respect for rights, are quite compatible with very great misery, and misery whose causes are not just individual misfortunes and psychic sickness, but social and moral impoverishment.

What Gilligan's older male subjects complain of is precisely this sort of alienation from some dimly glimpsed better possibility for human beings, some richer sort of network of relationships. As one of Gilligan's male subjects put it, "People have real emotional needs to be attached to something, and equality does not give you attachment. Equality fractures society and places on every person the burden of standing on his own two feet" (D.V., 167). It is not just the difficulty of self reliance which is complained of, but its socially "fracturing" effect. Whereas the younger men, in their college years, had seen morality as a matter of reciprocal non-interference, this older man begins to see it as reciprocal attachment. "Morality is . . . essential . . . for creating the kind of environment, interaction between people, that is a prerequisite to the fulfillment of individual goals. If you want other people not to interfere with your pursuit of whatever you are into, you have to play the game," says the spokesman for traditional liberalism (D.V. 98). But if what one is "into" is interconnexion, interdependence rather than an individual autonomy that may involve "detachment," such a version of morality will come to seem inadequate. And Gilligan stresses that the interconnexion that her mature women subjects, and some men, wanted to sustain was not merely freely chosen interconnexion; nor interconnexion between equals, but also the sort of interconnexion that can obtain between a child and her unchosen mother and father, or between a child and her unchosen older and younger siblings, or indeed between most workers and their unchosen fellow workers, or most citizens and their unchosen fellow citizens.

A model of a decent community different from the liberal one is involved in the version of moral maturity that Gilligan voices. It has in many ways more in common with the older religion-linked versions of morality and a good society than with the modern Western liberal ideal. That perhaps is why some find it so dangerous and retrograde. Yet it seems clear that it also has much in common with what we can call Hegelian versions of moral maturity and of social health and malaise, both with Marxist versions and with so-called right-Hegelian views.

Let me try to summarize the main differences, as I see them, between on the one hand Gilligan's version of moral maturity and the sort of social structures that would encourage, express and protect it, and on the other the orthodoxy she sees herself to be challenging. I shall from now on be giving my own interpretation of the significance of her challenges, not merely reporting them.[11] The most obvious point is the challenge to the individualism of the Western tradition, to the fairly entrenched belief in the possibility and desirability of each person pursuing his own good in his own way, constrained only by a minimal formal common good, namely a working legal apparatus that enforces contracts and protects individuals from undue interference by others. Gilligan reminds us that noninterference can, especially for the relatively powerless, such as the very young, amount to neglect, and even between

[11]I have previously written about the significance of her findings for moral philosophy in "What Do Women Want in a Moral Theory?" *Nous* 19 (March 1985); "Trust and Antitrust," *Ethics* 96 (1986); and in "Hume the Women's Moral Theorist" in *Women and Moral Theory, Kittay and Meyers*, ed., forthcoming.

equals can be isolating and alienating. On her less individualist version of individuality, it becomes defined by responses to dependency and to patterns of interconnexion, both chosen and unchosen. It is not something a person *has*, and which she then chooses relationships to suit, but something that develops out of a series of dependencies and inter-dependencies, and responses to them. This conception of individuality is not flatly at odds with, say, Rawls' Kantian one, but there is at least a difference of tone of voice between speaking as Rawls does of each of us having our own rational life plan, which a just society's moral traffic rules will allow us to follow, and which may or may not include close association with other persons, and speaking as Gilligan does of a satisfactory life as involving "progress of affiliative relationship" (D.V., 170) where "the concept of identity expands to include the experience of interconnexion" (D.V., 173). Rawls can allow that progress to Gilligan-style moral maturity may be *a* rational life plan, but not a moral constraint on every life-pattern. The trouble is that it will not do just to say "let this version of morality be an optional extra. Let us agree on the essential minimum, that is on justice and rights, and let whoever wants to go further, and cultivate this more demanding ideal of responsibility and care." For, first, it cannot be satisfactorily cultivated without closer cooperation from others than respect for rights and justice will ensure, and, second, the encouragement of some to cultivate it while others do not could easily lead to exploitation of those who do. It obviously *has* suited some in most societies well enough that others take on the responsibilities of care (for the sick, the helpless, the young) leaving them free to pursue their own less altruistic goods. Volunteer forces of those who accept an ethic of care, operating within a society where the power is exercised and the institutions designed, redesigned, or maintained by those who accept a less communal ethic of minimally constrained self-advancement, will not be the solution. The liberal individualists may be able to "tolerate" the more communally minded, if they keep the liberals' rules, but it is not so clear that the more communally minded can be content with just those rules, nor be content to be tolerated and possibly exploited.

For the moral tradition which developed the concept of rights, autonomy and justice is the same tradition that provided "justifications" of the oppression of those whom the primary rights-holders depended on to do the sort of work they themselves preferred not to do. The domestic work was left to women and slaves, and the liberal morality for rights-holders was surreptitiously supplemented by a different set of demands made on domestic workers. As long as women could be got to assume responsibility for the care of home and children, and to train their children to continue the sexist system, the liberal morality could continue to be the official morality, by turning its eyes away from the contribution made by those it excluded. The long unnoticed moral proletariat were the domestic workers, mostly female. Rights have usually been for the privileged. Talking about laws, and the rights those laws recognize and protect, does not in itself ensure that the group of legislators and rights-holders will not be restricted to some elite. Bills of rights have usually been proclamations of the rights of some in-group, barons, landowners, males, whites, non-foreigners. The "justice perspective," and the legal sense that goes with it, are shadowed by their patriarchal past. What did Kant, the great prophet of autonomy, say in his moral theory about women? He said they were incapable of legislation, not fit to vote, that they needed the guidance of more "rational" males.[12] Autonomy was not for them, only for first class, really rational, persons. It is ironic that Gilligan's original findings in a way confirm Kant's views—it seems that autonomy really may not be for women. Many of them reject that ideal (D.V., 48), and have been found not as good at making rules as are men. But where Kant concludes—"so much the worse for women," we can conclude—"so much the worse for the male fixation on the special skill of drafting legislation, for the bureaucratic mentality of rule worship, and for the male exaggeration of the importance of independence over mutual interdependence."

It is however also true that the moral theories that made the concept of a person's rights central were not just the instruments for excluding some persons, but also the instruments used by those who demanded that more and more persons be included in the favored group. Abolitionists, reformers, women, used the language of rights to assert their claims to inclusion in the group of full members of a community. The tradition of liberal moral theory has in fact developed so as to include the women it had for so long excluded, to include the poor as well as rich, blacks and whites, and so on. Women like Mary Wollstonecraft used the male moral theories to good purpose. So we should not be wholly ungrateful for those male moral theories, for all their objectionable earlier content. They were undoubtedly patriarchal, but they also contained the seeds of the challenge, or antidote, to this patriarchal poison.

But when we transcend the values of the Kantians, we should not forget the facts of history—that those values were the values of the oppressors of women. The Christian church, whose version of the moral law Aquinas codified, in his very legalistic moral theory, still insists on the maleness of the God it worships, and jealously reserves for males all the most powerful positions in its hierarchy. Its patriarchical prejudice is open and avowed. In the secular moral theories of men, the sexist patriarchal prejudice is today often

[12]Immanuel Kant, *Metaphysics of Morals*, sec. 46.

less open, not as blatant as it is in Aquinas, in the later natural law tradition, and in Kant and Hegel, but is often still there. No moral theorist today would say that women are unfit to vote, to make laws, or to rule a nation without powerful male advisors (as most queens had), but the old doctrines die hard. In one of the best male theories we have, John Rawls's theory, a key role is played by the idea of the "head of a household." It is heads of households who are to deliberate behind a "veil of ignorance" of historical details, and of details of their own special situation, to arrive at the "just" constitution for a society. Now of course Rawls does not think or say that "heads" are fathers rather than mothers. But if we have really given up the age-old myth of women needing, as Grotius put it, to be under the "eye" of a more "rational" male protector and master, then how do families come to have any one "head," except by the death or desertion of one parent? They will either be two-headed, or headless. Traces of the old patriarchal poison still remain in even the best contemporary moral theorizing. Few may actually say that women's place is in the home, but there is much muttering, when unemployment figures rise, about how the relatively recent flood of women into the workforce complicates the problem, as if it would be a good thing if women just went back home whenever unemployment rises, to leave the available jobs for the men. We still do not really have a wide acceptance of the equal right of women to employment outside the home. Nor do we have wide acceptance of the equal duty of men to perform those domestic tasks which in no way depend on special female anatomy, namely cooking, cleaning, and the care of weaned children. All sorts of stories (maybe true stories), about children's need for one "primary" parent, who must be the mother if the mother breast feeds the child, shore up the unequal division of domestic responsibility between mothers and fathers, wives and husbands. If we are really to transvalue the values of our patriarchal past, we need to rethink all of those assumptions, really test those psychological theories. And how will men ever develop an understanding of the "ethics of care" if they continue to be shielded or kept from that experience of caring for a dependent child, which complements the experience we all have had of being cared for as dependent children? These experiences form the natural background for the development of moral maturity as Gilligan's women saw it.

Exploitation aside, why would women, once liberated, not be content to have their version of morality merely tolerated? Why should they not see themselves as voluntarily, for their own reasons, taking on *more* than the liberal rules demand, while having no quarrel with the content of those rules themselves, nor with their remaining the only ones that are expected to be generally obeyed? To see why, we need to move on to three more differences between the Kantian liberals (usually contractarians) and their critics. These concern the relative weight put on relationships between equals, and the relative weight put on freedom of choice, and on the authority of intellect over emotions. It is a typical feature of the dominant moral theories and traditions, since Kant, or perhaps since Hobbes, that relationships between equals or those who are deemed equal in some important sense, have been the relations that morality is concerned primarily to regulate. Relationships between those who are clearly unequal in power, such as parents and children, earlier and later generations in relation to one another, states and citizens, doctors and patients, the well and the ill, large states and small states, have had to be shunted to the bottom of the agenda, and then dealt with by some sort of "promotion" of the weaker so that an appearance of virtual equality is achieved. Citizens collectively become equal to states, children are treated as adults-to-be, the ill and dying are treated as continuers of their earlier more potent selves, so that their "rights" could be seen as the rights of equals. This pretence of an equality that is in fact absent may often lead to desirable protection of the weaker, or more dependent. But it somewhat masks the question of what our moral relationships *are* to those who are our superiors or our inferiors in power. A more realistic acceptance of the fact that we begin as helpless children, that at almost every point of our lives we deal with both the more and the less helpless, that equality of power and interdependency, between two persons or groups, is rare and hard to recognize when it does occur, might lead us to a more direct approach to questions concerning the design of institutions structuring these relationships between unequals (families, schools, hospitals, armies) and of the morality of our dealings with the more and the less powerful. One reason why those who agree with the Gilligan version of what morality is about will not want to agree that the liberals' rules are a good minimal set, the only ones we need pressure *everyone* to obey, is that these rules do little to protect the young or the dying or the starving or any of the relatively powerless against neglect, or to ensure an education that will form persons to be *capable* of conforming to an ethics of care and responsibility. Put baldly, and in a way Gilligan certainly has not put it, the liberal morality, if unsupplemented, may *unfit* people to be anything other than what its justifying theories suppose them to be, ones who have no interest in each others' interests. Yet some must take an interest in the next generation's interests. Women's traditional work, of caring for the less powerful, especially for the young, is obviously socially vital. One cannot regard any version of morality that does not ensure that it gets well done as an adequate "minimal morality," any more than we could so regard one that left any concern for more distant future generations an optional extra. A moral theory, it can plausibly be claimed, cannot regard concern for new and future persons as an optional charity left for those with a taste for it. If the morality the theory endorses is to sustain itself, it must provide for its own continuers, not just take out a loan on a carefully encouraged maternal instinct or on the enthusiasm of a self-selected group of environmentalists, who make it their business or hobby to be concerned with what we are doing to mother earth.

The recognition of the importance for all parties of relations between those who are and cannot but be unequal, both of these relations in themselves and for their effect on personality formation and so on other relationships, goes along with a recognition of the plain fact that not all morally important relationships can or should be freely chosen. So far I have discussed three reasons women have not to be content to pursue their own values within the framework of the liberal morality. The first was its dubious record. The second was its inattention to relations of inequality or its pretence of equality. The third reason is its exaggeration of the scope of choice, or its inattention to unchosen relations. Showing up the partial myth of equality among actual members of a community, and of the undesirability of trying to pretend that we are treating all of them as equals, tends to go along with an exposure of the companion myth that moral obligations arise from freely *chosen* associations between such equals. Vulnerable future generations do not choose their dependence on earlier generations. The unequal infant does not choose its place in a family or nation, nor is it treated as free to do as it likes until some association is freely entered into. Nor do its parents always choose their parental role, or freely assume their parental responsibilities any more than we choose our power to affect the conditions in which later generations will live. Gilligan's attention to the version of morality and moral maturity found in women, many of whom had faced a choice of whether or not to have an abortion, and who had at some point become mothers, is attention to the perceived inadequacy of the language of rights to help in such choices or to guide them in their parental role. It would not be much of an exaggeration to call the Gilligan "different voice" the voice of the potential parents. The emphasis on care goes with a recognition of the often unchosen nature of the responsibilities of those who give care, both of children who care for their aged or infirm parents, and of parents who care for the children they in fact have. Contract soon ceases to seem the paradigm source of moral obligation once we attend to parental responsibility, and justice as a virtue of social institutions will come to seem at best only first equal with the virtue, whatever its name, that ensures that each new generation is made appropriately welcome and prepared for their adult lives.

This all constitutes a belated reminder to Western moral theorists of a fact they have always known, that as Adam Ferguson, and David Hume before him emphasized, we are born into families, and the first society we belong to, one that fits or misfits us for later ones, is the small society of parents (or some sort of child-attendants) and children, exhibiting as it may both relationships of near equality and of inequality in power. This simple reminder, with the fairly considerable implications it can have for the plausibility of contractarian moral theory, is at the same time a reminder of the role of human emotions as much as human reason and will in moral development as it actually comes about. The fourth feature of the Gilligan challenge to liberal orthodoxy is a challenge to its typical *rationalism*, or intellectualism, to its assumption that we need not worry what passions persons have, as long as their rational wills can control them. This Kantian picture of a controlling reason dictating to possibly unruly passions also tends to seem less useful when we are led to consider what sort of person we need to fill the role of parent, or indeed want in any close relationship. It might be important for father figures to have rational control over their violent urges to beat to death the children whose screams enrage them, but more than control of such nasty passions seems needed in the mother or primary parent, or parent-substitute, by most psychological theories. They need to love their children, not just to control their irritation. So the emphasis in Kantian theories on rational control of emotions, rather than on cultivating desirable forms of emotion, is challenged by Gilligan, along with the challenge to the assumption of the centrality of autonomy, or relations between equals, and of freely chosen relations.

The same set of challenges to "orthodox" liberal moral theory has come not just from Gilligan and other women, who are reminding other moral theorists of the role of the family as a social institution and as an influence on the other relationships people want to or are capable of sustaining, but also, as I noted at the start, from an otherwise fairly diverse group of men, ranging from those influenced by both Hegelian and Christian traditions (MacIntyre) to all varieties of other backgrounds. From this group I want to draw attention to the work of one philosopher in particular, namely Laurence Thomas, the author of a fairly remarkable article[13] in which he finds sexism to be a more intractable social evil than racism. In a series of articles, and a forthcoming book,[14] Thomas makes a strong case for the importance of supplementing a concern for justice and respect for rights with an emphasis on equally needed virtues, and on virtues seen as appropriate *emotional* as well as rational capacities. Like Gilligan (and unlike MacIntyre) Thomas gives a lot of attention to the childhood beginnings of moral and social capacities, to the role of parental love in making that possible, and to the emotional as well as the cognitive development we have reason to think both possible and desirable in human persons.

[13]Laurence Thomas, "Sexism and Racism: Some Conceptual Differences," *Ethics* 90 (1980), 239–50; republished in *Philosophy, Sex and Language*, Vetterling-Braggin, ed. (Totowa, NJ: Littlefield Adams 1980).

[14]See articles listed in note 6, above. The forthcoming book has the title *A Psychology of Moral Character*.

It is clear, I think, that the best moral theory has to be a cooperative product of women and men, has to harmonize justice and care. The morality it theorizes about is after all for all persons, for men and for women, and will need their combined insights. As Gilligan said (D.V., 174), what we need now is a "marriage" of the old male and the newly articulated female insights. If she is right about the special moral aptitudes of women, it will most likely be the women who propose the marriage, since they are the ones with more natural empathy, with the better diplomatic skills, the ones more likely to shoulder responsibility and take moral initiative, and the ones who find it easiest to empathize and care about how the other party feels. Then, once there is this union of male and female moral wisdom, we maybe can teach each other the moral skills each gender currently lacks, so that the gender difference in moral outlook that Gilligan found will slowly become less marked.

For Further Reflection

1. What are the two major approaches to ethics that Baier contrasts?
2. What criticisms does she lodge against justice-oriented moral theories? Do you agree with her?
3. What is her opinion of care-centered views offered by thinkers such as Alasdair MacIntyre and Susan Wolf?

The Ethics of Care

VIRGINIA HELD

Virginia Held has taught philosophy at Hunter College and The Graduate Center of the City University of New York. In this reading, she explores the moral perspective known as the ethics of care, identifying its central themes, showing how it relates to an "ethic of justice," and distinguishing it from virtue ethics.

The ethics of care is only a few decades old. Some theorists do not like the term "care" to designate this approach to moral issues and have tried substituting "the ethic of love," or "relational ethics," but the discourse keeps returning to "care" as the so far more satisfactory of the terms considered, though dissatisfactions with it remain. The concept of care has the advantage of not losing sight of the work involved in caring for people and of not lending itself to the interpretation of morality as ideal but impractical to which advocates of the ethics of care often object. Care is both value and practice.

By now, the ethics of care has moved far beyond its original formulations, and any attempt to evaluate it should consider much more than the one or two early works so frequently cited. It has been developed as a moral theory relevant not only to the so-called private realms of family and friendship but to medical practice, law, political life, the organization of society, war, and international relations.

The ethics of care is sometimes seen as a potential moral theory to be substituted for such dominant moral theories as Kantian ethics, utilitarianism, or Aristotelian virtue ethics. It is sometimes seen as a form of virtue ethics. It is almost always developed as emphasizing neglected moral considerations of at least as much importance as the considerations central to moralities of justice and rights or of utility and preference satisfaction. And many who contribute to the understanding of the ethics of care seek to integrate the moral considerations, such as justice, which other moral theories have clarified, satisfactorily with those of care, though they often see the need to reconceptualize these considerations.

FEATURES OF THE ETHICS OF CARE

Some advocates of the ethics of care resist generalizing this approach into something that can be fitted into the form of a moral theory. They see it as a mosaic of insights and value the way it is sensitive to contextual nuance and particular narratives rather than making the abstract and universal claims of more familiar moral theories. Still, I think one can discern among various versions of the ethics of care a number of major features.

First, the central focus of the ethics of care is on the compelling moral salience of attending to and meeting the needs of the particular others for whom we take responsibility. Caring for one's child, for instance, may well and defensibly be at the forefront of a person's moral concerns. The ethics of care recognizes that human beings are dependent for many years of their lives, that the moral claim of those dependent on us for the care they need is pressing, and that there are highly important moral aspects in developing the relations of caring that enable human beings to live and progress. All persons need care for at least their early years. Prospects for human progress and flourishing hinge fundamentally on the care that those needing it receive, and the ethics of care stresses the moral force of the responsibility to respond to the needs of the dependent. Many persons will become ill and dependent for some periods of their later lives, including in frail old age, and some who are permanently disabled will need care the whole of their lives. Moralities built on the image of the independent, autonomous, rational individual largely overlook the reality of human dependence and the morality for which it calls. The ethics of care attends to this central concern of human life and delineates the moral values involved. It refuses to relegate care to a realm "outside morality." How caring for particular others should be reconciled with the claims of, for instance, universal justice is an issue that needs to be addressed. But the ethics of care starts with the moral claims of particular others, for instance, of one's child, whose claims can be compelling regardless of universal principles.

Second, in the epistemological process of trying to understand what morality would recommend and what it would be morally best for us to do and to be, the ethics of care values emotion rather than rejects it. Not all emotion is valued, of course, but in contrast with the dominant rationalist approaches, such emotions as sympathy, empathy, sensitivity, and responsiveness are seen as the kind of moral emotions that need to be cultivated not only to help in the implementation of the dictates of reason but to better ascertain what morality recommends. Even anger may be a component of the moral indignation that should be felt when people are treated unjustly or inhumanely, and it may contribute to (rather than interfere with) an appropriate interpretation of the moral wrong. This is not to say that raw emotion can be a guide to morality; feelings need to be reflected on and educated. But from the care perspective, moral inquiries that rely entirely on reason and rationalistic deductions or calculations are seen as deficient.

The emotions that are typically considered and rejected in rationalistic moral theories are the egoistic feelings that undermine universal moral norms, the favoritism that interferes with impartiality, and the aggressive and vengeful impulses for which morality is to provide restraints. The ethics of care, in contrast, typically appreciates the emotions and relational capabilities that enable morally concerned persons in actual interpersonal contexts to understand what would be best. Since even the helpful emotions can often become misguided or worse—as when excessive empathy with others leads to a wrongful degree of self-denial or when benevolent concern crosses over into controlling domination—we need an *ethics* of care, not just care itself. The various aspects and expressions of care and caring relations need to be subjected to moral scrutiny and *evaluated*, not just observed and described.

Third, the ethics of care rejects the view of the dominant moral theories that the more abstract the reasoning about a moral problem the better because the more likely to avoid bias and arbitrariness, the more nearly to achieve impartiality. The ethics of care respects rather than removes itself from the claims of particular others with whom we share actual relationships. It calls into question the universalistic and abstract rules of the dominant theories. When the latter consider such actual relations as between a parent and child, if they say anything about them at all, they may see them as permitted and cultivating them a preference that a person may have. Or they may recognize a universal obligation for all parents to care for their children. But they do not permit actual relations ever to take priority over the requirements of impartiality. As Brian Barry expresses this view, there can be universal rules permitting people to favor their friends in certain contexts, such as deciding to whom to give holiday gifts, but the latter partiality is morally acceptable only because universal rules have already so judged it. The ethics of care, in contrast, is skeptical of such abstraction and reliance on universal rules and questions the priority given to them. To most advocates of the ethics of care, the compelling moral claim of the particular other may be valid even when it conflicts with the requirement usually made by moral theories that moral judgments be universalizeable, and this is of fundamental moral importance. Hence the potential conflict between care and justice, friendship and impartiality, loyalty and universality. To others, however, there need be no conflict if universal judgments come to incorporate appropriately the norms of care previously disregarded.

Annette Baier considers how a feminist approach to morality differs from a Kantian one and Kant's claim that women are incapable of being fully moral because of their reliance on emotion rather than reason. She writes, "Where Kant concludes 'so much the worse for women,' we can conclude 'so much the worse for the male fixation on the special skill of drafting legislation, for the bureaucratic mentality of rule worship, and for the male exaggeration of the importance of independence over mutual interdependence.' "

Margaret Walker contrasts what she sees as feminist "moral understanding" with what has traditionally been thought of as moral "knowledge." She sees the moral understanding she advocates as involving "attention, contextual and narrative appreciation, and communication in the event of moral deliberation." This alternative moral epistemology holds that "the adequacy of moral understanding decreases as its form approaches generality through abstraction."

The ethics of care may seek to limit the applicability of universal rules to certain domains where they are more appropriate, like the domain of law, and resist their extension to other domains. Such rules may simply be inappropriate in, for instance, the contexts of family and friendship, yet relations in these domains should certainly be *evaluated*, not merely described, hence morality should not be limited to abstract rules. We should be able to give moral guidance concerning actual relations that are trusting, considerate, and caring and concerning those that are not.

Dominant moral theories tend to interpret moral problems as if they were conflicts between egoistic individual interests on the one hand, and universal moral principles on the other. The extremes of "selfish individual" and "humanity" are recognized, but what lies between these is often overlooked. The ethics of care, in contrast, focuses especially on the area between these extremes. Those who conscientiously care for others are not seeking primarily to further their own *individual* interests; their interests are intertwined with the persons they care for. Neither are they acting for the sake of *all others or humanity in general*; they seek instead to preserve or promote an actual human relation between themselves and *particular others*. Persons in caring relations are acting for self-and-other together. Their characteristic stance is neither egoistic nor altruistic; these are the options in a conflictual situation, but the well-being of a caring relation involves the cooperative well-being of those in the relation and the well-being of the relation itself.

In trying to overcome the attitudes and problems of tribalism and religious intolerance, dominant moralities have tended to assimilate the domains of family and friendship to the tribal, or to a source of the unfair favoring of one's own. Or they have seen the attachments people have in these areas as among the nonmoral private preferences people are permitted to pursue if restrained by impartial moral norms. The ethics of care recognizes the *moral* value and importance of relations of family and friendship and the need for *moral* guidance in these domains to understand how existing relations should often be changed and new ones developed. Having grasped the value of caring relations in such contexts as these more personal ones, the ethics of care then often examines social and political arrangements in the light of these values. In its more developed forms, the ethics of care as a feminist ethic offers suggestions for the radical transformation of society. It demands not just equality for women in existing structures of society but equal consideration for the experience that reveals the values, importance, and moral significance, of caring.

A fourth characteristic of the ethics of care is that like much feminist thought in many areas, it reconceptualizes traditional notions about the public and the private. The traditional view, built into the dominant moral theories, is that the household is a private sphere beyond politics into which government, based on consent, should not intrude. Feminists have shown how the greater social, political, economic, and cultural power of men has structured this "private" sphere to the disadvantage of women and children, rendering them vulnerable to domestic violence without outside interference, often leaving women economically dependent on men and subject to a highly inequitable division of labour in the family. The law has not hesitated to intervene into women's private decisions concerning reproduction but has been highly reluctant to intrude on men's exercise of coercive power within the "castles" of their homes.

Dominant moral theories have seen "public" life as relevant to morality while missing the moral significance of the "private" domains of family and friendship. Thus the dominant theories have assumed that morality should be sought for unrelated, independent, and mutually indifferent individuals assumed to be equal. They have posited an abstract, fully rational "agent as such" from which to construct morality, while missing the moral issues that arise between interconnected persons in the contexts of family, friendship, and social groups. In the context of the family, it is typical for relations to be between persons with highly unequal power who did not choose the ties and obligations in which they find themselves enmeshed. For instance, no child can choose her parents yet she may well have obligations to care for them. Relations of this kind are standardly noncontractual, and conceptualizing them as contractual would often undermine or at least obscure the trust on which their worth depends. The ethics of care addresses rather than neglects moral issues arising in relations among the unequal and dependent, relations that are often laden with emotion and involuntary, and then notices how often these attributes apply not only in the household but in the wider society as well. For instance, persons do not choose which gender, racial, class, ethnic, religious, national, or cultural groups to be brought up in, yet these sorts of ties may be important aspects of who they are and how their experience can contribute to moral understanding.

A fifth characteristic of the ethics of care is the conception of persons with which it begins. This will be dealt with in the next section.

THE CRITIQUE OF LIBERAL INDIVIDUALISM

The ethics of care usually works with a conception of persons as relational, rather than as the self-sufficient independent individuals of the dominant moral theories. The dominant theories can be interpreted as importing into moral theory a concept of the person developed primarily for liberal political and economic theory, seeing the person as a rational, autonomous agent, or a self-interested individual. On this view, society is made up of "independent, autonomous units who cooperate only when the terms of cooperation are such as to make it further the ends of each of the parties," in Brian Barry's words. Or, if they are Kantians, they refrain from actions that they could not will to be universal laws to which all fully rational and autonomous individual agents could agree. What such views hold, in Michael Sandel's critique of them, is that "what separates us is in some important sense prior to what connects us—epistemologically prior as well as morally prior. We are distinct individuals first and *then* we form relationships." In Martha Nussbaum's liberal feminist morality, "the flourishing of human beings taken one by one is both analytically and normatively prior to the flourishing" of any group.

The ethics of care, in contrast, characteristically sees persons as relational and interdependent, morally and epistemologically. Every person starts out as a child dependent on those providing us care, and we remain interdependent with others in thoroughly fundamental ways throughout our lives. That we can think and act as if we were independent depends on a network of social relations making it possible for us to do so. And our relations are part of what constitute our identity. This is not to say that we cannot become autonomous; feminists have done much interesting work developing an alternative conception of autonomy in place of the liberal individualist one. Feminists have much experience rejecting or reconstituting relational ties that are oppressive. But it means that from the perspective of an ethics of care, to construct morality *as if* we were Robinson Crusoes, or, to use Hobbes's image, mushrooms sprung from nowhere, is misleading. As Eva Kittay writes, this conception fosters the illusion that society is composed of free, equal, and independent individuals who can choose to associate with one another or not. It obscures the very real facts of dependency for everyone when they are young, for most people at various periods in their lives when they are ill or old and infirm, for some who are disabled, and for all those engaged in unpaid "dependency work." And it obscures the innumerable ways persons and groups are interdependent in the modern world.

Not only does the liberal individualist conception of the person foster a false picture of society and the persons in it, it is, from the perspective of the ethics of care, impoverished also as an ideal. The ethics of care values the ties we have with particular other persons and the actual relationships that partly constitute our identity. Although persons often may and should reshape their relations with others—distancing themselves from some persons and groups and developing or strengthening ties with others—the autonomy sought within the ethics of care is a capacity to reshape and cultivate new relations, not to ever more closely resemble the unencumbered abstract rational self of liberal political and moral theories. Those motivated by the ethics of care would seek to become more admirable relational persons in better caring relations.

Even if the liberal ideal is meant only to instruct us on what would be rational in the terms of its ideal model, thinking of persons as the model presents them has effects that should not be welcomed. As Annette Baier writes, "Liberal morality, if unsupplemented, may *unfit* people to be anything other than what its justifying theories suppose them to be, ones who have no interest in each others' interests." There is strong empirical evidence of how adopting a theoretical model can lead to behavior that mirrors it. Various studies show that studying economics, with its "repeated and intensive exposure to a model whose unequivocal prediction" is that people will decide what to do on the basis of self-interest, leads economics students to be less cooperative and more inclined to free ride than other students.

The conception of the person adopted by the dominant moral theories provides moralities at best suitable for legal, political, and economic interactions between relative strangers, once adequate trust exists for them to form a political entity. The ethics of care is, instead, hospitable to the relatedness of persons. It sees many of our responsibilities as not freely entered into but presented to us by the accidents of our embeddedness in familial and social and historical contexts. It often calls on us to *take* responsibility, while liberal individualist morality focuses on how we should leave each other alone. The view of persons as embedded and encumbered seems fundamental to much feminist thinking about morality and especially to the ethics of care.

JUSTICE AND CARE

Some conceptions of the ethics of care see it as contrasting with an ethic of justice in ways that suggest one must choose between them. Carol Gilligan's suggestion of alternative perspectives in interpreting and organizing the elements of a moral problem lent itself to this implication; she herself used the metaphor of the ambiguous figure of the vase and the faces, from psychological research on perception, to illustrate how one could see a problem as either a problem of justice or a problem of care, but not as both simultaneously.

An ethic of justice focuses on questions of fairness, equality, individual rights, abstract principles, and the consistent application of them. An ethic of care focuses on attentiveness, trust, responsiveness to need, narrative nuance, and cultivating caring relations. Whereas an ethic of justice seeks a fair solution between competing individual interests and rights, an ethic of care sees the interests of carers and cared-for as importantly intertwined rather than as simply competing. Whereas justice protects equality and freedom, care fosters social bonds and cooperation.

These are very different emphases in what morality should consider. Yet both deal with what seems of great moral importance. This has led many to explore how they might be combined in a satisfactory morality. One can persuasively argue, for instance, that justice is needed in such contexts of care as the family, to protect against violence and the unfair division of labor or treatment of children. One can also persuasively argue that care is needed in such contexts of justice as the streets and the courts, where persons should be treated humanely, and in the way education and health and welfare should be dealt with as social responsibilities. The implication may be that justice and care should not be separated into different "ethics," that, in Sara Ruddick's proposed approach, "justice is always seen in tandem with care."

Few would hold that considerations of justice have no place at all in care. One would not be caring well for two children, for instance, if one showed a persistent favoritism toward one of them that could not be justified on the basis of some such factor as greater need. The issues are rather what constellation of values have priority and which predominate in the practices of the ethics of care and the ethics of justice. It is quite possible to delineate significant differences between them. In the dominant moral theories of the ethics of justice, the values of equality, impartiality, fair distribution, and noninterference have priority; in practices of justice, individual rights are protected, impartial judgments are arrived at, punishments are deserved, and equal treatment is sought. In contrast, in the ethics of care, the values of trust, solidarity, mutual concern, and empathetic responsiveness have priority; in practices of care, relationships are cultivated, needs are responded to, and sensitivity is demonstrated.

An extended effort to integrate care and justice is offered by Diemut Bubeck. She makes clear that she "endorse[s] the ethic of care as a system of concepts, values, and ideas, arising from the practice of care as an organic part of this practice and responding to its material requirements, notably the meeting of needs." Yet her primary interest is in understanding the exploitation of women, which she sees as tied to the way women do most of the unpaid work of caring. She argues that such principles as equality in care and the minimization of harm are tacitly, if not explicitly, embedded in the practice of care, as carers whose capacities and time for engaging in caring labor are limited must decide how to respond to various others in need of being cared for. She writes that "far from being extraneous impositions...considerations of justice arise from within the practice of care itself and therefore are an important part of the ethic of care, properly understood." The ethics of care must thus also concern itself with the justice (or lack of it) of the ways the tasks of caring are distributed in society. Traditionally, women have been expected to do most of the caring work that needs to be done; the sexual division of labor exploits women by extracting unpaid care labor from them, making women less able than men to engage in paid work. "Femininity" constructs women as carers, contributing to the constraints by which women are pressed into accepting the sexual division of labor. An ethic of care that extols caring but that fails to be concerned with how the burdens of caring are distributed contributes to the exploitation of women, and of the minority groups whose members perform much of the paid but ill-paid work of caring in affluent households, in day care centers, hospitals, nursing homes, and the like.

The question remains, however, whether justice should be thought to be incorporated into any ethic of care that will be adequate or whether we should keep the notions of justice and care and their associated ethics conceptually distinct. There is much to be said for recognizing how the ethics of care values interrelatedness and responsiveness to the needs of particular others, how the ethics of justice values fairness and rights, and how these are different emphases. Too much integration will lose sight of these valid differences. I am more inclined to say that an adequate, comprehensive moral theory will have to include the insights of both the ethics of care and the ethics of justice, among other insights, rather than that either of these can be incorporated into the other in the sense of supposing that it can provide the grounds for the judgments characteristically found in the other. Equitable caring is not necessarily better caring, it is fairer caring. And humane justice is not necessarily better justice, it is more caring justice.

Almost no advocates of the ethics of care are willing to see it as a moral outlook less valuable than the dominant ethics of justice. To imagine that the concerns of care can merely be added on to the dominant theories, as, for instance, Stephen Darwall suggests, is seen as unsatisfactory. Confining the ethics of care to the private sphere while holding it unsuitable for public life, as Nel Noddings did at first and as many accounts of it suggest, is also to be rejected. But how care and justice are to be meshed without losing sight of their differing priorities is a task still being worked on.

My own suggestions for integrating care and justice are to keep these concepts conceptually distinct and to delineate the domains in which they should have priority. In the realm of law, for instance, justice and the assurance of rights should have priority, although the humane considerations of care should not be absent. In the realm of the family and among friends, priority should be given to expansive care, though the basic requirements of justice surely should also be met. But these are the clearest cases; others will combine moral urgencies. Universal human rights (including the social and economic ones as well as the political and civil) should certainly be respected, but promoting care across continents may be a more promising way to achieve this than mere rational recognition. When needs are desperate, justice may be a lessened requirement on shared responsibility for meeting needs, although this rarely excuses violations of rights. At the level of what constitutes a society in the first place, a domain within which rights are to be assured and care provided, appeal must be made to something like the often weak but not negligible caring relations among persons that enable them to recognize each other as members of the same society. Such recognition must eventually be global; in the meantime, the civil society without which the liberal institutions of justice cannot function presumes a background of some degree of caring relations rather than of merely competing individuals. Furthermore, considerations of care provide a more fruitful basis than considerations of justice for deciding much about how society should be structured, for instance, how extensive or how restricted markets should be. And in the course of protecting the rights that ought to be recognized, such as those to basic necessities, policies that express the caring of the community for all its members will be better policies than those that grudgingly, though fairly, issue an allotment to those deemed unfit.

Care is probably the most deeply fundamental value. There can be care without justice: There has historically been little justice in the family, but care and life have gone on without it. There can be no justice without care, however, for without care no child would survive and there would be no persons to respect.

Care may thus provide the wider and deeper ethics within which justice should be sought, as when persons in caring relations may sometimes compete and in doing so should treat each other fairly, or, at the level of society, within caring relations of the thinner kind we can agree to treat each other for limited purposes as if we were the abstract individuals of liberal theory. But although care may be the more fundamental value, it may well be that the ethics of care does not itself provide adequate theoretical resources for dealing with issues of justice. Within its appropriate sphere and for its relevant questions, the ethics of justice may be best for what we seek. What should be resisted is the traditional inclination to expand the reach of justice in such a way that it is mistakenly imagined to be able to give us a comprehensive morality suitable for all moral questions.

IMPLICATIONS FOR SOCIETY

Many advocates of the ethics of care argue for its relevance in social and political and economic life. Sara Ruddick shows its implications for efforts to achieve peace. I argue that as we see the deficiencies of the contractual model of human relations within the household, we can see them also in the world beyond and begin to think about how society should be reorganized to be hospitable to care, rather than continuing to marginalize it. We can see how not only does every domain of society need transformation in light of the values of care but so would the relations between such domains if we took care seriously, as care would move to the center of our attention and become a primary concern of society. Instead of a society dominated by conflict restrained by law and preoccupied with economic gain, we might have a society that saw as its most important task the flourishing of children and the development of caring relations, not only in personal contexts but among citizens and using governmental institutions. We would see that instead of abandoning culture to the dictates of the marketplace, we should make it possible for culture to develop in ways best able to enlighten and enrich human life.

Joan Tronto argues for the political implications of the ethics of care, seeing care as a political as well as moral ideal advocating the meeting of needs for care as "the highest social goal." She shows how unacceptable are current arrangements for providing care: "Caring activities are devalued, underpaid, and disproportionately occupied by the relatively powerless in society." Bubeck, Kittay, and many others argue forcefully that care must be seen as a public concern, not relegated to the private responsibility of women, the inadequacy and arbitrariness of private charities, or the vagaries and distortions of the market. In her recent book *Starting at Home*, Noddings explores what a caring society would be like.

When we concern ourselves with caring relations between more distant others, this care should not be thought to reduce to the mere "caring about" that has little to do with the face-to-face interactions of caring labor and can easily become paternalistic or patronizing. The same characteristics of attentiveness, responsiveness to needs, and understanding situations from the points of view of others should characterize caring when the participants are more distant. This also requires the work of understanding and of expending varieties of effort.

Given how care is a value with the widest possible social implications, it is unfortunate that many who look at the ethics of care continue to suppose it is a "family ethics," confined to the "private" sphere. Although some of its earliest formulations suggested this, and some of its related values are to be seen most clearly in personal contexts, an adequate understanding of the ethics of care should recognize that it elaborates values as fundamental and as relevant to political institutions and to how society is organized, as those of justice. Perhaps its values are even more fundamental and more relevant to life in society than those traditionally relied on.

Instead of seeing the corporate sector, and military strength, and government and law as the most important segments of society deserving the highest levels of wealth and power, a caring society might see the tasks of bringing up children, educating its members, meeting the needs of all, achieving peace and treasuring the environment, and doing these in the best ways possible to be that to which the greatest social efforts of all should be devoted. One can recognize that something comparable to legal constraints and police enforcement, including at a global level, may always be necessary for special cases, but also that caring societies could greatly decrease the need for them. The social changes a focus on care would require would be as profound as can be imagined.

The ethics of care as it has developed is most certainly not limited to the sphere of family and personal relations. When its social and political implications are understood, it is a radical ethic calling for a profound restructuring of society. And it has the resources for dealing with power and violence.

THE ETHICS OF CARE AND VIRTUE ETHICS

Insofar as the ethics of care wishes to cultivate in persons the characteristics of a caring person and the skills of activities of caring, might an ethic of care be assimilated to virtue theory?

To some philosophers, the ethics of care is a form of virtue ethics. Several of the contributors to the volume *Feminists Doing Ethics* adopt this view. Leading virtue theorist Michael Slote argues extensively for the position that caring is the primary virtue and that a morality based on the motive of caring can offer a general account of right and wrong action and political justice.

Certainly there are some similarities between the ethics of care and virtue theory. Both examine practices and the moral values they embody. Both see more hope for moral development in reforming practices than in reasoning from abstract rules. Both understand that the practices of morality must be cultivated, nurtured, shaped.

Until recently, however, virtue theory has not paid adequate attention to the practices of caring in which women have been so heavily engaged. Although this might be corrected, virtue theory has characteristically seen the virtues as incorporated in various traditions or traditional communities. In contrast, the ethics of care as a feminist ethic is wary of existing traditions and traditional communities: Virtually all are patriarchal. The ethics of care envisions caring not as practiced under male domination, but as it should be practiced in postpatriarchal society, of which we do not yet have traditions or wide experience. Individual egalitarian families are still surrounded by inegalitarian social and cultural influences.

In my view, although there are similarities between them and although to be caring is no doubt a virtue, the ethics of care is not simply a kind of virtue ethics. Virtue ethics focuses especially on the states of character of individuals, whereas the ethics of care concerns itself especially with caring *relations*. Caring relations have primary value.

If virtue ethics is interpreted, as with Slote, as primarily a matter of motives, it may neglect unduly the labor and objective results of caring, as Bubeck's emphasis on actually meeting needs highlights. Caring is not only a question of motive or attitude or virtue. On the other hand, Bubeck's account is unduly close to a utilitarian interpretation of meeting needs, neglecting that care *also* has an aspect of motive and virtue. If virtue ethics is interpreted as less restricted to motives, and if it takes adequate account of the results of the virtuous person's activities for the persons cared for, it may better include the concerns of the ethics of care. It would still, however, focus on the dispositions of individuals, whereas the ethics of care focuses on social relations and the social practices and values that sustain them. The traditional Man of Virtue may be almost as haunted by his patriarchal past as the Man of Reason. The work of care has certainly not been among the virtuous activities to which he has adequately attended.

The ethics of care, in my view, is a distinctive ethical outlook, distinct even from virtue ethics. Certainly it has precursors, and such virtue theorists as Aristotle, Hume, and the moral sentimentalists contribute importantly to it. As a feminist ethic, the ethics of care is certainly not a mere description or generalization of women's attitudes and activities as developed under patriarchal conditions. To be acceptable, it must be a *feminist* ethic, open to both women and men to adopt. But in being feminist, it is different from the ethics of its precursors and different as well from virtue ethics.

The ethics of care is sometimes thought inadequate because of its inability to provide definite answers in cases of conflicting moral demands. Virtue theory has similarly been criticized for offering no more than what detractors call a "bag of virtues," with no clear indication of how to prioritize the virtues or apply their requirements, especially when they seem to conflict. Defenders of the ethics of care respond that the adequacy of the definite answers provided by, for instance, utilitarian and Kantian moral theories is illusory. Cost-benefit analysis is a good example of a form of utilitarian calculation that purports to provide clear answers to questions about what we ought to do, but from the point of view of moral understanding, its answers are notoriously dubious. So, too, often are casuistic reasonings about deontological rules. To advocates of the ethics of care, its alternative moral epistemology seems better. It stresses sensitivity to the multiple relevant considerations in particular contexts, cultivating the traits of character and of relationship that sustain caring, and promoting the dialogue that corrects and enriches the perspective of any one individual. The ethics of care is hospitable to the methods of discourse ethics, though with an emphasis on actual dialogue that empowers its participants to express themselves rather than on discourse so ideal that actual differences of viewpoint fall away.

For Further Reflection

1. Can an ethic of justice be plausibly combined with the ethics of care? Are they compatible at all? Explain.

2. Do you agree with the criticisms of the liberal individualist conception of a person? How does this conception compare with the ethics of care conception of a person? Is one better than the other—or does each capture a part of the truth?
3. Should the ethics of care be viewed as a type of virtue ethics? Why or why not?

Further Readings for Chapter 7

Simone De Beauvoir. *The Second Sex*. New York: Bantam, 1961.

Carol Gilligan. *In a Different Voice: Psychological Theory and Women's Development*. Cambridge, Mass.: Harvard University Press, 1982.

Virginia Held, ed. *Justice and Care: Essential Readings in Feminist Ethics*. Oxford: Westview Press, 1995.

———.*Feminist Morality*. Chicago: University of Chicago Press, 1993.

Nel Noddings. *Caring: A Female Approach to Ethics and Moral Education*. Berkeley: University of California Press, 1986.

Susan Moller Okin. *Justice, Gender, and the Family*. New York: Basic Books, 1989.

PART III

Moral Issues

In this part of our book we examine two related, vitally important issues in moral theory: egoism and the question "Why should we be moral?" (Chapter 8); and the question of whether life has meaning (Chapter 9). As you will see, these questions are related. If life has no meaning, it may not make sense to be moral all of the time or care about morality. But if life does have meaning, morality matters.

CHAPTER 8

Ethics and Egoism

Why Should We Be Moral?

Why should we be moral? That is, you may ask yourself, Why should I do what morality requires even when it may not be in my best interest? Or, Is it really in my best interest to be moral all the time, even if I fail to realize it? Or, Is morality only *sometimes* in my best interest—when it depends on group cooperation? For example, people can run up charges on their credit cards and not pay them, perhaps moving to a different country to escape the debt. So it might be in George's interest to charge up his credit card and then move to another country. But if it is not in his interest to move, he may get into trouble if he doesn't pay his credit card bill, and he will get a bad credit rating, which will affect his future prospects of obtaining loans. So in this case, it is in George's interest to comply with moral rules. But suppose he can cheat and get away with it? Say he obtains someone else's brilliant research paper and turns it in as his own. No one is likely ever to find out. Why shouldn't he cheat? Of course, he won't like it if other people do the same—and if enough people cheat, grades will become meaningless. But then, as he profits from his immorality, he can contribute some money back into moral reform, so that more people will be motivated to be good.

Is there anything wrong with this reasoning?

In our first reading, Glaucon, Plato's brother, asks Socrates why we should be moral. He then tells the story of the shepherd Gyges, who finds a ring that allows him to become invisible. What fun he can have! He can serve his interests with impunity and not be discovered. But Socrates rejects this view and argues that Gyges and his ilk never get away with immorality. Justice is intrinsically valuable, like health. The good is really good for you, so that if you act immorally, you really are harming yourself.

But many reject Socrates' way of looking at the matter. They accuse him of supposing an objective world of values or a divine law that ensures that those who act selfishly will be punished—through karma or by God. But take away the notion of God or karma and the picture breaks down.

Our second reading is a selection from Ayn Rand's *Atlas Shrugged* in which she argues that ethical egoism is the correct moral theory and that altruism is irrational: "Parasites, moochers, looters, brutes and thugs can be of no value to a human being—nor can he gain any benefit from living in a society that treats him as a sacrificial animal and penalizes him for his virtues in order to reward *them* or their vices, which means a society based on the ethics of altruism." Rand defines *altruism* as the ethics that tells one "to sacrifice one's life. Altruism erodes men's capacity to grasp the value of an individual's life; it reveals a mind from which the reality of a human being has been wiped out."

In our third reading, Louis P. Pojman criticizes Ayn Rand's philosophy of egoism as one-sided and oblivious to the importance of altruism. In particular, Rand fails to distinguish between *selfishness* and *self-interest*. *Selfishness* is enhancing your own welfare even to the detriment of others, whereas *self-interest* is the legitimate concern we have to satisfy our preferences and interests. Pojman argues for a moderate position that recognizes the moral validity of both limited egoism and reciprocal altruism.

In our final reading, James Rachels's "A Critique of Ethical Egoism," we examine a systematic critique of ethical egoism.

The Ring of Gyges

PLATO

The Greek philosopher Plato (427–347 B.C.) is considered one of the greatest thinkers who ever lived. He was the student of Socrates and the teacher of Aristotle. The following dialogue is from his masterpiece, the *Republic*, in which Plato's brother, Glaucon, asks Socrates whether justice is good in itself or only a necessary evil. That is, it is often thought that morality is simply a compromise between our longing to dominate and our fear of being dominated by others. Since we can't dominate everyone else and fear being dominated by others, we enter into a social contract to live by mutually coercive rules, which we name morality. To illustrate his point, Glaucon tells the story of a shepherd named Gyges who comes upon a ring, which at his behest makes him invisible. He uses the ring to escape the sanctions of society—its laws and punishments—and to serve his lust and greed. Glaucon asks whether anyone with such power would refrain from doing the sort of thing Gyges did. We enter the dialogue in the second book of the *Republic*. Socrates has just shown that the type of egoism advocated by the sophist Thrasymachus is contradictory. Socrates is speaking.

BOOK 2

With these words I was thinking that I had made an end of the discussion; but the end, in truth, proved to be only a beginning. For Glaucon, who is always the most pugnacious of men, was dissatisfied at Thrasymachus' retirement; he wanted to have the battle out. So he said to me: Socrates, do you wish really to persuade us, or only to seem to have persuaded us, that to be just is always better than to be unjust?

I should wish really to persuade you, I replied, if I could.

Then you certainly have not succeeded. Let me ask you now:—How would you arrange goods—are there not some which we welcome for their own sakes, and independently of their consequences, as, for example, harmless pleasures and enjoyments, which delight us at the time, although nothing follows from them?

I agree in thinking that there is such a class, I replied.

Is there not also a second class of goods, such as knowledge, sight, health, which are desirable not only in themselves, but also for their results?

Certainly, I said.

Reprinted from *The Dialogues of Plato,* translated by Benjamin Jowett (Charles Scribner's, 1889).

And would you not recognize a third class, such as gymnastic, and the care of the sick, and the physician's art; also the various ways of money-making—these do us good but we regard them as disagreeable; and no one would choose them for their own sakes, but only for the sake of some reward or result which flows from them?

There is, I said, this third class also. But why do you ask?

Because I want to know in which of the three classes you would place justice?

In the highest class, I replied, among those goods which he who would be happy desires both for their own sake and for the sake of their results.

Then the many are of another mind; they think that justice is to be reckoned in the troublesome class, among goods which are to be pursued for the sake of rewards and of reputation, but in themselves are disagreeable and rather to be avoided.

I know, I said, that this is their manner of thinking, and that this was the thesis which Thrasymachus was maintaining just now, when he censured justice and praised injustice. But I am too stupid to be convinced by him.

I wish, he said, that you would hear me as well as him, and then I shall see whether you and I agree. For Thrasymachus seems to me, like a snake, to have been charmed by your voice sooner than he ought to have been; but to my mind the nature of justice and injustice have not yet been made clear. Setting aside their rewards and results, I want to know what they are in themselves, and how they inwardly work in the soul. If you please, then, I will revive the argument of Thrasymachus. And first I will speak of the nature and origin of justice according to the common view of them. Secondly, I will show that all men who practice justice do so against their will, of necessity, but not as a good. And thirdly, I will argue that there is reason in this view, for the life of the unjust is after all better far than the life of the just—if what they say is true, Socrates, since I myself am not of their opinion. But still I acknowledge that I am perplexed when I hear the voices of Thrasymachus and myriads of others dinning in my ears; and, on the other hand, I have never yet heard the superiority of justice to injustice maintained by any one in a satisfactory way. I want to hear justice praised in respect of itself; then I shall be satisfied, and you are the person from whom I think that I am most likely to hear this; and therefore I will praise the unjust life to the utmost of my power, and my manner of speaking will indicate the manner in which I desire to hear you too praising justice and censuring injustice. Will you say whether you approve of my proposal?

Indeed I do; nor can I imagine any theme about which a man of sense would oftener wish to converse.

I am delighted, he replied, to hear you say so, and shall begin by speaking, as I proposed, of the nature and origin of justice.

They say that to do injustice is, by nature, good; to suffer injustice, evil; but that the evil is greater than the good. And so when men have both done and suffered injustice and have had experience of both, not being able to avoid the one and obtain the other, they think that they had better agree among themselves to have neither; hence there arise laws and mutual covenants; and that which is ordained by law is termed by them lawful and just. This they affirm to be the origin and nature of justice:—it is a mean or compromise, between the best of all, which is to do injustice and not be punished, and the worst of all, which is to suffer injustice without the power of retaliation; and justice, being at a middle point between the two, is tolerated not as a good, but as the lesser evil, and honoured by reason of the inability of men to do injustice. For no man who is worthy to be called a man would ever submit to such an agreement if he were able to resist; he would be mad if he did. Such is the received account, Socrates, of the nature and origin of justice.

Now that those who practice justice do so involuntarily and because they have not the power to be unjust will best appear if we imagine something of this kind: having given both to the just and the unjust power to do what they will, let us watch and see whither desire will lead them; then we shall discover in the very act the just and unjust man to be proceeding along the same road, following their interest, which all natures deem to be their good, and are only diverted into the path of justice by the force of law. The liberty which we are supposing may be most completely given to them in the form of such a power as is said to have been possessed by Gyges the ancestor of Croesus the Lydian. According to the tradition, Gyges was a shepherd in the service of the king of Lydia; there was a great storm, and an earthquake made an opening in the earth at the place where he was feeding his flock. Amazed at the sight, he descended into the opening, where, among other marvels, he beheld a hollow brazen horse, having doors, at which he stooping and looking in saw a dead body of stature, as appeared to him, more than human, and having nothing on but a gold ring; this he took from the finger of the dead and reascended. Now the shepherds met together, according to custom, that they might send their monthly report about the flocks to the king; into their assembly he came having the ring on his finger, and as he was sitting among them he chanced to turn the collet of the ring inside his hand, when instantly he became invisible to the rest of the company and they began to speak of him as if he were no longer present. He was astonished at this, and again touching the ring he turned the collet outwards and reappeared; he made several trials of the ring, and always with the same result—when he turned the collet inwards he became invisible, when outwards he reappeared. Whereupon he contrived to be chosen one of the messengers who were sent to the court; where as soon as he arrived he seduced the queen, and with her help conspired against the king and slew him, and took the kingdom. Suppose now that there were two such magic rings, and the just put on one of them and the unjust the other; no man can be imagined to be of such an iron nature that he would stand fast in justice. No man would keep his hands off what was not his own when he could safely take what he liked out of the market, or go into houses and lie with any one at his pleasure, or kill or release from prison whom he would, and in all respects be like a God among men. Then the actions of the just would be as the actions of the unjust; they would both come at last to the same point. And this we may truly affirm to be a great proof that a man is just, not willingly or because he thinks that justice is any good to him individually, but of necessity, for wherever any one thinks that he can safely be unjust, there he is unjust. For all men believe in their hearts that injustice is far more profitable to the individual than justice, and he who argues as I have been supposing, will say that they are right. If you could imagine any one obtaining this power of becoming invisible, and never doing any wrong or touching what was another's, he would be thought by the lookers-on to be a most wretched idiot, although they would praise him to one another's faces, and keep up appearances with one another from a fear that they too might suffer injustice. Enough of this.

Now, if we are to form a real judgment of the life of the just and unjust, we must isolate them; there is no other way; and how is the isolation to be effected? I answer: Let the unjust man be entirely unjust, and the just man entirely just; nothing is to be taken away from either of them, and both are to be perfectly furnished for the work of their respective lives. First, let the unjust be like other distinguished masters of craft; like the skillful pilot or physician, who knows intuitively his own powers and keeps within their limits, and who, if he fails at any point, is able to recover himself. So let the unjust make his unjust attempts in the right way, and lie hidden if he means to be great in his injustice (he who is found out is nobody): for the highest reach of injustice is: to be deemed just when you are not. Therefore I say that in the perfectly unjust man we must assume the most perfect injustice; there is to be no deduction, but we must allow him, while doing the most unjust acts, to have acquired the greatest reputation for justice. If he have taken a false step he must be able to recover himself; he must be one who can speak with effect, if any of his deeds come to light, and who can force his way where force is required by his courage and strength, and command of money and friends. And at his side let us place the just man in his nobleness and simplicity, wishing, as Aeschylus says, to be and not to seem good. There must be no seeming, for if he seem to be just he will be honoured and rewarded, and then we shall not know whether he is just for the sake of justice or for the sake of honours and rewards; therefore, let him be clothed in justice only, and have no other covering; and he must be imagined in a state of life the opposite of the former. Let him be the best of men, and let him be thought the worst; then he will have been put to the proof; and we shall see whether he will be affected by the fear of infamy and its consequences. And let him continue thus to the hour of death; being just and seeming to be unjust. When both have reached the uttermost extreme, the one of justice and the other of injustice, let judgment be given which of them is the happier of the two.

Heavens! my dear Glaucon, I said, how energetically you polish them up for the decision, first one and then the other, as if they were two statues.

I do my best, he said. And now that we know what they are like there is no difficulty in tracing out the sort of life which awaits either of them. This I will proceed to describe; but as you may think the description a little too coarse, I ask you to suppose, Socrates, that the words which follow are not mine.—Let me put them into the mouths of the eulogists of injustice: they will tell you that the just man who is thought unjust will be scourged, racked, bound—will have his eyes burnt out; and, at last, after suffering every kind of evil, he will be impaled: Then he will understand that he ought to seem only, and not to be, just; the words of Aeschylus may be more truly spoken of the unjust than of the just. For the unjust is pursuing a reality; he does not live with a view to appearances—he wants to be really unjust and not to seem only:—

His mind has a soil deep and fertile.
Out of which spring his prudent counsels.

In the first place, he is thought just, and therefore bears rule in the city; he can marry whom he will, and give in marriage to whom he will; also he can trade and deal where he likes, and always to his own advantage, because he has no misgivings about injustice; and at every contest, whether in public or private, he gets the better of his antagonists, and gains at their expense, and is rich, and out of his gains he can benefit his friends, and harm his enemies; moreover, he can offer sacrifices, and dedicate gifts to the gods abundantly and magnificently, and can honour the gods or any man whom he wants to honour in a far better style than the just, and therefore he is likely to be dearer than they are to the gods. And thus, Socrates, gods and men are said to unite in making the life of the unjust better than the life of the just. . . .

[We pick up the discussion in Book 9.]

BOOK 9

"Now that we've gotten this far," I said, "let's go back to that statement made at the beginning, which brought us here: that it pays for a man to be perfectly unjust if he appears to be just. Isn't that what someone said?"

"Yes."

"Then since we've agreed what power justice and injustice each have, let's have a discussion with him."

"How?"

"By molding in words an image of the soul, so that the one who said that will realize what he was saying."

"What kind of image?"

"Oh, something like those natures the myths tell us were born in ancient times—the Chimaera, Scylla, Cerberus, and others in which many different shapes were supposed to have grown into one."

"So they tell us," he said.

"Then mold one figure of a colorful, many-headed beast with heads of wild and tame animals growing in a circle all around it; one that can change and grow all of them out of itself."

"That's a job for a skilled artist. Still, words mold easier than wax or clay, so consider it done."

"And another of a lion, and one of a man. Make the first by far the biggest, the second second largest."

"That's easier, and already done."

"Now join the three together so that they somehow grow."

"All right."

"Next mold the image of one, the man, around them all, so that to someone who can't see what's inside but looks only at the container it appears to be a single animal, man."

"I have."

"Then shall we inform the gentleman that when he says it pays for this man to be unjust, he's saying that it profits him to feast his multifarious beast and his lion and make them grow strong, but to starve and enfeeble the man in him so that he gets dragged wherever the animals lead him, and instead of making them friends and used to each other, to let them bite and fight and eat each other?"

"That's just what he's saying by praising injustice."

"The one who says justice pays, however, would be saying that he should practice and say whatever will give the most mastery to his inner man, who should care for the many-headed beast like a farmer, raising and domesticating its tame heads and preventing the wild ones from growing, making the lion's nature his partner and ally, and so raise them both to be friends to each other and to him."

"That's exactly what he means by praising justice."

"So in every way the commender of justice is telling the truth, the other a lie. Whether we examine pleasure, reputation, or profit, we find that the man who praises justice speaks truly, the one who disparages it disparages sickly and knows nothing of what he disparages."

"I don't think he does at all."

"Then let's gently persuade him—his error wasn't intended—by asking him a question: 'Shouldn't we say that the traditions of the beautiful and the ugly have come about like this: Beautiful things are those that make our bestial parts subservient to the human—or rather, perhaps, to the divine—part of our nature, while ugly ones are those that enslave the tame to the wild?' Won't he agree?"

"If he takes my advice."

"On this argument then, can it pay for a man to take money unjustly if that means making his best part a slave to the worst? If it wouldn't profit a man to sell his son or his daughter into slavery—to wild and evil men at that—even if he got a fortune for it, then if he has no pity on himself and enslaves the most godlike thing in him to the most godless and polluted, isn't he a wretch who gets bribed for gold into a destruction more horrible than Euriphyle's, who sold her husband's life for a necklace?"

"Much more horrible," said Glaucon.

". . . [E]veryone is better off being ruled by the godlike and intelligent; preferably if he has it inside, but if not, it should be imposed on him from without so that we may all be friends and as nearly alike as possible, all steered by the same thing."

"Yes, and we're right," he said.

"Law, the ally of everyone in the city, clearly intends the same thing, as does the rule of children, which forbids us to let them be free until we've instituted a regime in them as in a city. We serve their best part with a similar part in us, install a like guardian and ruler in them, and only then set them free."

"Clearly."

"Then how, by what argument, Glaucon, can we say that it pays for a man to be unjust or self-indulgent or to do something shameful to get more money or power if by doing so he makes himself worse?"

"We can't," he said.

"And how can it pay to commit injustice without getting caught and being punished? Doesn't getting away with it make a man even worse? Whereas if a man gets caught and punished, his beastlike part is taken in and tamed, his tame part is set free, and his whole soul acquires justice and temperance and knowledge. Therefore his soul recovers its best nature and attains a state more honorable than the state the body attains when it acquires health and strength and beauty, by as much as the soul is more honorable than the body."

"Absolutely."

"Then won't a sensible man spend his life directing all his efforts to this end?"

For Further Reflection

1. Which would you choose to be, Glaucon's good but suffering person or his bad but successful person? Is there a third alternative?
2. Socrates' answer to Glaucon is that, despite appearances, we should choose the life of the "unsuccessful" just person because it is to our advantage to be moral. Socrates' answer depends on a notion of mental health. He contends that immorality corrupts the inner person, so that one is happy or unhappy in exact proportion to one's moral integrity. Is this a plausible reply?
3. Is the good always good for you?

In Defense of Ethical Egoism

AYN RAND

Ayn Rand (1908–1982) wrote several philosophical novels, including *We the Living* (1936), *The Fountainhead* (1943), and *Atlas Shrugged* (1959), from which the present selection is taken. Her works set forth a form of ethical egoism that is called *objectivism*, the philosophy that the proper life for rational beings is the pursuit of their happiness and that altruism and self-sacrifice are incompatible with rational morality. In this passage, she criticizes conventional altruistic morality ("the morality of sacrifice") and praises the morality of selfishness.

VALUE YOURSELF

"... Yes, this *is* an *age* of moral crisis. Yes, you *are* bearing punishment for your evil. But it is not man who is now on trial and it is not human nature that will take the blame. It is your moral code that's through, this time. Your moral code has reached its climax, the blind alley at the end of its course. And if you wish to go on living, what you now need is not to *return* to morality—you who have never known any—but to *discover* it.

"You have heard no concepts of morality but the mystical or the social. You have been taught that morality is a code of behavior imposed on you by whim, the whim of a supernatural power or the whim of society, to serve God's purpose or your neighbor's welfare, to please an authority beyond the grave or else next door—but not to serve *your* life or pleasure. Your pleasure, you have been taught, is to be found in immorality, your interests would best be served by evil, and any moral code must be designed not *for* you, but *against* you, not to further your life, but to drain it.

"For centuries, the battle of morality was fought between those who claimed that your life belongs to God and those who claimed that it belongs to your neighbors—between those who preached that the good is self-sacrifice for the sake of ghosts in heaven and those who preached that the good is self-sacrifice for the sake of incompetents on earth. And no one came to say that your life belongs to you and that the good is to live it.

"Both sides agreed that morality demands the surrender of your self-interest and of your mind, that the moral and the practical are opposites, that morality is not the province of reason, but the province of faith and force. Both sides agreed that no rational morality is possible, that there is no right or wrong in reason—that in reason there's no reason to be moral.

"Whatever else they fought about, it was against man's mind that all your moralists have stood united. It was man's mind that all their schemes and systems were intended to despoil and destroy. Now choose to perish or to learn that the anti-mind is the anti-life.

"Man's mind is his basic tool of survival. Life is given to him, survival is not. His body is given to him, its sustenance is not. His mind is given to him, its content is not. To remain alive, he must act, and before he can act he must know the nature and purpose of his action. He cannot obtain his food without a knowledge of food and of the way to obtain it. He cannot dig a ditch—or build a cyclotron—without a knowledge of his aim and of the means to achieve it. To remain alive, he must think.

"But to think is an act of choice. The key to what you so recklessly call 'human nature,' the open secret you live with, yet dread to name, is the fact that *man is a being of volitional consciousness.* Reason does not work automatically; thinking is not a mechanical process; the connections of logic are not made by instinct. The function of your stomach, lungs, or heart is automatic; the function of your mind is not. In any hour and issue of your life, you are free to think or to evade that effort. But you are not free to escape from your nature, from the fact that *reason* is your means of survival—so that for *you,* who are a human being, the question 'to be or not to be' is the question 'to think or not to think.'

"A being of volitional consciousness has no automatic course of behavior. He needs a code of values to guide his actions. 'Value' is that which one acts to gain and keep, 'virtue' is the action by which one gains and keeps it. 'Value' presupposes an answer to the question: of value to whom and for what? 'Value' presupposes a standard, a purpose and the necessity of action in the face of an alternative. Where there are no alternatives, no values are possible.

"There is only one fundamental alternative in the universe: existence or non-existence—and it pertains to a single class of entities: to living organisms. The existence of inanimate matter is unconditional, the existence of life is not: it depends on a specific course of action. Matter is indestructible, it changes its forms, but it cannot cease to exist. It is only a living organism that faces a constant alternative: the issue of life or death. Life is a process of self-sustaining and self-generated action. If an organism fails in that action, it dies; its chemical elements remain, but its life goes out of existence. It is only the concept of 'Life' that makes the concept of 'Value' possible. It is only to a living entity that things can be good or evil.

"A plant must feed itself in order to live; the sunlight, the water, the chemicals it needs are the values its nature has set it to pursue; its life is the standard of value directing its actions. But a plant has no choice of action; there are alternatives in the conditions it encounters, but there is no alternative in its function; it acts automatically to further its life, it cannot act for its own destruction.

"An animal is equipped for sustaining its life; its senses provide it with an automatic code of action, an automatic knowledge of what is good for it or evil. It has no power to extend its knowledge or to evade it. In conditions where its knowledge proves inadequate, it dies. But so long as it lives, it acts on its knowledge, with automatic safety and no power of choice, it is unable to ignore its own good, unable to decide to choose the evil and act as its own destroyer.

"Man has no automatic code of survival. His particular distinction from all other living species is the necessity to act in the face of alternatives by means of *volitional choice.* He has no automatic knowledge of what is good for him or evil, what values his life depends on, what course of action it requires. Are you prattling about an instinct of self-preservation? An *instinct* of self-preservation is precisely what man does not possess. An 'instinct' is an unerring and automatic form of knowledge. A desire is not an instinct. A desire to live does not give you the knowledge required for living. And even man's desire to live is not automatic: your secret evil today is that *that* is the desire you do not hold. Your fear of death is not a love for life and will not give you the knowledge needed to keep it. Man must obtain his knowledge and choose his actions by a process of thinking, which nature will not force him to perform. Man has the power to act as his own destroyer—and that is the way he has acted through most of his history.

"A living entity that regarded its means of survival as evil, would not survive. A plant that struggled to mangle its roots, a bird that fought to break its wings would not remain for long in the existence they affronted. But the history of man has been a struggle to deny and to destroy his mind.

"Man has been called a rational being, but rationality is a matter of choice—and the alternative his nature offers him is: rational being or suicidal animal. Man has to be man—by choice; he has to hold his life as a value—by choice; he has to learn to sustain it—by choice; he has to discover the values it requires and practice his virtues—by choice.

"A code of values accepted by choice is a code of morality.

"Whoever you are, you who are hearing me now, I am speaking to whatever living remnant is left uncorrupted within you, to the remnant of the human, to your *mind,* and I say: There *is* a morality of reason, a morality proper to man, and *Man's Life* is its standard of value.

"All that which is proper to the life of a rational being is the good; all that which destroys it is the evil.

"Man's life, as required by his nature, is not the life of a mindless brute, of a looting thug or a mooching mystic, but the life of a thinking being—not life by means of force or fraud, but life by means of achievement—not survival at any price, since there's only one price that pays for man's survival: reason.

"Man's life is the *standard* of morality, but your own life is its *purpose.* If existence on earth is your goal, you must choose your actions and values by the standard of that which is proper to man—for the purpose of preserving, fulfilling and enjoying the irreplaceable value which is your life.

"Since life requires a specific course of action, any other course will destroy it. A being who does not hold his own life as the motive and goal of his actions, is acting on the motive and standard of *death.* Such a being is a metaphysical monstrosity, struggling to oppose, negate and contradict the fact of his own existence, running blindly amuck on a trail of destruction, capable of nothing but pain.

"Happiness is the successful state of life, pain is an agent of death. Happiness is that state of unconsciousness which proceeds from the achievement of one's values. A morality that dares to tell you to find happiness in the renunciation of your happiness—to value the failure of your values—is an insolent negation of morality. A doctrine that gives you, as an ideal, the role of a sacrificial animal seeking slaughter on the altars of others, is giving you *death* as your standard. By the grace of reality and the nature of life, man—every man—is an end in himself, he exists for his own sake, and the achievement of his own happiness is his highest moral purpose.

"But neither life nor happiness can be achieved by the pursuit of irrational whims. Just as man is free to attempt to survive in any random manner, but will perish unless he lives as his nature requires, so he is free to seek his happiness in any mindless fraud, but the torture of frustration is all he will find, unless he seeks the happiness proper to man. The purpose of morality is to teach you, not to suffer and die, but to enjoy yourself and live.

"Sweep aside those parasites of subsidized classrooms, who live on the profits of the mind of others and proclaim that man needs no morality, no values, no code of behavior. They, who pose as scientists and claim that man is only an animal, do not grant him inclusion in the law of existence they have granted to the lowest of insects. They recognize that every living species has a way of survival demanded by its nature, they do not claim that a fish can live out of water or that a dog can live without its sense of smell—but man, they claim, the most complex of beings, man can survive in any way whatever, man has no identity, no nature, and there's no practical reason why he cannot live with his means of survival destroyed, with his mind throttled and placed at the disposal of any orders *they* might care to issue.

"Sweep aside those hatred-eaten mystics, who pose as friends of humanity and preach that the highest virtue man can practice is to hold his own life as of no value. Do they tell you that the purpose of morality is to curb man's instinct of self-preservation? It is for the purpose of self-preservation that man needs a code of morality. The only man who desires to be moral is the man who desires to live.

"No, you do not have to live; it is your basic act of choice; but if you choose to live, you must live as a man—by the work and the judgment of your mind.

"No, you do not have to live as a man: it is an act of moral choice. But you cannot live as anything else—and the alternative is that state of living death which you now see within you and around you, the state of a thing unfit for existence, no longer human and less than animal, a thing that knows nothing but pain and drags itself through its span of years in the agony of unthinking self-destruction.

"No, you do not have to think; it is an act of moral choice. But someone had to think to keep you alive; if you choose to default, you default on existence and you pass the deficit to some moral man, expecting him to sacrifice his good for the sake of letting you survive by your evil. . . .

"This much is true: the most *selfish* of all things is the independent mind that recognizes no authority higher than its own and no value higher than its judgment of truth. You are asked to sacrifice your intellectual integrity, your logic, your reason, your standard of truth—in favor of becoming a prostitute whose standard is the greatest good for the greatest number.

"If you search your code for guidance, for an answer to the question: 'What *is* the good?'—the only answer you will find is '*The good of others.*' The good is whatever others wish, whatever you feel they feel they wish, or whatever you feel they ought to feel. 'The good of others' is a magic formula that transforms anything into gold, a formula to be recited as a guarantee of moral glory and as a fumigator for any action, even the slaughter of a continent. Your standard of virtue is not an object, not an act, nor a principle, but an *intention.* You need no proof, no reasons, no success, you need not achieve *in fact* the good of others—all you need to know is that your motive was the good of others, *not* your own. Your only definition of the good is a negation: the good is the 'non-good for me.'

"Your code—which boasts that it upholds eternal, absolute, objective moral values and scorns the conditional, the relative and the subjective—your code hands out, as its version of the absolute, the following rule of moral conduct: If *you* wish it, it's evil; if others wish it, it's good; if the motive of your action is *your* welfare, don't do it; if the motive is the welfare of others, then anything goes.

"As this double-jointed, double-standard morality splits you in half, so it splits mankind into two enemy camps: one is *you,* the other is all the rest of humanity. *You* are the only outcast who has no right to wish or live. *You* are the only servant, the rest are the masters, *you* are the only giver, the rest are the takers, *you* are the eternal debtor, the rest are the creditors never to be paid off. You must not question their right to your sacrifice, or the nature of their wishes and their needs: their right is conferred upon them by a negative, by the fact that they are 'non-you.'

"For those of you who might ask questions, your code provides a consolation prize and booby-trap: it is for your own happiness, it says, that you must serve the happiness of others, the only way to achieve your joy is to give it up to others, the only way to achieve your prosperity is to surrender your wealth to others, the only way to protect your life is to protect all men except yourself—and if you find no joy in this procedure, it is your own fault and the proof of your evil; if you were good, you would find your happiness in providing a banquet for others, and your dignity in existing on such crumbs as *they* might care to toss you.

"You who have no standard of self-esteem, accept the guilt and dare not ask the questions. But you know the unadmitted answer, refusing to acknowledge what you see, what hidden premise moves your world. You know it, not in honest statement, but as a dark uneasiness within you, while you flounder between guiltily cheating and grudgingly practicing a principle too vicious to name.

"I, who do not accept the unearned, neither in values nor in *guilt,* am here to ask the questions you evaded. Why is it moral to serve the happiness of others, but not your own? If enjoyment is a value, why is it moral when experienced by others, but immoral when experienced by you? If the sensation of eating a cake is a value, why is it an immoral indulgence in your stomach, but a moral goal for you to achieve in the stomach of others? Why is it immoral for you to desire, but moral for others to do so? Why is it immoral to produce a value and keep it, but moral to give it away? And if it is not moral for you to keep a value, why is it moral for others to accept it? If you are selfless and virtuous when you give it, are they not selfish and vicious when they take it? Does virtue consist of serving vice? Is the moral purpose of those who are good, self-immolation for the sake of those who are evil? . . .

"Under a morality of sacrifice, the first value you sacrifice is morality; the next is self-esteem. When need is the standard, every man is both victim and parasite. As a victim, he must labor to fill the needs of others, leaving himself in the position of a parasite whose needs must be filled by others. He cannot approach his fellow men except in one of two disgraceful roles: he is both a beggar and a sucker.

"You fear the man who has a dollar less than you, that dollar is rightfully his, he makes you feel like a moral defrauder. You hate the man who has a dollar more than you, that dollar is rightfully yours, he makes you feel that you are morally defrauded. The man below is a source of your guilt, the man above is a source of your frustration. You do not know what to surrender or demand, when to give and when to grab, what pleasure in life is rightfully yours and what debt is still unpaid to others—you struggle to evade, as 'theory,' the knowledge that by the moral standard you've accepted you are guilty every moment of your life, there is no mouthful of food you swallow that is not *needed* by someone somewhere on earth—and you give up the problem in blind resentment, you conclude that moral perfection is not to be achieved *or desired,* that you will muddle through by snatching as snatch can and by avoiding the eyes of the young, of those who look at you as if self-esteem were possible and they expected you to have it. Guilt is all that you retain within your soul—and so does every other man, as he goes past, avoiding *your* eyes. Do you wonder why your morality has not achieved brotherhood on earth or the good will of man to man?

"The justification of sacrifice, that your morality propounds, is more corrupt than the corruption it purports to justify. The motive of your sacrifice, it tells you, should be *love*—the love you ought to feel for every man. A morality that professes the belief that the values of the spirit are more precious than matter, a morality that teaches you to scorn a whore who gives her body indiscriminately to all men—this same morality demands that you surrender your soul to promiscuous love for all comers.

"As there can be no causeless wealth, so there can be no causeless love or any sort of causeless emotion. An emotion is a response to a fact of reality, an estimate dictated by your standards. To love is to *value.* The man who tells you that it is possible to value without values, to love those whom you appraise as worthless, is the man who tells you that it is possible to grow rich by consuming without producing and that paper money is as valuable as gold.

"Observe that he does not expect you to feel a causeless fear. When his kind get into power, they are expert at contriving means of terror, at giving you ample cause to feel the fear by which they desire to rule you. But when it comes to love, the highest of emotions, you permit them to shriek at you accusingly that you are a moral delinquent if you're incapable of feeling causeless love. When a man feels fear without reason, you call him to the attention of a psychiatrist; you are not so careful to protect the meaning, the nature and the dignity of love.

"Love is the expression of one's values, the greatest reward you can earn for the moral qualities you have achieved in your character and person, the emotional price paid by one man for the joy he receives from the virtues of another. Your morality demands that you divorce your love from values and hand it down to any vagrant, not as response to his worth, but as response to his *need,* not as reward, but as alms, not as a payment for virtues, but as a blank check on vices. Your morality tells you that the purpose of love is to set you free of the bonds of morality, that love is superior to moral judgment, that true love transcends, forgives and survives every manner of evil in its object, and the greater the love the greater the depravity it permits to the loved. To love a man for his virtues is paltry and human, it tells you; to love him for his flaws is divine. To love those who are worthy of it is self-interest; to love the unworthy is sacrifice. You owe your love to those who don't deserve it, and the less they deserve it, the more love you owe them—the more loathsome the object, the nobler your love—the more unfastidious your love, the greater your virtue—and if you can bring your soul to the state of a dump heap that welcomes anything on equal terms, if you can cease to value moral values, you have achieved the state of moral perfection.

"Such is your morality of sacrifice and such are the twin ideals it offers: to refashion the life of your body in the image of a human stockyards, and the life of your spirit in the image of a dump. . . .

"Since childhood, you have been hiding the guilty secret that you feel no desire to be moral, no desire to seek self-immolation, that you dread and hate your code, but dare not say it even to yourself, that you're devoid of those moral 'instincts' which others profess to feel. The less you felt, the louder you proclaimed your selfless love and servitude to others, in dread of ever letting them discover your own self, the self that you betrayed, the self that you kept in concealment, like a skeleton in the closet of your body. And they, who were at once your dupes and your deceivers, they listened and voiced their loud approval, in dread of ever letting you discover that they were harboring the same unspoken secret. Existence among you is a giant pretense, an act you all perform for one another, each feeling that he is the only guilty freak, each placing his moral authority in the unknowable known only to others, each faking the reality he feels they expect him to fake, none having the courage to break the vicious circle.

"No matter what dishonorable compromise you've made with your impracticable creed, no matter what miserable balance, half-cynicism, half-superstition, you now manage to maintain, you still preserve the root, the lethal tenet: the belief that the moral and the practical are opposites. Since childhood, you have been running from the terror of a choice you have never dared fully to identify: If the *practical,* whatever you must practice to exist, whatever works, succeeds, achieves your purpose, whatever brings you food and joy, whatever profits you is evil—and if the good, the moral is the *impractical,* whatever fails, destroys, frustrates, whatever injures you and brings you loss or pain—then your choice is to be moral or to live.

"The sole result of that murderous doctrine was to remove morality from life. You grew up to believe that moral laws bear no relation to the job of living, except as an impediment and threat, that man's existence is an amoral jungle where anything goes and anything works. And in that fog of switching definitions which descends upon a frozen mind, you have forgotten that the evils damned by your creed were the virtues required for living, and you have come to believe that actual evils are the *practical* means of existence. Forgetting that the impractical 'good' was self-sacrifice, you believe that self-esteem is impractical; forgetting that the practical 'evil' was production, you believe that robbery is practical. . . .

"Accept the fact that the achievement of your happiness is the only *moral* purpose of your life, and that *happiness*—not pain or mindless self-indulgence—is the proof of your moral integrity, since it is the proof and the result of your loyalty to the achievement of your values. Happiness was the responsibility you dreaded, it required the kind of rational discipline you did not value yourself enough to assume—and the anxious staleness of your days is the monument to your evasion of the knowledge that there is no moral substitute for happiness, that there is no more despicable coward than the man who deserted the battle for his joy, fearing to assert his right to existence, lacking the courage and the loyalty to life of a bird or a flower reaching for the sun. Discard the protective rags of that vice which you called a virtue: humility—learn to value yourself, which means: to fight for your happiness—and when you learn that *pride* is the sum of all virtues, you will learn to live like a man.

"As a basic step of self-esteem, learn to treat as the mark of a cannibal any man's *demand* for your help. To demand it is to claim that your life is *his* property—and loathsome as such claim might be, there's something still more loathsome: your agreement. Do you ask if it's ever proper to help another man? No—if he claims it as his right or as a moral duty that you owe him. Yes—if such is your own desire based on your own selfish pleasure in the value of his person and his struggle."

For Further Reflection

1. Has Rand successfully defended her theory of ethical egoism? How does it relate to Socrates' idea that one ought never to harm anyone else? Could one reconcile Socrates' idea with Rand's theory? Socrates believes that one should never harm anyone else because doing so is never in one's own interest. What would be needed to get Rand's theory to agree with that conclusion?
2. Can the ethical egoist make his or her views public? If you follow Rand, should you let others know where you stand? Should you persuade them to be egoists? If the egoist cannot make his theory public, does this disqualify it as a genuine ethical theory?
3. Can the ethical egoist be a consistent egoist and have friends? If friendship entails loving another in such a way as to sacrifice one's own interest for the friend's, does this give the egoist difficulty?

Egoism and Altruism

A Critique of Ayn Rand

LOUIS P. POJMAN

In this essay Pojman criticizes Ayn Rand's version of ethical egoism for creating a false dilemma between (1) a self-demeaning altruism and (2) a consummate egoism in which people always put themselves first. He argues that Rand conflates *selfishness* with *self-interest,* but the two concepts are only superficially similar. He then draws from evolutionary ethologists who describe animal behavior, illustrating a middle way between self-degrading sacrifice and selfish egoism.

Universal ethical egoism is the theory that everyone ought always to serve his or her own self-interest. That is, everyone ought to do what will maximize one's own expected utility or bring about one's own greatest happiness, even if it requires harming others. Ethical egoism is utilitarianism reduced to the pinpoint of the single individual ego. Instead of advocating the greatest happiness for the greatest number, as utilitarianism does, it advocates the greatest happiness for myself, whoever I may be. It is a self-preoccupied prudence, urging one to postpone enjoyment today for long-term benefits. In its more sophisticated form, it compares life to a competitive game, perhaps a war-game, and urges each person to *try* to win in the game of life.

In her books *The Virtue of Selfishness* and *Atlas Shrugged,* Ayn Rand argues that selfishness is a virtue and altruism a vice, a totally destructive idea that leads to the undermining of individual worth. She defines *altruism* as the view that

> any action taken for the benefit of others is good, and any action taken for one's own benefit is evil. Thus, the *beneficiary* of an action is the only criterion of moral value—and so long as the beneficiary is anybody other than oneself, anything goes.[1]

As such, altruism is suicidal:

> If a man accepts the ethics of altruism, his first concern is not how to live his life, but how to sacrifice it. . . . Altruism erodes men's capacity to grasp the value of an individual life; it reveals a mind from which the reality of a human being has been wiped out.

Since finding happiness is the highest goal and good in life, altruism, which calls on us to sacrifice our happiness for the good of others, is contrary to our highest good.

Her argument seems to go like this:

1. The perfection of one's abilities in a state of happiness is the highest goal for humans. We have a moral duty to attempt to reach this goal.
2. The ethics of altruism prescribes that we sacrifice our interests and lives for the good of others.
3. Therefore, the ethics of altruism is incompatible with the goal of happiness.

[1] Ayn Rand, *The Virtue of Selfishness* (New American Library, 1964), pp. vii and 27–32; 80ff.

4. Ethical egoism prescribes that we seek our own happiness exclusively, and as such it is consistent with the happiness goal.
5. Therefore ethical egoism is the correct moral theory.

Ayn Rand's argument for the virtue of selfishness is flawed by the fallacy of a false dilemma. It simplistically assumes that absolute altruism and absolute egoism are the only alternatives. But this is an extreme view of the matter. There are plenty of options between these two positions. Even a predominant egoist would admit that (analogous to the paradox of hedonism) sometimes the best way to reach self-fulfillment is for us to forget about ourselves and strive to live for goals, causes, or other persons. Even if altruism is not required (as a duty), it may be permissible in many cases. Furthermore, self-interest may not be incompatible with other-regarding motivation. Even the Second Great Commandment set forth by Moses and Jesus states not that you must always sacrifice yourself for the other person, but that you ought to love your neighbor *as* yourself (Lev. 19:19; Matt. 23). Self-interest and self-love are morally good things, but not at the expense of other people's legitimate interests. When there is moral conflict of interests, a fair process of adjudication needs to take place.

But Rand's version of egoism is only one of many. We need to go to the heart of ethical egoism: the thesis that our highest moral duty is always to promote our individual interests. Let us focus on the alleged problems of this thesis.

FOUR CRITICISMS OF ETHICAL EGOISM

The Inconsistent Outcomes Argument

Brian Medlin argues that ethical egoism cannot be true because it fails to meet a necessary condition of morality, that of being a guide to action. He claims that it will be like advising people to do inconsistent things based on incompatible desires.[2] His argument goes like this:

1. Moral principles must be universal and categorical.
2. I must universalize my egoist desire to come out on top over Tom, Dick, and Harry.

[2]Brian Medlin, "Ultimate Principles and Ethical Egoism," *Australasian Journal of Philosophy* (1957), pp. 111–118; reprinted in Louis Pojman, *Ethical Theory*, pp. 91–95.

3. But I must also prescribe Tom's egoist desire to come out on top over Dick, Harry, and me (and so on).
4. Therefore I have prescribed incompatible outcomes and have not provided a way of adjudicating conflicts of desire. In effect, I have said nothing.

The proper response to this is that of Jesse Kalin, who argues that we can separate our beliefs about ethical situations from our desires.[3] He likens the situation to a competitive sports event, in which you believe that your opponent has a right to try to win as much as you, but you desire that you, not he, will in fact win. An even better example is that of the chess game in which you recognize that your opponent ought to move her bishop to prepare for checkmate, but you hope she won't see the move. Belief that A ought to do Y does not commit you to wanting A to do Y.

The Publicity Argument

On the one hand, in order for something to be a moral theory it seems necessary that its moral principles be publicized. Unless principles are put forth as universal prescriptions that are accessible to the public, they cannot serve as guides to action or as aids in resolving conflicts of interest. But on the other hand, it is not in the egoist's self-interest to publicize them. Egoists would rather that the rest of us be altruists. (Why did Nietzsche and Rand write books announcing their positions? Were the royalties taken in by announcing ethical egoism worth the price of letting the cat out of the bag?)

Thus it would be self-defeating for the egoist to argue for her position, and even worse that she should convince others of it. But it is perfectly possible to have a private morality that does not resolve conflicts of interest. So the egoist should publicly advocate standard principles of traditional morality—so that society doesn't break down—while adhering to a private, nonstandard, solely self-regarding morality. So, if you're willing to pay the price, you can accept the solipsistic-directed norms of egoism.

If the egoist is prepared to pay the price, egoism could be a consistent system that has some limitations. Although the egoist can cooperate with others in limited ways and perhaps even have friends—so long as their interests don't conflict with his—he has to be very careful about preserving his isolation. The egoist can't give advice or argue about his position—not sincerely at least. He must act alone, atomistically or solipsistically in moral isolation, for to announce his

[3]See Jesse Kalin, "In Defense of Egoism," in *Ethical Theory,* 4th ed., ed. Louis Pojman (Wadsworth, 2002), p. 95f.

adherence to the principle of egoism would be dangerous to his project. He can't teach his children the true morality or justify himself to others or forgive others.

The Paradox of Egoism

The situation may be even worse than the sophisticated, self-conscious egoist supposes. Could the egoist have friends? And if limited friendship is possible, could he or she ever be in love or experience deep friendship? Suppose the egoist discovers that in the pursuit of the happiness goal, deep friendship is in his best interest. Can he become a friend? What is necessary to deep friendship? A true friend is one who is not always preoccupied about his own interest in the relationship but who forgets about himself altogether, at least sometimes, in order to serve or enhance the other person's interest. "Love seeketh not its own." It is an altruistic disposition, the very opposite of egoism. So the *paradox of egoism* is that in order to reach the goal of egoism one must give up egoism and become (to some extent) an altruist, the very antithesis of egoism.

The Argument from Counterintuitive Consequences

The final argument against ethical egoism is that it is an absolute ethics that not only permits egoistic behavior but demands it. Helping others at one's own expense is not only not required, it is morally wrong. Whenever I do not have good evidence that my helping you will end up to my advantage, I must refrain from helping you. If I can save the whole of Europe and Africa from destruction by pressing a button, then so long as there is nothing for me to gain by it, it is wrong for me to press that button. The Good Samaritan was, by this logic, morally wrong in helping the injured victim and not collecting payment for his troubles. It is certainly hard to see why the egoist should be concerned about environmental matters if he or she is profiting from polluting the environment. (For example, if the egoist gains 40 hedons in producing P, which produces pollution that in turn causes others 1,000 dolors—units of suffering—but suffers only 10 of those dolors himself, then by an agent-maximizing calculus he is morally obligated to produce P.) There is certainly no obligation to preserve scarce natural resources for future generations. "Why should I do anything for posterity?" the egoist asks. "What has posterity ever done for me?"

In conclusion, we see that ethical egoism has a number of serious problems. It cannot consistently publicize itself, nor often argue its case. It tends towards solipsism and the exclusion of many of the deepest human values, such as love and deep friendship. It violates the principle of fairness, and, most of all, it entails an absolute prohibition on altruistic behavior, which we intuitively sense as morally required (or, at least, permissible).

EVOLUTION AND ALTRUISM

If sheer unadulterated egoism is an inadequate moral theory, does that mean we ought to aim at complete altruism, total self-effacement for the sake of others? What is the role of self-love in morality? An interesting place to start answering these queries is with the new field of sociobiology, which theorizes that social structures and behavioral patterns, including morality, have a biological base, explained by evolutionary theory.

In the past, linking ethics to evolution meant justifying exploitation. Social Darwinism justified imperialism and the principle that "Might makes right" by saying that survival of the fittest is a law of nature. This philosophy lent itself to a promotion of ruthless egoism. This is nature's law, "nature red in tooth and claw." Against this view ethologists such as Robert Ardrey and Konrad Lorenz argued for a more benign view of the animal kingdom—one reminiscent of Rudyard Kipling's, in which the animal kingdom survives by cooperation, which is at least as important as competition. On Ardrey's and Lorenz's view it is the group or the species, not the individual, that is of primary importance.

With the development of sociobiology—in the work of E. O. Wilson but particularly the work of Robert Trivers, J. Maynard Smith, and Richard Dawkins—a theory has come to the fore that combines radical individualism with limited altruism. It is not the group or the species that is of evolutionary importance but the gene, or, more precisely, the gene type. Genes—the parts of the chromosomes that carry the blueprints for all our natural traits (e.g., height, hair color, skin color, intelligence)—copy themselves as they divide and multiply. At conception they combine with the genes of a member of the opposite sex to form a new individual.

In his fascinating sociobiological study, Richard Dawkins describes human behavior as determined evolutionarily by stable strategies set to replicate the gene.[4] This is not done consciously, of course, but by the invisible hand that drives consciousness. We are essentially gene machines.

Morality—that is, successful morality—can be seen as an evolutionary strategy for gene replication. Here's an example: Birds are afflicted with life-endangering parasites. Because they lack limbs to enable them to pick the parasites off their heads, they—like much of the animal kingdom—depend on the ritual of mutual grooming. It turns out that nature has evolved two basic types of birds in this regard: those who are disposed to groom anyone (the nonprejudiced type?), and those who refuse to groom anyone but who present themselves for grooming. The former type of bird Dawkins calls "Suckers" and the latter "Cheaters."

[4]Richard Dawkins, *The Selfish Gene* (Oxford University Press, 1976), Ch. 10.

In a geographical area containing harmful parasites and where there are only Suckers or Cheaters, Suckers will do fairly well, but Cheaters will not survive, for want of cooperation. However, in a Sucker population in which a mutant Cheater arises, the Cheater will prosper, and the Cheater gene-type will multiply. As the Suckers are exploited, they will gradually die out. But if and when they become too few to groom the Cheaters, the Cheaters will start to die off too and eventually become extinct.

Why don't birds all die off, then? Well, somehow nature has come up with a third type, call them "Grudgers." Grudgers groom all and only those who reciprocate in grooming them. They groom each other and Suckers, but not Cheaters. In fact, once caught, a Cheater is marked forever. There is no forgiveness. It turns out then that unless there are a lot of Suckers around, Cheaters have a hard time of it—harder even than Suckers. However, it is the Grudgers that prosper. Unlike Suckers, they don't waste time messing with unappreciative Cheaters, so they are not exploited and have ample energy to gather food and build better nests for their loved ones.

J. L. Mackie argues that the real name for Suckers is "Christian," one who believes in complete altruism, even turning the other cheek to one's assailant and loving one's enemy. Cheaters are ruthless egoists who can survive only if there are enough naive altruists around. Whereas Grudgers are *reciprocal* altruists who have a rational morality based on cooperative self-interest, Suckers, such as Socrates and Jesus, advocate "turning the other cheek and repaying evil with good."[5] Instead of a Rule of Reciprocity, "I'll scratch your back if you'll scratch mine," the extreme altruist substitutes the Golden Rule, "If you want the other fellow to scratch your back, you scratch his—even if he won't reciprocate."

The moral of the story is this: Altruist morality (so interpreted) is only rational given the payoff of eternal life (with a scorekeeper, as Woody Allen says). Take that away, and it looks like a Sucker system. What replaces the "Christian" vision of submission and saintliness is the reciprocal altruist with a tit-for-tat morality, someone who is willing to share with those willing to cooperate.

Mackie may caricature the position of the religious altruist, but he misses the subtleties of wisdom involved (Jesus said, "Be as wise as serpents but as harmless as doves"). Nevertheless, he does remind us that there is a difference between core morality and complete altruism. We have duties to cooperate and reciprocate, but no duty to serve those who manipulate us nor an obvious duty to sacrifice ourselves for people outside our domain of special responsibility. We have a special duty of high altruism toward those in the close circle of our concern, namely, our family and friends.

[5]J. L. Mackie, "The Law of the Jungle: Moral Alternatives and Principles of Evolution," *Philosophy* 53 (1978).

CONCLUSION

Martin Luther once said that humanity is like a man who, when mounting a horse, always falls off on the opposite side, especially when he tries to overcompensate for his previous exaggerations. So it is with ethical egoism. Trying to compensate for an irrational, guilt-ridden, Sucker altruism of the morality of self-effacement, it falls off the horse on the other side, embracing a Cheater's preoccupation with self-exaltation that robs the self of the deepest joys in life. Only the person who mounts properly, avoiding both extremes, is likely to ride the horse of happiness to its goal.

For Further Reflection

1. Evaluate whether this statement, which I first encountered in a student paper, is true or false: "Everyone is an egoist, for everyone always tries to do what will bring them satisfaction."
2. What is the relationship between ethics and evolution? How does this relationship throw light on egoism? What is the significance of reciprocity for ethics?
3. Some philosophers, beginning with Plato, have argued that ethical egoism is irrational, since it precludes psychological health. In an article entitled "Ethical Egoism and Psychological Dispositions" (*American Philosophical Quarterly* 17[1], 1980), Laurence Thomas sets forth the following argument:

    P1. A true friend could never, as a matter of course, be disposed to harm or to exploit anyone with whom he is a friend [definition of a friend].

    P2. An egoist could never be a true friend to anyone [for the egoist must be ready to exploit others whenever it is in his or her interest].

    P3. Only someone with an unhealthy personality could never be a true friend to anyone [definition of a healthy personality; that is, friendship is a necessary condition for a healthy personality].

    P4. Ethical egoism requires that we have a kind of disposition which is incompatible with our having a healthy personality [from P1–P3].

    Conclusion: Therefore, from the standpoint of our psychological makeup, ethical egoism is unacceptable as a moral theory.

   Do you agree with Thomas? How might the ethical egoist respond?

A Critique of Ethical Egoism

JAMES RACHELS

James Rachels (1941–2003) was a professor of philosophy at the University of Alabama at Birmingham and the author of several books and articles on moral philosophy, including *The Elements of Moral Philosophy,* from which this selection is taken. In this essay, Rachels first distinguishes ethical egoism from psychological egoism, the doctrine that people always act out of their own perceived self-interest. Ethical egoism is the doctrine that states that it is always our duty to act exclusively in our self-interest. He examines three arguments in favor of ethical egoism, showing that each fails to support its conclusion, and he then examines three arguments against the doctrine. Rachels concludes that although only one of these three arguments is sound, it is enough to invalidate ethical egoism.

IS THERE A DUTY TO CONTRIBUTE FOR FAMINE RELIEF?

Each year millions of people die of malnutrition and related health problems. A common pattern among children in poor countries is death from dehydration caused by diarrhea brought on by malnutrition. James Grant, executive director of the United Nations Children's Fund (UNICEF), estimates that about 15,000 children die in this way *every day.* That comes to 5,475,000 children annually. Even if his estimate is too high, the number that die is staggering.

For those of us in the affluent countries, this poses an acute moral problem. We spend money on ourselves, not only for the necessities of life but for innumerable luxuries—for fine automobiles, fancy clothes, stereos, sports, movies, and so on. In our country, even people with modest incomes enjoy such things. The problem is that we *could* forgo our luxuries and give the money for famine relief instead. The fact that we don't suggests that we regard our luxuries as more important than feeding the hungry.

Why do we allow people to starve to death when we could save them? Very few of us actually believe our luxuries are that important. Most of us, if asked the question directly, would probably be a bit embarrassed, and we would say that we probably should do more for famine relief. The explanation of why we do not is, at least in part, that we hardly ever think of the problem. Living our own comfortable lives, we are effectively insulated from it. The starving people are dying at some distance from us; we do not see them, and we can

---

avoid even thinking of them. When we do think of them, it is only abstractly, as bloodless statistics. Unfortunately for the starving, statistics do not have much power to motivate action.

But leaving aside the question of *why* we behave as we do, what is our *duty?* What *should* we do? We might think of this as the "common-sense" view of the matter: morality requires that we balance our own interests against the interests of others. It is understandable, of course, that we look out for our own interests, and no one can be faulted for attending to his own basic needs. But at the same time the needs of others are also important, and when we can help others—especially at little cost to ourselves—we should do so. Suppose you are thinking of spending ten dollars on a trip to the movies, when you are reminded that ten dollars could buy food for a starving child. Thus you could do a great service for the child at little cost to yourself. Common-sense morality would say, then, that you should give the money for famine relief rather than spending it on the movies.

This way of thinking involves a general assumption about our moral duties: it is assumed that we have moral duties *to other people*—and not merely duties that we create, such as by making a promise or incurring a debt. We have "natural" duties to others *simply because they are people who could be helped or harmed by our actions.* If a certain action would benefit (or harm) other people, then that is a reason why we should (or should not) do that action. The common-sense assumption is that other people's interests *count,* for their own sakes, from a moral point of view.

But one person's common sense is another person's naive platitude. Some thinkers have maintained that, in fact, we have no "natural" duties to other people. *Ethical Egoism* is the idea that each person ought to pursue his or her own self-interest exclusively. It is different from Psychological Egoism, which is a theory of human nature concerned with how people *do* behave—Psychological Egoism says that people do in fact always pursue their own interests. Ethical Egoism, by contrast, is a normative theory—that is, a theory about how we *ought* to behave. Regardless of how we do behave, Ethical Egoism says we have no moral duty except to do what is best for ourselves.

It is a challenging theory. It contradicts some of our deepest moral beliefs—beliefs held by most of us, at any rate—but it is not easy to refute. We will examine the most important arguments for and against it. If it turns out to be true, then of course that is immensely important. But even if it turns out to be false, there is still much to be learned from examining it—we may, for example, gain some insight into the reasons why we *do* have obligations to other people.

But before looking at the arguments, we should be a little clearer about exactly what this theory says and what it does not say. In the first place, Ethical

Egoism does not say that one should promote one's own interests *as well as* the interests of others. That would be an ordinary, unexceptional view. Ethical Egoism is the radical view that one's *only* duty is to promote one's own interests. According to Ethical Egoism, there is only one ultimate principle of conduct, the principle of self-interest, and this principle sums up *all* of one's natural duties and obligations.

However, Ethical Egoism does not say that you should *avoid* actions that help others, either. It may very well be that in many instances your interests coincide with the interests of others, so that in helping yourself you will be aiding others willy-nilly. Or it may happen that aiding others is an effective *means* for creating some benefit for yourself. Ethical Egoism does not forbid such actions; in fact, it may demand them. The theory insists only that in such cases the benefit to others is not what makes the act right. What makes the act right is, rather, the fact that it is to one's own advantage.

Finally, Ethical Egoism does not imply that in pursuing one's interests one ought always to do what one wants to do, or what gives one the most pleasure in the short run. Someone may want to do something that is not good for himself or that will eventually cause himself more grief than pleasure—he may want to drink a lot or smoke cigarettes or take drugs or waste his best years at the race track. Ethical Egoism would frown on all this, regardless of the momentary pleasure it affords. It says that a person ought to do what *really is* to his or her own best advantage, *over the long run*. It endorses selfishness, but it doesn't endorse foolishness.

THREE ARGUMENTS IN FAVOR OF ETHICAL EGOISM

What reasons can be advanced to support this doctrine? Why should anyone think it is true? Unfortunately, the theory is asserted more often than it is argued for. Many of its supporters apparently think its truth is self-evident, so that arguments are not needed. When it *is* argued for, three lines of reasoning are most commonly used.

1. The first argument has several variations, each suggesting the same general point:

a. Each of us is intimately familiar with our own individual wants and needs. Moreover, each of us is uniquely placed to pursue those wants and needs effectively. At the same time, we know the desires and needs of other people only imperfectly, and we are not well situated to pursue them. Therefore, it is reasonable to believe that if we set out to be "our brother's keeper," we would often bungle the job and end up doing more mischief than good.

b. At the same time, the policy of "looking out for others" is an offensive intrusion into other people's privacy; it is essentially a policy of minding other people's business.

c. Making other people the object of one's "charity" is degrading to them; it robs them of their individual dignity and self-respect. The offer of charity says, in effect, that they are not competent to care for themselves; and the statement is self-fulfilling—they cease to be self-reliant and become passively dependent on others. That is why the recipients of "charity" are so often resentful rather than appreciative.

What this adds up to is that the policy of "looking out for others" is self-defeating. If we want to promote the best interests of everyone alike, we should *not* adopt so-called altruistic policies of behavior. On the contrary, if each person looks after his or her *own* interests, it is more likely that everyone will be better off, in terms of both physical and emotional well-being. Thus Robert G. Olson says in his book *The Morality of Self-Interest* (1965), "The individual is most likely to contribute to social betterment by rationally pursuing his own best long-range interests." Or as Alexander Pope said more poetically,

> Thus God and nature formed the general frame
> And bade self-love and social be the same.

It is possible to quarrel with this argument on a number of grounds. Of course no one favors bungling, butting in, or depriving people of their self-respect. But is this really what we are doing when we feed hungry children? Is the starving child in Ethiopia really harmed when we "intrude" into "her business" by supplying food? It hardly seems likely. Yet we can set this point aside, for considered as an argument for Ethical Egoism, this way of thinking has an even more serious defect.

The trouble is that it isn't really an argument *for Ethical Egoism* at all. The argument concludes that we should adopt certain policies of action; and on the surface they appear to be egoistic policies. However, the *reason* it is said we should adopt those policies is decidedly *un*egoistic. The reason is one that to an egoist shouldn't matter. It is said that we should adopt those policies because doing so will promote the "betterment of society"—but according to Ethical Egoism, that is something we should not be concerned about. Spelled out fully, with everything laid on the table, the argument says:

1. We ought to do whatever will promote the best interests of everyone alike.
2. The interests of everyone will best be promoted if each of us adopts the policy of pursuing our own interests exclusively.

3. Therefore, each of us should adopt the policy of pursuing our own interests exclusively.

If we accept this reasoning, then we are not ethical egoists at all. Even though we might end up *behaving* like egoists, our ultimate principle is one of beneficence—we are doing what we think will help everyone, not merely what we think will benefit ourselves. Rather than being egoists, we turn out to be altruists with a peculiar view of what in fact promotes the general welfare.

2. The second argument was put forward with some force by Ayn Rand, a writer little heeded by professional philosophers but who nevertheless was enormously popular on college campuses during the 1960s and 1970s. Ethical Egoism, in her view, is the only ethical philosophy that respects the integrity of the individual human life. She regarded the ethics of "altruism" as a totally destructive idea, both in society as a whole and in the lives of individuals taken in by it. Altruism, to her way of thinking, leads to a denial of the value of the individual. It says to a person: *your* life is merely something that may be sacrificed. "If a man accepts the ethics of altruism," she writes, "his first concern is not how to live his life, but how to sacrifice it." Moreover, those who would *promote* this idea are beneath contempt—they are parasites who, rather than working to build and sustain their own lives, leech off those who do. Again, she writes:

> Parasites, moochers, looters, brutes and thugs can be of no value to a human being—nor can he gain any benefit from living in a society geared to *their* needs, demands and protections, a society that treats him as a sacrificial animal and penalizes him for his virtues in order to reward *them* for their vices, which means: a society based on the ethics of altruism.

By "sacrificing one's life" Rand does not necessarily mean anything so dramatic as dying. A person's life consists (in part) of projects undertaken and goods earned and created. To demand that a person abandon his projects or give up his goods is also a clear effort to "sacrifice his life." Furthermore, throughout her writings Rand also suggests that there is a *metaphysical* basis for egoistic ethics. Somehow, it is the only ethics that takes seriously the *reality* of the individual person. She bemoans "the enormity of the extent to which altruism erodes men's capacity to grasp . . . the value of an individual life; it reveals a mind from which the reality of a human being has been wiped out."

What, then, of the starving people? It might be argued, in response, that Ethical Egoism "reveals a mind from which the reality of a human being has been wiped out"—namely, the human being who is starving. Rand quotes with approval the evasive answer given by one of her followers:

"Once, when Barbara Brandon was asked by a student: 'What will happen to the poor . . . ?'—she answered: 'If *you* want to help them, you will not be stopped.'"

All these remarks are, I think, part of one continuous argument that can be summarized like this:

1. A person has only one life to live. If we place any value on the individual—that is, if the individual has any moral worth—then we must agree that this life is of supreme importance. After all, it is all one has, and all one is.
2. The ethics of altruism regards the life of the individual as something one must be ready to sacrifice for the good of others.
3. Therefore, the ethics of altruism does not take seriously the value of the human individual.
4. Ethical Egoism, which allows each person to view his or her own life as being of ultimate value, *does* take the human individual seriously—in fact, it is the only philosophy that does so.
5. Thus, Ethical Egoism is the philosophy that ought to be accepted.

The problem with this argument, as you may already have noticed, is that it relies on picturing the alternatives in such an extreme way. "The ethics of altruism" is taken to be such an extreme philosophy that *nobody,* with the possible exception of certain monks, would find it congenial. As Ayn Rand presents it, altruism implies that one's own interests have *no* value, and that *any* demand by others calls for sacrificing them. If that is the alternative, then any other view, including Ethical Egoism, will look good by comparison. But this is hardly a fair picture of the choices. What we called the common-sense view stands somewhere between the two extremes. It says that one's own interests and the interests of others are both important and must be balanced against one another. Sometimes, when the balancing is done, it will turn out that one should act in the interests of others; other times, it will turn out that one should take care of oneself. So even if the Randian argument refutes the extreme "ethics of altruism," it does not follow that one must accept the other extreme of Ethical Egoism.

3. The third line of reasoning takes a somewhat different approach. Ethical Egoism is usually presented as a *revisionist* moral philosophy, that is, as a philosophy that says our common-sense moral views are mistaken and need to be changed. It is possible, however, to interpret Ethical Egoism in a much less radical way, as a theory that *accepts* common-sense morality and offers a surprising account of its basis.

The less radical interpretation goes as follows. In everyday life, we assume that we are obliged to obey certain rules. We must avoid doing harm to others, speak the truth, keep our promises, and so on. At first glance, these duties appear to be very different from one another. They appear to have little in common. Yet from a theoretical point of view, we may wonder whether there is not some hidden *unity* underlying the hodge-podge of separate duties. Perhaps there is some small number of fundamental principles that explain all the rest, just as in physics there are basic principles that bring together and explain diverse phenomena. From a theoretical point of view, the smaller the number of basic principles, the better. Best of all would be *one* fundamental principle, from which all the rest could be derived. Ethical Egoism, then, would be the theory that all our duties are ultimately derived from the one fundamental principle of self-interest.

Taken in this way, Ethical Egoism is not such a radical doctrine. It does not challenge common-sense morality; it only tries to explain and systematize it. And it does a surprisingly successful job. It can provide plausible explanations of the duties mentioned above, and more:

a. If we make a habit of doing things that are harmful to other people, people will not be reluctant to do things that will harm *us*. We will be shunned and despised; others will not have us as friends and will not do us favors when we need them. If our offenses against others are serious enough, we may even end up in jail. Thus it is to our own advantage to avoid harming others.

b. If we lie to other people, we will suffer all the ill effects of a bad reputation. People will distrust us and avoid doing business with us. We will often need for people to be honest with us, but we can hardly expect them to feel much of an obligation to be honest with us if they know we have not been honest with them. Thus it is to our own advantage to be truthful.

c. It is to our own advantage to be able to enter into mutually beneficial arrangements with other people. To benefit from those arrangements, we need to be able to rely on others to keep their parts of the bargains we make with them—we need to be able to rely on them to keep their promises to us. But we can hardly expect others to keep their promises to us if we are not willing to keep our promises to them. Therefore, from the point of view of self-interest, we should keep our promises.

Pursuing this line of reasoning, Thomas Hobbes suggested that the principle of Ethical Egoism leads to nothing less than the Golden Rule: we should "do unto others" *because* if we do, others will be more likely to "do unto us."

Does this argument succeed in establishing Ethical Egoism as a viable theory of morality? It is, in my opinion at least, the best try. But there are two serious objections to it. In the first place, the argument does not prove quite as much as it needs to prove. At best, it shows only that *as a general rule* it is to one's own advantage to avoid harming others. It does not show that this is *always* so. And it could not show that, for even though it may usually to be one's advantage to avoid harming others, sometimes it is not. Sometimes one might even *gain* from treating another person badly. In that case, the obligation not to harm the other person could *not* be derived from the principle of Ethical Egoism. Thus it appears that not all our moral obligations can be explained as derivable from self-interest.

But set that point aside. There is still a more fundamental question to be asked about the proposed theory. Suppose it is true that, say, contributing money for famine relief is somehow to one's own advantage. It does not follow that this is the only reason, or even the most basic reason, why doing so is a morally good thing. (For example, the most basic reason might be *in order to help the starving people.* The fact that doing so is also to one's own advantage might be only a secondary, less important, consideration.) A demonstration that one could *derive* this duty from self-interest does not prove that self-interest is the *only reason* one has this duty. Only if you accept an additional proposition—namely, the proposition that there is no reason for giving *other than* self-interest—will you find Ethical Egoism a plausible theory.

THREE ARGUMENTS AGAINST ETHICAL EGOISM

Ethical Egoism has haunted twentieth-century moral philosophy. It has not been a popular doctrine; the most important philosophers have rejected it outright. But it has never been very far from their minds. Although no thinker of consequence has defended it, almost everyone has felt it necessary to explain why he was rejecting it—as though the very possibility that it might be correct was hanging in the air, threatening to smother their other ideas. As the merits of the various "refutations" have been debated, philosophers have returned to it again and again.

The following three arguments are typical of the refutations proposed by contemporary philosophers.

1. In his book *The Moral Point of View* (1958), Kurt Baier argues that Ethical Egoism cannot be correct because it cannot provide solutions for conflicts of interest. We need moral rules, he says, only because our interests sometimes come into conflict. (If they never conflicted, then there would be no problems to solve and hence no need for the kind of guidance that morality provides.) But Ethical Egoism does not help to resolve conflicts of interest; it only exacerbates them. Baier argues for this by introducing a fanciful example:

> Let B and K be candidates for the presidency of a certain country and let it be granted that it is in the interest of either to be elected, but that only one can succeed. It would then be in the interest of B but against the interest of K if B

> were elected, and vice versa, and therefore in the interest of B but against the interest of K if K were liquidated, and vice versa. But from this it would follow that B ought to liquidate K, that it is wrong for B not to do so, that B has not "done his duty" until he has liquidated K; and vice versa. Similarly K, knowing that his own liquidation is in the interest of B and therefore, anticipating B's attempts to secure it, ought to take steps to foil B's endeavors. It would be wrong for him not to do so. He would "not have done his duty" until he had made sure of stopping B. . . .
>
> This is obviously absurd. For morality is designed to apply in just such cases, namely, those where interests conflict. But if the point of view of morality were that of self-interest, then there could never be moral solutions of conflicts of interest.

Does this argument prove that Ethical Egoism is unacceptable? It does, *if* the conception of morality to which it appeals is accepted. The argument assumes that an adequate morality must provide solutions for conflicts of interest in such a way that everyone concerned can live together harmoniously. The conflict between B and K, for example, should be resolved so that they would no longer be at odds with one another. (One would not then have a duty to do something that the other has a duty to prevent.) Ethical Egoism does not do that, and if you think an ethical theory should, then you will not find Ethical Egoism acceptable.

But a defender of Ethical Egoism might reply that *he* does not accept this conception of morality. For him, life is essentially a long series of conflicts in which each person is struggling to come out on top; and the principle he accepts—the principle of Ethical Egoism—simply urges each one to do his or her best to win. On his view, the moralist is not like a courtroom judge, who resolves disputes. Instead, he is like the Commissioner of Boxing, who urges each fighter to do his best. So the conflict between B and K will be "resolved" not by the application of an ethical theory but by one or the other of them winning the struggle. The egoist will not be embarrassed by this—on the contrary, he will think it no more than a realistic view of the nature of things.

2. Some philosophers, including Baier, have leveled an even more serious charge against Ethical Egoism. They have argued that it is a *logically inconsistent* doctrine—that is, they say it leads to logical contradictions. If this is true, then Ethical Egoism is indeed a mistaken theory, for no theory can be true if it is self-contradictory.

Consider B and K again. As Baier explains their predicament, it is in B's interest to kill K, and obviously it is in K's interest to prevent it. But, Baier says,

> if K prevents B from liquidating him, his act must be said to be both wrong and not wrong—wrong because it is the prevention of what B ought to do, his

duty, and wrong for B not to do it; not wrong because it is what K ought to do, his duty, and wrong for K not to do it. But one and the same act (logically) cannot be both morally wrong and not morally wrong.

Now, does *this* argument prove that Ethical Egoism is unacceptable? At first glance it seems persuasive. However, it is a complicated argument, so we need to set it out with each step individually identified. Then we will be in a better position to evaluate it. Spelled out fully, it looks like this:

1. Suppose it is each person's duty to do what is in his own best interests.
2. It is in B's best interest to liquidate K.
3. It is in K's best interest to prevent B from liquidating him.
4. Therefore B's duty is to liquidate K, and K's duty is to prevent B from doing it.
5. But it is wrong to prevent someone from doing his duty.
6. Therefore it is wrong for K to prevent B from liquidating him.
7. Therefore it is both wrong and not wrong for K to prevent B from liquidating him.
8. But no act can be both wrong and not wrong—that is a self-contradiction.
9. Therefore the assumption with which we started—that it is each person's duty to do what is in his own best interests—cannot be true.

When the argument is set out in this way, we can see its hidden flaw. The logical contradiction—that it is both wrong and not wrong for K to prevent B from liquidating him—does *not* follow simply from the principle of Ethical Egoism. It follows from that principle, *and* the additional premise expressed in step (5)—namely, that "it is wrong to prevent someone from doing his duty." Thus we are not compelled by the logic of the argument to reject Ethical Egoism. Instead, we could simply reject this additional premise, and the contradiction would be avoided. That is surely what the ethical egoist would want to do, for the ethical egoist would never say, without qualification, that it is always wrong to prevent someone from doing his duty. He would say, instead, that *whether one ought to prevent someone from doing his duty depends entirely on whether it would be to one's own advantage to do so.* Regardless of whether we think this is a correct view, it is, at the very least, a *consistent* view, and so this attempt to convict the egoist of self-contradiction fails.

3. Finally, we come to the argument that I think comes closest to an outright refutation of Ethical Egoism. It is also the most interesting of the arguments, because at the same time it provides the most insight into why the interests of other people *should* matter to a moral agent.

Before this argument is presented, we need to look briefly at a general point about moral values. So let us set Ethical Egoism aside for a moment and consider this related matter.

There is a whole family of moral views that have this in common: they all involve dividing people into groups and saying that the interests of some groups count for more than the interests of other groups. Racism is the most conspicuous example; it involves dividing people into groups according to race and assigning greater importance to the interests of one race than to others. The practical result is that members of the preferred race are to be *treated better* than the others. Anti-Semitism works the same way, and so can nationalism. People in the grip of such views will think, in effect: "*My* race counts for more," or "Those who believe in *my* religion count for more," or "*My* country counts for more," and so on.

Can such views be defended? Those who accept them are usually not much interested in argument—racists, for example, rarely try to offer rational grounds for their position. But suppose they did. What could they say?

There is a general principle that stands in the way of any such defense, namely: *We can justify treating people differently only if we can show that there is some factual difference between them that is relevant to justifying the difference in treatment.* For example, if one person is admitted to law school while another is rejected, this can be justified by pointing out that the first graduated from college with honors and scored well on the admissions test, while the second dropped out of college and never took the test. However, if *both* graduated with honors and did well on the entrance examination—in other words, if they are in all relevant respects equally well qualified—then it is merely arbitrary to admit one but not the other.

Can a racist point to any differences between, say, white people and black people that would justify treating them differently? In the past, racists have sometimes attempted to do this by picturing blacks as stupid, lacking in ambition, and the like. *If* this were true, then it might justify treating them differently, in at least some circumstances. (This is the deep purpose of racist stereotypes—to provide the "relevant differences" needed to justify differences in treatment.) But of course it is not true, and in fact there are no such general differences between the races. Thus racism is an *arbitrary* doctrine, in that it advocates treating some people differently even though there are no differences between them to justify it.

Ethical Egoism is a moral theory of the same type. It advocates that each of us divide the world into two categories of people—ourselves and all the rest—and that we regard the interests of those in the first group as more important than the interests of those in the second group. But each of us can ask, what is the difference between myself and others that justifies placing myself in this special category? Am I more intelligent? Do I enjoy my life more? Are my accomplishments greater? Do I have needs or abilities that are so different from the needs or abilities of others? *What is it that makes me so special?* Failing an answer, it turns out that Ethical Egoism is an arbitrary doctrine, in the same way that racism is arbitrary.

The argument, then, is this:

1. Any moral doctrine that assigns greater importance to the interests of one group than to those of another is unacceptably arbitrary unless there is some difference between the members of the groups that justifies treating them differently.
2. Ethical Egoism would have each person assign greater importance to his or her own interests than to the interests of others. *But there is no general difference between oneself and others, to which each person can appeal, that justifies this difference in treatment.*
3. Therefore, Ethical Egoism is unacceptably arbitrary.

And this, in addition to arguing against Ethical Egoism, also sheds some light on the question of why we should care about others.

We should care about the interests of other people *for the very same reason we care about our own interests;* for their needs and desires are comparable to our own. Consider, one last time, the starving people we could feed by giving up some of our luxuries. Why should we care about them? We care about ourselves, of course—if *we* were starving, we would go to almost any lengths to get food. But what is the difference between us and them? Does hunger affect them any less? Are they somehow less deserving than we? If we can find no relevant difference between us and them, then we must admit that if *our* needs should be met, so should *theirs.* It is this realization, that we are on a par with one another, that is the deepest reason why our morality must include some recognition of the needs of others, and why, then, Ethical Egoism fails as a moral theory.

For Further Reflection

1. Go over the three arguments for ethical egoism. Do you agree with Rachels's assessment that they all fail to establish the theory? Could a slight modification in any of them save the theory?
2. How does the third argument lead to the Golden Rule? Why is it the "best try"?
3. Identify the three arguments against ethical egoism. Which of them, if any, refutes ethical egoism?

Further Readings for Chapter 8

Axelrod, Robert M. *The Evolution of Cooperation.* New York: Basic Books, 1984. A brilliant study on the rationality of cooperation.

Dawkins, Richard. *The Selfish Gene.* 2nd ed. Oxford: Oxford University Press, 1989. One of the most fascinating studies on the subject, defending limited altruism.

Gauthier, David, ed. *Morality and Rational Self-Interest.* Englewood Cliffs, N.J.: Prentice-Hall, 1970.

———. *Morality by Agreement.* Oxford: Clarendon Press, 1986.

Hospers, John. *Human Conduct: An Introduction to the Problems of Ethics.* New York: Harcourt Brace Jovanovich, 1961.

MacIntyre, Alasdair. "Egoism and Altruism." In *The Encyclopedia of Philosophy,* edited by Paul Edwards. New York: Macmillan, 1967.

Nielsen, Kai. "Why Should I Be Moral?" *Methodos* 15, no. 59–60 (1963). This comprehensive article appears in several anthologies.

Olen, Jeffrey. *Moral Freedom.* Philadelphia: Temple University Press, 1988.

Rachels, James. *The Elements of Moral Philosophy.* New York: Random House, 1986. See chapters 5 and 6.

Rand, Ayn. *The Virtue of Selfishness.* New York: New American Library, 1964.

Singer, Peter. *The Expanding Circle: Ethics and Sociobiology.* New York: Farrar, Straus & Giroux, 1981. A good discussion of egoism in the light of sociobiology.

Taylor, Richard. *Good and Evil.* New York: Macmillan, 1970. See especially chapter 5.

CHAPTER 9

Does Life Have Meaning?

Here are the kinds of questions about life—serious, uneasy questions—that we all ask ourselves sooner or later, often despairing of ever finding answers while wondering if the questions themselves make any sense:

> What is the meaning of life? What, if anything, makes life meaningful? What would make *my* life meaningful? Is life worth living?
>
> Does life have a purpose? What is the purpose of *my* life? Why am I here? What is the point of it all?
>
> Does God give life purpose? How can humans have a purpose if there is no God to give them one? How can we matter if we are, as science seems to suggest, not part of some divine cosmic plan?
>
> What meaning can my life have if all my struggles, hopes, and schemes ultimately end in death? What meaning can anything I do have if it will inevitably be undone and forgotten?
>
> We are microscopic specks in a vast cosmos—ants on a tiny blue rock spinning around a star identical to billions of other stars strewn among billions of galaxies. So how can we think our lives are of any significance at all? How can anything we do matter?
>
> In a world darkened by suffering and loss—where children starve, despots enslave, disease kills, and injustice thrives—how can life have any meaning?
>
> To all of this, some people may be tempted to respond, "Who cares?"

But people do care. Successful people sometimes ponder such questions when, despite their many achievements, they begin to wonder what the point of all their work has been. They ask: What is the ultimate purpose of all this activity? Why should I go on? Happy people devoted to the pursuit of pleasure can gradually—or quite suddenly—come to believe that their lives are trivial and without value. People living well-planned and steady lives can find their blueprint for life to be humdrum, arbitrary, or aimless. Questions about life's meaning are forced to the surface by misfortune, tragedy, and heartbreak—by the death of a loved one, the failure of a career or business, disenchantment with a political or social cause, collapse of a worldview or belief system, devastating illness and disability, social isolation, poverty, racism, persecution. In such cases, life can seem bereft of meaning. And then a deeper question may arise unbidden: Why should I keep living?

Philosophy has plenty of useful things to say about meaning in life, although that has not always been the case. Philosophers have traditionally explored the goods that a life should contain if it is to matter, even though they did not usually apply the term "meaning of life." Some famous philosophers have even insisted that probing the meaning of life is the central task of philosophy. Albert Camus (1913–1960), for example, declared in his essay "The Myth of Sisyphus," "There is but one truly serious philosophical problem, and that is suicide. Judging whether life is or is not worth living amounts to answering the fundamental question of philosophy."[1] But only in the last three or four decades have Anglo-American philosophers begun to take the subject seriously and produce insightful work in this emerging field.

In most of the twentieth century, philosophers ignored or dismissed the question of life's meaning, even though many people (especially students) assumed that philosophy is *mostly* about the meaning of life. A lot of philosophers have insisted that the question is nonsensical because "meaning" is a term that typically refers to words and symbols, not objects, activities, and lives. To them, asking "What is the meaning of life?" was like asking "How heavy is the color blue?" Others have thought the question fundamentally unanswerable, that answering it is in principle not possible, or that even if answerable, no one knows or ever will know the answer.

This icy pessimism about meaning in life has been thawing. The thaw has taken the form of a growing number of philosophers probing two areas: (1) what the meaning-of-life question *means* (what we're really asking when we enquire about life's meaning) and (2) what, if anything, makes life *meaningful* (what things can give meaning to a person's life). The result has been greater understanding and clarity and a sense among

[1]Albert Camus, "The Myth of Sisyphus," from *The Myth of Sisyphus*, trans. Justin O'Brien (New York: Penguin, 1955).

those working in the field that—contrary to the pessimists—meaning in life is indeed possible.

Philosophers agree that life's meaning is a vitally important intrinsic value. That is, it is valuable for its own sake, not just as a means to something else. They also distinguish between meaning of life *in general* (or meaning of the universe or the human species) and meaning *in individual lives*. People usually call the former "meaning *of* life," and sometimes they refer to the latter as "meaning *in* life." For many, "meaning of life" is about meaning derived from God or religion or some spiritual or sacred order. They tend to ask questions like "What's it all about?" or "What does it all mean?" For others, "meaning in life" is about meaning that they find or create for themselves. They might ask "Is my life meaningful?" or "What things give my life meaning?"

Mixing up these two senses of meaning can cause confusion. When people assert that life is meaningless, they may be saying only that life as a whole has no meaning, not that individual lives are meaningless. And when they say that life has meaning, they may be referring only to the meaning that their own lives exhibit.

The majority of the philosophical investigations of life's meaning have focused on meaning *in* life, on the quality or qualities that make an individual life worth living. Philosophers differ on these questions, but there are some common themes and even consensus on some matters.

Most in the field argue that meaning in life is not about just one thing. This monist (one thing only) idea about meaning is a misunderstanding encouraged by the word *the* in "the meaning of life." Having a meaningful life is not, they insist, *only* about achieving worthwhile goals, or *only* being involved with something greater than yourself, or *only* attaining choice-worthy purposes. Meaning in life is pluralistic; it has to do with several different elements. The philosopher Thaddeus Metz, author of *Meaning in Life: An Analytic Study*, offers this pluralistic account:

> Specifically, I advance a family resemblance approach, according to which enquiry into life's meaning is, roughly, about a cluster of ideas that overlap with one another. To ask about meaning, I submit, is to pose questions such as: which ends, beside one's own pleasure as such, are most worth pursuing for their own sake; how to transcend one's animal nature; and what in life merits great esteem and admiration.[2]

[2]Thaddeus Metz, *Meaning in Life: An Analytic Study* (Oxford: Oxford University Press, 2013), 34.

Joshua Seachris, editor of *Exploring the Meaning of Life: An Anthology and Guide*, also takes the pluralistic approach:

> Indeed, when you ask both nonphilosophers and philosophers what they take the question [of life's meaning] to mean, you will likely hear it explicated in terms of value, worth, significance, or purpose. . . . "Around what purposes should I order my life?" or "Does my life achieve some good purpose?" "What confers value on my life?" or "What makes my life worthwhile and not irredeemably futile?" or "What brings narrative coherence and intelligibility to my life (or some subset of its parts)?" or "In virtue of what is my life worthy of great esteem?"[3]

One way to understand the pluralistic perspective is to see the different manifestations of meaning as aspects of a single quality—value. According to the philosopher Iddo Landau,

> The meaning of life, then, has to do primarily with value . . . Complaints that there is no meaning in life are complaints that there is insufficient value in life. Questions about the meaning of life are questions about what is of sufficient worth in life. A meaningful life is one in which there is sufficient number of aspects of sufficient value, and a meaningless life is one in which there is not a sufficient number of aspects of sufficient value. This is one reason why people who take their lives to be meaningless sometimes say that they sense emptiness, although they occasionally find it difficult to explain what their lives are empty of. When asked in discussions, they sometimes reach the view that their lives are empty of issues of sufficiently high value.[4]

If the pluralistic standpoint is correct, then "What is *the* meaning of life?" is the wrong question.

The consensus among philosophers is that meaning in life is not only multidimensional, it can also vary in intensity or quality. The meaningfulness of a life is not an all-or-nothing business. As Metz explains,

> Nearly all those writing on meaning in life believe that it comes in degrees, so that, say, some lives as a whole are more meaningful that others . . . Note that calling someone's life "more important" or "more significant"

[3]Joshua Seachris, ed., *Exploring the Meaning of Life: An Anthology and Guide* (Malden, MA: John Wiley and Sons, 2013), 10.
[4]Iddo Landau, *Finding Meaning in an Imperfect World* (New York: Oxford University Press, 2017), 15–16.

than another's might be thought to imply some kind of assessment from a moral perspective, but in the present context it does not. One can coherently hold the view that some people's lives are less meaningful, important, etc. than others, or even downright meaningless, and still maintain that people have an equal moral status grounding obligations to help and not to harm.[5]

People tend to equate meaningfulness in life with happiness, but most who study meaning think this is a mistake. Philosophers have much to say about the relationship between meaningfulness and happiness or pleasure. For now, we can let the philosopher John Martin Fischer make the most salient point:

> We certainly want to be happy. But meaningfulness is not the same as happiness, although we would expect a connection between them. If one's life is meaningful, then probably the individual would be happy. But we can certainly imagine people with meaningful lives—scientists, artists, poets, philosophers, and so on—who struggle in their fields and are thus not very happy (if they are happy at all). Or we can consider people whose careers are deeply engaging and meaningful, but whose personal lives are troubled and who are thus not very happy. The recent suicides of the enormously successful fashion designer Kate Spade and the famous chef and television personality Anthony Bourdain illustrate this point.
>
> We can also imagine a very happy individual whose happiness comes from what we would consider trivial or superficial activities—maybe a life devoted to crossword puzzles, Sudoku, or counting the bulbs in the banks of lights at Dodger Stadium. We shouldn't be elitist and perhaps these lives are *to some degree* meaningful. But meaning in life is *not* the same a happiness. One can have a very happy life that is only somewhat meaningful, and a very meaningful life that is not very happy.[6]

To be meaningful (however *meaning* is defined), what features must a life have? What activities, attitudes, or pursuits must a life comprise? Philosophers have investigated and critiqued particular meaning-conferring features and devised theories to explain how those can or should fit together. They, like the rest of us, have an intuitive sense of what these features might be. They identify many activities and experiences as meaningful, although they differ about the comparative worth of these

[5]Metz, *Meaning in Life*, 4.

[6]John Martin Fischer, *Death, Mortality, and Meaning in Life* (New York: Oxford University Press, 2020), 2–3.

factors and how they are related. Unsurprisingly, the list includes loving and caring relationships, friendship, creativity, beauty, personal excellence, moral goodness, helping others, knowledge, transcendence, and achievement.

Is there a principle or theory that identifies a common thread that runs through all or most of these sources of meaning? Is there a theme that unites them? Philosophers have offered several different possibilities. They have argued that the elements that give meaning to life are those that involve: living according to your vision of life; recognizing the value of love; loving the good in everything; filling life with objective moral goods (love, loyalty, trust, etc.); exercising your capacity for creative activity; using or advancing your rational nature in exceptional ways; actively engaging in projects of objective worth; creating a world where happiness and love can thrive; or transcending yourself through moral, intellectual, and artistic achievement.

Any honest examination of life's meaning must take into account the views of philosophical nihilists (or pessimists) who deny that life has any meaning or value. They have argued, among other things, that nothing matters because life is unremitting struggle, dissatisfaction, and pointless repetition; because in a thousand years nothing we do now will matter; because our lives will end in death and the cosmos in annihilation; because from the cosmic perspective life is absurd, arbitrary, and insignificant; because there is no God to give our lives purpose; and because there is no objective morality. Are the nihilists right? Contemporary philosophers acknowledge that there is truth in some nihilist claims, but they have also challenged them and argued for the possibility of meaningful lives.

Most people seem to think meaning in life is some grand, towering truth. Or a deep mystery revealed only to the fortunate few, some esoteric wisdom that must be extracted from gurus and sages who live in caves or temples. This chapter should convince you otherwise—and demonstrate that with the help of philosophy, you can find your own way.

Consider this odd fairytale. A graduate student with a master's in business pays a visit to a philosophy professor. The student has come seeking something that she has so far failed to acquire in her studies: the ultimate secret, the meaning of life. The professor pauses, then answers in his best guru-like voice, "The meaning of life is . . . a big purple thing." Silence. The professor chuckles; the student doesn't know whether to laugh or sigh.

With his absurd answer the professor means to make a point, or several. There is no great secret concerning the meaning of life, no cryptic bit of knowledge that, once known, will reveal all. There is no slogan or incantation or parable that will ensure your life is worth living. Moreover, no one can simply hand you the meaning of life as if it were a gift basket. The process of examining the question of life's meaning or purpose is *personal.* You have to make that journey yourself. No one can bestow upon you what you must find for yourself, no more than a friend can tell you what your favorite foods are supposed to be.

The Good Brahmin

VOLTAIRE

Voltaire (1694–1778) was one of the greatest French philosophers of the eighteenth century and the author of several works, including *Candide* (1759), *Treatise on Tolerance* (1763), and *Philosophical Dictionary* (1764). The story of the Good Brahmin has to do with despair and the meaning of life.

On my travels I met an old Brahmin, a very wise man, of marked intellect and great learning. Furthermore, he was rich and, consequently, all the wiser, because, lacking nothing, he needed to deceive nobody. His household was very well managed by three handsome women who set themselves out to please him. When he was not amusing himself with his women, he passed the time in philosophizing. Near his house, which was beautifully decorated and had charming gardens attached, there lived a narrow-minded old Indian woman: she was a simpleton, and rather poor.

Said the Brahmin to me one day: "I wish I had never been born!" On my asking why, he answered: "I have been studying forty years, and that is forty years wasted. I teach others and myself am ignorant of everything. Such a state of affairs fills my soul with so much humiliation and disgust that my life is intolerable. I was born in Time, I live in Time, and yet I do not know what

"Story of a Good Brahmin" from *The Portable Voltaire* by Voltaire, edited by Ben Ray Redman,

Time is. I am at a point between two eternities, as our wise men say, and I have no conception of eternity. I am composed of matter: I think, but I have never been able to learn what produces my thought. I do not know whether or not my understanding is a simple faculty inside me, such as those of walking and digesting, and whether or not I think with my head as I grip with my hands. Not only is the cause of my thought unknown to me; the cause of my actions is equally a mystery. I do not know why I exist, and yet every day people ask me questions on all these points. I have to reply, and as I have nothing really worth saying I talk a great deal, and am ashamed of myself afterward for having talked.

"It is worse still when I am asked if Brahma was born of Vishnu or if they are both eternal. God is my witness that I have not the remotest idea, and my ignorance shows itself in my replies. 'Ah, Holy One,' people say to me, 'tell us why evil pervades the earth.' I am in as great a difficulty as those who ask me this question. Sometimes I tell them that everything is as well as can be, but those who have been ruined and broken in the wars do not believe a word of it—and no more do I. I retire to my home stricken at my own curiosity and ignorance. I read our ancient books, and they double my darkness. I talk to my companions: some answer me that we must enjoy life and make game of mankind; others think they know a lot and lose themselves in a maze of wild ideas. Everything increases my anguish. I am ready sometimes to despair when I think that after all my seeking I do not know whence I came, whither I go, what I am nor what I shall become."

The good man's condition really worried me. Nobody was more rational or more sincere than he. I perceived that his unhappiness increased in proportion as his understanding developed and his insight grew.

The same day I saw the old woman who lived near him. I asked her if she had ever been troubled by the thought that she was ignorant of the nature of her soul. She did not even understand my question. Never in all her life had she reflected for one single moment on one single point of all those which tormented the Brahmin. She believed with all her heart in the metamorphoses of Vishnu and, provided she could obtain a little Ganges water wherewith to wash herself, thought herself the happiest of women.

Struck with this mean creature's happiness, I returned to my wretched philosopher. "Are you not ashamed," said I, "to be unhappy when at your very door there lives an old automaton who thinks about nothing, and yet lives contentedly?"

"You are right," he replied. "I have told myself a hundred times that I should be happy if I were as brainless as my neighbor, and yet I do not desire such happiness."

My Brahmin's answer impressed me more than all the rest. I set to examining myself, and I saw that in truth I would not care to be happy at the price of being a simpleton.

I put the matter before some philosophers, and they were of my opinion. "Nevertheless," said I, "there is a tremendous contradiction in this mode of thought, for, after all, the problem is—how to be happy. What does it matter whether one has brains or not? Further, those who are contented with their lot are certain of their contentment, whereas those who reason are not certain that they reason correctly. It is quite clear, therefore," I continued, "that we must choose not to have common sense, however little common sense may contribute to our discomfort." Everyone agreed with me, but I found nobody, notwithstanding, who was willing to accept the bargain of becoming a simpleton in order to become contented. From which I conclude that if we consider the question of happiness we must consider still more the question of reason.

But on reflection it seems that to prefer reason to felicity is to be very senseless. How can this contradiction be explained? Like all the other contradictions. It is matter for much talk.

For Further Reflection

1. Discuss the sense of meaninglessness and despair that the good, but unhappy, Brahmin feels. Why does he experience such emptiness in life?
2. Compare the Brahmin with the old and contented woman. Why would people prefer to be the Brahmin rather than the unreflective woman? Would you rather be a happy simpleton than a sometimes sad but rational person who must live with a sense of the absurd? Consider animals, so long as they are fed, as the epitome of contentment. They never ask about the meaning of life. Is the sense of the absurd a hallmark of our superior rationality?

Hedonism

EPICURUS

The Greek philosopher Epicurus (341–271 B.C.) founded the school of philosophy named after himself, *epicureanism*, a hedonistic theory wherein good is identified with pleasure and evil with pain. In this respect his philosophy is the precursor of Bentham's utilitarianism (Chapter 4). But contrary to popular opinion, Epicurus's version of hedonism is nothing like the modern ideas connected with his name—sensuality, profligacy, and decadence. On the contrary, he believed that the good life consists in simple but deep pleasures and the absence of pain, in an attitude of imperturbable emotional tranquility. We should seek pleasure in conversation, friendship, a good but simple diet, and a prudent life. Since only good and bad sensations should concern us, and since death is not a sensation, we should not fear death. We should not even think very much about it.

Become accustomed to the belief that death is nothing to us. For all good and evil consists in sensation, but death is deprivation of sensation. And therefore a right understanding that death is nothing to us makes the mortality of life enjoyable, not because it adds to it an infinite span of time, but because it takes away the craving for immortality. For there is nothing terrible in life for the man who has truly comprehended that there is nothing terrible in not living. So that the man speaks but idly who says that he fears death not because it will be painful when it comes, but because it is painful in anticipation. For that which gives no trouble when it comes, is but an empty pain in anticipation. So death, the most terrifying of ills, is nothing to us, since so long as we exist, death is not with us; but when death comes, then we do not exist. It does not then concern either the living or the dead, since for the former it is not, and the latter are no more.

But the many at one moment shun death as the greatest of evils, at another yearn for it as a respite from the evils in life. But the wise man neither seeks to escape life nor fears the cessation of life, for neither does life offend him nor does the absence of life seem to be any evil. And just as with food he does not seek simply the larger share and nothing else, but rather the most pleasant, so he seeks to enjoy not the longest period of time, but the most pleasant.

And he who counsels the young man to live well, but the old man to make a good end, is foolish, not merely because of the desirability of life, but also because it is the same training which teaches to live well and to die well. Yet much worse still is the man who says it is good not to be born, but

> once born make haste to pass the gates of Death.

For if he says this from conviction why does he not pass away out of life? For it is open to him to do so, if he had firmly made up his mind to this. But if he speaks in jest, his words are idle among men who cannot receive them.

We must then bear in mind that the future is neither ours, nor yet wholly not ours, so that we may not altogether expect it as sure to come, nor abandon hope of it, as if it will certainly not come.

We must consider that of desires some are natural, others vain, and of the natural some are necessary and others merely natural; and of the necessary some are necessary for happiness, others for the repose of the body, and others for very life. The right understanding of these facts enables us to refer all choice and avoidance to the health of the body and the soul's freedom from disturbance, since this is the aim of the life of blessedness. For it is to obtain this end that we always act, namely, to avoid pain and fear. And when this is once secured for us, all the tempest of the soul is dispersed, since the living creature has not to wander as though in search of something that is missing, and to look for some other thing by which he can fulfil the good of the soul and the good of the body. For it is then that we have need of pleasure, when we feel pain owing to the absence of pleasure; but when we do not feel pain, we no longer need pleasure. And for this cause we call pleasure the beginning and end of the blessed life. For we recognize pleasure as the first good innate in us, and from pleasure we begin every act of choice and avoidance, and to pleasure we return again, using the feeling as the standard by which we judge every good.

And since pleasure is the first good and natural to us, for this very reason we do not choose every pleasure, but sometimes we pass over many pleasures, when greater discomfort accrues to us as the result of them: and similarly we think many pains better than pleasures, since a greater pleasure comes to us when we have endured pains for a long time. Every pleasure then because of its natural kinship to us is good, yet not every pleasure is to be chosen: even as every pain also is an evil, yet not all are always of a nature to be avoided. Yet by a scale of comparison and by the consideration of advantages and disadvantages we must form our judgement on all these matters. For the good on certain occasions we treat as bad, and conversely the bad as good.

And again independence of desire we think a great good—not that we may at all times enjoy but a few things, but that, if we do not possess many, we may enjoy the few in the genuine persuasion that those have the sweetest pleasure in luxury who least need it, and that all that is natural is easy to be obtained, but that which is superfluous is hard. And so plain savours bring us pleasure equal to a luxurious diet, when all the pain due to want is removed; and bread and water produce the highest pleasure, when one who needs them puts them to his lips. To grow accustomed therefore to simple and not luxurious diet gives us health to the full, and makes a man alert for the needful employments of life, and when after long intervals we approach luxuries, disposes us better towards them, and fits us to be fearless of fortune.

When, therefore, we maintain that pleasure is the end, we do not mean the pleasures of profligates and those that consist in sensuality, as is supposed by some who are either ignorant or disagree with us or do not understand, but freedom from pain in the body and from trouble in the mind. For it is not continuous drinkings and revellings, nor the satisfaction of lusts, nor the enjoyment of fish and other luxuries of the wealthy table, which produce a pleasant life, but sober reasoning, searching out the motives for all choice and avoidance, and banishing mere opinions, to which are due the greatest disturbance of the spirit.

Of all this the beginning and the greatest good is prudence. Wherefore prudence is a more precious thing even than philosophy: for from prudence are sprung all the other virtues, and it teaches us that it is not possible to live pleasantly without living prudently and honourably and justly, nor, again, to live a life of prudence, honour, and justice without living pleasantly. For the virtues are by nature bound up with the pleasant life, and the pleasant life is inseparable from them. For indeed who, think you, is a better man than he who holds reverent opinions concerning the gods, and is at all times free from fear of death, and has reasoned out the end ordained by nature? He understands that the limit of good things is easy to fulfil and easy to attain, whereas the course of ills is either short in time or slight in pain: he laughs at destiny, whom some have introduced as the mistress of all things. He thinks that with us lies the chief power in determining events, some of which happen by necessity and some by chance, and some are within our control; for while necessity cannot be called to account, he sees that chance is inconstant, but that which is in our control is subject to no master, and to it are naturally attached praise and blame. For, indeed, it were better to follow the myths about the gods than to become a slave to the destiny of the natural philosophers: for the former suggests a hope of placating the gods by worship, whereas the latter involves a necessity which knows no placation. As to chance, he does not regard it as a god as most men do (for in a god's acts there is no disorder), nor as an uncertain cause of all things: for he does not believe that good and evil are given by chance to man for the framing of a blessed life, but that opportunities for great good and great evil are afforded by it. He therefore thinks it better to be unfortunate in reasonable action than to prosper in unreason. For it is better in a man's actions that what is well chosen should fail, rather than that what is ill chosen should be successful owing to chance.

Meditate therefore on these things and things akin to them night and day by yourself, and with a companion like to yourself, and never shall you be disturbed waking or asleep, but you shall live like a god among men. For a man who lives among immortal blessings is not like to a mortal being.

PRINCIPAL DOCTRINES

I. The blessed and immortal nature knows no trouble itself nor causes trouble to any other, so that it is never constrained by anger or favour. For all such things exist only in the weak.

II. Death is nothing to us: for that which is dissolved is without sensation; and that which lacks sensation is nothing to us.

III. The limit of quantity in pleasures is the removal of all that is painful. Wherever pleasure is present, as long as it is there, there is neither pain of body nor of mind, nor of both at once.

IV. Pain does not last continuously in the flesh, but the acutest pain is there for a very short time, and even that which just exceeds the pleasure in the flesh does not continue for many days at once. But chronic illnesses permit a predominance of pleasure over pain in the flesh.

V. It is not possible to live pleasantly without living prudently and honourably and justly, nor again to live a life of prudence, honour, and justice without living pleasantly. And the man who does not possess the pleasant life, is not living prudently and honourably and justly, and the man who does not possess the virtuous life, cannot possibly live pleasantly.

VI. To secure protection from men anything is a natural good, by which you may be able to attain this end.

VII. Some men wished to become famous and conspicuous, thinking that they would thus win for themselves safety from other men. Wherefore if the life of such men is safe, they have obtained the good which nature craves; but if it is not safe, they do not possess that for which they strove at first by the instinct of nature.

VIII. No pleasure is a bad thing in itself: but the means which produce some pleasures bring with them disturbances many times greater than the pleasures.

IX. If every pleasure could be intensified so that it lasted and influenced the whole organism or the most essential parts of our nature, pleasures would never differ from one another.

X. If the things that produce the pleasures of profligates could dispel the fears of the mind about the phenomena of the sky and death and its pains, and also teach the limits of desires and of pains, we should never have cause to blame them: for they would be filling themselves full with pleasures from every source and never have pain of body or mind, which is the evil of life.

XI. If we were not troubled by our suspicions of the phenomena of the sky and about death, fearing that it concerns us, and also by our failure to grasp the limits of pains and desires, we should have no need of natural science.

XII. A man cannot dispel his fear about the most important matters if he does not know what is the nature of the universe but suspects the truth of some mythical story. So that without natural science it is not possible to attain our pleasures unalloyed.

XIII. There is no profit in securing protection in relation to men, if things above and things beneath the earth and indeed all in the boundless universe remain matters of suspicion.

XIV. The most unalloyed source of protection from men, which is secured to some extent by a certain force of expulsion, is in fact the immunity which results from a quiet life and the retirement from the world.

XV. The wealth demanded by nature is both limited and easily procured; that demanded by idle imaginings stretches on to infinity.

XVI. In but few things chance hinders a wise man, but the greatest and most important matters reason has ordained and throughout the whole period of life does and will ordain.

XVII. The just man is most free from trouble, the unjust most full of trouble.

XVIII. The pleasure in the flesh is not increased, when once the pain due to want is removed, but is only varied: and the limit as regards pleasure in the mind is begotten by the reasoned understanding of these very pleasures and of the emotions akin to them, which used to cause the greatest fear to the mind.

XIX. Infinite time contains no greater pleasure than limited time, if one measures by reason the limits of pleasure.

XX. The flesh perceives the limits of pleasure as unlimited and unlimited time is required to supply it. But the mind, having attained a reasoned understanding of the ultimate good of the flesh and its limits and having dissipated the fears concerning the time to come, supplies us with the complete life, and we have no further need of infinite time: but neither does the mind shun pleasure, nor, when circumstances begin to bring about the departure from life, does it approach its end as though it fell short in any way of the best life.

XXI. He who has learned the limits of life knows that that which removes the pain due to want and makes the whole of life complete is easy to obtain; so that there is no need of actions which involve competition.

XXII. We must consider both the real purpose and all the evidence of direct perception, to which we always refer the conclusions of opinion; otherwise, all will be full of doubt and confusion.

XXIII. If you fight against all sensations, you will have no standard by which to judge even those of them which you say are false.

XXIV. If you reject any single sensation and fail to distinguish between the conclusion of opinion as to the appearance awaiting confirmation and that which is actually given by the sensation or feeling, or each intuitive apprehension of the mind, you will confound all other sensations as well with the same groundless opinion, so that you will reject every standard of judgement. And if among the mental images created by your opinion you affirm both that which awaits confirmation and that which does not, you will not escape error, since you will have preserved the whole cause of doubt in every judgement between what is right and what is wrong.

XXV. If on each occasion instead of referring your actions to the end of nature, you turn to some other nearer standard when you are making a choice or an avoidance, your actions will not be consistent with your principles.

XXVI. Of desires, all that do not lead to a sense of pain, if they are not satisfied, are not necessary, but involve a craving which is easily dispelled, when the object is hard to procure or they seem likely to produce harm.

XXVII. Of all the things which wisdom acquires to produce the blessedness of the complete life, far the greatest is the possession of friendship.

XXVIII. The same conviction which has given us confidence that there is nothing terrible that lasts for ever or even for long, has also seen the protection of friendship most fully completed in the limited evils of this life.

XXIX. Among desires some are natural and necessary, some natural but not necessary, and others neither natural nor necessary, but due to idle imagination.

XXX. Wherever in the case of desires which are physical, but do not lead to a sense of pain, if they are not fulfilled, the effort is intense, such pleasures are due to idle imagination, and it is not owing to their own nature that they fail to be dispelled, but owing to the empty imaginings of the man.

For Further Reflection

1. Epicureanism is often thought of as a shallow, gluttonous, profligate life of undifferentiated pleasure, whose motto is "Eat, drink, and be merry, for tomorrow we die" ("the pig philosophy"). Does one get this impression from Epicurus's writings?
2. Consider his view on the fact of death: You ought not fear what never touches you. Death never touches you, for when you are, it is not; and when it is, you are not. Is this a reasonable argument against the fear of death? Why do we consider death an evil? What is the proper attitude toward death, and why?

Life Is Absurd

ALBERT CAMUS

Albert Camus (1913–1960) was born in French colonial Algeria into a poor working-class family. He was a French journalist, novelist, and philosopher who fought in the French underground during World War II and argued for courage and integrity in public life. He is most famous for his novels *The Stranger* (1942), *The Plague* (1947), and *The Fall* (1956), for which he received a Nobel Prize for literature. He was killed in a car crash in 1960. His rival existentialist, Jean-Paul Sartre, fittingly called it "an absurd death."

In this selection we see Camus' overall assessment that life is absurd, meaningless. The only important philosophical question is, Why not commit suicide? Life is compared with the myth of Sisyphus, wherein that man is condemned by the gods to roll a huge stone up a mountain, watch it roll back down, and retrieve it, only to repeat the process again endlessly. Despite the threat of meaninglessness, Camus says, there is reason to continue living, for we are free to create our own fates and to take solace in our noble struggles against the absurd.

ABSURDITY AND SUICIDE

There is but one truly serious philosophical problem, and that is suicide. Judging whether life is or is not worth living amounts to answering the fundamental question of philosophy. All the rest—whether or not the world has three dimensions, whether the mind has nine or twelve categories—comes afterwards. These are games; one must first answer. And if it is true, as Nietzsche claims, that a philosopher, to deserve our respect, must preach by example, you can appreciate the importance of that reply, for it will precede the definitive act. These are facts the heart can feel; yet they call for careful study before they become clear to the intellect.

If I ask myself how to judge that this question is more urgent than that, I reply that one judges by the actions it entails. I have never seen anyone die for the ontological argument. Galileo, who held a scientific truth of great importance, abjured it with the greatest of ease as soon as it endangered his life. In a certain sense, he did right.[1] That truth was not worth the stake. Whether the earth or the sun revolves around the other is a matter of profound indifference.

From *The Myth of Sisyphus and Other Essays* by Albert Camus, translated by Justin O'Brien.

[1]From the point of view of the relative value of truth. On the other hand, from the point of view of virile behavior, this scholar's fragility may well make us smile.

To tell the truth, it is a futile question. On the other hand, I see many people die because they judge that life is not worth living. I see others paradoxically getting killed for the ideas or illusions that give them a reason for living (what is called a reason for living is also an excellent reason for dying). I therefore conclude that the meaning of life is the most urgent of questions. How to answer it? On all essential problems (I mean thereby those that run the risk of leading to death or those that intensify the passion of living) there are probably but two methods of thought: the method of La Palisse and the method of Don Quixote. Solely the balance between evidence and lyricism can allow us to achieve simultaneously emotion and lucidity. In a subject at once so humble and so heavy with emotion, the learned and classical dialectic must yield, one can see, to a more modest attitude of mind deriving at one and the same time from common sense and understanding.

Suicide has never been dealt with except as a social phenomenon. On the contrary, we are concerned here, at the outset, with the relationship between individual thought and suicide. An act like this is prepared within the silence of the heart, as is a great work of art. The man himself is ignorant of it. One evening he pulls the trigger or jumps. Of an apartment-building manager who had killed himself I was told that he had lost his daughter five years before, that he had changed greatly since, and that that experience had "undermined" him. A more exact word cannot be imagined. Beginning to think is beginning to be undermined. Society has but little connection with such beginnings. The worm is in man's heart. That is where it must be sought. One must follow and understand this fatal game that leads from lucidity in the face of existence to flight from light. . . .

But it is hard to fix the precise instant, the subtle step when the mind opted for death, it is easier to deduce from the act itself the consequences it implies. In a sense, and as in melodrama, killing yourself amounts to confessing. It is confessing that life is too much for you or that you do not understand it. Let's not go too far in such analogies, however, but rather return to everyday words. It is merely confessing that that "is not worth the trouble." Living, naturally, is never easy. You continue making the gestures commanded by existence for many reasons, the first of which is habit. Dying voluntarily implies that you have recognized, even instinctively, the ridiculous character of that habit, the absence of any profound reason for living, the insane character of that daily agitation, and the uselessness of suffering.

What, then, is that incalculable feeling that deprives the mind of the sleep necessary to life? A world that can be explained even with bad reasons is a familiar world. But, on the other hand, in a universe suddenly divested of illusions and lights, man feels an alien, a stranger. His exile is without remedy since he is deprived of the memory of a lost home or the hope of a promised land. This divorce between man and his life, the actor and his setting, is properly the feeling of absurdity. All healthy men having thought of their own suicide, it can be seen, without further explanation, that there is a direct connection between this feeling and the longing for death.

The subject of this essay is precisely this relationship between the absurd and suicide, the exact degree to which suicide is a solution to the absurd. The principle can be established that for a man who does not cheat, what he believes to be true must determine his action. Belief in the absurdity of existence must then dictate his conduct. It is legitimate to wonder, clearly and without false pathos, whether a conclusion of this importance requires forsaking as rapidly as possible an incomprehensible condition. I am speaking, of course, of men inclined to be in harmony with themselves. . . .

All great deeds and all great thoughts have a ridiculous beginning. Great works are often born on a street-corner or in a restaurant's revolving door. So it is with absurdity. The absurd world more than others derives its nobility from that abject birth. In certain situations, replying "nothing" when asked what one is thinking about may be pretense in a man. Those who are loved are well aware of this. But if that reply is sincere, if it symbolizes that odd state of soul in which the void becomes eloquent, in which the chain of daily gestures is broken, in which the heart vainly seeks the link that will connect it again, then it is as it were the first sign of absurdity.

It happens that the stage sets collapse. Rising, streetcar, four hours in the office or the factory, meal, streetcar, four hours of work, meal, sleep, and Monday Tuesday Wednesday Thursday Friday and Saturday according to the same rhythm—this path is easily followed most of the time. But one day the "why" arises and everything begins in that weariness tinged with amazement. "Begins"—this is important. Weariness comes at the end of the acts of a mechanical life, but at the same time it inaugurates the impulse of consciousness. It awakens consciousness and provokes what follows. What follows is the gradual return into the chain or it is the definitive awakening. At the end of the awakening comes, in time, the consequence: suicide or recovery. In itself weariness has something sickening about it. Here, I must conclude that it is good. For everything begins with consciousness and nothing is worth anything except through it. . . .

But what does life mean in such a universe? Nothing else for the moment but indifference to the future and a desire to use up everything that is given. Belief in the meaning of life always implies a scale of values, a choice, our preferences. Belief in the absurd, according to our definitions, teaches the contrary. But this is worth examining.

Knowing whether or not one can live *without appeal* is all that interests me. I do not want to get out of my depth. This aspect of life being given me, can I adapt myself to it? Now, faced with this particular concern, belief in the absurd is tantamount to substituting the quantity of experiences for the quality. If I convince myself that this life has no other aspect than that of the absurd, if I feel that its whole equilibrium depends on that perpetual opposition between my conscious revolt and the darkness in which it struggles, if I admit that my freedom has no meaning except in relation to its limited fate, then I must say that what counts is not the best of living but the most living. . . .

On the one hand the absurd teaches that all experiences are unimportant, and on the other it urges toward the greatest quantity of experiences. How, then, can one fail to do as so many of those men I was speaking of earlier—choose the form of life that brings us the most possible of that human matter, thereby introducing a scale of values that on the other hand one claims to reject?

But again it is the absurd and its contradictory life that teaches us. For the mistake is thinking that that quantity of experiences depends on the circumstances of our life when it depends solely on us. Here we have to be oversimple. To two men living the same number of years, the world always provides the same sum of experiences. It is up to us to be conscious of them. Being aware of one's life, one's revolt, one's freedom, and to the maximum, is living, and to the maximum. Where lucidity dominates, the scale of values becomes useless. . . .

THE MYTH OF SISYPHUS

The gods had condemned Sisyphus to ceaselessly rolling a rock to the top of a mountain, whence the stone would fall back of its own weight. They had thought with some reason that there is no more dreadful punishment than futile and hopeless labor.

If one believes Homer, Sisyphus was the wisest and most prudent of mortals. According to another tradition, however, he was disposed to practice the profession of highwayman. I see no contradiction in this. Opinions differ as to the reasons why he became the futile laborer of the underworld. To begin with, he is accused of a certain levity in regard to the gods. He stole their secrets. Ægina, the daughter of Æsopus, was carried off by Jupiter. The father was shocked by that disappearance and complained to Sisyphus. He, who knew of the abduction, offered to tell about it on condition that Æsopus would give water to the citadel of Corinth. To the celestial thunderbolts he preferred the benediction of water. He was punished for this in the underworld. Homer tells us also that Sisyphus had put Death in chains. Pluto could not endure the sight of his deserted, silent empire. He dispatched the god of war, who liberated Death from the hands of her conqueror.

It is said also that Sisyphus, being near to death, rashly wanted to test his wife's love. He ordered her to cast his unburied body into the middle of the public square. Sisyphus woke up in the underworld. And there, annoyed by an obedience so contrary to human love, he obtained from Pluto permission to return to earth in order to chastise his wife. But when he had seen again the face of this world, enjoyed water and sun, warm stones and the sea, he no longer wanted to go back to the infernal darkness. Recalls, signs of anger, warnings were of no avail. Many years more he lived facing the curve of the gulf, the sparkling sea, and the smiles of earth. A decree of the gods was necessary. Mercury came and seized the impudent man by the collar and, snatching him from his joys, led him forcibly back to the underworld, where his rock was ready for him.

You have already grasped that Sisyphus is the absurd hero. He *is*, as much through his passions as through his torture. His scorn of the gods, his hatred of death, and his passion for life won him that unspeakable penalty in which the whole being is exerted toward accomplishing nothing. This is the price that must be paid for the passions of this earth. Nothing is told us about Sisyphus in the underworld. Myths are made for the imagination to breathe life into them. As for this myth, one sees merely the whole effort of a body straining to raise the huge stone, to roll it and push it up a slope a hundred times over; one sees the face screwed up, the cheek tight against the stone, the shoulder bracing the clay-covered mass, the foot wedging it, the fresh start with arms outstretched, the wholly human security of two earth-clotted hands. At the very end of his long effort measured by skyless space and time without depth, the purpose is achieved. Then Sisyphus watches the stone rush down in a few moments toward that lower world whence he will have to push it up again toward the summit. He goes back down to the plain.

It is during that return, that pause, that Sisyphus interests me. A face that toils so close to stones is already stone itself! I see that man going back down with a heavy yet measured step toward the torment of which he will never know the end. That hour like a breathing-space which returns as surely as his suffering, that is the hour of consciousness. At each of those moments when he leaves the heights and gradually sinks toward the lairs of the gods, he is superior to his fate. He is stronger than his rock.

If this myth is tragic, that is because its hero is conscious. Where would his torture be, indeed, if at every step the hope of succeeding upheld him? The workman of today works every day in his life at the same tasks, and this fate is no less absurd. But it is tragic only at the rare moments when it becomes conscious. Sisyphus, proletarian of the gods, powerless and rebellious, knows the whole extent of his wretched condition: it is what he thinks of during his descent. The lucidity that was to constitute his torture at the same time crowns his victory. There is no fate that cannot be surmounted by scorn.

If the descent is thus sometimes performed in sorrow, it can also take place in joy. This word is not too much. Again I fancy Sisyphus returning toward his rock, and the sorrow was in the beginning. When the images of earth cling too tightly to memory, when the call of happiness becomes too insistent, it happens that melancholy rises in man's heart: this is the rock's victory, this is the rock itself. The boundless grief is too heavy to bear. These are our nights of Gethsemane. But crushing truths perish from being acknowledged. Thus, Œdipus at the outset obeys fate without knowing it. But from the moment he knows, his tragedy begins. Yet at the same moment, blind and desperate, he realizes that the only bond linking him to the world is the cool hand of a girl. Then a tremendous remark rings out: "Despite so many ordeals, my advanced age and the nobility of my soul make me conclude that all is well." Sophocles' Œdipus, like Dostoevsky's Kirilov, thus gives the recipe for the absurd victory. Ancient wisdom confirms modern heroism.

One does not discover the absurd without being tempted to write a manual of happiness. "What! by such narrow ways—?" There is but one world, however. Happiness and the absurd are two sons of the same earth. They are inseparable. It would be a mistake to say that happiness necessarily springs from the absurd discovery. It happens as well that the feeling of the absurd springs from happiness. "I conclude that all is well," says Œdipus, and that remark is sacred. It echoes in the wild and limited universe of man. It teaches that all is not, has not been, exhausted. It drives out of this world a god who had come into it with dissatisfaction and a preference for futile sufferings. It makes of fate a human matter, which must be settled among men.

All Sisyphus' silent joy is contained therein. His fate belongs to him. His rock is his thing. Likewise, the absurd man, when he contemplates his torment, silences all the idols. In the universe suddenly restored to its silence, the myriad wondering little voices of the earth rise up. Unconscious, secret calls, invitations from all the faces, they are the necessary reverse and price of victory. There is no sun without shadow, and it is essential to know the night. The absurd man says yes and his effort will henceforth be unceasing. If there is a personal fate, there is no higher destiny, or at least there is but one which he concludes is inevitable and despicable. For the rest, he knows himself to be the master of his days. At that subtle moment when man glances backward over his life, Sisyphus returning toward his rock, in that slight pivoting he contemplates that series of unrelated actions which becomes his fate, created by him, combined under his memory's eye and soon sealed by his death. Thus, convinced of the wholly human origin of all that is human, a blind man eager to see who knows that the night has no end, he is still on the go. The rock is still rolling.

I leave Sisyphus at the foot of the mountain! One always finds one's burden again. But Sisyphus teaches the higher fidelity that negates the gods and raises rocks. He too concludes that all is well. This universe henceforth without a master seems to him neither sterile nor futile. Each atom of that stone, each mineral flake of that night-filled mountain, in itself forms a world. The struggle itself toward the heights is enough to fill a man's heart. One must imagine Sisyphus happy.

For Further Reflection

1. Is life absurd, as Camus insists? Does Camus give good reasons for this claim? What leads him to this pessimistic conclusion?
2. Is Camus being irreverent in asking such an outrageous question as "Why not commit suicide"?
3. Why does Camus say that Sisyphus must be imagined to be happy?
4. Compare Camus with Epicurus. In what ways are their views similar? In what ways different?

The Human Search for Meaning

Reflections on Auschwitz

VIKTOR FRANKL

Viktor Frankl (1905–1997) was a professor of psychiatry and neurology at the University of Vienna Medical School and is the founder of logotherapy, the psychological therapy based on the idea that human beings must find a meaning to their lives in order to function. This idea is based on Nietzsche's dictum "He who has a why to live for, can bear with almost any how." Frankl spent three years in Nazi concentration camps, including Auschwitz.

His entire family was exterminated by the Nazis. In this selection Frankl reflects on the search for meaning in the concentration camp.

What did the prisoner dream about most frequently? Of bread, cake, cigarettes, and nice warm baths. The lack of having these simple desires satisfied led him to seek wish-fulfillment in dreams. Whether these dreams did any good is another matter; the dreamer had to wake from them to the reality of camp life, and to the terrible contrast between that and his dream illusions.

I shall never forget how I was roused one night by the groans of a fellow prisoner, who threw himself about in his sleep, obviously having a horrible nightmare. Since I had always been especially sorry for people who suffered from fearful dreams or deliria, I wanted to wake the poor man. Suddenly I drew back the hand which was ready to shake him, frightened at the thing I was about to do. At that moment I became intensely conscious of the fact that no dream, no matter how horrible, could be as bad as the reality of the camp which surrounded us, and to which I was about to recall him. . . .

When the last layers of subcutaneous fat had vanished, and we looked like skeletons disguised with skin and rags, we could watch our bodies beginning to devour themselves. The organism digested its own protein, and the muscles disappeared. Then the body had no powers of resistance left. One after another the members of the little community in our hut died. . . .

In attempting this psychological presentation and a psychopathological explanation of the typical characteristics of a concentration camp inmate, I may give the impression that the human being is completely and unavoidably influenced by his surroundings. (In this case the surroundings being the unique structure of camp life, which forced the prisoner to conform his conduct to a certain set pattern.) But what about human liberty? Is there no spiritual freedom in regard to behavior and reaction to any given surroundings? Is that theory true which would have us believe that man is no more than a product of many conditional and environmental factors—be they of a biological, psychological or sociological nature? Is man but an accidental product of these? Most important, do the prisoners' reactions to the singular world of the concentration camp prove that man cannot escape the influences of his surroundings? Does man have no choice of action in the face of such circumstances?

We can answer these questions from experience as well as on principle. The experiences of camp life show that man does have a choice of action. There were enough examples, often of a heroic nature, which proved that apathy could be overcome, irritability suppressed. Man *can* preserve a vestige of spiritual freedom, of independence of mind, even in such terrible conditions of psychic and physical stress.

We who lived in concentration camps can remember the men who walked through the huts comforting others, giving away their last piece of bread. They may have been few in number, but they offer sufficient proof that everything can be taken from a man but one thing: the last of the human freedoms—to choose one's attitude in any given set of circumstances, to choose one's own way.

And there were always choices to make. Every day, every hour, offered the opportunity to make a decision, a decision which determined whether you would or would not submit to those powers which threatened to rob you of your very self, your inner freedom; which determined whether or not you would become the plaything of circumstance, renouncing freedom and dignity to become molded into the form of the typical inmate.

Seen from this point of view, the mental reactions of the inmates of a concentration camp must seem more to us than the mere expression of certain physical and sociological conditions. Even though conditions such as lack of sleep, insufficient food and various mental stresses may suggest that the inmates were bound to react in certain ways, in the final analysis it becomes clear that the sort of person the prisoner became was the result of an inner decision, and not the result of camp influences alone. Fundamentally, therefore, any man can, even under such circumstances, decide what shall become of him—mentally and spiritually. He may retain his human dignity even in a concentration camp. Dostoevski said once, "There is only one thing that I dread: not to be worthy of my sufferings." These words frequently came to my mind after I became acquainted with those martyrs whose behavior in camp, whose suffering and death, bore witness to the fact that the last inner freedom cannot be lost. It can be said that they were worthy of their sufferings; the way they bore their suffering was a genuine inner achievement. It is this spiritual freedom—which cannot be taken away—that makes life meaningful and purposeful.

An active life serves the purpose of giving man the opportunity to realize values in creative work, while a passive life of enjoyment affords him the opportunity to obtain fulfillment in experiencing beauty, art, or nature. But there is also purpose in that life which is almost barren of both creation and enjoyment and which admits of but one possibility of high moral behavior: namely, in man's attitude to his existence, an existence restricted by external forces. A creative life and a life of enjoyment are banned to him. But not only creativeness and enjoyment are meaningful. If there is a meaning in life at all, then there must be a meaning in suffering. Suffering is an ineradicable part of life, even as fate and death. Without suffering and death human life cannot be complete.

The way in which a man accepts his fate and all the suffering it entails, the way in which he takes up his cross, gives him ample opportunity—even under the most difficult circumstances—to add a deeper meaning to his life. It may remain brave, dignified and unselfish. Or in the bitter fight for self-preservation he may forget his human dignity and become no more than an animal. Here lies the chance for a man either to make use of or to forego the opportunities of attaining the moral values that a difficult situation may afford him. And this decides whether he is worthy of his sufferings or not.

Do not think that these considerations are unworldly and too far removed from real life. It is true that only a few people are capable of reaching such high moral standards. Of the prisoners only a few kept their full inner liberty and obtained those values which their suffering afforded, but even one such example is sufficient proof that man's inner strength may raise him above his outward fate. Such men are not only in concentration camps. Everywhere man is confronted with fate, with the chance of achieving something through his own suffering. . . .

A man who let himself decline because he could not see any future goal found himself occupied with retrospective thoughts. In a different connection, we have already spoken of the tendency there was to look into the past, to help make the present, with all its horrors, less real. But in robbing the present of its reality there lay a certain danger. It became easy to overlook the opportunities to make something positive of camp life, opportunities which really did exist. Regarding our "provisional existence" as unreal was in itself an important factor in causing the prisoners to lose their hold on life; everything in a way became pointless. Such people forgot that often it is just such an exceptionally difficult external situation which gives man the opportunity to grow spiritually beyond himself. Instead of taking the camp's difficulties as a test of their inner strength, they did not take their life seriously and despised it as something of no consequence. They preferred to close their eyes and to live in the past. Life for such people became meaningless.

Naturally only a few people were capable of reaching great spiritual heights. But a few were given the chance to attain human greatness even through their apparent worldly failure and death, an accomplishment which in ordinary circumstances they would never have achieved. To the others of us, the mediocre and the half-hearted, the words of Bismarck could be applied: "Life is like being at the dentist. You always think that the worst is still to come, and yet it is over already." Varying this, we could say that most men in a concentration camp believed that the real opportunities of life had passed. Yet, in reality, there was an opportunity and a challenge. One could make a victory of those experiences, turning life into an inner triumph, or one could ignore the challenge and simply vegetate, as did a majority of the prisoners.

Any attempt at fighting the camp's psychopathological influence on the prisoner by psychotherapeutic or psychohygienic methods had to aim at giving him inner strength by pointing out to him a future goal to which he could look forward. Instinctively some of the prisoners attempted to find one on their own. It is a peculiarity of man that he can only live by looking to the future—*sub specie aeternitatis.* And this is his salvation in the most difficult moments of his existence, although he sometimes has to force his mind to the task. . . .

The prisoner who had lost faith in the future—his future—was doomed. With his loss of belief in the future, he also lost his spiritual hold; he let himself decline and became subject to mental and physical decay. Usually this happened quite suddenly, in the form of a crisis, the symptoms of which were familiar to the experienced camp inmate. We all feared this moment—not for ourselves, which would have been pointless, but for our friends. Usually it began with the prisoner refusing one morning to get dressed and wash or to go out on the parade grounds. No entreaties, no blows, no threats had any effect. He just lay there, hardly moving. If this crisis was brought about by an illness, he refused to be taken to the sick-bay or to do anything to help himself. He simply gave up. There he remained, lying in his own excreta, and nothing bothered him any more.

I once had a dramatic demonstration of the close link between the loss of faith in the future and this dangerous giving up. F—, my senior block warden, a fairly well-known composer and librettist, confided in me one day: "I would like to tell you something, Doctor. I have had a strange dream. A voice told me that I could wish for something, that I should only say what I wanted to know, and all my questions would be answered. What do you think I asked? That I would like to know when the war would be over for me. You know what I mean, Doctor—for me! I wanted to know when we, when our camp, would be liberated and our sufferings come to an end."

"And when did you have this dream?" I asked.

"In February, 1945," he answered. It was then the beginning of March.

"What did your dream voice answer?"

Furtively he whispered to me, "March thirtieth."

When F— told me about his dream, he was still full of hope and convinced that the voice of his dream would be right. But as the promised day drew nearer, the war news which reached our camp made it appear very unlikely that we would be free on the promised date. On March twenty-ninth, F— suddenly became ill and ran a high temperature. On March thirtieth, the day his prophecy had told him that the war and suffering would be over for him, he became delirious and lost consciousness. On March thirty-first, he was dead. To all outward appearances, he had died of typhus.

Those who know how close the connection is between the state of mind of a man—his courage and hope, or lack of them—and the state of immunity of his body will understand that the sudden loss of hope and courage can have a deadly effect. The ultimate cause of my friend's death was that the expected liberation did not come and he was severely disappointed. This suddenly lowered his body's resistance against the latent typhus infection. His faith in the future and his will to live had become paralyzed and his body fell victim to illness—and thus the voice of his dream was right after all.

The observations of this one case and the conclusion drawn from them are in accordance with something that was drawn to my attention by the chief doctor of our concentration camp. The death rate in the week between Christmas, 1944, and New Year's, 1945, increased in camp beyond all previous experience. In his opinion, the explanation for this increase did not lie in the harder working conditions or the deterioration of our food supplies or a change of weather or new epidemics. It was simply that the majority of the prisoners had lived in the naïve hope that they would be home again by Christmas. As the time drew near and there was no encouraging news, the prisoners lost courage and disappointment overcame them. This had a dangerous influence on their powers of resistance and a great number of them died.

As we said before, any attempt to restore a man's inner strength in the camp had first to succeed in showing him some future goal. Nietzsche's words, "He who has a *why* to live for can bear with almost any *how*," could be the guiding motto for all psychotherapeutic and psychohygienic efforts regarding prisoners. Whenever there was an opportunity for it, one had to give them a *why*—an aim—for their lives, in order to strengthen them to bear the terrible *how* of their existence. Woe to him who saw no more sense in his life, no aim, no purpose, and therefore no point in carrying on. He was soon lost. The typical reply with which such a man rejected all encouraging arguments was, "I have nothing to expect from life any more." What sort of answer can one give to that?

What was really needed was a fundamental change in our attitude toward life. We had to learn ourselves and, furthermore, we had to teach the despairing men, that it did not really matter what we expected from life, but rather what life expected from us. We needed to stop asking about the meaning of life, and instead to think of ourselves as those who were being questioned by life—daily and hourly. Our answer must consist, not in talk and meditation, but in right action and in right conduct. Life ultimately means taking the responsibility to find the right answer to its problems and to fulfill the tasks which it constantly sets for each individual.

These tasks, and therefore the meaning of life, differ from man to man, and from moment to moment. Thus it is impossible to define the meaning of life in a general way. Questions about the meaning of life can never be answered by sweeping statements. "Life" does not mean something vague, but something very real and concrete, just as life's tasks are also very real and concrete. They form man's destiny, which is different and unique for each individual. No man and no destiny can be compared with any other man or any other destiny. No situation repeats itself, and each situation calls for a different response. Sometimes the situation in which a man finds himself may require him to shape his own fate by action. At other times it is more advantageous for him to make use of an opportunity for contemplation and to realize assets in this way. Sometimes man may be required simply to accept fate, to bear his cross. Every situation is distinguished by its uniqueness, and there is always only one right answer to the problem posed by the situation at hand.

When a man finds that it is his destiny to suffer, he will have to accept his suffering as his task; his single and unique task. He will have to acknowledge the fact that even in suffering he is unique and alone in the universe. No one can relieve him of his suffering or suffer in his place. His unique opportunity lies in the way in which he bears his burden.

For us, as prisoners, these thoughts were not speculations far removed from reality. They were the only thoughts that could be of help to us. They kept us from despair, even when there seemed to be no chance of coming out of it alive. Long ago we had passed the stage of asking what was the meaning of life, a naïve query which understands life as the attaining of some aim through the active creation of something of value. For us, the meaning of life embraced the wider cycles of life and death, of suffering and of dying.

Once the meaning of suffering had been revealed to us, we refused to minimize or alleviate the camp's tortures by ignoring them or harboring false illusions and entertaining artificial optimism. Suffering had become a task on which we did not want to turn our backs. We had realized its hidden opportunities for achievement, the opportunities which caused the poet Rilke to write, "*Wie viel ist aufzuleiden!*" (How much suffering there is to get through!) Rilke spoke of "getting through suffering" as others would talk of "getting through work." There was plenty of suffering for us to get through. Therefore, it was necessary to face up to the full amount of suffering, trying to keep moments of weakness and furtive tears to a minimum. But there was no need to be ashamed of tears, for tears bore witness that a man had the greatest of courage, the courage to suffer. Only very few realized that. Shamefacedly some confessed occasionally that they had wept, like the comrade who answered my question of how he had gotten over his edema, by confessing, "I have wept it out of my system." . . .

Freedom . . . is not the last word. Freedom is only part of the story and half of the truth. Freedom is but the negative aspect of the whole phenomenon whose positive aspect is responsibility. In fact, freedom is in danger of degenerating into mere arbitrariness unless it is lived in terms of responsibility. That is why *I recommend that the Statue of Liberty on the East Coast be supplemented by a Statue of Responsibility on the West Coast.*

For Further Reflection

1. What, according to Frankl, are the important ingredients in living a truly human life? Do you agree? Frankl's ideas are relevant to concentration camp experience, but are they the best ones for everyday existence?
2. Frankl believes that we must discover a meaning to our lives in order to endure great evil. But could that meaning itself be an evil?

The Ascent of Meaning

JOHN MESSERLY

John Messerly is an American philosopher who taught at St. Louis University, Ursuline College, and the University of Texas at Austin. In this essay, he argues that we may play an important role in a process of emerging cosmic meaning. While we cannot know this, we have reasons to hope that it may be true.

1. DOES LIFE HAVE MEANING?

Life is difficult. It includes physical pain, mental anguish, loneliness, war, and death. Life is good too. There is truth, beauty, goodness, joy, and love. But it seems that the cosmos will eventually perish—with all our cares and concerns, all our lives and longings, vanishing in the dark, cold, stillness of space. It will be as if we never were. How then does life have meaning?

This essay was commissioned exclusively for this edition.

2. MEANING *IN* LIFE AND MEANING *OF* LIFE

We distinguish between two basic questions concerning life and meaning.

The first is: What is the meaning *of* life? It might also be expressed: Does the universe have a purpose? Does anything matter? Why does anything exist? What is it all about? This is the *cosmic* dimension of the question. It asks if there is a deep explanation or universal narrative that would make sense of everything, including us.

The second is: Can I find meaning *in* life? It might also be expressed: Does my life matter? What is the point of my life? Should I go on living? How should I live? This is the *individual* dimension of the question. It asks if there is a valuable, significant, or worthwhile way to live that prevents life from being futile, pointless, or absurd.

Note that our two main questions are related. So the cosmos and our individual lives may both be meaningful or meaningless; the cosmos meaningful but our lives still meaningless; or the cosmos meaningless but our lives still meaningful. Moreover, the cosmos or an individual life may become more or less meaningful over time. And while we cannot precisely define the concept of meaning, we claim that either individual lives or the cosmos are meaningful if they have value, purpose, or significance. Meaning may not be synonymous with these terms, but they serve as an approximation. What we can state with confidence is that *meaning is a positive value that is good for its own sake.*

Notice too that questions about meaning arise naturally within us and penetrate to our core. We cannot live long without wondering why we all must suffer; we cannot love passionately without asking why we and our loved ones die; we cannot think deeply without recognizing our apparent insignificance in the vastness of space and time. We wonder where it all came from, where it is all going, and what it is all about. Such questions may seem superfluous in our troubled world but without some understanding of life and meaning, we are all lost, adrift on life's journey. For answers many turn to religion.

3. WESTERN RELIGIONS: ARE THEY TRUE?

Western monotheistic religions answer both the meaning *in* life and the meaning *of* life questions with an overarching worldview. Here are two examples from Christianity. The *Westminster Shorter Catechism* answers the question: "What is the chief end of Man?" with "Man's chief end is to glorify God, and enjoy him forever." The *Baltimore Catechism* answers, "Why did God make you?" with "God made me to know Him, to love Him, and to serve Him in this world, and to be happy with Him forever in heaven." We find similar ideas in Judaism and Islam.

But such answers are problematic. For one thing they largely rest on a medieval worldview that has been unraveled by the Renaissance, Reformation, and the Scientific Revolution, especially Darwinism. Moreover, the philosophical arguments for the existence of a god are notoriously weak, the concept of soul scientifically superfluous, and the evidence of an afterlife almost nil and contradicted by our usual experience. Religious beliefs are often superstitious, implausible, or mutually contradictory, both an affront to the intellect and an insult to our best scientific knowledge. Some sophisticated theologies may be more intellectually palatable, but they are usually still tethered to dubious claims about the supernatural or they are philosophically obscure. As a result, most Western philosophers today doubt that answers to questions of meaning come from a supernatural dimension; in fact, atheism is the default position in Western philosophy today.

Nevertheless, many persons derive meaning from their tenaciously held, emotionally satisfying religious beliefs. The desire to believe in spiritually grounded truth, beauty, goodness, justice, immortality, and meaning is strong, and the comfort religious beliefs provide is probably the best argument for accepting them. For some, religious answers suffice. Still, believing something fervently does not make it true. And remember that we pay a price for religious consolation. Religions often promote zealotry, intolerance, and theocracy; they are usually anti-progressive, anti-scientific, misogynistic, and authoritarian; and they typically encourage credulity and conspiratorial thinking, which oppose the rational thinking we so desperately need.

4. WESTERN RELIGIONS: DO GODS MAKE LIFE MEANINGFUL?

But even if some religious claims *are* true it is unclear how they answer questions of meaning. For example, suppose that a god exists, has a plan for us, and we know the plan. Even granting these questionable assumptions, how does being a part of that god's plan give *your* life meaning? Being a part of your parent's plan does not do that. Do you not want to freely choose your own plan?

Now you may reply that your god's plan or love is better than their worldly equivalents. But while we can imagine that a god somehow mysteriously makes sense of everything this is merely an article of faith, a placeholder for our ignorance. It is just as easy to imagine that this god enjoys our suffering, laughs at our efforts, and is entertained by our foibles. Maybe life is the cruel joke of an immature, capricious, or malevolent god. Or we might conclude, after looking at the evidence, that god is imaginary.

Consider just the staggering amount of evil in the world. Do we really need so many earthquakes and hurricanes, so much cancer and ebola, to appreciate the good things of life? What is the point of all the non-human animal pain that characterizes the natural world? Is the suffering and death of newborns from Tay Sachs, Lesch Nyhan, Necrotizing Enterocolitis, or Anencephaly justified, as some theologians argue, because reacting to such tragedies builds our souls, or helps us to appreciate good or is *somehow* part of a god's plan? Such explanations strain credulity. It appears that the world these gods supposedly created is both seriously flawed and not especially conducive to meaning.

Put simply, Western religious answers to the questions of meaning are suspect because 1) the truth of religion is doubtful; and 2) it is not clear how or if gods, assuming they exist, make life meaningful. Today, religious answers to questions of meaning are unavailable for most philosophers.

5. EASTERN RELIGIONS AND MEANING IN LIFE

Eastern religions also make use of metaphysically dubious notions—karma, nirvana, reincarnation, moksha, etc. To the extent they use these ideas to explain life's meaning, then those explanations are suspect; I doubt that anyone will be reincarnated or experience nirvana. However, Eastern religions generally emphasize self-transformation rather than belief, humility and compassion instead of creed and dogma. The idea that salvation depends on being a certain type of person rather than on believing specific propositions—for instance, that Jesus is the savior—is typical in the self-salvation traditions of the East. Thus Eastern religions are more immune to criticism about having false beliefs.

Put differently, Eastern religions focus more on finding meaning *in* life rather than the meaning *of* life. Even if they state a meaning of life—say, attaining nirvana—they tend to emphasize how to achieve this rather than having faith in it. Activities such as being compassionate, reducing desires, or experiencing bliss, liberation, or oneness with reality exemplify this approach. Of the eastern religions, Buddhism is especially anti-dogmatic, anti-metaphysical, and practical. It provides instructions about ending suffering, cultivating compassion, and achieving mindfulness. Furthermore, its central tenets—that reality is radically impermanent and that we lack a core self—are compatible with modern science. So Buddhism seemingly provides insights concerning living well and finding meaning *in* life.

6. WESTERN PHILOSOPHY AND MEANING IN LIFE

Western philosophers typically ignore the question of the meaning *of* life as they regard it as unanswerable or incoherent. Regarding meaning *in* life, most contemporary Western philosophers adopt some variant of one of three basic approaches—nihilism, objective naturalism, or subjective naturalism.

Nihilists argue that neither the cosmos nor individual lives have meaning inasmuch as nothing has value, nothing matters, and all is futile. Some believe this because a god would be necessary for meaning and no god exists, while others argue that life would be pointless even if a god were real. Still others maintain that life is too boring, unsatisfactory, or ephemeral to be meaningful, or that there is no universal morality to give life meaning. Nihilism haunts us but why accept such a depressing conclusion if we cannot know it is true? Do we not have good reason to believe that caring for vulnerable children and protecting them from harm confers meaning on our lives?

Objective naturalists reject supernaturalism and argue that meaning can be found in the natural world by connecting with mind-independent, objective, intrinsic goods like truth, beauty, joy, justice, and love. They claim we must both want and choose objectively good things for our lives to be meaningful. In this view, lives counting paper clips or memorizing long lists of phone numbers are meaningless whereas lives spent searching for truth, creating beauty, or helping others are paradigms of meaning. Problems with this view revolve around questions about the source and reality of objective goods.

Subjective naturalists reject supernaturalism and argue that meaning is created by getting what we want or by achieving our goals. In this view, meaning varies from person to person and can be found in any subjective desire. Its rallying cry is "create your own meaning." But apparently, it does not matter if we find meaning by collecting coins, writing philosophy books, helping the homeless, or torturing innocent children. The problem here is how to exclude finding meaning in doing *anything* we desire—including what is generally thought to be trivial or immoral.

Perhaps by combining the subjective and objective approaches—by directing our subjective desires toward objectively good things—we can find meaning in life. While this approach holds promise, we still need to explain why some things are objectively good. But does science have anything to say about this?

7. SCIENCE AND MEANING IN LIFE

Positive psychology studies what makes life good, fulfilling, or meaningful. This research has found that we experience meaning and life satisfaction by 1) fully engaging in activities; 2) mastering challenging tasks; 3) increasing our understanding; 4) enjoying satisfying relationships and social connections; 5) possessing skills valued by others; 6) experiencing mindfulness; 7) having a sense of purpose; 8) being optimistic; or 9) feeling concern with something larger than the self—nature, family, social justice, progress, belief systems, political causes, cosmic evolution, etc. Research also shows that having purpose and meaning in our lives predicts better physical and mental health outcomes. Apparently, *it is in our self-interest to live meaningful lives.* Research about purpose and meaning also reveals that neither is related to age, sex, gender, physical attractiveness, educational level, or material possessions or excess wealth (after one's basic needs are met).

These results overlap somewhat with what philosophers have said for millennia—that certain universal human goods provide the deepest fulfillment and meaning. These goods include knowledge, friendship, health, love, fulfilling work, and aesthetic enjoyment. The idea that happy and meaningful lives involve universal human goods of which wealth and material possessions are only a small part goes back at least to Aristotle. Contrast this view of meaningful lives with, for example, those spent merely in search of momentary pleasure.

Putting this all together provides a basic conception of good or meaningful lives. They are lives in which our fundamental needs for food, clothing, shelter, love, education, health-care, and physical safety are met; we are not obsessed with wealth or material possessions; we engage in freely-chosen productive work that allows for creativity, mastery, and purpose; we care for and love both ourselves and others; and we show concern for objective goods like truth, beauty, goodness, justice, joy, and love. We may even say that by living a meaningful life we experience self-transcendence—we transcend the narrow confines of the ego.

8. IS MEANING IN LIFE ENOUGH?

Nevertheless, many claim their lives lack meaning. Maybe these people do not know what truly gives life meaning, or perhaps they lack life's necessities, purposeful work, loving relationships, personal freedom, or physical and mental health. Or perhaps they must focus on survival to the exclusion of all other concerns. Many obstacles exist to finding meaning in life and *if we find meaning we are indeed fortunate.*

But should we be satisfied with the meaning life offers or should we want more? On the one hand, if we are too satisfied with our lives' meaning then we limit the meaning we may otherwise experience. On the other hand, if we are too dissatisfied with our lives' meaning then we will miss the meaning life does offer. I would argue that we should be content enough to experience the meaning life provides while discontent enough to want there to be more. In other words, we should adopt an attitude between satisfaction and dissatisfaction.

So, while we should be grateful to be able to find meaning *in* life, we may still wish that this meaning connects with some larger meaning. We envisage—and we desire—that there is a meaning *of* life too. For if everything we love, know, create, and care about ultimately vanishes, then the meaning we find in life is ephemeral. Against the backdrop of eternal oblivion, meaning in life is too fleeting to satisfy our hunger for cosmic meaning. We may find truth, create beauty, attain moral virtue, have a loving family and engaging work, but so what? How does this matter if it all ultimately ends? What most of us want then is for our lives to connect with some larger cosmic meaning. And that seemingly demands that something is eternal. Could that something be us?

9. IS THERE A HEAVEN?

Belief in personal immortality is widespread, yet there is no evidence for it. We do not personally know anyone who came back from the dead and told us about an afterlife, and after people die they appear . . . well . . . dead. Yet people cling to any indirect evidence they can—near-death experiences, reincarnation, communication with the dead, proclamations from preachers, etc. Modern science generally rejects the supposed evidence for an afterlife for multiple reasons: none of the so-called evidence withstands critical scrutiny; the idea of an immortal soul plays no explanatory or predictive role in the scientific study of human beings; and overwhelming evidence supports the view that consciousness ceases when brain functioning does. If souls or disembodied spirits exist, then some of the most basic ideas of modern science are mistaken—which is extraordinarily unlikely.

Now this cursory treatment does not show that an afterlife is impossible. For that, we would need answers to philosophical questions about personal identity and the mind-body problem. But explaining either the dualistic theory of life after death—where souls (if they are real) somehow separate from bodies at death and live forever—or the monist theory—where a new body related to the earthly body is raised at the last judgment and lives forever (the orthodox Christian view)—is extraordinarily difficult. In the first case, substance dualism must be defended and in the second, the miraculous idea of the new body must be explained.

Either way, the philosophical task is daunting and the scientific winds blow against these ancient beliefs. Personal immortality may be possible, but it does not seem very plausible. The consensus in cognitive science, neurology, and other sciences is that consciousness depends on a functioning brain—when our brains cease to function so too does our consciousness. When my body dies, I doubt that I will move to a better neighborhood.

10. DEATH IS BAD

But maybe death is not bad. After all, there are undoubtedly fates worse than death. A state of eternal, conscious torment is much worse and more meaningless than oblivion, and I prefer death to even some relatively short periods of incarceration, dementia, or pain. Nonetheless, death is usually bad because being dead deprives us of our lives. If we find our lives valuable, then we are harmed by being dead even if being dead is devoid of experience. But it is not just self-preservation that motivates us to oppose death. We also do not want others to die, thereby revealing our fidelity to the intrinsic value of those we care about.

Now some people gainsay our worries about death. They argue that we should no more worry about our future non-existence than we do now about not existing before we were born. But those situations are asymmetrical. While many of us want to be conscious indefinitely into the future almost no one cares that they were not alive in the long-ago past. We just care more about future experiences than past ones. We prefer a day's suffering in the past to an hour's suffering in the future; we prefer an hour's pleasure in the future to a day's pleasure in the past.

Others claim that death is really good for us because immortality would be boring, hopeless, or meaningless. But people who say such things either really want to die or they deceive themselves. I think it is usually the latter—they adapt their preferences to what seems inescapable. Generally, people do not want to die and are despondent upon receiving a death sentence. People cry at the funerals of their loved ones, accepting death only because they think it is inevitable. I doubt they would be so accepting if they thought death was avoidable. So here's our situation. After all the books and knowledge, memories and dreams, effort and struggle, voices and places and faces, then suddenly . . . nothing. Is that really desirable? No. Death is bad. Death should be optional.

11. INDIVIDUAL DEATH AND MEANING

What makes being dead especially bad is that it deprives us of the possibility of any future meaning. While death may not completely extinguish the meaning we find in life, it detracts significantly from that meaning by limiting the duration of our lives. This is easy to see. A life of a thousand years provides the possibility for more meaning than a life of fifty years, and the latter provides the possibility for more meaning than a life of five years. All other things being equal, a longer life is potentially more meaningful than a shorter one.

Nonetheless, many persons claim that the prospect of our deaths makes life more meaningful by stimulating an urgency within us to live meaningfully. But this is not always true. Some people know their lives will be relatively short and they still live meaningless lives, while others believe their lives will be relatively long and they still live meaningfully. Furthermore, even if our imminent deaths led us to live more meaningfully that does not justify all the meaning lost by our being dead.

However, while our individual deaths limit or destroy the meaning we find *in* life, it is still possible for there to be a meaning *of* life even if we die. If what ultimately matters is not our little egos but some larger purpose, and if our deaths somehow serve that purpose, then individual death may be acceptable. If this is true, then we can take comfort knowing that, after we have gone, others will pick up where we left off. By contrast, notice how most of us recoil at the thought that shortly after we die all human life will go extinct. Our deaths then—while bad for us and others—do not necessarily undermine the possibility of there being a meaning *of* life.

12. COSMIC DEATH AND MEANING

However, cosmic death apparently eliminates all meaning. The meaning we find *in* life might have had some small significance while we were living but cosmic death largely if not completely undermines that meaning. As for the meaning *of* life, it is impossible to see how there can be any if all life and consciousness end forever. Now we might avoid universal death if, for example, the death of our universe brings about the birth of another one; the many-worlds interpretation of quantum mechanics is true; other universes exist in a multiverse; or, if all descend into nothingness, a quantum fluctuation brings about something from nothing. Or maybe nothingness is impossible as Parmenides argued long ago.

Such speculative scenarios lead us back to the idea that something must be eternal for there to be a meaning *of* life. For if cosmic death is inevitable then all seems futile. We may have experienced meaning while alive, and the cosmos may have been meaningful while it existed, but if everything ends forever then it all seems pointless. And, unfortunately, according to our best physics, cosmic death is nearly certain. How then to avoid feeling forlorn?

13. SCIENTIFIC IMMORTALITY: INDIVIDUAL AND COSMIC

While a supernatural afterlife is highly unlikely, science and technology may eventually defeat death. We may eventually stop the aging process; run ancestor simulations; reanimate cryogenically preserved brains; upload consciousness into robotic bodies or virtual realities; or defeat death through some combination of nanotechnology, genetic engineering, artificial intelligence, or robotics. Individual immortality is plausible, perhaps assured, if science and technology continue to progress. Maybe our individual deaths are not inevitable after all.

As for the cosmos, perhaps our posthuman descendants will use superintelligence to avoid cosmic death by altering the laws of physics or escaping to other universes. If superintelligence pervades the universe, it could become so powerful as to ultimately decide the fate of the cosmos. Or other intelligent creatures in the universe or multiverse may be able to perpetuate life indefinitely in ways we cannot now imagine. When imagining the far future we cannot rule out such possibilities. Maybe cosmic death is not foreordained either.

There are then speculative scenarios in which individual and cosmic death might be avoided. Yet, even if we could escape individual and cosmic death, eternal life does not guarantee meaningfulness, as the idea of everlasting suffering illustrates. Immortality may be necessary for individual or cosmic meaning but it is not sufficient.

14. CEASELESSLY ASCENDING MEANING

Besides being long-lasting, an individual life or the cosmos are maximally meaningful if they are infused with things like truth, goodness, beauty, joy, and love. In other words, a maximally meaningful life is the best one that we can live and a maximally meaningful cosmos is the best one that can be. However, this does *not* imply that there is a fully or completely meaningful endpoint for the cosmos. Instead, perhaps a maximally meaningful cosmos continually approaches some limit of meaning—like an asymptote, where the curve gets gradually closer to the line indefinitely without ever reaching it.

In this view, no matter where we are on the timeline, only a finite amount of meaning will have been created and there will always be an infinite amount of meaning yet to be realized. In other words, no matter how meaningful the cosmos becomes, it can always become infinitely more meaningful. So a maximally meaningful cosmos is one that is always getting more meaningful, forever transcending itself. Walt Whitman provides the imagery,

> This day before dawn I ascended a hill and look'd at the
> crowded heaven,
> And I said to my spirit *When we become the enfolders of*
> *those orbs, and the pleasure and knowledge of every thing*
> *in them, shall we be fill'd and satisfied then?*
> And my spirit said *No, we but level that lift to pass and*
> *continue beyond.*[1]

[1]Walt Whitman. "Song of Myself" from *Leaves of Grass* (Originally published in 1855.)

This cosmos of ceaselessly ascending meaning probably depends, among many other things, on the enlargement of our consciousness, the perfection of our moral natures, and the overcoming of all our limitations—as well as similar developments in other consciousness that exists in the cosmos. The philosophy which advocates that we overcome the constraints of our nature is called *transhumanism.*

15. TRANSHUMANISM AND MEANING

Transhumanism is an intellectual movement that aims to transform and improve the human condition by developing and utilizing sophisticated technologies to greatly enhance human intellectual, physiological, and moral functioning. It is based on the idea that humanity is now in an early phase of its potential evolutionary development. A common transhumanist theme is that humans may eventually transform themselves into beings with such greatly expanded abilities that they will have become *posthuman.*

Transhumanists want to transcend human nature because they yearn to rise above their current intellectual, physical, and psychological constraints; they want to increase their capacity for joy, love, and serenity and to experience new states of consciousness; and they long to think, feel, mature, discover, create, enjoy, and love beyond what one can do in a mere seventy or eighty years. Transhumanists believe there is a moral imperative to overcome the inherited biological traits that cause so much suffering and impede progress and to enhance those traits that make life better and more meaningful.

Notice that if we become posthuman, religion will lose its raison d'être—to soothe suffering by promising a heavenly afterlife. For who will die hoping for such rewards when science and technology offers immortality? If in a thousand or a million years our posthuman descendants travel through an infinite cosmos or virtual realities with augmented minds, do you really think they will cling to ancient mythologies that once satisfied more primitive brains?

Yes, we may fail to become posthuman—succumbing to asteroids, pandemics, climate change, nuclear annihilation, hostile aliens, vacuum decay, malevolent artificial intelligence, religious or political zealotry, or scenarios we cannot now fathom. However, if we augment our intellectual and moral faculties, and conquer individual and universal death, then we can transcend our evolutionary heritage. However, if we remain dependent on brains forged in the Pleistocene, on ice-aged adaptations, then we will surely perish—the mismatch between our reptilian brains and what we need to survive and flourish is just too great.

Thus, we should take control of our destiny and become the protagonists of the evolutionary epic. Yes, it is risky to direct our own evolution, but with no risk-free way to proceed, we either evolve or we will die. We know what we are, but we can become much more. This is the transhumanist message. But does the past indicate that the future could be better and more meaningful?

16. COSMIC EVOLUTION AND THE MEANING OF LIFE

A study of cosmic evolution supports the idea that the cosmos has become increasingly meaningful. Where there once was no meaning—in a universe without mind—there now are meanings and purposes. These meanings have their origin in the matter which coalesced into stars and planets, at least one of which, in turn, supported organisms that evolved large brains and created culture. Meaning emerged when complex brains intermingled with physical and then, much later, cultural environments. The result of this interaction was a reality that became, among other things, infused with meaning.

And, since the minds from which meanings emerge are a part of the universe, *a part of the universe now has meaning.* This has a further profound implication. Cosmic evolution is the story of a universe slowly coming to perceive itself through the conscious perceptions of the minds that emerged from it. So when we contemplate the universe, *a part of the universe is conscious.*

But will cosmic evolution lead to greater meaning and consciousness? We cannot say for certain but there is a trajectory to past evolution: molecules organized into cells; cells into organisms; and human organisms into families, tribes, cities, and nations. This could lead someday to interstellar cooperatives, along with an increase in intelligence that might lead to a near-omnipotent command of matter and energy. Think of it this way. If the infinitesimally small elementary particles existing immediately after the Big Bang became a universe almost a hundred billion light-years across; if some of the atoms in stars became living beings; and if biological evolution eventually gave rise to consciousness—all without conscious input—then who knows what is possible if consciousness *directs* evolution?

17. THE MEANING OF LIFE

If the cosmos gradually actualizes its potential for greater meaning, based to some extent on our conscious efforts, then we would have been part of something larger and more enduring than ourselves. Our lives would have helped create an increasingly meaningful cosmos. In that case, the meaning *in* our lives would unite with the meaning *of* life; *individual* meaning and *cosmic* meaning would be interfused; the part and the whole giving each other meaning.

Some might still find it distressing to think that their individual consciousness, despite its role in creating cosmic meaning, will have faded into oblivion long before new heights of meaning are reached. But maybe this view of time is mistaken and future meaning is already a part of us, and we are a part of it . . . now. After all, Einstein's theory of special relativity implies that objects and events from the past, present, and future all exist eternally and are all equally real. Regardless, we can take comfort from the idea that a meaningful life at least partly endures through its connection with the emergence of a meaningful cosmos.

Here then is our cosmic vision. In our imagination, we are as links in a chain leading onward and upward toward more advanced levels of being, consciousness, joy, love, and meaning. We are an integral part of a never-ending, endlessly striving, continually ascending process of emerging meaning. And we find individual meaning by hastening the gradual emergence of cosmic meaning. *The meaning of life, of all being and consciousness, is to actively create a better and more meaningful reality.*

18. SKEPTICISM

Yet, as we ascend these mountains of thought, we fall back to earth. Looking to the past we see that wisdom, goodness, and meaning have emerged in cosmic evolution but so too have ignorance, cruelty, and loneliness. The arrow of time moves forward but we might be heading toward human extinction, universal death, or eternal misery. So, while we can imagine a ceaselessly ascending cosmos that becomes increasingly meaningful, we do not know if we live in one. Quite simply, our brains, wired by evolution to survive and reproduce, are probably not that well-suited to make grand claims about an inconceivably large, incredibly old, unimaginably mysterious, and ever-evolving cosmos.

We cannot then erase all our doubts or allay all our fears. Intellectual integrity demands that we admit that life might be utterly meaningless. All of reality heading . . . nowhere. Our lives, our cares, our loves, our dreams . . . all for naught. But then again we do not *know* that life is meaningless. So we cannot unequivocally either affirm or reject claims about life's meaning—the honest and brave must tolerate ambiguity. Ultimately, we are uncertain of our place, if any, in the cosmos. And *the challenge of life is to live and die in a world that we do not fully understand.*

19. HOPE

In response to this ultimate uncertainty, I advocate hope. Hope that it all makes sense; that things ultimately matter; that our lives and universal life are meaningful; that our cosmic vision becomes a reality. But what do I mean by hope? As I use the term, hope does *not* refer to future expectations. I neither have faith that, nor am I optimistic about, the objects of my hopes being realized. Instead, *hope is an attitude that spurs action.*

To better understand this, contrast hope with its opposite—despair. When we despair, we no longer care; we give up because our actions seemingly do not matter. But a hopeful attitude rejects despair. It cares although it might not matter; strives against obstacles; acts in the face of the unknown. I do not know if my actions are ultimately meaningful, but I can choose to hope, care, and strive nonetheless. However, if the objects of our hopes are unattainable, then we are bound to be disappointed. That is false hope and it can be devastating. True hope, on the other hand, consists of both a belief in an outcome's possibility and a desire for that outcome. And, since life becoming more meaningful is both possible and desirable, hoping for it is *not* a false hope.

Still, any of us can lose hope and succumb to despair. Some people are in hopeless situations—in unremitting pain, persistent vegetative states, tortured by a life in prison or solitary confinement. For them hope is no salve and their lives perhaps no longer worth living. This fills me with irredeemable sadness. But, for those of us not presently in such dire circumstances, we can carry on, braving the struggle of human life. As James Fitzjames Stephens taught me long ago:

> We stand on a mountain pass in the midst of whirling snow and blinding mist, through which we get glimpses now and then of paths which may be deceptive. If we stand still we shall be frozen to death. If we take the wrong road we shall be dashed to pieces. We do not certainly know whether there is any right one. What must we do? "Be strong and of a good courage." Act for the best, hope for the best, and take what comes . . . If death ends all, we cannot meet death better.[2]

20. GOING FORWARD

We have discovered that we can find meaning *in* life, and that meaning may join with a meaning *of* life. Our meaningful lives may play a significant role in a grand cosmic story of emerging meaning. We cannot know this,

[2]James Fitzjames Stephen. *Liberty, Equality, Fraternity.* (Originally published 1873.)

but if we reject illusory nonsense, accept our ignorance in this unimaginably mysterious cosmos, overcome our limitations, and act and hope for the best, then perhaps our lives are truly connected with the increasing beauty, goodness, joy, love, and meaning of an endlessly striving, ceaselessly ascending cosmos.

I will end by echoing the poetry of the great biologist Julian Huxley:

I turn the handle and the story starts:
Reel after reel is all astronomy,
Till life, enkindled in a niche of sky,
Leaps on the stage to play a million parts.
Life leaves the slime and through the oceans darts;
She conquers earth, and raises wings to fly;
Then spirit blooms, and learns how not to die,
Nesting beyond the grave in others' hearts.
I turn the handle; other men like me
Have made the film; and now I sit and look
In quiet, privileged like Divinity
To read the roaring world as in a book.

If this thy past, where shall thy future climb,
O Spirit, built of Elements and Time![3]

I thank Jason Abshire, Caspar Addyman, Darrell Arnold, Gary Bartlett, Thierry Joffrain, Jane Messerly, Jennifer Messerly, Thaddeus Metz, and Larry Rifkin for their comments and suggestions. I would especially like to thank Joshua Shrode for spending countless hours discussing this essay with me.

[3]Julian Huxley. Evolution: At the Mind's Cinema (1922), in *The Captive Shrew and Other Poems of a Biologist,* Basil Blackwell (1932), 55.

Reflections on Suffering

BERTRAND RUSSELL

The British philosopher Bertrand Russell (1872–1970) was someone who thought deeply about the question of the meaning of life. Russell says in his *Autobiography* that his youth was very unhappy and that only the love of mathematics kept him from committing suicide. Gradually, he learned to find happiness. In these two short selections from his *Autobiography*, Russell first tells of an experience that greatly affected his life and then goes on to summarize what gives him meaning in life.

SPRING 1901

When we came home, we found Mrs. W undergoing an unusually severe bout of pain. She seemed cut off from everyone and every thing by walls of agony; and the sense of the solitude of each human soul suddenly overwhelmed me. Ever since my marriage, my emotional life had been calm and superficial. I had forgotten all the deeper issues, and had been content with flippant cleverness. Suddenly the ground seemed to give way beneath me, and I found myself in quite another region. Within five minutes I went thru some such reflections as the following: the loneliness of the human soul is unendurable; nothing can penetrate it except the highest intensity of the sort of love that religious teachers have preached; whatever does not spring from this motive is harmful, or at best useless; it follows that war is wrong, that a public school education is abominable, that the use of force is to be deprecated, and that in human relations one should penetrate to the core of loneliness in each person and speak to that. [The writer then describes his sudden awareness of Mrs. W's three-year-old son with whom he then and there found an affinity.] . . . At the end of those five minutes, I had become a completely different person. For a time, a sort of mystic illumination possessed me. I felt that I knew the inmost thoughts of everybody that I met in the street, and though this was, no doubt, a delusion, I did in actual fact find myself *in far closer touch* than previously with all my friends, and many of my acquaintances. Having been an Imperialist, I became during those five minutes . . . a Pacificist. Having for years cared only for exactness and analysis, I found myself filled with semi-mystical feelings about beauty, and with an intense interest in children and with a desire almost as profound as that of the Buddha to find some philosophy which should make human life endurable. A strange excitement possessed me, containing intense pain but also some element of triumph through the fact that I could dominate pain, and make it, as I thought, a gateway to wisdom. The mystic insight which I then imagined myself to possess has largely faded, and the habit of analysis has reasserted itself. But something of what I thought I saw in that moment has remained always with me, *causing* my attitude during the first war, my interest in my children, my indifference to minor misfortunes and a certain emotional tone in all my human relations.

EPILOGUE

Love, Knowledge, and Pity

Three passions, simple but overwhelmingly strong, have governed my life: the longing for love, the search for knowledge, and unbearable pity for the suffering of mankind. These passions, like great winds, have blown me hither and thither, in a wayward course, over a deep ocean of anguish, reaching to the very verge of despair.

I have sought love, first, because it brings ecstasy—ecstasy so great that I would often have sacrificed all the rest of life for a few hours of this joy. I have sought it, next, because it relieves loneliness—that terrible loneliness in which one shivering consciousness looks over the rim of the world into the cold unfathomable lifeless abyss. I have sought it, finally, because in the union of love I have seen, in a mystic miniature, the prefiguring vision of the heaven that saints and poets have imagined. This is what I sought, and though it might seem too good for human life, this is what—at last—I have found.

With equal passion I have sought knowledge. I have wished to understand the hearts of men. I have wished to know why the stars shine. And I have tried to apprehend the Pythagorean power by which number holds sway above the flux. A little of this, but not much, I have achieved.

Love and knowledge, so far as they were possible, led upward toward the heavens. But always pity brought me back to earth. Echoes of cries of pain reverberate in my heart. Children in famine, victims tortured by oppressors, helpless old people a hated burden to their sons, and the whole world of loneliness, poverty, and pain make a mockery of what human life should be. I long to alleviate the evil, but I cannot, and I too suffer.

This has been my life. I have found it worth living, and would gladly live it again if the chance were offered me.

For Further Reflection

1. Compare the first passage with the second. Do you see any differences?
2. How does your set of values compare with Russell's? Do you think that Russell's philosophy of life is adequate for happiness and the good life? Compare it with the other readings in this part.

The Meaning of Life

RICHARD TAYLOR

Richard Taylor (1919–2003) was an American philosopher who taught at major universities and wrote several influential books, including *Metaphysics* (1963), *Good and Evil* (1970), and *Virtue Ethics* (1991). In this essay, he rejects the notion that meaning in life is assigned to us from a source outside us. "The meaning of life," he says, "is from within us, it is not bestowed from without, and it far exceeds in both its beauty and permanence any heaven of which men have ever dreamed or yearned for."

The question whether life has any meaning is difficult to interpret, and the more you concentrate your critical faculty on it the more it seems to elude you, or to evaporate as any intelligible question. You want to turn it aside, as a source of embarrassment, as something that, if it cannot be abolished, should at least be decently covered. And yet I think any reflective person recognizes that the question it raises is important, and that it ought to have a significant answer.

If the idea of meaningfulness is difficult to grasp in this context, so that we are unsure what sort of thing would amount to answering the question, the idea of meaninglessness is perhaps less so. If, then, we can bring before our minds a clear image of meaningless existence, then perhaps we can take a step toward coping with our original question by seeing to what extent our lives, as we actually find them, resemble that image, and draw such lessons as we are able to from the comparison.

From Richard Taylor, *Good and Evil: A New Direction* (Amherst, NY: Prometheus Books, 1984), pp. 19–27.

MEANINGLESS EXISTENCE

A perfect image of meaninglessness, of the kind we are seeking, is found in the ancient myth of Sisyphus. Sisyphus, it will be remembered, betrayed divine secrets to mortals, and for this he was condemned by the gods to roll a stone to the top of a hill, the stone then immediately to roll back down, again to be pushed to the top by Sisyphus, to roll down once more, and so on again and again, *forever.* Now in this we have the picture of meaningless, pointless toil, of a meaningless existence that is absolutely *never* redeemed. It is not even redeemed by a death that, if it were to accomplish nothing more, would at least bring this idiotic cycle to a close. If we were invited to imagine Sisyphus struggling for a while and accomplishing nothing, perhaps eventually falling from exhaustion, so that we might suppose him then eventually turning to something having some sort of promise, then the meaninglessness of that chapter of his life would not be so stark. It would be a dark and dreadful dream, from which he eventually awakens to sunlight and reality. But he does not awaken, for there is nothing for him to awaken to. His repetitive toil is his life and reality, and it goes on forever, and it is without any meaning whatever. Nothing ever comes of what he is doing, except simply, more of the same. Not by one step, nor by a thousand, nor by ten thousand does he even expiate by the smallest token the sin against the gods that led him into this fate. Nothing comes of it, nothing at all.

This ancient myth has always enchanted people, for countless meanings can be read into it. Some of the ancients apparently thought it symbolized the perpetual rising and setting of the sun, and others the repetitious crashing of the waves upon the shore. Probably the commonest interpretation is that it symbolizes our eternal struggle and unquenchable spirit, our determination always to try once more in the face of overwhelming discouragement. This interpretation is further supported by that version of the myth according to which Sisyphus was commanded to roll the stone *over* the hill, so that it would finally roll down the other side, but was never quite able to make it.

I am not concerned with rendering or defending any interpretation of this myth, however. I have cited it only for the one element it does unmistakably contain, namely, that of a repetitious, cyclic activity that never comes to anything. We could contrive other images of this that would serve just as well, and no myth-makers are needed to supply the materials of it. Thus, we can imagine two persons transporting a stone—or even a precious gem, it does not matter—back and forth, relay style. One carries it to a near or distant point where it is received by the other; it is returned to its starting point, there to be recovered by the first, and the process is repeated over and over. Except in this relay nothing counts as winning, and nothing brings the contest to any close; each step only leads to a repetition of itself. Or we can imagine two groups of prisoners, one of them engaged in digging a prodigious hole in the ground that is no sooner finished than it is filled in again by the other group, the latter then digging a new hole that is at once filled in by the first group, and so on and on endlessly.

Now what stands out in all such pictures as oppressive and dejecting is not that the beings who enact these roles suffer any torture or pain, for it need not be assumed that they do. Nor is it that their labors are great, for they are no greater than the labors commonly undertaken by most people most of the time. According to the original myth, the stone is so large that Sisyphus never quite gets it to the top and must groan under every step, so that his enormous labor is all for nought. But this is not what appalls. It is not that his great struggle comes to nothing, but that his existence itself is without meaning. Even if we suppose, for example, that the stone is but a pebble that can be carried effortlessly, or that the holes dug by the prisoners are but small ones, not the slightest meaning is introduced into their lives. The stone that Sisyphus moves to the top of the hill, whether we think of it as large or small, still rolls back every time, and the process is repeated forever. Nothing comes of it, and the work is simply pointless. That is the element of the myth that I wish to capture.

Again, it is not the fact that the labors of Sisyphus continue forever that deprives them of meaning. It is, rather, the implication of this: that they come to nothing. The image would not be changed by our supposing him to push a different stone up every time, each to roll down again. But if we supposed that these stones, instead of rolling back to their places as if they had never been moved, were assembled at the top of the hill and there incorporated, say, in a beautiful and enduring temple, then the aspect of meaninglessness would disappear. His labors would then have a point, something would come of them all, and although one could perhaps still say it was not worth it, one could not say that the life of Sisyphus was devoid of meaning altogether. Meaningfulness would at least have made an appearance, and we could see what it was.

That point will need remembering. But in the meantime, let us note another way in which the image of meaninglessness can be altered by making only a very slight change. Let us suppose that the gods, while condemning Sisyphus to the fate just described, at the same time, as an afterthought, waxed perversely merciful by implanting in him a strange and irrational impulse; namely, a compulsive impulse to roll stones. We may if we like, to make this more graphic, suppose they accomplish this by implanting in him some substance that has this effect on his character and drives. I call this perverse, because from our point of view there is clearly no reason why anyone should have a persistent and insatiable desire to do something so pointless as that.

Nevertheless, suppose that is Sisyphus' condition. He has but one obsession, which is to roll stones, and it is an obsession that is only for the moment appeased by his rolling them—he no sooner gets a stone rolled to the top of the hill than he is restless to roll up another.

Now it can be seen why this little afterthought of the gods, which I called perverse, was also in fact merciful. For they have by this device managed to give Sisyphus precisely what he wants—by making him want precisely what they inflict on him. However it may appear to us, Sisyphus' fate now does not appear to him as a condemnation, but the very reverse. His one desire in life is to roll stones, and he is absolutely guaranteed its endless fulfillment. Where otherwise he might profoundly have wished surcease, and even welcomed the quiet of death to release him from endless boredom and meaninglessness, his life is now filled with mission and meaning, and he seems to himself to have been given an entry to heaven. Nor need he even fear death, for the gods have promised him an endless opportunity to indulge his single purpose, without concern or frustration. He will be able to roll stones *forever.*

What we need to mark most carefully at this point is that the picture with which we began has not really been changed in the least by adding this supposition. Exactly the same things happen as before. The only change is in Sisyphus' view of them. The picture before was the image of meaningless activity and existence. It was created precisely to be an image of that. It has not lost that meaninglessness, it has now gained not the least shred of meaningfulness. The stones still roll back as before, each phase of Sisyphus' life still exactly resembles all the others, the task is never completed, nothing comes of it, no temple ever begins to rise, and all this cycle of the same pointless thing over and over goes on forever in this picture as in the other. The *only* thing that has happened is this: Sisyphus has been reconciled to it, and indeed more, he has been led to embrace it. Not, however, by reason or persuasion, but by nothing more rational than the potency of a new substance in his veins.

THE MEANINGLESSNESS OF LIFE

I believe the foregoing provides a fairly clear content to the idea of meaninglessness and, through it, some hint of what meaningfulness, in this sense might be. Meaninglessness is essentially endless pointlessness, and meaningfulness is therefore the opposite. Activity, and even long, drawn out and repetitive activity, has a meaning if it has some significant culmination, some more or less lasting end that can be considered to have been the direction and purpose of the activity. But the descriptions so far also provide something else; namely, the suggestion of how an existence that is objectively meaningless, in this sense, can nevertheless acquire a meaning for him whose existence it is.

Now let us ask: Which of these pictures does life in fact resemble? And let us not begin with our own lives, for here both our prejudices and wishes are great, but with the life in general that we share with the rest of creation. We shall find, I think, that it all has a certain pattern, and that this pattern is by now easily recognized.

We can begin anywhere, only saving human existence for our last consideration. We can, for example, begin with any animal. It does not matter where we begin, because the result is going to be exactly the same.

Thus, for example, there are caves in New Zealand, deep and dark, whose floors are quiet pools and whose walls and ceilings are covered with soft light. As you gaze in wonder in the stillness of these caves it seems that the Creator has reproduced there in microcosm the heavens themselves, until you scarcely remember the enclosing presence of the walls. As you look more closely, however, the scene is explained. Each dot of light identifies an ugly worm, whose luminous tail is meant to attract insects from the surrounding darkness. As from time to time one of these insects draws near it becomes entangled in a sticky thread lowered by the worm, and is eaten. This goes on month after month, the blind worm lying there in the barren stillness waiting to entrap an occasional bit of nourishment that will only sustain it to another bit of nourishment until. . . . Until what? What great thing awaits all this long and repetitious effort and makes it worthwhile? Really nothing. The larva just transforms itself finally to a tiny winged adult that lacks even mouth parts to feed and lives only a day or two. These adults, as soon as they have mated and laid eggs, are themselves caught in the threads and are devoured by the cannibalistic worms, often without having ventured into the day, the only point to their existence having now been fulfilled. This has been going on for millions of years, and to no end other than that the same meaningless cycle may continue for another millions of years.

All living things present essentially the same spectacle. The larva of a certain cicada burrows in the darkness of the earth for seventeen years, through season after season, to emerge finally into the daylight for a brief flight, lay its eggs, and die—this all to repeat itself during the next seventeen years, and so on to eternity. We have already noted, in another connection, the struggles of fish, made only that others may do the same after them and that this cycle, having no other point than itself, may never cease. Some birds span an entire side of the globe each year and then return, only to insure that others may follow the same incredibly long path again and again. One is led to wonder what the point of it all is, with what great triumph this ceaseless effort, repeating itself through millions of years, might finally culminate, and why it should go on and on for so long, accomplishing nothing, getting nowhere. But then you realize that there is no point to it at all, that it really culminates in nothing, that each of these cycles, so filled with toil, is to be followed only by more of the same. The point of any living thing's life is, evidently, nothing but life itself.

This life of the world thus presents itself to our eyes as a vast machine, feeding on itself, running on and on forever to nothing. And we are part of that life. To be sure, we are not just the same, but the differences are not so great as we like to think; many are merely invented, and none really cancels the kind of meaninglessness that we found in Sisyphus and that we find all around, wherever anything lives. We are conscious of our activity. Our goals, whether in any significant sense we choose them or not, are things of which we are at least partly aware and can therefore in some sense appraise. More significantly, perhaps, we have a history, as other animals do not, such that each generation does not precisely resemble all those before. Still, if we can in imagination disengage our wills from our lives and disregard the deep interest we all have in our own existence, we shall find that they do not so little resemble the existence of Sisyphus. We toil after goals, most of them—indeed every single one of them—of transitory significance and, having gained one of them, we immediately set forth for the next, as if that one had never been, with this next one being essentially more of the same. Look at a busy street any day, and observe the throng going hither and thither. To what? Some office or shop, where the same things will be done today as were done yesterday, and are done now so they may be repeated tomorrow. And if we think that, unlike Sisyphus, these labors do have a point, that they culminate in something lasting and, independently of our own deep interests in them, very worthwhile, then we simply have not considered the thing closely enough. Most such effort is directed only to the establishment and perpetuation of home and family; that is, to the begetting of others who will follow in our steps to do more of the same. Everyone's life thus resembles one of Sisyphus's climbs to the summit of his hill, and each day of it one of his steps; the difference is that whereas Sisyphus himself returns to push the stone up again, we leave this to our children. We at one point imagined that the labors of Sisyphus finally culminated in the creation of a temple, but for this to make any difference it had to be a temple that would at least endure, adding beauty to the world for the remainder of time. Our achievements, even though they are often beautiful, are mostly bubbles; and those that do last, like the sand-swept pyramids, soon become mere curiosities while around them the rest of human-kind continues its perpetual toting of rocks, only to see them roll down. Nations are built upon the bones of their founders and pioneers, but only to decay and crumble before long, their rubble then becoming the foundation for others directed to exactly the same fate. The picture of Sisyphus is the picture of existence of the individual man, great or unknown, of nations, of the human race, and of the very life of the world.

On a country road one sometimes comes upon the ruined hulks of a house and once extensive buildings, all in collapse and spread over with weeds. A curious eye can in imagination reconstruct from what is left a once warm and thriving life, filled with purpose. There was the hearth, where a family once talked, sang, and made plans; there were the rooms, where people loved, and babes were born to a rejoicing mother; there are the musty remains of a sofa, infested with bugs, once bought at a dear price to enhance an ever-growing comfort', beauty, and warmth. Every small piece of junk fills the mind with what once, not long ago, was utterly real, with children's voices, plans made, and enterprises embarked upon. That is how these stones of Sisyphus were rolled up, and that is how they became incorporated into a beautiful temple, and that temple is what now lies before you. Meanwhile other buildings, institutions, nations, and civilizations spring up all around, only to share the same fate before long. And if the question "What for?" is now asked, the answer is clear: so that just this may go on forever.

The two pictures—of Sisyphus and of our own lives, if we look at them from a distance—are in outline the same and convey to the mind the same image. It is not surprising, then, that we invent ways of denying it, our religions proclaiming a heaven that does not crumble, their hymnals and prayer books declaring a significance to life of which our eyes provide no hint whatever.[1] Even our philosophies portray some permanent and lasting good at which all may aim, from the changeless forms invented by Plato to the beatific vision of St. Thomas and the ideals of permanence contrived by the moderns. When these fail to convince, then earthly ideals such as universal justice and brotherhood are conjured up to take their places and give meaning to our seemingly endless pilgrimage, some final state that will be ushered in when the last obstacle is removed and the last stone pushed to the hilltop. No one believes, of course, that any such state will be final, or even wants it to be in case it means that human existence would then cease to be a struggle; but in the meantime such ideas serve a very real need.

THE MEANING OF LIFE

We noted that Sisyphus' existence would have meaning if there were some point to his labors, if his efforts ever culminated in something that was not just an occasion for fresh labors of the same kind. But that is precisely the

[1]A popular Christian hymn, sung often at funerals and typical of many hymns, expresses this thought:

Swift to its close ebbs out life's little day;
Earth's joys grow dim, its glories pass away:
Change and decay in all around I see:
O thou who changest not, abide with me.

meaning it lacks. And human existence resembles his in that respect. We do achieve things—we scale our towers and raise our stones to the hilltops—but every such accomplishment fades, providing only an occasion for renewed labors of the same kind.

But here we need to note something else that has been mentioned, but its significance not explored, and that is the state of mind and feeling with which such labors are undertaken. We noted that if Sisyphus had a keen and unappeasable desire to be doing just what he found himself doing, then, although his life would in no way be changed, it would nevertheless have a meaning for him. It would be an irrational one, no doubt, because the desire itself would be only the product of the substance in his veins, and not any that reason could discover, but a meaning nevertheless.

And would it not, in fact, be a meaning incomparably better than the other? For let us examine again the first kind of meaning it could have. Let us suppose that, without having any interest in rolling stones, as such, and finding this, in fact, a galling toil, Sisyphus did nevertheless have a deep interest in raising a temple, one that would be beautiful and lasting. And let us suppose he succeeded in this, that after ages of dreadful toil, all directed at this final result, he did at last complete his temple, such that now he could say his work was done, and he could rest and forever enjoy the result. Now what? What picture now presents itself to our minds? It is precisely the picture of infinite boredom! Of Sisyphus doing nothing ever again, but contemplating what he has already wrought and can no longer add anything to, and contemplating it for an eternity! Now in this picture we have a meaning for Sisyphus' existence, a point for his prodigious labor, because we have put it there; yet, at the same time, that which is really worthwhile seems to have slipped away entirely. Where before we were presented with the nightmare of eternal and pointless activity, we are now confronted with the hell of its eternal absence.

Our second picture, then, wherein we imagined Sisyphus to have had inflicted on him the irrational desire to be doing just what he found himself doing, should not have been dismissed so abruptly. The meaning that picture lacked was no meaning that he or anyone could crave, and the strange meaning it had was perhaps just what we were seeking.

At this point, then, we can reintroduce what has been until now, it is hoped, resolutely pushed aside in an effort to view our lives and human existence with objectivity; namely, our own wills, our deep interest in what we find ourselves doing. If we do this we find that our fives do indeed still resemble that of Sisyphus, but that the meaningfulness they thus lack is precisely the meaningfulness of infinite boredom. At the same time, the strange meaningfulness they possess is that of the inner compulsion to be doing just what we were put here to do, and to go on doing it forever. This is the nearest we may hope to get to heaven, but the redeeming side of that fact is that we do thereby avoid a genuine hell.

If the builders of a great and flourishing ancient civilization could somehow return now to see archaeologists unearthing the trivial remnants of what they had once accomplished with such effort—see the fragments of pots and vases, a few broken statues, and such tokens of another age and greatness—they could indeed ask themselves what the point of it all was, if this is all it finally came to. Yet, it did not seem so to them then, for it was just the building, and not what was finally built, that gave their life meaning. Similarly, if the builders of the ruined home and farm that I described a short while ago could be brought back to see what is left, they would have the same feelings. What we construct in our imaginations as we look over these decayed and rusting pieces would reconstruct itself in their very memories, and certainly with unspeakable sadness. The piece of a sled at our feet would revive in them a warm Christmas. And what rich memories would there be in the broken crib? And the weed-covered remains of a fence would reproduce the scene of a great herd of livestock, so laboriously built up over so many years. What was it all worth, if this is the final result? Yet, again, it did not seem so to them through those many years of struggle and toil, and they did not imagine they were building a Gibraltar. The things to which they bent their backs day after day, realizing one by one their ephemeral plans, were precisely the things in which their wills were deeply involved, precisely the things in which their interests lay, and there was no need then to ask questions. There is no more need of them now—the day was sufficient to itself, and so was the life.

This is surely the way to look at all of life—at one's own life, and each day and moment it contains; of the life of a nation; of the species; of the life of the world; and of every thing that breathes. Even the glow worms I described, whose cycles of existence over the millions of years seem so pointless when looked at by us, will seem entirely different to us if we can somehow try to view their existence from within. Their endless activity, which gets nowhere, is just what it is their will to pursue. This is its whole justification and meaning. Nor would it be any salvation to the birds who span the globe every year, back and forth, to have a home made for them in a cage with plenty of food and protection, so that they would not have to migrate anymore. It would be their condemnation, for it is the doing that counts for them, and not what they hope to win by it. Flying these prodigious distances, never ending, is what it is in their veins to do, exactly as it was in Sisyphus's veins to roll stones, without end, after the gods had waxed merciful and implanted this in him.

You no sooner drew your first breath than you responded to the will that was in you to live. You no more ask whether it will be worthwhile, or whether anything of significance will come of it, than the worms and the birds. The point of living is simply to be living, in the manner that it is your nature to be living. You go through life building your castles, each of these beginning to fade into time as the next is begun; yet it would be no salvation to rest from all this. It would be a condemnation, and one that would in no way be redeemed were you able to gaze upon the things you have done, even if these were beautiful and absolutely permanent, as they never are. What counts is that you should be able to begin a new task, a new castle, a new bubble. It counts only because it is there to be done and you have the will to do it. The same will be the life of your children, and of theirs; and if the philosopher is apt to see in this a pattern similar to the unending cycles of the existence of Sisyphus, and to despair, then it is indeed because the meaning and point he is seeking is not there—but mercifully so. The meaning of life is from within us, it is not bestowed from without, and it far exceeds in both its beauty and permanence any heaven of which men have ever dreamed or yearned for.

For Further Reflection

1. According to Taylor, does the fact that our lives are short and that the results of our labors will soon disappear prevent us from having a meaningful life? Explain.
2. Can the life of Sisyphus ever be meaningful to him? Why or why not?
3. In Taylor's view, how can the meaning of life come from within us? Do you agree? Why or why not?

Further Readings for Chapter 9

Baggini, Julian. *What's It All About? Philosophy and the Meaning of Life*. New York: Oxford University Press, 2004.

Barrett, William. *Irrational Man.* New York: Doubleday, 1958.

Bretall, Robert, ed. *A Kierkegaard Anthology.* Princeton, N.J.: Princeton University Press, 1946.

Camus, Albert. *The Myth of Sisyphus and Other Essays.* Translated by J. O. O'Brien. New York: Random House, 1955.

———. *The Plague.* New York: Random House, 1948.

Frankl, Viktor. *Man's Search for Meaning.* New York: Beacon Press, 1963.

Kaufmann, Walter. *Existentialism from Dostoevsky to Sartre.* New York: New American Library, 1975.

———, ed. and trans. *A Portable Nietzsche.* New York: Viking, 1954.

Kierkegaard, Søren. *Fear and Trembling.* Translated by Walter Lowrie. Princeton, N.J.: Princeton University Press, 1954.

Klemke, E. D. *The Meaning of Life.* Oxford: Oxford University Press, 1981.

Nietzsche, Friedrich. *The Will to Power.* New York: Random House, 1967.

Russell, Bertrand. *The Conquest of Happiness.* New York: New American Library, 1930.

Sanders, Steven, and David Cheney, eds. *The Meaning of Life.* Englewood Cliffs, N.J.: Prentice-Hall, 1980.

Sartre, Jean-Paul. *Existentialism and Human Emotions.* New York: Philosophical Library, 1948.

Schopenhauer, Arthur. *The Will to Live: Selected Writings of Arthur Schopenhauer.* Edited by Richard Taylor. London: Ungar, 1967.

Tolstoy, Leo. *My Confessions.* Translated by Leo Wiener. London: Dent, 1905.

PART IV

Applied Ethics

Moral Problems

> What is the use of studying philosophy if all that it does for you is enable you to talk with some plausibility about some abstruse questions of logic, etc., and if it does not improve your thinking about the important questions of everyday life?
>
> —*Ludwig Wittgenstein*

In this fourth part of our book, we turn to six sets of moral problems facing students every day: (1) sexism and misogyny; (2) racism, equity, and privilege; (3) free speech and hate speech; (4) pandemic ethics; (5) food ethics; and (6) the ethics of climate change. Can philosophical analysis illuminate these issues, supplying appropriate guidance for living? In this part, we attempt to answer that question in the affirmative, even as we offer opposing points of view.

CHAPTER 10

Sexism and Misogyny

Now, in the twenty-first century, after all the obvious advancements of women in the workplace, government, education, politics, and sports, it can seem strange to some ears to hear that sexism and misogyny still exist and are significant problems for society. But that's exactly what scientists, scholars, and social observers are saying—and have been saying for a long time.

Sexism is oppression, prejudice, or discrimination based on sex or gender, usually directed against girls and women. It is an ideology that justifies or rationalizes unequal treatment of women. According to the philosophers Ann E. Cudd and Leslie E. Jones,

> sexism is a systematic, pervasive, but often subtle, force that maintains the oppression of women, and that is at work through institutional structures, in interpersonal interactions and the attitudes that are expressed in them, and in the cognitive, linguistic, and emotional processes of individual minds. In short, sexism structures our very experience of the world, and makes that world on the whole worse for women than for men.[1]

By a host of measures—health, wealth, education, political rights, sexual and domestic violence, wages and salaries, burdens of childrearing and housework, availability of contraception, access to high government offices, and more—women are valued far less than men. As Cudd and Jones say,

> When we compare the life prospects of women and men, we find that a woman is far more likely to be poor, unhealthy, abused, and politically

[1]Ann E. Cudd and Leslie E. Jones, "Sexism," in A *Companion to Applied Ethics*, edited by R. G. Frey and Christopher Heath Wellman. Malden, MA: Blackwell, 2003, 105–106.

> disenfranchised, even while she works longer hours and is largely responsible for the primary care of future generations.[2]

Misogyny is hatred or hostility toward women because they are women. Kate Manne, author of *Down Girl: The Logic of Misogyny*, broadens this definition:

> [On the naïve conception of the term] misogyny is primarily a property of individual misogynists who are prone to hate women qua women, that is, because of their gender, either universally or at least very generally. . . . [We] should instead understand misogyny as primarily a property of social environments in which women are liable to encounter hostility due to the enforcement and policing of patriarchal norms and expectations—often, though not exclusively, insofar as they violate patriarchal law and order. Misogyny hence functions to enforce and police women's subordination and to uphold male dominance.[3]

Both sexism and misogyny are everywhere and all the more damaging because they are so often invisible, insidious, and unacknowledged.

[2]Cudd and Jones, "Sexism," 102.
[3]Kate Manne, *Down Girl: The Logic of Misogyny*. New York: Oxford University Press, 2018, 18–19.

Sexism

ANN E. CUDD AND LESLIE E. JONES

Cudd and Jones see sexism as a "historically and globally pervasive form of oppression against women" that involves systematic inequality. They observe that sexism operates at three levels: (1) institutional sexism, which exerts its influence through social institutions; (2) interpersonal sexism, which works through relationships among individuals outside institutional structures; and (3) unconscious sexism, which arises from the beliefs, attitudes, and feelings of persons. Institutional sexism is built into the explicit and implicit norms and rules of institutions. In interpersonal sexism, a person needs no intend to act in sexist ways; sexism can be intentional and unintentional. Unconscious sexism is often denied, but Cudd and Jones point out that it is a "real, documented, psychological phenomenon." They contend that sexism is a serious form of oppression throughout the world and that "it is incumbent on decent people to oppose it."

It is a pervasive, long-standing, and deeply disturbing fact that, by many ways of measuring well-being, women around the globe live lesser lives than men. In much of the world they are less well nourished, less healthy, and less well educated (UNIFEM, 2000). Everywhere they are vulnerable to violence and abuse by men. It has been estimated that as a result of these facts, and because in many places girl babies are disproportionately aborted or killed, there are one billion missing women (Drèze and Sen, 1989). Many more women in the world lack access to education and many more are illiterate. Jobs that are high paying are much less likely to be held by women. Tedious and menial work is much more likely to be done by women. Women in the workforce are paid less than their male counterparts, are more often harassed and intimidated in work, and are far more often responsible for childcare and housework "after work." Independently of their participation in the paying workforce, women suffer from domestic violence at much greater rates, bear primary responsibility for childrearing and housework, and are much more likely to be sick and poor in their old age. In much of the world women do not have access to safe abortion, or sometimes even to contraception, further putting women's health and well-being at risk. Women everywhere bear almost the full burden of unplanned pregnancies. Women in many nations of the world lack full formal equality under the law. Where they have it, they are less likely to be able to access the judicial system, and so still lack substantive equality.

Ann E. Cudd and Leslie E. Jones, "Sexism," in *A Companion to Applier Ethics*, edited by R. G. Fvey and Christopher Heath Wellman (Malden, MA: Blackwell, 2003), 102–117.

And almost nowhere in the world do women hold high government offices at anywhere near the rates of men. In short, when we compare the life prospects of women and men, we find that a woman is far more likely to be poor, unhealthy, abused, and politically disenfranchised, even while she works longer hours and is largely responsible for the primary care of future generations.

Two general explanations could account for this remarkable disparity in life prospects: (1) women are by nature inferior to men, and so less worthy of concern or less able to benefit from equal concern, or (2) women are systematically disadvantaged by society. Under the first we include explanations based on psychology, biology, socio-biology, and so on that maintain that natural differences between men and women are sufficient to justify the comparatively sadder life prospects of women. As we will discuss below in "Objections," we suspect that many such claims depend on truant evidence (Fausto-Sterling, 1985), and that any immediate normative implications follow from whatever differences might exist between men and women.

In what follows we proceed on the assumption that the more plausible course is to take some version of the second as true. To follow this line in investigating the ways in which women are systematically disadvantaged is to investigate sexism. We begin with a characterization of sexism. We then offer a brief history of its social recognition. We turn then to the levels at which sexism conditions human social life, and discuss some paradigm examples of sexism. We then set out the two principal types of feminist theories of sexism, and conclude with a brief discussion of three objections to struggles against sexism.

WHAT IS SEXISM?

It is important to note at the outset that sexism is a highly complex notion. It is thus much easier to define conceptually, though this is no small task, than to concretely and unequivocally identify. Though there are certainly patent cases of sexism, on many definitions sexism is often only identifiable by its symptoms or consequences. We can quite readily explain that, if some distribution of opportunities systematically deprives women of what is offered to men, and there is no apparent overriding reason which justifies such a distribution, then we have a clear prima facie case of sexism. As a general claim this seems to us both undeniable and unassailable. The idea that sexism involves systematic inequality is, in short, a commonly recognized working definition. Yet those who deny that there is (much) sexism in the world, or in a particular case, often demand clear, ostensible evidence. Objective, operational criteria would be helpful here, and helpful for doing research or making policy as well. The task of finding such criteria is often quite difficult and comes from a wide array of theories covering the gamut of the social and psychological world. For sexism happens not only in explicitly institutionally structured settings, such as, for example, the denial of equal opportunity for jobs, but also in the daily and presumably much more spontaneous interactions between persons. As these latter interactions involve a wide variety of motives and causes, they may appear to be idiosyncratic and individualized rather than socially constructed. In such cases the charge of sexism might then appear less apt because less than obvious. Thus, the conceptual work of clarifying the nature of sexism is a far easier task than the practical work of showing that some particular concrete instance involving the mistreatment of women is the result of sexism or an instance of sexism. It is for this reason that much feminist work focuses on conceptual clarification and the organization of women's experience.

In its widest sense the term "sexism" can be used to refer to anything that creates, constitutes, promotes, sustains, or exploits an unjustifiable distinction between the sexes (Frye, 1983: 18). In this wide sense the term "sexism" (and its nominative "sexist") can be used to refer to any purported though mistaken difference between the sexes. This neutral descriptive use of the term, however, is deeply unsatisfactory. First, because the history of the term (brief as it is) shows it to have been intentionally modeled on "racism." As "racism" does not merely describe attempts to differentiate between races, but instead refers to pernicious distinctions between races, the term "sexism" is better understood as referring to pernicious distinctions between the sexes. Second, a neutral use of the term implicitly denies its conceptual role in binding together and illuminating the various faces of women's social difference, and the ways in which these differences are harmful. Again, just as racism is most accurately used to refer to various forms of oppression against non-Caucasians (at least in Western societies), in the more accurate and more specific sense with which we will be concerned here, "sexism" refers to a historically and globally pervasive form of oppression against women. It is this more specific and explicitly normative sense of sexism that is the subject of feminist inquiry.

One catalyst for the identification of sexism was women's participation in struggles against racism. In fact, the first wave of the women's movement began with the participation of a number of thoughtful women in the abolition movement of the nineteenth century (Stanton and Anthony, 1981), and the "second wave" can likewise trace its resurgence to the women of the civil rights movement in the twentieth century (Evans, 1979). When contemplating a name for "the problem that has no name," as Betty Friedan (1983: ch.1) put it, there is little doubt that for many feminists the parallels with racism made the term "sexism" appealing. In some ways it might seem that this was an unfortunate start, for the differences between racism and sexism are sometimes obscured by the easy way in which they form lists of social wrongs. Perhaps the most important difference is that racism is based on dubious theories about the differences between the races, while sexual difference can hardly be denied. Racism seems often to be motivated by a hatred or fear of the other from which the conclusion comes that other "races" than one's own are inferior, a kind of racism that Kwame Anthony Appiah has called "intrinsic racism." Sexism, by contrast, is typically akin to what he calls "extrinsic racism," where the judgment that the other is inferior derives from the judgment that aspects or abilities of the other are inferior (Appiah, 1990). Thus, many sexist men when so-charged can truly object that "I am not sexist; I love women," but this only means, at best, that they are not intrinsic sexists. However, there are many parallels between racism and sexism. For one thing, both are pervasive and have a high human cost. But, more importantly, the psychological mechanisms that make sexism and racism possible and desirable are similar: namely, our penchant for categorizing by social group, and making invidious distinctions between in-group and out-group members (Cudd, 1998). Furthermore, the social mechanisms that maintain sexism and racism are similar. Both sexism and racism are maintained through systematic violence and economic disadvantage. Both are difficult to pinpoint, but can be statistically documented and are much more readily perceived by the victims than by the respective dominant social groups. Both sexism and racism can have devastating psychological effects on individuals. And both inspire enormously powerful backlash when they are publicly challenged. Considerable work remains to be done, however, on the relationship between the concepts of sexism and racism (Alcoff, 1998).

If one holds, as we do, that sexism is pervasive, both historically and globally, then it will be no surprise that its ground will be both wide and deep. Institutions that are sexist will be both causes and effects of sexism. When regarded as a result of past sexism, such institutions will then carry on a tradition of, say, excluding women from available high-paying work. Managers and others who carry on this tradition may, of course, overtly maintain extrinsic sexism. They may sincerely, but falsely, believe women to be incapable of carrying on this work. This *intentional extrinsic sexism* should be distinguished from what might be called *individuated extrinsic sexism,* which maintains that while women (as a group) are capable of carrying on this work, no individual woman is. In either case it will be extremely difficult to persuasively establish such trenchant attitudes as sexist. In the latter case though women in general are held to be able to do this work, the technique of holding that each one now applying cannot do the job will effectively, if unintentionally, maintain the sexist tradition. Within that tradition such judgments are considered to be matters of keeping high standards, not sexism. As this practice requires an increasingly high degree of dubious judgment the longer it continues, over time it becomes correspondingly less reasonable to attribute to managers and others the sincere belief that women (as a group) are equally capable. In the case of intentional extrinsic sexism the fact that there are currently no or few women in the field contributes to the view that women cannot or do not want to do the work. The tradition of excluding women is, in this case, *intentional,* but is labeled by those who practice it "realism," not "sexism."

One important effect of the practice of excluding women in these ways is, of course, that women are made more dependent on others, usually men. By reducing the opportunities women have available to them, women are less able to clearly establish, both to themselves and to others, their general ability to accomplish high-paying (or high-status) tasks. Where these patterns are left unchallenged there is thus little to counter the claim that women are, by nature, more dependent. Moreover, these effects of sexist hiring practices are reinforced in a number of ways. They are reinforced by patterns of language which mark and delimit appropriate activities and attitudes on the basis of sex, and relegate the activities and attitudes of women to a lower status (i.e. sexist language). And they are reinforced by systems of education and enculturation which support, if not create and coerce, discrete proclivities for girls and boys, and relegate the proclivities of girls to a lower status. These social aspects of sexism are further mirrored in psychological dispositions, desires, and self-concepts. Accepting the activities, attitudes, and proclivities which are typically associated with men as "normal" or "standard" for human beings (i.e. the man standard) would render the activities, attitudes, and proclivities which are typically associated with women, when different, abnormal or substandard. For instance, women will appear "highly emotional" or "hysterical" when they display more emotion and concern than men, or "brooding" and "moody" when less. More pertinently, recognition of the man standard enables us to make as much sense as one can of the characterization of pregnancy as a form of illness or a temporary disability.

We stated earlier that sexism involves systematic inequality. Our discussion to this point has attempted to elucidate this notion. On our view sexism is a systematic, pervasive, but often subtle, force that maintains the oppression of women, and that is at work through institutional structures, in interpersonal interactions and the attitudes that are expressed in them, and in the cognitive, linguistic, and emotional processes of individual minds. In short, sexism structures our very experience of the world, and makes that world on the whole worse for women than for men.

BACKGROUND: LANGUAGE, EXPERIENCE, AND RECOGNITION

Though sexism is a pervasive form of oppression, the term "sexism" is of surprisingly recent coinage, first appearing in print in 1968 (Shapiro, 1985). Language and recognition are close allies when identifying social problems and investigating the possibility of social transformation. In naming this social phenomenon, and thus drawing attention to it, the second-wave feminists of the 1970s provided the conceptual space within which to recognize and reorganize long-standing moral, social, and political structures based on and affecting gender and biological sex. The resulting explorations into sexism have yielded considerable insights, and a number of difficulties.

Prior to the very recent coining of "sexism" there was simply no term to refer to the concept of women's oppression. Instead, authors identified various ways in which women seemed to be mistreated. Authors writing on this subject generally described fairly "local" forms of mistreatment. The primary focus of feminist arguments in the eighteenth and nineteenth centuries, for example, concerned the importance of education for women and an opposition to the absolute sovereignty of men within marriage (Astell, 1694, 1700). These arguments, however, commonly held that any change in the position of women depended largely, if not solely, on a change in women. They also often agreed with the popular view that women had a naturally limited rational capacity (when compared with men), and that domestic life was women's naturally proper sphere.

At the end of the eighteenth century Mary Wollstonecraft focused on a comparatively greater variety of social factors contributing to women's subordinate position. Taking the radical stance that women are not inferior by nature, she held that women are naturally deserving of equal rights, and could, if properly educated, participate in "the theatre of politics." Like her predecessors, she held that women in general had an underdeveloped rational capacity. The vices that misogynist satires commonly attributed to women were, in her view, quite generally deserved: "it is your own conduct, O ye foolish women! which throws an odium on your sex!" (Wollstonecraft, [1792] 1988: 302). Unlike them, however, she argued that it was not nature, but a lack of education that had contributed to women's focus on relatively trivial matters. Importantly, however, Wollstonecraft did not think that education would be sufficient to rectify women's subordinate position. She recognized that what she called the "stream of popular opinion" had an even stronger effect on women's social standing than did any characteristics actually possessed by individual women (Wollstonecraft, [1792] 1988: 102). For bolstered by the stream of popular opinion and a socially produced reprehensible female character, she agreed that women's behavior often did "justify the authority that chains such a weak being to her duty" (Wollstonecraft, [1792] 1988: 319). However, as women were just as capable as men of acquiring "human virtues," she argued that they were a social resource that was being squandered.

Like Wollstonecraft, J. S. Mill argued in the mid-nineteenth century that the various forms of mistreatment women suffered were contrary to general utility (Mill, 1869). According to Mill, the opportunities offered to women and men should be based on a perfect equality of opportunity. That is, there should be nothing that is offered to men that is denied to women because they are women. Women, like men, will differ in aptitude and interest, but, like men, they should be allowed to win their social positions through fair and appropriate competition. On this position, the aim is to secure gender-neutral standards for all. As women have not been provided with the resources (for example, education, employment opportunities, political access, and social standing) to meet these standards, what is needed is a social transformation, which will give them the levels of access usually accorded men.

In 1949 Simone de Beauvoir reiterated the argument that women were not inferior to men by nature. However, de Beauvoir was interested in explaining not only the subordinate position of women in society, but also forms of female subjectivity that contribute to the durability of women's subordination. She thus gave greater weight to organizing "the lived experience" of women than did any of her predecessors. In her view both men's and women's natures have been socially constructed. However, the social construction of women has created a "second sex" in which women do not even regard themselves as a locus of dignity, as a self (de Beauvoir, 1952). Instead, they regard themselves as "other," and, like men, reserve the notion of selfhood for men. The creation of a second sex is, moreover, the result of a primarily unconscious "desire for self-justification." That is, even the choices a woman believes she makes authentically, i.e. for herself, are the result of her constructed nature, the construction of which is for another, i.e. men. Alternatively, as the notion of "being a man" involves superiority, specifically superiority over women, men have a stake in maintaining women's inferiority. Women's subordination is thus explained and reinforced by men's and women's ways of experiencing the world. Though instructive in delineating aspects of female subjectivity, her work faces serious interpretive difficulties that mirror the main lines of feminist inquiry. These difficulties turn on the question of whether her position can be reconciled with some concept of gender-neutral standards. On the one hand, unless we can make sense of a self which is deeper than a constructed self, any notion of gender-neutral standards will be suspect. In other words, without an Archimedean point of view, gender neutrality will mean "equality with men" (i.e. the man standard) and women's differences will be detrimental to their well-being. On the other hand, if there is no deeper self, and the constructed differences between men and women must none the less be taken as "brute differences," then we are left with the difficult and somewhat uncomfortable goal of establishing "separate but equal" standards. To a large measure, feminist work on sexism has engaged in exploring, developing, and critically evaluating these complex lines of thought.

It would be difficult to deny that a sincere recognition of sexism will transform one's self-conception and one's conception of the world. Plato's allegory of the cave is a story of such experiential transformation, of coming to recognize something one would have not seen, and of coming to realize that what seems real is not real. For many women the recognition of sexism is just such a transformation. For like the cave-dwellers' first glimpse of the sun, the recognition of sexism is both revelatory and disorienting. Women sometimes describe their first recognition of sexism as a moment of realization, a "click" in which many previously disparate experiences, problems, reports, and issues become unified. What seemed previously to be simply one's own experiences, become a woman's experiences. What seemed previously to be personal problems, become women's problems. What were reports about others, or issues concerning others, become stories and issues about women like oneself. The recognition of sexism thus involves both a new way of conceptualizing experience and an identification with other women. It is also, unsurprisingly, a bewildering recognition (Bartky, 1990). For once made it is difficult to determine which of one's reactions are, and which are not, the result of one's own idiosyncrasies. As the world of personal experience fades and the pervasiveness of sexism becomes more clear, few aspects of one's life remain in place. Fear, anger, and resentment at being insulted or threatened (however subtly) can no longer be regarded as simply personal reactions to personal affronts. They may, and often are, better apprehended as part of a system of oppression, in which individual perpetrators, perhaps even unknowingly, reaffirm the boundaries resulting from sexism.

The recognition of sexism for men is and has been both a slower and seemingly quite different process (Segal, 1990). Few men report the recognition of sexism as a "click." It is more likely to take the form of a ploddingly arduous reconstruction of their own experience, which will require that they take responsibility for participation in sexist practices, and re-evaluate many of their beliefs and desires. Forms of male social interactions (e.g. jokes, chiding) come to be recognized as a mutual devaluing of women. Aspects and images of masculinity come to be recognized as compelling yet inconsistent with an aspiration for both inclusive social justice and uncoerced interpersonal cooperation. The recognition of sexism can thus also be transformative. As it is accompanied by an awareness that by forgoing forms of power and privilege the exercise of which determines one's relative social standing, the transformation carries considerable personal risk. As it is accompanied by a realization of complicity the intentional nature of which is not always clear, it carries considerable moral risk. Different accounts of sexism will affect the degree of moral risk men face and the degree of personal risk which they ought to undertake.

Though the dynamics may be different, what is clear for both men and women is that the recognition of sexism, and its corresponding personal transformation, is a prerequisite for social transformation. Sexism, as noted above, works at a number of different levels whose interaction is, again, in need of further clarification.

LEVELS OF SEXISM

Sexism can be seen as a force responding to and molding human interactions. As a force, it can be seen, roughly, to operate at three levels: institutional sexism, which works on and through the level of social institutions; interpersonal sexism, which works on and through interactions among individuals who are not explicitly mediated by institutional structures; and unconscious sexism, which works at the personal level of the cognitive and affective processes of individuals. It is helpful to sort out these levels in order to explain why some charges of sexism are relatively uncontroversial, while others are difficult to see or evidence conclusively.

Institutional sexism

Institutional sexism refers to invidious sexual inequalities in the explicit rules and implicit norms governing and structuring social institutions. Religious institutions provide a useful example of how explicit rules and implicit norms structure institutions. In the Catholic Church, for instance, it is an explicit rule that all priests are men and all nuns are women. Only priests can run the church hierarchy, and priests outrank nuns in most decision-making situations. While it is clear how explicit rules can govern and structure institutions, this example can also help us to see that implicit norms also structure Catholic experience and create sexual inequality. While it is no longer widely accepted as an explicit rule that in heterosexual marriage the man is the head of the household and the woman is the helpmeet, it is implied by the relative rank of priests and nuns in the church and by its sacred writings. This implicit norm positions men above women in marriage (as in all other social institutions in which both sexes are present), clearly an invidious sexual inequality. In addition to the more explicitly rule-governed institutions of government, religion, family, health care, and education, there are crucially important informally or implicitly structured institutions prime among them being language, and the sites of cultural and artistic production. To say that sexism is a systematic social injustice based on one's sex (Radcliff Richards, 1980), or a discriminatory sex-role differentiation (Bartky, 1990), is to speak of institutional sexism. Sexism, then, must be understood as a part of the social order, similar to the economic order of capitalism or the political order of liberalism.

Interpersonal sexism

Whereas institutional sexism involves the explicit rules and their implicit norms that sustain oppressive social institutions, interpersonal sexism involves interactions between persons that are not governed by explicit rules. Interpersonal sexism comprises actions and other expressions between persons that create, constitute, promote, sustain, and/or exploit invidious sexual inequalities.

The person who is acting in a sexist way or making a sexist expression need not intend sexism; there are intentional and unintentional forms of interpersonal sexism. Here are some examples from our experiences:

- As a child, the girl is not allowed the free play of her brothers; she is prevented by her parents and teachers from engaging in rough-and-tumble play, not included in activities involving building, transportation, etc., not encouraged to try or expected to succeed at sports, mathematics, or leadership activities, and required, unlike her brothers, to do domestic chores.
- In school the teachers require her to speak less and restrain her behavior more than boys. Teachers reward her with better grades for her passivity, but boys exclude her from their games and begin to take the superior attitudes of their fathers.
- In sports she sees males and manhood extolled, females and womanhood ridiculed. Coaches and team-mates insult male athletes by calling them "woman" or "girl," and praise them with the term "man."
- When a man and a woman negotiate a car loan or a home loan, or buy an expensive machine, the salesperson speaks only to the man. Supermarket ads are aimed, meanwhile, at women as housewives.
- In conversations between colleagues men are routinely deferred to while women's remarks are ignored. When a male colleague repeats what a female has said, he is complimented for his good idea.

Sexism is a key motif that unifies this otherwise seemingly disparate set of personal experiences. This list could, of course, be greatly expanded, and much feminist work has been devoted to increasing our stock of example experiences. This work is important because sexism is such an integral but unspoken part of the everyday world that both men and women have a difficult time recognizing it. For society's ground of legitimacy seems to require that injustice be recognized and socially opposed. Yet the injustice of sexism is built into the very fabric of everyone's everyday experiences from infancy on.

Unconscious sexism

"Unconscious sexism" refers to the psychological mechanisms and tacit beliefs, emotions, and attitudes that create, constitute, promote, sustain, and/or exploit invidious sexual inequalities. This category will be denied by many as vague, unprovable, or too easily invoked. But there are both conceptual and empirical arguments in favor of its existence. The conceptual argument is that the statistical evidence concerning the lesser lives that women live would be completely puzzling given the legal guarantees of equality for men and women in many countries were it not for the possibility of such unconscious sexism. Institutional and interpersonal sexism cannot alone account for all the data. That implies that there are unconscious attitudes and beliefs that allow persons in positions of power unconsciously to prefer men to women when social rewards are distributed, and yet not to see themselves or be seen as applying sexist standards.

The empirical argument is widely diffused, but accessible. It consists first of all in evidence for the existence of unconscious motivations, which is vast in the psychological literature. Second, there is evidence that when the same work is attributed to a woman it is judged of less value than when attributed to a man (Valian, 1998). Third, there is evidence that women find it more painful to think of themselves as oppressed, and men find it more painful to think of themselves as the privileged gender. Thus, there is motivation for neither women nor men to think of women as oppressed and men as dominant (Branscombe, 1998). Fourth, there is a great deal of evidence from social cognitive psychology to suggest that persons make invidious distinctions among salient social categories, that we tend to amplify them well beyond the real differences between individuals in those categories, and that sex is one of those categories (Tajfel, 1981). Now since it surely cannot be argued that men get the worse end of this deal, this fact constitutes evidence for the claim that such cognitive processes tend to create unconscious sexist attitudes and beliefs. There is, no doubt, a great deal more evidence that could be cited, but this much should be sufficient to make the point that unconscious sexism is a real, documented, psychological phenomenon.

Having demonstrated its reality, however, some discussion and examples will be helpful to see how unconscious sexism is manifested and how one might go about discovering it. The key to recognizing unconscious motivations, especially unsavory ones that persons are reluctant to acknowledge in themselves, is to look for decisions or actions that could not be justified by a reasonable assessment of the available evidence. What counts as "reasonable" and "available" are crucial issues here, of course. By "reasonable" we mean consistent with one's other explicitly held beliefs and widely shared, non-sexist, knowledge in the community. We insist on explicit beliefs here because, of course, if one has tacit sexist beliefs the action could be reasonable but sexist, and yet not counted as unconscious. By "available evidence" we are referring to reports that would be made by a member of the community who does not have sexist beliefs or attitudes, or whose sexist beliefs played no role in the reports, or to widely shared, non-sexist, knowledge in the community. Of course, there may be no non-sexist members of any community. The practices of sexism affect one's self-conception. Internal critique may not be enough to free oneself from identification with those practices. But we must begin to identify sexist practices somewhere. Granting that it is possible that we will not recognize all unconscious (or, indeed, all conscious) sexism, we can still begin by finding the more obvious cases. Consider the following examples:

- A philosophy department is looking to hire a new faculty member. One-third of the applicants are women. One-third of the interview list is made up of women. In the interviews the women are judged as doing worse than the men. The comments afterwards are that they don't seem "as polished" or "professional" as the men. The fact is that the women do not meet the interviewers' expectations of what a philosopher or a faculty member is supposed to look like, a stereotype that includes being a man.
- A department is considering how to advise a female colleague and a male colleague concerning their chances for tenure. They have equal but modest publishing records, and roughly equal but modest teaching records. However, the female colleague has far more service. Both colleagues have been active participants in the departmental politics and have voiced strong opinions in departmental meetings. The male is judged to be an excellent colleague, while the female is judged to be uncollegial. They give the male colleague a very positive report for his tenure prospects, and the female is warned that she must publish more and improve her teaching to get tenure. In fact, the department has judged her to be worse because they feel uncomfortable with a strong, active woman, while the man is judged to have leadership qualities.
- A drug is being tested for its effectiveness in preventing heart disease. All the research subjects are men. When asked to account for this the research team leader responds that women's hormones would interfere

> with the study. While it is surely true that the drug could affect women differently from men as a result of female hormones, it is equally true that it could affect men differently from women as a result of male hormones. This symmetry is lost on the research team, who, like most of us, tend to think of women as the ones with the "interfering" or abnormal hormones.

Unconscious sexism often seems to be innocent, in the sense that the beliefs or feelings that make it up are never voiced, and often based on widely shared stereotypes. Whether or not it is innocent surely depends on the degree to which the individual has access to information that counters the unconscious sexist beliefs and attitudes, a condition that depends on larger social factors. Although we do believe that "sexism" names not only a mistake but a prima facie wrong, there are cases where one can commit this wrong and yet not be culpable.

These levels of sexism are, of course, interrelated. Understood as institutional discrimination, sexism concerns the interactions between men and women only as symptoms of a more pervasive problem. Social institutions guide, and on some accounts cause, our interpersonal attitudes. Our self-conceptions and our conception of others are at least partially a product of the social structures through which we interact with one another. How they are interrelated is a central question within feminism, feminist philosophy, and feminist social science. Different ways of understanding the interrelations between these levels result in different, and sometimes quite divergent, accounts. Two types of account are prominent in the feminist literature. In the next section we discuss these two types.

TWO FEMINIST VIEWS OF SEXISM

Though feminists agree that sexism structures our very experience of the world, feminist theories of sexism vary considerably. None the less, they can be very roughly divided into two categories. First, what can be labeled "equality feminism" maintains that social institutions are the primary medium of sexism. Men and women do not differ markedly in their potential capacities, interests, and abilities. Given similar training, men and women would develop fairly similar talents, at least as similar as those between men or between women. Thus if we are to transform society it will require that we resist and undermine those institutions that enforce sex differences and disproportionately deprive women of opportunities to develop highly valued social skills. Equality feminists need not accept what we have above called "the man standard." Rather, most contemporary equality feminists employ measures of social value such as utility, respect for human rights, or hypothetical agreement in order to develop gender-neutral standards by which to judge the opportunities, activities, and proclivities of men and women.

Alternatively, "difference feminists" maintain that unconscious desires are the primary medium of sexism. Accordingly, social institutions are the result, rather than the cause, of sexism. Recently a variety of feminists holding this view have attempted to both articulate the differences between men and women and re-evaluate equality feminism. Some, like Carol Gilligan (1982), Nel Noddings (1984), and Sara Ruddick (1989), have argued that women's "different voice" involves a greater emphasis on responsiveness, caring, and the maintenance of particular, concrete relationships. This voice is undervalued in society, they argue, because of the dominance of "responsibility"—a notion which involves a strict adherence to principle and which, they argue, typifies the male point of view. Others skeptical of gender neutrality are also skeptical of the idea that caring and relationship maintenance best characterize women's difference. They thus seek to identify a different difference. Catherine MacKinnon (1987: 39) writes: "women value care because men have valued us according to the care we give them, and we could probably use some." In her view, since women's subordinate position in society informs their experience of the world, and so requires concrete critical evaluation, it can also give them a unique, and privileged, position from which to criticize our social traditions. Somewhat similarly, Luce Irigaray argues that the critical revaluation of women should neither reassert what has traditionally been taken to be women's nature, nor strive for equality with men. She maintains that the law has a duty to "offer justice to *two genders that differ* in their needs, their desires, their properties" (Irigaray, 1993: 4).

Both views aim to transform institutional sexism, interpersonal sexism, and unconscious sexism. They differ, however, over just what form such a transformation would take. For equality feminists the notion that there is a significant difference between men and women, a difference that makes a difference, seems more likely to sustain the global disparity existing between men and women since this disparity has been built on the basis of sex differentiation. For difference feminists, on the other hand, the notion that there is no significant difference between men and women, seems likely to undermine women's emancipation. Since women have been defined and have defined themselves in relation to men, as subordinate to dominant, women's independence depends on discovering, or perhaps imaginatively inventing, a different identity. Importantly, both equality feminists and difference feminists have the same worry. For both, the idea that an attempted transformation of society will result in a mere modification of sexism rather than its elimination is, given its evident though under-acknowledged depth and pervasiveness, a predominant, reasonable, and clearly practical concern.

OBJECTIONS

Three kinds of objections have been raised to feminist struggles against sexism, which we shall call the objections from *essentialism*, *skepticism*, and *defeatism*. The objection from *essentialism* maintains that there are essential biological or psychological differences between men and women such that true equality or even equal evaluation of men and women will ultimately be impossible or will too greatly restrain our liberty. Such objections to feminist efforts to remedy the ravages of sexism have a long history, from Aristotle's view of woman as partial man through biological theories of inferiority propagated in the nineteenth and twentieth centuries to Freudian psychoanalytic theories of femininity. A recent and currently influential version of this objection appeals to evolutionary psychology to explain the differences between the status of men and women. According to evolutionary psychology, there are distinct male and female psychologies because of the different reproductive strategies that each sex pursues, and the resulting psychologies make males more competitive, independent, and aggressive, while females are more nurturing and concerned about interpersonal relations. In addition, at least one proponent of evolutionary psychology has claimed that male psychology makes it inevitable that men will "run to extremes—or, in other words, that men are disproportionately represented in the top and bottom of many measurements" (Guyot, 2001: B15). Thus, the best lawyers, artists, politicians, businessmen, and so on must be men. So, Guyot argues, it would be inefficient and morally wrong to bring about parity in gender representation of these fields.

To this objection we have three responses. First, specifically regarding evolutionary psychology, it is a highly theorized but largely untested hypothesis at this point. Given its genealogy as another in a string of allegedly scientific proofs of women's inferiority, it is important to be skeptical until and unless it scores empirical successes. Second, and this response applies to any scientific theory about sexual difference, normative implications of difference are never directly implied by any descriptive differences. That is, it is fallacious to infer from the fact of sexual difference that women should therefore not have equal chances for social success. Finally, the ideals of liberal individualism and equality require each individual to be treated as a unique person, deserving of praise or social rewards based on his or her actual individual merit, and not based on the average merits of her class, caste, race, or gender. So even if it were true that women on average are less well suited to be lawyers, or whatever, it does not follow that there should be no safeguards in place to ensure that women are not discriminated against because of their sex. In fact, if women are on average less well suited to various occupations, it raises the likelihood that employers will unfairly judge individual women by their sex rather than their individual merits.

The objection from *skepticism* maintains that sexism is admittedly a serious problem in some other countries, but, though it has been a problem in our society in the past, sexism has largely been overcome. Women are not prevented from gaining an education, entering the workforce, or asserting their equal right to vote, to own property, or to divorce. In some cases women are treated preferentially and sometimes even outperform men. Therefore, there is no reason to pursue any remedies to sexism—it is already gone. This sort of objection has been leveled by Christina Hoff Sommers (2000). However, this objection overlooks a wealth of statistical information that proves that women's well-being is still compromised in contemporary American society. The gender wage gap hovers around 75 percent (Institute for Women's Policy Research, 1997b)—up considerably from the 59 percent of the late 1970s, but still hardly something to be satisfied with. According to the Joint Center for Poverty Research, although the overall rate of poverty in the United States in 1997 was 13.3 percent, the rate for women was 24 percent. Women suffer from domestic violence at roughly four times the rate of men (US Department of Justice, 2000). In 2001, 73 women served in the US Congress (13.6 percent): thirteen in the Senate, and 60 in the House, both all-time highs. Of course, no woman has ever been US President, and only two women are now and have ever been Justices of the Supreme Court. Women in state legislatures compose only 22.4 percent even of those bodies (Center for American Women in Politics, 2001). Women own businesses at approximately half the rate of men, and of the top one hundred wealthiest people in *Forbes Magazine*'s list for 2001, only ten were women. And this is only a partial list of the great inequalities suffered by women in contemporary US society. Finally, it is also important to point out to the skeptic that the fact that women are suffering from sexism in much of the world is itself harmful to all women. Women form a social group—a non-voluntary social group. They thereby share each other's fate to an extent. If women are harassed on the streets of Kabul, then American women who travel there will be harassed. If women are subjected to humiliating or violent treatment in East Asia, then American women who travel there will be as well. If women are not taken seriously in a country, then how can a woman diplomat from America hope to do her job there? The skeptic thus underestimates both the degree to which sexism still exists in Western society and the effects that sexism worldwide has on all women.

The *defeatist* argues that there is nothing that he or anyone personally can do to fight sexism. Defeatists often continue by arguing that since they are not themselves mistreating women, do not dislike women or hold them to be inferior, they should not therefore be required to do anything to combat sexism; nor do they think that anything constructive can be done to eliminate it. Defeatists overlook the existence of institutional and unconscious sexism. They fail to recognize that they can participate in sexism even without overt, conscious sexist attitudes. If they take seriously the problem of sexism, then they should examine their behaviors, choices, and preferences for what those express to the world. Perhaps they will find underneath a dislike of a certain co-worker, say, a prejudice against assertive women that they do not harbor against assertive men. This would be an example of unconscious sexism (made conscious). They should also examine how they respond to other people's overt interpersonal sexism. Do they laugh at wife jokes? Look the other way from sexual harassment in the office? Such behaviors support sexism, and thus injustice. Finally, the defeatist who acknowledges institutional sexism has the obligation not to support it: not to vote for it, not to buy from it, not to encourage it. The defeatist has no real defense, in other words, as long as he admits that there may be unconscious sexism, interpersonal sexism among others, or institutional sexism.

In conclusion, sexism is alive and well in contemporary Western society, and to an even greater degree in much of the rest of the world. Sexism is a serious form of oppression, and, as such, it is incumbent on decent people to oppose it, though the form that opposition should take remains a serious matter for theorists and activists alike.

References

Alcoff, Linda Martin (1998) Racism. In *A Companion to Feminist Philosophy.* Maiden, MA: Blackwell.

Appiah, A. (1990) Racisms. In D. T. Goldberg (ed.). *Anatomy of Racism.* Minneapolis: University of Minnesota Press.

Astell, M. (1694) *A Serious Proposal to the Ladies for the Advancement of their True and Greatest Interest.* New York: New York University Press, 1997.

—— (1700) *Some Reflections on Marriage.* New York: Source Book Press, 1970.

Bartky, S. L. (1990) *Femininity and Domination.* New York: Routledge.

de Beauvoir, S. (1952) *The Second Sex.* trans. H. M. Parshley. New York: Random House (orig. pub. 1949).

Branscombe, N. (1998) Thinking about one's gender group's privileges or disadvantages: consequences for well-being in women and men. *British Journal of Social Psychology*, 37: 167–84.

Center for American Women in Politics (2001) www.rci.rutgers.edu/~cawp/facts/cawpfs.html

Cudd, A. E. (1998) Psychological explanations of oppression. In C. Willett (ed.). *Theorizing Multiculturalism.* Maiden, MA: Blackwell.

Drèze, J. and Sen, A. (1989) *Hunger and Public Action.* Oxford: Clarendon Press.

Evans, S. (1979) *Personal Politics: The Roots of Women's Liberation in the Civil Rights Movement and the New Left.* New York: Vintage Books.

Fausto-Sterling, Anne (1985) *Myths of Gender: Biological Theories about Women and Men.* New York: Basic Books.

Friedan, B. (1983) *The Feminine Mystique.* 20th anniv. edn. New York: Dell.

Frye, M. (1983) *The Politics of Reality*. Trumansburg, NY: The Crossing Press.

Gilligan, C. (1982) *In a Different Voice: Psychological Theory and Women's Development*. Cambridge, MA: Harvard University Press.

Guyot, J. F. (2001) The defining moment for gender equity. *The Chronicle of Higher Education*. April 20.

Institute for Women's Policy Research (1997a) *The Status of Women in the States: Highlights*. Research-in-Brief. Washington, DC.

—— (1997b) *The Wage Gap: Men's and Women's Earnings*. Briefing Paper. Washington, DC.

Irigaray, L. (1993) *Sexes and Genealogies*, trans. Gillian Gill. New York: Columbia University Press.

MacKinnon, C. (1987) *Feminism Unmodified: Discourses on Life and Law*. Cambridge, MA: Harvard University Press.

Mill, J. S. (1869) *The Subjection of Women*. New York: Source Books, 1970.

Noddings, N. (1984) *Caring: A Feminine Approach to Ethics and Moral Education*. Berkeley, CA: University of California Press.

Radcliff Richards, J. (1980) *The Sceptical Feminist*. London: Routledge and Kegan Paul.

Ruddick, S. (1989) *Maternal Thinking: Toward a Politics of Peace*. New York: Basic Books.

Segal, L. (1990) Slow *Motion: Changing Masculinities, Changing Men*. New Brunswick, NJ: Rutgers University Press.

Shapiro, F. R. (1985) Historical notes on the vocabulary of the Women's Movement. *American Speech*, 1: 3–16.

Sommers. C. H. (2000) *The War Against Boys: How Misguided Feminism is Harming our Young Men*. New York: Simon and Schuster.

Stanton, E. C. and Anthony, S. B. (1981) *Correspondence. Writings, Speeches*, ed. E. C. DuBois. New York: Schocken Books.

Tajfel, H. (1981) *Human Groups and Social Categories*. Cambridge: Cambridge University Press.

UNIFEM (2000) *Progress of the World's Women 2000*. New York: United Nations.

US Department of Justice, Office of Justice Programs (2000) *Extent, Nature, and Consequences of Intimate Partner Violence: Findings from the National Violence against Women Survey*. Washington, DC.

Valian, V. (1998) *Why So Slow? The Advancement of Women*. Cambridge, MA: MIT Press.

Wollstonecraft, M. (1792) *Vindication of the Rights of Woman*. New York: Penguin, 1988.

For Further Reflection

1. What examples do Cudd and Jones provide of unconscious sexism at work?
2. Why do they reject the neutral sense of the term "sexism" and prefer to use the "more accurate and more specific sense" of the word?
3. What do they mean by their assertion that for many women the recognition of sexism is a transformation?

What We Get Wrong About Misogyny

KATE MANNE WITH SEAN ILLING

Kate Manne teaches at the Sage School of Philosophy at Cornell University. She argues for distinguishing carefully between sexism and misogyny. The former, she says, is an ideology that exists to justify inequality. The latter is a manifestation of sexist ideology—social systems that react to women with hostility and hatred when male privilege or status is threatened. Here she is interviewed by Sean Illing at *Vox*.

What is misogyny? How is it different from sexism? And why does the male-dominated status quo seem to persist?

A new book by Cornell philosophy professor Kate Manne has answers. She argues that misogyny is *not* about male hostility or hatred toward women—instead, it's about controlling and punishing women who challenge male dominance. Misogyny rewards women who reinforce the status quo and punishes those who don't.

In this interview, we explore how sexism and misogyny are different, how misogyny is embedded in our customs and institutions, and what Trump's election and our current moment reveal about our future.

SEAN ILLING Can you sum up your argument in this book?

KATE MANNE There's a tendency to define misogyny as this deep hatred in the heart, harbored by men toward girls and women. I define misogyny as social systems or environments where women face hostility and hatred because they're women in a man's world—a historical patriarchy.

SEAN WING I always thought of misogyny as an ideology: a body of ideas that exists to justify social relations. But you argue that this is sexism, and that misogyny is better understood as a moral manifestation of sexist ideology.

KATE MANNE Yeah, that's really well put. One way of looking at it is we have these patriarchal social structures, bastions of male privilege where a dominant man might feel entitled to (and often receive) feminine care and attention from women.

I think of misogyny and sexism as working hand-in-hand to uphold those social relations. Sexism is an ideology that says, "These arrangements just make sense. Women are just more caring, or nurturing, or empathetic," which is only true if you prime people by getting them to identify with their gender.

So sexism is the ideology that *supports* patriarchal social relations, but misogyny *enforces* it when there's a threat of that system going away.

SEAN ILLING Misogyny, the way you define it, is something we practice almost unconsciously. We're embedded in a culture and we internalize the customs and social mores that define that culture—and thus perpetuate it. We're all implicated, even if we're not aware of it.

KATE MANNE There are relatively few misogynists as brazen or as unapologetic as Donald Trump, partly because misogynists often think they're taking the moral high ground by preserving a status quo that feels right to them. They want to be socially and morally superior to the women they target.

I think most misogynistic behavior is about hostility toward women who violate patriarchal norms and expectations, who aren't serving male interests in the ways they're expected to. So there's this sense that women are doing something wrong: that they're morally objectionable or have a bad attitude or they're abrasive or shrill or too pushy. But women only appear that way because we expect them to be otherwise, to be passive.

SEAN ILLING This book calls attention to the roles we all play in society, roles that we're assigned at birth and rarely question, and how we punish people—especially women—when they defy those roles.

KATE MANNE I'm less interested in assignments of blame or holding people accountable in direct ways for their perpetuation of misogyny, and I'm more interested in having us understand the ways in which most, if not all of us, tend to be complicit in misogynistic social systems.

I wanted to know how we police women, how we keep them in their place, in their designated lane. We can combat this, and it's not like we all have to purify ourselves or something. But we have to be aware of the unconscious biases and cultural norms that sustain all of this.

SEAN ILLING So you want people to think of misogyny as a kind of enforcement strategy; it's not the patriarchy itself but the thing that preserves the patriarchy.

KATE MANNE Yes. Misogyny is the law enforcement branch of patriarchy. If you think about someone like Donald Trump claiming he's the law enforcement president, I think that's right. It's the law of patriarchy, among other things, that he's enforcing. It's the law that polices and punishes women who transgress or threaten dominant men.

SEAN ILLING Did the election of Donald Trump, an open misogynist, change your thinking in any way?

KATE MANNE No, it actually crystallized it. Since August 2015, my prediction was that Trump would be elected over Clinton, and the reason would be low voter turnout for Clinton, because that's just the way these things work: the lack of enthusiasm for a woman who's up against a male candidate who talks and acts like he's the last hurrah for patriarchy. I just saw it coming the whole way through.

On election night, I wasn't shocked, but it hurts to know that the most incompetent, morally bankrupt, and ignorant white man can be elected over a woman about whom reasonable people can disagree but who was obviously more qualified than Trump.

SEAN ILLING Every day, it seems, there is another scandal, another revelation about some asshole who used his power to exploit, assault, or harass women. We're having a cultural moment here. What's your read on what's happened since the Harvey Weinstein story broke?

KATE MANNE It seems to be mostly a good thing. It's certainly better than the alternative, which is these men getting away with it. But the thing that bothers me is their age. These are all men in their 50s, mostly 60s, sometimes 70s, who are being taken down well past the age of commercial viability, so they're not paying the price that they should.

The point is, we have this image of these old, predatory, powerful monsters. They totally exist, but they didn't start out that way. They started in adolescence. We are seeing this reluctance to face up to the fact that young men, even boys, can do the damage of their much older counterparts.

I wrote this book partly because I went to an all-boys school. I was one of the first three girls who attended the school the year it integrated, and while my experiences weren't harrowing, they were, to put it mildly, unpleasant. And the institution just saw these boys as innocent, and didn't intervene in any meaningful way. That happens all too often.

SEAN ILLING What will it take to change things?

KATE MANNE I wish I knew. This time last year, I was in New York. I spent a week alone trying to write the conclusion of my book. My editor had asked me to write a prescriptive conclusion. What do we do about misogyny? I just couldn't, because I don't know. I just don't know.

I think one thing that will help is undoing the ties that bind people falsely, the false sense of moral obligation that keeps women with abusers and makes us reluctant to try to educate, to really morally educate young men not to participate in and enact rape culture.

The good news is it's becoming really obvious that women are not inferior to men in masculine-coded pursuits like math and physics and philosophy. Women are funny. Women are writers. It takes an enormous amount of willful denialism not to see that women are free-minded and creative beings just as much as men are.

SEAN ILLING Culture can change pretty quickly. We've seen it happen with same-sex marriage and drug laws. But what we're talking about here is power relations—and that seems to be a different kind of challenge altogether.

KATE MANNE When people are attached to positions they believe are their birthright, you get huge amounts of backlash. When men think women are taking opportunities and privileges away from them, when they think women are challenging male dominance, you get backlash. But we have to deal with that. Women cannot—and should not—internalize patriarchal values and give and give and give until we're nothing.

What would need to change is for men in positions of power to accept that women can surpass them without having wronged them.

For Further Reflection

1. According to Manne, what is most misogynist behavior about?
2. What does Manne mean by "Misogyny is the law enforcement branch of patriarchy"?

The Yellow Wallpaper

CHARLOTTE PERKINS GILMAN

Charlotte Perkins Gilman (1860–1935) was a prominent feminist and author of a number of nonfiction books, including *Women and Economics* (1898) and *Man-Made World* (1911), and several short stories, "The Yellow Wallpaper" being the best-known. The story has now been told on film, TV, and stage and is regarded as an early feminist masterpiece. It is a tale of an intelligent woman who is a victim of the constraints imposed on her by a conventional nineteenth-century middle-class marriage. She is relegated to the domestic realm where she is expected to remain docile, childlike, uneducated, and intellectually comatose. The result is a disastrous descent into mental illness—and a disturbing look at the social realities that caused it.

It is very seldom that mere ordinary people like John and myself secure ancestral halls for the summer.

A colonial mansion, a hereditary estate, I would say a haunted house, and reach the height of romantic felicity—but that would be asking too much of fate!

Still I will proudly declare that there is something queer about it.

Else, why should it be let so cheaply? And why have stood so lone untenanted?

John laughs at me, of course, but one expects that in man. John is practical in the extreme. He has no patience with faith, an intense horror of superstition, and he scoffs openly at any talk of things not to be felt and seen and put down in figures.

John is a physician, and *perhaps*—(I would not say it to a living soul, of course, but this is dead paper and a great relief to my mind)—*perhaps* that is one reason I do not get well faster.

You see he does not believe I am sick! And what can one do?

If a physician of high standing, and one's own husband, assures friends and relatives that there is really nothing the matter with one but temporary nervous depression—a slight hysterical tendency—what is one to do?

My brother is also a physician, and also of high standing, and he says the same thing.

So I take phosphates or phosphites—whichever it is—and tonics, and journeys, and air, and exercise, and am absolutely forbidden to "work" until I am well again.

Personally, I disagree with their ideas.

Personally, I believe that congenial work, with excitement and change, would do me good.

But what is one to do?

I did write for a while in spite of them; but it *does* exhaust me a good deal—having to be so sly about it, or else meet with heavy opposition.

I sometimes fancy that in my condition if I had less opposition and more society and stimulus—but John says the very worst thing I can do is to think about my condition, and I confess it always makes me feel bad.

So I will let it alone and talk about the house.

The most beautiful place! It is quite alone, standing well back from the road, quite three miles from the village. It makes me think of English places that you read about, for there are hedges and walls and gates that lock, and lots of separate little houses for the gardeners and people.

There is a *delicious* garden! I never saw such a garden—large and shady, full of box-bordered paths, and lined with long grape-covered arbors with seats under them.

There were greenhouses, too, but they are all broken now. There was some legal trouble, I believe, something about the heirs and co-heirs; anyhow, the place has been empty for years.

That spoils my ghostliness, I am afraid, but I don't care—there is something strange about the house—I can feel it.

I even said so to John one moonlight evening, but he said what I felt was a draught, and shut the window.

I get unreasonably angry with John sometimes. I'm sure I never used to be so sensitive. I think it is due to this nervous condition.

But John says if I feel so I shall neglect proper self-control; so I take pains to control myself—before him, at least, and that makes me very tired.

I don't like our room a bit. I wanted one downstairs that opened on the piazza and had roses all over the window, and such pretty old-fashioned chintz hangings! But John would not hear of it.

He said there was only one window and not room for two beds, and no near room for him if he took another.

He is very careful and loving, and hardly lets me stir without special direction.

I have a schedule prescription for each hour in the day; he takes all care from me, and so I feel basely ungrateful not to value it more.

He said we came here solely on my account; that I was to have perfect rest and all the air I could get. "Your exercise depends on your strength, my dear," said he, "and your food somewhat on your appetite; but air you can absorb all the time." So we took the nursery at the top of the house.

It is a big, airy room, the whole floor nearly, with windows that look all ways, and air and sunshine galore. It was nursery first and then playroom and gymnasium, I should judge; for the windows are barred for little children, and there are rings and things in the walls.

The paint and paper look as if a boys' school had used it. It is stripped off—the paper—in great patches all around the head of my bed, about as far as I can reach, and in a great place on the other side of the room low down. I never saw a worse paper in my life.

One of those sprawling flamboyant patterns committing every artistic sin.

It is dull enough to confuse the eye in following, pronounced enough constantly to irritate and provoke study, and when you follow the lame uncertain curves for a little distance they suddenly commit suicide—plunge off at outrageous angles, destroy themselves in unheard of contradictions.

The color is repellant, almost revolting; a smouldering unclean yellow, strangely faded by the slow-turning sunlight.

It is a dull yet lurid orange in some places, a sickly sulphur tint in others.

No wonder the children hated it! I should hate it myself if I had to live in this room long.

There comes John, and I must put this away—he hates to have me write a word.

We have been here two weeks, and I haven't felt like writing before, since that first day.

I am sitting by the window now, up in this atrocious nursery, and there is nothing to hinder my writing as much as I please, save lack of strength.

John is away all day, and even some nights when his cases are serious.

I am glad my case is not serious!

But these nervous troubles are dreadfully depressing.

John does not know how much I really suffer. He knows there is no *reason* to suffer, and that satisfies him.

Of course it is only nervousness. It does weigh on me so not to do my duty in any way!

I meant to be such a help to John, such a real rest and comfort, and here I am a comparative burden already!

Nobody would believe what an effort it is to do what little I am able—to dress and entertain, and order things.

It is fortunate Mary is so good with the baby. Such a dear baby! And yet I *cannot* be with him, it makes me so nervous. I suppose John never was nervous in his life. He laughs at me so about this wallpaper!

At first he meant to repaper the room, but afterwards he said that I was letting it get the better of me, and that nothing was worse for a nervous patient than to give way to such fancies.

He said that after the wallpaper was changed it would be the heavy bedstead, and then the barred windows, and then that gate at the head of the stairs, and so on.

"You know the place is doing you good," he said, "and really, dear, I don't care to renovate the house just for a three months' rental."

"Then do let us go downstairs," I said, "there are such pretty rooms there."

Then he took me in his arms and called me a blessed little goose, and said he would go down cellar, if I wished, and have it whitewashed into the bargain.

But he is right enough about the beds and windows and things. It is an airy and comfortable room as any one need wish, and, of course, I would not be so silly as to make him uncomfortable just for a whim.

I'm really getting quite fond of the big room, all but that horrid paper.

Out of one window I can see the garden, those mysterious deep-shaded arbors, the riotous old-fashioned flowers, and bushes and gnarly trees.

Out of another I get a lovely view of the bay and a little private wharf belonging to the estate. There is a beautiful shaded lane that runs down there from the house. I always fancy I see people walking in these numerous paths and arbors, but John has cautioned me not to give way to fancy in the least. He says that with my imaginative power and habit of story-making, a nervous weakness like mine is sure to lead to all manner of excited fancies, and that I ought to use my will and good sense to check the tendency. So I try.

I think sometimes that if I were only well enough to write a little it would relieve the press of ideas and rest me.

But I find I get pretty tired when I try.

It is so discouraging not to have any advice and companionship about my work. When I get really well, John says we will ask Cousin Henry and Julia down for a long visit; but he says he would as soon put fireworks in my pillowcase as to let me have those stimulating people about now.

I wish I could get well faster.

But I must not think about that. This paper looks to me as if it *knew* what a vicious influence it had!

There is a recurrent spot where the pattern lolls like a broken neck and two bulbous eyes stare at you upside down.

I get positively angry with the impertinence of it and the everlastingness. Up and down and sideways they crawl, and those absurd, unblinking eyes are everywhere. There is one place where two breadths didn't match, and the eyes go all up and down the line, one a little higher than the other.

I never saw so much expression in an inanimate thing before, and we all know how much expression they have! I used to lie awake as a child and get more entertainment and terror out of blank walls and plain furniture than most children could find in a toy-store.

I remember what a kindly wink the knobs of our big, old bureau used to have, and there was one chair that always seemed like a strong friend.

I used to feel that if any of the other things looked too fierce I could always hop into that chair and be safe.

The furniture in this room is no worse than inharmonious, however, for we had to bring it all from downstairs. I suppose when this was used as a playroom they had to take the nursery things out, and no wonder! I never saw such ravages as the children have made here.

The wallpaper, as I said before, is torn off in spots, and it stick-eth closer than a brother—they must have had perseverance as well as hatred.

Then the floor is scratched and gouged and splintered, the plaster itself is dug out here and there, and this great heavy bed which is all we found in the room, looks as if it had been through the wars.

But I don't mind it a bit—only the paper.

There comes John's sister. Such a dear girl as she is, and so careful of me! I must not let her find me writing.

She is a perfect and enthusiastic housekeeper, and hopes for no better profession. I verily believe she thinks it is the writing which made me sick!

But I can write when she is out, and see her a long way off from these windows.

There is one that commands the road, a lovely shaded winding road, and one that just looks off over the country. A lovely country, too, full of great elms and velvet meadows.

This wallpaper has a kind of sub-pattern in a different shade, a particularly irritating one, for you can only see it in certain lights, and not clearly then.

But in the places where it isn't faded and where the sun is just so—I can see a strange, provoking, formless sort of figure, that seems to skulk about behind that silly and conspicuous front design.

There's sister on the stairs!

Well, the Fourth of July is over! The people are all gone and I am tired out. John thought it might do me good to see a little company, so we just had mother and Nellie and the children down for a week.

Of course I didn't do a thing. Jennie sees to everything now. But it tired me all the same.

John says if I don't pick up faster he shall send me to Weir Mitchell in the fall.

But I don't want to go there at all. I had a friend who was in his hands once, and she says he is just like John and my brother, only more so!

Besides, it is such an undertaking to go so far.

I don't feel as if it was worth while to turn my hand over for anything, and I'm getting dreadfully fretful and querulous.

I cry at nothing, and cry most of the time.

Of course I don't when John is here, or anybody else, but when I am alone.

And I am alone a good deal just now. John is kept in town very often by serious cases, and Jennie is good and lets me alone when I want her to.

So I walk a little in the garden or down that lovely lane, sit on the porch under the roses, and lie down up here a good deal.

I'm getting really fond of the room in spite of the wallpaper. Perhaps *because* of the wallpaper.

It dwells in my mind so!

I lie here on this great immovable bed—it is nailed down, I believe—and follow that pattern about by the hour. It is as good as gymnastics, I assure you. I start, we'll say, at the bottom, down in the corner over there where it has not been touched, and I determine for the thousandth time that I *will* follow that pointless pattern to some sort of a conclusion.

I know a little of the principle of design, and I know this thing was not arranged on any laws of radiation, or alternation, or repetition, or symmetry, or anything else that I ever heard of.

It is repeated, of course, by the breadths, but not otherwise.

Looked at in one way each breadth stands alone, the bloated curves and flourishes—a kind of "debased Romanesque" with delirium tremens—go waddling up and down in isolated columns of fatuity.

But, on the other hand, they connect diagonally, and the sprawling outlines run off in great slanting waves of optic horror, like a lot of wallowing sea-weeds in full chase.

The whole thing goes horizontally, too, at least it seems so, and I exhaust myself trying to distinguish the order of its going in that direction.

They have used a horizontal breadth for a frieze, and that adds wonderfully to the confusion.

There is one end of the room where it is almost intact, and there, when the crosslights fade and the low sun shines directly upon it, I can almost fancy radiation after all,—the interminable grotesques seem to form around a common centre and rush off in headlong plunges of equal distraction.

It makes me tired to follow it. I will take a nap I guess.

I don't know why I should write this.

I don't want to.

I don't feel able.

And I know John would think it absurd. But I *must* say what I feel and think in some way—it is such a relief!

But the effort is getting to be greater than the relief.

Half the time now I am awfully lazy, and lie down ever so much.

John says I mustn't lose my strength, and has me take cod liver oil and lots of tonics and things, to say nothing of ale and wine and rare meat.

Dear John! He loves me very dearly, and hates to have me sick. I tried to have a real earnest reasonable talk with him the other day, and tell him how I wish he would let me go and make a visit to Cousin Henry and Julia.

But he said I wasn't able to go, nor able to stand it after I got there; and I did not make out a very good case for myself, for I was crying before I had finished.

It is getting to be a great effort for me to think straight. Just this nervous weakness I suppose.

And dear John gathered me up in his arms, and just carried me upstairs and laid me on the bed, and sat by me and read to me till it tired my head.

He said I was his darling and his comfort and all he had, and that I must take care of myself for his sake, and keep well.

He says no one but myself can help me out of it, that I must use my will and self-control and not let any silly fancies run away with me.

There's one comfort, the baby is well and happy, and does not have to occupy this nursery with the horrid wallpaper.

It we had not used it, that blessed child would have! What a fortunate escape! Why, I wouldn't have a child of mine, an impressionable little thing, live in such a room for worlds.

I never thought of it before, but it is lucky that John kept me here after all, I can stand it so much easier than a baby, you see.

Of course I never mention it to them any more—I am too wise—but I keep watch for it all the same.

There are things in that paper that nobody knows but me, or ever will.

Behind that outside pattern the dim shapes get clearer every day.

It is always the same shape, only very numerous.

And it is like a woman stooping down and creeping about behind that pattern. I don't like it a bit. I wonder—I begin to think—I wish John would take me away from here!

It is so hard to talk with John about my case, because he is so wise, and because he loves me so.

But I tried it last night.

It was moonlight. The moon shines in all around just as the sun does.

I hate to see it sometimes, it creeps so slowly, and always comes in by one window or another.

John was asleep and I hated to waken him, so I kept still and watched the moonlight on that undulating wallpaper till I felt creepy.

The faint figure behind seemed to shake the pattern, just as if she wanted to get out.

I got up softly and went to feel and see if the paper *did* move, and when I came back John was awake.

"What is it, little girl?" he said. "Don't go walking about like that—you'll get cold."

I thought it was a good time to talk so I told him that I really was not gaining here, and that I wished he would take me away.

Why darling! said he, our lease will be up in three weeks, and I can't see how to leave before.

"The repairs are not done at home, and I cannot possibly leave town just now. Of course if you were in any danger, I could and would, but you really are better, dear, whether you can see it or not. I am a doctor, dear, and I know. You are gaining flesh and color, your appetite is better, I feel really much easier about you."

"I don't weigh a bit more," said I, "nor as much; and my appetite may be better in the evening when you are here, but it is worse in the morning when you are away!"

"Bless her little heart!" said he with a big hug, "she shall be as sick as she pleases! But now let's improve the shining hours by going to sleep, and talk about it in the morning!"

"And you won't go away? I asked gloomily.

"Why, how can I, dear? It is only three weeks more and then we will take a nice little trip of a few days while Jennie is getting the house ready. Really, dear, you are better!"

"Better in body perhaps—" I began, and stopped short, for he sat up straight and looked at me with such a stern, reproachful look that I could not sav another word.

"My darling," said he, "I beg of you, for my sake and for our child's sake, as well as for your own, that you will never for one instant let that idea enter your mind! There is nothing so dangerous, so fascinating, to a temperament like yours. It is a false and foolish fancy. Can you not trust me as a physician when I tell you so?"

So of course I said no more on that score, and we went to sleep before long. He thought I was asleep first, but I wasn't, and lay there for hours hying to decide whether that front pattern and the back pattern really did move together or separately.

On a pattern like this, by daylight, there is a lack of sequence, a defiance of law, that is a constant irritant to a normal mind.

The color is hideous enough, and unreliable enough, and infuriating enough, but the pattern is torturing.

You think you have mastered it, but just as you get well underway in following, it turns a back-somersault and there you are. It slaps you in the face, knocks you down, and tramples upon you. It is like a bad dream.

The outside pattern is a florid arabesque, reminding one of a fungus. If you can imagine a toadstool in joints, an interminable string of toadstools, budding and sprouting in endless convolutions—why, that is something like it.

That is, sometimes!

There is one marked peculiarity about this paper, a thing nobody seems to notice but myself, and that is that it changes as the light changes.

When the sun shoots in through the east window—I always watch for that first, long, straight ray—it changes so quickly that I never can quite believe it.

That is why I watch it always.

By moonlight—the moon shines in all night when there is a moon—I wouldn't know it was the same paper.

At night in any kind of light, in twilight, candlelight, lamplight, and worst of all by moonlight, it becomes bars! The outside pattern I mean, and the woman behind it is as plain as can be.

I didn't realize for a long time what the thing was that showed behind, that dim sub-pattern, but now I am quite sure it is a woman.

By daylight she is subdued, quiet. I fancy it is the pattern that keeps her so still. It is so puzzling. It keeps me quiet by the hour.

I lie down ever so much now. John says it is good for me, and to sleep all I can.

Indeed he started the habit by making me lie down for an hour after each meal.

It is a very bad habit I am convinced, for you see I don't sleep. And that cultivates deceit, for I don't tell them I'm awake—O, no!

The fact is I am getting a little afraid of John.

He seems very queer sometimes, and even Jennie has an inexplicable look.

It strikes me occasionally, just as a scientific hypothesis, that perhaps it is the paper!

I have watched John when he did not know I was looking, and come into the room suddenly on the most innocent excuses, and I've caught him several times *looking at the paper!* And Jennie too. I caught Jennie with her hand on it once.

She didn't know I was in the room, and when I asked her in a quiet, a very quiet voice, with the most restrained manner possible, what she was doing with the paper—she turned around as if she had been caught stealing, and looked quite angry—asked me why I should frighten her so!

Then she said that the paper stained everything it touched, that she had found yellow smooches on all my clothes and John's, and she wished we would be more careful!

Did not that sound innocent? But I know she was studying that pattern, and I am determined that nobody shall find it out but myself!

Life is very much more exciting now than it used to be. You see I have something more to expect, to look forward to, to watch. I really do eat better, and am more quiet than I was.

John is so pleased to see me improve! He laughed a little the other day, and said I seemed to be flourishing in spite of my wallpaper.

I turned it off with a laugh. I had no intention of telling him it was *because* of the wallpaper—he would make fun of me. He might even want to take me away.

I don't want to leave now until I have found it out. There is a week more, and I think that will be enough.

I'm feeling ever so much better! I don't sleep much at night, for it is so interesting to watch developments; but I sleep a good deal in the daytime.

In the daytime it is tiresome and perplexing.

There are always new shoots on the fungus, and new shades of yellow all over it. I cannot keep count of them, though I have tried conscientiously.

It is the strangest yellow, that wallpaper! It makes me think of all the yellow things I ever saw—not beautiful ones like buttercups, but old foul, bad yellow things.

But there is something else about that paper—the smell! I noticed it the moment we came into the room, but with so much air and sun it was not bad. Now we have had a week of fog and rain, and whether the windows are open or not, the smell is here.

It creeps all over the house.

I find it hovering in the dining-room, skulking in the parlor, hiding in the hall, lying in wait for me on the stairs.

It gets into my hair.

Even when I go to ride, if I turn my head suddenly and surprise it—there is that smell!

Such a peculiar odor, too! I have spent hours in trying to analyze it, to find what it smelled like.

It is not bad—at first, and very gentle, but quite the subtlest, most enduring odor I ever met.

In this damp weather it is awful, I wake up in the night and find it hanging over me.

It used to disturb me at first. I thought seriously of burning the house—to reach the smell.

But now I am used to it. The only thing I can think of that it is like is the *color* of the paper! A yellow smell.

There is a very funny mark on this wall, low down, near the mopboard. A streak that runs round the room. It goes behind every piece of furniture, except the bed, a long, straight, even *smooch*, as if it had been rubbed over and over.

I wonder how it was done and who did it, and what they did it for. Round and round and round—round and round and round—it makes me dizzy!

I really have discovered something at last.

Through watching so much at night, when it changes so, I have finally found out.

The front pattern *does* move—and no wonder! The woman behind shakes it!

Sometimes I think there are a great many women behind, and sometimes only one, and she crawls around fast, and her crawling shakes it all over.

Then in the very bright spots she keeps still, and in the very shady spots she just takes hold of the bars and shakes them hard.

And she is all the time trying to climb through. But nobody could climb through that pattern—it strangles so; I think that is why it has so many heads.

They get through, and then the pattern strangles them off and turns them upside down, and makes their eyes white!

If those heads were covered or taken off it would not be half so bad.

I think that woman gets out in the daytime!

And I'll tell you why—privately—I've seen her!

I can see her out of every one of my windows!

It is the same woman, I know, for she is always creeping, and most women do not creep by daylight.

I see her in that long shaded lane, creeping up and down. I see her in those dark grape arbors, creeping all around the garden.

I see her on that long road under the trees, creeping along, and when a carriage comes she hides under the blackberry vines.

I don't blame her a bit. It must be very humiliating to be caught creeping by daylight!

I always lock the door when I creep by daylight, i can't do it at night, for I know John would suspect something at once.

And John is so queer now, that I don't want to irritate him. I wish he would take another room! Besides, I don't want anybody to get that woman out at night but myself.

I often wonder if I could see her out of all the windows at once. But, turn as fast as I can, I can only see out of one at one time. And though I always see her, she *may* be able to creep faster than I can turn!

I have watched her sometimes away off in the open country, creeping as fast as a cloud shadow in a high wind.

If only that top pattern could be gotten off from the under one! I mean to try it, little by little.

I have found out another funny thing, but I shan't tell it this time! It does not do to trust people too much.

There are only two more days to get this paper off, and I believe John is beginning to notice. I don't like the look in his eyes.

And I heard him ask Jennie a lot of professional questions about me. She had a very good report to give.

She said I slept a good deal in the daytime.

John knows I don't sleep very well at night, for all I'm so quiet!

He asked me all sorts of questions, too, and pretended to be very loving and kind.

As if I couldn't see through him!

Still, I don't wonder he acts so, sleeping under this paper for three months.

It only interests me, but I feel sure John and Jennie are secretly affected by it.

Hurrah! This is the last day, but it is enough. John is to stay in town over night, and won't be out until this evening.

Jennie wanted to sleep with me—the sly thing! but I told her I should undoubtedly rest better for a night all alone.

That was clever, for really I wasn't alone a bit! As soon as it was moonlight and that poor thing began to crawl and shake the pattern, I got up and ran to help her.

I pulled and she shook, I shook and she pulled, and before morning we had peeled off yards of that paper.

A strip about as high as my head and half around the room.

And then when the sun came and that awful pattern began to laugh at me, I declared I would finish it to-day!

We go away to-morrow, and they are moving ail my furniture down again to leave things as they were before.

Jennie looked at the wall in amazement, but I told her merrily that I did it out of pure spite at the vicious thing.

She laughed and said she wouldn't mind doing it herself, but I must not get tired.

How she betrayed herself that time!

But I am here, and no person touches this paper but Me—not *alive!*

She tried to get me out of the room—it was too patent! But I said it was so quiet and empty and clean now that I believed I would lie down again and sleep all I could; and not to wake me even for dinner—I would call when I woke.

So now she is gone, and the servants are gone, and the things are gone, and there is nothing left but that great bedstead nailed down, with the canvas mattress we found on it.

We shall sleep downstairs to-night, and take the boat home tomorrow.

I quite enjoy the room, now it is bare again.

How those children did tear about here!

This bedstead is fairly gnawed!

But I must get to work.

I have locked the door and thrown the key down into the front path.

I don't want to go out, and I don't want to have anybody come in, till John comes.

I want to astonish him.

I've got a rope up here that even Jennie did not find. If that woman does get out, and tries to get away, I can tie her!

But I forgot I could not reach far without anything to stand on! This bed will *not* move!

I tried to lift and push it until I was lame, and then I got so angry I bit off a little piece at one corner—but it hurt my teeth.

Then I peeled off all the paper I could reach standing on the floor. It sticks horribly and the pattern just enjoys it! All those strangled heads and bulbous eyes and waddling fungus growths just shriek with derision!

I am getting angry enough to do something desperate. To jump out of the window would be admirable exercise, but the bars are too strong even to try.

Besides I wouldn't do it. Of course not. I know well enough that a step like that is improper and might be misconstrued.

I don't like to *look* out of the windows even—there are so many of those creeping women, and they creep so fast.

I wonder if they all come out of that wallpaper as I did?

But I am securely fastened now by my well-hidden rope—you don't get *me* out in the road there!

I suppose I shall have to get back behind the pattern when it comes night, and that is hard!

It is so pleasant to be out in this great room and creep around as I please!

I don't want to go outside. I won't, even if Jennie asks me to.

For outside you have to creep on the ground, and everything is green instead of yellow.

But here I can creep smoothly on the floor, and my shoulder just fits in that long smooch around the wall, so I cannot lose my way.

Why there's John at the door!

It is no use, young man, you can't open it!

How he does call and pound!

Now he's crying for an axe.

It would be a shame to break down that beautiful door! "John dear!" said I in the gentlest voice, "the key is down by the front steps, under a plantain leaf!"

That silenced him for a few moments.

Then he said, very quietly indeed, "Open the door, my darling!" "I can't," said I. "The key is down by the front door under a plantain leaf!"

And then I said it again, several times, very gently and slowly, and said it so often that he had to go and see, and he got it of course, and came in. He stopped short by the door.

"What is the matter?" he cried. "For God's sake, what are you doing!"

I kept on creeping just the same, but I looked at him over my shoulder.

"I've got out at last," said I, "in spite of you and Jane. And I've pulled off most of the paper, so you can't put me back!"

Now why should that man have fainted? But he did, and right across my path by the wall, so that I had to creep over him every time!

For Further Reflection

1. This story is lauded by modern feminists and many others concerned about the social oppression of women. Why do you think that is?
2. The ending can be seen as a woman slipping into insanity or as a woman asserting her power—her own kind of resistance—in an impossible situation. Which interpretation do you prefer and why? Or do you prefer another view?
3. The narrator's husband John is neither violent nor abusive toward her, but his actions are nevertheless coercive. How are they coercive?

Further Readings for Chapter 10

Anderson, Kristin J. *Modern Misogyny: Anti-Feminism in a Post-Feminist Era*. New York: Oxford University Press, 2015.

Cudd, Ann E., and Leslie E. Jones. "Sexism," in *A Companion to Applied Ethics*, edited by R. G. Frey and Christopher Heath Wellman. Malden, MA: Blackwell, 2003, 105–106.

Cudd, Ann E., and Robin O. Andreasen, eds. *Feminist Theory: A Philosophical Anthology*. Malden, MA: Blackwell, 2005.

de Beauvoir, Simone. *The Second Sex*. New York: Vintage Books, 1974.

Friedan, Betty. *The Feminine Mystique*. New York: Dell, 1983.

Held, Virginia. *Feminist Morality: Transforming Culture, Society, and Politics*. Chicago: University of Chicago Press, 1993.

Kelly, Conor. "Sexism in Practice: Feminist Ethics Evaluating the Hookup Culture." *Journal of Feminist Studies in Religion* 28, no. 2 (2012): 27–48.

Manne, Kate. *Down Girl: The Logic of Misogyny*. New York: Oxford University Press, 2018.

Mill, John Stuart. *The Subjection of Women*. New York: Source Books, 1970.

Nussbaum, Martha C. *Sex and Social Justice*. Oxford: Oxford University Press, 1999.

CHAPTER 11

Racism, Equity, and Privilege

Issues of race and racial justice have been simmering on campuses for decades, but they have recently boiled over as many students demanded racial equity and as incidents outside the university have shown that racial reckonings in America are way past due. The most infamous of these recent incidents was the May 2020 death of George Floyd, a 46-six-year-old black man killed by a Minneapolis police officer who pinned him to the street by jamming a knee into his neck for almost nine minutes as Floyd gasped, "I can't breathe." His death launched massive public protests in thousands of U.S. cities and provoked demonstrations throughout the world. On many campuses minority students have reported a culture of racism, encounters with students using racial slurs, widespread acceptance of racial stereotypes, and racial inequities in the way colleges and universities function.

To understand such racial ills and to try to remedy them, we must be clear about the non-moral facts of racism and race as well as the right and wrong of racial beliefs, actions, and motivations. What is racism? Why is it morally wrong? Does systemic racism exist? Do races even exist? Who is guilty of racism? Philosophers, sociologists, and other scholars have been carefully examining these questions and are articulating coherent answers.

RACE AND RACISM

The basic presupposition of racism is that there are in fact such things as races—the notion that there are discrete groups of people who share certain essential, inherent characteristics. The traditional idea is that race is a matter of heritable *biological* features common to all members of a racial group and that these features explain the psychological and cultural traits of those members.

Race scholar Lawrence Blum points out that the popular idea of race generally omits the biological element but keeps the idea of *inherency*—the notion that "certain traits of mind, character, and temperament are inescapably part of a racial group's 'nature' and hence define its racial fate."[1] A group's nature is supposed to be permanent and unchanging. On this conception of race, whites are just naturally that way; blacks are naturally this way; Jews have these inherent traits; Asians have these inherent characteristics; Native Americans have this inherent disposition. Racism, then, presupposes the idea that distinct races exist and that important, inherent differences among them can be distinguished. This presupposition alone, however, does not constitute racism. *Racism* is the additional belief that some races are inferior in these important ways or are otherwise deserving of dislike or hostility.

The two essential elements in this definition are what Blum calls *inferiorization* and *antipathy*. All forms of racism, he says, can be identified by reference to one or both of these concepts:

> Inferiorization is linked to historical racist doctrine and racist social systems. Slavery, segregation, imperialism, apartheid, and Nazism all treated certain groups as inferior to other groups . . .
>
> Though race-based antipathy is less related to the original concept of "racism," today the term unequivocally encompasses racial bigotry, hostility, and hatred. Indeed, the racial bigot is many people's paradigm image of a "racist." . . .
>
> Historical systems of racism did of course inevitably involve racial antipathy as well as inferiorization. Hatred of Jews was central to Nazi philosophy; and it is impossible to understand American racism without seeing hostility to blacks and Native Americans as integral to the nexus of attitudes and emotions that shored up slavery and segregation.[2]

Racism is morally wrong, and shortly we'll examine exactly why that is. But racism is also empirically wrong—it is based on assumptions about the world that science has shown to be unfounded. The consensus among scientists and scholars is that the traditional view of races—that there are distinct groups of people sharing significant biological characteristics—is false. Race, in other words, has no physical scientific basis. Sociologist Tanya Maria Golash-Boza explains:

> Race is a social construction, an idea we endow with meaning through daily interactions. It has no biological basis. This might seem odd to read, as the

[1]Lawrence Blum, *"I'm Not a Racist But . . .": The Moral Quandary of Race* (Ithaca, NY: Cornell University Press, 2002), 133.
[2]Blum, *"I'm Not a Racist But,"* 8–9.

> physical differences between a Kenyan, a Swede, and a Han Chinese, for example, are obvious. However, these physical differences do not necessarily mean that the world can be divided into discrete racial groups. If you were to walk from Kenya to Sweden to China, you would note incremental gradations in physical differences between people across space, and it would be difficult to decide where to draw the line between Africa and Europe and between Europe and Asia. There may be genetic differences between Kenyans and Swedes, but the genetic variations within the Kenyan population are actually greater than those between Swedes and Kenyans. Although race is a social, as opposed to a biological, construction, it has a wide range of consequences in our society, especially when used as a sorting and stratifying mechanism.[3]

Many people assume that the idea of race has been around since the dawn of history, but this assumption is incorrect. Historically, the idea that people can be divided into discrete groups based on their common biological and cultural traits is relatively new. In the ancient world, people did not think to categorize humanity into exclusive racial groups. They recognized that cultures might differ in various ways—in skin color, for example—but they did not lump all persons of a particular skin tone into a single social classification. The idea of race arose in different forms over time beginning only around the sixteenth century. Historians and sociologists maintain that as Europeans subjugated and enslaved Africans and native peoples in the Americas, the idea of inferior and superior races developed and was used to rationalize the unequal status and ill treatment of whole cultures.

So if race is a social construction, should we discard the concept of race altogether? Many who have studied this question are reluctant to do that. The political scientist Michael James, for example, says,

> Race constructivists accept the skeptics' dismissal of biological race but argue that the term still meaningfully refers to the widespread grouping of individuals into certain categories by society, indeed often by the very members of such racial ascriptions. Normatively, race constructivists argue that since society labels people according to racial categories, and since such labeling often leads to race-based differences in resources, opportunities, and well-being, the concept of race must be conserved, in order to facilitate race-based social movements or policies, such as affirmative action, that compensate for socially constructed but socially relevant racial differences.[4]

[3]Tanya Maria Golash-Boza, *Race and Racisms: A Critical Approach* (New York: Oxford University Press, 2016), 3.
[4]Michael James, "Race," in *Stanford Encyclopedia of Philosophy*, Spring 2017, ed. Edward N. Zalta, https://plato.stanford.edu/archives/spr2017/entries/race/.

Even though races in the biological sense don't exist, "racialized groups"—groups that people *believe* are discrete races and treat as such—do. Scholars contend that despite the nonexistence of biological race, giving up entirely our ability to talk and think about racialized groups and racial realities would have disastrous effects—which is why so many observers condemn the notion of racial color blindness.

Racism is morally wrong. But why?

Inferiorizing racism is morally wrong mainly because it is a violation of fundamental moral principles. It violates the principle of *respect for persons*, the precept that persons are possessors of ultimate inherent worth and should be treated as such. Persons have rights—the rights of free expression, choice, and privacy, the right not to be coerced, enslaved, cheated, or discriminated against. This form of racism also violates the *principle of justice*, the idea that people should get what is fair or what is their due or, more generally, that equals should be treated equally. People should be treated the same unless there is a morally relevant reason for treating them differently—and racial difference is *not* morally relevant.

Having racist beliefs and attitudes is wrong, and acting on them is, of course, morally worse. According to Blum, these wrongs take on an additional weight of immorality because they are racial:

> What is it about racially-based violations of these human norms that intensifies the moral wrong involved?
>
> The additional opprobrium is racism's integral tie to the social and systematic horrors of slavery, apartheid, Nazism, colonialism, segregation, imperialism, and the shameful treatment of Native Americans in the United States—all race-based systems of oppression. U.S. law recognizes that racially based wrongs are more serious than other similar wrongs by calling race a particularly "invidious" distinction.[5]

Antipathy racism is morally blameworthy because hatred, hostility, and bigotry are vices, especially when they are directed against people who have been made to suffer solely because of their membership in a racial group. Antipathy racism, like the inferiorizing kind, has led to, and still leads to, racial conflict, suffering, injustice, and violence.

For many ethicists, racism is morally wrong simply because it hurts people. This is an appeal to another moral principle, the principle of *utility*, which says we should produce the most favorable balance of benefit over harm for

[5]Blum, *"I'm Not a Racist But,"* 27.

all concerned. It is obvious that racist beliefs, words, and actions can do harm or lead to harm, and the harm is magnified when racism operates through organizations, corporations, governments, and the law.

For many people, racism is basically *individual racism*, person-to-person acts of intolerance or discrimination. But a prevalent, seldom-acknowledged kind of racism is *institutional* or *structural racism*, unequal treatment that arises from the way organizations, institutions, and social systems operate. This is inferiorizing or antipathy racism that functions almost unseen in corporations, government agencies, schools, the labor market, and systems of health care, housing, and criminal justice. The people who work within such systems may or may not be racially prejudiced, but the systems themselves cause racial discrimination and inequality through their policies and procedures.

Overt, individual racism (the kind voiced publicly in racial slurs, for example) may be less common these days, but scholars insist that institutional or structural racism is common and nearly invisible. According to race scholar Eduardo Bonilla-Silva:

> Contemporary racial inequality is reproduced through "new racism" practices that are subtle, institutional, and apparently nonracial. In contrast to the Jim Crow era, where racial inequality was enforced through overt means (e.g., signs saying "No Niggers Welcomed Here" or shotgun diplomacy at the voting booth), today racial practices operate in a "now you see it, now you don't" fashion. For example, residential segregation, which is almost as high today as it was in the past, is no longer accomplished through overtly discriminatory practices. Instead, covert behaviors such as not showing all the available units, steering minorities and whites into certain neighborhoods, quoting higher rents or prices to minority applicants, or not advertising units at all are the weapons of choice to maintain separate communities. In the economic field, "smiling face" discrimination ("We don't have jobs now, but please check later"), advertising job openings in mostly white networks and ethnic newspapers, and steering highly educated people of color into poorly remunerated jobs or jobs with limited opportunities for mobility are the new ways of keeping minorities in a secondary position. Politically, although the civil rights struggles have helped remove many of the obstacles for the electoral participation of people of color, racial gerrymandering, multimember legislative districts, election runoffs, annexation of predominately white areas, at-large district elections, and anti-single-shot devices (disallowing concentrating votes [on] one or two candidates in cities using at-large elections) have become standard practices to disenfranchise people of color.[6]

[6]Eduardo Bonilla-Silva, *Racism without Racists* (Lanham, MD: Rowman and Littlefield, 2014), 3.

Today blacks fare much worse than whites in income, wealth, education, employment, health, and home ownership. These inequalities are caused by racist policies and conditions of the past, and they have in most cases been allowed to continue or been made worse by inequalities in the present.

RACIST OR NOT?

On campus and off, the term "racist" is being applied to numerous individuals, actions, policies, institutions, and systems. We are morally obligated to be clear about exactly who or what deserves the label. As Blum argues, racism involves either antipathy or inferiorization directed at a racial group. Racial antipathy is revealed in attitudes and actions expressing contempt, disrespect, and hostility, and racial inferiorization is embodied in attitudes and actions that treat one racial group as somehow inferior to another. Actions (like statements) can be racist, and attitudes (like motives) can be racist, but racism in the former does not necessarily involve racism in the latter.

If this analysis of racism is correct, then many things are clearly racist, but many other things are clearly not. As Blum says,

> Some feel that the word [racist] is thrown around so much that anything involving "race" that someone does not like is liable to castigation as "racist." . . . A local newspaper called certain blacks "racist" for criticizing other blacks who supported a white over a black candidate for mayor. A white girl in Virginia said that it was "racist" for an African American teacher in her school to wear African attire. . . . Merely mentioning someone's race (or racial designation), using the word "Oriental" for Asians without recognizing its origins and its capacity for insult, or socializing only with members of one's own racial group are called "racist.". . .
>
> Not every instance of racial conflict, insensitivity, discomfort, miscommunication, exclusion, injustice, or ignorance should be called "racist." Not all *racial* incidents are *racist* incidents. We need a more varied and nuanced moral vocabulary for talking about the domain of race. . . . All forms of racial ills should elicit concern from responsible individuals. If someone displays racial insensitivity, but not racism, people should be able to see that for what it is.[7]

Many statements are unequivocally racist: a white person calls a black person the n-word, a white man tells a racist joke that demeans blacks, an Asian American blurts out "goddamn white people," a black person says Latinos are lazy, a white woman asserts that Mexicans are rapists and murderers.

[7]Blum, *"I'm Not a Racist But,"* 1–2.

These statements would be racist even if the person making them did not bear any antipathy or inferiorizing attitude toward the targeted group. Whether the person making the racist statement is in fact a racist is a separate issue. Someone who harbors no animosity or inferiorizing attitude toward a racial group but who nevertheless utters a racist statement is no racist—but instead may be racially insensitive, ignorant, uncomfortable, or self-deceived.

Racism should be of concern to everyone, but we must be morally mature enough to recognize that racism comes in degrees. The most evil manifestations of racism are slavery, segregation, apartheid, massacres, lynchings, and mass incarcerations. But beyond these extremes, there are gradations to take into account. Clearly, racist violence is worse than preaching racist violence. Believing that another race is inferior or that it deserves to be hated is not as morally heinous as trying to harm that group. Having unexpressed racist attitudes is not as morally bad as trying to convince others to have them. Telling a racist joke about a racial group is not as bad as discriminating against that group in business or employment. An artistic creation—a movie, painting, song, or book—can be slightly racist or savagely racist in the way it depicts people of color. Racism is a serious moral matter, but we need to address each instance with the degree of seriousness and moral censure that it deserves. Otherwise, we risk treating racism simplistically and distorting much needed conversations about it.

WHITE PRIVILEGE

White privilege refers to the advantages or benefits that whites enjoy simply because they are white. These advantages of racial privilege can seem almost invisible. As Golash-Boza says,

> If you are white, it can be difficult to notice that you are not being followed around the store [by security]; that people are smiling at you on the street instead of clutching their purses; that no one asks you if you speak English; that you are not asked for identification when paying with a credit card. Instead, you are likely to think that these things are normal—that this is simply how things are.[8]

Philosopher and race scholar Shannon Sullivan concurs:

> One of the main features of racial inequality after the end of de jure Jim Crow is its relative invisibility. Today white advantages often are subtle, even hidden, and they frequently are difficult to prove empirically or pinpoint

[8]Golash-Boza, *Race and Racisms*, 3.

> with certainty. When they can be demonstrated, as in the case of institutional racial biases against people of color, they often are explained away as the result of something other than racial bias. . . . In other cases, racial inequalities benefitting white people operate without explicitly mentioning race or whiteness at all. K-12 school suspension rates, for example, tend to be extremely imbalanced, penalizing black students disproportionately, but they often are discussed as race-neutral matters of "zero tolerance" of "disruptive" and "insubordinate" behavior. . . . Practices such as these tend to camouflage race and white advantage, making it all too easy for white (and other) people to deny that they exist and for racial inequality to hum along unchallenged.[9]

Does having or benefiting from white privilege make you a racist? Blum argues that it's a mistake to conflate white privilege with personal racism:

> The whole point of the idea of white privilege is that it does *not* depend on the attitudes of its beneficiaries toward disadvantaged racial groups; nonracists still partake of white privilege. . . . What is so disturbing about white privilege is that you need not be in any way personally blameworthy for having it, but it is still unfair that you do. It is not personally racist to have white privilege. . . . White privilege is a different sort of racial ill than personal racism. But it is morally wrong to be complacent about or accepting of racial privileges once one knows one possesses them; one is (often) thereby being complicit with injustice.[10]

White privilege can help us identify a type of racial ill, scholars say, but the concept is easily misused. Sullivan argues that it can, unfortunately, distract white people from the more important task of working toward racial justice.

[9]Shannon Sullivan, "White Privilege," in *The Oxford Handbook of Philosophy and Race*, ed. Naomi Zack (New York: Oxford University Press, 2019), 332.
[10]Blum, *"I'm Not a Racist But,"* 73, 76.

Racism: What It Is and Isn't

LAWRENCE BLUM

Lawrence Blum is emeritus professor of philosophy and distinguished professor of liberal arts and education at the University of Massachusetts Boston. He argues that the terms *racist* and *racism* have been massively overused and misunderstood and that they have been unhelpfully used to refer to almost anything that is problematic with race. We need a broader vocabulary for referring to racial ills, for not every event or situation that is racial is also racist. Racism concerns two things—either antipathy or inferiorizing. This clarification helps us see that that not every racially objectionable action is done from a racist motive, and not all racial stereotypes are racist.

We in the United States are notoriously poor at communicating about racial matters. David Shipler, in his informative and insightful book *A Nation of Strangers*, rightly says, "Blacks and whites do not listen well to each other" (Shipler, 1997, p. 447). Native Americans, Latinos, Chicanos, and Asian-Americans are not all that much better. We find honest discussion about race across racial lines especially difficult. Ironically, race is the subject of scores of books and articles. And one often hears impatience expressed about race. "Race is talked to death," it is said.

There may be a lot of words written about race. But there is a good deal less honest, open, and productive conversation about it among persons of different races than there needs to be. For the past several years I have taught courses on race and racism to undergraduates, graduate students in education, and high school students. Most of my classes are quite racially and ethnically diverse. In my experience a range of reasons accounts for the lack of productive conversation. People are afraid of giving offense. They are afraid of revealing prejudices they know are not socially acceptable. They are afraid of *appearing* prejudiced, even if they are actually not. They feel ignorant of groups other than their own and are afraid to risk revealing their ignorance and trying to remedy it. The whole idea of "race" just carries unpleasant associations with them, and they would rather avoid it. They may think we should all be "color-blind," that it is somehow wrong even to take notice of or make reference to other people's racial identity. This idea of color-blindness is both particularly strong, yet also particularly misplaced, among teachers, especially

Studies in Philosophy and Education 21: 203–218, 2002. Printed in the Netherlands.

at the pre-college level. Teachers can not serve their students fully unless they are aware of the full range of factors affecting their lives, and race is very likely to be one of those factors (Schofield, 1989).

Some reasons for reluctance to engage in race discussions are more race-specific. Blacks, and to a lesser extent other people of color, may want to avoid what they assume will be offensive or at least annoying remarks from others. Or they might not want to have to be in a position of correcting others' (especially whites') ignorance. Latinos, Native Americans, and Asian-Americans may not be certain how to insert themselves into a discourse which seems to them dominated by "black/white" issues, or they may feel resentful of this dominance, and assume their specific concerns will not be adequately attended to. Notwithstanding these obstacles, I have also found a great deal of good will among students, and an anxious desire for their teachers to create contexts that facilitate constructive interracial interchange.

Each of the cited obstacles is deserving of further attention. However, I wish in this lecture to focus on a different obstacle, though one that bears on several of those just mentioned. It is the idea of "racism" itself. There is a great deal of confusion surrounding the meaning of "racism" and "racist." Yet one thing is clear—few people wish to be, or to be thought of as, "racists." Fear of being thought racist, together with a good deal of confusion as to, "what" being racist consists in, is a potent formula for inhibition regarding discussing racial matters, most especially for whites who are, understandably, in most danger of being thought to be, and indeed of actually being, racists.

Clarifying meanings is the professional task of the philosopher, and I think that if we become clearer about what "racism" actually consists in, and what lies outside of the scope of racism yet may still be morally problematic, we will be better equipped to engage in productive discussions about race. Of course I have no illusions that merely clarifying meanings will bring about either racial justice or racial harmony, or even the more minimal goal of producing helpful conversations about these matters. But it seems an essential first step.

The words "racism" and "racist" have become deeply entrenched in the moral vocabulary of the United States and Western Europe. "Is television a racist institution?" asks an article concerning the NAACP's criticizing the fall 1999 prime-time network shows for having no "minority" actors in lead roles in twenty-seven new series (Weinraub, 1999, pp. A1, A14). Blacks who criticized other blacks for supporting a white over a black candidate in a mayoral race were called racist. A white girl in Virginia said that it was racist for an African-American teacher in her school to wear African attire (Shipler, p. 92). The Milton, Wisconsin, school board voted to retire its "Redmen" name and logo depicting a Native American wearing a headdress, because they have been criticized as racist. "Racist" has become the standard way to condemn and deplore people, actions, policies, symbols, and institutions for malfeasance in the racial domain.

In serving as a term of moral reproach, "racism" has joined more time-honored vices such as "dishonesty," "cruelty," "cowardice," and "hypocrisy." Apart from a small number of avowed white supremacists, most Americans wish very much to avoid being called "racist." In this regard, "racist" operates similarly to "cruel." Few admit to being cruel. Persons who are cruel might say the target of their cruelty deserved it, or they might simply fail to recognize the harm caused by their actions. Similarly, no one admits to being racist. Those who are, or are thought to be, might say their remarks were just a joke; they did not intend any harm; people are just being oversensitive; it was a personal, not a racial, thing; and the like. One expects people who are accused of being racist to deny it and newspapers should stop regarding this as newsworthy.

OVERUSING "RACISM"

Yet the widely-shared reproach carried by "racist" is threatened by a current tendency to overuse the term. Some feel that the word is thrown around so much that anything involving "race" that someone does not like is liable to castigation as "racist"—for example, merely mentioning someone's race (or racial designation),[1] using the word "Oriental" for Asians without recognizing its origins and its capacity for insult, or socializing only with members of one's own racial group. Many people would not agree, or would not be sure, that any of the four examples in the paragraph before the previous one constitute "racism." A few observers go even further and suspect that the word has lost all significant meaning. "Racism is . . . what black activists define it to be. . . . When words lose coherent meaning, they also lose the power to shame. 'Racism,' 'sexism,' and 'homophobia' have become such words. Labels that should horrify are simply shrugged off (Nuechterlein, 1996, p. B9). *Time* columnist Lance Morrow sees social damage in this same development: "The words 'racism' and 'racist' are a feckless indulgence, corrosive to blacks and whites alike and to relations between them" (Morrow, 1996, p. 18).

A major reason for what Robert Miles calls the "conceptual inflation" (Miles, 1989, pp. 41–68), to which the idea of "racism" has been subject is its having become the central or even only notion used to mark morally suspect

[1]I do not believe that there are races in the sense in which "races" is generally understood in popular discourse, so I regard it as misleading to say that someone "is of a certain race." It is more accurate to say that someone has, or has been assigned, a racial designation, or that she is a member of a racial group; I will generally use the latter expression.

behavior, attitude, and social practice regarding race. The result—either something is racist, or it is morally in the clear. In Boston a white police officer, as a bizarre joke and apparently with no malice intended, placed a hangman's noose on the motorcycle of a black police officer. "Police probe sees no racism in noose prank," says the headline of an article reporting the findings of an investigation into the incident. Perhaps the white officer was not "a racist," nor operating from racist motives; but, as the victim in the incident said, "You cannot hang a noose like that near any black man who knows his history and say it does not have tremendous significance" (Boston Globe, p. B1).[2] If our only choices are to label an act "racist" or "nothing to get too upset about," those who seek to garner moral attention to some racial malfeasance will be tempted to call it "racist." That overuse in turn feeds a diminishing of "racism's" moral force, and thus contributes to weakened concern about racism and other racial ills.

Not all racial incidents are racist incidents. Not every instance of racial conflict, insensitivity, discomfort, miscommunication, exclusion, injustice, or ignorance should be called "racist." This more varied and nuanced moral vocabulary needs to be more fully utilized, complementing "racist" and "racism." All forms of racial ills should elicit concern from responsible citizens. If someone displays racial insensitivity, but not racism, people should be able to see that straightforwardly as a matter of moral concern. In a soccer game, a nine-year-old white boy said "Boy, pass the ball over here" to one of his back teammates, and "was virtually accused of being a racist by the father of one of his teammates," says an article on the incident. (That description may itself reflect the loss of an evaluative vocabulary other than "racist" and "racism," rather than what the black boy's father actually said.) In any case, the white boy was almost surely not "a racist" and the article itself goes on to express more accurately the racial ill involved in his remark: "The word 'boy' is a tripwire attached to so much charged racial baggage that it is no longer safely used as a term for a prepubescent male."

If a policy has a racially unjust effect, or unequally affects already unequally placed racial groups, this too should be reason for concern, even if there is no suggestion that it arises from racist motives, or is part of the sort of entrenched pattern strongly rooted in historical racism. For example, school lunch programs have been criticized for relying too strongly on milk, in light of the African-Americans' substantial propensity toward lactose intolerance; but no untoward motives, or failures of sensitivity, need have prompted the original policies favoring milk for them to be of concern. Similarly, it is troubling if prime-time TV fails adequately to reflect its viewers', and the society's,

[2]The black officer seemed clearly to be referring to lynching.

ethnoracial diversity; but it is not necessarily "racist."[3] Someone who exhibits a culpable ignorance about racial matters bearing on an interaction with an acquaintance or co-worker should feel a degree of shame about this, and be motivated to correct that ignorance—without her having to think she has been "racist." We should not be faced with the choice of "racism or nothing."

"Racism's" conceptual inflation and moral overload can arise from another source as well—designating as "racism" any prejudice, injustice, domination, inferiorizing, bigotry, and the like, against human groups defined in <u>any</u> manner, for example, by gender, disability, nationality. In *The Decent Society*, Avishai Margalit, an Israeli philosopher, defines racism as the denying of dignity to *any human group*, and uses as a particular test case "retarded" persons (Margalit, 1996, pp. 80–83). This inflated use of racism pays indirect tribute to the centrality of racism as a form of oppression and denial of dignity in contemporary Western consciousness. That centrality is reflected also in later coinages, such as "sexism," "ableism" (discrimination against the disabled), "racism," and "hetero-sexism"—all consciously modeled on "racism," and attempting to draw on racism's moral opprobrium to condemn other phenomena seen as in important ways analogous to racism.[4] This "racism"-influenced proliferation of other "isms" at least avoids the confusion wrought by Margalit's conflating all of them with "racism" itself. At least it encourages us to explore the similarities between discrimination, exploitation, and denials of dignity based on race, and those based on other human attributes, such as gender, sexual orientation, disability, national membership, and the like, thereby allowing the possibility of significant *disanalogies.* Margalit's subsuming all these moral ills under "racism" cuts off that inquiry at the starting line, and, in so doing, contribute to a counterproductive inflation of the term "racism."

RACIST JOKES AND RACIST PERSONS

A different source of confusion and moral overload regarding racism concerns what one might call racism's location. Many different kinds of entity can be racist – actions, institutions, practices, symbols, statements, jokes, persons, to name a few. The moral significance of an attribution of racism differs depending on its location. Take racist jokes for instance. A person who

[3]It is noteworthy that it was the newspaper article, rather than the NAACP itself, that called the networks "racist," or framed the issue as one of racism. Kweisi Mfume, the president of the NAACP, said only that the programming was "a vitual whitewash." *New York Times*, Sept 20, 1991, A1.

[4]Of those listed, only "sexism" has fully succeeded in attaching moral condemnation to its referent—discrimination against, or the denial of dignity to, women, or discrimination on the basis of sex in general—in popular thought and speech.

tells a racist joke is not necessarily "a racist," in the sense of a person who harbors pervasive racial animosity or inferiorizing attitudestoward a racially defined group. He may tell the joke without sharing the racist sentiments the joke expresses. People often tell jokes as a way of trying to win acceptance; they might tell whatever they think will bring a laugh. Imagine, for example, someone telling a joke that makes fun of Asian-Americans in a particularly demeaning manner, in order to gain acceptance in a group. (The group could consist of any ethnoracial group, except Asian-Americans. I am not assuming that only whites tell racist jokes [or are racists, for that matter].)[5] This individual does not necessarily hold racist views of Asians or Asian-Americans. The joke is racist, but the teller of the joke is not. Of course, this does not mean that, as long as one does not share the racist views a joke expresses, it is perfectly fine to tell such a joke. To think that it is all right is to reason in precisely the all-or-nothing manner I have been criticizing. It is a very bad thing to tell a racist joke. One often hears public figures who have been caught out telling a racist joke or making a racist remark defending themselves by saying that they did not intend any offense to the group in question, that they are not racist. Often this defense is quite disingenuous, and the individual in fact does hold the racist attitudes implied in the joke. But even when it is not, this is a feeble defense from a moral point of view. It is bad to tell a racist joke, whether one means to offend, or holds racist attitudes, or not. Jokes, and humor more generally, raise a common locational issue about racism—the difference between intention and effect—illustrated in two examples of racist humor that came to public attention in the late 1990's. One was a fraternity party, in which the fraternity members dressed up in Native American warrior attire and wielded tomahawks. A second, again a fraternity, involved staging a mock slave auction. In both cases, members of the fraternities in question defended themselves by saying that they did not mean to offend anyone. But the moral shortcoming in both cases did not lie in setting out to deliberately demean native Americans and African-Americans. It lay in their failing to realize that what they were doing *was* demeaning to Native Americans and African-Americans, whether they *intended* this or not. It is not even clear that ignorance of the affront would be morally more acceptable them an intention to affront.

Still, engaging in racist humor does not make one a racist. More generally, clarity and racial understanding would be advanced if people attempted to take greater care in locating the racism they allege in a situation. Is it a practice that is racist, whether the persons who participate in the practice are

[5]In "I'm Not a Racist, But . . ." I argue that members of any group can be racist. Forinstance, I counter the view that only whites can be racist because only whites hold poweras a racial group.

racist or not? Is it the motive of an act that is racist? Is it an attitude taken to be expressed in a remark, or the remark itself? Is it a person about whom one knows enough to say that he or she is "a racist?"

To help us avoid the first form of confusion about racism—conceptual inflation—I will suggest a core meaning rooted in the history of its use, that confines "racism" to phenomena deserving of the severest moral condemnation (within the appropriately located type, that is, act, statement, joke, person, and so on). Fixing on such a definition should encourage us to make use of the considerable other resources our language affords us for describing and evaluating race-related ills that do not characteristically rise to the level of racism—racial insensitivity, racial conflict, racial injustice, racial ignorance, racial discomfort, and others. Such an agreed-upon meaning for "racism" should facilitate interracial communication, at least in diminishing a free-floating and pervasive fear of the dreaded charge of "racism"—by making clearer what is and what is not to be counted as racism—while at the same time encouraging a wider scope of moral concern to race-related phenomena. In doing so, my suggested definition of racism should stanch the creeping loss of moral cachet of the term "racism" itself, with its attendant undermining of moral concern toward racism and other race-related ills.

DEFINING "RACISM"

In proffering a definition of racism, it would be folly to claim that one was doing no more than articulating "our concept" of racism. Even apart from inflationary usages, it is not likely that all employments of that concept cohere in an overall, self-consistent whole. Nevertheless, especially in fight of the history of this concept, I hope my proposal can reasonably be viewed as a plausible candidate for a core meaning.

"Racism" was first used by German social scientists in the 1930s to refer to the ideology of race superiority central to Nazism, and its core historical meaning broadened out to other systems of racial domination and oppression, such as segregation, South African apartheid, and European colonialism. In this light, I want to suggest that all forms of racism can be related to either of two general "themes"—*inferiorization*, and *antipathy*. Inferiorizing is treating the racial other as inferior or of lesser value and, secondarily, viewing the racial other as inferior. Racial antipathy is simply a strong dislike, often tinged with hostility, toward individuals or groups because of their race. Of the two modes, inferiorization is more obviously linked to historical racist doctrines and social systems. Slavery, segregation, imperialism, apartheid, and Nazism all involved certain groups being regarded as and treated as inferior to other groups.

But race-based hatred was also central to the ideological and attitudinal components of Nazism, and, for whatever reason, racial bigotry, hostility, and hatred are now securely linked to the contemporary idea of "racism" in both Europe and the United States. Indeed, the racial bigot is many people's paradigm image of "a racist," and few would now deny application of the appellation "racist" to such persons. A disturbing but illuminating example of contemporary antipathy racism occurred in Washington state in 1999. The Makah tribe of the Olympic Peninsula announced its intention to hunt for whales as a way of instilling pride and tradition in the tribe's youth. The hunt was permitted by the government, and the tribe killed a whale in May of that year. Many non-Native American Washington residents were outraged by this act. Amidst arguably reasonable objections to the whale hunting were expressions of outright antipathy racism toward the Makah, and toward Native Americans more generally. One letter to the Seattle Times, for example, said, "I have a very real hatred for Native Americans now. It's embarrassing, but I would be lying if I said it wasn't the truth" (Tizon, 1999).

Inferiorizing and antipathy racism are distinct. Some superiority racists do not hate the target of their beliefs. They may have a paternalistic concern and feelings of kindness for persons they regard as their human inferiors. This form of racism was prevalent among slave owners, and characterized many whites' views of blacks during the segregation era in the United States. The concern and kindness are misdirected, and demeaning, because the other is not seen as an equal, or even as a full human being; it is a racist form of concern. Nevertheless such attitudes are distinct from antipathy and hatred.

On the other side, not every race hater regards the target of her hatred as inferior. In the U.S. antipathy toward Asians and Jews often accompanies, and is in part driven by, a kind of resentment of those seen as in some ways superior (e.g. more successful). And some whites who hate blacks do not really regard blacks as inferior; they may fear and be hostile to them, but fear and hostility are not the same as contempt and other forms of inferiorizing. (Again, antipathy and contempt may accompany one another). Survey research suggests that pure superiority racism toward blacks has substantially decreased since segregation, more so than hostility-based racism (Schuman et al., pp. 156–157). Nevertheless, the great and persistent racial inequalities in our society provide a standing encouragement to advantaged groups to see disadvantaged groups as somehow deserving their lower status.

However, antipathy and inferiorizing racism are not entirely separate either. The paternalistic inferiorizing racist (e.g. a white segregationist) often hates those members of the racial group who do not accept the inferior social position he regards as appropriate to their inferior natures—for example, blacks who do not engage in the deference behavior the paternalistic racist expects.

Emmett Till was lynched in 1955 out of hatred directed toward a young black man who had transgressed the rules of racial deference and constraint defining him as an inferior being. In addition, many racists both hate *and* regard as inferior members of a particular racial group (and not only a particular subcategory of such members, such as those who do not "stay in their place").

RACIAL AND RACIST STEREOTYPES

If we confine racism to manifestations or representations of racial antipathy or racial inferiorizing, we can see that many things can go wrong in the area of race without being racist. Consider two objectionable stereotypes of blacks, for instance—blacks as intellectually deficient, and blacks as good dancers. The first is a straightforwardly racist stereotype; it portrays blacks as inferior in regard to a fundamental human attribute. The second, however, is not racist, on my account. It attributes a positive rather than a negative quality. It is a far less objectionable stereotype than the inferiority stereotype.

Nevertheless, the stereotype of blacks as good dancers is still an objectionable one. Like any stereotype, it wildly overgeneralizes about a group; it blinds us to the internal diversity of the group—some blacks are bad dancers, some are good, some are so-so (and this is so of every racial group). Also, all stereotyping discourages recognizing the individuality of members of the group.

The stereotype of blacks as good dancers is also objectionable in a more specific, historically contextual sense, which can be recognized in the more variegated moral vocabulary revealed by loosening our fixation on "racism" and "racist." This stereotype hearkens back to the slave era, when viewing blacks as good dancers was bound up with their being seen as mentally inferior. While this direct implication is no longer clearly attached to the "good dancer" stereotype, stereotypes must be viewed historically as well as contemporarily, and a given stereotype's resonance with a much more distinctly racist stereotype renders it objectionable in a way that stereotypes without such historical resonance would not be. Other stereotypes lacking such historical resonance are, for example, Asians as poor drivers, blacks as poor swimmers, and whites as not being able to jump. All are objectionable, racial (race-based) stereotypes. But it is moral overload to call them *racist* stereotypes, and to do so contributes to a cheapening of the moral force of the idea of "racism."

RACIAL DISCOMFORT OR ANXIETY

Another application of the definition of racism is the difference between racial antipathy and what I will call "racial discomfort" or "racial anxiety." Consider the following example.

Ms. Verano is a white fourth grade teacher. She feels comfortable with all the children in her very racially-mixed class. She holds all students to equally high standards of performance. But, though she has never admitted this to herself, she is not really comfortable with most of the black parents. She does not dislike blacks, nor does she think they are inferior. However, she is not particularity familiar with African-American culture, knows very few blacks other than her students, and is not confident about her ability to communicate with black other than her students, and is not confident about her ability to communicate with black adults. As a result Ms. Verano is somewhat defensive when speaking with black parents in parent conferences, and is not able to listen to their concerns and viewpoints about their children as well as she does with parents in other racial groups. Because she does not glean as much information from the black parents about their children as she does from the other parents, she is not able to serve these children as well as the other children in her class. Ms. Verano does not have antipathy or inferiorizing attitudes toward blacks. To call her a "racist" would be conceptual inflation. She bears no antipathy toward blacks; I have built this feature into the example. Nor does she regard blacks as inferior. Ms. Verano's situation is best described by saying that she is uncomfortable with black adults (not children). She has "racial discomfort" or "racial anxiety."

Racial anxiety is quite common in the United States, especially, I believe, among whites, although it can be found in any racial group. Racial anxiety can stem from different sources, and one of them can be anxiety that one's racist prejudices be revealed. In this case racial anxiety would be a manifestation of racism. However, racial anxiety is not always racist in its genesis. We can realize that a group of persons is different from us in some socially important way, and we can feel that we are just not knowledgeable enough about this group to feel comfortable in the presence of its members. We can be anxious that we will embarrass ourselves by saying or doing the "wrong thing." We may worry that the group will dislike or reject us if we attempt to approach it. This social anxiety is perfectly familiar regarding cultural differences; the individual is anxious approaching a culture about with she lacks knowledge. Members of different racial groups are also often quite ignorant of one anothers' modes of life (sometimes but not always because cultural and racial differences correspond), even if they interact in schools and workplaces. In a sense racial anxiety is even *more* likely than mere cultural anxiety, since differences in "race" are more socially charged than are cultural differences. If one is equally ignorant of the other group, there is more reason to be anxious that one will violate some unforeseen norm with regard to a racially different group than a culturally different one.

In itself, racial anxiety or discomfort is not racism. Nor is racial discomfort the sort of thing for which its possessor is subject to moral criticism. It is not morally bad to be racially anxious, as it is morally bad to be racially prejudiced. However, racial discomfort is still a bad thing, and an individual who recognizes her racial anxiety should not rest content with it just because it is not a moral blot on her character. This is so, in part, because, as in Ms. Verano's case, it can lead to acts of a discriminatory character, Ms. Verano is unlikely to be able to educate her black pupils to the same degree as she does her other students, since she will lack information pertinent to them.

In addition racial anxiety reinforces a sense of separateness and "otherness" concerning those of other racial groups. It makes it difficult to recognize internal diversity in such groups, and to appreciate the individuality of members of the group. It feeds into (in addition to drawing on) the homogenizing of racial groups that is a typical pitfall in the racial arena.

Racial discomfort is also inimical to the development of interracial community and other forms of productive interracial relationship. It inhibits a sense of identification across racial lines, and reinforces a sense (particularly found among high school and some college students) that it is somehow more "natural" to socialize with members of one's own racial group than of other groups. We should strive for a society in which people feel as comfortable as possible interacting in all public and private venues with members of ethnic and racial groups other than their own. Such comfort would not only make social existence more pleasant, varied, and interesting for members of all groups, but would serve the purposes of civic attachment and civic engagement as well. Teachers in a position to do so would do well to make an effort to decrease racial discomfort and anxiety in their classes, for example by forming interracial groups for various tasks, encouraging interracial communication, explicitly discussing its importance and pitfalls, and the like.[6] Individuals are well advised to look for signs of racial discomfort in themselves and, if they discover them, do what they can to relieve this discomfort, for example by reaching out to persons of other racial groups or by becoming more familiar with and knowledgeable about the modes of life of those groups.

Furthermore, the fact that it is generally difficult to tell whether reluctance to engage with racial others is a product of antipathy or mere discomfort itself takes a toll on racial minorities who have to worry and wonder about the source of some troubling racial interaction. "'In waiting rooms or lobbies . . . I've tried to initiate a conversation [with whites], and I could tell they don't want to talk,' says Sharon Walter, an African-American. 'But when a white

[6]Stephan 1999 provides a wealth of information about how to improve intergroup relations in schools.

person walks in, conversation begins. I don't want to think it's racism . . . The better part of me wants to think otherwise'" (Shipler, p. 448). Merely having such thoughts is itself a psychic cost.

In summary, then, racial anxiety or discomfort is not, in itself, racist (although it *can* be a manifestation of underlying racism). Yet it is still a bad thing, destructive to interracial relationships.

RACE, IDENTITY, AND RECOGNITION

Another race-related ill distinct from racism is illustrated in the following example. A Haitian-American girl is one of two black students in her class. When a race-related issue arises in discussion, the teacher turns to her and asks her what "the black point of view" is on the question at hand.

There seem several distinct though related wrongs this teacher has committed. He has failed to recognize Haitian-Americans as a distinct ethnic group within the larger "black" umbrella. He has treated a racial group in an overly homogeneous manner, implying that there could be something that could coherently be called "the black point of view" on an issue. Finally, he has failed to recognize the student as an individual, with her own individual views.

These three related forms of misrecognition are directed toward an individual or a group of which the individual is a member. The latter two—racial homogenization, and not acknowledging individuality—are particularly serious failings in a teacher. However, that is not to say that they are "racist." The teacher's behavior need not imply that he harbors animus toward black, or regards them as inferior.

RACIAL MOTIVES AND RACIAL STEREOTYPES

Confusion about both the location and the meaning of racism infected public understanding of a particularly tragic event that took place in Providence, Rhode Island, in January, 2000. Several women were fighting in a late-night diner. The night manager threw the patrons out of the diner, at which point some male friends got involved, one of whom drew a gun. Inside the diner, an off-duty patrolman, Cornel Young, Jr., an African-American, was waiting for a take-out order. Meanwhile, the police had been called to the scene outside. Officer Young, after warning the patrons to get down, rushed outside to help the two officers on the scene, his gun drawn. (Providence police are required to carry their firearms when off duty.)

The two officers had ordered the male friend to drop his gun, which he did, and they then turned to Officer Young and ordered him to do so as well. It is not clear whether Young heard the order, but in any case he did not comply, and the two officers, who were white, shot and killed him. It emerged that, despite the officers' failing to recognize Officer Young, one of the officers had been a police academy classmate of Young's, and both had graduated in the same class three years earlier.

The killing sparked community outrage and anguish. Charges of racism were made. It was said that the killing was "racially motivated." Eventually a federal civil rights investigation took place, and the two officers were cleared of having intended to deprive Officer Young of his civil rights, or of acting out of racial animosity.

It is impossible to know whether the two officers were racially biased against blacks. However, their behavior is perfectly consistent with their lacking any form of racial prejudice or racial motivation. It is not likely that they shot at Young because they disliked black people. Some people, recognizing this, then felt some relief. The incident turned from one involving racism to a (mere) "tragic accident."

But this response oversimplifies. Racism may be absent in motivations and attitudes but be present elsewhere. In this situation, it is much more plausible to think that it lay in the stereotypes that the officers carried in their minds about blacks. That is why, or part of why, they reacted to a black man with a gun in plainclothes as if he were a perpetrator, even though they actually knew him as a fellow officer. In another widely-reported case around the same time, four white officers in New York city killed an innocent black man whom they wrongly took to be reaching for a gun. Treating blackness as if it were an indicator of suspiciousness or criminality is referred to as "racial profiling" and has come in for a good deal of public criticism as a result of these and similar incidents, not only ones involving fatalities.

The white officers who killed Officer Young were apparently genuinely remorseful and upset by their having unwittingly killed a fellow officer. But this does not mean they were not prey to racial stereotypes linking blackness to criminality. Officer Young's mother was surely correct when she said that her son would be unlikely to have been shot had he been white. But it is important to be careful about what we mean if we say that he was killed "because he was black." If does not necessarily mean "out of hostility or animosity toward black persons." It could mean "because he was seen in the moment as a dangerous person and this was so in part because he was black." I believe it is also plausible to refer to this racial stereotype as "racist." But my point here is not so much to defend that position as to encourage clarity as to the location of what is, or was, racially objectionable in the situation. It was in the stereotype, not in the motives of the white officers. And it shows the tremendous danger that can accompany racist stereotypes even in the absence of racial antipathy; they can be life threatening.

I have given a stripped down version of this complex racial situation, and want to mention only two other points. First, some members of the community placed some of the blame on the Providence police department's failure to educate its police force about the dangers and wrong of racial stereotyping and racial profiling. That is, they have seen the fault in a kind of institutional irresponsibility regarding race, in the context of a recognition that antiblack stereotypes are particularly troubling in a police force that is meant to be protectors of their community.

The second race-related matter is more speculative on my part. Even though the white officers, and especially the one who graduated from the police academy with Office Young, knew him, it is possible that a form of racial homogenization was involved in their failure to recognize him. Perhaps the officer in some sense still saw all blacks, or black men, as "looking alike." Perhaps in the heat of the moment the image of blackness blocked his seeing Officer Young as an individual person. Racial thinking does, in general, inhibit the perception of others as individuals; the case of the teacher asking the black student for "the black point of view" would be another version of this same homogenization. Perhaps—again I am speculating—although the white officer did know Officer Young, whites and blacks did not interact much on or off the job; if so this social segregation might have contributed to the racial homogenization that in turn contributed to his failing to recognize Officer Young.

CONCLUSION

Gaining some clarity about what "racism" means will help us engage in productive conversations about racial matters—conversations that are too infrequent, both inside and outside classroom settings. We have seen three ways by which we might gain that clarity. First, within a given category (actions, jokes, stereotypes, remarks, stereotypes, persons), we should confine "racism" to especially egregious wrongs in that category. Not every stereotype is racist. Not every remark that is racially offensive is racist. Not every racially insensitive action is a racist action. I have suggested that the distinct opprobrium attaching to "racism" and "racist" can be retained and protected if we recognize that racism refers to racial inferiorization or racial antipathy, and that the different categorical forms of racism can all be related to either of those two definitions.

Second, we should not confuse racism in one category with racism in another. A person who is prey to a racist stereotype is not necessarily "a racist"; nor does she necessarily operate from racist motives. A remark can be unquestionably racist without the person making the remark being a racist, or making the remark for a racist reason, or motive.

Finally, in endeavoring to protect the distinct moral opprobrium of the accusation of "racism" from conceptual inflation and moral overload, as well as from categorical drift and confusion, we must at the same time recognize that "racism" by no means captures all of what can go wrong in the domain of race. There is a much larger terrain of moral ills in the racial domain than racism itself, and we should draw on our manifold linguistic resources—racial insensitivity, failure to recognize racial identity, racial ignorance, racial anxiety, racial injustice, racial homogenization, and so on—to express and describe moral disvalue in this domain. Moral concern is appropriately directed toward this wider domain, and should not be confined to racism appropriately so called.

References

Black, White Officers Cited in Noose Incident, *Boston Globe,* April 29, 1999, B1.

Blum, L. (2002). *I'm not a racist, but . . .: The moral quandary of race.* Ithaca: Cornell University Press.

Margalit, A. (1996). *The decent society.* Cambridge: Harvard University Press.

Miles, R. (1989). *Racism.* London: Routledge.

Morrow, L. (1994). *Time, b*[12/5/94] cited in *Extra!*, vol. 9, #2, March/April 1996.

Nuechterlein, J., in *First things*, August-September, 1996, from *Chronicle of Higher Education*, September 6.

Schofield, J.W. (1989). *Black and white in school: Trust, tension, or tolerance?* New York: Teachers College Press.

Schuman, H., Steeh, C., Bobo, L. & Krysan, M. (1997). *Racial attitudes in America: Trends and interpretation*, revised edn. Cambridge: Harvard University Press.

Shipler, D.K. (1997). *A country of strangers: Blacks and whites in America.* New York: Vintage Books.

Stephan, W. (1999). *Reducing prejudice and stereotyping in schools.* New York: Teachers College Press.

Tizon, A., Whale killing uncovers anti-Indian hatred, *Boston Globe*, May 30, 1999.

Weinraub, B., Stung by criticism of fall shows, TV Networks add minority roles, *New York Times*, 1999.

For Further Reflection

1. How does Lawrence Blum define racism? In his definition, what is inferiorization? What is antipathy?
2. Identify two actions that are commonly thought to be racist but that, according to Blum's definition of racism, are not.
3. Do you believe that having or benefiting from white privilege makes you a racist? Why or why not?
4. Does uttering a racist statement make you a racist? Explain.

Uses and Abuses of the Discourse of White Privilege

NAOMI ZACK

Naomi Zack is emeritus professor of philosophy at the University of Oregon and the editor of the *Oxford Companion of Philosophy and Race*. She declares that white privilege is a real phenomenon but that discussions about it are problematic. She argues that contemporary "*discourse* of white privilege . . . goes too far in blaming all whites for all forms of racism and it does not go far enough in directly addressing injustice against nonwhites."

White privilege in real life is something real that exists. White privilege *discourse* is thought, talk, and writing about white privilege—it is not the thing itself.

Our present idea of white privilege was introduced by Peggy Mcintosh in 1989: "White privilege is like an invisible weightless knapsack of special provisions, maps, passports, codebooks, visas, clothes, tools and blank checks." The idea lives on in exhortations to *Check your privilege!* on college campuses and through broader public and social media. But the *discourse* of white privilege is problematic from two angles—it goes too far in blaming all whites for all forms of racism and it does not go far enough in directly addressing injustice against nonwhites. Both perspectives are worth consideration but the second is more important because it involves violations of fundamental human rights.

Whites cannot call or email or log onto a Bureau of White Privilege to check their white accounts, draw on their white assets, withdraw white funds, or use white credits to make purchases. But whites are generally better off than nonwhites—in health, wealth, freedom, education, longevity, and a host of other human goods. That is, although overt oppression expressed by an official ideology of white supremacy is largely past in our post-civil rights era of formal equality, racist historical effects persist. White (European and American) "privileges" endure. White privilege is a network of dispositions in society whereby individuals behave differently, that is, better to whites than nonwhites, solely because whites are white. Attitudes, beliefs, and emotions are the internal psychic component of white privilege and they include freedom from worrying about or suffering from racism.

Naomi Zack "Uses and Abuses of the Discourse of White Privilege," Philosopher (blog), 24 June 2016, politicalphilosophar.net.

However, not all whites, all of the time, enjoy privileges compared to nonwhites or are responsible for the comparative disadvantages of nonwhites. And even though some whites may be complicit with the racism of others, their expressed non-racist views and cultural contributions should not be dismissed solely on the grounds of their race. That is, to shut down speech just because it is uttered by a white person would be unfair and when racial *ad hominem* is robustly denounced on behalf of people of color, the fallacy should be recognized in an even-handed way. (We continue to be shocked by Kant's, "This fellow was quite black . . . a clear proof that what he said was stupid.") Still, "Check your privilege!" or white privilege discourse has more serious pitfalls than such insults to white people. The discourse seems to be incapable of addressing injustice against people of color.

In progressive, left-liberal society, it is virtuous not to exaggerate one's disadvantage or ignore unfair or unearned advantage. The motivation for white privilege discourse is that the person being asked or told to check her privilege will be ashamed after recognizing that she has unfair or unearned advantages solely due to being white—and that insight will serve social justice. It's as though the discourse of foodies about their abundant culinary choices and self-indulgent practices could correct the problems of world hunger!

White privilege discourse is largely about the facts of white racial advantage and what white people think and feel about that. Building awareness of racial imbalances is progressive. But as a leading response to contemporary injustice, white privilege discourse may miss the importance of racial injustice and degenerate into just another display of the advantages that white people have of not being required to respond to racial injustice against their racial group. After all, and for the most part, whites are treated justly, in wealthy, democratic, capitalistic societies.

Awareness by whites of their privilege, in an ongoing discourse that whites conduct, is neither cognitively nor rhetorically adequate for addressing injustice. If black people can be killed or executed by police officers, without trial or even the appearance of criminal action, while white people are left alone, this is not wholly or solely a matter of white privilege. Yes, white people are better off, but to confine resistance to the injustice done to nonwhites to discourse about how whites are privileged in being left alone (i.e., to only talk about white privilege), minimizes or trivializes the injustice against nonwhites. This injustice could only be wholly or solely a matter of white privilege if we lived in and accepted the norms of a maximally repressive totalitarian society where it was customary for government officials to execute anyone without trial or even the appearance of criminal action. Against that background, we could say that those who were not treated that way were privileged. They would be privileged in enjoying that perk of exceptional leniency.

But we do not live in such a system or accept a normative totalitarian description of the system we do live in. We live in a system where everyone, regardless of race is supposed to have the same basic rights. That nonwhites are not recognized as having these rights is not a privilege of whites, but a violation of the rights of nonwhites.

Nevertheless, human rights have only an ideal status. Philosophically they are only posits and morally those who are outraged by the injustice of rights violation have little power. But, the basis for outrage concerning the recent high profile cases of summary execution of unarmed young black men by police officers is a *legal* issue, a matter of positive law in U.S. jurisdictions. US citizens are constitutionally protected by certain rights that most, especially whites, still correctly assume are in force for them: the right to privacy from unjustified government search and seizure (where death is a form of seizure); the right to due process; the right to equal protection by government officials.

The Fourth Amendment states that "the people" have a right "to be secure in their persons, houses, papers, and effects, against unreasonable searches and seizures . . . but upon probable cause." The Fourteenth Amendment reads in part that that no state shall "deny to any person within its jurisdiction the equal protection of the laws." Police racial profiling followed by summary execution violates both amendments. However, these constitutional rights have been steadily eroded by the U.S. Supreme Court in recent decades. In *Graham v. Connor* in 1989, the Justices ruled that claims that police have used excessive force must be analyzed under an "objective reasonableness" standard referring to officer behavior, rather than rales of due process or probable cause. In *Plumhoff et al. v. Richard* (2012), the Court ruled that Fourth Amendment rights must be balanced against the "qualified immunity" of officers. These rulings and similar ones come to bear in cases like the shooting of Michael Brown, where all an officer need do to avoid indictment or conviction for manslaughter or murder is claim that he believed his life was in danger.

To protect the rights of minorities against police—really everyone's rights, but the recent killings of unarmed young men concern minorities—it will likely be necessary to revisit at least *Graham* and *Plumhoff*. The civil rights movements of the 1950s and 60s were led by impassioned and brilliant lawyers, constantly bringing cases before the courts. These days, the legal cases that get the most attention are those aimed at dismantling affirmative action. Yes, whites are privileged, but no amount of exhortation to "check" their privilege or confessional discourse in response, will correct the legal injustice of police homicide based on racial profiling.

Police racial profiling and its attendant violence is not the only form of rights violation that corresponds to nonwhite race in the United States and is neglected by white privilege discourse. Unequal educational resources in materials and teacher skills have persisted after *Brown v. Board of Education* called for integrated education "with all deliberate speed" in 1954. But K-12 schools are funded by local property taxes that are directly related to real estate values. It's been widely publicized since the 1970s that the differences in tax-based educational resources per child are as much as 1000 percent between mainly white neighborhoods and mainly black and brown neighborhoods, as residential racial segregation has persisted due to differences in wealth and income, along with social preferences regarding the race of neighbors. All modem democracies uphold public education as a fundamental right at this time, but that right cannot be fully implemented in the United States given the disparities in opportunities for children that result from ongoing residential segregation. No amount of positive descriptions of the privileges of white middle class school children mitigates the deprivations of poor nonwhite children who do not have comparable learning opportunities. Needed is egalitarian educational reform to enlarge those opportunities. No amount or intensity of discourse about the privilege of white children a few blocks away could fill in for what poor nonwhite children lack. And again, if equal adequate education is a right, a structure in which nonwhite children are deprived of that right is a problem of injustice in and of itself. And that problem is not addressed by talking about the fact that white children enjoy the right! (That there are structural inequalities that perpetuate rights violations of nonwhites underscores the importance of resistance that attends to rights instead of privileges.)

For Further Reflection

1. What does Zack mean by her assertion that the discourse of white privilege goes too far in blaming all whites for all forms of racism?
2. Why does Zack think that as a leading response to racial injustice, white privilege discourse may not be very helpful?

Racism Without Racists

EDUARDO BONILLA-SILVA

Eduardo Bonilla-Silva is professor of sociology at Duke University and the author of *Racism without Racists: Color-Blind Racism and the Persistence of Racial Inequality in America.* He asks, "How is it possible to have this tremendous degree of racial inequality in a country where most whites claim that race is no longer relevant?" He argues that racial inequality is now reproduced not by the overt methods of the Jim Crow era, but by what he calls "new racism" practices that are subtle, institutional, and apparently nonracial.

Nowadays, except for members of white supremacist organizations, few whites in the United States claim to be "racist." Most whites assert they "don't see any color, just people"; that although the ugly face of discrimination is still with us, it is no longer the central factor determining minorities' life chances; and, finally, that, like Dr. Martin Luther King Jr., they aspire to live in a society where "people are judged by the content of their character, not by the color of their skin." More poignantly, most whites insist that minorities (especially blacks) are the ones responsible for whatever "race problem" we have in this country. They publicly denounce blacks for "playing the race card," for demanding the maintenance of unnecessary and divisive race-based programs, such as affirmative action, and for crying "racism" whenever they are criticized by whites. Most whites believe that if blacks and other minorities would just stop thinking about the past, work hard, and complain less (particularly about racial discrimination), then Americans of all hues could "all get along."

But regardless of whites' "sincere fictions,“ racial considerations shade almost everything in America. Blacks and dark-skinned racial minorities lag well behind whites in Virtually every area of social life; they are about three times more likely to be poor than whites, earn about 40 percent less than whites, and have about an eighth of the net worth that whites have. They also receive an inferior education compared to whites, even when they attend integrated institutions. In terms of housing, black-owned units comparable to white-owned ones are valued at 35 percent less. Blacks and Latinos also have less access to the entire housing market because whites, through a variety of exclusionary practices by white realtors and homeowners, have

Eduardo Bonilla-Silva, *Racism Without Racists* (Lanham, MD: Rowman and Littlefield, 2014). 1–4.

been successful in effectively limiting their entrance into many neighborhoods. Blacks receive impolite treatment in Stores, in restaurants, and in a host of other commercial transactions. Researchers have also documented that blacks pay more for goods such as cars and houses than do whites. Finally, blacks and dark-skinned Latinos are the targets of racial profiling by the police, which, combined with the highly racialized criminal court system, guarantees their over-representation among those arrested, prosecuted, incarcerated, and if charged for a capital crime, executed. Racial profiling on the highways has become such a prevalent phenomenon that a term has emerged to describe it: driving while black. In short, blacks and most minorities are "at the bottom of the well."

How is it possible to have this tremendous degree of racial inequality in a country where most whites claim that race is no longer relevant? More important, how do whites explain the apparent contradictions between their professed color blindness and the United States' color-coded inequality? In this book I attempt to answer both of these questions. I contend that whites have developed powerful explanations—which have ultimately become justifications—for contemporary racial inequality that exculpate them from any responsibility for the status of people of color. These explanations emanate from a new racial ideology that I label *color-blind racism*. This ideology, which acquired cohesiveness and dominance in the late 1960s, explains contemporary racial inequality as the outcome of nonracial dynamics. Whereas Jim Crow racism explained blacks' social standing as the result of their biological and moral inferiority, color-blind racism avoids such facile arguments. Instead, whites rationalize minorities' contemporary status as the product of market dynamics, naturally occurring phenomena, and blacks' imputed cultural limitations. For instance, whites can attribute Latinos' high poverty rate to a relaxed work ethic ("the Hispanics are mañana, mañana, mañana—tomorrow, tomorrow, tomorrow") or residential segregation as the result of natural tendencies among groups ("Does a cat and a dog mix? I can't see it. You can't drink milk and scotch, Certain mixes don't mix.").

Color-blind racism became the dominant racial ideology as the mechanisms and practices for keeping blacks and other racial minorities "at the bottom of the well" changed. I have argued elsewhere that contemporary racial inequality is reproduced through "new racism" practices that are subtle, institutional, andapparently nonracial. In Contrast to the Jim Crow era, where racial inequality was enforced through overt means (e.g., signs saying "No Niggers Welcomed Here" or shotgun diplomacy at the voting booth), today racial practices operate in a "now you see it, now you don't" fashion. For example, residential segregation, which is almost as high today as it was in the past, is no longer accomplished through overtly discriminatory practices.

Instead, covert behaviors such as not showing all the available units, steering minorities and whites into certain neighborhoods, quoting higher rents or prices to minority applicants, or not advertising units at all are the weapons of choice to maintain separate communities. In the economic field, "smiling face" discrimination ("We don't have jobs now, but please check later"), advertising job openings in mostly white networks and ethnic newspapers, and steering highly educated people of color into poorly remunerated jobs or jobs with limited opportunities for mobility are the new ways of keeping minorities in a secondary position. Politically, although the civil rights struggles have helped remove many of the obstacles for the electoral participation of people of color, "racial gerrymandering, multimember legislative districts, election runoffs, annexation of predominantly white areas, at-large district elections, and anti-single-shot devices (disallowing concentrating votes in one or two candidates in cities using at-large elections) have become standard practices to disenfranchise" people of color. Whether in banks, restaurants, school admissions, or housing transactions, the maintenance of white privilege is done in a way that defies facile racial readings. Hence, the contours of color-blind racism fit America's new racism quite well.

Compared to Jim Crow racism, the ideology of color blindness seems like "racism lite." Instead of relying on name calling (niggers, spics, chinks), color-blind racism otherizes softly ("these people are human, too"); instead of proclaiming that God placed minorities in the world in a servile position, it suggests they are behind because they do not work hard enough; instead of viewing interracial marriage as wrong on a straight racial basis, it regards it as "problematic" because of concerns over the children, location, or the extra burden it places on couples. Yet this new ideology has become a formidable political tool for the maintenance of the racial order. Much as Jim Crow racism served as the glue for defending a brutal and overt system of racial oppression in the pre-civil rights era, color-blind racism serves today as the ideological armor for a covert and institutionalized system in the post-civil rights era. And the beauty of this new ideology is that it aids in the maintenance of white privilege without fanfare, without naming those who it subjects and those who it rewards. It allows a president to state things such as, "I strongly support diversity of all kinds, including racial diversity in higher education," yet, at the same time, to characterize the University of Michigan's affirmation action program as "flawed" and "discriminatory" against whites. Thus whites enunciate positions that safeguard their racial interests without sounding "racist." Shielded by color blindness, whites can express resentment toward minorities; criticize their morality, values, and work ethic; and even claim to be the victims of "reverse racism." This is the thesis I will defend in this book to explain the curious enigma of "racism without racists."

For Further Reflection

1. What are three "new racism" practices that Bonilla-Silva identifies?
2. How does Bonilla-Silva define "color-blind racism"? What examples of this phenomenon does he give?
3. According to Bonilla-Silva, why is the ideology of color blindness a problem?

Good White Liberals

SHANNON SULLIVAN

Shannon Sullivan is professor of philosophy and health psychology at the University of North Carolina Charlotte and the author of several books on racism, sexism, and white privilege. She observes that white domination of people of color is strong and persistent in the twenty-first century, perpetuated by white class hierarchies and white class biases that help middle-class white people avoid taking responsibility for remedying the harms of white privilege. Many white middle-class people, she argues, expend enormous energy not on stamping out racial injustice but on trying to prove to themselves and to people of color that they are not racist, that they are morally good white liberals.

What can white people do to help end racial injustice? This is a question with a complicated history in the United States, in large part because most white people haven't wanted to ask, much less answer it. The question dates back at least until antebellum America when a small number of white people participated in the Underground Railroad, which enabled black slaves to escape their white masters, and helped work to end legalized slavery. It's a question that can be found in twentieth-century civil rights struggles when some—again, not many—white people engaged in lunch counter sit-ins alongside African Americans and traveled to the South to help register African Americans to vote. More recently, it's a question that operated in the historic 2008 election of the first African American to the presidency of the United States,

Shannon Sullivan, *Good White People* (Albany: State University of New York Press, Albany, 2014), 1–11.

which was possible in part because approximately 43 percent of white voters supported Barack Obama.

It's also a question that assumes that white people can do something positive with regard to racial justice. Not everyone would agree with this assumption. Perhaps most famously, Malcolm X recounts in his autobiography that when a white college girl heard him speak on white racism and agonizingly asked him "What can I *do*?" he dismissed her with the terse reply "Nothing." Up until the last year of his life, Malcolm X argued that the white "man" was the devil, destroying black lives, families, and communities, and thus there was nothing that white people could do to help the United States achieve racial justice for black people and other people of color. White people inevitably were the problem, according to Malcolm X, and the only positive thing they could do was stay out of black people's way.

White people *are* a big part of the problem. So too, of course, are white privileging institutions, tax codes, and other societal structures that help sustain white domination. But not all white domination operates on an impersonal level. A great deal of it functions through the practices and habits of individual white people and the predominantly white families and communities to which they belong. This does not mean that white people are atomistic individuals, sealed off from the world around them. On the contrary: like all human beings (and other living organisms), white people are constituted in and through transactional relationships with their environments. Their experiences, beliefs, and behaviors both are shaped by and contribute to a white-dominated world. And so the personal question of what white people can do still needs to be asked and answered. To say that white people can do nothing is to let them off the hook too easily. It says that they do not have to respond to the racist damage that white people historically have and presently continue to cause, and it countenances their continued negligence and inaction with regard to white domination of people of color.

Racial justice movements are not dependent on white people for their success. The struggles, protests, and demands of people of color have been and most likely will continue to be the main motor driving racial justice movements. But white people can play a positive role in those movements as well. In fact, I think they have a small, but somewhat unique role to play given the persistence of de facto racial segregation in work places, neighborhoods, school systems, places of worship, and so on. Just as feminist movements need men who are willing to speak out against sexism and male privilege—especially in all-male settings such as locker rooms and fraternity houses—racial justice movements need white people who are willing to speak and act against white racism when they encounter it in their families, neighborhoods, workplaces, and elsewhere. important as women are to feminist change, eliminating sexism should not be reduced to "women's work." Likewise, white people who care about racial justice should not sit back and wait for people of color to clean up the mess that white people have made. White people need to make a positive contribution to racial justice even though their contributions will be secondary to those of people of color.

The question of what white people can do is important even though there are no such things as stable racial categories or universal racial essences. Racial categories, including whiteness, are historical and political products of human activity, and for that reason the human racial landscape has changed over time and likely will continue to change. Perhaps at some point in the future, racial categories no longer will exist. I don't think any of us today can know for sure. At this point in history, however, they do exist and cannot be quickly eliminated by pretending or simply declaring that they don't. This means that, for better or worse, whiteness also is not going anywhere anytime soon even though its meaning and effects are not set in stone. The "beige supremacy" that the Latin Americanization of race in the United States is likely to produce, for example, would still be a racial hierarchy that privileges whites over mixed-race and light-skinned Asians and Latinos, the latter of which would share in beige people's domination over dark-skinned people, including most African Americans, who would count as black. "The whiteness question," as Linda Martín Alcoff has called it, thus doggedly persists: what can white people do to promote racial justice?

For all the urgency of the whiteness question, however, white people have done a miserable job of answering it. The few positive examples given above shouldn't mislead anyone: white people generally don't know how to live their racial identities in ways that promote racial justice. Even worse, their ignorance often poses as knowledge, making it all the more insidious. This is particularly true in the early twenty-first century, and it's true of the majority of white people, not just a small subset of them. I'm not merely speaking here of the avowed white supremacist who clearly has no interest in eliminating racial injustice. I am, primarily, addressing the bulk of white people in the post-Jim Crow United States and other similar white-dominated nations who consider themselves to be non or anti-racist. These are the white liberals of which Lerone Bennett speaks, the "good" white people whose goodness is marked by their difference from the "bad" white people who are considered responsible for any lingering racism in a progressive, liberal society. ("White liberal" here thus does not designate a member of a particular political party. Both white Republicans and white Democrats in the United States often are white liberals.) What is particularly interesting and frightening about white liberals is that, unlike white supremacists, they usually think they know what white people can do to fight white racism. "Act like you know" has been the mantra of proper white identity after all, even as what good white people know or think they know has shifted over time. Good white people today should, for example, refrain from making derogatory remarks about race, support multicultural celebrations in their communities, and so on. For white liberals, knowing and acting according to these answers ensures that a sharp, bright line is drawn between good anti-racist white people and bad white supremacists.

But white liberals and white supremacists are not as different as white liberals would like to believe and would like others to believe. They grow from the same tree of white domination, as Bennett suggests, and this means that many of the "anti-racist" habits, practices, and beliefs of the white liberal also are rooted in and help nourish white racism. White domination of people of color is alive and well in the twenty-first century, and most white people don't want to acknowledge their complicity with it. The oft-recited progressive narrative about improved racial justice in the United States from the days of slavery to the so-called Obama era is something of a convenient fiction that serves to reassure white people that significant problems of racial injustice no longer exist. Let me be clear: by no means am I advocating a retreat from the hard-won victories of civil rights and other racial justice movements. But white domination of people of color didn't end when the United States became more "enlightened" about race. It instead has tended to change its form to operate with and through liberal enlightenment. A great deal of change has taken place in the United States since the days of chattel slavery and Jim Crow; at the same time, a great deal of white domination has been maintained through those changes. White liberalism generally doesn't aim to end white domination. Quite the opposite: it aims to render it more tolerable, both to its beneficiaries and its victims, and so to perpetuate itself indefinitely—an aim it shares with its "enemy" white supremacy.

Having the same roots doesn't mean that white liberalism and white supremacy are identical, however. Understanding how white domination could continue after white supremacy became passé means understanding the particularities of white liberalism's style of white racism. (While some contemporary scholars have reappropriated the term *white supremacy* to refer to systematic racial oppression and privilege, I will continue to use it, as Bennett does, to refer to overt white racism. I accordingly will use *white privilege* to refer to the seemingly invisible, often unconscious forms of white racism that pervade the United States' post–Jim Crow era, and *white domination* and *white racism* as general terms covering both white supremacy and white privilege.) The most obvious difference between white liberalism and white supremacy is that the racial biases of white supremacists tend to be much more overt than those of white liberals, an observation that is not necessarily to the credit of white liberals. The racial biases of white liberals often are more difficult to detect (at least by white people), especially as they tend to operate in the name of non- or anti-racism, and thus they can be much more difficult to challenge than the racial biases of white supremacists.

Perhaps less acknowledged about white liberal anti-racism is its use of white class hierarchies to perpetuate white domination of people of color. The pernicious tangle of race and class oppression will be the primary focus of this book. Intra-white class biases might seem to have nothing to do with people of color, but as I will argue, they are one of the central ways by which middle-class white people avoid taking responsibility for and fighting against white privilege. White liberals' answers to the whiteness question tend to be covert attempts to maintain and secure their race-class status. These attempts might not always be consciously designed; in fact, many of them probably operate unconsciously. But they nonetheless exist and are effective in maintaining white domination of people of color.

One of the main ways that white class hierarchies operate is through the production and display of white middle-class moral goodness. This is achieved by establishing the moral badness of poor and lower-class white people. Lower-class white people supposedly are the retrograde white people who still believe and act in racist ways; they are the real problem when it comes to lingering racism in our enlightened times. Knowing this, white middle-class liberals know and/or take steps to ensure that they are different in kind than the white lower class, and this process of othering secures white liberals' status as good. *Those* white people (the lower class) are racist; we middle-class whites are not like them; therefore we are not racist. At the heart of this anti-racism, however, is not necessarily an attempt to eliminate racial injustice—which, to be successful, might involve strategies or tactics that don't make white people look or feel morally good—but a desire to be recognized as Not Racist^ perhaps especially by people of color. As Steve Biko Has argued in the context of racial struggles in South Africa, "instead of involving themselves in an all-out attempt to stamp out racism from their white society, liberals waste lots of time trying to prove to as many blacks as they can find that they are liberal." A similar situation holds in the United States and many other white-dominated liberal nations. George Yancy provides an excellent example of this sad fact when he recounts being on an academic job interview and having to endure a white philosopher's hour-long speech about *his* anti-racism. The white person spent so much time explaining and illustrating his own racial goodness that there was virtually no time in the interview to talk about Yancy's accomplishments and achievements. Class hierarchies, racial oppression, and moral sanctimoniousness are intertwined in much of white liberal anti-racism, and for that reason critical philosophy of race needs different answers to the whiteness question than the ones liberalism tends to offer. Liberal political projects may be well intended, but as Wendy Brown has argued, they often "inadvertently redraw the very configurations and effects of power that they seek to vanquish."

The quest of middle-class white people for their moral redemption tends to be especially, though not uniquely attractive to white middle-class women. As feminist sociologist Sarita Srivastava has documented in her research on white feminists in anti-racist organizations, white women in particular tend to "become mired in self-examination and stuck in deliberations on morality and salvation. Not surprisingly, this ethical self-transformation is still framed by the poles of good versus evil, newly interpreted as the fraudulent nonracist versus the authentic antiracist." Here I wish to highlight what Srivastava-calls the "desire for innocence" in the face of racist "sin," which characterizes a great deal of white people's, and perhaps especially white women's involvement in anti-racist-activities. Srivastava's research supports María Lugones's observation that white women often want to see themselves as innocently ignorant of, or at least confused about the nasty operations of racism. Whether gender-inflected or not, the white desire for innocence is implicated in the middle-class dumping of responsibility for racism on lower- and working-class white people, who are posited as the true source of ongoing racial injustice. Lower-class white people allegedly are the bad white people who are too unintelligent or unenlightened to know that people of color aren't inferior to white people. With their disdain, scorn, and even hatred of lower-class white people, good white liberals often use their guilt and shame to exploit class differences among whites, which allows them to efface their own complicity in white racism and white domination. . . .

I will use the term, *middle-class* very broadly to include wealthy people that might be considered upper-class. In this sense, my use of "middle-class" could be understood as "middle and middle-to-upper class." I will stick with the shorter term, not just for simplicity's sake but because of the ideological hegemony of the middle class in the United States. While some people in the United States clearly make enough money to be considered something other than middle-class—think here of the top 1 percent who are estimated to control 35 percent of the United States' total wealth—across the income/wealth spectrum in the United States, the rhetoric of the middle class holds sway. It's inseparable from the American Dream and the Protestant work ethic: everyone who works hard can succeed. There supposedly are no social barriers or caste systems that would block a person's ability to change her status in life. This is assumed to be different from Great Britain, for example, where royalty still exists and class analyses often operate with more explicit considerations of a ruling class, in addition to the working and middle class. In an odd way, then, the middle class represents the supposed lack of a class system in the United States. Whatever the reality, the perception in America is that virtually everyone in the country is middle-class. The exception might be a small minority of very poor people and an even smaller number of very rich people, but even the rich are said to have made it the way that anyone could if they tried hard enough. Likewise, the poor are assumed to be at fault for their poverty, getting (or not) what they deserved. The middle class in the United States thus is less a precise economic category than a broad rhetorical designation for the vast majority of Americans who see themselves as the moral norm: hard workers who deserve their success and who have endless possibilities for improving their lives even further.

The four main chapters of this book will focus on four central strands of white liberal anti-racism, demonstrating how intra-white class biases operate within white anti-racism to shore up the racial goodness of white liberals. I'll call the first strand dumping on "white trash." Through a process of abjection, white middle-class anxieties about the failures of poor whites are managed by expelling white trash from the realm of proper whiteness. Conflating white lower-class status with white supremacy, middle-class white people use class etiquette to posit poor whites and the white working class as irremediably racist. Middle-class white people thus are able to deflect their responsibility for and complicity with white domination onto white trash, thereby ensuring their own racial innocence and goodness.

The second strand of white liberal anti-racism also involves a process of othering, this time with respect to white people's history and ancestry. We could call this strand demonizing the past, making white slaveholders in particular seem incomprehensible to white people today. How could white people in the eighteenth and nineteenth centuries have owned, whipped, starved, raped, and abused other people the way they did? It's inconceivable, so the response goes, and thus the only answer is that white slaveholders were so evil as to be inhuman. As I will argue, slaveholders surely did these horrific things, but demonizing them takes their actions and lives out of the realm of the human, reassuring good white people today that they would never be capable of doing anything similar. Functioning hand in hand with a progressive narrative of whiteness, demonizing slaveholders allows contemporary white liberals to congratulate themselves on their racial enlightenment and moral superiority, relieving them of the need to examine the different ways in which they too might be participating in racist evil.

Both of these strands of white anti-racism serve to distance good white people from racism. Whoever the real racists are—white slaveholders, white supremacists, poor white people—they are over there, not here where the middle-class white people are. The third strand of middle-class whiteness also distances good white people from complicity with white racism, in this case by distancing them from race altogether. This strand is white color blindness. . . . Color blindness entails not seeing race and seeing "just people" instead. Racism requires the existence of racial categories; therefore, racists are the people who use those categories, not non- or anti-racist people. On this logic, good white parents and teachers should not use or recognize racial categories on pain of being or appearing as one of the bad racists. As good white children are taught, color blindness supposedly is a marker of a white person's evolution beyond racism, demonstrating that she is so racially advanced that she isn't even aware of the racial categories on which racism depends.

The fourth strand of middle-class whiteness on which I will focus is cultivating the emotions of white guilt, shame, and betrayal, the latter in the figure of white "race traitor." These tend to be the recommended attitudes toward whiteness that contemporary white people should embody. The best way for a good white person to ensure that she isn't mistaken for one of the bad white people is to display guilt and shame about her racial identity and history and to distance herself from whiteness by traitorously calling for its abolition. These affects are not equally available or deployable by all white people, however. They tend to function as forms of cultural capital for middle-class white people in particular. Wielding forms of emotional class privilege, middle-class white liberals help ensure that they are (seen as) different from lower-class white people, who don't feel properly guilty about white racism.

What are some alternatives to these four strands of middle-class whiteness? . . . Love can be thought of as an affect that binds a person to that which she loves, and in that way love can counter the distancing tendencies that many good white people have toward their whiteness. I will argue that rather than try to create distance between themselves and their racial identity, white people need a closer, more intimate relationship with it if they are going to be effective in racial justice movements. Rather than try to flee their whiteness, white people need to embrace it more tightly. Rather than despise their whiteness, white people need to learn to love it.

I have in mind here the kind of white love well described by James Baldwin nearly fifty years ago. As he claimed about the United States, "White people in this country will have quite enough to do in learning how to accept and love themselves and each other, and when they have achieved this—which will not be tomorrow and may very well be never—the Negro problem will no longer exist, for it will no longer be needed." Baldwin brilliantly captures the relationship between the lack of white self-love—white self-loathing—and white oppression of people of color. The so-called Negro problem is really a problem of white domination, and that problem is connected to white people's inability to acknowledge, accept, and even affirm themselves as white.

This affirmation is not a way to let white people off the racist hook that they've hung themselves on. Love is consistent with and even requires a willingness to be severely, yet constructively critical of what one loves, and white people are in need of a great deal of criticism. As I understand it, the loving acceptance called for by Baldwin isn't necessarily an enjoyable experience. Love is an emotion, but not always in the sense of being a pleasant sentiment. It can be and often is discontent, especially with situations, actions, and passions that separate people from one another, for example, through oppression and domination. A white person's loving herself as a white person means her critically caring enough about the effects whiteness has in the world to work to make it something different and better than what it is today. Although likely a difficult experience to undergo, this loving transformation of white identity would be to the benefit of both people of color and white people.

As I explore both white middle-class goodness and alternatives to it based in self-love, I often will take up relationships between white family members, such as white children, white parents, and white grandparents. I do so because one of my primary motivations for writing this book is to grapple with the down-to-earth, real life question of how to live as a white person. That real life question means for me, as it does for many other white people, how to live day to day with white family members for and to which one is responsible. For example, how can I honor and respect my elders if many of them were or are openly racist? How can I rear my children in ways that effectively challenge rather than unconsciously replicate white domination? As feminists demonstrated when they argued that the personal is political, family is where a number of important social and political issues hit home. The problem of ongoing white domination is no exception. In the words of one cultural anthropologist, family "is perhaps the most critical site for the generation and reproduction of racial formations," and "the meaning of race depends to a large degree on whether particular families reproduce homogenous or heterogeneous racial categories." The whiteness question thus isn't merely a theoretical issue. It's also a down-to-earth practical matter enacted in daily experiences, conversations, and interactions that often involve close family members.

Of course, some white people have family members that aren't white. Many white people in the United States and Great Britain, for example, are not considered mixed race but have black ancestry (often without knowing or acknowledging it). Some white people also have contemporary family members who are not white, and in particular the legalization of interracial marriage in the United States in 1967 resulted in an increase in mixed-race children. All people can have family members from more than one race, but the facts of mixed-race identities and multiracial families do not erase the simple truth that a large number of white people also have family members who count as white. Those personal relationships should not be ceded to white domination. They are too socially valuable and personally meaningful to too many people to discard them as trivial. "The revolution of the American family," as Ronald Sundstrom argues, "is an important condition of social justice," and so white people need to critically and creatively wrestle with how to live family in ways that don't reproduce white racism.

Because of my concerns about the harmfulness of so-called white anti-racism, I will describe a white person-whose racial identity and habits challenge white domination as a "white ally," rather than the more obvious "anti-racist white person." I also will use phrases such as "racial justice struggles" and "racial justice movements" rather than "anti-racism" to describe the activities that white allies pursue. It's important to note that the figure of the white ally is more ideal than real. I'm not sure if many white allies yet exist, and perhaps they never will. The white ally nonetheless can serve as an ideal for which white people might strive even if they never achieve it. In fact, the white ally might need always to be considered an unachieved ideal and never a fait accompli. Given the monumental history of white domination, which will never disappear even if white domination someday does, a white person's relationship to her whiteness must always be a critical one. This means that the process of creating a white allied identity necessarily will be ongoing and capable of improvement.

I also choose "white ally" because I see white people who fight for racial justice as allied with people of color who are doing the same. A relationship of alliance is not necessarily the same thing as friendship. As I will elaborate in the book's conclusion, I'm somewhat suspicious of some efforts of white people to befriend or develop close personal relationships with people of color. Too often white efforts to make non-white friends can have more to do with making guilty white people feel better about themselves or with white people's accumulation of cultural credit, than with promoting racial justice. A white ally may or may not have close, affectionate relationships with people of color, but she can be aligned with them and their interests in that she struggles for racial justice.

For Further Reflection

1. According to Sullivan, what is one of the main ways that white middle-class people produce and display "white middle-class moral goodness"?
2. What are the "four central strands of white liberal anti-racism" that Sullivan identifies?
3. How does Sullivan distinguish between *white privilege* and *white supremacy*?

Further Readings for Chapter 11

Alexander, Michelle. *The New Jim Crow*. New York: The New Press, 2012.

Altman, Andrew. "Discrimination," in *Stanford Encyclopedia of Philosophy*, Winter 2016 ed., edited by Edward N. Zalta. https://plato.stanford.edu/archives/win2016/entries/discrimination/.

Appiah, Kwame Anthony. "Racisms," in *Anatomy of Racism*, edited by David Theo Goldberg. Minneapolis: University of Minnesota Press, 1990.

Blum, Lawrence. *"I'm Not a Racist But . . ." : The Moral Quandary of Race*. Ithaca, NY: Cornell University Press, 2002.

Bonilla-Silva, Eduardo. *Racism without Racists*, 5th ed. Lanham, MD: Rowman and Littlefield, 2018.

Golash-Boza, Tanya Maria. *Racism and Racisms: A Critical Approach*. New York: Oxford University Press, 2016.

Rattansi, Ali. *Racism: A Very Short Introduction*. Oxford: Oxford University Press, 2007.

Sullivan, Shannon. *Good White People: The Problem with Middle-Class White Anti-Racism*. Albany: SUNY Press, 2014.

Zack, Naomi. *The Ethics and Mores of Race: Equality after the History of Philosophy*. Lanham, MD: Rowman and Littlefield, 2011.

Zack, Naomi, ed. *The Oxford Handbook of Philosophy and Race*. New York: Oxford University Press, 2017.

CHAPTER 12

Free Speech and Hate Speech

We have had good reason to be concerned about the state of free speech on America's college campuses. In recent years, the political and moral tensions that have poisoned public discourse nationally have spread to the academy. The symptoms are disconcerting: extreme political polarization, increased racial tensions, profound intolerance of opposing views, the weaponization of internet speech, social media-stoked outrage, and hate-inspired words and intimidation. The hate comes through in political tirades, racist invective, racist and anti-Semitic symbols, hate crimes, white-supremacist rants, anti-LGBTQ diatribes, and a profusion of other less subtle forms of loathing.

In such disputes the flashpoints vary, but the heart of the matter is often a clash between two essential values: (1) the need to make campuses equally inclusive and welcoming for all students, and (2) the importance of safeguarding freedom of expression, without which free inquiry and open-ended learning is impaired. In the name of the former value, students insist that free speech be curbed to shield marginalized groups from harm; moved by the latter, students claim the right to express and hear offensive views.

Freedom of speech or expression is the right to express, either verbally or non-verbally, opinions or ideas without onerous limitations imposed by government or society. "Speech" or "expression" refers not just to spoken words, but to writing, shouting, creating works of art, acting on stage, singing, carrying signs, waving or burning flags, and much more. Free speech is a cherished value essential to freedom of thought, democratic self-government, pursuit of knowledge, and moral deliberation. It is recognized as a bedrock principle in liberal democracies throughout the world, codified as a human right by international bodies, and inscribed in the U.S. Constitution's First Amendment as a guard against government attempts to constrain what people say.

The right of free speech, though extremely important, is not absolute. Like any other right, speech can be legitimately restricted when it conflicts with other important values in society. The U.S. Supreme Court, for example, has consistently ruled that the government may punish certain kinds of speech that it deems harmful. The narrowly defined types of speech considered worthy of punishment include true threats, punishable incitement, harassment, fighting words, and expression that facilitates criminal conduct.

The First Amendment was devised as a shield against *government* restraints on our basic rights. With few exceptions, it does not restrict the actions of *private* persons or organizations. As far as the Constitution is concerned, employees do not have a right to free speech in the workplace. In general, a private company is free to fire employees who espouse views at work that the company doesn't like. State colleges and universities are legal extensions of the government and are thus bound by the First Amendment. Nonstate schools are not constrained in the same way but may still try to align themselves with First Amendment requirements. In any case, free speech is widely regarded as a *moral* right, whatever its legal or political status.

Historically, the right of free speech has been the supreme ally of citizens who demand justice while governments try to silence them—marginalized, vulnerable minority groups, dissenters, nonconformists, the unpopular, the disdained. Over the last half century, the Supreme Court has affirmed again and again that speech may not be censored or punished just because it is disfavored, disturbing, or feared. This interpretation of free speech rights has had profound effects in American history:

The U.S. Constitution as interpreted by the Supreme Court asserts unequivocally that most speech is immune from censorship or punishment—that is, it is *Constitutionally protected* (unregulated). People are free to say, write, depict, or circulate all sorts of opinions, ideas, feelings, and expressions in almost any type of media. But some forms of speech, a very short list, can be censored or punished—they are *Constitutionally unprotected.* The Court has argued that censoring speech because it is disfavored or disturbing would violate the "viewpoint neutrality rule," the foundation of the nation's right of free speech. As the Court sees it, to punish speech because of these features is to punish the speech's message, and that's poison to democratic government. In addition, the Court has consistently ruled that speech cannot be deemed unprotected just because it provokes a fear of possible harmful behavior. As Justice Louis Brandeis asserted in his opinion in *Whitney v. California* (1927), "Fear of serious injury cannot alone justify suppression of free speech. . . . Men feared witches and burnt women." Banning fear-provoking speech would violate the "emergency test," which says fearful speech can only be punished when it poses a danger of directly causing certain specific, imminent, serious harms.

The Court's distinctions between Constitutionally protected and unprotected speech directly pertain to the volatile issue of hate speech. *Hate speech* has no precise legal definition but generally refers to hateful, abusive, or discriminatory speech directed against a person or group because of their race, religion, sexual orientation, gender identity, ethnicity, or national origin. The Court's decisions make it clear that under the Constitution, *it is not the case that all hate speech is fully protected, nor is it the case that all hate speech is unprotected.*

What about hate speech that is protected? Can't it cause harms? And if it causes harms, shouldn't it also be censored or punished? These questions get to the heart of debates about hate speech on campus and in the larger society. They call for a thoughtful examination of the possible harms of hate speech and what should or should not be done about them.

First we should acknowledge that speech can indeed affect people in profound ways. Words are not physical things, but neither are they inert. Sticks and stones can hurt us, but words can wound just as well. Words can lead to laughter or tears, spread fear or comfort, promote peace or discord, humiliate or elevate, and engender love or hate. More to the point, hate speech, both protected and unprotected, can inflict harm on its targeted victims.

Scholars point out that hate speech can harm its intended victims both psychologically and physiologically. It is unclear, however, whether hateful, ugly words always cause psychic or emotional harms. There is no doubt that hate speech can cause stress and that chronic stress—long-term, continuing stress like the kind caused by nonstop bullying—can be physically and psychologically damaging. Stress caused by hate speech is not always chronic in this sense but is often sporadic and brief. More importantly, research shows that the stressful impact of disturbing messages can be altered, lessened, and even negated by many factors. Whether speech is harmful depends on where the speech happens, the speech's apparent purpose, the reactions of bystanders, the body language and tone of the speaker, the speaker's and listener's relationship, the traits and past experiences of the listener, and more. When confronted with disparaging, subordinating speech, listeners have reacted with anger and hurt but also with quiet defiance, calm retorts, contemptuous disregard, and empowering determination to work against hate and bigotry.

In the campus controversies involving free speech, three positions have dominated. The first takes free speech to be the overriding value at stake. It's the view (sometimes called "free speech absolutism") that the right of free speech must be preserved above all else and that any perceived harms, offense, or emotional distress caused by protected speech are irrelevant. For many proponents of this view, protecting students from contrary, challenging views (through speech codes, for example) undermines democracy, promotes emotional immaturity, and leads to intellectual weakness (or, as some have alleged, "snowflake" fragility).

A second position, directly opposed to the first, says speech that deliberately demeans or offends vulnerable groups should be banned to protect those groups from harm. Those who take this view favor speech codes that forbid certain kinds of offensive language, especially hate speech. They take the possible harms of speech very seriously and are less impressed by arguments about the benefits of unfettered speech.

A third position represents a middle way. It recognizes the need to protect free speech to preserve democracy and to advance knowledge while ensuring that all voices, all races, and all genders have an equal opportunity to be heard. It says that free speech is too important to be restricted and yet we can't ignore the harm that it can do. It calls for conscientious efforts to make campuses safe for *both* the free and uninhibited exchange of ideas as well as the full and equal participation of all students in the expression and debate of those ideas. From this perspective, the free speech absolutists as well as those who want to protect minorities from harmful speech have missed the point—which is to try to accommodate both these important demands.

Free Speech on Campus

SIGAL R. BEN-PORATH

Sigal R. Ben-Porath is professor of education, political science, and philosophy at the University of Pennsylvania. She argues that in the campus free speech debates, it is possible to both protect the free and open exchange of ideas in the pursuit of knowledge and ensure that all members of the campus community are able to participate in this free and open exchange.

A call for creating an inclusive environment in which all members are respected and where all voices can be heard should be framed and recognized as furthering rather than impeding the realization of a free and open campus. Students sometimes call on campus administrators to support inclusion and diversity by limiting speech, and they refer to harms caused to them by instances in which open expression allows for hurtful speech to take center stage. But an inclusive and welcoming campus is one that must recognize the necessity of free speech.

To see how inclusion and free speech can coincide rather than stand in opposition, a closer look is needed at what "harm" means in the context of the free speech cases discussed here. In order to bridge the divide between those who seek to protect speech from attacks by advocates of inclusion and those who seek to protect minority groups from attacks by proponents of free speech, we need to clarify what is the harm that the latter are aiming to avoid.

The notion of harm has been central to the liberal debate at least since it was articulated by John Stuart Mill, who famously noted that "the only purpose for which power can be rightfully exercised over any member of a civilized community, against his will, is to prevent harm to others." Harm to others is thus to him the only justified reason to limit the freedom of any member in a democratic community, although Mill is sometimes understood to have claimed that you still have a right to speak even if your words harm others. As articulated after the Middlebury events [where the speech of Charles Murray was violently protected] by Cornel West and Robert P. George, two eminent scholars who represent opposing ideological views, "All of us should be willing—even eager—to engage with anyone who is prepared to do business in the currency of truth-seeking discourse by offering reasons, marshaling evidence, and making arguments." By this view, very few instances

Sigal R. Ben-Porath, *Free Speech on Campus* (Philadelphia: University of Pennsylvania press, 2017), 37–44.

of speech can constitute harm, if harm even remains a relevant aspect of the debate. There are cases for limiting free speech in the name of preventing harm to others—yelling "fire" in a crowded theater and publicizing libelous statements about another person are famous examples. But for the most part, when views and opinions are expressed as part of an open, democratic exchange, they should be permissible.

However, this expansive view of free speech as rarely causing harm and therefore usually not being subject to censure can reasonably be put into question in the context of the diversifying campus. . . . For now, it will suffice to clarify: recognizing that some forms of speech are harmful and that these harms compound other (historical and current) harms does not mean that speech should be more commonly censored or curtailed. Rather, attention to speech is called for by issues surrounding it, such as the possible motivations of speakers, including "the troll problem"—speakers who intend merely to be provocative rather than to inform, challenge, or generate dialogue. In addition, the possible impact of words can be part of the consideration, both immediately and in the aggregate accumulation of small harms. Again, while the response should not be to shut down or avoid speech, additional steps can reasonably be taken by other student groups and sometimes even by the campus leadership. Forms of expression (and behavior) that were seen as mainstream when the campus was all-male, all-white, or presumed to be all-straight—such as using casual sexist, racist, and antigay language—are being challenged by some as preventing members of newer groups from being recognized as full members of the campus community.

Advocates' calls to give "no platform" to such speakers miss the mark because they seek to avoid perspectives that deserve or, at the very least, require dialogue—if some or many in society hold certain views, even reprehensible ones, avoiding them does nothing to challenge them. For liberals of different races who hold clear views on racial equality, for example, speaking to Charles Murray would surely provide an opportunity to challenge his views without risking their own intellectual integrity or sense of self-worth. Shortly after the events at Middlebury, Murray was scheduled to speak at the invitation of a professor at Notre

Dame, who wrote, "Notre Dame is one of Charles Murray's first post-Middlebury campus lectures. It makes our event a referendum on free speech and how universities handle controversial speakers. I didn't intend for his visit to address these issues, but it now does. Given the trends of cancelled lectures, ever-increasing calls to disinvite speakers, and ideological bullying on college campuses, we must take a stand for civil discourse and reasoned engagement. We must show that universities can host respectful conversations among people who disagree." But clearly intellectual exchange is not the focus for everyone. Rather, progressive activists are concerned that voicing what they perceive—possibly correctly—as racially charged or even racist views would harm members of racial minority groups on campus and therefore should be silenced. For them, standing for civil discourse and reasoned engagement, and even more so the commitment to respectful conversation, requires that speakers respect all their audience members, a stance that misogyny, homophobia, and racism preclude.

Like the Yale case, which started off with advice against donning hurtful costumes, many speech cases in recent years have been framed as issues related to causing and avoiding harm or searching for safety in the face of potential or actual harm. For opponents of this view, the demand to avoid harm is tantamount to an attack on a core value of the university, as outlined in the 2016 letter to freshmen from the University of Chicago, which declared that safe spaces and trigger warnings would not be provided. But in fact the collective effort to avoid harm is an important step in constructing a free and equal community of inquiry, which is the shared goal in this debate, and should thus be taken seriously by those on both sides of the free speech divide.

In response to the attack on Charles Murray at Middlebury, its student government association issued a statement recommending that departments and student organizations "respect the boundaries of the College's community standards . . . in order to create a better learning environment." This line of response is typical to the frame of mind that sees free speech mostly through the lens of offense and that presumes an inherent tension between protecting free expression and protecting vulnerable groups from (further) harm. Some progressives and liberals have come to fear that, by hosting speakers like Murray, conservative student groups are invoking free speech to cover up an insidious attempt to promote hate-based and evidence-free speech and to incite anger rather than to create a meaningful opportunity for learning and dialogue. This is a reasonable concern in the context of an educational institution, but nonetheless it should not be used to curtail free speech. Curtailing free speech based on content or—even worse—the presumed motivation of the speaker, raises the risk of creating some version of thought police—namely, a regulatory mechanism for deciding which views and opinions warrant an invitation to campus and which do not. This is not to say that there is no space for response, and some options are suggested below, but it does mean that the liberal concern about hate based and evidence-free or inciting events, even if justified, should not result in a call for censoring or curtailing events and speakers.

Polarized views on free speech produced the Chicago "no trigger warnings here" letter, assuming that if professors provide trigger warnings as a way to protect vulnerable students from potential harm, they will be compromising their commitment to open-minded research and the spirit and principles of free expression. On the other side, they produced the call from Middlebury students "to articulate some parameters for which viewpoints are worthy" of the process of free inquiry, asserting that a stricter limitation on permissible speech on campus would give rise to a more inclusive community.

This perceived tension is mostly misguided, and the framework that presumes an opposition between free inquiry on the one hand and inclusion on the other juxtaposes views that could potentially overlap through a shared commitment to protect free and inclusive speech. The presumed tension between free speech and protection from harm is the result of a rigid and inaccurate description of both, and a charitable and close reading of the above statements that articulate both sides shows a commitment to similar values. The University of Chicago seemed to be blindsided by the backlash to their letter, and in response they took pains to clarify their commitment to an open and equitable campus where all are welcome and respected. The Middlebury students who circulated the "Broken Inquiry" statement after the Murray event expressed a sense of dismay at his invitation and perspective, but they still articulated as their first principle the view that "genuine higher learning is possible only where free, reasoned, and civil speech and discussion are respected." There seems to be an agreement—even if thin, even if only as lip service—that free speech and inquiry are central tenets of university or college life and its mission, and that diversity, equity, and inclusion need to be respected. Not often enough is it acknowledged that equity and inclusion do not have to stand in the way of free speech and open-minded inquiry and that the two can go hand in hand in promoting the key mission of higher education institutions.

Moreover, both sides fail to take account of how their views can readily become self-defeating. When social justice advocates call for the curtailment of free speech through censoring speakers and canceling events, they neglect to recognize the historical reality that curtailing free speech might harm vulnerable groups. Once censorship based on content is possible, what is to stop people in power—administrators, religious majority groups, or other established centers of power—from limiting speech by dissenters, opponents, or anyone who threatens the status quo?

On the other hand, free speech advocates who insist that unfettered free speech is a necessary condition for the open-minded free inquiry that makes a university worth its name sidestep the fact that when many on campus are effectively silenced, inquiry is in fact neither free nor open-minded. It remains the prerogative of those who have tools and support to join the conversation and to participate in the main activities on campus, including research, active learning, and established social roles. Many women, racial and sexual minorities, first-generation students, and other individuals who may not see themselves (or be seen by others) as belonging or possess the tools required to hit the ground running remain outside the conversation, impoverishing the conversation and hindering the search for truth and knowledge.

It is commonly said that the only cure for inaccurate or even harmful speech is more and better speech. Inclusive freedom is aligned with this stance in one sense: colleges should not aim to enforce civility or regulate speech but should focus, rather, on providing ample opportunities for students to develop and express their views, question, and even rebel. Curtailing speech to prevent controversy is both unjustified and ineffective; instead, colleges should aim to enable multiple forms of expressive and political speech, guided by no more than broad legal requirements and a thin, flexible commitment to an inclusive atmosphere. The latter should be used not to limit speech but to support students in developing opportunities for further speech and the capacity to productively respond to speech that they find offensive rather than to look for ways to shut it down.

For Further Reflection

1. Should campus speech be censored or punished if it offends or upsets members of marginalized groups? Why or why not?
2. What is Ben-Porath's attitude toward free speech and inclusion?
3. Why does she think both the views of social justice advocates and free speech advocates can become self-defeating?

Two Views of Speech Laws

RICHARD STENGEL AND CONOR FRIEDERSDORF

Richard Stengel, a former editor of *Time* and the State Department's former undersecretary for public diplomacy and public affairs, argues that America needs a hate speech law. Conor Friedersdorf, staff writer at *The Atlantic*, disagrees. Here are brief excerpts from their dueling essays.

Richard Stengel, "Why America Needs a Hate Speech Law," *Washington Post*, October 29, 2019, https://www.washingtonpost.com/opinions/2019/10/29/why-america-needs-hate-speech-law/; Conor Friedersdorf, "Bad Arguments for Limiting Speech," *The Atlantic*, October 31, 2019, https://www.theatlantic.com/ideas/archive/2019/10/arguments-limiting-speech/601066/.

STENGEL

Yes, the First Amendment protects the "thought that we hate," but it should not protect hateful speech that can cause violence by one group against another. In an age when everyone has a megaphone, that seems like a design flaw.

It is important to remember that our First Amendment doesn't just protect the good guys; our foremost liberty also protects any bad actors who hide behind it to weaken our society. . . .

That's partly because the intellectual underpinning of the First Amendment was engineered for a simpler era. The amendment rests on the notion that the truth will win out in what Supreme Court Justice William O. Douglas called "the marketplace of ideas." This "marketplace" model has a long history going back to 17th-century English intellectual John Milton, but in all that time, no one ever quite explained how good ideas drive out bad ones, how truth triumphs over falsehood. . . .

The presumption has always been that the marketplace would offer a level playing field. But in the age of social media, that landscape is neither level nor fair.

On the Internet, truth is not optimized. On the Web, it's not enough to battle falsehood with truth; the truth doesn't always win. In the age of social media, the marketplace model doesn't work. . . .

Since World War II, many nations have passed laws to curb the incitement of racial and religious hatred. These laws started out as protections against the kinds of anti-Semitic bigotry that gave rise to the Holocaust. . . .

I think it's time to consider these statutes. . . . Domestic terrorists such as Dylann Roof and Omar Mateen and the El Paso shooter were consumers of hate speech. Speech doesn't pull the trigger, but does anyone seriously doubt that such hateful speech creates a climate where such acts are more likely?

Let the debate begin. Hate speech has a less violent, but nearly as damaging, impact in another way: It diminishes tolerance. It enables discrimination. Isn't that, by definition, speech that undermines the values that the First Amendment was designed to protect: fairness, due process, equality before the law? Why shouldn't the states experiment with their own version of hate speech statutes to penalize speech that deliberately insults people based on religion, race, ethnicity and sexual orientation?

All speech is not equal. And where truth cannot drive out lies, we must add new guardrails. I'm all for protecting "thought that we hate," but not speech that incites hate. It undermines the very values of a fair marketplace of ideas that the First Amendment is designed to protect.

FRIEDERSDORF

"Yes, the First Amendment protects the 'thought that we hate,'" Stengel grants in his op-ed, "but it should not protect hateful speech that can cause violence by one group against another." But if the U.S. outlaws speech that causes violence, that will create a perverse incentive—anyone who wants a viewpoint outlawed need only stoke violence to get his way. If Islamist radicals react with violence to feminist speech or Hollywood movies that portray two men kissing, will Stengel advocate for laws that infringe on the ability of Americans to so express themselves? . . .

The First Amendment is as important and as salutary in its effects now as ever, giving the United States an extra bulwark against authoritarians at a moment when their power is ascendant in dozens of countries. . . .

But there is no reason to believe that the truth was simpler to figure out in 1789 than in 2019. The First Amendment was adopted to limit federal power—to protect vigorous self-governance by the people—without any presumption that truth would always win out. . . .

Liberal free-speech regimes are better than any alternative ever tried at subjecting all ideas to scrutiny, and at preventing powerful actors from quashing truth seekers. . . .

There was never a time when truth always won, but let's set that aside. How strange to simultaneously believe that it's more difficult than ever to tell truths from falsehoods, that many citizens do not, in fact, possess the *ability* to do so, *and* to imply that elected officials chosen by those citizens should make determinations about what is true and false and punish people for the latter. . . .

But laws against hate speech don't necessarily create a climate where such acts are less likely, because any law narrow enough to avoid punishing a lot of innocent people is broad enough to permit hateful bigots to convey information that a tiny number of people respond to with violence. . . .

In his conclusion, Stengel poses a question . . . Why shouldn't the states experiment with their own version of hate speech statutes to penalize speech that deliberately insults people based on religion, race, ethnicity and sexual orientation?

Because it is immoral to marshal state violence to punish people for expressing their beliefs. Because laws against speech that insults people based on religion, race, ethnicity, and sexual orientation would have punished essayists like Christopher Hitchens, comedians like Eddie Murphy, hip-hop artists, feminist radicals like Andrea Dworkin, and radical gay activists who dislike "breeders."

For Further Reflection

1. Outline Stengel's argument for hate speech laws. Do you find it convincing? Why or why not?
2. Outline Friedersdorf argument against hate speech laws. Do you think it successfully refutes Stengel's argument? Explain.
3. Do you agree with Friedersdorf about why states should not experiment with their own versions of hate speech statutes? Give reasons for your answer.

Hate Speech

ERWIN CHEMERINSKY AND HOWARD GILLMAN

Chemerinsky and Gillman acknowledge that the harm caused by hate speech is real and serious, but they argue against using speech codes to try to curtail hate speech. They point out that speech codes have been consistently ruled unconstitutional by the courts, that they have proven to be impermissibly vague and overbroad, and that they often result in the punishment of people for their political viewpoints or worldviews.

THE EXPERIENCE WITH HATE SPEECH CODES

By the early 1990s, over 350 colleges and universities adopted hate speech codes. A number of these were challenged in court, and all to be challenged were declared unconstitutional.

One of the most prominent examples involved the University of Michigan, which was motivated to devise a hate speech code after some truly horrendous events on campus. In 1987, flyers were distributed that declared "open season" on blacks. Blacks were referred to as "saucer lips," "porch monkeys," and "jigaboos." A student disc jockey allowed racist jokes to be broadcast on

---

Erwin Chemerinsky and Howard Gillman, *Free Speech on Campus* (New Haven, CT: Yale University Press, 97-110).

the campus radio station, and student demonstrations were interrupted by the display of a KKK uniform from a nearby dorm window. Another flyer proclaimed, "Niggers get off campus" and "Darkies don't belong in classrooms—they belong hanging from trees." The university had to respond to such horrific expression.

The challenge was how to translate the natural desire to eliminate such egregious behavior into a policy that was consistent with the First Amendment. This proved extremely difficult. The policy adopted by the university in 1988 prohibited:

> Any behavior, verbal or physical, that stigmatizes or victimizes an individual on the basis of race, ethnicity, religion, sex, sexual orientation, creed, national origin, ancestry, age, marital status, handicap or Vietnam-era veteran status, and that
>
> a. Involves an express or implied threat to an individual's academic efforts, employment, participation in University sponsored extra-curricular activities or personal safety; or
> b. Has the purpose or reasonably foreseeable effect of interfering with an individual's academic efforts, employment, participation in University sponsored extra-curricular activities or personal safety; or
> c. Creates an intimidating, hostile, or demeaning environment for educational pursuits, employment or participation in University sponsored extra-curricular activities.

Shortly after this policy went into effect, in the fall of 1988, the University Office of Affirmative Action issued an interpretive guide entitled *What Students Should Know about Discrimination and Discriminatory Harassment by Students in the University Environment.* The examples of what was prohibited included:

> A flyer containing racist threats distributed in a residence hall.
>
> Racist graffiti written on the door of an Asian student's study carrel.
>
> A male student makes remarks in class like "Women just aren't as good in this field as men," thus creating a hostile learning atmosphere for female classmates.
>
> Students in a residence hall have a floor party and invite everyone on their floor except one person because they think she might be a lesbian.
>
> A black student is confronted and racially insulted by two white students in a cafeteria.
>
> Male students leave pornographic pictures and jokes on the desk of a female graduate student.
>
> Two men demand that their roommate in the residence hall move out and be tested for AIDS.

Commenting on the breadth of this code, Kent Greenawalt observed that it "seemed to reach into the realm of obnoxious ideas civilly expressed."

In practice, the code was used not against the kinds of purely hateful slurs that inspired its passage, but against people who expressed opinions that others objected to.

Complaints were filed against a student who stated that Jewish people used the Holocaust to justify Israel's policies toward the Palestinians. Another student found himself facing punishment for saying that he had heard that minorities had a difficult time in a particular course. A graduate student in social work was subjected to formal disciplinary procedures for asserting that homosexuality was a disease. As the court noted, "On at least three separate occasions, students were disciplined or threatened with discipline for comments made in a classroom setting." Eventually, a graduate student challenged the policy in federal court by claiming that the hate speech code put him at risk of punishment for studying certain controversial theories in his field of psychobiology, including the study of individual and group differences in personality traits and cognitive abilities.

A federal judge struck down the policy on the grounds that the University of Michigan's definition of what was prohibited speech was so broad and vague that it was "simply impossible to discern any limitation" on the policy's reach. Any controversial or critical comment could put someone at risk for punishment. To qualify as prohibited under the code, the judge wrote, language must "'stigmatize' or 'victimize' an individual. However, both of these terms are general and elude precise definition. Moreover, it is clear that the fact that a statement may victimize or stigmatize an individual does not, in and of itself, strip it of protection under the accepted First Amendment tests."

This was not an isolated outcome. Between 1989 and 1995, every court that examined a university speech code found the code unconstitutional. The hate speech code passed by the University of Wisconsin, for instance, provided that the university could discipline a student in nonacademic matters in the following situations:

> For racist or discriminatory comments, epithets or other expressive behavior directed at an individual or on separate occasions at different individuals, or for physical conduct, if such comments, epithets or other expressive behavior or physical conduct intentionally:
>
> 1. Demean the race, sex, religion, color, creed, disability, sexual orientation, national origin, ancestry or age of the individual or individuals; and
> 2. Create an intimidating, hostile or demeaning environment for education, university-related work, or other university-authorized activity.

The federal district court found this regulation unconstitutionally overbroad and vague, mostly because a great deal of speech that people might consider "demeaning" was clearly protected by the First Amendment.

When George Mason University suspended a fraternity in 1991 after it conducted an "ugly woman contest" with racist and sexist overtones, the United States Court of Appeals struck down the sanctions, explaining that the First Amendment protected even offensive and juvenile expression. The court declared: "We agree wholeheartedly that it is the University officials' responsibility, even their obligation, to achieve the goals they have set. On the other hand, a public university has many constitutionally permissible means to protect female and minority students. We must emphasize, as have other courts, that 'the manner of [its action] cannot consist of selective limitations upon speech.'"

The invalidation of hate speech codes was not limited to public universities. In May 1990, the Stanford Student Conduct Legislative Council adopted a student conduct code, drafted by law professor and constitutional scholar Thomas Grey, that prohibited "discrirninatory harassment," including "personal vilification of students on the basis of their sex, race, color, handicap, religion, sexual orientation or national and ethnic origin." Personal vilification was defined as intentional, personally directed "fighting words or non-verbal symbols . . . commonly understood to convey direct and visceral hatred or contempt for human beings" on the basis of their membership in those groups.

In February 1995, a California Superior Court judge invalidated the Stanford code as violating a California statute, the Leonard Law, which provides that "no private postsecondary educational institution shall make or enforce any rule subjecting any student to disciplinary sanctions solely on the basis of conduct that is speech . . . that, when engaged in outside the campus or facility of a private postsecondary institution, is protected from governmental restriction by the First Amendment." The Leonard Law thus says that private schools cannot punish speech that would be deemed protected in a public institution. The court declared: "Defendants' Speech Code does violate Plaintiffs' 1st Amendment rights since the Speech Code proscribes more than just 'fighting words' as denned in *Chaplinsky*, and the later lines of case law. To this extent, therefore, Defendants' Speech Code is overbroad. In addition, however, the Speech Code also targets the content of certain speech [and] . . . is an impermissible content-based regulation."

The motivations behind the desire to punish hateful speech are laudable. So far, however, the legal and definitional challenges of translating these motivations into workable codes have proven impossible to overcome. After watching so many universities lose in court, some, such as the University of

Pennsylvania, withdrew their hate speech codes; others, such as Yale, said they would not be enforced.

SHOULD HATE SPEECH ON CAMPUSES BE PROHIBITED?

We believe, with legal scholars Delgado, Lawrence, Matsuda, and Waldron, that hate speech causes great harm and that colleges and universities must act to protect students from harm. Their advocacy was instrumental in causing many schools to adopt policies prohibiting such expression. But the courts have ruled that the First Amendment clearly prohibits public colleges and universities from using hate speech codes to achieve this goal.

This is the law. But should it be? After all, many countries punish speech that disparages or incites hatred against a person or group on the basis of race, religion, sex, ethnicity, or sexual orientation. Even if public colleges and universities are limited by First Amendment restrictions, there might still be good reasons why private colleges and universities should adopt such codes.

We think not. There are strong reasons why campuses should resist calls to censor and punish people who express ideas, considered offensive, hateful, or demeaning.

First, decades and decades of efforts—by state governments, local municipalities, and campuses—have demonstrated that all such codes are impermissibly vague and overbroad. They all risk punishing people based on political viewpoint or worldview. Any rule that seeks to punish people for their speech must state specifically what is prohibited and what is allowed. Otherwise, too many people will be afraid to say anything controversial for fear that they will be singled out for arbitrary punishment based on unclear standards. There are no examples of codes that both are sufficiently specific, and that apply only to unprotected speech. The Michigan code, for instance, prohibited "any behavior, verbal or physical, that stigmatizes or victimizes an individual on the basis of race, ethnicity, religion, sex, sexual orientation, creed." The Stanford code provided that "Speech or other expression constitutes harassment by vilification if it: a) is intended to insult or stigmatize an individual or individuals on the basis of their sex, race, color, handicap, religions-sexual orientation, or national and ethnic origin." The University of Wisconsin code prohibited speech that was "demeaning" based on "race, sex, religion, color, creed, disability, sexual orientation, national origin, ancestry or age of the individual or individuals." Jeremy Waldron defined hate speech as "the use of words which are deliberately abusive and/or insulting and/or threatening and/or demeaning directed at members of vulnerable minorities, calculated to stir up hatred against them."

These codes have an intentionally broad sweep, but precisely for that reason, they inevitably prohibit the expression of ideas that might be seen as "stigmatizing," "demeaning," or "insulting." In addition to being inherently vague, these concepts are also inherently politically charged. Much of what we debate as a society—including on college campuses—relates to whether certain forms of expression should be considered demeaning or insulting, and these disagreements often run deep. Many anti-racism and anti-sexism advocates make powerful arguments for why seemingly innocuous speech acts, and many forms of cultural expression, should be considered exclusionary and demeaning. Some even embrace the view that cultural reproduction of racism and patriarchy is built into the very foundation of our social order. Opponents of these positions sometimes claim the critics are too quick to find oppression, that they are humorless, or that their concerns, while sometimes legitimate, are overstated. Others argue that what the critics consider demeaning (such as sexualized depictions of women or certain examples of cultural appropriation) are actually empowering. The arguments are endless.

Given this level of disagreement, any hate speech code can, in theory, either lead to the punishment of very many people (who may not think they are demeaning anyone) or result in a refusal to punish many arguably stigmatizing speech acts. The upshot is that people will inevitably be punished for their political views, with arbitrary and often surprising results. Given the definitional problems, how could it be otherwise? Suppose gay and lesbian students complain that they are demeaned by a Christian student's expressed belief that traditional heterosexual marriage is the only true marriage. Should the university deny that this belief is demeaning, or punish the student? What if the Christian student then complains that the gay students' complaint demeans and stigmatizes her religious beliefs? The door is open to an endless succession of claims and counterclaims. Justice Clarence Thomas believes that affirmative action programs stigmatize minorities on the basis of race and "stamp minorities with a badge of inferiority." Could a student's advocacy of affirmative action be taken as stigmatizing minorities as inferior? What of Laura Kipnis's argument that overly protective approaches to sex on campus stigmatize women? Or the claim that some anti-racism rhetoric demeans whites and is calculated to stir up hatred against them? These challenges are inherent to the entire enterprise. They cannot be solved with better definitions.

This brings us to our second argument against such codes: they are often used to punish the speech of people who were not their intended targets. Vague and overbroad laws inherently risk discriminatory enforcement, and that is exactly what has happened with hate speech codes. As Nadine Strossen observes: "One ironic, even tragic, result of this discretion is that members of minority groups themselves—the very people whom the law is intended to protect—are likely targets of punishment. For example, among the first individuals prosecuted under the British Race Relations Act of 1965 were black power leaders." Although the English law was adopted in response to a rise in anti-Semitic incidents on campus, it was used against those who advocated on behalf of Israel, by people who argued that according to United Nations General Assembly resolution no. 3379, Zionism was a form of racism.

That has also been the experience with hate speech codes in the United States. As Henry Louis Gates Jr. notes:

> During the years in which Michigan's speech code was enforced, more than twenty blacks were charged—by whites—with racist speech. Not a single instance of white racist speech was punished. . . . A full disciplinary hearing was conducted only in the case of a black social work student who was charged with saying, in a class discussion of research projects, that he believed that homosexuality was an illness, and that he was developing a social work approach to move homosexuals toward heterosexuality.

Hate speech codes around the world have often been applied in politically charged ways. In 2006, individuals in Sweden were convicted for distributing leaflets to high school students saying homosexuality was a "deviant sexual proclivity," had "a morally destructive effect on the substance of society," and was responsible for the development of HIV and AIDS. In 2009, a member of the Belgian Parliament was convicted of distributing leaflets with the slogans "Stand up against the Islamification of Belgium," "Stop the sham integration policy," and "Send non-European job seekers home." The European Court of Human Rights affirmed these convictions, rejecting defenses based on freedom of speech. In Poland, a Catholic magazine was fined $11,000 for mating "contempt, hostility and malice" by comparing a woman's abortion to the medical experiments at Auschwitz. In 2008, film star Brigitte Bardot was convicted by French authorities for placing online a letter to president Nicolas Sarkozy in which she complained about the Islamic practice of ritual animal slaughter. It was her fifth conviction for hate speech. In 2011, Scottish football fan Stephen Birrell was sentenced to eight months in prison for insulting Celtic F.C. fans, Catholics, and the pope on a Facebook page. During sentencing, the sheriff, Bill Totten, told Birrell that his views would not be tolerated by "the right-thinking people of Glasgow and Scotland." In Kenya, hate speech laws are used only against those who speak out against the ruling party's Jubilee Alliance, including a movement leader who contested the 2013 election results, a student activist who criticized the president on Twitter, and a blogger who said the president was "adolescent."

We come back to a central point: protecting hate speech is necessary because the alternative—granting governments the power to punish speakers they don't like—creates even more harm. The argument in favor of hate speech laws is essentially an argument for granting people in authority the power to censor or punish individuals who insult, stigmatize, or demean others, and it is inevitable that such vague and broad authority will be abuse or used in ways that were not contemplated by censorship advocates.

Even if one could punish exactly the hateful speakers one hopes to punish, the entire process risks making martyrs and rallying support for those sanctioned. For example, the Dutch government's hate speech prosecutions of far-right politician Geertz Wilders led to more attention to his anti-Muslim sentiments and his criticisms of Moroccan immigrants. It allowed him to motivate the increasing ranks of his supporters by claiming that "If speaking about this is punishable, then the Netherlands is no longer a free country but a dictatorship." (One of his tweets reads, "Prosecuted for what millions think.") Moreover, as Strossen notes, these bans can stultify "the candid intergroup dialogue concerning racism and other forms of bias that constitutes an essential precondition for reducing discrimination" and can "generate litigation and other forms of controversy that will exacerbate intergroup tensions."

There is also no evidence that the presence or absence of hate speech laws results in more tolerant attitudes toward vulnerable groups or in less discrimination. In the United States, even without hate speech laws, we have moved from only 4 percent of Americans approving of interracial marriage in 1958 to 86 percent approval in 2011, with about 15 percent of all new marriages in 2015 between persons of different races. According to FBI statistics, the total number of U.S. hate crime incidents decreased from 8,759 in 1996 to 6,628 in 2010 and to 5,928 in 2015. Even without punishing anti-gay sentiment, acceptance of same-sex marriage has dramatically increased between 2001 (when 57 percent of people opposed it) to 2016 (when 55 percent favored it), mostly because of the greater presence of gay and lesbian voices and experiences in American culture and politics. By contrast, in Europe, the Anti-Defamation League's survey of anti-Semitism reports higher levels in all European countries surveyed, despite their having hate speech laws, than in the United States. A report from the EU Fundamental Rights Agency reports an increase in hate crimes between 2000 and 2009 in eleven out of fourteen surveyed EU nations. As one commentator puts it in his review of Waldron's discussion of hate speech, "Waldron demands that defenders of current First Amendment protections answer the question of whether the targets of abuse 'can [lead their lives], can their children be brought up, can their hopes be maintained and their worst fears dispelled, in a social environment polluted by [hate speech]?' The answer seems to-be an emphatic 'yes.'"

Finally, although advocates for speech codes claim that hate speech plays no part in the legitimate expression of ideas, we believe that censorship of words leads inevitably to the censorship of ideas. It is tempting to say that campuses should at the very least be able to prohibit epithets; words like "nigger" and "faggot" cause great harm. But it is not difficult to imagine contexts—in scholarly analysis, popular culture, or casual conversation—where the use of any given word would be considered appropriate. As Justice Harlan eloquently explained: "We cannot indulge the facile assumption that one can forbid particular words without also running a substantial risk of suppressing ideas in the process. Indeed, governments might soon seize upon the censorship of particular words as a convenient guise for banning the expression of unpopular views. " Hate speech codes inescapably ban the expression of unpopular ideas and views, which never is tolerable in colleges and universities.

But even if colleges and universities can't and shouldn't try to ban hate speech, they still must act to create a conducive learning environment for all students. The question becomes: what can they do?

For Further Reflection

1. What was the court's verdict in the case of the University of Michigan's speech code? What do the terms "overbreadth" and "vagueness" refer to in speech code cases?
2. Why do Chemerinsky and Gillman say that speech codes will inevitably be used to punish political views?
3. Do you believe that hate speech codes do more harm than good? Explain.

Further Readings for Chapter 12

Baer, Ulrich. *What Snowflakes Get Right: Free Speech, Truth, and Equality on Campus*. New York: Oxford University Press, 2019.

Ben-Porath, Sigal R. *Free Speech on Campus*. Philadelphia: University of Pennsylvania Press, 2017.

Chemerinsky, Erwin, and Howard Gillman. *Free Speech on Campus*. New Haven, CT: Yale University Press, 2017.

Fish, Stanley. *There's No Such Thing as Free Speech, and It's a Good Thing, Too*. New York: Oxford University Press, 1994.

Knight Foundation. "Free Expression on College Campuses." May 2019, https://kf-site-production.s3.amazonaws.com/media_elements/files/000/000/351/original/Knight-CP-Report-FINAL.pdf.

Lackey, Jennifer, ed. *Academic Freedom*. New York: Oxford University Press, 2018.

Majeed, Azhar. "Defying the Constitution: The Rise, Persistence, and Prevalence of Campus Speech Codes." *Georgetown Journal of Law & Public Policy* 7, no. 2 481 (2009): 483–544.

Matsuda, Mari J. "Public Response to Racist Speech: Considering the Victim's Story." *Michigan Law Review* 87, no. 8, Legal Storytelling (Aug. 1989): 2320–2381.

Strossen, Nadine. *Hate: Why We Should Resist It with Free Speech, Not Censorship*. New York: Oxford University Press, 2018.

Waldron, Jeremy. *The Harm of Hate Speech*. Cambridge, MA: Harvard University Press, 2012.

Zimmerman, Jonathan. *Campus Politics: What Everyone Needs to Know*. New York: Oxford University Press, 2016.

CHAPTER 13

Pandemic Ethics

The COVID-19 pandemic is both a worldwide human tragedy and a moral catastrophe. As of this writing, globally it has infected over 116 million people and killed more than 2.5 million. In the United States there have been almost 29 million cases and well over a half million deaths with many more likely before the virus is subdued. The moral upheaval comes from the life-and-death decisions that this plague has forced upon us, decisions that have arisen on several levels at once and that have often left us at a loss to deal with them.

To fully understand the moral questions involved, we have to understand the nature of the danger. The latest scientific research has established that COVID-19 is a coronavirus that hasn't been seen in humans before. It causes mild symptoms in most people but severe illness and even death in others. It provokes more serious illness than the flu and spreads faster. Those most likely to have very serious symptoms are older people and people with existing medical conditions like cancer, chronic kidney disease, diabetes, and sickle cell disease, but young people have been hit hard too. The virus is transmitted very easily from one person to another, mainly through respiratory droplets produced by people with COVID-19 when they cough, sneeze, talk, sing, or breathe. The infected person need not be showing any symptoms to spread the virus. Anyone can get COVID-19, and anyone can spread it.

One person can spread the virus to another just by talking or laughing while standing within six feet of them. This unsettling fact—and several others—has led the Centers for Disease Control and Prevention (CDC) to issue guidelines for slowing the spread of the virus: wear a mask, stay six feet from others who don't live with you, and avoid crowds.

Vaccines are available that have been proven safe and highly effective in preventing COVID-19. The CDC says,

- Based on what we know about vaccines for other diseases and early data from clinical trials, experts believe that getting a COVID-19 vaccine may also help keep you from getting seriously ill even if you do get COVID-19.
- Getting vaccinated yourself may also protect people around you, particularly people at increased risk for severe illness from COVID-19. . . .
- COVID-19 can have serious, life-threatening complications, and there is no way to know how COVID-19 will affect you. And if you get sick, you could spread the disease to friends, family, and others around you.[1]

Many moral questions about COVID-19 appear when health care workers try to decide how to allocate scarce medical resources—ventilators, ICU hospital beds, personnel, masks, personal protective equipment (PPE), medications, and vaccines. The decisions that must be made involve balancing principles of fairness, justice, equity, autonomy, respect for persons, and utility. And they are far from academic, for lives are weighing in the balance, and often every choice, whether right or wrong, brings anguish, dread, uncertainty, and grief.

Imagine a hospital that is overwhelmed by seriously ill COVID-19 patients. Without proper treatment, many of them will die. Ventilators (lifesaving machines that act as bellows to move air in and out of the lungs), hospital beds, testing, and PPE are scarce. The hospital is understaffed, and the workers are stressed, many of them near exhaustion. Some of the patients are young adults, some are over seventy, some were healthy before getting the virus, some have underlying medical conditions, some can afford any level of care, many are poor. In situations like this when resources are extremely limited, how do you decide how those resources should be used? What moral considerations apply?

Ethicists agree that some approaches should *not* be used. A person's wealth should not figure into decisions about who lives or dies. Wealthy, famous, or politically powerful people should not get priority over first responders and medical staff. When deciding who gets treatment, a first-come, first-served approach should not be used. Such a process would give unfair preference to patients living closer to the hospital, and it would unjustly exclude patients who become ill later because they were conscientious—because they wore

[1]CDC, "COVID-19," https://cdc.gov/coronavirus/2019-ncov/vaccines.

masks, maintained social distancing, and adhered to other safety guidelines. Society's perception of a person's moral worth should not be a factor.

When resources are limited, a primary moral value is maximizing benefits to patients, which can mean either saving the most lives or saving the most "life-years" (prioritizing patients likely to live longest after treatment). Ethicists say we should aim at both. But in practice, doing this is rarely straightforward or easy. Leading ethicists explain why:

> Operationalizing the value of maximizing benefits means that people who are sick but could recover if treated are given priority over those who are unlikely to recover even if treated and those who are likely to recover without treatment. Because young, severely ill patients will often comprise many of those who are sick but could recover with treatment, this operationalization also has the effect of giving priority to those who are worst off in the sense of being at risk of dying young and not having a full life.[2]

By this moral reckoning, the one available ventilator and bed might go to the seriously ill 25-year-old woman who is likely to recover and not to the 80-year-old who is likely to recover but unlikely to live much longer.

COVID-19 has also exposed fundamental moral issues relating to minority and poor communities, where there has been both unfair allocation of medical resources and unequal impact of the pandemic on health and well-being. For example, experts say segregation and other social and economic inequities have led to higher rates of African Americans contracting the coronavirus, as opposed to any genetic or biological predisposition. In addition, research has shown that the quality of health care that African Americans receive is much lower than that for whites.

In the COVID-19 pandemic, moral decisions are not just general, focusing on interventions and allocations; they are also personal. Consider the practice of mask-wearing, which has been proven to greatly reduce your chances of transmitting the virus to others and can provide you with some protection as well. Yet many people refuse to wear them. Many don't trust science or experts, or they believe that the dangers of the pandemic have been hyped. For others, refusing to wear a mask is a political act, a way to reject liberal values or to show solidarity with their political tribe. Some reject masks in the name of freedom, on grounds of individual liberty. They don't want the government or anyone else telling them what to do.

[2]Ezekiel J. Emanuel, M.D., Govind Persad, Ross Upshur, Beatriz Thome, Michael Parker, Aaron Glickman, Cathy Zhang, Connor Boyle, Maxwell Smith, and James P. Phillips, "Fair Allocation of Scarce Medical Resources in the Time of COVID-19," *New England Journal of Medicine*, 2020; 382:2049-2055, https://www/nejm.org/doi/full/10.1056/nejmsb2005114.

This latter claim rests on the moral principle of autonomy, a person's rational capacity for self-governance or self-determination—the ability to direct one's own life and choose for oneself. Philosophers contend, however, that no moral principle is absolute; each principle must be balanced against others. Another principle to consider here is justice, which refers to people getting what is fair or what is their due. It can be argued that in a seriously threatening pandemic, because those who refuse to wear masks are putting others at risk, they are treating them unfairly. People are entitled to freedom, but not if exercising that freedom treats others unjustly. Another principle is respect for persons, which says that persons are possessors of ultimate inherent worth and must be treated as such. Some have argued that by going without a mask, we expose others to the risk of contracting a deadly disease—a most grievous form of disrespect.

Many ethicists would agree. One of them is Laurie Zoloth at the University of Chicago:

> Social solidarity is the most precious tenet of our democracy. It begins with the notion that you should care about others, even strangers. And the idea that you should love your neighbor as profoundly as you love yourself—even placing their concerns and needs ahead of your own—is the great moral lesson and the core of justice in many religions. . . .
>
> Freedom should not come at the expense of justice. In America, we once had a vision of freedom in which sacrifice was inherent: People sacrificed their very lives for the freedom of others. We've let that vision devolve into one of mere personal preference.[3]

[3]Quoted in Max Witynski, "Ethicist Laurie Zoloth Says It's Our Duty to Get a COVID-19 Vaccine and Wear Masks," *UChicago News*, January 26, 2021.

Why Some Americans Refuse to Social Distance and Wear Masks

MICHAEL SANDEL WITH COLLEEN WALSH

It might seem that threatened by a menacing worldwide plague like COVID-19, people would do what scientists and health experts suggest they should do to stop the virus. But that's naïve. Many refuse to wear masks, social distance, or get the vaccine, often on the grounds that taking those precautions would violate their rights. But what does morality ask us to do? Michael Sandel, Harvard professor of government and author of *Justice: What's the Right Thing to Do?*, discusses our obligations in this interview in *The Harvard Gazette.*

GAZETTE: So many people have chosen not to wear masks or to keep their distance from others, despite the data that those simple measures help save lives. Why is there such resistance?

SANDEL: The wearing of masks has become a flashpoint of partisan disagreement, a new front in the culture wars. On one level, this seems puzzling. Why doesn't everyone simply wear a mask for the sake of public health? For two reasons: First, many Americans consider mask mandates a violation of individual liberty. They don't want the government to force them to wear a mask. Second, many Americans resent governing elites who claim to derive their authority from science. Here, the debate over masks is similar to the partisan disagreement on climate change. Many supporters of President Trump share his resentment of elites and experts. They don't trust experts who tell them they should wear a mask to reduce the spread of the coronavirus any more than they trust experts who say they should pay a carbon tax to alleviate climate change. The resistance to wearing a mask is not about public health; it's about politics.

GAZETTE: What are our ethical obligations in the middle of a pandemic?

SANDEL: Our ethical obligations are, first of all, to minimize the possibility that our behavior will expose others to the risk of contracting the virus. This means wearing masks and social distancing. Beyond this, those of us who are fortunate enough to work from the safety of our homes have a responsibility to support those who take risks on our behalf—not only doctors, nurses, and hospital workers, but delivery workers, grocery-store

Colleen Walsh, "Why Some Americans Refuse to Social Distance and Wear Masks," *The Harvard Gazette*, August 28, 2020.

clerks, maintenance workers, child-care workers, home health care workers. This support should take the form of public appreciation for such workers, but also tangible, material support, such as health care, paid sick leave, and wage support.

GAZETTE: There are periods in American history—like World War II—when nearly everyone spent years voluntarily sacrificing in service to a national cause. Why isn't that happening now? What has changed?

SANDEL: The question reminds me of an internet meme early in the pandemic: "Your grandparents were called to war. You are called to sit on your couch. You can do this." Even as the pandemic highlights our mutual dependence, it is striking how little solidarity and shared sacrifice it has called forth. Why do we seem incapable of solidarity at the time we need it most? The answer goes back to the social unraveling that preceded this crisis. The pandemic caught us unprepared—logistically and medically, but also morally unprepared. It arrived at a time of deep polarization and partisan rancor. Four decades of deepening inequality have driven us apart. Resentment of the elites whose policies produced these inequalities led to a populist backlash. The pandemic arrived at just the wrong moment—amid toxic politics, incompetent leadership, and fraying social bonds.

GAZETTE: How might Americans be the same or different from people in other societies in taking these types of individual steps to help society as a whole? Are there examples from COVID that you can point to?

SANDEL: Sadly, the U.S. has handled the COVID crisis worse than most affluent countries. We've had more than 4½ times the number of deaths per capita as Germany, 60 times the number in Japan, and more than 80 times as many as South Korea. Our poor performance is due partly to failed leadership at the federal level and the lack of an adequate public health system. But I think you are right to suggest that social habits and cultural factors come into play. Our ardent individualism is a strength in some settings but not in contending with a pandemic. In Japan, the ready acceptance of face masks seems to have reduced the spread of the virus. In Germany, the electorate supported far greater investment in wage replacement and public health spending than the U.S. government could muster. In South Korea, a single-payer health system made testing easier and more widespread. In addition, a social movement among landlords to reduce or freeze rents helped keep small businesses afloat.

GAZETTE: What role do leaders have in supporting this social contract?

SANDEL: Trust matters in a pandemic—not only trust in the scientific information and medical advice the government provides, but trust among citizens. Perhaps the single greatest responsibility of leaders in times of crisis is to inspire such trust. Angela Merkel in Germany and Jacinda Ardern in

New Zealand are examples of leaders who have led their countries through the crisis effectively, in part by fostering trust. In this country, by contrast, we've seen how evading responsibility and sowing discord undermines the trust and solidarity we need to contend with the pandemic.

GAZETTE: What does this say, when we are all so culturally siloed, about the future of shared American values and what we owe to each other?

SANDEL: From the outset of this crisis, we've heard the slogan, "We are all in this together." We hear it from politicians, advertisers, and celebrities. It evokes our mutual dependence and vulnerability in the face of COVID-19. It points to an inspiring ideal. But it rings hollow, because we know it doesn't describe the facts on the ground. Some of us work from home and hold meetings on Zoom. Others have little choice but to risk their health and lives serving the public and delivering things to our doorsteps, enabling us to avoid risk. The people we now celebrate as "essential workers" are not the best-paid or most-honored workers in our society. This is a moment to ask how to reconfigure the economy to bring the rewards of such workers into better alignment with the importance of the work they do. This moment makes vivid the need for a broader public debate about the inequality this crisis has highlighted and a reconsideration of what we owe one another as citizens.

For Further Reflection

1. According to Sandel, why do so many Americans resist mask wearing and social distancing?
2. What moral obligations does Sandel say we have in the pandemic?
3. What point does he make about the importance of trust?

Fair Allocation of Scarce Medical Resources in the Time of COVID-19

EZEKIEL J. EMANUEL, GOVIND PERSAD, ROSS UPSHUR, BEATRIZ THOME, MICHAEL PARKER, AARON GLICKMAN, CATHY ZHANG, CONNOR BOYLE, MAXWELL SMITH, AND JAMES P. PHILLIPS

Ezekiel Emanuel and his colleagues remind us that a society's systematic unequal distribution of power, money, and resources results in avoidable differences in health outcomes—health inequities. Part of the problem is that medical resources are not always allocated in morally plausible ways. These thinkers ask what moral values should guide us in avoiding and correcting inequities, and they agree on four essential principles.

Previous proposals for allocation of resources in pandemics and other settings of absolute scarcity, including our own prior research and analysis, converge on four fundamental values: maximizing the benefits produced by scarce resources, treating people equally, promoting and rewarding instrumental value, and giving priority to the worst off. Consensus exists that an individual person's wealth should not determine who lives or dies. Although medical treatment in the United States outside pandemic contexts is often restricted to those able to pay, no proposal endorses ability-to-pay allocation in a pandemic.

Each of these four values can be operationalized in various ways. Maximization of benefits can be understood as saving the most individual lives or as saving the most life-years by giving priority to patients likely to survive longest after treatment. Treating people equally could be attempted by random selection, such as a lottery, or by a first-come, first-served allocation. Instrumental value could be promoted by giving priority to those who can save others, or rewarded by giving priority to those who have saved others in the past. And priority to the worst off could be understood as giving priority

Ezekiel J. Emanuel, M.D., Govind Persad, Ross Upshur, Beatriz Thome, Michael Parker, Aaron Glickman, Cathy Zhang, Connor Boyle, Maxwell Smith, and James P. Phillips, "Fair Allocation of Scarce Medical Resources in the Time of COVID-19," *New England Journal of Medicine*, 2020; 382:2049-2055, https://www/nejm.org/doi/full/10.1056/nejmsb2005114.

either to the sickest or to younger people who will have lived the shortest lives if they die untreated.

The proposals for allocation discussed above also recognize that all these ethical values and ways to operationalize them are compelling. No single value is sufficient alone to determine which patients should receive scarce resources. Hence, fair allocation requires a multivalue ethical framework that can be adapted, depending on the resource and context in question.

WHO GETS HEALTH RESOURCES IN A COVID-19 PANDEMIC?

These ethical values—maximizing benefits, treating equally, promoting and rewarding instrumental value, and giving priority to the worst off—yield six specific recommendations for allocating medical resources in the Covid-19 pandemic: maximize benefits; prioritize health workers; do not allocate on a first-come, first-served basis; be responsive to evidence; recognize research participation; and apply the same principles to all Covid-19 and non–Covid-19 patients.

Recommendation 1: In the context of a pandemic, the value of maximizing benefits is most important. This value reflects the importance of responsible stewardship of resources: it is difficult to justify asking health care workers and the public to take risks and make sacrifices if the promise that their efforts will save and lengthen lives is illusory. Priority for limited resources should aim both at saving the most lives and at maximizing improvements in individuals' post-treatment length of life. Saving more lives and more years of life is a consensus value across expert reports. It is consistent both with utilitarian ethical perspectives that emphasize population outcomes and with nonutilitarian views that emphasize the paramount value of each human life. There are many reasonable ways of balancing saving more lives against saving more years of life; whatever balance between lives and life-years is chosen must be applied consistently.

Limited time and information in a Covid-19 pandemic make it justifiable to give priority to maximizing the number of patients that survive treatment with a reasonable life expectancy and to regard maximizing improvements in length of life as a subordinate aim. The latter becomes relevant only in comparing patients whose likelihood of survival is similar. Limited time and information during an emergency also counsel against incorporating patients' future quality of life, and quality-adjusted life-years, into benefit maximization. Doing so would require time-consuming collection of information and would present ethical and legal problems. However, encouraging all patients, especially those facing the prospect of intensive care, to document in an advance care directive what future quality of life they would regard as acceptable and when they would refuse ventilators or other life-sustaining interventions can be appropriate.

Operationalizing the value of maximizing benefits means that people who are sick but could recover if treated are given priority over those who are unlikely to recover even if treated and those who are likely to recover without treatment. Because young, severely ill patients will often comprise many of those who are sick but could recover with treatment, this operationalization also has the effect of giving priority to those who are worst off in the sense of being at risk of dying young and not having a full life.

Because maximizing benefits is paramount in a pandemic, we believe that removing a patient from a ventilator or an ICU bed to provide it to others in need is also justifiable and that patients should be made aware of this possibility at admission. Undoubtedly, withdrawing ventilators or ICU support from patients who arrived earlier to save those with better prognosis will be extremely psychologically traumatic for clinicians—and some clinicians might refuse to do so. However, many guidelines agree that the decision to withdraw a scarce resource to save others is not an act of killing and does not require the patient's consent. We agree with these guidelines that it is the ethical thing to do. Initially allocating beds and ventilators according to the value of maximizing benefits could help reduce the need for withdrawal.

Recommendation 2: Critical Covid-19 interventions—testing, PPE, ICU beds, ventilators, therapeutics, and vaccines—should go first to front-line health care workers and others who care for ill patients and who keep critical infrastructure operating, particularly workers who face a high risk of infection and whose training makes them difficult to replace. These workers should be given priority not because they are somehow more worthy, but because of their instrumental value: they are essential to pandemic response. If physicians and nurses are incapacitated, all patients—not just those with Covid-19—will suffer greater mortality and years of life lost. Whether health workers who need ventilators will be able to return to work is uncertain, but giving them priority for ventilators recognizes their assumption of the high-risk work of saving others, and it may also discourage absenteeism. Priority for critical workers must not be abused by prioritizing wealthy or famous persons or the politically powerful above first responders and medical staff—as has already happened for testing. Such abuses will undermine trust in the allocation framework.

Recommendation 3: For patients with similar prognoses, equality should be invoked and operationalized through random allocation, such as a lottery, rather than a first-come, first-served allocation process. First-come, first-served is used for such resources as transplantable kidneys, where scarcity is long-standing and patients can survive without the scarce resource. Conversely, treatments for coronavirus address urgent need, meaning that a first-come, first-served approach would unfairly benefit patients living nearer to health facilities. And first-come, first-served medication or vaccine distribution would encourage crowding and even violence during a period when social distancing is paramount. Finally, first-come, first-served approaches mean that people who happen to get sick later on, perhaps because of their strict adherence to recommended public health measures, are excluded from treatment, worsening outcomes without improving fairness. In the face of time pressure and limited information, random selection is also preferable to trying to make finer-grained prognostic judgments within a group of roughly similar patients.

Recommendation 4: Prioritization guidelines should differ by intervention and should respond to changing scientific evidence. For instance, younger patients should not be prioritized for Covid-19 vaccines, which prevent disease rather than cure it, or for experimental post- or pre-exposure prophylaxis. Covid-19 outcomes have been significantly worse in older persons and those with chronic conditions. Invoking the value of maximizing saving lives justifies giving older persons priority for vaccines immediately after health care workers and first responders. If the vaccine supply is insufficient for patients in the highest risk categories—those over 60 years of age or with coexisting conditions—then equality supports using random selection, such as a lottery, for vaccine allocation. Invoking instrumental value justifies prioritizing younger patients for vaccines only if epidemiologic modeling shows that this would be the best way to reduce viral spread and the risk to others.

Epidemiologic modeling is even more relevant in setting priorities for coronavirus testing. Federal guidance currently gives priority to health care workers and older patients, but reserving some tests for public health surveillance (as some states are doing) could improve knowledge about Covid-19 transmission and help researchers target other treatments to maximize benefits.

Conversely, ICU beds and ventilators are curative rather than preventive. Patients who need them face life-threatening conditions. Maximizing benefits requires consideration of prognosis—how long the patient is likely to live if treated—which may mean giving priority to younger patients and those with fewer coexisting conditions. This is consistent with the Italian guidelines that potentially assign a higher priority for intensive care access to younger patients with severe illness than to elderly patients. Determining the benefit-maximizing allocation of antivirals and other experimental treatments, which are likely to be most effective in patients who are seriously but not critically ill, will depend on scientific evidence. These treatments may produce the most benefit if preferentially allocated to patients who would fare badly on ventilation.

Recommendation 5: People who participate in research to prove the safety and effectiveness of vaccines and therapeutics should receive some priority for Covid-19 interventions. Their assumption of risk during their participation in research helps future patients, and they should be rewarded for that contribution. These rewards will also encourage other patients to participate in clinical trials. Research participation, however, should serve only as a tie-breaker among patients with similar prognoses.

Recommendation 6: There should be no difference in allocating scarce resources between patients with Covid-19 and those with other medical conditions. If the Covid-19 pandemic leads to absolute scarcity, that scarcity will affect all patients, including those with heart failure, cancer, and other serious and life-threatening conditions requiring prompt medical attention. Fair allocation of resources that prioritizes the value of maximizing benefits applies across all patients who need resources. For example, a doctor with an allergy who goes into anaphylactic shock and needs life-saving intubation and ventilator support should receive priority over Covid-19 patients who are not frontline health care workers.

IMPLEMENTING RATIONING POLICIES

The need to balance multiple ethical values for various interventions and in different circumstances is likely to lead to differing judgments about how much weight to give each value in particular cases. This highlights the need for fair and consistent allocation procedures that include the affected parties: clinicians, patients, public officials, and others. These procedures must be transparent to ensure public trust in their fairness.

The outcome of these fair allocation procedures, informed by the ethical values and recommendations delineated here, should be the development of prioritization guidelines that ensure that individual physicians are not faced with the terrible task of improvising decisions about whom to treat or making these decisions in isolation. Placing such burdens on individual physicians could exact an acute and life-long emotional toll. However, even well-designed guidelines can present challenging problems in real-time decision making and implementation. To help clinicians navigate these challenges, institutions may employ triage officers, physicians in roles outside direct patient care, or committees of experienced physicians and ethicists, to help apply guidelines, to assist with rationing decisions, or to make and implement choices outright—relieving the individual front-line clinicians of that burden. Institutions may also include appeals processes, but appeals should be limited to concerns about procedural mistakes, given time and resource constraints.

CONCLUSIONS

Governments and policy makers must do all they can to prevent the scarcity of medical resources. However, if resources do become scarce, we believe the six recommendations we delineate should be used to develop guidelines that can be applied fairly and consistently across cases. Such guidelines can ensure that individual doctors are never tasked with deciding unaided which patients receive life-saving care and which do not. Instead, we believe guidelines should be provided at a higher level of authority, both to alleviate physician burden and to ensure equal treatment. The described recommendations could shape the development of these guidelines.

For Further Reflection

1. Why do Emanuel and his colleagues say critical Covid-19 interventions should go first to front-line health care workers and others who care for ill patients and who keep critical infrastructure operating?
2. Why do they recommend against using a first-come, first-served rule to allocate medical resources?
3. When do they say it is appropriate to use random selection (lottery, for example) to distribute interventions?
4. How can prioritization guidelines help relieve the emotional toll on physicians?

Further Readings for Chapter 13

Krakt, Austin. "Who Should Be Saved First? Experts Offer Ethical Guidance." *New York Times*, March 24, 2020.

Mounk, Yascha. "The Extraordinary Decisions Facing Italian Doctors." *Atlantic*, March 11, 2020, https://www.theatlantic.com/ideas/archive/2020/03/who-gets-hospital-bed/607807/.

Persad, Govind, Alan Wertheimer, and Ezekiel J. Emanuel. "Principles for Allocation of Scarce Medical Interventions." *Lancet* 373 (2009): 423–431.

Tolchin, Benjamin, Sarah C. Hull, and Katherine Kraschel. "Triage and Justice in an Unjust Pandemic: Ethical Allocation of Scarce Medical Resources in the Setting of Racial and Socioeconomic Disparities." *Journal of Medical Ethics* 47 (2021): 200–202.

Witynski, Max. "Ethicist Laurie Zoloth Says It's Our Duty to Get a COVID-19 Vaccine and Wear Masks." *UChicago News*, January 26, 2021Our ethical duty to get a COVID-19 vaccine and wear masks | University of Chicago News (uchicago.edu).

CHAPTER 14

Food Ethics

What does ethics have to do with food? It has a lot to do with food, on several levels, in multiple spheres of life, in countless ways that involve us in fraught moral choices. Consider:

> Billions of animals are given painful, short lives and then killed to be eaten. Is that ethically permissible? What, if anything, should be done about it?
>
> Nearly a billion people worldwide are malnourished. Is that ethically permissible? What, if anything, should be done about it?
>
> Large numbers of badly paid agricultural workers work back-breaking, tenuous jobs so that much better-off people can enjoy cheap produce. Is that ethically permissible? What, if anything, should be done about it?
>
> These workers and the food they produce for industrialized countries are part of an economic framework that stretches all over the globe with effects on both the best-off and the worst-off. Indeed, food policy in America operates within that framework and also puts huge amounts of dollars here, withholding huge amounts of dollars there. Is that framework just? What, if anything, should be done about it? Who should be doing it?[1]

As momentous as these situations are, the kind of food we eat and how we produce it is having even larger effects on the planet in the form of climate change:

> As our climate continues to heat up and the impacts of that warming grow more frequent and severe, farmers and farm communities around the world

[1]Anne Barnhill, Mark Budolfson, and Tyler Doggett, *Food, Ethics, and Society* (New York: Oxford University Press, 2017), 1.

will be increasingly challenged. And US farmers won't be spared the damage that climate change is already beginning to inflict.

In fact, the industrial model that dominates our nation's agriculture—a model that neglects soils, reduces diversity, and relies too heavily on fertilizers and pesticides—makes US farms susceptible to climate impacts in several ways.

The combination of advancing climate change and an already-vulnerable industrial system is a "perfect storm" that threatens farmers' livelihoods and our food supply.[2]

The world's food system is responsible for about one-quarter of the planet-warming greenhouse gases that humans generate each year. That includes raising and harvesting all the plants, animals and animal products we eat—beef, chicken, fish, milk, lentils, kale, corn and more—as well as processing, packaging and shipping food to markets all over the world. If you eat food, you're part of this system. . . .

When forests are cleared to make room for farms and livestock—this happens on a daily basis in some parts of the world—large stores of carbon are released into the atmosphere, which heats up the planet. When cows, sheep and goats digest their food, they burp up methane, another potent greenhouse gas contributing to climate change. Animal manure and rice paddies are also big methane sources. Finally, fossil fuels are used to operate farm machinery, make fertilizer and ship food around the globe, all of which generate emissions.[3]

For many people, the most vexing—and personal—questions have to do with the morality of eating meat, the main focus of this chapter. Millions of people are vegetarians; they refrain from eating meat. Many of these exclude meat from their diets for religious, cultural, or medical reasons. But some vegetarians are *moral vegetarians*—they refuse to eat meat because they believe it is morally wrong to do so. They usually take this stand because they are aware of the horrendous cruelty and painful deaths that are an integral part of the meat industry, or they believe that animals have rights.

Moral arguments for and against eating meat are numerous, many of them more sophisticated than you might expect. Most of them will be covered in the following readings.

[2]Union of Concerned Scientists, "Climate Change and Agriculture: A Perfect Storm in Farm Country," March 20, 2019, https://www.ucsusa.org/resources/climate-change-and-agriculture.
[3]Julia Moskin, Brad Plumer, Rebecca Lieberman, and Eden Weingart, "Your Questions about Food and Climate Change, Answered," *New York Times*, April 30, 2019, https://www.nytimes.com/interactive/2019/04/30/dining/climate-change-food-eating-habits.html.

Shooting an Elephant

GEORGE ORWELL

George Orwell, pseudonym of Eric Arthur Blair (1903–1950), novelist and essayist, was born in India and served in the Indian imperial police. He rejected the imperialism connected with his position and went to live as a beggar in the East End of London. This experience became the subject of his book *Down and Out in Paris and London* (1933). His best-known works are *Animal Farm* (1945) and *Nineteen Eighty-Four* (1949), a pessimistic satire about future political tyranny.

This essay, written in the 1930s, is based on Orwell's experience in the imperial police in Burma.

In Moulmein, in Lower Burma, I was hated by large numbers of people—the only time in my life that I have been important enough for this to happen to me. I was sub-divisional police officer of the town, and in an aimless, petty kind of way anti-European feeling was very bitter. No one had the guts to raise a riot, but if a European woman went through the bazaars alone somebody would probably spit betel juice over her dress. As a police officer I was an obvious target and was baited whenever it seemed safe to do so. When a nimble Burman tripped me up on the football field and the referee (another Burman) looked the other way, the crowd yelled with hideous laughter. This happened more than once. In the end the sneering yellow faces of young men that met me everywhere, the insults hooted after me when I was at a safe distance, got badly on my nerves. The young Buddhist priests were the worst of all. There were several thousands of them in the town and none of them seemed to have anything to do except stand on street corners and jeer at Europeans. All this was perplexing and upsetting. For at that time I had already made up my mind that imperialism was an evil thing and the sooner I chucked up my job and got out of it the better. Theoretically—and secretly, of course—I was all for the Burmese and all against their oppressors, the British. As for the job I was doing, I hated it more bitterly than I can perhaps make clear. In a job like that you see the dirty work of Empire at close quarters. The wretched prisoners huddling in the stinking cages of the lock-ups, the grey, cowed faces of the long-term convicts, the scarred buttocks of the men who had been flogged with bamboos—all these oppressed me with an intolerable sense of guilt.

But I could get nothing into perspective. I was young and ill-educated and I had had to think out my problems in the utter silence that is imposed on every Englishman in the East. I did not even know that the British Empire is dying, still less did I know that it is a great deal better than the younger empires that are going to supplant it. All I knew was that I was stuck between my hatred of the empire I served and my rage against the evil-spirited little beasts who tried to make my job impossible. With one part of my mind I thought of the British Raj as an unbreakable tyranny, as something clamped down, in *saecula saeculorum,* upon the will of prostrate peoples; with another part I thought that the greatest joy in the world would be to drive a bayonet into a Buddhist priest's guts. Feelings like these are the normal by-products of imperialism; ask any Anglo-Indian official, if you can catch him off duty.

One day something happened which in a roundabout way was enlightening. It was a tiny incident in itself, but it gave me a better glimpse than I had had before of the real nature of imperialism—the real motives for which despotic governments act. Early one morning the sub-inspector at a police station the other end of town rang me up on the 'phone and said that an elephant was ravaging the bazaar. Would I please come and do something about it? I did not know what I could do, but I wanted to see what was happening and I got on to a pony and started out. I took my rifle, an old .44 Winchester and much too small to kill an elephant, but I thought the noise might be useful *in terrorem.* Various Burmans stopped me on the way and told me about the elephant's doings. It was not, of course, a wild elephant, but a tame one which had gone "must." It had been chained up, as tame elephants always are when their attack of "must" is due, but on the previous night it had broken its chain and escaped. Its mahout, the only person who could manage it when it was in that state, had set out in pursuit, but had taken the wrong direction and was now twelve hours' journey away, and in the morning the elephant had suddenly reappeared in the town. The Burmese population had no weapons and were quite helpless against it. It had already destroyed somebody's bamboo hut, killed a cow and raided some fruit-stalls and devoured the stock; also it had met the municipal rubbish van and, when the driver jumped out and took to his heels, had turned the van over and inflicted violences upon it.

The Burmese sub-inspector and some Indian constables were waiting for me in the quarter where the elephant had been seen. It was a very poor quarter, a labyrinth of squalid bamboo huts, thatched with palm-leaf, winding all over a steep hillside. I remember that it was a cloudy, stuffy morning at the beginning of the rains. We began questioning the people as to where the elephant had gone and, as usual, failed to get any definite information. That is invariably the case in the East; a story always sounds clear enough at a distance, but the nearer you get to the scene of events the vaguer it becomes.

Some of the people said that the elephant had gone in one direction, some said that he had gone in another, some professed not even to have heard of any elephant. I had almost made up my mind that the whole story was a pack of lies, when we heard yells a little distance away. There was a loud, scandalized cry of "Go away, child! Go away this instant!" and an old woman with a switch in her hand came around the corner of a hut, violently shooing away a crowd of naked children. Some more women followed, clicking their tongues and exclaiming; evidently there was something that the children ought not to have seen. I rounded the hut and saw a man's dead body sprawling in the mud. He was an Indian, a black Dravidian coolie, almost naked, and he could not have been dead many minutes. The people said that the elephant had come suddenly upon him round the corner of the hut, caught him with its trunk, put its foot on his back and ground him into the earth. This was the rainy season and the ground was soft, and his face had scored a trench a foot deep and a couple of yards long. He was lying on his belly with arms crucified and head sharply twisted to one side. His face was coated with mud, the eyes wide open, the teeth bared and grinning with an expression of unendurable agony. (Never tell me, by the way, that the dead look peaceful. Most of the corpses I have seen looked devilish.) The friction of the great beast's foot had stripped the skin from his back as neatly as one skins a rabbit. As soon as I saw the dead man I sent an orderly to a friend's house nearby to borrow an elephant rifle. I had already sent back the pony, not wanting it to go mad with fright and throw me if it smelt the elephant.

The orderly came back in a few minutes with a rifle and five cartridges, and meanwhile some Burmans had arrived and told us that the elephant was in the paddy fields below, only a few hundred yards away. As I started forward practically the whole population of the quarter flocked out of the houses and followed me. They had seen the rifle and were all shouting excitedly that I was going to shoot the elephant. They had not shown much interest in the elephant when he was merely ravaging their homes, but it was different now that he was going to be shot. It was a bit of fun to them, as it would be to an English crowd; besides they wanted the meat. It made me vaguely uneasy. I had no intention of shooting the elephant—I had merely sent for the rifle to defend myself if necessary—and it is always unnerving to have a crowd following you. I marched down the hill, looking and feeling a fool, with the rifle over my shoulder and an evergrowing army of people jostling at my heels. At the bottom, when you got away from the huts, there was a metalled road and beyond that a miry waste of paddy fields a thousand yards across, not yet ploughed but soggy from the first rains and dotted with coarse grass. The elephant was standing eight yards from the road, his left side towards us. He took not the slightest notice of the crowd's approach. He was tearing up bunches of grass, beating them against his knees to clean them and stuffing them into his mouth.

I had halted on the road. As soon as I saw the elephant I knew with perfect certainty that I ought not to shoot him. It is a serious matter to shoot a working elephant—it is comparable to destroying a huge and costly piece of machinery—and obviously one ought not to do it if it can possibly be avoided. And at that distance, peacefully eating, the elephant looked no more dangerous than a cow. I thought then and I think now that his attack of "must" was already passing off; in which case he would merely wander harmlessly about until the mahout came back and caught him. Moreover, I did not in the least want to shoot him. I decided that I would watch him for a little while to make sure that he did not turn savage again, and then go home.

But at that moment I glanced round at the crowd that had followed me. It was an immense crowd, two thousand at the least and growing every minute. It blocked the road for a long distance on either side. I looked at the sea of yellow faces above the garish clothes—faces all happy and excited over this bit of fun, all certain that the elephant was going to be shot. They were watching me as they would watch a conjurer about to perform a trick. They did not like me, but with the magical rifle in my hands I was momentarily worth watching. And suddenly I realized that I should have to shoot the elephant after all. The people expected it of me and I had to do it; I could feel their two thousand wills pressing me forward, irresistibly. And it was at this moment, as I stood there with the rifle in my hands, that I first grasped the hollowness, the futility of the white man's dominion in the East. Here was I, the white man with his gun, standing in front of the unarmed native crowd—seemingly the leading actor of the piece; but in reality I was only an absurd puppet pushed to and fro by the will of those yellow faces behind. I perceived in this moment that when the white man turns tyrant it is his own freedom that he destroys. He becomes a sort of hollow, posing dummy, the conventionalized figure of a sahib. For it is the condition of his rule that he shall spend his life in trying to impress the "natives," and so in every crisis he has got to do what the "natives" expect of him. He wears a mask, and his face grows to fit it. I had got to shoot the elephant. I had committed myself to doing it when I sent for the rifle. A sahib has got to act like a sahib; he has got to appear resolute, to know his own mind and do definite things. To come all that way, rifle in hand, with two thousand people marching at my heels, and then to trail feebly away, having done nothing—no, that was impossible. The crowd would laugh at me. And my whole life, every white man's life in the East, was one long struggle not to be laughed at.

But I did not want to shoot the elephant. I watched him beating his bunch of grass against his knees, with that preoccupied grandmotherly air that elephants have. It seemed to me that it would be murder to shoot him. At that age I was not squeamish about killing animals, but I had never shot an elephant and never wanted to. (Somehow it always seems worse to kill a *large* animal.) Besides, there was the beast's owner to be considered. Alive, the elephant was worth at least a hundred pounds; dead, he would only be worth the value of his tusks, five pounds, possibly. But I had got to act quickly. I turned to some experienced-looking Burmans who had been there when we arrived, and asked them how the elephant had been behaving. They all said the same thing: he took no notice of you if you left him alone, but he might charge if you went too close to him.

It was perfectly clear to me what I ought to do. I ought to walk up to within, say, twenty-five yards of the elephant and test his behavior. If he charged, I could shoot; if he took no notice of me, it would be safe to leave him until the mahout came back. But also I knew that I was going to do no such thing. I was a poor shot with a rifle and the ground was soft mud into which one would sink at every step. If the elephant charged and I missed him, I should have about as much chance as a toad under a steamroller. But even then I was not thinking particularly of my own skin, only of the watchful yellow faces behind. For at that moment, with the crowd watching me, I was not afraid in the ordinary sense, as I would have been if I had been alone. A white man mustn't be frightened in front of "natives"; and so, in general, he isn't frightened. The sole thought in my mind was that if anything went wrong those two thousand Burmans would see me pursued, caught, trampled on and reduced to a grinning corpse like that Indian up the hill. And if that happened it was quite probable that some of them would laugh. That would never do. There was only one alternative. I shoved the cartridges into the magazine and lay down on the road to get a better aim.

The crowd grew very still, and a deep, low, happy sigh, as of people who see the theatre curtain go up at last, breathed from innumerable throats. They were going to have their bit of fun after all. The rifle was a beautiful German thing with cross-hair sights. I did not then know that in shooting an elephant one would shoot to cut an imaginary bar running from ear-hole to ear-hole. I ought, therefore, as the elephant was sideways on, to have aimed straight at his ear-hole; actually I aimed several inches in front of this, thinking the brain would be further forward.

When I pulled the trigger I did not hear the bang or feel the kick—one never does when a shot goes home—but I heard the devilish roar of glee that went up from the crowd. In that instant, in too short a time, one would have thought, even for the bullet to get there, a mysterious, terrible change had come over the elephant. He neither stirred nor fell, but every line of his body had altered. He looked suddenly stricken, shrunken, immensely old, as though the frightful impact of the bullet had paralysed him without knocking him down. At last, after what seemed a long time—it might have been five seconds, I dare say—he sagged flabbily to his knees. His mouth slobbered. An enormous senility seemed to have settled upon him. One could have imagined him thousands of years old. I fired again into the same spot. At the second shot he did not collapse but climbed with desperate slowness to his feet and stood weakly upright, with legs sagging and head drooping. I fired a third time. That was the shot that did for him. You could see the agony of it jolt his whole body and knock the last remnant of strength from his legs. But in falling he seemed for a moment to rise, for as his hind legs collapsed beneath him he seemed to tower upward like a huge rock toppling, his trunk reaching skywards like a tree. He trumpeted, for the first and only time. And then down he came, his belly towards me, with a crash that seemed to shake the ground even where I lay.

I got up. The Burmans were already racing past me across the mud. It was obvious that the elephant would never rise again, but he was not dead. He was breathing very rhythmically with long rattling gasps, his great mound of a side painfully rising and falling. His mouth was wide open—I could see far down into caverns of pale pink throat. I waited a long time for him to die, but his breathing did not weaken. Finally I fired my two remaining shots into the spot where I thought his heart must be. The thick blood welled out of him like red velvet, but still he did not die. His body did not even jerk when the shots hit him, the tortured breathing continued without a pause. He was dying, very slowly and in great agony, but in some world remote from me where not even a bullet could damage him further. I felt that I had got to put an end to that dreadful noise. It seemed dreadful to see the great beast lying there, powerless to move and yet powerless to die, and not even to be able to finish him. I sent back for my small rifle and poured shot after shot into his heart and down his throat. They seemed to make no impression. The tortured gasps continued as steadily as the ticking of a clock.

In the end I could not stand it any longer and went away. I heard later that it took him half an hour to die. Burmans were bringing dahs and baskets even before I left, and I was told they had stripped his body almost to the bones by the afternoon.

Afterwards, of course, there were endless discussions about the shooting of the elephant. The owner was furious, but he was only an Indian and could do nothing. Besides, legally I had done the right thing, for a mad elephant has to be killed, like a mad dog, if its owner fails to control it. Among the Europeans opinion was divided. The older men said I was right, the younger men said it was a damn shame to shoot an elephant for killing a coolie, because an elephant was worth more than any damn Coringhee coolie. And afterwards I was very glad that the coolie had been killed; it put me legally in the right and it gave me a sufficient pretext for shooting the elephant. I often wondered whether any of the others grasped that I had done it solely to avoid looking a fool.

For Further Reflection

1. What is the message you get out of this story?
2. How does Orwell connect imperialism with the shooting of the elephant? Can you elaborate on the few hints he offers?
3. Why does Orwell say he knows with perfect certainty that he ought not to shoot the elephant? Why is it wrong? Why does he shoot him? Can you identify with the dilemma Orwell feels?

How to Argue for (and Against) Ethical Veganism

TRISTRAM MCPHERSON

Tristram McPherson is an associate professor in the department of philosophy at Ohio State University. In this article, he does two things at once: (1) he argues that it is wrong both to kill animals and to eat meat, and (2) he shows by example how to write a well-reasoned philosophy essay.

This paper has two goals. The first is to offer a carefully reasoned argument for *ethical veganism:* the view that it is (at least typically) wrong to eat or otherwise use animal products. The second goal is to give you, the reader, some important tools for developing, evaluating, and replying to reasoned arguments for ethical conclusions. I begin by offering you a brief essay, arguing that it is wrong to eat meat. This essay both introduces central elements of my case for veganism, and serves as one helpful model of a short ethics essay. In the remainder of this paper, I use the model essay as a target, to illustrate important strategies for developing objections to ethical arguments. I will also illustrate a range of important ways for the vegan to reply to these objections. You can use the models and skills I illustrate here in your own essays, and in your reasoned evaluation of ethical arguments. I conclude that the arguments and replies offered in this paper add up to a powerful reasoned case for ethical veganism. You can practice the skills I illustrate here to decide for yourself—in a reasoned way—whether my conclusion is correct.

I begin with the promised model essay:

IT IS WRONG TO EAT MEAT

Most of us think that it would be wrong to adopt a puppy from a shelter, in order to take it home and torture it until it dies. However, we do not think it is wrong to eat a steak for dinner. In this essay, I will argue that these views are hard to square with each other, and that the second view is false: it is wrong to eat meat. My argument has the following structure:

1. It is wrong to make animals suffer
2. If it is wrong to make animals suffer, then it is wrong to kill animals
3. If it is wrong to kill animals, then it is wrong to eat meat

C. It is wrong to eat meat.

This argument is *valid*. This means that the conclusion must be true if all of the premises are true. I will defend each of these premises in turn.

First, why think that it is wrong to make animals suffer? To begin, think about why it is wrong to make another person suffer. Part of the most plausible explanation is that because suffering is awful to experience, it is wrong to inflict suffering. Because an animal's suffering is awful for it, this explanation entails that it is wrong to make an animal suffer.

This premise of my argument assumes that animals *can* suffer, which is mildly controversial. For example, René Descartes suggested that animals are just complicated machines with no inner lives (1991 [1640], 148). However, Descartes' views are scientifically indefensible (see Allen and Trestman 2014, §7.1), so I set them aside.

You might object to my case for my first premise that it is only wrong to make a creature suffer if that creature is an ethical agent: the sort of being who can be morally responsible for its actions. But this is false. It is wrong to make babies suffer, and they are not ethical agents. You might object that it is only wrong to make *human beings* suffer. This is implausible for several reasons. First, think about torturing a baby: what is wrong with this is surely the nature of the suffering inflicted, not the fact that the baby has a human genetic code. Second, imagine a non-human animal with a miraculous mutation, which has the ability to speak, reason, and feel as much as you or I do. Surely the mere fact that such an animal is not genetically human does not make it okay to torture it (compare Peter Singer's argument against such "speciesism" in his 1977). And, finally, think again about the case I began this essay with: it is wrong to torture a puppy. But surely the central explanation here is just the same as with a human victim: torture will inflict horrible suffering on the puppy, and it is wrong to inflict such suffering.

Some authors, like Carl Cohen (1986, 867), insist that all suffering is not equal: human suffering is much more ethically important than animal suffering. My argument is compatible with this thesis. I am not arguing that torturing a puppy is just as bad as torturing a human being. I think the latter is typically much worse. My claim is only that making the puppy suffer is wrong, and that the pleasure a human being might take from torturing it does not justify inflicting that suffering.

Next, I argue that if it is wrong to make animals suffer, it is wrong to kill them. Some people find the idea that it is wrong to kill animals much less intuitive than the idea that it is wrong to make them suffer. However, an example shows that this combination of views—that it is wrong to make animals suffer, but not to kill them—is difficult to defend. Suppose that there is a cow that has a disease that will be fatal unless treated by giving the cow a painful medical operation. If the cow would go on to have a long and pleasant life after the operation, performing this operation seems good, not wrong. This shows that an ordinarily wrongful act—inflicting suffering on a cow—can be permissible if it is necessary to save the cow's life. But if *saving* an animal's life can justify inflicting suffering that would otherwise be wrong, it is hard to understand how *taking* that animal's life could be a matter of ethical indifference.

We can bolster this initial argument by combining it with a plausible explanation of why it is wrong to kill animals. One important reason why killing a *person* is typically wrong is that killing typically deprives the victim of an objectively valuable future. That is, killing someone deprives them of the valuable experiences activities, projects, etc. that they would otherwise have had (compare Marquis 1989, §11; I do not claim, with Marquis, that this is the "primary" thing wrong with killing). This principle applies to animals as well: just as suffering can make an animal's life go badly, pleasant experiences can make it go well. So, just as with humans, it is plausible that it is (typically) wrong to kill animals because doing so deprives them of a valuable future.

Finally, I argue that if it is wrong to kill animals, it is wrong to eat meat. Killing and eating are, obviously, not the same thing: in our economically specialized society, many meat-eaters never even see the animals they eat alive, let alone make them suffer or kill them. However, this doesn't mean that eating meat is okay. To see why, consider an analogy.

There is a new restaurant in town: the food is sensational, and the prices are very low. How do they do it? Here's how: the owner kidnaps world-class chefs, and enslaves them at the restaurant. Suppose that the owner is connected with the mob, and going to the police would just get you killed. Your patronizing the restaurant does not enslave anyone, but it still seems wrong. The explanation for why it is wrong is roughly that by patronizing the restaurant, you would be *complicit* in wrongdoing: you would be benefiting from a wrongful act (enslavement), while economically supporting the wrongdoer (the slaver).

Making animals suffer may be less awful than enslaving another human being. But the same form of explanation applies to eating meat. The raising of animals for food causes those animals a horrifying amount of suffering, and early death (see Mason and Singer 1990 for some of the literally grisly details). If it is wrong to kill animals and to cause them to suffer, then the industry that produces our meat acts wrongly on a massive scale. It is wrong to eat meat because in doing so you are complicit with that massive and systematic wrongdoing.

In this essay I have argued that it is wrong to eat meat. One clarification of this conclusion is in order: like many ethical claims, it should be read as a claim about what is *typically* true. It is typically wrong for you to break all of my fingers, but if doing so is the only way to prevent nuclear catastrophe, break away! Similarly, there may be unusual circumstances in which it is permissible or even required to eat meat. Nonetheless, if my argument is sound, each of us does wrong almost every time we sit down to a meal that contains meat.

I have written "It is Wrong to Eat Meat" as a model short philosophy essay. Unless your professor tells you otherwise, you would do well to emulate several of the stylistic features of this essay:

- The introduction offers a brief clear motive for the question addressed, states the essay's thesis, and previews the argument to come;
- The argument of the paper is summarized in valid premise/conclusion form;
- The essay does not waste words: every sentence is dedicated to developing the central argument, explaining a concept, introducing an objection or replying to it, or doing other important work. Even the conclusion does important work, introducing a crucial clarification of the argument.
- The essay does not use lengthy quotes from its sources: instead, it cites those sources after stating (in my own words) key claims that I take from them.

The argument of this essay is also an excellent target for reasoned objections. I now discuss how to offer such objections.

First, let's back up a bit and think about the activity that we are engaged in. We are seeking to make and to evaluate reasoned arguments about ethics. For example, the model essay did not just disagree with the claim that it is okay to eat meat; it offered reasons for thinking that claim is incorrect, and it organized those reasons into an argument. Making an argument does not simply aim to persuade your reader. I know, for example, that no reasoned argument is as likely to change eating habits as grisly video footage of life inside the animal factories that produce our meat. If philosophers aimed simply to persuade, we would write clever advertising, rather than carefully argued essays. Instead, my aim as a philosopher is to seek the truth together with my audience, in a way that respects the ability of each person involved to find the truth herself, using her own ability to reason. My aim now is to offer you some tools to enable you to skillfully engage in this sort of respectful argumentation.

For many of you, the conclusion of the model essay is a challenge to your ethical views. You may be tempted to reply to this sort of challenge by simply disagreeing with the conclusion. Resist this temptation: if an author offers you an argument, and you ignore the argument and simply reject their conclusion, it is very difficult to seek the truth together with you. So, when you are presented with an argument, your central question should be: does this argument give me good reason to accept its conclusion? The model argument appears to be *valid*: the truth of its premises would logically ensure the truth of the conclusion. When you object to a valid argument, you should focus on objecting to its premises, not the conclusion. This is because the argument purports to offer you reasons to accept its conclusion, and if you cannot explain why you should reject those reasons, you aren't providing a compelling reply to the argument.[1] On the other hand, if you can identify a good reason to reject one of the premises of an argument, you have made an important and constructive contribution, by explaining why a reasonable person should not be persuaded by the argument. This is why it is important to learn how to offer reasoned objections to the premises of an argument.

Developing reasoned objections is in part a creative task, and there is no recipe for doing it well. However, there are several useful general strategies for finding good objections. Taking the model essay as a target, I will introduce some of these strategies, and illustrate them with exemplary objections to the model essay. Another important philosophical skill is to assess the import of

[1]This paragraph simplifies in several ways. First, in some arguments the premises (even if true) simply fail to support the conclusion, even given a charitable interpretation. Clearly demonstrating that fact can be a powerful way of objecting to such an argument. Second, some philosophers have argued that it can be legitimate to object to certain arguments as a whole, without criticizing either specific premises or the logical structure of the argument. For discussion relevant to our topic, see McPherson 2014 and *2016-a*.

potential objections. Because of this, when I consider each objection I will discuss whether it can be answered, whether it calls for some amendment to the model essay's argument, or whether it constitutes a promising line of objection to the overall strategy of the model argument. The point of carefully exploring objections and replies is to arrive ultimately at the best arguments that can be made on each side of an ethical issue, like the issue of whether it is wrong to eat meat. Because objections should target the premises of an argument (as I have emphasized), I will organize my discussion by focusing on each premise in turn.

PREMISE ONE: INFLICTING SUFFERING

Premise One of the model argument says:

1. It is wrong to make animals suffer

In this section, I consider objections to this principle that are instances of three general strategies for identifying objections: looking to extreme cases, appealing to an obscured distinction, and appealing to a competing ethical principle.

One excellent way to find objections to ethical principles is to look to extreme cases (Hájek *forthcoming-b,* §4; this and Hájek *forthcoming-a* are excellent sources of heuristics for doing philosophy, although they are most suited for somewhat advanced philosophy students). There are several relevant *types* of extreme cases. One type of extreme case involves *raising the stakes.* Suppose, for example, that some generic supervillain will incinerate the earth unless you torture this puppy. It is surely required (and not wrong) to torture the puppy in that case. So it is not *always* wrong to cause animals to suffer.

It is not enough to find an objection: you should also think about how someone sympathetic to the argument that you are objecting to should reply to your objection. In this case, there is a decisive reply to this objection: the conclusion of the model essay already granted that it is only *typically* wrong to eat meat. Because scenarios involving comic-book supervillains are extremely atypical, this is not an effective objection to the argument of the model essay. There is an important lesson here: make sure that you interpret the argument you are objecting to accurately and fairly. Failure to do this is so common it has its own name: the *straw man* fallacy.

A different sort of extreme case is more potent. If we arranged animals on a continuum of cognitive sophistication, we would notice that puppies (which featured in the model argument) are relatively close to us on that continuum.

So: what happens to the model argument as we move to animals farther away from us on that continuum? Here is one salient example: oysters and other bivalves lack brains, and so are almost certainly incapable of suffering. Because one cannot make an oyster suffer, it cannot be wrong to eat an oyster for the reasons suggested in the model essay.[2] Because there is nothing atypical about eating oysters, this case is an important objection to the argument in the model essay.

One important way to reply to an objection is to concede that it requires one to modify one's argument. This objection to the model argument is powerful, and the best reply is thus concessive. I grant that the model argument does not explain why it is wrong to eat oysters, and so I conclude that the conclusion of the model argument should be restricted to apply only to eating animals that can suffer.

This in turn raises a further question: *which* animals, exactly, can suffer? Here there are formidable methodological barriers to investigation (Allen and Trestman 2014, §4). The core problem is that we have no direct access to animals' experiential states, so we must reason about their inner lives on the basis of behavioral, functional, neurobiological and evolutionary considerations. Unsurprisingly, the strongest case for suffering can be made for mammals, where the evolutionary and neurobiological parallels with humans are closest. However, we should not assume that only mammals can experience pain; some have argued that there is evidence for pain experience in all vertebrates (Varner 2003), and in many cases we may simply lack adequate empirical knowledge to be able to assess the issue. Especially hard cases include cephalopods such as squid, which are behaviorally very sophisticated but evolutionarily distant from us. My approach to this issue invokes a modest sort of precautionary principle: Because we are not in a position to be confident about whether birds, fish, and cephalopods can suffer, we are not in a position to know whether we act wrongly when we eat them. Indifference to the possibility that we act wrongly is a vice, and we should avoid eating these animals on that basis.

A second powerful way to find objections to a premise is to identify an important distinction that the argument for that premise ignores. For example, one could argue that Premise One of the model essay becomes less plausible once we make the distinction between *being in pain* and *suffering*. Some philosophers grant that many animals can be in pain. However, they suggest that suffering requires something in addition to being in pain that most non-human animals lack. For example, perhaps it requires

[2]There might, however, be other arguments that count against eating animals that cannot suffer: for example, one could offer environmental objections to how some such animals are raised or harvested, or appeal to the idea that simply being a fellow animal is morally significant.

a conscious belief: that *I am having this pain* (for discussion, see Akhtar 2011, 496–499). An objector might argue that it is suffering in this sense—and not merely being in pain—that is ethically significant. If this were true, then my argument would at very least be incomplete: I would need to discuss the nature of suffering more carefully, and then explore which animals can experience it.

The best reply to this objection begins by emphasizing that the important issue here is not how we should use the word *suffering* (in philosophy you should usually avoid fighting about how to use words). It is rather whether conscious belief (or something like it) is required for pain to be ethically significant. If we are clear on this point, another extreme case shows why this objection fails. The most intense pains tend to fully occupy us: one is unlikely to be thinking anything—let alone *I am having this pain*—when in utter agony. But surely it is wrong to inflict utter agony on someone, because of how awful it feels (compare Rachels 2011, 898). This shows that it can be wrong to inflict pain that does not count as suffering in the objector's stipulated sense. If this is true of agonizing pains, it should be true of less intense pains. And if it is true for our own case, it should be true for animals as well. I thus conclude that this objection fails.

A third way to object to an ethical premise is to identify and defend an independently plausible ethical principle that conflicts with it. You may have encountered such a principle in your previous study of ethics, or you might be able to develop one yourself. One example of this strategy is to argue against Premise One of the model argument by appealing to contractualism, which is one of the most influential contemporary approaches to ethics and political philosophy. The basic idea of contractualism is that moral (or political) principles are principles that reasonable persons would agree to as rules to govern their lives together. So understood, contractualism can seem to cast serious doubt on the ethical significance of animals. As Peter Carruthers notes, according to the contractualist, "Morality is viewed as constructed *by* human beings, in order to facilitate interactions *between* human beings . . ." (1992, 102, emphasis his). Because it is hard to see how a principle like Premise One would help to facilitate such interactions, contractualism may seem to give us good reasons to reject this premise.

I have two interlocking replies to this objection. First, the most plausible forms of contractualism do not have the implications that the objector claims. Exemplary here is T. M. Scanlon's extremely influential contractualist ethical theory. Scanlon is careful to argue that his theory can be extended to protect animals (1998,177–84). Further, Scanlon is clear that we have strong reasons that are not based in the contractual principle, so his view is compatible with the idea that we might have such reasons not to harm animals. Other philosophers have been more ambitious, offering contractualist arguments on behalf of animals (Rowlands 2002, Ch. 3; Talbert 2006).

Of course, there are some contractualist theories that have the implications that Carruthers suggests. But these are controversial views among contractualists, and contractualism itself is only one of a number of controversial and competing general ethical theories. Because of this controversy, however, it is unlikely that we should be confident in the truth of these contractualist theories. Without such confidence, however, it is hard to see how these theories could give us good reasons to reject Premise One. Further, the case of animals is exactly one where these theories appear implausible. Because it is obviously wrong for me to torture puppies just for fun, it counts against a moral theory that implies otherwise. This sort of case is part of a deep and more general challenge. As Martha Nussbaum (2006) and others have argued, many of our most important moral concerns address the interests of distinctively vulnerable parties (such as children, the severely mentally handicapped, and animals), and not simply the interactions between equally capable adult humans. A contractualism that ignores these interests is indefensible. In light of these considerations, it will be very difficult to mount a compelling case against Premise One of my argument that appeals to contractualism.

In this section I have considered three kinds of objections to Premise One of my argument. An important part of my reply has been concessive, refining the premise that I want to defend: so refined, the thesis states that it is typically wrong to inflict pain on a range of animals, including at least all mammals. So refined, I have suggested that it is very difficult to reasonably reject this premise.

PREMISE TWO: KILLING ANIMALS

Premise Two of the model argument says:

2. If it is wrong to make animals suffer, then it is wrong to kill animals

This premise is *conditional.* In order to successfully object to a conditional, one would need to find a reasonable way to accept the *antecedent* (i.e. the first part) of the conditional, while rejecting the *consequent* (i.e. the second part). Here, this would mean granting that it is wrong to make animals suffer, and arguing that it is nonetheless okay to kill them. I will consider three strategies for objecting to this premise. These strategies all target my explanation of why we should accept this premise. This was the idea that the wrongness of killing is well-explained by the fact that killing deprives the victim of a valuable future. The first strategy appeals to a competing explanation, the second strategy objects that my explanation is incomplete, and the third objects that my explanation has a false presupposition.

Just as a promising objection can be based in a competing ethical principle, so we can base an objection in a competing ethical explanation. In arguing for Premise Two, I offered a general explanation of the wrongness of killing: that killing can be wrong because it deprives the victim of a valuable future. One seemingly competing explanation is that killing you would be wrong because it would violate your autonomy. *Violation* here includes two important and separable ideas. First, killing you would interfere with your exercise of your autonomy. You cannot live your life in the way you choose if you are dead. Second, killing you would be a way of failing to respect your autonomy: if I take myself to be licensed to kill you, I take myself to have the right to ride roughshod over your own view of how your life should go.

In certain cases, this explanation of the wrongness of killing may seem markedly superior to the "valuable future" explanation offered in the model essay. For example, suppose that Alice is near death and in pain, but wishes to continue living. If I inject her with a lethal dose of morphine, I wrongly kill her. (Notice that this is another instance of using an extreme case to make a point.) The best explanation here is that I have wrongly failed to respect her right to autonomously determine whether she continues to live. By contrast, it is not clear that I deprive her of a valuable future at all. Because most non-human animals are not autonomous agents (there may be borderline cases of non-human agency, such as chimpanzees), this competing explanation suggests that Premise Two is false.

To see why this objection is not promising, notice that the autonomy-violation explanation also clearly fails in some cases. Because you are an autonomous agent, I should not force you to go to bed at a certain time, even if it is good for you to do so. By contrast, I act *rightly* when I paternalistically force my three-year-old son to go to bed at an appropriate time. This is because he is not an autonomous agent, It would obviously be very wrong to kill my son, but since he is not an autonomous agent, this cannot be explained in terms of autonomy violation.

You might think that this leaves us at an impasse: we have two candidate explanations of the wrongness of killing (valuable future-deprivation and autonomy-violation) and counter-examples to each. Does this show that both must be bad explanations? No. A better diagnosis is that each of these accounts provides a *typically sufficient but not necessary* explanation of the wrongness of killing. That is: killing can be wrong *either* because it violates autonomy, *or* because it deprives the victim of a valuable future (or both). On this account, one of the reasons why it is uncontroversial that it is wrong to kill an adult human in a range of ordinary circumstances is that there are several different things wrong with such killing. Because Premise Two of the model argument requires only that the valuable future-deprivation explanation is typically sufficient, this reply vindicates that premise.

Another important way to object to an ethical principle or explanation is to argue that it is *incomplete.* Whenever someone offers a principle or explanation, it is always a good idea to ask: is that *all* that is doing the important explanatory work here? Or have I only been given a part of the best ethical principle that applies to this sort of case? For example, one might think that a future's merely *being valuable* is not sufficient to explain why we must not eliminate it. Suppose that my wife and I were debating whether to have another child. If we did, that child would almost certainly have a valuable future. But it seems clear that I do no wrong simply by preventing that future: my having had a vasectomy does not make me akin to a murderer. Michael Tooley (1972) proposes an explanation of this fact: in order for it to be wrong to deprive an entity of a valuable future, that entity needs to have the capacity to care about its own continued existence. Because the child I do not conceive does not currently exist, it cannot care about its future existence, and hence I do not wrong it by preventing its future, on Tooley's view. One might appeal to Tooley's view to argue that it is not wrong to kill most animals because they are not cognitively sophisticated enough to care about their continued existence.

It is not obvious whether some animals can care about their futures in the relevant way. However, I set this aside, and instead focus on arguing against Tooley's explanatory claim (notice that I do so by appealing to extreme cases reasoning). Suppose that artificial intelligence research advances to the point that we are capable of creating intelligent and autonomous androids, capable of almost everything humans are: sophisticated reasoning, love, physical and emotional pain, etc. Suppose this type of android is programmed to be simply incapable of caring about its own continued existence, although it can and typically does care deeply about particular others. In light of this programming, such androids would be predictably prone to certain tragic behavior: they would sometimes lay down their lives to save others from inconsequential harms. It would be obviously wrong to kill such an android—even with its consent—to save yourself from a splinter. The android's inability to care about its future is a rational imperfection, but not one that licenses killing it.

We can square our judgments about the nonexistent child and the android if we suggest that the android is (imagined to be) an ethically significant being that now exists, while the non-existent child is a merely possible entity. We can then amend our ethical explanation as follows: it is wrong to deprive existing creatures of valuable futures, but it is not wrong to prevent non-existing entities from coming into existence. This explanation implies that it is wrong to kill existing animals, and so supports Premise Two.

A third way to object to an explanation is to argue that it has a false presupposition. That is: it works only by implicitly assuming some false claim. One crucial presupposition of my explanation of the wrongness of killing animals is that if I refrain from killing a cow today, there is a single moral patient—the cow—that will enjoy various pleasant cow experiences in the future. The objector suggests that we have reason to doubt this, if we think carefully about the conditions for the continued existence of a given moral patient.

The objection can be initially motivated by another extreme case: suppose that a mad scientist was able to map the neural structure of our brains, and then *swap* those structures: your brain is "wiped" and then rebuilt in accordance with the map of my brain, so that your body is now the home of beliefs, desires, and "memories" near identical to mine (pre-operation), and vice-versa. Suppose that the mad scientist performs this swap shortly after I injected my own heart with a slow-acting but lethal poison. Arguably, thanks to the mad scientist's intervention, I will have survived, and succeeded in killing you, rather than myself.

Some philosophers use cases like these to argue that *psychological continuity* is required for personal identity or ethically significant survival. In the case above, the idea is that I survive the operation because the surviving body houses a psychology that is continuous with my pre-operation psychology. This sort of case matters to my argument for the following reason. Suppose that the psychological connections across the life of a cow are not very rich. Then, in killing the cow now, I may be depriving *it* of only an inconsequential amount of valuable future. I will also be preventing a series of future "cows" from coming into existence and enjoying life. But as we saw from the non-existent child case, it appears not to be wrong to refrain from bringing into existence beings with valuable futures.

This leads us to the central issue: do animals have rich enough psychological connections to underwrite the intuitive thought that a given cow (e.g.) is the same moral patient over time? I am cautiously optimistic that they do, in at least many cases. For example, many animals appear capable of various forms of memory (Allen and Trestman 2014, §7.4). However, as with questions about animal pain and suffering, answers here are likely to vary substantially across species in ways that require careful empirical work to tease out.

It is worth making two further points. First, theories of personal identity—and related claims about the persistence of a given moral patient—are extremely difficult to assess. The view that psychological continuity is the criterion of ethically significant survival is controversial. And on many competing views—on which organism continuity, or brain continuity can underwrite ethically significant survival, for example—the objection will fail immediately. Second, the precautionary approach to practical ethics that I advocated in the preceding section is again relevant here. This objection certainly reveals deep complexities ignored by the argument of the model essay. However, we should only be content to reject that argument if these complexities lead us to be confident that it is not wrong to kill animals.

In this section I have argued that the appeal to autonomy-violation complements—rather than competes with—the valuable future-deprivation account of the wrongness of killing. I also argued that it can be wrong to kill a being that is incapable of caring about its own continued existence. In discussing this issue, I amended the ethical principle I endorse to claim that it is wrong to deprive an *existing* moral patient of the valuable future that it would otherwise have. And I argued that many animals are probably the same moral patient across time (although I granted that the issues here are quite complex).

PREMISE THREE: USING ANIMAL PRODUCTS

Premise Three of the model argument is the claim that:

3. If it is wrong to kill animals, then it is wrong to eat meat

I argued for this claim by defending another ethical principle: that it is wrong to be complicit in wrongdoing, that is to benefit from that wrongdoing, and to support it. Here we can ask two questions: should we accept this principle, and does it really support Premise Three? In this section I begin by considering an objection to the idea that this principle supports Premise Three, before considering whether this principle is objectionably incomplete.

It is always wise to consider whether an ethical principle really supports the conclusion it is intended to. Consider a case that illustrates this sort of objection to Premise Three. Suppose Alice is driving carefully on a country road, when a deer jumps in front of her truck without warning. The deer is killed instantly, and Alice moves its carcass to the side of the road and leaves. Zoe, who lives nearby, sees all of this. Zoe knows how to dress a deer carcass and has a taste for venison. She takes the carcass home, dresses it, cooks some, and eats it (compare Bruckner 2016 for further discussion of cases like this one). In this scenario, Zoe knowingly prepared and ate meat. But in doing so, Zoe is not complicit in any wrongdoing: Alice's killing of the deer was neither malicious nor negligent, so it is hard to see how it could be wrong. This is a case where eating meat is not complicit in wrongful killing, so it is a case where Premise Three fails to hold, even if the principle I offer is true.

I am happy to grant the objector this case. Recall that my conclusion is that eating meat is *typically* wrong. This case helpfully brings out another atypical exception. The objection lacks more general force exactly because in the overwhelming majority of cases, the meat that we eat *is* wrongfully produced (at least if the arguments for Premises One and Two are sound).

We saw in the previous section that a good strategy for finding objections to an explanation is to challenge its completeness. The same is true for ethical principles like my complicity principle. We can challenge the completeness of my principle by arguing that complicity with the wrongful treatment of animals could only be wrong if it tended to make a difference to how much wrongful treatment there was (see Appiah 1986–7 for a version of this view about complicity). I will call this the *efficacy objection.* This objection has significant force: one might wonder what the point of avoiding complicity is, if it makes no difference to how much animal suffering occurs.

Because I take this to be the single most important challenge to the argument of the model paper, I will offer three potentially complementary replies. (Please note that I offer multiple replies to help illustrate the issues here. In general you should focus on developing the single strongest reply to an objection as clearly as you can, rather than offering multiple replies.)

The first reply accepts the objection, and claims that it is wrong to eat meat because doing so *does* tend to make a difference to the amount of mistreatment of animals. This might seem absurd: by the time I buy a chicken at the store (for example) it is already dead. And the idea that every chicken bought will cause another one to be raised, made to suffer, and then killed, is plainly false. Peter Singer (1980, 335–6, and following him, Norcross 2004, Kagan 2011, and Rachels 2011) has replied to this challenge in the following way: There must be some change in demand for chicken that the market would notice. For example, Singer imagines that for every 10,000 vegetarians, there would be one fewer 20,000-bird broiler factory, harming and killing 100,000 chickens a year. He imagines further that if we were just below the threshold—if, for example, 1,009,999 people were vegetarians—the last 9,999 vegetarians would save no chickens, because demand for chicken would be just above the threshold that triggers a change in supply. Given these assumptions, and given that we do not know exactly how many other vegetarians there are, someone becoming vegetarian has only a 1/10,000 chance of making any difference to the number of chickens made to suffer and die.

That sounds depressing. But Singer argues that we should pay attention to the other numbers: if one *is* that 1/10,000, one will save 100,000 chickens a year. In light of this, the *expected* effect of becoming vegetarian is the effect you would have if you make a difference divided by your chance of making that difference; in the example, saving 100,000/10,000 = 10 chickens a year from short but awful lives. Of course, these precise numbers are merely illustrative; Singer grants that we do not know where exactly the thresholds are. But he suggests that the structure of probable effects will be similar on any reasonable hypothesis about these thresholds. So, according to Singer, while any reduction or increase in one's meat consumption has a tiny chance of making a difference to the amount of wrongful animal suffering and death, the difference you will make if you do make a difference will be correspondingly huge. And this, it might be claimed, is what makes it wrong to eat meat. If Singer's reasoning is sound, it answers the efficacy objection: complicity is wrong in part because it has an ethically significant chance of making an ethically significant difference. While Singer's reply is promising, his argument is somewhat complex, and relies on some controversial assumptions (see Budolfson *forthcoming* for an important reply). In light of this, I will explore alternative ways of replying to the efficacy objection.

Singer's argument illustrates two important ideas worth keeping in mind in your ethical reasoning. First, sometimes the *expected* effects of your actions are ethically significant, and not just their actual effects. (In this case, the alleged expected effect of being a vegetarian is sparing ten chickens a year from short and awful lives, even if for most vegetarians, there is no actual effect on chicken well-being.) Second, in thinking about the effects of an action, it is sometimes important to step back from focusing on the particular act, and think about how that act fits into overall patterns.

A second response to the efficacy objection appeals to these patterns in another way, by focusing on the ethical significance of what groups of people do together. One advantage of this approach is that it is uncontroversial that meat-eaters as a group *do* make a difference to the amount of animal suffering: if there were no omnivores there would be no factory farms.

I will introduce the key idea with another example. Suppose that there are two small cities, Upstream and Downstream, along the same river. The river is the only available source of water for the households in each city. Each household in each city draws its water from the river as the river comes into the city, and dumps its sewage in the river as it flows out of the city. The sewage dumped in the river in Upstream flows down the river and pollutes the drinking water drawn from the river in Downstream. As a result, the people in Downstream are constantly getting seriously ill and dying. Suppose that each household in Upstream could, at small cost, bury their sewage instead of dumping it in the river. If everyone in Upstream did this, it would end the health catastrophe in Downstream. However, given the number of other households that are actually polluting, a single person in Upstream burying his sewage would not save anyone in Downstream from illness or death.

It seems plausible that the sewage-dumpers in Upstream *together* wrongfully cause massive amounts of suffering and death in Downstream. Anyone in Upstream who dumps her sewage in the river is thus part of a group that acts wrongly. It is easy to cease to be part of that group, however: one need only bury one's sewage. It seems plausible that one should bury one's sewage in this situation, rather than dump it into the river. We could explain this by appealing to the following ethical principle: if one can avoid being part of a group that together does serious wrong, then one acts wrongly by continuing to be a member of that group. This principle applies neatly to eating meat. Together, the meat-eaters make a tremendous difference: without their demand for meat, no one would cause animals to suffer and die in order to produce it. So the meat-eaters together make vast amounts of wrongful pain and death happen to animals. So, by the ethical principle just proposed, one acts wrongly by continuing to be a member of that group.

This reply answers the efficacy objection by appealing to group efficacy. However, the issue of when exactly it is wrong to remain a part of an ethically objectionable group is very complicated. (Sometimes, for example, it is only by being part of such a group that one can mitigate the bad things the group does.) So I will explore another alternative response to the efficacy objection, which is the one I find most promising.

This response directly rejects the efficacy objection, and defends the claim that complicity with wrongdoing can be a sufficient explanation for wrongdoing, even if it has no expected bad effects. I will defend this response in three ways: by appealing to a plausibly analogous ethical principle, by clarifying the anti-complicity principle, and by appealing to a variant on an earlier case that helps to distinctively motivate it.

The first thing to notice is that there are other plausible ethical principles that require us to act even when our doing so will not make a difference. For example, the duty of *fair play* requires that one not benefit from successful cooperative institutions without making a fair contribution to them; i.e., that one not *freeride* (see e.g. Klosko 2004). Consider, as an example, sneaking onto a public bus without paying the fare.

Second, it may be useful to more precisely state the principle that I endorse (see McPherson *2016-b* for more detailed discussion):

> **Anti-Complicity** It is typically wrong to aim to benefit by cooperating with the wrongful elements of others' plans

When introducing a principle, it is often useful to briefly explain each of the elements of that principle. I now do this for Anti-Complicity. My talk of "plans" here should not be taken to apply only to patterns of explicit reasoning; rather it should include the pattern of goals that explain an individual's or institution's behavior. If my unconscious desire to humiliate my rival explains all of my behavior, humiliating my rival counts as my pla n, even if I would never consciously admit this is what I am up to. My talk of "benefit" should similarly be read in an expansive way: smoking does more harm than good, but if one seeks the enjoyment of a cigarette, one is aiming at benefit in the sense I am interested in. We should understand "cooperating" in the following way: our plans often call for others to act in certain ways. For example, if I make widgets for sale, my plan includes others' buying those widgets. Of course, it is not crucial that any particular person buys my widgets. So anyone who buys a widget counts as cooperating with my plan. Finally plans can be disjunctive: someone can plan to read the newspaper, buy some tools at the store, and then use the tools to torture a puppy. The clearly wrongful part here is the puppy torturing. Buying the tools is instrumental to the wrongful behavior, and is arguably wrongful for that reason, and reading the newspaper is not a wrongful part of the plan. It is most clear that we should not cooperate with the wrongful part of the plan.

Anti-Complicity is plausible in part because it can explain the wrongness of certain acts that cannot be explained by either the group or individual efficacy explanations. Return to the example in the model essay: the restaurant that kidnaps and enslaves chefs to make its food. Suppose the restaurant is *demand-insensitive:* it's partly a money-laundering operation, and so it will remain in business even if no one ever patronizes it. This means that neither an individual, nor the whole group of patrons, have any chance of reducing the amount of slavery in the restaurant by refusing to patronize it. Still, it seems wrong to go to the restaurant and enjoy the fruits of the slave chefs' unwilling labors. Anti-Complicity can explain why, while principles that demand that the individual or group make a difference cannot.

If the arguments earlier in the paper are correct, the meat industry has a wrongful plan: to produce meat in a way that involves egregious amounts of pain and early death, and then to sell that meat, They do not, of course, typically sell it directly to consumers. But consumers buying meat is clearly part of their plan: for if consumers do not buy, then wholesalers will not either, and the meat industry's plan would not be economically viable. (This is why meat-industry groups sometimes advertise directly to consumers: to increase consumer-level demand for their goods.) So, in buying meat, one is cooperating with their wrongful plan. And Anti-Complicity suggests that doing so is typically wrong.

Of the three explanations that I have discussed here (individual efficacy, group efficacy, and Anti-Complicity), I prefer the last. However, it is worth emphasizing that, as with explanation of the wrongness of killing, it is not clear that these explanations compete. Rather, if each is sound, they could be complementary explanations of the wrongness of eating meat. This means that the objector has her work cut out for her. For each of the three explanations that I have discussed, she must either debunk the relevant explanatory principle, or argue that the principle does not entail that it is wrong to eat meat. For example, one might insist that individual efficacy is required for wrongdoing in these cases, and then argue against the Singer-style reasoning. I take this to be the most promising way to reject the argument, but to nonetheless be a very difficult task.

THE IMPLICATIONS OF THE ARGUMENT: VEGANISM

In the previous three sections, I have considered several objections to each of the three premises of the model argument, and refined that argument in light of those objections. I now want to consider the broader implications of the argument, as refined. I will begin by considering two objections to the argument that target gaps between the premises and my overall thesis: ethical veganism.

An obvious but important objection at this stage notes that my aim in this paper is to argue for ethical veganism: the view that it is (at least typically) wrong to eat or otherwise use animal products. However, the model argument concludes only that it is wrong to eat *meat*. The model argument itself thus fails to establish ethical veganism. I grant this objection. However, the argument I have developed in this paper naturally extends to support ethical veganism.

The first point to notice is that it is possible to imagine farming with animals in a way that does not involve shortening their lives or making them suffer.' My argument does not suggest any objection to using animal products made on such farms. However, when we turn from possible to actual animal farming, we find that my case against killing animals and making them suffer applies to almost all of the institutions that produce animal products (with the exceptions of some shellfish farms). The reasons lie in the interaction between biology and economics. Consider a single example: even the most humane dairy farm will typically produce as many male calves as female, and almost all of the males will be killed early, so as not to be an economic burden. That means that the central plan of almost any economically viable dairy farming operation involves raising cows to be killed (or to be sold to another operation, knowing the latter operation will kill them), a practice that I have argued above is typically wrong. And this in turn means that the overall argument I have proposed applies here: the core plan of economically viable dairy farms involves systematic wrongdoing, and I have argued that it is wrong to be complicit with such wrongdoing. But one would be complicit with such wrongdoing if one were to buy and consume the milk (e.g.) produced on such farms, and hence buying and consuming such milk would be wrong. This example generalizes to the institutions that produce almost all of our animal products: eggs, cheese, leather, etc. And for this reason I think that my argument supports ethical veganism as opposed to a requirement to be a vegetarian who merely refrains from eating meat.

A second worry about my overall argument is that the initial simple statement of the argument in premise and conclusion form in the model essay is misleading. In the preceding sections, I have emphasized various ways that this argument should be refined, but there is a general worry that should be explored. The conclusion of the model argument emphasized that it is only *typically* wrong to eat meat. And as I explained in my initial discussion of Premise One, this qualifier should be read back into the premises. So the argument should look like this:

1. It is typically wrong to make animals suffer
2. If it is typically wrong to make animals suffer, then it is typically wrong to kill animals
3. If it is typically wrong to kill animals, then it is typically wrong to eat meat

C. It is typically wrong to eat meat.

The first thing to do is to verify that this statement of the argument, like the statement in the model essay, is valid. It is: the addition of the word "typically" does not alter the logical form of the argument, which is: *P, if P then Q, if Q then R, so R,* which is a slightly more complex variant of the classic *modus ponens* argument form. However, there are two connected worries about the argument as given. First, the reference to typicality points us at a range of ordinary cases, but every sort of exception that we have identified for each premise is an exception that must hold for the argument as a whole. The discussion has identified a raft of "atypical" exception cases: cases of making animals suffer to avoid ethically awful alternatives, cases of eating oysters and other animals incapable of experiencing pain, and cases of eating meat (like some roadkill) that was not wrongfully produced.

These cases do not exhaust the set of potential exceptions that the argument permits. And one might worry that as a result, the argument might be far too weak to support anything resembling veganism. To begin to see the force of this worry, notice that I have granted that human suffering and death may tend to be substantially more ethically significant than the suffering and death of non-human animals. This is because, as we saw above, killing you or making you suffer would be wrong for multiple reasons: some have to do with the awfulness of suffering, and the deprivation of your future, and others have to do with the ethical significance of your autonomy.

In light of this, my argument at least suggests that the most central and pressing human interests should typically take priority over the welfare of non-human animals. For example, my conclusion is compatible with the idea that we should typically harm or kill a non-human animal if doing so is needed to prevent suffering or death to a human being. This is practically relevant: in various times and places, animal products have been an essential element of the only feasible nutritionally adequate human diets. For example, in many parts of the world, owning a cow—or even a handful of chickens—can offer crucial protection against certain forms of malnutrition. I take it to be a virtue of my argument that it is compatible with cases like these counting as legitimate exceptions to the vegan principle.

At this point, however, one may wonder whether the case for veganism has any practical bite at all. After all, becoming a vegan involves a non-trivial sacrifice of real goods. Consider three sorts of examples. First, there is a sea of delicious animal-involving food, so as a vegan one sacrifices access to a range of interesting aesthetic goods. Second, food is deeply meaningful to many people, and animal products are centrally involved in many important cultural traditions and occasions. To be a vegan is thus to complicate one's relationship to those traditions and meanings. Finally, because shared values are central to many personal and professional relationships, veganism could be an impediment to such relationships, especially in cultural contexts where veganism is seen as threatening.

If the fact that veganism required one to sacrifice goods like these typically rendered omnivorism permissible, then veganism would not typically be ethically required, as I claim. Instead, it would be an admirable but non-obligatory ideal. However, I do not think that the sorts of sacrifices just mentioned suffice to make omnivorism permissible. The core issue here is how weighty the considerations in favor of veganism that I have developed in this paper are. The issue is complex, but I think that a reasonable heuristic can be derived from the initial example in the model paper: *some circumstances* would warrant torturing the stray puppy imagined in that example. But those circumstances would be comparatively dire. I contend that only similarly dire circumstances would warrant ordering the sirloin steak for dinner. And the sacrifices typically involved in becoming vegan, while significant, fall well below this threshold.

Challenging this heuristic would be yet another natural way to object to the argument of this paper. However, I think the heuristic is basically sound. And if it is, the argument of the paper suggests that we ought to eschew almost all animal products in almost all ordinary circumstances. We ought, in other words, to be vegan.

PEDAGOGICAL CODA

I conclude this paper by returning to my pedagogical aims: to aid you in thinking about how to make (and critically examine) philosophical arguments in ethics. In order to do so, I will review the basic elements of philosophical argument that I have sought to explain and illustrate in this paper.

The argument of the model essay began with a vivid *example:* the claim that it would be wrong to torture a puppy in a specific scenario. This case supported a *general principle:* that it is wrong to make animals suffer. The case supported the principle in part because the case seems *representative* of the principle. It does not seem that there is some unique feature of puppies that explains why it is wrong to torture them, for example. This principle was also supported by an underlying *ethical explanation:* it is wrong to cause animals to suffer, *because of how awful it is to experience suffering.* Although general principles themselves appear explanatorily illuminating, explanations and general principles can be different. One way to see this is to notice that there can be multiple good explanations of a single ethical principle, as in the case of the future-deprivation and autonomy-violation explanations of the wrongness of killing. In making arguments, cases, general principles, and explanations are likely to be the most important elements to develop. These elements should fit together in a rationally compelling way, and one good way to do that is to put these elements together into a valid argument, as I again did in the model essay.

In critically examining an argument, you might in principle target the structure of the argument itself: for example, showing that the argument contains some fallacious reasoning. Or you might challenge the ethical claims the argument makes about specific cases: for example, you could try to argue that there is nothing wrong with torturing puppies. (But I really hope you don't do that!) It is far more common for it to be useful to challenge the general principles and explanations offered in an argument. I have discussed several important ways of executing these challenges. First, it can be useful to look to extreme cases, to see if principles are really generally applicable. For example, the model argument appeals to suffering to explain why it is wrong to eat meat. But some animals (such as oysters) cannot suffer. So the model argument cannot explain why it is wrong to eat them. Second, it can be useful to see if an argument only works because it obscures an ethically important distinction. I discussed this issue using the example of the contrast between being in pain and suffering. Third, it is always a good idea to ask if there is a superior competitor to the general principle or ethical explanation offered in an argument. Examples of this strategy discussed above were the objection from contractualism, and the objection that autonomy violation is the best explanation of why killing is typically wrong. Fourth, a very natural objection to an explanation or principle is that it is *incomplete.* For example, I considered the idea that it is only wrong to deprive a creature of its valuable future i/that creature is capable of caring about that future. And I discussed the idea that complicity with wrongdoing is only morally objectionable if such complicity can make a difference to the extent of the underlying wrongdoing. Fifth, another important type of objection to some explanations is that those explanations rest on false presuppositions. For example, I considered the possibility that most animals do not have valuable futures in the ethically relevant sense, because most animals lack rich enough psychological connections to remain the same moral patient from one day to the next. Finally, another important way to challenge an argument is to show that there is a gap between an explanation offered in support of an ethical principle, and the principle itself. For example, the case of eating blamelessly produced roadkill suggests that there is a gap between its being wrong to kill animals, and its being wrong to eat meat, because some meat does not come from animals that were wrongfully killed.

I take these to be some of the most important tools for critically analyzing philosophical arguments. However, there are many more to be discovered. One very good habit to get into when reading philosophical papers is to ask: what kind of argument is this? How is this author objecting to that argument? If you do that consistently, you will soon have a very rich repertoire of tools for evaluating others' arguments, and making your own. One final note about how to use these tools. Probably the most important place to use the tools I have discussed in this paper is in revising your own paper. Once you have a draft of your paper in hand, you should be merciless in carefully reading through it, asking: how compelling is this argument? How could someone reasonably object to it? Are their objections sound? In my view, it is most important to use these tools to examine arguments for the conclusions that you most care about. Only by doing so can you determine whether these conclusions are reasonable, or whether you are guilty of wishful thinking, only accepting them *because* you care about them.[3]

[3]One final bit of guidance: you should always recognize help you have received in writing a paper! I am indebted to many people for helpful comments and discussion of ideas related to this paper. These include Mark Budolfson, David Plunkett, Tyler Doggett, Andrew Chignell, Sean Walsh, Derek Baker, Tom Dougherty, Gideon Rosen, and Katie Batterman, to audiences at Rhodes College, Bowling Green State University, Charles Sturt University, and Virginia Commonwealth University, and to many of my students for discussion. I am also indebted to Liz Harman, whose talk about ethical vegetarianism first started me thinking systematically about it. Parts of this paper draw significantly on my 2014, and especially my *2016-b.*

Works Cited

Akhtar, Sahar. "Animal Pain and Welfare: Can Pain Sometimes Be Worse for Them Than for Us?" *Oxford Handbook of Animal Ethics.* Eds. Tom Beauchamp and R. G. Frey. Oxford University Press, 2011. 495–518.

Allen, Colin, and Michael Trestman. "Animal Consciousness." *The Stanford Encyclopedia of Philosophy* (Summer 2014 Edition). Ed. Edward N. Zalta. <http://plato.stanford.edu/archives/sum2014/entries/consciousness-animal/>.

Appiah, Kwame Anthony. "Racism and Moral Pollution." *Philosophical Forum* 18.2–3 (1986). 185–202.

Bruckner, Donald W. "Strict Vegetarianism is Immoral" in *The Moral Complexities of Eating Meat,* Eds. Robert Fischer and Ben Bramble. Oxford University Press: 2016. 30–47.

Budolfson, Mark. "The Inefficacy Objection and the Problem with the Expected Consequences Response", *Philosophical Studies, forthcoming.*

Carruthers, Peter. *The Animals Issue.* Cambridge: Cambridge University Press, 1992.

Cohen, Carl. "The Case for the Use of Animals in Biomedical Research." *The New England Journal of Medicine* 315,1986. 865–869.

Descartes, René. *The Philosophical Writings of Descartes Vol. III.* Ed. and Tr. John Cottingham, Robert Stoothoff, Dugald Murdoch, and Anthony Kenny. Cambridge, Cambridge University Press, 1991.

Hájek, Alan. "Heuristics for Philosophical Creativity." *forthcoming* in *The Philosophy of Creativity.* Eds. Elliot Samuel Paul and Scott Barry Kaufman. Oxford: Oxford University Press. *Cited as forthcoming-a.*

———. "Philosophical Heuristics and Philosophical Methodology." *forthcoming* in *The Oxford Handbook of Philosophical Methodology.* Eds. Herman Cappelen, Tamar Gendler, and John Hawthorne. Oxford: Oxford University Press. *Cited as forthcoming-b.*

Kagan, Shelly. "Do I Make a Difference?" *Philosophy and Public Affairs* 39.2 (2011). 105–141.

Klosko, George. The Principle of Fairness and Political Obligation (New Edition). Rowman and Littlefield, 2004.

McPherson, Tristram. "A Case for Ethical Veganism." *Journal of Moral Philosophy* 11(6), 2014. 677–703.

———. "A Moorean Defense of the Omnivore?" in *The Moral Complexities of Eating Meat,* Eds. Robert Fischer and Ben Bramble. Oxford University Press: 2016. 118–134. *Cited as 2016-a.*

———. "Why I am a Vegan (and You Should be One Too)." in *Philosophy Comes to Dinner,* Eds. Andrew Chignell, Terence Cuneo, and Matthew Halterman. Routledge: 2016. 73–91. Cited as *2016-b.*

Marquis, Don. "Why Abortion is Immoral." *Journal of Philosophy* 86.4, April 1989. 183–202.

Mason, Jim and Peter Singer. *Animal Factories* Revised and Updated Edition. Harmony: 1990.

Norcross, Alasdair. "Puppies, Pigs, and People: Eating Meat and Marginal Cases." *Philosophical Perspectives* 18 (Ethics), 2004. 229–245.

Nussbaum, Martha. *Frontiers of Justice.* Harvard: Belknap, 2006.

Rachels, Stuart. "Vegetarianism." *Oxford Handbook of Animal Ethics.* Eds. Tom Beauchamp and R. G. Frey. Oxford: Oxford University Press, 2011. 877–905.

Rowlands, Mark. *Animals Like Us.* Verso: 2002.

Scanlon, T. M. *What We Owe to Each Other.* Cambridge, MA: Belknap: 1998.

Singer, Peter. *Animal Liberation.* New York: Avon, 1977.

———. "Utilitarianism and Vegetarianism." *Philosophy and Public Affairs.* 9.4 (Summer 1980), 325–337.

Talbert, Matthew. "Contractualism and Our Duties to Nonhuman Animals." *Environmental Ethics* 28 (Summer 2006). 202–215.

Tooley, Michael. "Abortion and Infanticide." *Philosophy and Public Affairs* 2.1 (August 1972). 37–65.

Varner, Gary. *In Nature's Interests.* Oxford: Oxford University Press, 1998.

For Further Reflection

1. What is the basic structure of McPherson's essay (what are the premises and conclusion)?
2. Summarize each objection to his argument.
3. What is his Anti-Complicity principle? Does it adequately explain what is wrong about being complicit in a wrongful act? Explain.
4. Do you think McPherson's argument is sound? That is, does the conclusion follow from the premises, and are the premises true? On what grounds do you judge the argument sound or unsound?

Animal Welfare

JOEL SALATIN

Joel Salatin calls himself "a Christian libertarian environmentalist capitalist lunatic farmer." He has authored nine books, including *Everything I Want to Do Is Illegal: War Stories from the Local Food Front*, from which this excerpt is taken. He offers several arguments for why free-range farming is morally permissible.

From *Everything I Want to Do is Illegal: War Stories from the Local Food Front* (Swoope, Va.: Polyface, 2011), pp. 321–324, 328–331.

. . . Unlike a cat, which relishes the chance to play with a mouse for a long time before finally killing and eating it, I do not scratch, beat, and paw animals before killing them. We honor and respect them both in life and in death. And just for the record, humans are not animals. Animals don't sin. Animals don't have souls.

This notion that modern humankind has evolved beyond killing animals is simply the result of too many people being totally disconnected from life. Anyone connected to life understands the cycles of life, which include death, decay, and regeneration. We've raised a generation on Bambi and Thumper rather than Thanksgiving hog killin' and the Christmas goose. Those who say they've achieved a spiritual Nirvana by being at one with the animals are only showing just how disconnected they are from real life cycles.

To be sure, I have no problem with vegans or vegetarians. I have no problem with animal worshippers—the ones who say a person is a cat is a fly is a grasshopper. The problem comes when they try to use the political process to outlaw meat consumption. Interestingly, these folks vilify the religious right for trying to impose their ideas on others, but have no problem when the shoe is on the other foot.

This became quite apparent to me in the early 1990s when I was asked by the Humane Society of the U.S. to help write the humane standards for a wonderful book they put together called *The Humane Consumer and Producer Guide*. In my mind, this is still one of the best national directories ever compiled to connect humane farmers with people who want to buy their food from these kinds of farmers. Anyway, in the standards, it was considered inhumane to abort a fetus from a heifer in the third trimester of the pregnancy.

If a heifer is not going to be used for breeding, farmers will sometimes abort the calves in order for the heifer to gain faster as a beef animal. Early in the pregnancy, drugs can be used. Often heifers are spayed. But if a heifer enters a feedlot already heavy with calf, farmers will induce abortions in order to simplify their operation and put the calories on back-fat rather than into milk and a baby calf. Amazingly, the people who are so concerned about abortions in the third trimester of a bovine pregnancy tend to support that action in humans. Isn't that incredible?

It's as inconsistent as the pro-lifers eating disrespected, factory-farmed meat out of Costco. I agree with Matthew Scully, author of *Dominion:* The people who should be most concerned about respecting and honoring animals are the members of the religious right. Instead these folks defend the right to abuse animals, to disrespect their chickenness and pigness. And they even applaud their own ability to find the cheapest food. I wonder if they think the best church comes from hiring the cheapest pastor.

Invariably, when animal rights advocates come to the farm and we begin talking about things like castration or embryo abortion, they always assume that I'm a fellow rabid human baby abortionist. As a farmer who has helped many cows deliver calves, the moment of ecstasy is when you reach in and the calf pulls away. That's when you know the calf is alive. And no farmer ever looks at his assistant and says, "Oh, good, this fetal mass is moving."

Rather, we exclaim, "Oh boy! It's alive! Let's get this little guy out of here." And if it's alive then, was it alive yesterday? How about the day before that? And the day before that? If any animal welfare groups want my respect, they will have to come out passionately in favor of a human pro-life position. In my soul, I cannot see how a person wanting desperately to save a tree or save a baby whale has no remorse at snuffing out a wiggling, very much alive human baby in what should be its safest environment, a mother's womb. The rise of the abortion movement coincided perfectly with our culture's disconnection to the land.

The wonder of life, the mystery and majesty of chicks hatching and pigs farrowing creates a deep appreciation for new life. Even the satisfaction of seeing cows get bred—knowing the value of that developing calf—makes farmers want to protect these developing babies. We farmers know they are the future. They are our survival. We do everything possible to bring those babies to term. People who don't see that routinely, who don't experience that, can easily lose that sense of awe. And when babies no longer instill awe, we've not become a higher developed society, we've become crass and harsh.

I don't know how many people have said to me, "How can you butcher those animals? I just don't think I could do it. They're so cute." I could just as easily turn the question around: "How could you live in a townhouse divorced from fields and woods and vibrant life? I just don't think I could do it. It's so sterile and dead."

A lot of this is just in the way we've been brought up, what we've experienced. I've grown up on the farm, battling possums and raccoons. And rats. Oh, I hate rats. When you find a hundred half-dead chicks stuffed down a hole under the brooder house, you develop a keen distaste for rats.

We had a guy come to one of our seminars sporting a PETA bumper sticker. That stands for People for the Ethical Treatment of Animals. Out here in farmland, we call it People Eating Tasty Animals. My favorite is this rendition: PETA—Indian word for poor hunter. Anyway, this fellow decided that if he couldn't kill it, he shouldn't eat it. Because every time we eat meat, we are vicariously taking an animal's life. He had been a vegetarian for several years.

The first morning of the seminar, we gave him a knife and let him kill some chickens. He appreciated our honoring them in life, and our honoring them in death. It was quite an epiphany for him, and he ate chicken the next night. Can you imagine a Tyson slaughter plant allowing this guy to come in and kill chickens? They have all sorts of no trespassing and security signs posted. This is part of the problem with the food system. We have made it unfriendly to people, to the extent that people can't be connected to it even if they wanted to. This inherently breeds disconnect, misunderstanding, and mistrust.

On our farm, we've changed the name of our pastured shelters from pens to shelters, partly as a response to this animal welfare movement. Pens sound like a shortened version of penitentiary. It has all sorts of negative connotations. In farm country, pens do not carry that kind of negativity. When we put animals in a pen, it's usually because they are receiving special care. If they aren't in a pen, they are just out there on the range so to speak, fighting the elements and surviving with minimal care. But in a pen, that's where they get special attention.

For urbanites, however, pen holds an entirely different meaning. They think it smacks of confinement, being enslaved, penned up and not free to move. In fact, some animal welfare folks visited us and castigated me for having the broilers out in these pens. They thought it was awful. I assured them that if the birds were not in a pen, they would be destroyed by predators and weather. And if one happens to get out, all it does is run around and around trying to get back in. They instinctively know that the pen means safety. And they don't want to be away from their buddies.

As we began realizing our language liability, we changed the word to shelter. Shelter sounds more like nurturing and care. Of course, it's a lot harder to say and we had to work hard at going to all this extra speech effort, but it has paid big dividends. We haven't had any complaints for some time now. . . .

Another blind spot in the animal welfare community is horse slaughter. I have been deeply chagrined with the effort to prohibit horse slaughter for human consumption in the U.S. I expect that by the time this book comes out, the final abattoir will be out of business. What legislation couldn't do, the judiciary has done. And it's a shame. I couldn't disagree more with my friends in the animal welfare movement over this issue. Although horse meat is not a staple of the American diet, it is consumed, with relish, in other cultures.

To deny farmers the extra value created by a vibrant horse meat sales option just because I don't like the idea of eating the Black Stallion is myopic to the extreme. Talk about the religious right. Give me a break. Since when did horses become sacred over llamas or cows or pigs? I guess since Flicka. A slaughtered horse is a slaughtered horse. Just because the meat goes to dog and cat food, does that make the killing act more noble?

Horses get old and stiff and crotchety. Allowing a useful market when they no longer can stay healthy is only reasonable. To what animal will we ascribe this non-human food status next? Squid? Lobster? And this is what concerns me. When I read the arguments these folks are putting out, it is clear to me that their real agenda is to make all animal slaughter illegal. All of it.

To do that, philosophically, a person must equate animals with humans. And that is an untenable position. Let me explain why from an ecologist's point of view. Tillage is generally destructive to soil. Historically, all sustainable tillage schemes are on a 5–7 year rotation, in which the land is tilled only about 2 years out of 7. The in between years of grass rebuild the soil.

Grass is nature's most efficient soil builder. It's also the most efficient carbon sequestration mechanism. Much better even than forest. Planting annual crops year after year requires large off-field inputs in both organic and conventional chemical systems. In all sustainable systems, tillage only 2 out of 7 years is all the soil can stand without hefty imported amendments. From a land healing and atmosphere cleaning perspective, nothing is as efficacious as grass. Grass value only increases on marginal lands. Millions of acres on the planet are not suitable for crop production, but they grow wonderful forages.

In fact, now we know that today's dense eastern forests did not exist before Europeans came to the continent. The Indians maintained savannahs by lighting routine fires to beat back encroaching trees. This manipulation encouraged more grass to grow stimulating herbivore populations. Manure is magic. Always has been; always will be. Even with all we know about soil fertility, we still don't know what the X factor is in manure that makes it better than the artificially reconstituted elements found in manure.

Without perennial meadows and grasses, we would have a more eroding landscape and a dirtier atmosphere. How do grasslands stay healthy? They regenerate and proliferate through routine mowing. That mowing is most efficiently performed by animals. Certainly some folks would say that animals on the landscape do not necessitate carnivorous humans. And while that may be true, part of the human responsibility is to steward the landscape to make it capture more solar energy, to sequester more atmospheric carbon, and to make it more productive than it would be if left to its natural devices.

Grass-based meat is a whole different nutritional item than grain-based meat. The recent discoveries regarding the B vitamins, conjugated linoleic acid, and the polyunsaturated fats, including the omega 3:omega 6 ratio, are proving that all of the alleged human health problems associated with meat consumption are a result of artificially producing that meat. We've had numerous customers who return to meat after a decade of vegetarianism destroys their health. I suggest skeptics contact the Weston A. Price Foundation for corroboration, or log onto <eatwild.com> for cutting-edge nutritional findings.

Whatever is wrong with eating meat and poultry is a result of producing it in factory farms and feedlots. Whatever environmental degradation, human health problems, or animal welfare issues impugn meat and poultry consumption can be rectified and turned into positives with a fundamentally different production style.

Beautifully, this fundamentally different production style would result in the 70 percent of North America's tilled farmland being converted to perennial grasslands. Only 30 percent of the grain acreage is for people, pigs, and poultry.

If we really want to heal the land, atmosphere, and our bodies on a massive scale—not to mention getting the petroleum out of agriculture—the fastest way to accomplish that is to increase demand for 100 percent grass finished beef and milk in this country. That is far more healing than anything else.

Finally, I actually have more respect for true vegans than I do vegetarians if the issue is animals equal humans. Vegetarians who eat eggs and dairy but refuse to eat meat because killing animals is wrong have no understanding of animal life cycles. Where do they think eggs and cheese come from? They certainly don't come from geriatric livestock. They come from productive, virile, breeding-age animals. And as those animals age, they must be culled from the herd before they become unproductive.

The symbiotic relationship between grasslands, ecology, and herds of herbivores is a natural principle. It has been functioning for millennia. For anyone to suggest that eliminating these relationships could be normal is to not recognize historical principles. When we begin looking at nutrient density, nothing beats meat, dairy, and poultry. Extricating animals from the landscape is not healthy for anyone or anything.

Certainly some people thrive on a vegetarian diet. I don't know anyone who thrives on a vegan diet. I've met many folks who are on a vegan diet, but I've never met a healthy one. Many times the diet works great as a cleansing or detoxifying regimen, but just because something works great as a temporary curative doesn't mean that continuing it is better. Antibiotics that knock out infection are great, but continuing to take them beyond the point of cure isn't healthy. Virtually all of the supposed animal-protein-induced toxicities are the result of factory farming. Grass-based changes everything.

Anyone wanting to invoke religious reasons for not eating animals should realize that Jesus certainly ate meat. So did Mohammed. So did Indians. I realize that in the Garden of Eden the lion didn't eat the lamb, but we haven't been in Eden for a long time. And it won't return because of our imposition; it will return only because outside spiritual forces intervene in our world.

I am all about caring for animals. On our farm, we do chores before we eat breakfast. Always. I would much rather deny myself rather than my animals. But that doesn't mean I worship them, or that they are human.

A chef was out one time to see the pigs and we walked up to the pig pasture. He had never seen live pigs before. His only acquaintance with pigs was pork. These pigs were scratching on trees, rooting in the dirt, lounging under bushes, nibbling at weeds and grass. He stood quietly for a while, mesmerized by the theater before him and the actors enjoying their parts. Finally he said, "I don't know anything about pigs. But I think if I were a pig, this is the way I'd like to live."

To me, that said it all. And that is the attitude we take toward the animals. I don't pay much attention to the folks who think children are dogs are rats are crickets. And I wish politicians wouldn't either. If our culture continues to destroy direct farmer-consumer local food commerce, people will continue to become more and more unreasonable in their thinking. Supposing themselves to become wise, they've become fools. And fools often pass laws.

That is one reason why we invite and encourage people to come out to our farm to visit, to touch, to see, to smell. Real husbandry on a real place in a real time helps to punch through the academic and theoretical disconnects pontificated by the radical animal welfare elite. I am native. That should not be illegal.

For Further Reflection

1. Salatin highlights what he considers the hypocrisy or inconsistency of those he disagrees with. Does he thereby show that their views are without merit?
2. Evaluate Salatin's environmental argument for free-range farming. Does he prove his case?
3. How does he argue that free-range farming is humane and respectful to animals? Is his argument a good one?
4. How does he argue that free-range farming is good for human health? Is his argument a good one?
5. Overall, does Salatin prove that free-range farming is morally permissible? Explain.

Further Readings for Chapter 14

Frey, R. G. *Rights, Killing and Suffering.* Oxford: Basil Blackwell, 1983.

Rachels, James. *Created from Animals: The Moral Implications of Darwinism.* Oxford: Oxford University Press, 1990.

Regan, Tom. *The Case for Animal Rights.* Berkeley: University of California Press, 1983. The most comprehensive philosophical treatise in favor of animal rights.

Regan, Tom, and Peter Singer, eds. *Animal Rights and Human Obligations.* Englewood Cliffs, N.J.: Prentice-Hall, 1976.

Robbins, John. *Diet for a New America: How Your Food Choices Affect Your Health, Happiness, and the Future of Life on Earth.* Walpole, N.H.: Stillpoint, 1987. A strong case for vegetarianism.

Rohr, Janelle, ed. *Animal Rights: Opposing Viewpoints.* San Diego: Greenhaven Press, 1989.

Singer, Peter. *Animal Liberation.* 2nd ed. New York: New York Review of Books, 1990.

VandeVeer, D., and Pierce, C., eds. *People, Penguins, and Plastic Trees.* Belmont, Calif.: Wadsworth, 1990.

Puppies, Pigs, and People: Eating Meat and Marginal Cases

ALASTAIR NORCROSS

Norcross argues that factory farming as it is currently practiced is highly immoral and that those who eat meat share in the blame for this immorality. He rebuts several arguments against this view, advances the popular "marginal cases" argument against eating meat, and contends that because animals are "moral patients," they are worthy of the kind of respect that should shield them from the cruelties of factory farming.

1. FRED'S BASEMENT

Consider the story of Fred, who receives a visit from the police one day. They have been summoned by Fred's neighbors, who have been disturbed by strange sounds emanating from Fred's basement. When they enter the basement they are confronted by the following scene: Twenty-six small wire cages, each containing a puppy, some whining, some whimpering, some howling. The puppies range in age from newborn to about six months. Many of them show signs of mutilation. Urine and feces cover the bottoms of the cages and the basement floor. Fred explains that he keeps the puppies for twenty-six weeks, and then butchers them while holding them upside-down. During their lives he performs a series of mutilations on them, such as slicing off their noses and their paws with a hot knife, all without any form of anesthesia. Except for the mutilations, the puppies are never allowed out of the cages, which are barely big enough to hold them at twenty-six weeks. The police are horrified, and promptly charge Fred with animal abuse. As details of the case are publicized, the public is outraged. Newspapers are flooded with letters demanding that Fred be severely punished. There are calls for more severe penalties for animal abuse. Fred is denounced as a vile sadist.

Finally, at his trial, Fred explains his behavior, and argues that he is blameless and therefore deserves no punishment. He is, he explains, a great lover of chocolate. A couple of years ago, he was involved in a car accident, which resulted in some head trauma. Upon his release from hospital, having apparently suffered no lasting ill effects, he visited his favorite restaurant and ordered their famous rich dark chocolate mousse. Imagine his dismay when he

Alastair Norcross, "Puppies, Pigs, and People: Eating Meat and Marginal Cases," *Philosophical Perspectives*, 18, 2004.

discovered that his experience of the mousse was a pale shadow of its former self. The mousse tasted bland, slightly pleasant, but with none of the intense chocolaty flavor he remembered so well. The waiter assured him that the recipe was unchanged from the last time he had tasted it, just the day before his accident. In some consternation, Fred rushed out to buy a bar of his favorite Belgian chocolate. Again, he was dismayed to discover that his experience of the chocolate was barely even pleasurable. Extensive investigation revealed that his experience of other foods remained unaffected, but chocolate, in all its forms, now tasted bland and insipid. Desperate for a solution to his problem, Fred visited a renowned gustatory neurologist, Dr. T. Bud. Extensive tests revealed that the accident had irreparably damaged the godiva gland, which secretes cocoamone, the hormone responsible for the experience of chocolate. Fred urgently requested hormone replacement therapy. Dr. Bud informed him that, until recently, there had been no known source of cocoamone, other than the human godiva gland, and that it was impossible to collect cocoamone from one person to be used by another. However, a chance discovery had altered the situation. A forensic veterinary surgeon, performing an autopsy on a severely abused puppy, had discovered high concentrations of cocoamone in the puppy's brain. It turned out that puppies, who don't normally produce cocoamone, could be stimulated to do so by extended periods of severe stress and suffering. The research, which led to this discovery, while gaining tenure for its authors, had not been widely publicized, for fear of antagonizing animal welfare groups. Although this research clearly gave Fred the hope of tasting chocolate again, there were no commercially available sources of puppy-derived cocoamone. Lack of demand, combined with fear of bad publicity, had deterred drug companies from getting into the puppy torturing business. Fred appeals to the court to imagine his anguish, on discovering that a solution to his severe deprivation was possible, but not readily available. But he wasn't inclined to sit around bemoaning his cruel fate. He did what any chocolate lover would do. He read the research, and set up his own cocoamone collection lab in his basement. Six months of intense puppy suffering, followed by a brutal death, produced enough cocoamone to last him a week, hence the twenty-six cages. He isn't a sadist or an animal abuser, he explains. If there were a method of collecting cocoamone without torturing, puppies, he would gladly employ it. He derives no pleasure from the suffering of the puppies itself. He sympathizes with those who are horrified by the pain and misery of the animals, but the court must realize that human pleasure is at stake. The puppies, while undeniably cute, are mere animals. He admits that he would be just as healthy without chocolate, if not more so. But this isn't a matter of survival or health. His life would be unacceptably impoverished without the experience of chocolate.

End of story. Clearly, we are horrified by Fred's behavior, and unconvinced by his attempted justification. It is, of course, unfortunate for Fred that he can no longer enjoy the taste of chocolate, but that in no way excuses the imposition of severe suffering on the puppies. I expect near universal agreement with this claim (the exceptions being those who are either inhumanly callous or thinking ahead, and wish to avoid the following conclusion, to which such agreement commits them). No decent person would even contemplate torturing puppies merely to enhance a gustatory experience. However, billions of animals endure intense suffering every year for precisely this end. Most of the chicken, veal, beef, and pork consumed in the US comes from intensive confinement facilities, in which the animals live cramped, stress-filled lives and endure unanaesthetized mutilations.[1] The vast majority of people would suffer no ill health from the elimination of meat from their diets. Quite the reverse. The supposed benefits from this system of factory farming, apart from the profits accruing to agribusiness, are increased levels of gustatory pleasure for those who claim that they couldn't enjoy a meat-free diet as much as their current meat-filled diets. If we are prepared to condemn Fred for torturing puppies merely to enhance his gustatory experiences, shouldn't wc similarly condemn the millions who purchase and consume factory-raised meat? Are there any morally significant differences between Fred's behavior and their behavior?

2. FRED'S BEHAVIOR COMPARED WITH OUR BEHAVIOR

The first difference that might seem to be relevant is that Fred tortures the puppies himself, whereas most Americans consume meat that comes from animals that have been tortured by others. But is this really relevant? What if Fred had been squeamish and had employed someone else to torture the puppies and extract the cocoamone? Would we have thought any better of Fred? Of course not.

Another difference between Fred and many consumers of factory-raised meat is that many, perhaps most, such consumers are unaware of the treatment of the animals, before they appear in neatly wrapped packages on supermarket shelves. Perhaps I should moderate my challenge, then. If we are prepared to condemn Fred for torturing puppies merely to enhance his gustatory experiences, shouldn't we similarly condemn those who purchase

[1]For information on factory farms, see, for example, Jim Mason and Peter Singer, *Animal Factories*, 2d ed. (New York: Harmony Books, 1990), Karen Davis, *Prisoned Chickens, Poisoned Eggs: An Inside Look at the Modern Poultry Industry* (Summertown, TN: Book Publishing Co., 1996), John Robbins, *Diet for a New America* (Walpole, NH: Stillpoint, 1987).

and consume factory-raised meat, in full, or even partial, awareness of the suffering endured by the animals? While many consumers are still blissfully ignorant of the appalling treatment meted out to meat, that number is rapidly dwindling, thanks to vigorous publicity campaigns waged by animal welfare groups. Furthermore, any meat-eating readers of this article are now deprived of the excuse of ignorance.

Perhaps a consumer of factory-raised animals could argue as follows: While I agree that Fred's behavior is abominable, mine is crucially different. If Fred did not consume his chocolate, he would not raise and torture puppies (or pay someone else to do so). Therefore Fred could prevent the suffering of the puppies. However, if I did not buy and consume factory-raised meat, no animals would be spared lives of misery. Agribusiness is much too large to respond to the behavior of one consumer. Therefore I cannot prevent the suffering of any animals. I may well regret the suffering inflicted on animals for the sake of human enjoyment. I may even agree that the human enjoyment doesn't justify the suffering. However, since the animals will suffer no matter what I do, I may as well enjoy the taste of their flesh.

There are at least two lines of response to this attempted defense. First, consider an analogous case. You visit a friend in an exotic location, say Alabama. Your friend takes you out to eat at the finest restaurant in Tuscaloosa. For dessert you select the house specialty, "Chocolate Mousse à la Bama," served with a small cup of coffee, which you are instructed to drink before eating the mousse. The mousse is quite simply the most delicious dessert you have ever tasted. Never before has chocolate tasted so rich and satisfying. Tempted to order a second, you ask your friend what makes this mousse so delicious. He informs you that the mousse itself is ordinary, but the coffee contains a concentrated dose of cocoamone, the newly discovered chocolate-enhancing hormone. Researchers at Auburn University have perfected a technique for extracting cocoamone from the brains of freshly slaughtered puppies, who have been subjected to lives of pain and frustration. Each puppy's brain yields four doses, each of which is effective for about fifteen minutes, just long enough to enjoy one serving of mousse. You are, naturally, horrified and disgusted. You will certainly not order another serving, you tell your friend. In fact, you are shocked that your friend, who had always seemed to be a morally decent person, could have both recommended the dessert to you and eaten one himself, in full awareness of the loathsome process necessary for the experience. He agrees that the suffering of the puppies is outrageous, and that the gain in human pleasure in no way justifies the appalling treatment they have to endure. However, neither he nor you can save any puppies by refraining from consuming cocoamone. Cocoamone production is now Alabama's leading industry, so it is much too large to respond to the behavior of one or two consumers. Since the puppies will suffer no matter what either of you does, you may as well enjoy the mousse.

If it is as obvious as it seems that a morally decent person, who is aware of the details of cocoamone production, couldn't order Chocolate Mousse a la Bama, it should be equally obvious that a morally decent person, who is aware of the details of factory farming, can't purchase and consume factory-raised meat. If the attempted excuse of causal impotence is compelling in the latter case, it should be compelling in the former case. But it isn't.

The second response to the claim of causal impotence is to deny it. Consider the case of chickens, the most cruelly treated of all animals raised for human consumption, with the possible exception of veal calves. In 1998, almost 8 billion chickens were slaughtered in the US,[2] almost all of them raised on factory farms. Suppose that there are 250 million chicken eaters in the US, and that each one consumes, on average, 25 chickens per year (this leaves a fair number of chickens slaughtered for nonhuman consumption, or for export). Clearly, if only one of those chicken eaters gave up eating chicken, the industry would not respond. Equally clearly, if they all gave up eating chicken, billions of chickens (approximately 6.25 billion per year) would not be bred, tortured, and killed. But there must also be some number of consumers, far short of 250 million, whose renunciation of chicken would cause the industry to reduce the number of chickens bred in factory farms. The industry may not be able to respond to each individual's behavior, but it must respond to the behavior of fairly large numbers. Suppose that the industry is sensitive to a reduction in demand for chicken equivalent to 10,000 people becoming vegetarians. (This seems like a reasonable guess, but I have no idea what the actual numbers are, nor is it important.) For each group of 10,000 who give up chicken, a quarter of a million fewer chickens are bred per year. It appears, then, that if you give up eating chicken, you have only a one in ten thousand chance of making any difference to the lives of chickens, unless it is certain that fewer than 10,000 people will ever give up eating chicken, in which case you have no chance. Isn't a one in ten thousand chance small enough to render your continued consumption of chicken blameless? Not at all. While the chance that your behavior is harmful may be small, the harm that is risked is enormous. The larger the numbers needed to make a difference to chicken production, the larger the difference such numbers would make. A one in ten thousand chance of saving 250,000 chickens per year from excruciating lives is morally and mathematically equivalent to the certainty of saving 25 chickens per year. We commonly accept that even small risks of great harms

[2]*Livestock Slaughter 1998 Summary*, NASS, USD A (Washington, D.C.: March 1999), 2; and *Poultry Slaughter*, NASS, USDA (Washington, D.C.: February 2, 1999), If.

are unacceptable. That is why we disapprove of parents who fail to secure their children in car seats or with seat belts, who leave their small children unattended at home, or who drink or smoke heavily during pregnancy. Or consider commercial aircraft safety measures. The chances that the oxygen masks, the lifejackets, or the emergency exits on any given plane will be called on to save any lives in a given week, are far smaller than one in ten thousand. And yet we would be outraged to discover that an airline had knowingly allowed a plane to fly for a week with nonfunctioning emergency exits, oxygen masks, and lifejackets. So, even if it is true that your giving up factory raised chicken has only a tiny chance of preventing suffering, given that the amount of suffering that would be prevented is in inverse proportion to your chance of preventing it, your continued consumption is not thereby excused.

But perhaps it is not even true that your giving up chicken has only a tiny chance of making any difference. Suppose again that the poultry industry only reduces production when a threshold of 10,000 fresh vegetarians is reached. Suppose also, as is almost certainly true, that vegetarianism is growing in popularity in the US (and elsewhere). Then, even if you are not the one, newly converted vegetarian, to reach the next threshold of 10,000, your conversion will reduce the time required before the next threshold is reached. The sooner the threshold is reached, the sooner production, and therefore animal suffering, is reduced. Your behavior, therefore, does make a difference. Furthermore, many people who become vegetarians influence others to become vegetarian, who in turn influence others, and so on. It appears, then, that the claim of causal impotence is mere wishful thinking, on the part of those meat lovers who are morally sensitive enough to realize that human gustatory pleasure does not justify inflicting extreme suffering on animals.

Perhaps there is a further difference between the treatment of Fred's puppies and the treatment of animals on factory farms. The suffering of the puppies is a necessary means to the production of gustatory pleasure, whereas the suffering of animals on factory farms is simply a by-product of the conditions dictated by economic considerations. Therefore, it might be argued, the suffering of the puppies is *intended as a means* to Fred's pleasure, whereas the suffering of factory raised animals is merely *foreseen* as a side-effect of a system that is a means to the gustatory pleasures of millions. The distinction between what is intended, either as a means or as an end in itself, and what is "merely" foreseen is central to the Doctrine of Double Effect. Supporters of this doctrine claim that it is sometimes permissible to bring about an effect that is merely foreseen, even though the very same effect could not permissibly be brought about if intended. (Other conditions have to be met in order for the Doctrine of Double Effect to judge an action permissible, most notably that there be an outweighing good effect.) Fred acts impermissibly, according to this line of argument, because he intends the suffering of the puppies as a means to his pleasure. Most meat eaters, on the other hand, even if aware of the suffering of the animals, do not intend the suffering.

In response to this line of argument, I could remind the reader that Samuel Johnson said, or should have said, that the Doctrine of Double Effect is the last refuge of a scoundrel.[3] I won't do that, however, since neither the doctrine itself, nor the alleged moral distinction between intending and foreseeing can justify the consumption of factory-raised meat. The Doctrine of Double Effect requires not merely that a bad effect be foreseen and not intended, but also that there be an outweighing good effect. In the case of the suffering of factory-raised animals, whatever good could plausibly be claimed to come out of the system clearly doesn't outweigh the bad. Furthermore, it would be easy to modify the story of Fred to render the puppies' suffering "merely" foreseen. For example, suppose that the cocoamone is produced by a chemical reaction that can only occur when large quantities of drain-cleaner are forced down the throat of a conscious, unanaesthetized puppy. The consequent appalling suffering, while not itself a means to the production of cocoamone, is nonetheless an unavoidable side-effect of the means. In this variation of the story, Fred's behavior is no less abominable than in the original.

One last difference between the behavior of Fred and the behavior of the consumers of factory-raised meat is worth discussing, if only because it is so frequently cited in response to the arguments of this paper. Fred's behavior is abominable, according to this line of thinking, because it involves the suffering of *puppies*. The behavior of meat-eaters, on the other hand, "merely" involves the suffering of chickens, pigs, cows, calves, sheep, and the like. Puppies (and probably dogs and cats in general) are morally different from the other animals. Puppies *count* (morally, that is), whereas the other animals don't, or at least not nearly as much.

So, what gives puppies a higher moral status than the animals we eat? Presumably there is some morally relevant property or properties possessed by puppies but not by farm animals. Perhaps puppies have a greater degree of rationality than farm animals, or a more finely developed moral sense, or at least a sense of loyalty and devotion. The problems with this kind of approach are obvious. It's highly unlikely that any property that has even an outside chance of being ethically relevant[4] is both possessed by puppies and not possessed by any farm animals. For example, it's probably true that most puppies

[3]For a fine critique of the Doctrine of Double Effect, see Jonathan Bennett, *The Act Itself*, (Oxford 1995), ch. 11.

[4]If someone were to assert that "puppyishness" or simply "being a puppy" were ethically relevant, I could do no more than favor them with an incredulous stare.

have a greater degree of rationality (whatever that means) than most chickens, but the comparison with pigs is far more dubious. Besides, if Fred were to inform the jury that he had taken pains to acquire particularly stupid, morally obtuse, disloyal and undevoted puppies, would they (or we) have declared his behavior to be morally acceptable? Clearly not. This is, of course, simply the puppy version of the problem of marginal cases (which I will discuss later). The human version is no less relevant. If their lack of certain degrees of rationality, moral sensibility, loyalty, devotion, and the like makes it permissible to torture farm animals for our gustatory pleasure, it should be permissible to do the same to those unfortunate humans who also lack those properties. Since the latter behavior isn't permissible, the lack of such properties doesn't justify the former behavior.

Perhaps, though, there *is* something that separates puppies, even marginal puppies (and marginal humans) from farm animals—our sympathy. Puppies count more than other animals, because we care more about them. We are outraged to hear of puppies abused in scientific experiments, but unconcerned at the treatment of laboratory rats or animals on factory farms. Before the 2002 World Cup, several members of the England team sent a letter to the government of South Korea protesting the treatment of dogs and cats raised for food in that country. The same players have not protested the treatment of animals on factory farms in England. This example, while clearly illustrating the difference in attitudes towards cats and dogs on the one hand, and farm animals on the other, also reveals one of the problems with this approach to the question of moral status. Although the English footballers, and the English (and US) public in general, clearly care far more about the treatment of cats and dogs than of farm animals, the South Koreans, just as clearly, do not. Are we to conclude that Fred's behavior would not be abominable were he living in South Korea, where dogs and cats are routinely abused for the sake of gustatory pleasure? Such relativism is, to put it mildly, hard to swallow. Perhaps, though, we can maintain the view that human feelings determine the moral status of animals, without condoning the treatment of dogs and cats in South Korea (and other countries). Not all human feelings count. Only the feelings of those who have achieved exactly the right degree of moral sensibility. That just so happens to be those in countries like the US and Britain who care deeply for the welfare of dogs and cats, but not particularly for the welfare of cows, chickens, pigs, and other factory-raised animals. Dog and cat eaters in South Korea are insufficiently sensitive, and humane farming advocates in Britain and the US are overly so. But, of course, it won't do simply to insist that this is the right degree of moral sensibility. We need an explanation of why this is the right degree of sensibility. Moral sensibility consists, at least in part, in reacting differently to different features of situations, actions, agents, and patients. If the right degree of moral sensibility requires reacting differently to puppies and to farm animals, there must be a morally relevant difference between puppies and farm animals. Such a difference can't simply consist in the fact that (some) people do react differently to them. The appeal to differential human sympathy illustrates a purely descriptive psychological difference between the behavior of Fred and that of someone who knowingly consumes factory-raised meat. It can do no serious moral work.

I have been unable to discover any morally relevant differences between the behavior of Fred, the puppy torturer, and the behavior of the millions of people who purchase and consume factory-raised meat, at least those who do so in the knowledge that the animals live lives of suffering and deprivation. If morality demands that we not torture puppies merely to enhance our own eating pleasure, morality also demands that we not support factory farming by purchasing factory-raised meat.

3. THE TEXAN'S CHALLENGE

Perhaps what I have said thus far is enough to convince many that the purchase and consumption of factory-raised meat is immoral. It is clear that the attribution of a different (and elevated) moral status to puppies from that attributed to farm animals is unjustified. But, one philosopher's *modus ponens*, as they say, is another Texan's *modus tollens*. Here is the *modus ponens* I have been urging:

(1) If it's wrong to torture puppies for gustatory pleasure, it's wrong to support factory farming.
(2) It is wrong to torture puppies for gustatory pleasure.
(3) Therefore it's wrong to support factory farming.

But some may be so convinced that supporting factory farming is not wrong that they may substitute that conviction for the second premise, and conclude that it is not wrong to torture puppies for gustatory pleasure. Thus we are confronted with the Texan's *modus tollens:*

(T1) If it's wrong to torture puppies for gustatory pleasure, then it's wrong to support factory farming.
(T2) It's not wrong to support factory fanning.
(T3) Therefore it's not wrong to torture puppies for gustatory pleasure.

I'm not saying that there is a large risk that many people, even Texans, will start breeding puppies for food (outside of those countries where it is already accepted practice). What they may do (and have done when I have presented them with this argument) is explain their reluctance to do so as a mere sentimental preference, as opposed to a morally mandated choice. They may claim, in a somewhat Kantian spirit, that someone who can treat puppies like that may be more likely to mistreat humans. They may agree that all animals deserve equal consideration of their interests. They may then justify their different treatment of animals either on the grounds that they are simply giving some animals *more* than they deserve, or that they are attending to their own interests. If the former, they could claim that morality mandates minimal standards of conduct, but that nothing prevents us from choosing to go beyond the requirements of morality when we feel like it. If the latter, they could claim that their sentimental attachment to puppies, kittens, and the like, makes it in their own interests not to raise and kill them for food. Nonetheless, they may insist, in terms of moral status, there is a clear difference between humans and other animals. Humans have a moral status so far above that of other animals that we couldn't even consider raising humans for food (even humanely), or experimenting on them without their consent, even though we routinely do such things to other animals.

4. HUMANS' VERSUS ANIMALS' ETHICAL STATUS—THE RATIONALITY GAMBIT

For the purposes of this discussion, to claim that humans have a superior ethical status to animals is to claim that it is morally right to give the interests of humans greater weight than those of animals in deciding how to behave. Such claims will often be couched in terms of rights, such as the rights to life, liberty or respect, but nothing turns on this terminological matter. One may claim that it is generally wrong to kill humans, but not animals, because humans are rational, and animals are not. Or one may claim that the suffering of animals counts less than the suffering of humans (if at all), because humans are rational, and animals are not. These claims may proceed through the intermediate claim that the rights of humans are more extensive and stronger than those (if any) of animals. Alternatively, one may directly ground the judgment about the moral status of certain types of behavior in claims about the alleged natural properties of the individuals involved. Much of the debate over the moral status of abortion proceeds along these lines. Many opponents of abortion appeal to features that fetuses have in common with adult humans, in order to argue that it is, at least usually, just as seriously wrong to kill them as it is to kill us. For example, John Noonan claims that it is the possession of a full human genetic code that grounds the attribution to fetuses of this exalted ethical status. Such an argument may, but doesn't have to, proceed through the intermediate claim that anything that possesses a full human genetic code has a right to life. Many proponents of the moral permissibility of abortion, on the other hand, claim features such as self-consciousness or linguistic ability as necessary conditions of full moral status, and thus deny such status to fetuses.

What could ground the claim of superior moral status for humans? Just as the defender of a higher moral status for puppies than for farm animals needs to find some property or properties possessed by puppies but not by farm animals, so the defender of a higher moral status for humans need to find some property or properties possessed by humans but not by other animals. The traditional view, dating back at least to Aristotle, is that rationality is what separates humans, both morally and metaphysically, from other animals. With a greater understanding of the cognitive powers of some animals, recent philosophers have often refined the claim to stress the kind and level of rationality required for moral reasoning. Let's start with a representative sample of three. Consider first these claims of Bonnie Steinbock:

> While we are not compelled to discriminate among people because of different capacities, if we can find a significant difference in capacities between human and non-human animals, this could serve to justify regarding human interests as primary. It is not arbitrary or smug, I think, to maintain that human beings have a different moral status from members of other species because of certain capacities which are characteristic of being human. We may not all be equal in these capacities, but all human beings possess them to some measure, and non-human animals do not. For example, human beings are normally held to be responsible for what they do. . . . Secondly, human beings can be expected to reciprocate in a way that non-human animals cannot . . . Thirdly, . . . there is the "desire for self-respect."[5]

Similarly, Mary Anne Warren argues that "the rights of persons are generally stronger than those of sentient beings which are not persons." Her main premise to support this conclusion is the following:

> [T]here is one difference [between human and non-human nature] which has a clear moral relevance: people are at least sometimes capable of being moved to action or inaction by the force of reasoned argument.[6]

[5]Bonnie Steinbock, "Speciesism and the Idea of Equality," *Philosophy* 53, no. 204 (April 1978). Reprinted in *Contemporary Moral Problems*, 5th edition, James E. White (ed.) (West, 1997) 467–468.

[6]Mary Anne Warren, "Difficulties with the Strong Animal Rights Position," *Between the Species* 2, no. 4, 1987. Reprinted in *Contemporary Moral Problems*, 5th edition, James E. White (ed.) (West. 1997), 482.

Carl Cohen, one of the most vehement modern defenders of what Peter Singer calls "speciesism" states his position as follows:

> Between species of animate life, however—between (for example) humans on the one hand and cats or rats on the other—the morally relevant differences are enormous, and almost universally appreciated. Humans engage in moral reflection; humans are morally autonomous; humans are members of moral communities, recognizing just claims against their own interest. Human beings do have rights, theirs is a moral status very different from that of cats or rats.[7]

So, the claim is that human interests and/or rights are stronger or more important than those of animals, because humans possess a kind and level of rationality not possessed by animals. How much of our current behavior towards animals this justifies depends on just how much consideration should be given to animal interests, and on what rights, if any, they possess. Both Stein-bock and Warren stress that animal interests need to be taken seriously into account. Warren claims that animals have important rights, but not as important as human rights. Cohen, on the other hand, argues that we should actually *increase* our use of animals.

5. THE CHALLENGE OF MARGINAL CASES

One of the most serious challenges to this defense of the traditional view involves a consideration of what philosophers refer to as "marginal cases." Whatever kind and level of rationality is selected as justifying the attribution of superior moral status to humans will either be lacking in some humans or present in some animals. To take one of the most commonly-suggested features, many humans are incapable of engaging in moral reflection. For some, this incapacity is temporary, as is the case with infants, or the temporarily cognitively disabled. Others who once had the capacity may have permanently lost it, as is the case with the severely senile or the irreversibly comatose. Still others never had and never will have the capacity, as is the case with the severely mentally disabled. If we base our claims for the moral superiority of humans over animals on the attribution of such capacities, won't we have to exclude many humans? Won't we then be forced to the claim that there is at least as much moral reason to use cognitively deficient humans in

[7]Carl Cohen, "The Case for the Use of Animals in Biomedical Research," *The New England Journal of Medecine*, vol. 315, 1986. Reprinted in *Social Ethics*, 4th edition, Thomas A. Mappes and Jane S. Zembaty, (eds.) (New York: McGraw-Hill, 1992) 463.

experiments and for food as to use animals? Perhaps we could exclude the only temporarily disabled, on the grounds of potentiality, though that move has its own problems. Nonetheless, the other two categories would be vulnerable to this objection.

I will consider two lines of response to the argument from marginal cases. The first denies that we have to attribute different moral status to marginal humans, but maintains that we are, nonetheless, justified in attributing different moral status to animals who are just as cognitively sophisticated as marginal humans, if not more so. The second admits that, strictly speaking, marginal humans are morally inferior to other humans, but proceeds to claim pragmatic reasons for treating them, at least usually, *as if* they had equal status.

As representatives of the first line of defense, I will consider arguments from three philosophers, Carl Cohen, Alan White, and David Schmidtz. First, Cohen:

> [the argument from marginal cases] fails; it mistakenly treats an essential feature of humanity as though it were a screen for sorting humans. The capacity for moral judgment that distinguishes humans from animals is not a test to be administered to human beings one by one. Persons who are unable, because of some disability, to perform the full moral functions natural to human beings are certainly not for that reason ejected from the moral community. The issue is one of kind . . . What humans retain when disabled, animals have never had.[8]

Alan White argues that animals don't have rights, on the grounds that they cannot intelligibly be spoken of in the full language of a right. By this he means that they cannot, for example, claim, demand, assert, insist on, secure, waive, or surrender a right. This is what he has to say in response to the argument from marginal cases:

> Nor does this, as some contend, exclude infants, children, the feeble-minded, the comatose, the dead, or generations yet unborn. Any of these may be for various reasons empirically unable to fulfill the full role of right-holder. But . . . they are logically possible subjects of rights to whom the full language of rights can significantly, however falsely, be used. It is a misfortune, not a tautology, that these persons cannot exercise or enjoy, claim, or waive, their rights or do their duty or fulfil their obligations.[9]

[8]Cohen, op. cit. 461.
[9]Alan White, *Rights*, (OUP 1984). Reprinted in *Animal Rights and Human Obligations*, 2nd edition, Tom Regan and Peter Singer (eds.) (Prentice Hall, 1989), 120.

David Schmidtz defends the appeal to typical characteristics of species, such as mice, chimpanzees, and humans, in making decisions on the use of different species in experiments. He also considers the argument from marginal cases:

> Of course, some chimpanzees lack the characteristic features in virtue of which chimpanzees command respect as a species, just as some humans lack the characteristic features in virtue of which humans command respect as a species. It is equally obvious that some chimpanzees have cognitive capacities (for example) that are superior to the cognitive capacities of some humans. But whether every human being is superior to every chimpanzee is beside the point. The point is that we can, we do, and we should make decisions on the basis of our recognition that mice, chimpanzees, and humans are relevantly different *types*. We can have it both ways after all. Or so a speciesist could argue.[10]

There is something deeply troublesome about the line of argument that runs through all three of these responses to the argument from marginal cases. A particular feature, or set of features is claimed to have so much moral significance that its presence or lack can make the difference to whether a piece of behavior is morally justified or morally outrageous. But then it is claimed that the presence or lack of the feature in any *particular* case is not important. The relevant question is whether the presence or lack of the feature is *normal*. Such an argument would seem perfectly preposterous in most other cases. Suppose, for example, that ten famous people are on trial in the afterlife for crimes against humanity. On the basis of conclusive evidence, five are found guilty and five are found not guilty. Four of the guilty are sentenced to an eternity of torment, and one is granted an eternity of bliss. Four of the innocent are granted an eternity of bliss, and one is sentenced to an eternity of torment. The one innocent who is sentenced to torment asks why he, and not the fifth guilty person, must go to hell. Saint Peter replies, "Isn't it obvious Mr. Ghandi? You are male. The other four men—Adolph Hitler, Joseph Stalin, George W. Bush, and Richard Nixon—are all guilty. Therefore the normal condition for a male defendant in this trial is guilt. The fact that you happen to be innocent is irrelevant. Likewise, of the five female defendants in this trial, only one was guilty. Therefore the normal condition for female defendants in this trial is innocence. That is why Margaret Thatcher gets to go to heaven instead of you."

As 1 said, such an argument is preposterous. Is the reply to the argument from marginal cases any better? Perhaps it will be claimed that a biological

[10]David Schmidtz, "Are all Species Equal?", *Journal of Applied Philosophy*, Vol. 15, no. 1 (1998), 61, my emphasis.

category such as a species is more "natural," whatever that means, than a category like "all the male (or female) defendants in this trial." Even setting aside the not inconsiderable worries about the conventionality of biological categories, it is not at all clear why this distinction should be morally relevant. What if it turned out that there were statistically relevant differences in the mental abilities of men and women? Suppose that men were, on average, more skilled at manipulating numbers than women, and that women were, on average, more empathetic than men. Would such differences in what was "normal" for men and women justify us in preferring an innumerate man to a female math genius for a job as an accountant, or an insensitive woman to an ultra-sympathetic man for a job as a counselor? I take it that the biological distinction between male and female is just as real as that between human and chimpanzee.

A second response to the argument from marginal cases is to concede that cognitively deficient humans really do have an inferior moral status to normal humans. Can we, then, use such humans as we do animals? I know of no-one who takes the further step of advocating the use of marginal humans for food (though R. G. Frey has made some suggestive remarks concerning experimentation). How can we advocate this second response while blocking the further step? Warren suggests that "there are powerful practical and emotional reasons for protecting non-rational human beings, reasons which are absent in the case of most non-human animals."[11] It would clearly outrage common human sensibilities, if we were to raise retarded children for food or medical experiments.[12] Here is Steinbock in a similar vein:

> I doubt that anyone will be able to come up with a concrete and morally relevant difference that would justify, say, using a chimpanzee in an experiment rather than a human being with less capacity for reasoning, moral responsibility, etc. Should we then experiment on the severely retarded? Utilitarian considerations aside, we feel a special obligation to care for the handicapped members of our own species, who cannot survive in this world without such care. . . . In addition, when we consider the severely retarded, we think, "That could be me." It makes sense to think that one might have been born retarded, but not to think that one might have been born a monkey. . . . Here we are getting away from such things as "morally relevant differences" and are talking about something much more difficult to articulate, namely, the role of feeling and sentiment in moral thinking.[13]

[11]Warren, op. cit. 483.
[12]For a similar argument, see Peter Carruthers, *The Animals Issue: Moral Theory in Practice* (Cambridge University Press, 1992.)
[13]Steinbock, op. cit. 469–470.

This line of response clearly won't satisfy those who think that marginal humans really do deserve equal moral consideration with other humans. It is also a very shaky basis on which to justify our current practices. What outrages human sensibilities is a very fragile thing. Human history is littered with examples of widespread acceptance of the systematic mistreatment of some groups who didn't generate any sympathetic response from others. That we do feel a kind of sympathy for retarded humans that we don't feel for dogs is, if true, a contingent matter. To see just how shaky a basis this is for protecting retarded humans, imagine that a new kind of birth defect (perhaps associated with beef from cows treated with bovine growth hormone) produces severe mental retardation, green skin, and a complete lack of emotional bond between parents and child. Furthermore, suppose that the mental retardation is of the same kind and severity as that caused by other birth defects that don't have the other two effects. It seems likely that denying moral status to such defective humans would not run the same risks of outraging human sensibilities as would the denial of moral status to other, less easily distinguished and more loved defective humans. Would these contingent empirical differences between our reactions to different sources of mental retardation justify us in ascribing different direct moral status to their subjects? The only difference between them is skin color and whether they are loved by others. Any theory that could ascribe moral relevance to differences such as these doesn't deserve to be taken seriously.[14]

Finally, perhaps we could claim that the practice of giving greater weight to the interests of all humans than of animals is justified on evolutionary grounds. Perhaps such differential concern has survival value for the species. Something like this may well be true, but it is hard to see the moral relevance. We can hardly justify the privileging of human interests over animal interests on the grounds that such privileging serves human interests!

6. AGENT AND PATIENT—THE SPECIESIST'S CENTRAL CONFUSION

Although the argument from marginal cases certainly poses a formidable challenge to any proposed criterion of full moral standing that excludes animals, it doesn't, in my view, constitute the most serious flaw in such attempts to justify the status quo. The proposed criteria are all variations on the Aristotelian criterion of rationality. But what is the moral relevance of rationality? Why should we think that the possession of a certain level or kind of

[14]Certain crude versions of the so-called ethics of care do seem to entail that the mere fact of being loved gives a different ethical status.

rationality renders the possessor's interests of greater moral significance than those of a merely sentient being? In Bentham's famous words "The question is not, Can they reason? nor Can they talk? But, Can they suffer?".[15]

What do defenders of the alleged superiority of human interests say in response to Bentham's challenge? Some, such as Carl Cohen, simply reiterate the differences between humans and animals that they claim to carry moral significance. Animals are not members of moral communities, they don't engage in moral reflection, they can't be moved by moral reasons, *therefore* (?) their interests don't count as much as ours. Others, such as Steinbock and Warren, attempt to go further. Here is Warren on the subject:

> Why is rationality morally relevant? It does not make us "better" than other animals or more "perfect." . . . But it is morally relevant insofar as it provides greater possibilities for cooperation and for the nonviolent resolution of problems.[16]

Warren is certainly correct in claiming that a certain level and kind of rationality is morally relevant. Where she, and others who give similar arguments, go wrong is in specifying what the moral relevance amounts to. If a being is incapable of moral reasoning, at even the most basic level, if it is incapable of being moved by moral reasons, claims, or arguments, then it cannot be a moral agent. It cannot be subject to moral obligations, to moral praise or blame. Punishing a dog for doing something "wrong" is no more than an attempt to alter its future behavior. So long as we are undeceived about the dog's cognitive capacities, we are not, except metaphorically, expressing any moral judgment about the dog's behavior. (We may, of course, be expressing a moral judgment about the behavior of the dog's owner, who didn't train it very well.) All this is well and good, but what is the significance for the question of what weight to give to animal interests? That animals can't be moral *agents* doesn't seem to be relevant to their status as moral *patients.* Many, perhaps most, humans are both moral agents and patients. Most, perhaps all, animals are only moral patients. Why would the lack of moral agency give them diminished status as moral patients? Full status as a moral patient is not some kind of reward for moral agency. I have heard students complain in this regard that it is *unfair* that humans bear the burdens of moral responsibility, and don't get enhanced consideration of their interests in return. This is a very strange claim. Humans are subject to moral obligations, because they are the kind of creatures who *can* be. What grounds moral agency is simply

[15]Jeremy Bentham, *Introduction to the Principles of Morals and Legislation*, (Various) chapter 17.
[16]Warren, op. cit. 482.

different from what grounds moral standing as a patient. It is no more unfair that humans and not animals are moral agents, than it is unfair that real animals and not stuffed toys are moral patients.

One other attempt to justify the selection of rationality as the criterion of full moral standing is worth considering. Recall the suggestion that rationality is important insofar as it facilitates cooperation. If we view the essence of morality as reciprocity, the significance of rationality is obvious. A certain twisted, but all-too-common, interpretation of the Golden Rule is that we should "do unto others in order to get them to do unto us." There's no point, according to this approach, in giving much, if any, consideration to the interests of animals, because they are simply incapable of giving like consideration to our interests. In discussing the morality of eating meat, I have, many times, heard students claim that we are justified in eating meat, because "the animals would eat us, if given half a chance." (That they say this in regard to our practice of eating cows and chickens is depressing testimony to their knowledge of the animals they gobble up with such gusto.) Inasmuch as there is a consistent view being expressed here at all, it concerns self-interest, as opposed to morality. Whether it serves my interests to give the same weight to the interests of animals as to those of humans is an interesting question, but it is not the same question as whether it is *right* to give animals' interests equal weight. The same point, of course, applies to the question of whether to give equal weight to my interests, or those of my family, race, sex, religion, etc. as to those of other people.

Perhaps it will be objected that I am being unfair to the suggestion that the essence of morality is reciprocity. Reciprocity is important, not because it serves *my* interests, but because it serves the interests of all. Reciprocity facilitates cooperation, which in turn produces benefits for all. What we should say about this depends on the scope of "all." If it includes all sentient beings, then the significance of animals' inability to reciprocate is in what it tells us about *how* to give their interests equal consideration. It certainly can't tell us that we should give less, or no, consideration to their interests. If, on the other hand, we claim that rationality is important for reciprocity, which is important for cooperation, which is important for benefiting humans, which is the ultimate goal of morality, we have clearly begged the question against giving equal consideration to the interests of animals.

It seems that any attempt to justify the claim that humans have a higher moral status than other animals by appealing to some version of rationality as the morally relevant difference between humans and animals will fail on at least two counts. It will fail to give an adequate answer to the argument from marginal cases, and, more importantly, it will fail to make the case that such a difference is morally relevant to the status of animals as moral patients as opposed to their status as moral agents.

I conclude that our intuitions that Fred's behavior is morally impermissible are accurate. Furthermore, given that the behavior of those who knowingly support factory farming is morally indistinguishable, it follows that their behavior is also morally impermissible.[17]

For Further Reflection

1. What is the argument from marginal cases? What is Norcross's final assessment of it?
2. Why does he think meat-eaters are not blameless in their consumption of meat produced by highly immoral factory farming?
3. What is Norcross's distinction between being a moral agent and a moral patient? How does he use it to argue against the practices of factory farming?

Further Readings for Chapter 14

Frey, R. G. *Rights, Killing and Suffering.* Oxford: Basil Blackwell, 1983.
Rachels, James. *Created from Animals: The Moral Implications of Darwinism.* Oxford: Oxford University Press, 1990.
Regan, Tom. *The Case for Animal Rights.* Berkeley: University of California Press, 1983.
Regan, Tom, and Peter Singer, eds. *Animal Rights and Human Obligations.* Englewood Cliffs, NJ: Prentice-Hall, 1976.
Robbins, John. *Diet for a New America: How Your Food Choices Affect Your Health, Happiness, and the Future of Life on Earth.* Walpole, NH: Stillpoint, 1987.
Rohr, Janelle, ed. *Animal Rights: Opposing Viewpoints.* San Diego: Greenhaven Press, 1989.
Singer, Peter. *Animal Liberation.* 2nd ed. New York: New York Review of Books, 1990.
VandeVeer, D., and Pierce, C., eds. *People, Penguins, and Plastic Trees.* Belmont, CA: Wadsworth, 1990.
Warren, Mary Anne. "Difficulties with the Strong Animal Rights Position." *Between the Species* 2, no. 4 (Fall 1987): 433–441.

[17]This paper, in various forms, has been presented in more places than I can remember, and has benefited from the comments of more people than I can shake a stick at. I particularly wish to thank, for their helpful comments, Doug Ehring, Mylan Engel, Mark Heller, and Steve Sverdlik.

CHAPTER 15

The Ethics of Climate Change

The first thing to understand about the issue of climate change is that it is both a *scientific* question (whether it's happening and, if so, why) and a *moral* question (what, if anything, we should do about it). An elementary mistake in thinking comes from letting your views on the latter dictate your assessment of the former.

For years, scientists throughout the world have been issuing unsettling reports and dire warnings about changes in Earth's climate. The Climate Science Special Report (CSSR), one of many statements issued by scientific organizations worldwide, says, "Global annually averaged surface air temperature has increased by about 1.8 degrees Fahrenheit (1.0 degrees C) over the last 115 years (1901–2016). This period is now the warmest in the history of modern civilization."[1]

Such a rise may seem small, but it can lead to huge, potentially cataclysmic effects worldwide. According to the Intergovernmental Panel on Climate Change (IPCC), a group of 1300 independent scientific experts worldwide,

> Each of the last three decades has been successively warmer at the Earth's surface than any preceding decade since 1850. The period from 1983 to 2012 was likely the warmest 30-year period of the last 1400 years in the Northern Hemisphere, where such assessment is possible (medium confidence).[2]

[1]U.S. Global Change Research Program, "Climate Science Special Report," Fourth National Climate Assessment (NCA4), Volume I, July 15, 2019, https://science2017.globalchange.gov/chapter/executive-summary/.

[2]Intergovernmental Panel on Climate Change (IPCC), *Climate Change 2014: Synthesis Report, Summary for Policymakers*, July 15, 2019, https://www.ipcc.ch/site/assets/uploads/2018/02/AR5_SYR_FINAL_SPM.pdf, 2.

Climate scientists say the planet is heating up because of the greenhouse effect: the heat of solar radiation is being trapped in the lower atmosphere by so-called greenhouse gases. These include carbon dioxide (CO_2), methane, and nitrous oxide, all of which have increased dramatically in the atmosphere since before the Industrial Revolution. Some of the increase comes from natural sources like volcanic eruptions, but most of it has been traced to human activity such as the burning of fossil fuels (coal, oil, and gas), as well as to deforestation and land use changes. The IPCC asserts,

> Anthropogenic [human-caused] greenhouse gas emissions have increased since the pre-industrial era, driven largely by economic and population growth, and are now higher than ever. This has led to atmospheric concentrations of carbon dioxide, methane and nitrous oxide that are unprecedented in at least the last 800,000 years. Their effects, together with those of other anthropogenic drivers, have been detected throughout the climate system and are extremely likely to have been the dominant cause of the observed warming since the mid-20th century.[3]

This global warming has already had powerful effects on the planet. These have been both positive and negative but, on balance, mostly negative. NASA declares in its report "Global Climate Change: Vital Signs of the Planet,"

> Glaciers have shrunk, ice on rivers and lakes is breaking up earlier, plant and animal ranges have shifted and trees are flowering sooner.
>
> Effects that scientists had predicted in the past would result from global climate change are now occurring: loss of sea ice, accelerated sea level rise and longer, more intense heat waves.[4]

According to the U.S. Global Change Research Program, there are many effects of climate change that are happening now in the United States and are likely to continue:

> **Northeast.** Heat waves, heavy downpours and sea level rise pose growing challenges to many aspects of life in the Northeast. Infrastructure, agriculture, fisheries and ecosystems will be increasingly compromised. Many states and cities are beginning to incorporate climate change into their planning.
>
> **Northwest.** Changes in the timing of streamflow reduce water supplies for competing demands. Sea level rise, erosion, inundation, risks to infrastructure and increasing ocean acidity pose major threats. Increasing wildfire, insect outbreaks and tree diseases are causing widespread tree die-off.

[3]IPCC, *Climate Change 2014*, 4.

[4]NASA, *Global Climate Change*, "Global Climate Change: Vital Signs of the Planet," July 15, 2019, https://climate.nasa.gov/.

Southeast. Sea level rise poses widespread and continuing threats to the region's economy and environment. Extreme heat will affect health, energy, agriculture and more. Decreased water availability will have economic and environmental impacts.
Midwest. Extreme heat, heavy downpours and flooding will affect infrastructure, health, agriculture, forestry, transportation, air and water quality, and more. Climate change will also exacerbate a range of risks to the Great Lakes.
Southwest. Increased heat, drought and insect outbreaks, all linked to climate change, have increased wildfires. Declining water supplies, reduced agricultural yields, health impacts in cities due to heat, and flooding and erosion in coastal areas are additional concerns.[5]

Climate change and global warming are controversial mostly because of their political and policy implications. If the planet really is becoming overheated, and if the main cause of the warming is increased levels of greenhouse gases produced by the burning of fossil fuels, then it seems that the obvious solution is to implement major reductions in the burning of these fuels. Such reductions would disrupt or alter the economic, commercial, and industrial systems that now run on the fuels—changes that many people strongly oppose.

But the scientific facts are clear: global warming is happening, and human activity is the cause. An enormous number of scientific studies and observations demonstrate that Earth is getting warmer, and the evidence that this warming is human-caused is extensive, consistent, and multidimensional. From 1800 to 2012, major greenhouse gas carbon dioxide has increased in the atmosphere by about 40 percent—from about 280 parts per million by volume to about 380 parts per million. As carbon dioxide has increased, so has global surface temperature, and scientists have been able to link the carbon dioxide directly to human activities.

Most actively publishing climate scientists—97 percent—affirm that global warming is happening now and that humans are causing it. Eighteen American scientific societies and 11 international science academies concur. A joint statement from the American scientific organizations says,

> Observations throughout the world make it clear that climate change is occurring, and rigorous scientific research demonstrates that the greenhouse gases emitted by human activities are the primary driver.[6]

[5]U.S. Global Change Research Program, "Climate Science Special Report."
[6]American Association for the Advancement of Science (AAAS) , "AAAS Reaffirms Statements on Climate Change and Integrity," December 4, 2009. AAAS Reaffirms Statement on Climate Change | American Association for the Advancement of Science.

The moral questions that climate change provokes are momentous. They confront both governments and international organizations as well as individuals. Given that climate change is real, humans are causing it, and the harm caused is and will be enormous, what are we morally obligated to do about it? Given that what we do or don't do now will affect future generations, what should we do, if anything, about that? What do we owe the future? What do rich countries owe the poorer people of the world whose lives and livelihoods are adversely affected by the tremendous amounts of greenhouse gas emissions produced by the rich? Can the actions of one person matter morally? If we agree that we have a duty to help prevent climate change, what exactly should we do? What *can* we do?

What Has Posterity Ever Done for Me?

ROBERT HEILBRONER

Robert Heilbroner (1919–2005) was for many years a professor of economics at the New School for Social Research in New York. He is the author of several books, including *The Worldly Philosophers and Marxism: For and Against.*

Heilbroner asks why we should care about future people or whether humanity survives into the distant future. Citing fellow economists who argue that we have no reason to sacrifice for the unknown future, Heilbroner expresses outrage at this callous disregard for future people. Admitting that he cannot give a rational argument for this view, he appeals to Adam's Smith's principle of sentiment or inner conscience, which urges us to work for the long-range survival of humanity.

Will mankind survive? Who knows? The question I want to put is more searching: Who cares? It is clear that most of us today do not care—or at least do not care enough. How many of us would be willing to give up some minor convenience—say, the use of aerosols—in the hope that this might extend the life of man on earth by a hundred years? Suppose we also knew with a high degree of certainty that humankind could not survive a thousand years unless we gave up our wasteful diet of meat, abandoned all pleasure driving, cut back on every use of energy that was not essential to the maintenance of a bare minimum. Would we care enough for posterity to pay the price of its survival?

I doubt it. A thousand years is unimaginably distant. Even a century far exceeds our powers of empathetic imagination. By the year 2075, I shall probably have been dead for three quarters of a century. My children will also likely be dead, and my grandchildren, if I have any, will be in their dotage. What does it matter to me, then, what life will be like in 2075, much less 3075? Why should I lift a finger to affect events that will have no more meaning for me seventy-five years after my death than those that happened seventy-five years before I was born?

There is no rational answer to that terrible question. No argument based on reason will lead me to care for posterity or to lift a finger in its behalf. Indeed, by every rational consideration, precisely the opposite answer is thrust upon us with irresistible force. As a Distinguished Professor of political economy at the University of London has written in the current winter issue of *Business and Society Review:*

> Suppose that, as a result of using up all the world's resources, human life did come to an end. So what? What is so desirable about an indefinite continuation of the human species, religious convictions apart? It may well be that nearly everybody who is already here on earth would be reluctant to die, and that everybody has an instinctive fear of death. But one must not confuse this with the notion that, in any meaningful sense, generations who are yet unborn can be said to be better off if they are born than if they are not.

Thus speaks the voice of rationality. It is echoed in the book *The Economic Growth Controversy* by a Distinguished Younger Economist from the Massachusetts Institute of Technology:

> ... Geological time [has been] made comprehensible to our finite human minds by the statement that the 4.5 billion years of the earth's history [are] equivalent to once around the world in an SST.... Man got on eight miles before the end, and industrial man got on six feet before the end.... Today we are having a debate about the extent to which man ought to maximize the length of time that he is on the airplane.
>
> According to what the scientists think, the sun is gradually expanding and 12 billion years from now the earth will be swallowed up by the sun. This means that our airplane has time to go round three more times. Do we want man to be on it for all three times around the world? Are we interested in man being on for another eight miles? Are we interested in man being on for another six feet? Or are we only interested in man for a fraction of a millimeter—our lifetimes?
>
> That led me to think: Do I care what happens a thousand years from now? ... Do I care when man gets off the airplane? I think I basically [have come] to the conclusion that I don't care whether man is on the airplane for another eight feet, or if man is on the airplane another three times around the world.

Is it an outrageous position? I must confess it outrages me. But this is not because the economists' arguments are "wrong"—indeed, within their rational framework they are indisputably right. It is because their position reveals the limitations—worse, the suicidal dangers—of what we call "rational argument" when we confront questions that can only be decided by an appeal to an entirely different faculty from that of cool reason. More than that, I suspect that if there is cause to fear for man's survival it is because the calculus of logic and reason will be applied to problems where they have as little validity, even as little bearing, as the calculus of feeling or sentiment applied to the solution of a problem in Euclidean geometry.

If reason cannot give us a compelling argument to care for posterity—and to care desperately and totally—what can? For an answer, I turn to another distinguished economist whose fame originated in his profound examination of moral conduct. In 1759, Adam Smith published "The Theory of Moral Sentiments," in which he posed a question very much like ours, but to which he gave an answer very different from that of his latter-day descendants.

Suppose, asked Smith, that "a man of humanity" in Europe were to learn of a fearful earthquake in China—an earthquake that swallowed up its millions of inhabitants. How would that man react? He would, Smith mused, "make many melancholy reflections upon the precariousness of human life, and the vanity of all the labors of man, which could thus be annihilated in a moment. He would, too, perhaps, if he was a man of speculation, enter into many reasonings concerning the effects which this disaster might produce upon the commerce of Europe, and the trade and business of the world in general." Yet, when this fine philosophizing was over, would our "man of humanity" care much about the catastrophe in distant China? He would not. As Smith tells us, he would "pursue his business or his pleasure, take his repose for his diversion, with the same ease and tranquillity as if nothing had happened."

But now suppose, Smith says, that our man were told he was to lose his little finger on the morrow. A very different reaction would attend the contemplation of this "frivolous disaster." Our man of humanity would be reduced to a tormented state, tossing all night with fear and dread—whereas "provided he never saw them, he will snore with the most profound security over the ruin of a hundred millions of his brethren."

Next, Smith puts the critical question: Since the hurt to his finger bulks so large and the catastrophe in China so small, does this mean that a man of humanity, given the choice, would prefer the extinction of a hundred million Chinese in order to save his little finger? Smith is unequivocal in his answer. "Human nature startles at the thought," he cries, "and the world in its greatest depravity and corruption never produced such a villain as would be capable of entertaining it."

But what stays our hand? Since we are all such creatures of self-interest (and is not Smith the very patron saint of the motive of self-interest?), what moves us to give precedence to the rights of humanity over those of our own immediate well-being? The answer, says Smith, is the presence within us all of a "man within the beast," an inner creature of conscience whose insistent voice brooks no disobedience: "It is the love of what is honorable and noble, of the grandeur and dignity, and superiority of our own characters."

It does not matter whether Smith's eighteenth-century view of human nature in general or morality in particular appeals to the modern temper. What matters is that he has put the question that tests us to the quick. For it is one thing to appraise matters of life and death by the principles of rational self-interest and quite another *to take responsibility for our choice.* I cannot imagine the Distinguished Professor from the University of London personally consigning humanity to oblivion with the same equanimity with which he writes off its demise. I am certain that if the Distinguished Younger Economist from M.I.T. were made responsible for determining the precise length of stay of humanity on the SST, he would agonize over the problem and end up by exacting every last possible inch for mankind's journey.

Of course, there are moral dilemmas to be faced even if one takes one's stand on the "survivalist" principle. Mankind cannot expect to continue on earth indefinitely if we do not curb population growth, thereby consigning billions or tens of billions to the oblivion of nonbirth. Yet, in this case, we sacrifice some portion of life-to-come in order that life itself may be preserved. This essential commitment to life's continuance gives us the moral authority to take measures, perhaps very harsh measures, whose justification cannot be found in the precepts of rationality, but must be sought in the unbearable anguish we feel if we imagine ourselves as the executioners of mankind.

This anguish may well be those "religious convictions," to use the phrase our London economist so casually tosses away. Perhaps to our secular cast of mind, the anguish can be more easily accepted as the furious power of the biogenetic force we see expressed in every living organism. Whatever its source, when we ask if mankind "should" survive, it is only here that we can find a rationale that gives us the affirmation we seek.

This is not to say we will discover a religious affirmation naturally welling up within us as we careen toward Armageddon. We know very little about how to convince men by recourse to reason and nothing about how to convert them to religion. A hundred faiths contend for believers today, a few perhaps capable of generating that sense of caring for human salvation on earth. But, in truth, we do not know if "religion" will win out. An appreciation of the magnitude of the sacrifices required to perpetuate life may well tempt us to opt for "rationality"—to enjoy life while it is still to be enjoyed on relatively easy terms, to write mankind a shorter ticket on the SST so that some of us may enjoy the next millimeter of the trip in first-class seats.

Yet I am hopeful that in the end a survivalist ethic will come to the fore—not from the reading of a few books or the passing twinge of a pious lecture, but from an experience that will bring home to us, as Adam Smith brought home to his "man of humanity," the personal responsibility that defies all the homicidal promptings of reasonable calculation. Moreover, I believe that the coming generations, in their encounters with famine, war, and the threatened life-carrying capacity of the globe, may be given just such an experience. It is a glimpse into the void of a universe without man. I must rest my ultimate faith on the discovery by these future generations, as the ax of the executioner passes into their hands, of the transcendent importance of posterity for them.

For Further Reflection

1. Why should we care about future generations? How would you answer Heilbroner's question, "Why should I lift a finger to affect events that will have no more meaning for me seventy-five years after my death than those that happened seventy-five years before I was born?"
2. Do you agree with Heilbroner that there is "no rational answer to that terrible question"? Defend your answer.
3. Do you think "religious convictions" or simply well-thought-out humanistic concerns (Adam Smith's "man of humanity") should have more weight than logic and rational argument when considering issues such as obligations to posterity? How do you decide?

A Perfect Moral Storm: The Ethical Tragedy of Climate Change

STEPHEN M. GARDINER

Stephen Gardiner makes the case that climate change—a global environmental tragedy—is at its core mostly an ethical failure on the part of humanity. It is, in fact, a threefold "perfect moral storm." The storms are: (1) global, in which rich nations have the power to act to benefit themselves to the detriment of poorer nations, (2) intergenerational, because earlier generations have pronounced power over the prospects of future generations, and (3) theoretical, due to a lack of general theories to guide us in dealing with the first two storms.

Stephen M. Gardiner, *A Perfect Moral Storm: The Ethical Tragedy of Climate Change* (Oxford: Oxford University Press, 2011), 3–13.

I. MY APPROACH

In my view, the global environmental tragedy is most centrally an ethical failure, and one that implicates our institutions, our moral and political theories, and ultimately ourselves, considered as moral agents. In a moment, I will introduce my explanation of how the tragedy comes about through the metaphor of the perfect moral storm. But first let me say something about the kind of project I am engaged in, some of the assumptions I am making, and the audience for which this book is intended.

Much work in moral and political philosophy, and especially in its more applied or practical areas, takes the form of announcing, developing, and defending a set of principles (or norms) for guiding institution building or policy decisions in a particular area. This is a worthy endeavor; however, it is not my aim in this book. Instead, my goal is to get clearer about the nature of the problem itself, as a preliminary to generating and assessing potential solutions.[1]

Such a project has precedents in at least two traditions of moral and political theorizing. The first is perhaps best exemplified by the social contract tradition in political philosophy in general, and the work of Thomas Hobbes in particular.[2] Hobbes sets out to say what the basic problem of political organization really is. (Infamously, he claims that it is to avoid the scenario of continual war in a state of nature where life is "nasty, brutish and short.") He then treats this account as the background against which potential solutions should be formulated and judged. As it happens, Hobbes's statement of the problem has turned out to be of more enduring interest than his own attempt at a solution. Still, his contribution is not regarded as any less important because of that. Sometimes clearly identifying the problem is a crucial step.[3]

The second tradition is most clearly evident in what might broadly be called virtue theory, although it is also present in other approaches to normative ethics, as well as in some areas of professional ethics, and in literature. This tradition seeks to identify the characteristic "temptations" present in certain situations, positions, or ways of life, where these are understood as vulnerabilities to behaving badly to which many are likely to be susceptible. Such work is helpful not only for thinking about how to resist acting badly,

[1]For solution-oriented material, see chapter 11, Gardiner et al. 2010, Garvey 2008, Page 2006, and Vanderheiden 2008a, 2008b.

[2]Locke 1988, Rousseau 1997, Rawls 1999, Dworkin 2000, and Nozick 1974 also fit into the more general tradition, even though not all are contract theorists.

[3]A similar point might be made in epistemology about Descartes s method of doubt. This is set up as the criterion against which solutions to the problem of knowledge should be judged. Again, Descartes's own solution has not been influential; but his effort to set out the problem provides the backdrop for centuries of further work.

but also in coming to understand ourselves as moral agents.[4] "Who we are," morally speaking, is a significant ethical issue, and one which . . . has considerable bearing on the global environmental tragedy.

Let us turn now to assumptions. In setting out my account of the global environmental tragedy I will be taking for granted a number of claims that I shall not attempt to justify within the confines of this book. These include that we have strong reason to believe that climate change poses a real and potentially catastrophic threat to human and other life on this planet,[5] that scientific concern about the threat is robust and not driven by some kind of left-wing or green conspiracy, and that people in all nations have a shared responsibility to act together to address the threat.[6] I shall also assume that ethical concerns matter in deciding exactly why and how we must act; and that it is not only inaction mat might be morally wrong (in ways to be discussed), but also inappropriate action(such as, a retreat of the affluent into, their own "fortress world," or predatory geoengineering). Nevertheless, in keeping with the goal of clearly identifying the problem, I will try to couch the ethical risks of our current predicament in the broadest possible terms. My hope is to specify the global environmental tragedy in language that almost all morally serious people can accept, and so I will try not to beg any contentious theoretical questions. Presumably, potential solutions to the tragedy will have to go further, and make claims that are more controversial. Still, in my view, it is better not to build in such assumptions at the beginning. As we shall see, one of my main claims is that we are already vulnerable to distraction from the imperative to act, and act well. . . .

In my view, the issue is one that concerns all of us, simply as moral agents. The future of our own societies, of humanity, and of many of the earth's species is at stake, and with them our own moral legacy. Hence, I have tried to make my discussion accessible to as many people as possible, avoiding as much tangential complexity as I can. This is not a time for purely parochial concerns, or local academic niceties. . . .

But I want to stress right from the start that my objective is not to vilify any particular individuals, groups, classes, or nations. Indeed, the point is not really to apportion blame at all, but rather to help us understand our own predicament. This is a tragedy in which most of the world's more affluent people play a part. Hence, almost all those able to read this book are ethically vulnerable to at least some extent, in many parts of our lives, and

[4]Consider, for example, Plato's discussion of conflicts between the three parts of the soul, Aristotle's account of the excess and deficiency related to each virtue, and Hume's analysis of the "monkish" and other virtues. Some recent writings on "moral psychology" also fit this mold.
[5]IPCC 2007a; Oreskes 2005.
[6]See chapter 11.

through membership in a wide range of social and political communities. If the moral quality of our lives is not to be compromised, we must seek to address it together.

II. INTRODUCING THE PERFECT STORM METAPHOR

The global environmental tragedy has many causes and aspects. But in this book I will highlight three central contributions through invoking the metaphor of "a perfect moral storm." I borrow the phrase "a perfect storm" from Sebastian Junger's book of that name, and the subsequent Hollywood film.[7] lunger recounts the true story of the *Andrea Gail*, a fishing vessel caught at sea during the rare convergence of three particularly bad storms, and ultimately destroyed as a result. Given this, I take a perfect storm to involve the unusual intersection of a number of serious, and mutually reinforcing, problems, which creates an unusual and perhaps unprecedented challenge. In my metaphor of the perfect moral storm, the three problems (or "storms") are all obstacles to our ability to behave ethically. Like the Andrea Gail, we are beset by forces that are likely at least to throw us off course, and may even sink us into the bargain.

Each of the first two storms involves a serious asymmetry of power, where the possibility of some taking undue advantage[8] of others is pronounced. The first storm is global. Its key feature is that the world's most affluent nations, and especially the rich within those nations, have considerable power to shape what is done, and to do so in ways which favor their own concerns, especially over those of the world's poorer nations, and poor people within those nations.

The second storm is intergenerational. Its key feature is that the current generation has similar, but more pronounced, asymmetric power over the prospects of future generations: roughly speaking, earlier generations can affect the prospects of future generations, but not vice versa. In my view, the intergenerational storm is the most prominent of the three. Here the possibilities for taking advantage are deep.

The third storm is theoretical. In dealing with the first two storms, it would be nice if we had robust general theories to guide us. Unfortunately, this is not the case. In particular, existing theories are extremely underdeveloped in

[7] Junger 1999.

[8] In keeping with my aim of begging as few theoretical questions as possible, I shall use the phrase "taking undue advantage" (or just "taking advantage") as a placeholder, to be filled in by a more nuanced philosophical account of the moral wrong at stake. (I take it that this is often the function of that phrase.) For example, one might try to flesh it out with notions such as "exploitation" (Bertram 2009) or "domination" (Nolt 2011), or by appeal to violations of the principles of a particular moral or political theory, such as Rawls's (cf. Gardiner 2011a).

many of the relevant areas, including intergenerational ethics, international justice, scientific uncertainty, and the human relationship to animals and the rest of nature. This not only complicates the task of behaving well, but also renders us more vulnerable to the first two storms.

Each of the three storms hampers the cause of ethical action, and threatens to blow it seriously off course. But taken together they are mutually reinforcing, and the challenge becomes profound. Moreover, this interaction also brings on new problems. Most prominently, the perfect storm puts pressure on the very terms in which we discuss the environmental crisis, tempting us to distort our moral sensibilities in order to facilitate the exploitation of our global and intergenerational position. I call this "the problem of moral corruption."

III. CLIMATE CHANGE

In this book, I explore the perfect moral storm through a discussion of one central example, that of global climate change. I do so both because this is the leading environmental problem of our age, and because it is an especially good example of the storm.

First, the sources and impacts of climate change are spread across space, time, and species. The temporal aspect is particularly striking. Once emitted, molecules of the main greenhouse gas, carbon dioxide, typically persist in the atmosphere and contribute to warming for centuries. Moreover, a significant percentage of these emissions remains for thousands, and even tens of thousands, of years. Given this, the full impacts of our current activities are realized over a very long period, making the problem they pose profoundly intergenerational.

Second, climate change provides a compelling case study of how the storm can undermine effective policy. On the matter of substance, there is a serious problem of political inertia. Leaders and their countries have been promising to act for nearly two decades now. But this has been a sad history of delay, obstruction, and broken promises. . . .

In the early 1990s, the nations of the world announced the objective of avoiding dangerous climate change for the sake of protecting current and future generations against its impacts, and with the understanding that ecosystems should not be pushed beyond their capacities to adapt. In line with this, many industrialized countries (including the United States, Canada, Japan, New Zealand, and Norway) said that they would voluntarily stabilize their emissions at 1990 levels by 2000. As it turned out, almost no one did so, and most had risen by around 10% by that time.[9]

[9]Marland 2008. Germany and the United Kingdom did post reductions, although these were for unrelated economic reasons.

Moreover, subsequent negotiations around the Kyoto Protocol have at best had only limited effect Despite a few notable efforts, emissions in most countries continued to grow through the next decade, even as the science suggested that reductions were becoming much more urgent. The United States, for example, saw growth of just over 20% in the period 1990–2005, while global emissions increased by almost 30%.

More recently, in the period 2007–09, much energy was invested in the idea that a United Nations meeting in Copenhagen in December 2009 would produce a new, more ambitious, and binding global treaty to replace Kyoto. However, as things turned out, that gathering delivered only a vague and weak political accord, accompanied by widespread dismay and angry recriminations.

It is difficult to see this experience as anything other than a geopolitical disaster. As Connie Hedegaard, the Danish Minister for Climate and Energy (and subsequently EU commissioner on climate action), put it two months before Copenhagen: "If the whole world comes to Copenhagen and leaves without making the needed political agreement, then I think it's a failure that is not just about climate. Then it's the whole global democratic system not being able to deliver results in one of the defining challenges of our century, And that . . . should not be a possibility."[10]

As a matter of public discourse, the geopolitical disaster has been facilitated by the fact that the current generation in the developed countries has spent much of the last two decades conveniently distracted and confused about the problem. On the one hand, governments have persistently had "other priorities," and citizens have failed to see climate change even as a serious environmental problem, let alone one of humanity's largest problems per se.[11] On the other hand, we have seen much hand wringing about the soundness of the science (albeit almost all by nonscientists, or scientists who don't work on climate), active campaigns of misinformation, and a tendency to reduce the issue to tangential matters such as recycling. In short, few seem interested in really dealing with the problem despite its catastrophic potential. All of this seems difficult to explain away in any normal way. Unfortunately, in a perfect moral storm, it makes perfect sense. The temptation to pass the buck on to the future, the poor, and nature is very strong. So, the incentive to disengage is high.

In my view, then, the perfect moral storm poses a very serious and deep ethical challenge, and one that is manifest in the climate policy of the last two decades. Still, mine is not a council of despair. First even given the theoretical storm, the broad outlines of what must be done are relatively clear

[10]Von Bulow 2009.

[11]Leiserowitz 2005, 2009; Pew 2005; see also Jamieson 2006.

and well-known, especially in the short- to medium-term. . . . Even lacking robust theory, intermediate guidance is possible using indirect methods, such as identifying intuitively clear cases of failure, trying to articulate ethical constraints based on those cases, searching for levels of overlapping consensus across existing theories, and defending such benchmarks against the forces of moral corruption. Such strategies suggest two things. To begin with, global emissions must be put onto a sensible pathway that takes seriously the needs and aspirations of both present and future people. Given the extreme risk facing future generations, this mandates that they must peak sometime in the next few decades and then decline significantly for the foreseeable future. In addition, the developed nations are morally required to take the lead, and the heaviest burdens, at least in the short- to medium-term.

Second, though achieving the broad outlines will be a serious challenge, the more central problem seems to be with engaging and then making operative the motivations that can bring it about. However, this is within our control. If climate change is a perfect moral storm, it is concerns about what we are doing to the poor, future generations, and nature justify most of what needs to be done. I am optimistic that most of us have such concerns, and take them seriously. (Others are less so, but that is another story.) Still, what seems clear is that we lack the appropriate institutions to make these concerns effective in the world of policy. Markets and democratic elections may be good at registering short-term and local interests, but they look more dubious in the face of the perfect storm. We must find new ways to engage such institutions, and probably also develop additional institutions to help.

Third, here it is useful to recognize that the biggest obstacles to effective action may be our own complacency. Much of what passes for even the most progressive discussion of climate change these days is devoted to persuading us that dealing with the problem will not be costly in terms of our current lifestyles, and so is compatible with ways of living that many take to be in their best interests. This is comforting talk, and I am hopeful that at least some of it may turn out to be true. Nevertheless, it seems to me that this is the wrong discussion to be having. The primary reasons for acting on climate change are not that doing so will be good (or at least not bad) *for us*; they are deeper and more morally serious than that. In my view, seeing this should make it easier for us to act. To dither when one might prevent moderate harms to oneself by taking modest precautionary action is folly to be sure, but its moral import is limited. By contrast, to engage in willful self-deception and moral corruption when the lives of future generations, the world's poor, and even the basic fabric of life on the planet is at stake is a much more serious business. We should wake up to that fact, and demand more of our institutions, our leaders, and ourselves.

IV. THE WIDER RELEVANCE OF THE MODEL

The focus of this book is on climate change. This is a vitally important topic. Still, I want to emphasize that the perfect moral storm analysis does not stand or fall with this case alone. In my view, the analysis is relevant to environmental affairs more generally, and indeed beyond them to other areas of human life. Importantly, other manifestations of the perfect moral storm are not only possible, but also likely over the coming decades and centuries. Presumably, as humanity's activities become ever more extensive, the potential for the global and intergenerational problems to manifest themselves also increases. Some suggestion of this may come from the fact that climate change is already the second genuinely global environmental problem to come along in just a few decades (after ozone depletion), and another (ocean acidification) comes fast on its heels.[12] Another indication comes from the thought that we may have already seen degenerate forms[13] of the storm in other areas—such as nuclear proliferation, and financial deregulation prior to the Great Depression and current recession.

One way to see the wider relevance of the perfect storm is by contrasting it with the traditional "tragedy of the commons" analysis originally made popular by Garrett Hardin. This model is ubiquitous in discussions of environmental (and many other) problems. But, for reasons which should become clear, I believe that the perfect moral storm is sometimes more fundamental, and the intergenerational storm often so. This has practical consequences. Hardin's model, though useful in many contexts and respects, would underestimate the seriousness of some problems, and misdirect our energies in searching for solutions.[14] Given this, it should sometimes give way.

Another reason that the perfect storm analysis has more general relevance is that ultimately we are in need of a political philosophy and an ethic to

[12]Ozone depletion does not seem to fit the perfect moral storm model, partly because it has substantial intragenerational effects that seem sufficient to motivate action. But ocean acidification may share some of the crucial characteristics.

[13]For example, we might see the convergence of the intergenerational and theoretical storms at a national or regional level. At first glance, this would not be a perfect moral storm in my sense, since it is not global in scope. Still, it might retain many of the same characteristics, so that much of what we say about the perfect storm remains apt. More deeply, from the theoretical point of view the crucial features of what I have been calling the "global" storm are not essentially tied to a single planet considered as such (let alone this planet), but rather to certain kinds of systems that are largely self-contained. I call the storm "global" since, at this stage in human history, the earth is such a system for humanity, and because many of our prominent political and theoretical problems are at this level (see chapter 7). I say more about the idea of degenerate forms in chapter 5.

[14]On Hardin's application of the commons metaphor to world population, see Appendix 1.

address it, and especially its intergenerational aspect. This is especially so if, as I suggest elsewhere, the challenge of the storm is in some ways more fundamental than the one much conventional theory tries to address.[15] Surely philosophy would be remiss if it did not try to rise to the challenge and provide an "ideal theory" to resolve this deep problem.[16]

In the case of climate change, of course, the problem is too urgent to wait, so we must muddle through without strong theory, and within existing institutions. Hence, as well as ideal theory, we must also seek an "ethics for the transition." As already mentioned, here we are fortunate that the basic parameters of what needs to be done morally-speaking are fairly clear, at least in the short- to medium-term. Nevertheless, there remains work to be done in fleshing out the details, and in defending this ethical consensus against the forces of moral corruption. Moreover, how to get existing political institutions to act, or how to create and fashion new (even transitional) ones, is not obvious. Hence, in addition to pointing in the general direction we should be heading, it would be useful for the ethics of the transition to offer some guidance in how to get there, and what to do while we figure out both of these things.

. . . Here my aim is to clearly identify the problem, trusting that in the current context this is itself a contribution to progress. If we persistently see global environmental problems in general, and climate change in particular, through other lenses (e.g., the scientific, economic, or short-term geopolitical), this may prevent us from reaching a solution. As Henry Shue likes to say, "sometimes sunlight is the best antiseptic."[17] I hope that in this case it is.

For Further Reflection

1. According to Gardiner, why is the intergenerational second storm a moral problem? What moral choices does it entail?
2. What are Gardiner's views about the reality of climate change?
3. Give two reasons why Gardiner does not counsel despair in the face of the perfect moral storm.

[15]Gardiner 2009a, 2011a.
[16]Rawls 1999.
[17]Shue 1980, 341.

The Public and Private Morality of Climate Change

JOHN BROOME

John Broome contends that climate change presents profound challenges to both public and private morality and that in each sphere we must identify obligations of justice and goodness. He argues that individuals do harm to others through their emissions of greenhouse gases, that we each have a duty of justice not to cause this harm, and that this duty is not as onerous as it may first appear.

We as individuals are subject to various moral duties. We have a duty to be kind to strangers, to keep our promises, to look after our parents when they are old, and so on. Collective entities, including our governments, are also subject to moral duties, or so I assume. I assume that a government should not imprison innocent people, it should protect refugees, it should support the destitute, and so on, and that these are moral duties.

The moral duties of governments—whatever they are—I call "public morality." They generate derivative moral duties for citizens: we should do what is appropriate to get our government to act rightly, and support it when it does. These duties I call "civic morality." By "private morality," I mean the morality of our private lives; private morality does not include our civic duties.

Climate change creates duties within both public and private morality. I shall describe some of them.

DUTIES OF JUSTICE AND DUTIES OF GOODNESS

Moral duties fall into two broad classes: duties of justice and duties of goodness or beneficence. There may be other sorts of moral duties, too, but I shall be concerned only with these two. I start by making the distinction between them.

The duty of goodness is to make the world better. Some libertarians deny that people as individuals have this duty. I disagree with those libertarians, but I have no need to argue with them here. My conclusions about private morality will not call on this duty of goodness. However, I shall assume that governments have a duty of goodness; I assume they have a duty to make the

John Broome, "The Public and Private Morality of Climate Change," The Tanner Lectures, University of Michigan, 2012.

world better for their own citizens at least. For instance, they should create their country's economic infrastructure and design their banking regulations with that aim in mind.

Improving the world is not our only moral duty. When an action of yours would improve the world, you are not necessarily morally required to do it, and sometimes you are not even morally permitted to do it. A famous example is the case of a surgeon who has five patients, each needing an organ in order to survive: one needs a heart, another a liver, a third a kidney, and so on. Suppose the surgeon kills an innocent visitor to the hospital and distributes her organs to the five patients, thereby saving five lives at the expense of one. That leads to a net benefit; it improves the world. Yet this surgeon s act is not morally permissible.

So there must be some other source of moral duties that can oppose the duty of goodness. There is evidently some sort of a moral duty not to harm people, even for the sake of the greater overall good. This is not merely a duty to take account of as a harm, as a negative good, in the course of performing your duty to improve the world. If it were, the surgeon I described would not be acting wrongly, whereas actually she is. On the other hand, the duty not to harm is not unlimited; there are occasions when it is morally permissible to harm someone. For instance, you may do harm in self-defense, and you may harm a person when you are inflicting a deserved punishment on her. I am sorry to say I cannot accurately delineate the boundaries of the duty not to harm, but I hope soon to identify one instance of it convincingly.

I take this duty not to harm to be a duty of justice. Other philosophers may classify it differently, and nothing will turn on the classification. It does have at least one feature that is characteristic of justice. It is a duty *owed* to a particular person, or to particular people. If you breach a duty of justice, you are doing an injustice, and there is always someone to whom you do it. To express this fact, we often say that the person has a *right* to your performing the duty. Rights go along with justice. When you have a duty of justice to do something, someone has a right to your doing it.

By contrast, duties of goodness are not owed to particular people. The difference is nicely illustrated by the views of the eighteenth-century philosopher William Godwin. Godwin thought that the duty to promote good is indeed owed to the people whose good you should promote.[1] He explicitly classified it as a duty of justice. For instance, he thought that if someone else can make better use of your horse than you can, she has a right to it. He thought you do her an injustice if you do not let her have it. Few of us agree with Godwin

[1]William Godwin, *Enquiry Concerning Political Justice*, 3rd ed. (1798; reprint, Harmondsworth: Penguin Press, 1976).

about that. Most of us think we have a duty to promote goodness, but we think the duty is not owed to particular people, and we therefore do not take it to be a duty of justice.

JUSTICE AND GOODNESS IN PUBLIC AND PRIVATE MORALITY

I am now going to apply this distinction among sorts of duty to the moral duties that arise from climate change. My first point is that the relative importance of justice and goodness differs between private morality and public morality. Justice is relatively more important for private morality, goodness relatively more important for public morality. Indeed, I shall argue that the private morality of climate change is governed entirely by the duty of justice, whereas public morality is also aimed at goodness.

Why do I say this? For two main reasons. The first is known as the "nonidentity problem." It was made prominent by the philosopher Derek Parfit.[2] Remember that a duty of justice is owed to particular people, who have a right to its performance. Take a particular person who is alive 150 years from now—call her "Sarah." Suppose Sarah's life is not very good because we, the current generation, allow climate change to go unchecked. Could she claim we do her an injustice by our profligacy? Could she say she has a right to a better life, which we deny her by emitting so much greenhouse gas? She could not, for a reason I shall now explain.

Suppose we were instead to take the trouble to reduce our emissions. By "we" I am referring to the present generation either in the whole world or within a particular nation. We would live lives of a different sort. The richer among us would travel less by car and plane and buy fewer consumer goods. The poorer would find farming easier and find less need to migrate to the cities; they would also find less need to move to higher ground to escape from the rising sea. There would be many other differences. Indeed, everyone's life would be different. Consequently, many people would have babies with different partners. Even those who would have the same partner as they actually do have would conceive their babies at different times.

The identity of a person depends on the sperm and egg she originates from. No one could have come from a different egg or a different sperm from the one she actually does come from. To put it differently: anyone who originated

[2]Derek Parfit, *Reasons and Persons* (Oxford: Oxford University Press, 1984), chap. 16. I think it was Douglas MacLean who brought me to see the importance of it for justice in particular, in bis "A Moral Requirement for Energy Policy," in *Energy and the Future*, edited by Douglas MacLean and Peter G. Brown (Totowa, NJ: Rowman and Littlefield, 1983), 180–97.

from a different sperm or a different egg would be a different person. Consequently, even the slightest variation in the timing of conception makes a different person. A slight change in a couple 5 lives means that they conceive different people. Were we to significantly reduce our emissions of greenhouse gas, it would change the lives of nearly everyone in the world. Within a couple of generations, the entire population of the world would consist of different people. Call this the "nonidentity effect."

Our Sarah would therefore not exist at all, were we to take the trouble to reduce our emissions. If she would not even exist were we to reduce our emissions, she cannot plausibly claim she had a right to a better life, which we violate by not doing so. We could not give Sarah a better life by emitting less gas, so we do not violate a right of hers by emitting profligately. Suppose we did owe a duty to Sarah to reduce emissions. Were we to carry out this duty, there would be no Sarah and therefore no duty. It would be a duty that cannot be satisfied. That makes no sense. We can conclude that our emissions do no injustice to Sarah. The same goes for nearly everyone in her generation.

In a way, the nonidentity effect excuses us as a generation from a charge of injustice toward future generations. Please do not think it excuses us from every moral duty to reduce emissions. Our continued emissions make the lives of future generations much less good than they could be. So they constitute a serious violation of our duty of goodness. This is not in any way a minor violation of morality; making the world less good is a serious moral fault. But it is not a violation of justice.

The nonidentity effect of a generations or a country's emissions will obviously be much bigger than the nonidentity effect of a single person's emissions. If you reduce your own emissions of greenhouse gas, that will affect the identity of some people in the next few generations, but probably not very many. So the nonidentity effect provides individuals with little excuse against a charge of injustice to future generations. That is the first reason justice is relatively more important for individuals than it is for nations and their governments.

THE HARM DONE BY AN INDIVIDUAL

The second reason justice is relatively more important in the private morality of climate change is that the duty of goodness demands very little of an individual. It requires you to reduce your greenhouse gas emissions only insofar as you can do so at a very small cost. Probably it requires you to turn off the light when you leave a room—that sort of thing. The reason is quantitative, and to explain it I need to start by giving you some idea of the quantity of harm a person's emissions do.

I shall use a calculation shown to me by David Frame, now of Victoria University in New Zealand.[3] I must emphasize that Frame means it to be very rough. The figures are intended only to show you the order of magnitude of the harm you do, nothing more. Frame calculates that an average person from a rich country, if she was born in 1950, will emit during the course of her whole life about 800 tonnes of carbon dioxide. This will warm the atmosphere by about half a billionth of a degree. A major part of the harm climate change will do is the killing of people. The World Health Organization has published predictions of the number who will be killed, and on that basis we can estimate that this 800 tonnes will shorten people's lives in total by some months. Each year of a rich person's emissions shortens lives by one or two days. We will not shorten any single person's life that much, but each of us shortens lives in total by that amount.

This is a serious harm. None of us would want to be responsible for shortening people's lives to that extent. This figure shows you, read conversely, how much good you could do by reducing your emissions. Some people despair in the face of climate change. They think the problem is so huge that nothing they can do as individuals will do any good. But they are wrong. By reducing your emissions, you can do significant good through extending people's lives. If you stop your emissions, each year you will extend lives by a day or two.

But the main point I want to make is that the good you can do by reducing your emissions, though significant, is small compared with other opportunities you have. Suppose you reduce your annual emissions to zero in the cheapest possible way (which is by offsetting them, as I shall explain later). It will cost you a few hundred dollars per year. For that you will extend people's lives by one or two days each year. But for a few hundred dollars, a charity that treats tuberculosis can cure a persons infection, and thereby extend her life for many years or decades. Of course, reducing emissions will do good in other ways as well as by saving lives, but they are not enough to close this very large gap in benefits. So if you aim to use your resources to improve the world, reducing emissions of greenhouse gas is not the way to do it. To improve the world, you should carry on emitting, and send the money you save by doing so to a tuberculosis charity. This is why I say that the duty of goodness does not require you to reduce your emissions significantly.

Why does the same argument not apply to governments? It's because governments—at least the governments of large countries—control more resources. Like individuals, they have more effective ways of using resources to do good, by treating tuberculosis, controlling malaria and polio, providing clean drinking water around the world, and so on. But even if they were to

[3]David Frame, "Personal and Intergenerational Carbon Footprints" (forthcoming).

do all those things, they could *still* improve the world further by using their power to reduce greenhouse gas emissions. A government's duty of goodness requires it to treat tuberculosis, control malaria, provide clean water, and so on, *and* control climate change. That is not so for an individual. If you were to devote all your resources to improving the world, even when they were completely exhausted, the need for tuberculosis treatment would still be more pressing than the need to reduce greenhouse gas emissions.

THE INJUSTICE OF EMISSIONS

The private morality of climate change therefore does not arise from the duty of goodness. It arises instead from the duty of justice. What justice does justice require of individuals?

I am concerned with the particular duty of justice not to harm. I have already said that each person's emissions of greenhouse gas do harm. I have even given a rough estimate of the amount of one particular harm they do: the harm of shortening lives. Earlier I pointed out that not all harms are necessarily unjust, but next I shall argue that the harm done by emissions is indeed an injustice. I cannot do this conclusively, because I am not able to identify exactly where the boundary lies between harms that are unjust and those that are not. But I shall mention seven different characteristics of the harm done by our emissions, and by the time I have reached the end of the list, I think it will be clear that this harm lies on the side of injustice. Several points beside the seven are so obvious that I do not include them in the list: the harm caused by emissions is not a merited punishment, it is done without the consent of the person harmed, and so on. Here is the list.

First, the harm done by our emissions is the result of something we *do*. Many of us make a distinction between doing harm and failing to prevent harm. If you fail to donate to a charity that relieves poverty, you fail to prevent the harm of poverty, but many of us do not think this failure is an injustice. Emitting greenhouse gas is different. In living our lives, we *act* in ways that cause greenhouse gases to be emitted. We *cause* carbon dioxide to spew from our chimneys and the exhaust pipes of our cars. These are consequences of things we do, rather than of things we omit to do.

Second, the harm we do by our emissions is serious. It may be permissible to do a trivial amount of harm, but this harm is far from trivial. I have given an idea of its size.

Third, the harm we do is not accidental. Indeed, we do it knowingly, though not deliberately. Few people in the developed world are ignorant of the greenhouse effect. Accidental harms are not an injustice, but emissions are not in that category.

Fourth, we do not compensate the victims of our harm. An injustice can sometimes be canceled by compensation, but our emissions are not canceled in this way.

Fifth, most of us make our emissions for our own benefit. That is not true of all of us. Some people are exceptionally altruistic and act for the sake of others. They may use the money they save by not cutting their emissions to benefit mankind. I am addressing not them, but the less altruistic majority. I said that justice normally prohibits you from harming other people even in order to make the world better. It more strongly prohibits you from harming other people in order to benefit yourself.

Sixth, the harms done by the emissions of the rich are not fully reciprocated. Some environmental harms are reciprocal. Traffic congestion is an example. If you drive to work, the presence of your car on the roads impedes other people on their way to work. They equally impede you. Each of you is significantly harming others by delaying them, but because the harm is reciprocal, we do not think that each of you is doing an injustice to others. Climate change is different. It is mostly a one-way transaction in which the present rich harm the present poor and future generations and are not much harmed in return. When I say that greenhouse gas emissions are an injustice, I am referring to the emissions of the present rich.

A seventh characteristic of greenhouse gas emissions is that we could easily reduce them. I shall soon explain that this is easier than you may think. You might be excused for causing harms that it would be very hard to avoid causing, but emitting greenhouse gas is not in that category.

I conclude from all these considerations that our emissions of greenhouse gas are an injustice.

THE INDIVIDUAL DUTY NOT TO CAUSE EMISSIONS

It follows that each of us is under a duty of justice not to cause the emission of greenhouse gas, at least without compensating the people who are harmed as a result. Your carbon footprint ought to be zero unless you make restitution. This is strong advice, but I find I cannot avoid drawing this conclusion. It puts me in a unusual position for a moral philosopher. Normally, moral philosophers talk in generalities. We avoid preaching to people about particular moral demands. But here I am doing that. Fortunately, you will see in a moment that this duty turns out to be less onerous than it may at first appear.

By what means should you perform this duty of justice? You might try to do it by compensating the people you harm. Doing so would be remarkably cheap. Most of the harm you cause will not happen till far in the future. This means that if you put aside money now to compensate the victims of your harm, you can exploit the power of compound interest before you have to pay it over. William Nordhaus calculates that if you are lucky enough to be able to invest your money at 5.5 percent per year, $7.40 is enough to compensate for the harm done by a tonne of carbon dioxide.[4] Since you emit perhaps twenty or thirty tonnes in a year, a couple of hundred dollars a year will suffice.

However, I do not recommend this means of trying to achieve justice, because it will fail. Remember that duties of justice are owed to particular people. "Your emissions of greenhouse gas are an injustice done to a large fraction of the world's population over a long period of time. You will not be able to compensate each of them individually.

You might try to make restitution through a collective international scheme of some sort. That way, you will not compensate all the individuals you harm, but you might manage some sort of surrogate compensation, by compensating large populations rather than individuals. Possibly you might satisfy justice by other means. But there remains another problem. You do not know how much compensation you actually owe. None of us knows how much harm we cause by our emissions. We may be able to compute how much gas we emit, but the harm that gas does is very uncertain. Predictions of the effects of climate change are recognized to be very uncertain indeed. I have mentioned Nordhaus figure, but I do not think he would claim it is particularly reliable.

You would do much better not to make the emissions in the first place; no compensation will then be required. This is possible. We all know some steps we might take: do not live wastefully, be frugal with energy in particular, switch off lights, do not waste water, eat less meat, eat local food, and so on. Many of these are steps you can take at little or no cost to yourself, and you should take those ones. However, you could not live in a way that does not cause the emission of any greenhouse gas at all. Virtually anything you buy has been produced using energy from fossil fuels. You can certainly reduce your emissions. But your most effective way of reducing your emissions to zero is to cancel or *offset* the emissions that you will still be causing after you have taken the obvious steps. Offsetting is a good way to fulfill your duty of justice. I shall explain how it works in a moment.

I am not telling you that offsetting is a way to solve the problem of climate change. I have already said that reducing your individual emissions of greenhouse gas—by offsetting or in other ways—is not the most effective way for you to improve the world. Your duty to have a zero carbon footprint does not derive from your duty of goodness. You must do it to avoid committing an injustice to other people—simply that. So far as solving the problem of climate change is concerned, your best route is through political action to induce your government to do what it should.

[4]William Nordhaus, *A Question of Balance* (New Haven, CT: Yale University Press, 2008), 15, 178.

OFFSETTING

Offsetting your emissions means ensuring that for every unit of greenhouse gas you cause to be added to the atmosphere, you also cause a unit to be subtracted from it. If you offset, on balance you add nothing. Offsetting does not remove the very molecules that you emit, but the climate does not care which particular molecules are warming it. If you offset all your emissions, you make sure that your presence in the world causes no addition to the greenhouse gas in the atmosphere. You do not contribute to warming the atmosphere, so you do no harm through climate change. It is not that you do harm, which you then compensate for; offsetting is not a sort of compensation. It is a way to avoid harming in the first place.

It will not be easy to calculate the offset you need. You must make sure you offset not just the gas that is directly emitted by your own actions, but also the gas that supplied the energy used in making everything you consume. The average emissions in your own country will not be a good guide, because much of what you consume will have been manufactured abroad. It would be safest to overestimate. But in any case, this calculation is much less pervaded by uncertainty than trying to calculate how much harm your emissions do, with the aim of compensating people for them. This adds to the reasons for preferring offsetting to compensating.

How do you offset in practice? You may be able to subtract gas from the atmosphere yourself. One way of doing so is to grow trees. As they grow, trees remove carbon from the air to build their bodies: they take in carbon dioxide molecules, keep the carbon, and release the oxygen. But you would need to make sure that your trees' carbon is permanently kept out of the air, and that would be hard to achieve. Eventually, your trees will die and decompose, and their carbon will return to the air. Somehow you will have to ensure your forest will be replanted again and again perpetually even after your death. For that reason, effective do-it-yourself offsetting is difficult.

More easily practicable means of offsetting are "preventive," as I call them. Instead of taking carbon dioxide out of the atmosphere, they prevent it from getting into the atmosphere in the first place.

Plenty of commercial organizations offer to prevent carbon emissions on your behalf. You pay them a fee per tonne of offsetting you ask them to do. They use your money to finance projects that diminish emissions somewhere in the world. Most projects create sources of renewable energy. For instance, they build hydroelectric power stations or wind farms. Others promote the efficient use of energy. One installs efficient cooking stoves in people's homes in Africa and Asia. Cooking with firewood is an important cause of carbon emissions, and efficient stoves reduce the quantity that is emitted.

Preventive offsetting is cheap. Responsible companies will offset a tonne of emissions for around ten dollars. This means you can offset all your emissions for a few hundred dollars. That is why I said you can easily avoid harming people through your emissions.

Many environmentalists are strongly opposed to offsetting. Greenpeace is opposed, for example. One of its arguments is: "The truth is, once you've put a tonne of CO_2 into the atmosphere, there's nothing off-setting can do to stop it changing our climate."[5] I do not think this is true. It at the same time you put a tonne of carbon dioxide into the atmosphere, you subtract another tonne, your actions together do not change the climate. So, since the climate does not change, the tonne you emit does not change it. Certainly, *you* do not change the climate, which is what matters.

Still, I recognize there are significant moral and practical problems connected with offsetting. One of them is that it is difficult to be sure that the reduction in emissions you pay for really happens. But I prefer to leave these for our discussion, because I want to get on to public morality.

GOVERNMENTS' DUTIES OF GOODNESS

Governments, like individuals, bear duties of justice. However, in responding to climate change, they also have duties of goodness. I am going to concentrate on those because I have already talked about justice. I want to survey a different part of the morality of climate change.

When governments try to promote goodness, they must generally do some complex calculations. Their actions, especially over climate change, benefit many people and also impose costs on many people. Different benefits have to be aggregated together somehow, and so do different costs. Then benefits have to be weighed against costs. Cost-benefit analysis of some sort is inevitable. Climate change is a problem on a vast scale, affecting the whole world for centuries, and the quantitative methods of economics are necessary for coping with it.

Cost-benefit analysis also calls for ethical analysis, because the valuing and weighing of benefits and costs raise moral questions of many sorts. How should benefits to the rich be weighed against benefits to the poor? How should we value the loss of a person's life against the mundane good things that life contains? How should we take account of the huge uncertainty that surrounds climate change, including the small chance of total catastrophe? How should we weigh distant future benefits against present costs? How should we take into account the changes in the world's population that climate change will

[5]Statement by Charlie Kronick of Greenpeace, January 17, 2007.

undoubtedly cause, including the small chance that our population will collapse to small numbers or even to extinction?

EFFICIENCY

All of those questions are fertile sources of disagreement and argument. But I have decided to leave them aside and take up one subject that does not involve weighing and aggregating. Instead, it involves what economists call efficiency. Having spent most of this lecture talking about private duties of justice that particularly do not aim to solve the problem of climate change, I am going to spend the rest of it on something that perhaps might solve it. It is a point that I have come to think is extremely important for the practical politics of climate change.

Oddly enough, it is a point of simple economics. When a person engages in some activity that emits greenhouse gas, the gas spreads around the globe and delivers small harms everywhere. These harms are among the costs of what the person does, but the person who causes the gas to be emitted does not bear this cost. It is borne by all people who suffer the harm. In economists' terminology, it is an "external cost" of the activity. Emissions of greenhouse gas constitute an "externality," as economists put it.

Externalities cause *inefficiency*. From the point of view of economics, this is what principally makes climate change a problem. Inefficiency here is what is sometimes called more specifically "Pareto inefficiency." It is defined as a situation in which it would be technically possible to make some people better off without making anyone worse off; a change of this sort is called a "Pareto improvement." Because emissions are an externality, they cause inefficiency in this sense, so a Pareto improvement is possible. I can go further. It would be technically possible to go so far as to remove the externality through a Pareto improvement.

This is a consequence of very elementary economic theory, though I admit I had to be reminded of its implications for climate change by my onetime teacher Duncan Foley.[6] The elementary economics needs to be modified to take account of the nonidentity effect, but it is nevertheless true that no one needs to make any sacrifice to solve the problem caused by the externality of greenhouse gas emissions.

I can describe in broad terms how the externality could be solved without any sacrifices. Although we are bequeathing to our successors a dirty atmosphere, we are doing quite a lot of good things for them in other ways.

[6]See Duncan Foley, "The Economic Fundamentals of Global Warming," in *Twenty-First Century Macroeconomics: Responding to the Climate Challenge*, edited by Jonathan M. Harris and Neva R. Goodwin (Cheltenham, UK: Edward Elgar, 2009), 115–26.

We are leaving them a lot of resources: cities, economic infrastructure, cultivated land, knowledge, and also those natural resources that we do not use up. Suppose we reduce our emissions of greenhouse gas. Other things being equal, that would require a sacrifice on our part. But we could fully compensate ourselves for the sacrifice by consuming more of other resources and leaving less to future generations in other ways. We could compensate ourselves to the extent that we are no worse off on balance. In macroeconomic terms, we could keep our own consumption constant and redirect our investment toward reducing greenhouse gas emissions. Future generations would receive from us fewer resources of other sorts, but they would have a cleaner atmosphere, and they would end up better off on balance.

Here is a slightly more concrete example of how this could be done. We could impose a carbon tax equal to the external damage done by emissions. Then we could compensate each person in some way for the carbon tax she pays. For example, we could reduce her income tax to the extent that she is just as well off as she was before. The carbon tax itself would finance some of the compensation, but it will not be enough to finance full compensation for everybody. The balance could be financed by a loan that will be repaid by future generations.

The externality of climate change could be removed without anyone's making a sacrifice. This raises a puzzle. When delegates come each year to meetings of the United Nations Framework Convention on Climate Change, at Copenhagen or Durban or somewhere else, they take themselves to be negotiating about how to distribute among the nations the burden of reducing climate change. No government will agree to accept a burden—to impose a sacrifice on its people—so the meetings regularly fail to achieve the reductions in emissions that are required. Yet I am saying that eliminating the problem of climate change requires no sacrifices at all. What is going on?

EFFICIENCY VERSUS OPTIMIZATION

I am telling the truth. It would indeed be possible in principle to eliminate the externality without any sacrifices. Doing so would be an improvement on the present situation, since some people would be better off and no one would be worse off. But it does not follow that this is the best thing that can be done about climate change. Most of the economists who work on climate change have chosen to look for this best thing, and their thinking has influenced the political process. These economists approach the problem as one of *optimization*. They look for the *best* way of managing our resources: the way that will do the most good. They work out how the international community can best meet its duty of goodness. This involves weighing benefits and costs in the way I have described. It turns out that, if their calculations are correct and founded on correct ethical principles, it would be best if the present generation did make some sacrifices for the future. This is the conclusion of the *Stern Review*, and William Nordhaus agrees, though he thinks there should be much less sacrifice than Stern does.[7]

Compare these three options:

> Business as usual. ("BAU")
>
> Reduce emissions and fully compensate ourselves for doing so, so there is no sacrifice. ("Compensation")
>
> Reduce emissions and do not fully compensate ourselves for doing so, so there is sacrifice. ("Optimum")
>
> We are told that Optimum is better than Compensation, which is better than BAU. . . .

Compensation is unattractive. Not only is it worse than Optimum, but it also incorporates injustice. BAU is an unjust situation: the present rich harm the present poor by our emissions of greenhouse gas, and that is unjust. If we move from there to Compensation, the rich are paid for reducing their emissions by those who suffer from them. This is an improvement for those who suffer, but it nevertheless perpetuates the injustice. If someone unjustly hurts you every day, you may be able to improve your situation by paying her to stop it, but that does not remove the injustice.

So I understand why the political process aims toward Optimum rather than Compensation. But the constant failure of the political process has made me cynical. National leaders will not commit their presently living people—in most cases their electorate—to the sacrifices they must make to achieve Optimum. I no longer think Optimum can be reached through negotiation, and I now favor aiming instead at Compensation. The issue at stake would then be how to distribute the *benefits* of controlling climate change—not the burdens—among the nations. Putting the question in this optimistic form might break the political logjam.

The difference between Compensation and Optimum is a matter of the distribution of resources between people: between the rich and the poor and between present and future generations. This distribution is not primarily determined by climate change, and dealing with climate change need not involve putting it right.[8] If you aim for the very best outcome, you are aiming

[7] Nicholas Stern et al., *The Economics of Climate Change: The Stem Review* (Cambridge: Cambridge University Press, 2007). A remark by William Nordhaus on page 180 of *A Question of Balance* implies agreement.

[8] Here I agree with Eric Posner and David Weisbach in *Climate Change Justice* (Princeton, NJ: Princeton University Press, 2010).

to correct all the present ills of the world. For example, suppose you think that the correct rate for discounting future commodities is below the interest rate in the market. By implication, you think the market does not pass as many resources to the future as it should; present people are consuming too much and not leaving enough for our successors. If, in dealing with climate change, you choose policies that are optimal according to your lower discount rate, you will find yourself making up for this general failure, as well as for the particular problem of climate change. Now that I have become cynical, I think we should concentrate on solving the particular problem and temporarily leave aside the general one.

PUBLIC MORALITY

Should we understand this as a moral duty of goodness, resting on governments and the international community? It could be argued that promoting efficiency is not even a moral duty at all. It is in everyone's interests. We could think of this task of government as merely one of coordinating people s activities in pursuing their own interests. We might even think a government in this domain acts not as an agent in its own right, but as a mere mechanism through which individual people coordinate their activities by mutual agreement. Many economists claim that ethics has nothing to do with economics, and many of those same economists claim that economics is concerned with efficiency only. I think this idea may be the basis of their thinking.

But governments have too many of the characteristics of agency for this to be plausible. For example, governments clearly have intentions. After two centuries, the Monroe Doctrine still expresses one of the US government's intentions, even though the personnel who constitute the government have changed many times. True, it remains a topic for philosophical research how a collective entity can have intentions, but it is a fact. As agents, governments are potentially bearers of moral duties, and improving the world is one duty they actually bear. Moreover, they cannot be merely a forum where agents coordinate their interests, since many of the relevant interests belong to people who are not yet born. Governments have a moral responsibility toward those people.

If governments cannot achieve the best outcome, Optimum, their duty of goodness requires them at least to aim for Compensation.

This sets a task for the economics profession. The theory tells us that Compensation, where no one makes a sacrifice, is possible. But to make it possible in practice requires some work. We are to reduce our emissions, financing the cost of doing so by loans that will be repaid by future people. But we know well that there is a limit to the amount that governments can borrow, and several governments seem to have already reached their limit. We therefore need new economic institutions that are robust enough to support enough borrowing to achieve Compensation. Economists must design these institutions.

I hope institutions can be created that will make Compensation possible. If so, I hope it will allow progress to be made on climate change. But remember that Compensation is not a good solution. If Compensation can be achieved, Optimum still remains a possibility. Getting from Compensation to Optimum is a matter of the distribution of resources between generations. It could be achieved by canceling the debt that builds up under Compensation. I hope that by making Compensation a real possibility, we might achieve something more like Optimum in the end. In taking the cynical position, I have not abandoned the aim of doing the best.

For Further Reflection

1. What is John Broome's distinction between "public morality," "civic morality," and "private morality"?
2. What does he say are our duties of justice and goodness regarding climate change?
3. What is offsetting? What is Broome's view of its use in meeting our moral obligations?

Further Readings for Chapter 15

Broome, John. *Counting the Cost of Global Warming.* Isle of Harris, UK: White Horse Press, 1992.

DesJardins, Joseph. *Environmental Ethics.* 2nd ed. Belmont, CA: Wadsworth, 1997.

Garvey, James. *Ethics and Climate Change.* London: Continuum, 2008.

Newton, Lisa H., and Catherine K. Dillingham. *Watersheds 2: Ten Cases in Environmental Ethics.* Belmont, CA: Wadsworth, 1997.

Passmore, John. *Man's Responsibility for Nature.* 2nd ed. London: Duckworth, 1980.

Schlosberg, David. 2007. *Environmental Justice.* Oxford: Oxford University Press.

Sterba, James, ed. *Earth Ethics.* Englewood Cliffs, NJ: Prentice-Hall, 1994.

VanDeVeer, Donald, and Christine Pierce, eds. *The Environmental Ethics and Policy Book.* Belmont, CA: Wadsworth, 1994.

Zimmerman, Michael, ed. *Environmental Philosophy.* Englewood Cliffs, NJ: Prentice-Hall, 1993.

APPENDIX

How to Read and Write Philosophy Papers

LEWIS VAUGHN

READING

In some ways, reading philosophy is like reading the literature of many other fields. It requires a good deal of abstract thought, often involves difficult concepts or extraordinary propositions, and can be intimidating to those who approach the subject for the first time. But in other ways, reading philosophy is fairly distinctive. When you read a philosophical essay, you are not simply trying to glean some facts from it as you might if you were reading a science text or technical report. Neither are you following a storyline as if you were reading a mystery novel (though philosophy papers sometimes contain their share of mysteries). In most cases, you are tracing the steps in an argument, trying to see what conclusion the writer wants to prove and whether she succeeds in proving it. Along the way, you may encounter several premises with their accompanying analyses, clarifications, explanations, and examples. You may even run into a whole chain of arguments. In the end, if you have read well and the writer has written well, you are left not with a new set of data or a story ending, but a realization—maybe even a revelation—that a conclusion is, or is not, worthy of belief.

The best way to learn how to read philosophy well is to read philosophy often. You will probably get plenty of chances to do that in your current philosophy course. Having a few rules to guide you in your reading, however, may help shorten the learning curve. As you read, keep the following in mind.

1. Approach the text with an open mind.

If you are studying philosophy for the first time, you are likely—at least at first—to find a good bit of the material difficult, strange, or exasperating, sometimes all three at once. That's normal. Philosophy is an exploration of the rugged frontiers of our knowledge of fundamental things, so much of this new territory is likely to seem daunting or unfamiliar. There's also an excellent chance that your first visits to this terrain will be vexing, perhaps even infuriating, because you may sometimes disagree with what you read.

There is no shame in experiencing any of these reactions. They come with the territory. But if you are to make any headway in philosophy and write good papers, you need to try your best to counteract these attitudes and feelings. Remember, philosophy at its best is a fair-minded, fearless search for truth. Anything that interferes with this noble quest must be overcome and cast aside.

Avoid making a judgment about an essay's ideas or arguments until you fully understand them and have fairly considered them. Make sure you are not reading with the intent to prove the conclusions false (or true). Be open to the possibility that the essay could give you good reasons to change your mind about something.

Try to maintain a neutral attitude toward the writer, presuming neither that she is right nor wrong, neither sinner nor saint. Don't assume that everything a renowned philosopher says must be true, and don't presuppose that everything a philosopher you dislike says must be false. Give the writer the same attention and respect that you would give a friend who is discussing a serious issue with you.

If you are reading the work of a famous philosopher and you find yourself thinking that his or her ideas are obviously silly or ridiculous, think again. The odds are good that you are misunderstanding what you read. It is wiser to assume that the text offers something of value (even if you disagree with it) and that you need to read more carefully.

2. Read actively and critically.

Philosophical reading is intense. It cannot be rushed. It cannot be crammed. It cannot be done while your mind is on automatic pilot.

Philosophical reading is *active* reading. Instead of reading just to get through a piece of writing, you must take your time and ask yourself what key terms and passages mean, how the argument is structured, what the central thesis is, where the premises are, how certain key ideas are related, whether the main conclusion conflicts with propositions you know are true, even how the material compares with other philosophical writing on the same subject.

Philosophical reading is also *critical* reading. In critical reading, you ask not what something means but whether a statement is true and if the reasoning is solid. You ask if the conclusion really follows from the premises, whether the premises are true, if the analysis of a term really makes sense, if an argument has been overlooked, if an analogy is weak, whether there are counterexamples to key claims, and whether the claims agree with other things you have good reason to believe.

3. Identify the conclusion first, then the premises.

When you first begin reading philosophical texts, they may seem to you like dark thickets of propositions into which you may not enter without losing your way. But your situation is really not that bad. As we have seen, in argumentative writing (the kind you are most likely to encounter in philosophy), you can depend on there being, well, an argument, a conclusion backed by premises. There could, of course, be several arguments that support the main argument, and the arguments could be complex, but these sets of conclusion-plus-premises will all serve as recognizable guideposts. If you want to penetrate the thicket, then, you must first identify the argument (or arguments). And the key to doing that is to *find the conclusion first, then look for the premises.*

When you find the main conclusion, you thereby identify the main point of the essay, and you then have the number-one clue to the function of all the rest of the text. Once you uncover the point that the writer is trying to prove, finding the supporting premises becomes much easier. And when you isolate the premises, locating the text that explains and amplifies the premises gets easier too. Therefore, the first—and most important—question you can ask about a philosophical essay is, *"What claim is the writer trying to prove?"*

4. Outline, paraphrase, or summarize the argument.

Understanding an essay's argument is so important that testing whether you really "get it" is crucial. You can test your grasp of the argument by outlining, paraphrasing, or summarizing it. If you can lay out an argument's premises and conclusion in an outline, or if you can accurately paraphrase or summarize the argument, you probably have a pretty good understanding of it. Very often students who think they comprehend an argument are surprised to see that they cannot devise an adequate outline or summary of it. Such failures suggest that, although outlining, paraphrasing, or summarizing may seem to some to be unnecessary, it is not—at least not to those new to philosophy.

5. Evaluate the argument and formulate a tentative judgment.

When you read philosophy, understanding it is just the first step. You also must do something that many beginners find both difficult and alien: You must make an informed judgment about what you read. Simply reiterating what the writer has said will not do. *Your* judgment is what matters here. Mainly, this judgment is your evaluation of the argument presented by the writer—an assessment of (1) whether the conclusion follows from the premises and (2) whether the premises are true. Only when the answer is *yes* to both these questions can you say that the conclusion of the argument is worthy of acceptance. This kind of evaluation is precisely what your instructor expects when she asks you to critique an argumentative essay in philosophy.

A philosophical text, of course, contains more than just a bare-bones argument. Often a considerable amount of space is devoted to explaining the background or history of the topic being addressed, elaborating on each of the premises, discussing the implications of the argument's conclusion, and answering possible criticisms of the essay's main points. Certainly you must take these into account when you are reading and evaluating a philosophical text. But your primary task is to arrive at an honest and well-reasoned assessment of the text's central claim.

WRITING

In conversations, letters to the editor, or online discussions, have you ever taken a position on an issue and offered reasons why your view is correct? If so, then you have defended a thesis. You have presented an argument, giving reasons for accepting a particular thesis, or conclusion. If you elaborate on your argument in a written paper, you create something even more valuable—a *thesis defense (or argumentative) essay*. In a thesis defense essay, you try to show the reader that your view is worthy of acceptance by offering reasons that support it. Your thesis may assert your position on a philosophical, social, or political issue; or on the arguments or claims of other writers (including some famous or not-so-famous philosophers); or on the interpretation of a single work or several. In every case, you affirm a thesis and give reasons for your affirmation.

This type of essay is not merely an analysis of claims, or a summary of points made by someone else, or a reiteration of what other people believe or say—though a good thesis defense essay may contain some of these elements. A thesis defense essay is supposed to be a demonstration of what you believe and why you believe it. What other people think is, ultimately, beside the point.

Basic Essay Structure

Thesis defense essays usually contain the following elements, though not necessarily in this order:

I. *Introduction (or opening)*
   A. *Thesis statement (the claim to be supported)*
   B. *Plan for the paper*
   C. *Background for the thesis*
II. *Argument supporting the thesis*
III. *Assessment of objections*
IV. *Conclusion*

Introduction

The introduction often consists of the paper's first paragraph, sometimes just a sentence or two. Occasionally it is longer, perhaps several paragraphs. The length depends on how much ground you must cover to introduce the argument. Whatever the length, the introduction should be no longer than necessary. In most cases the best introductions are short.

If there is a rule of thumb for what the introduction must contain, it is this: *The introduction should set forth the thesis statement.* The thesis statement usually appears in the first paragraph. It is the claim that you hope to support or prove in your essay, the conclusion of the argument that you intend to present. You may want to pose the thesis statement as the answer to a question that you raise, or as the solution to a problem that you wish to discuss. However presented, your thesis statement is the assertion you must support with reasons. It is like a compass to your readers, guiding them from paragraph to paragraph, premise to premise, showing them a clear path from introduction to conclusion. It also helps you stay on course. It reminds you to relate every sentence and paragraph to your one controlling idea.

Your thesis statement should be restricted to a claim that you can defend in the space allowed. You want to state it in a single sentence and do so as early as possible. You may need to add a few words to explain or elaborate on the statement if you think its meaning or implications unclear.

The other two parts of an introduction—the plan for the paper (B) and background information for the thesis (C)—may or may not be necessary, depending on your thesis and your intent. In more formal essays, you will need not only to state your thesis but also to spell out how you intend to argue for it. You will have to summarize your whole argument—each of your premises and conclusion—or, if your argument is long or complex, at least the most important points. Providing background information for your thesis is a matter of explaining what your thesis means (which includes defining terms and clarifying concepts), what its implications are, why the issue is so important or pressing, or why you have decided to address it. Sometimes the needed background information is so extensive that you must supply much of it after the introduction. At any rate, by adding the right kind of background information, you give your readers good reason to care about what you are saying and to continue reading.

In many philosophy papers, the background information includes a summary or sketch of the views of other philosophers—what they have said that is relevant to the issue or to your thesis. Providing this kind of material can help the reader understand why your topic is worth exploring and why your argument is relevant.

Argument Supporting the Thesis

Between your paper's introduction and conclusion is the *body* of the essay. The basic components of the body are (1) the premises of your argument plus the material that supports or explains them and (2) an evaluation of objections to your thesis. Each premise must be clearly stated, carefully explained and illustrated, and properly backed up by examples, statistics, expert opinion, argument, or other reasons or evidence. You may be able to adequately develop the essay by devoting a single paragraph to each premise, or you may have to use several paragraphs per premise.

Whatever tack you take, you must stick to the central rule of paragraph development: Develop just one main point in each paragraph, embodying that point in a topic sentence. Make sure that each paragraph in turn relates to your thesis statement.

If your essay is a critique of someone else's arguments, you should examine them in the body, explaining how they work and laying out the author's response to any major criticisms of them. Your account of the arguments should be accurate and complete, putting forth the author's best case and providing enough detail for your readers to understand the import of your own argument. After the presentation of the author's side of things, you can then bring in your critique, asserting and explaining each premise.

Some premises, of course, may be so obvious that they do not require support. The determining factor is whether your readers would be likely to question them. If your readers are likely to accept a premise as it is, no backup is required. If they are not, you need to support the premise. A common mistake is to assume that a premise would be accepted by everyone when in fact it is controversial.

Recall that in a good argument the conclusion logically follows from the premises, and the premises are true. Your task in the body of your essay is to put forth such an argument and to do so plainly—to demonstrate clearly to your readers that your premises are properly related to your conclusion and that they are true. You should leave no doubt about what you are trying to prove and how you are trying to prove it. In longer papers, you may want to back up your thesis with more than one argument. This is an acceptable way to proceed, providing you make the relationships between the separate arguments and your thesis clear.

Assessment of Objections

Very often an argumentative essay includes an *assessment of objections*—a sincere effort to take into account any objections or doubts that readers are likely to have about points in your essay. (In some cases, however, there may be no significant objections to assess.) You must show your readers that the objections are unfounded, that your argument is not fatally wounded by likely criticisms. Contrary to what some may think, when you deal effectively with objections in your essay, *you do not weaken it—you strengthen it.* You lend credibility to it by making an attempt to be fair and thorough. You make your position stronger by removing doubts from your readers' minds. If you don't confront likely objections, your readers may conclude that you are either ignorant of the objections or you don't have a good reply to them. An extra benefit is that in dealing with objections, you may see ways to make your argument stronger.

On the other hand, you may discover that you do not have an adequate answer to the objections. Then what? Then you look for ways to change your arguments or thesis to overcome the criticisms. You can weaken your thesis by making it less sweeping or less probable. Or you may need to abandon your thesis altogether in favor of one that is stronger. Discovering that your beloved thesis is full of holes is not necessarily a setback. You have increased your understanding by finding out which boats will float and which will not.

Conclusion

Unless your essay is very short, it should have a *conclusion*. The conclusion usually appears in the last paragraph. Many conclusions simply reiterate the thesis statement and then go on to emphasize how important it is. Others issue a call to action, present a compelling perspective on the issue, or discuss further implications of the thesis statement. Some conclusions contain a summary of the essay's argument. A summary is always a good idea if the argument is complex, long, or formal.

Writing the Essay: Step by Step

Now we examine the steps involved in crafting a good thesis defense essay. You have the best chance of writing a good essay if you try to follow these steps. Just remember that the process is not linear. You may not be able to follow the steps in the sequence suggested. You may have to backtrack or rearrange the order of the steps. This kind of improvising on the fly is normal—and often necessary. At any stage in the process, you may discover that your argument is not as good as you thought, or that you did not take an important fact into account, or that there is a way that you can alter the essay to make it stronger. You may then want to go back and rework your outline or tinker with the draft you are working on—and your essay will be better for it. Rethinking and revising are normal procedures for even the best writers.

Here are the steps:

1. *Select a topic and narrow it to a specific issue.*
2. *Research the issue.*
3. *Write a thesis statement.*
4. *Create an outline.*
5. *Write a first draft.*
6. *Study and revise your first draft.*
7. *Produce a final draft.*

Step 1. Select a topic and narrow it to a specific issue.

This step is first for a reason. It is here to help inexperienced writers avoid a tempting but nasty trap: picking a thesis out of the air and writing their paper on it. Caution: *Any thesis that you dream up without knowing anything about it is likely to be unusable*—and a waste of time. It is better to begin by selecting a topic or issue and narrowing it through research and hard thinking to a manageable thesis.

A topic is simply a broad category of subject matter, such as *human cloning, the mind, capital punishment*, and *God*. Within topics there lurk an infinite number of issues—that is, questions that are in dispute. From the topic of capital punishment, for example, countless issues arise: whether executing criminals deters crime, whether executing a human being is ever morally permissible, whether it is ethical to execute people who are insane or mentally impaired, whether the system of capital punishment in the United States is unfair, whether the death penalty should be mandatory for serial killers, whether executing juveniles is immoral . . . the list could go on and on. The basic idea is to select from the roster of possibilities an issue that (1) you are interested in and (2) you can adequately address in the space allowed.

Step 2. Research the issue.

The main reason for researching an issue is to find out what viewpoints and arguments are involved. Often your instructor will suggest good sources to research for a particular writing assignment. Your assigned reading may be the only source you need to check. Otherwise, you can read articles and books, talk to people who have studied the issue or at least thought about it carefully, or go online to review topical or philosophical sites.

Step 3. Write a thesis statement.

The conclusion of your selected argument will serve as the basis for your thesis statement. Often the conclusion *is* your thesis statement. Writing a good thesis statement is an essential step because the entire essay is built on it. An imprecise or clumsy thesis statement can lead to an imprecise or clumsy argument, which can wreck any argumentative essay.

At this stage, you should try to get the wording of your statement just right, even though you may revise it later on. Its scope should be restricted to what you can handle in the space you have. It should also be focused on just one idea, not several. A good thesis statement must be clear. No one should have to guess about the meaning of your thesis. The thesis "Same-sex marriages are intolerable," for example, is intolerably vague since there are many ways that something can be intolerable. It gives us very little information about what will be discussed in the essay.

It is possible to devise a thesis statement that is restricted, focused, clear—and trivial. A trivial thesis statement is one that either concerns an insignificant issue or makes an insignificant claim. People generally don't care about insignificant issues, and few would bother to disagree with an insignificant claim. Who cares whether pens are better than pencils, or whether gambling is more fun than beachcombing? And who would care to contest the claim that pleasure is better than pain? An essay built on a trivial thesis statement wastes your readers' time (if they bother to read it at all), and you learn nothing and change nothing by writing it. Thesis statements should be worthy.

Here are some thesis statements that meet the above criteria:

- *Jeremy Bentham's moral theory known as act-utilitarianism conflicts with our commonsense ideas about human rights.*
- *The U.S. government should be allowed to arrest and indefinitely imprison without trial any American citizen who is suspected of terrorism.*
- *Subjective relativism—the view that truth depends on what someone believes—is self-refuting.*
- *Racial profiling should not be used to do security screening of airline passengers.*

Step 4. Create an outline of the whole essay.

If you can write out your thesis statement and outline the argument used to defend it, you have already come far. Your argument and thesis statement will constitute the skeleton of your essay. The next step is to flesh out the bones with introductory or explanatory material, responses to objections, and support for the premises (which may consist of subordinate arguments, examples, explanations, analogies, statistics, scientific research, expert opinion, or other evidence). Producing a detailed, coherent outline of the whole essay is the best way to manage this task, and if you already have an outline of your argument, creating an outline for the whole essay will be easy. An outline helps you fill out your argument in an orderly fashion, showing you how the pieces fit together, and whether any parts are missing or misaligned. This filling-out process will probably require you to research your thesis further—to check the truth of premises, examine alternative arguments, look for additional evidence, or assess the strength of objections to your argument.

Do not be afraid to alter your outline at any stage. As you write, you may realize that your thesis is weak, your argument flawed, or your premises vague. If so, you should go back and adjust the outline before writing any further. Writing is an act of exploration, and good writers are not afraid to revise when they find something amiss.

When you outline your essay, include your full thesis statement in the introduction. Then as you work on the outline, you can refer to the statement for guidance. The major points of your outline will include the premises, conclusion, objections, and responses to objections.

You will find that as you tweak the outline, you may need to adjust the thesis statement. And as you perfect the thesis statement, you may need to adjust the outline. In the end, you want to satisfy yourself that the outline is complete, accurate, and structurally sound, tracing a clear and logical progression of points.

Step 5. Write a first draft.

Good writers revise . . . and revise and revise. They either write multiple drafts, revising in successive passes, or they revise continuously as they write. They know that their first tries will always be in need of improvement. Inexperienced writers, on the other hand, too often dash off a first draft without a second look—then turn it in! A much more reasonable approach (and the best one for most students) is to at least write a first draft and a final draft or—better—several drafts and a final one.

In argumentative essays, because of the importance of articulating an argument carefully, and the difficulty of writing later drafts of the essay unless the first one is in reasonable shape, the first draft should be fairly solid. That is, in your first draft, you should write a tentative version of each paragraph, and the wording of your thesis statement and all premises should be at least close to final form.

Give your draft a good introduction that lays out your thesis statement, provides background information on the issue, and draws your readers into the essay. Make it interesting, informative, and pertinent to the question at hand. Do not assume that your readers will automatically see that your paper is worth reading.

Every paragraph in your paper should relate to the thesis; every sentence in each paragraph should relate to a topic sentence. Delete any sentence that does not serve the essay's purpose. Ensure that paragraphs appear in a logical sequence and are clearly linked by transitional words and phrases or references to material in preceding paragraphs. Your readers should never have to wonder what the connection is between parts of your paper.

Step 6. Study and revise your first draft.

Your first draft is likely to have problems both big and small. At this stage, though, you should scrutinize mostly the big ones. This is no time for proofreading (correcting spelling, fixing punctuation, repairing typos, and the like). This is the time to make substantive changes.

Step 7. Produce a final draft.

After completing all substantive changes, you should generate a final draft, the one you will turn in. The final draft should reflect not only the big changes, but the corrections of all minor errors as well—misspellings, typos, grammatical errors, misplaced words, faulty punctuation, and documentation mistakes. This task should be primarily a proofreading job. At this stage, you should also format the manuscript according to your instructor's requirements.

The key to producing a clean final draft is *down time*—an interim in which you leave the last draft alone and focus on something else. Coming back to your paper after a day or so away from it can help you see errors that passed right by you before. You may be surprised how many mistakes this fresh look can reveal. If you cannot set the essay aside, ask a friend to read it and give you some constructive criticism.

INDEX